Henry Bordwin
87 Hillside Rd
Newton Hglds
MA 02461

617 244-0019
244-6964

WITH AN
AIR
Debonair

WITH AN AIR *Debonair*

MUSICAL THEATRE IN AMERICA

1785 – 1815

SUSAN L. PORTER

Smithsonian Institution Press
Washington and London

Editor: Duke Johns
Designer: Janice Wheeler

Library of Congress Cataloging-in-Publication Data
Porter, Susan L., 1941–
    With an air debonair : musical theatre in America, 1785–1815 / Susan L. Porter.
    p. cm.
    Includes bibliographical references and index.
    ISBN 1-56098-063-X
    1. Musical theater—United States—History—18th century. 2. Musical
theater—United States—History—19th century.
I. Title.
ML1711.P67 1991
792.6'0973'09034—dc20   90-24921

British Library Cataloguing-in-Publication Data is available

Manufactured in the United States of America
98 97 96 95 94 93 92 91   5 4 3 2 1

∞The paper used in this publication meets the minimum requirements of the American National Standard for Permanence of Paper for Printed Library Materials z39.48-1984

For permission to reproduce illustrations appearing in this book, please correspond directly with the owners of the works, as listed in the individual captions. The Smithsonian Institution Press does not retain reproduction rights for these illustrations individually, or maintain a file of addresses for photo sources.

To my sons, Mark and Lael, who have grown up along with this book

CONTENTS

7.
Melpomene, Mirth, and Melody: Acting Traditions   231

8.
The Singer and the Song   305

9.
The Orchestra in the Theatre   361

10.
The Modern Performance   407

PREFACE

The history of the beginnings of American musical theatre has been told from many viewpoints. Contemporary periodicals provided the first descriptions and reviews. In 1810, in *The Mirror of Taste and Dramatic Censor,* Stephen Cullen Carpenter began the process of memorializing the actors and actresses who sang and acted in those early works. Shortly afterward, in 1814, James Fennell followed the lead of his English contemporaries when he wrote the first of many self-histories and reminiscences by Americans associated with the stage. In 1832 William Dunlap's *History of the American Theatre* launched a parade of theatrical histories, some broad in scope, some dealing with a particular geographical area.

These early histories and reviews dealt with the American stage as a whole—and indeed there was no separation of function in the early theatre. The same facilities, the same personnel, the same techniques were used in the performance of all theatrical genres. It was not until the early twentieth century, with Oscar Sonneck's *Early Opera in America,* that musical theatre began to be considered apart from other traditions, and its special genres and traditions differentiated. Although Sonneck touched on all aspects of musical theatre, his volume is particularly valuable in its tracings of companies and repertory. He laid the groundwork with a survey of such detailed accuracy and insight that it has remained unequaled for the period before 1800.

Since that time much work has been done in the field. Julian Mates provided additional detail for the period covered by Sonneck, although with little emphasis on the music itself, in *The American Musical Stage Before 1800*. Roger Fiske's *English Theatre Music in the Eighteenth Century* met and surpassed Sonneck's standards in an exhaustive survey that has direct bearing on the study of American musical theatre. Patricia Virga expanded knowledge of ballad operas and pastiches written in America before 1790, with a thorough study of the texts and music. In various articles David P. McKay has contributed to the literature on ballad opera, and Ann Dhu Shapiro has broken new ground in the study of pantomime and melodrama. Charlotte Kaufman and her Friends of Dr. Burney have added practical performance experience through the re-creation of eighteenth-century English works.

Though this present study provides a brief overview of the early history of American musical theatre, it begins its substantial coverage with the period following the end of the American Revolution, when American theatre began the evolutionary process that made its finest houses and troupes the equal of the best British houses. The survey continues into the early nineteenth century, through the period of the War of 1812, as America took its first tentative steps toward theatrical independence. The year 1815 ended the war with a burst of Americanism; it also began a burst of expansion to the frontier.

This period from approximately 1785 to 1815 also includes the best and most characteristic of the English and American operas, many of which have been short-changed by artificial divisions of style, considering only one of the two centuries involved. Most earlier studies have dealt only with the musical theatre of the eighteenth century. Those that have acknowledged the early years of the nineteenth century have either glossed over them quickly as a preliminary to "genuine" American styles later in the century, or have concentrated on specific genres or cities. Many of the most useful periodical sources, however, date from the early years of the nineteenth century and provide a wealth of hitherto neglected information about performance styles and practices, which not only illuminate the first decades of the new century but retrospectively shed new light on aspects of eighteenth-century musical theatre.

This book deals almost exclusively with opera in English, as a continuation of English theatrical tradition. Its aims are fourfold:

(a) to review this vibrant, rapidly changing, comprehensive period of theatrical history through the eyes and ears of contemporary observers, highlighting the place of musical theatre in early American life;

(b) to offer substantial documentation of musical performance practice, using primarily American records and descriptions but also considering material from European (particularly English) sources when it clarifies points of performance practice or demonstrates interrelationships;

(c) to serve as a touchstone for modern performances of these works, by assembling a wealth of well-documented material from as many primary sources as possible, allowing performers and directors to locate information pertinent to a specific performance situation; and

(d) to make all the information available in a well-organized, readable format useful to musical and theatrical scholars, performers, and amateurs.

ACKNOWLEDGMENTS

Many persons have assisted with this study from its inception sixteen years ago. Among those who have assisted most are Jenny Neeley and Ruth Ann Loar, typists; William Kearns, Gillian Anderson, Nicholas Tawa, Kate Van Winkle Keller, Robert Sedoris, and Alan Luhring, who provided expert professional advice at various stages; James Biddle and Philip Heath of the Ohio State University at Lima, who provided institutional support; Ed Stephens, preliminary reading; Betty Milum, Kathy Stedke, and Anna Selfridge, special local library services; and Angie Hays and Bob and Kitty Keller, who generously provided the hiding places I needed for writing the final draft.

Special thanks go to the staffs of the Music Division and the Newspaper and Current Periodicals Division of the Library of Congress, whose familiar, smiling faces and exceptional service were beyond price. Special thanks, too, to the American Antiquarian Society, for the Associateship that enabled me to spend a long, fruitful fall luxuriating in their periodical collections, and to Georgia Barnhill and all the other helpful staff members who have always done more than I had any right to expect. Other libraries that have proven especially helpful are Harvard University's Theatre Collection, Music Library, and Widener Library; the Rare Books Collection at the Boston Public Library; and the Music and Theatre Divisions of the Performing Arts Library of the New York Public Library at Lincoln Center.

In particular I'd like to acknowledge all the anonymous or pseudonymous editors and critics who contributed to newspapers and periodicals between 1785 and 1815, and who supplied such a great part of the raw material for this book. Finally, I gratefully acknowledge the exceptional skills of my own editor, Duke Johns, who often knew better than I did what I wanted to say and how to say it.

The title of this book is taken from an air in Samuel Arnold's *The Son in Law* (1779).

I

THE ESTABLISHMENT OF MUSICAL THEATRE IN AMERICA

A Brief Historical Overview

The first theatrical performances in America were six decades before the American Revolution; a century later, American theatre was fully established along the Eastern seaboard from Maine to Georgia and had made its way westward as far as the Ohio Valley. By the turn of the nineteenth century, theatrical entertainment was available in most communities, and acceptable for most people.

In its early years the theatre served as the most important single place of amusement in American cities. Open three—later, four—nights each week during the season, a well-regulated theatre provided a reliable and reasonably comfortable, if often repetitious, place of entertainment. It provided a never-ending series of revivals of old favorites, with the occasional spice of a new piece or the excitement of a major new production, and it was the best place in town to hear one's favorite songs, which were interpolated before, between, and even during the evening's plays. A city's best professional musicians were almost always to be found at the theatre.

The members of the acting company were like an extended family, each known by name. They were scolded for their misdeeds, welcomed with applause on their first appearance at the beginning of a season or after a long absence, and if deserving, rewarded generously with the profits of a benefit at the end of a guest appearance or a season. Their activities were important enough to be news at a time when there were no social columns or "color sections" in newspapers, and when all the latest international, national, and local news was reported in one or two pages. Not only was news of the marriages, travels, successful benefits, and deaths of favorite actors and actresses reported in local papers, but it would be repeated in papers in other cities.

The theatre was far more than a place of amusement. It served as a gathering place where one might see and be seen, with various sections of the house considered appropriate for one's social class, race, and sex. Young bucks strutted, maidens coquetted, businessmen relaxed, sailors caroused, stagestruck youths critiqued, and society matrons reigned. It was the place to hear the latest news, with important events like the naval victories of the War of 1812 or the peace that ended it announced from the stage. It provided a focal point for community holidays and celebrations such as the Fourth of July or Washington's Birthday. It was the site of mourning at the death of Washington, the rallying point for patriotism, the center of information on Election Day, and the place to see one's favorite celebrities. Presidents' or generals' or naval heroes' attendance at the theatre was often announced in advance, and the populace would throng to share the occasion.

Along with many other niceties and necessities, theatre in early America was imported from England. It altered in response to local events and preferences, but it remained as English as if it had been performed in England, reflecting the interests, tastes, and experiences of the English emigrants who formed the majority of settlers in eighteenth-century America. As late as 1810, Philadelphian Stephen Cullen Carpenter spoke of "the English stage, by which we mean every stage where the English language is spoken."[1]

Music had always been an important part of the tradition of the English playhouse, but in the eighteenth century a process began that enlarged music's role as an adjunct to comedy, tragedy, and pantomime and placed it at the heart of such genres as ballad opera and its successors, English comic opera, melodrama, and musical romance. In contrast to the Italian opera that prevailed at London's opera houses, ballad opera had its beginnings in the playhouse. Italian opera required highly trained musicians and attracted a limited, aristocratic audience in the metropolis of London. Ballad opera in English spread quickly throughout the English provinces, in Ireland, and in America, performed by nearly every thespian in every troupe and finding an audience that came from every stratum of society.

THE COLONIAL PERIOD

Theatre companies performed in America as early as 1716, when the first theatre was built in Williamsburg. The season at the Courtroom in Charleston, South Carolina, in 1735 included both the first pantomime and the first opera known to be performed in America. The pantomime *The Adventures of Harlequin and Scaramouch* was performed there on February 4 as an afterpiece to Thomas Otway's tragedy *The Orphan*. On February 18 the ballad opera *Flora, or Hob in the Well* was presented, with the same pantomime as an afterpiece. Other ballad operas presented in this era of irregular troupes and occasional performances include *The Devil to Pay,* presented in Charleston in 1736; *The Mock Doctor,* New York, 1750; *The Beggar's Opera,* New York, 1750; *Damon and Phillida,* New York, 1751; *The Virgin Unmask'd,* New York, 1751; *Colin and Phoebe,* New York, 1751; and *The Honest Yorkshireman,* New York, 1752.

America's most permanent early theatrical troupe made its first appearance in 1752 at Williamsburg as Hallam's London Company of Comedians. As the American Company, under the management of Lewis Hallam, Sr., and later David Douglass, the troupe continued to present theatrical entertainments from Virginia to New York until the Revolution. (By this time, theatre was already banned in Boston. An act passed in 1750 outlawed "public stage-plays; interludes and other theatrical entertainments" throughout the Commonwealth of Massachusetts; it was enforced until 1793.[2]) Like its English counterparts, Hallam's strolling company performed in makeshift theatres, using whatever ingenuity was needed to present its adaptations of the day's most popular English stage works. The troupe built its first New York theatre on Nassau Street in 1753; other temporary quarters were built in Annapolis, Maryland (1760), and Newport and Providence, Rhode Island (1761). (Rhode Island authorities promptly passed an anti-theatre law that stood, not without evasion, until 1793.)

More permanent structures were built in New York and Philadelphia in the 1760s. The Southwark Theatre in Philadelphia was erected by Douglass's troupe in 1766, and the John Street Theatre in New York in 1767; each served for more than three decades. Thereafter the company performed regularly in New York and in Philadelphia, with occasional forays into Virginia and Maryland. The first season at the Southwark included performances of Thomas A. Arne's *Thomas and Sally* and William Boyce's *The Chaplet,* both all-sung operas, Henry Carey's *The Contrivances,* an all-composed opera in ballad-opera style, and the pantomime *The Witches.* The first season at the John Street included all of the above works plus the pantomime *Harlequin Collector* and the ballad operas *Flora, The Devil to Pay, The Honest Yorkshireman,* and *Damon and Phillida.*[3]

The repertoire was still almost entirely English. During the 1760s popular English operas were performed in America only a year or two after their first London performances. Both Samuel Arnold's pastiche *Maid of the Mill* (1765) and Charles Dibdin's *The Padlock* (1768) were performed in New York in 1769. Americans, too, were becoming interested in writing and composing operas. One opera by an American had already been performed in London.[4] It is quite likely that Americans had prepared new editions of the English operas performed here, and in 1767 an American "comic opera," *The Disappointment; or, The Force of Credulity* by Andrew Barton, was advertised for performance in Philadelphia. The work was actually a ballad opera, typical both in its satirical text and in its use of music. The satire seems to have been too pointed for some prominent Philadelphians; the work was withdrawn before its first performance. Barton was responsible for the text; the name of the arranger of the music was not mentioned. The music included eighteen airs and a dance, ranging in style from "Yankee Doodle" to Arne's "My Fond Shepherds"; the great majority (thirteen) were ballad tunes.[5]

The Continental Congress put an end to playgoing in America on October 24, 1774, when it passed a resolution discouraging "every species of extravagance and dissipation, especially horse-racing, and all kinds of gaming, cock-fighting, exhibition of shows, plays and other expensive diversions and entertainments."[6] This "discouragement" was strengthened further on October 16, 1778:

Whereas frequenting Play Houses and theatrical entertainments, has a fatal tendency to divert the minds of the people from a due attention to the means necessary for the defence of their country and preservation of their liberties: Resolved, that any person holding an office under the United States who shall act, promote, encourage or attend such plays, shall be deemed unworthy to hold such office and shall be accordingly dismissed.[7]

Six months later the Pennsylvania legislature enacted a law prohibiting not only acting but being "in any way concerned [with] any play house, theatre, stage or scaffold for acting, showing or exhibiting any tragedy, comedy or tragicomedy, farce, interlude or any other play or any part of a play whatsoever."[8] The law remained in effect until 1789.

As a result of these laws, legitimate theatre suffered a decade-long hiatus in America. In 1774 the American Company sailed to a season in Charleston, and then into safe exile in Jamaica until the end of the Revolutionary War. The most notable efforts at drama during the war years were those by British soldiers in New York and Philadelphia. These players presented several ballad operas and, in 1780, William Shield's *Flitch of Bacon* (London, 1778); William Dunlap reported that their orchestra (composed of fourteen players from the regimental bands) was better than that of the Old American Company.[9] Their repertory probably included *The Blockheads, or Fortunate Contractor,* a political pastiche published in London in 1782 with the notation "performed in New York."

AFTER THE WAR: TRADITION AND DEVELOPMENT

American theatre began the slow process of reestablishing and enhancing its institutions, personnel, and audiences as the Revolution ended, though theatrical exhibitions were still prohibited in many states and cities. Various small companies began performing again as early as June 1781, when former American Company actor and singer Thomas Llewellyn Wall and his family began performing "A Medley of Theatrical Trifles" or "A Farrago of Theatrical Amusements" at Annapolis and Baltimore. These mixtures of song, recitations, and dramatic scenes were at first presented by Mr. and Mrs. Wall, with singing by Miss Wall, "a child of seven years," accompanied by her father on the mandolin. Performances at the Theatre in Annapolis (apparently a brick structure erected by the American Company in 1771) alternated with performances in the Baltimore area, first at George James L'Argeau's dancing room, then at Mr. Johnson's Sail-Warehouse and Adam Lindsay's Coffee-House, both at Fell's Point. L'Argeau augmented the performances with several airs on the "musical glasses" at his dancing room on June 23. Notations in pen (presumably by Thomas Wall) at the bottom of the bills for the September 18 and 20 Annapolis performances made clear that this was *not* post-revolutionary, or even entirely American, theatre. On September 20, the notice "N.B. A band of Music is provided." was printed on the bill, and Wall added in pen: "N.B. The Band of Music that was provided for this night's performance belong'd to the Regiment of the Count De Chalour [Charlus], who with the French Army were on their March to Virginia, to attack Lord Cornwallis, posted at York Town."[10]

During the fall of 1781, the company was augmented by various amateurs, who were identified by Wall with his penned notations on the bills: Serj^t Morgan of the Artillery, in the Continental Service; Mr.

Bentley, a gentleman who sang for his amusement; several gentlemen who acted for their amusement, including Adam Lindsay (the proprietor of the coffee-house), William Tilyard, Mr. Shakespear (very possibly a pseudonym!), and Dr. Harrison; and "a PERSON who never appeared before on the stage," Lieu[t] Street of the Maryland Line.[11] On January 15, 1782, Thomas Wall and Adam Lindsay and their Maryland Company of Comedians opened the New Theatre in Baltimore for a full season of performances, with a few professional actors gradually augmented by further gentlemen and amateurs. During this season (which lasted until July 9, including benefits), five operas—*The Contrivances, The Honest Yorkshireman, The Padlock, Thomas and Sally,* and *The Devil to Pay*—were performed as afterpieces, a total of eighteen performances.

The revival of regular theatre in America was signaled by the return of the American Company. In 1784 Lewis Hallam, Jr., son of the original manager, brought the remnants of his company back to America, reopening the Southwark Theatre in Philadelphia in December as the Opera House, Southwark, with a series of "lectures," "entertainments," and "concerts" designed to outwit the antitheatre law. Though Edward Moore's tragedy *The Gamester* might be presented as a "Serious and Moral Lecture (in five parts) on the Vice of Gaming," introduced between the parts of a concert, musical pieces were unabashedly introduced as operas, which were presumably considered exempt from the antitheatre law.[12] The company moved to New York in August 1785 and, joined by John Henry and his troupe, reopened the John Street Theatre. Hallam and Henry rechristened their group the Old American Company to distinguish it from the many "young" troupes that appeared after the war, including Dennis Ryan's "American Company," which had succeeded Wall in Baltimore in 1783.

For the next seven years, under Hallam and Henry, the Old American Company enjoyed an "almost complete and uninterrupted monopoly . . . and controlled the amusement field from New York to Annapolis."[13] As antitheatre laws were gradually repealed, a regular circuit including New York, Philadelphia, Baltimore, and Annapolis

was established. Americans from all levels of the new egalitarian society attended the performances; the stage box at the Southwark was
"decorated with suitable emblems for the reception of *President* Washington, whenever he delighted the audience by his presence."[14]

America's colonial era was ended; when theatrical performances resumed in the new nation, however, artistic independence was not yet
secured. Styles in musical theatre had changed in England during the
war, and American theatres made haste to bring themselves into fashion by importing the latest English plays and music. Operas and pantomimes were a regular part of the repertory, and Americans quickly
caught up on recent English comic operas. In that season of 1786,
residents of New York saw Thomas Linley's *The Duenna* (London,
1775) and William Shield's *Rosina* (London, 1782) and *Poor Soldier*
(London, 1783).

American playwrights and composers remained conservative, and
continued to produce pastiches in the latter years of the 1780s. In
general, these works were a means for political or social statements;
the borrowed music served as a vehicle rather than a focus. Royall
Tyler's opera *May Day in Town, or New-York in an Uproar,* with
"Music compiled from the most eminent Masters," was performed on
May 19, 1787.[15] William Hill Brown's *The Better Sort, or The Girl of
Spirit* was published in Boston in 1789, but was not performed until
the twentieth century.[16] William Dunlap produced a sequel to Shield's
Poor Soldier in 1789; this work, *Darby's Return,* was first performed
on November 24 in New York, and owed its success to the perfor-
mance of Thomas Wignell as Darby and to the popularity of the origi-
nal. *The Reconciliation, or The Triumph of Nature,* by Peter Markoe,
was printed in Philadelphia in 1790, and three airs appeared in *The
Universal Asylum and Columbian Magazine* (the first music from an
American opera to be published), but it was not performed.

In the 1790s American opera reached new levels of abundance,
creativity, and performance quality. Antitheatrical laws were repealed
in Philadelphia (1789) and Boston (1793); Charleston had maintained
a brisk theatrical business since 1785. New York, Philadelphia, Bos-

ton, and Charleston were established as major theatrical centers. Roomy, well-equipped theatres were built in all four cities, while competent, efficiently managed resident companies were established in each. These major companies and many smaller troupes toured most of the remaining cities in the United States, building theatres and establishing regular seasons in Baltimore; Washington, D.C.; Richmond, Norfolk, and Petersburg, Virginia; Savannah, Georgia; Hartford, Connecticut; Portsmouth, New Hampshire; Portland, Maine; and Newport and Providence, Rhode Island, before the end of the century. During these years, major American companies became the equals of companies in comparably sized English cities outside London, with similar repertories and facilities.

Philadelphia was the first city to threaten the virtual monopoly of the Old American Company. Thomas Wignell, a comic actor, broke with the company in 1791 in a disagreement over standards and variety of performance. He traveled to England in 1792 and recruited a company of excellent actors and singers. Meanwhile, his partner, composer and harpsichordist Alexander Reinagle, superintended the construction of the New Theatre in Philadelphia. The theatre was ready for occupancy early in 1793, but misunderstandings about the completion date and a yellow fever epidemic kept the company from performing there that year; instead they made their American debut in Annapolis in December 1793. On February 17, 1794, the New Theatre opened with great acclaim, and thus began a great rivalry between the two companies headquartered in New York and Philadelphia. For the next thirty years the Philadelphia company excelled in the presentation of English opera in America. Wignell and Reinagle soon added Baltimore to their circuit and divided their time between those two theatres, with occasional trips to Annapolis and later to Washington, D.C.

The Old American Company had realized its need to improve its acting standards and repertory in order to compete with the new troupe. John Henry therefore traveled to England in 1792, hiring a highly qualified company that included John Hodgkinson, "a host in himself,"[17] who purchased Henry's interest in the company in 1794. The *New York Magazine* reported in the fall of 1794 that the company "was truly formidable—altogether superior to anything the citizens of New York have seen before, and in our opinion, unrivalled by any force upon the continent."[18] The Old American Company ventured once more to Philadelphia in the fall of 1794, while the Wignell-Reinagle company was in Baltimore; they played until December and then closed their Southwark Theatre for the last time.[19] The company thereafter made occasional tours to other cities, but was always identified principally with the John Street and later the Park Street theatres in New York.

Particularly important in Charleston was the Virginia Company of John Bignall and Thomas Wade West, which toured throughout the southern states for a number of years; they built a theatre on Broad Street in 1793. In 1794 a troupe of French refugees occupied the City Theatre on Church Street and presented a few plays, a great many pantomimes, and probably some complete operas in French. In October 1794 the two companies combined, and thereafter the histories of these companies and theatres were intermingled until the end of the century. The Charleston Theatre company dominated the field in that city during the first third of the nineteenth century, often traveling to Richmond, Norfolk, or Savannah.

Boston's first postwar theatre performances were presented by Joseph Harper in defiance of the antitheatre laws. He performed for several months in 1792 before he was arrested and the performances stopped. When the antitheatre laws were repealed by the Massachusetts legislature in 1793, preparations were immediately begun for the construction of a theatre on Federal Street, which opened early in 1794. Charles Stuart Powell's company played there until 1795. When Powell failed financially, the company was taken over by Col. John S. Tyler, who invited Hodgkinson and the Old American Company to play in Boston in the fall of 1795. Since New York was in the midst of a yellow fever epidemic, the company was happy to oblige. In December 1796 Powell opened a second Boston theatre, the Haymarket, in direct competition with the Federal Street company, now managed by J. Brown Williamson. In July 1797 Hodgkinson and a contingent from the New York company opened the Haymarket, and for several years thereafter it was the custom to use the Boston Theatre on Federal Street during the winter season and the Haymarket in the summer. The Boston Theatre burned on January 26, 1798; when it reopened in October, it was leased by Hodgkinson.

William Dunlap joined Hodgkinson in the management of the New York Theatre in 1796 and became sole manager in 1798; with this addition and the completion of New York's Park Theatre in 1798, the major troupes, theatrical centers, and circuits of early American theatre had been established. When John Bernard arrived in America in 1797, he reported:

There were three leading managements at this time in America, conducting three distinct circuits—in the North, South, and centre: that of Hodgkinson and Dunlap, who had succeeded Henry and Hallam, in the direction of what was called the "Old American Company," and whose principal cities were New York and Boston; that of Mons. Solee, whose headquarters was Charleston, but who migrated northward to Newberne and Richmond; and that of Wignell and Reinagle, whose home was Philadelphia, but who also paid visits to Baltimore and Annapolis.[20]

Thereafter, though actors, managers, and support staff changed frequently, the principal theatrical centers themselves remained relatively stable.

The story of American theatre from this point is one of continual expansion. Small troupes continued to push back the frontiers of American theatre, moving down the rivers and over the mountains, north to Canada, southwest to New Orleans, and west to Lexington, Louisville, Cincinnati, and St. Louis.

After the Revolution, every major new work performed in London was imported for performance in the States. Some were brought as printed libretto and score copies; others came in manuscript form or in memory only with immigrants or with American visitors returning from London. Not only did this flood of new materials provide an ever-increasing repertory for the flourishing playhouses, it also provided a boost for the fledgling American music publishing industry. While publishing

of secular music prior to the revolution was slight . . . The opening of the first Congress in 1789 marked the turning point . . . and in this very year secular music publishing took a start in Boston and Philadelphia, while New York became active in 1793.[21]

"Favorite songs" from the operas were published singly or in various collections, and complete librettos were reprinted from London versions, reset in new type and often including phrases like "as performed at the Theatre, New York." A typical ad for librettos appeared in Hartford in 1796:

PLAYS
Just received, and for sale by J. Babcock
a variety of Plays, among which are
. . . the Poor Soldier, the Agreeable Surprize, the Farmer, the Quaker, the Doctor and the Apothecary, the Children in the Wood, Rosina, the Padlock, the Deserter, Lionel and Clarisa, or the School for Fathers, Inkle and Yarico, No Song, No Supper . . . &c.[22]

In the 1790s the first works by non-English playwrights began to be heard in American theatres. French pantomimes, ballets, and operas were performed by (and sometimes for) French immigrants, often refugees from the French Revolution. Translations of works by German playwrights began to form an increasing part of the repertory. Whatever their origin and however they were acquired, a great many musical works were performed in American theatres in the last decade of the century. Sonneck reports that from 1793 to 1800, 128 "musical entertainments, musical dramas, operas, musical farces, ballad operas, speaking pantomimes or ballets" were performed in New York, many of them straight from London. The Philadelphia New Theatre produced 157 musical entertainments from its 1794 opening to 1800;

during the same years the Boston Federal Street Theatre produced 96; the Boston Haymarket produced 62 between 1796 and 1800; in Charleston the various theatres produced 97 from 1793 till 1800.[23] In the next decade, musical theatre works were still more popular; 226 were performed in New York, 235 in Philadelphia, 192 in Boston, and 185 in Charleston.[24]

Most of the theatrical composers of the postwar period were European immigrants: Victor Pelissier from France, Gottlieb Graupner from Germany, Benjamin Carr, Alexander Reinagle, James Hewitt, and Rayner Taylor from England. They provided the accompaniments for the English works imported as piano-vocal scores, and wrote their own works in a similar style. Just as earlier American composers had emulated their English counterparts by producing pastiches and ballad operas, these composers created unified theatrical works with the bulk of the music for each piece "newly composed" by a single musician. No longer described as ballad operas, these works were called musical entertainments, musical dramas, comic operas, or simply operas.

Several comic operas vie for the distinction of being the first composed in America. Elihu Hubbard Smith wrote *Edwin and Angelina; or, The Banditti,* with music by Victor Pelissier, in 1791, though it did not have its first (and only) performance until December 19, 1796. Its principal claim to fame is that it was the "first opera of which all parts are known to have been created in America, and which then came to production."[25] The libretto, adapted from Goldsmith, survives, along with two musical numbers.

An opera on an American subject was *Tammany; or The Indian Chief,* with libretto by Anne Julia Hatton and music by James Hewitt. This was a highly political work that offended some of the audience and even some of the actors with its anti-Federalist message. It was first performed on March 3, 1794, in New York. Both score and libretto are lost, but the words to some of the songs survive, along with music to one song.

William Dunlap's *The Archers: or, the Mountaineers of Switzerland* has sometimes been called the first American opera. It premiered in

New York on April 8, 1796, with music by Benjamin Carr. Though Dunlap's libretto survives complete, the music is lost except for two pieces: "Why Huntress, Why" and a Rondo, which were published separately.[26]

Unfortunately, none of these earliest examples exists with sufficient music to mount a reasonably authentic modern performance, and none achieved great or lasting popularity. *Tammany* received eight performances in three cities; *The Archers* was performed just four times.

One of the first important changes at the turn of the century was the development of a star system. It altered the accepted eighteenth-century concept of the "stock company," with its layers of "first line" and "second line" roles, to one in which the best-qualified actors moved from city to city, engaged for a few days or weeks at a time, skimming the cream not only from the available parts but from the season's profits. Sometimes stars received only a benefit (but within the most desirable and profitable part of the season), sometimes they were given a fixed stipend for a given number of performances, and sometimes they received both. Managers and company members complained, but audiences loved the system, and attendance dropped off when no star was present. This led to the importation of even bigger stars, with the advent of George Frederick Cooke and Joseph Holman, major London celebrities, setting the pattern for the nineteenth century.

When no star was present, managers attempted to capture the public attention with ever more elaborately produced musical pieces. In these early years of the nineteenth century, American opera came increasingly under the influence of the melodrama and the musical romance. Terms like "grand dramatic romance," "grand heroic panto-mimical romance," "historical melodrama," and even "grand opera" were used in an attempt to convey the difference between the new works being performed and the works that had been popular at the end of the eighteenth century. These terms reflected a continually expanding use of spectacular effects, scenery, costumes, and background music.

One such work composed in 1808 has the distinction of being the first American work known to be performed in England after being performed in America. John Bray's *The Indian Princess, or La Belle Sauvage,* an "Operatic MeloDrame" with text by James Nelson Barker, was first performed in Philadelphia in 1808, and premiered in London in 1820.[27]

Another important change at the turn of the century was the increasing trend toward the establishment of second companies in major cities. During the 1790s, the Old American Company and the Wignell-Reinagle company had accepted the fact that they could not compete in each other's territory, and each had established reliable circuits of its own. The Charleston and City theatres quickly joined forces. It took longer for the Haymarket Theatre to fail in Boston, but fail it did, in spite of the political controversy that fueled its existence. Other companies, however, continued to try to establish theatres, such as the short-lived Grove Theatre on Bedlow Street in New York in 1804.

The first successful competition came from the circuses, first established in America in 1792, when Alexander Placide and his troupe of French acrobats, ropedancers, dancers, and pantomimists arrived fresh from Sadler's Wells. Placide and his troupe were quickly integrated into the mainstream of American theatre. In 1793 John William Ricketts built more or less permanent circus facilities in Philadelphia and New York, offering primarily equestrian exhibitions but eventually adding slackrope and tightrope dancing, tumbling, and other feats of agility and strength. Circuses frequently boasted some sort of "band of music," and it was perhaps inevitable that some sort of pantomime entertainment would be added to the circus. In the summer of 1796 Ricketts began presenting pantomimes—usually standard harlequinades—as the closing part of the evening's entertainment. By the second decade of the nineteenth century, this had become fairly standard practice at various circuses, such as Pepin and Breschard's establishments in major cities, and all were equipped with a proscenium stage, constructed on one side of the ring, which could be used not only for pantomimes but for "legitimate" theatre as well. Frequently an evening at the circus included an equestrian exhibition followed by a pantomime or comic opera. Imagine the difficulties of singing in an atmosphere full of the dust and odors of a just-completed horseback show! Assuming that the ring was the standard forty-two feet, the audience was normally separated from the stage by a considerable distance during these musical afterpieces.

The circuses often scheduled their performances during the parts of the year when the theatres were closed, or performed on the nights when the theatres were dark, but eventually the facilities constructed for the circuses helped second companies obtain a toehold in several major cities. Small companies, such as the Theatrical Commonwealth established by disgruntled actors in Philadelphia and New York in 1813–14, or displaced actors, such as those from Charleston during the War of 1812, could rent a circus building, easily convert the ring into a pit by adding seating, and have a rough-and-ready venue for all kinds of theatrical fare.

These second companies usually held on by a shoestring, but while they lasted they often posed a genuine financial threat for the regular houses. Nevertheless, the new theatres served to stress the legitimacy and regularity of the established houses, which by now possessed not only a company of experienced, qualified actors, but also an established orchestra, a full technical support staff, and a supply of stock scenery, costumes, and decorations. New companies found it difficult to compete and tended toward more repetition of standard repertoire. They used the simpler comic operas of the eighteenth century as afterpieces, for example, and only an occasional melodrama or musical romance, with their greater demands for special scenery and costumes. When they did present melodramas or romances, they frequently included battle scenes or processions that could be performed on horseback. The Olympic Theatre, which opened in Philadelphia on January 1, 1812, used the circus building just down the street from the Chestnut Street theatre; various other companies offered a similar mixture of equestrian entertainment, pantomime, musical theatre, and drama. When the Chestnut Street theatre performed the melodrama

Timor the Tartar for the first time in 1813, it stressed its own legitimacy by noting in the bills that there would be no horses (as there had been in the earlier production at the Olympic).[28]

The War of 1812 brought increased American nationalism, but considerable ambivalence persisted about the traditional close ties to Britain that had been reestablished following the Revolution. There was no sudden break of connections with English theatre because of the war, and managers lamented the impediment to the free exchange of actors and repertory. Most of the works performed continued to be imported from England and altered for American performance; others were written in America but based on works popular in France, Germany, or England. In 1814, for example, Rayner Taylor provided new music for a "Grand Romantic Drama" called *The Æthiop*,[29] with text by William Dimond, which had originally been performed at Covent Garden (1812) with music by Henry Rowley Bishop. William Dunlap had regularly borrowed from the works of European dramatists for the librettos of musical works for the New York stage, such as *Count Benyowsky, Pizarro, Wildgoose Chase,* and *The Stranger* (all based on Kotzebue). John Bray, Charles E. Smith, and others continued this trend of providing new translations from German works rather than using those provided by English playwrights. Immigrants of other nationalities, particularly the French, continued to contribute specific works as well as stylistic influences.

In spite of this continuing dependence on European traditions and genius, American theatre had begun to come into its own, with the best available talent devoted to theatrical music. Without question, theatre held a central place in American society, and music held a central place in theatrical entertainment in this post-Revolutionary period. Introduced into all theatrical genres, music also entertained the audience before the performance began, between the acts of the play, and between the various pieces that made up the evening's fare. American performers, writers, composers, and arrangers were vigorously and ardently producing, promoting, and promulgating the music of the American theatre.

2

MUSICAL ENTERTAINMENTS

Genres and Styles

To understand the stylistic elements of English opera and re-lated genres in America, it is essential to trace several important developments on the English stage. English opera developed as a part of the strong tradition of English drama, which in the eighteenth century produced such dramatists as Oliver Goldsmith and Richard Brinsley Sheridan. Not only did opera share its stage—and its performers—with the masterpieces of English drama, but it shared many of its stylistic characteristics as well. The English playgoer expected a variety of entertainment at the playhouse, and any respectable troupe included the instrumentalists (called the musicians or the band) and the singers needed for the musical additions essential to plays of all kinds. The company performed in dramatic works ranging from tragedy to opera; the musicians provided introductory concerts, interludes, appropriate music in the course of the play (marches, dirges, and so on), and accompaniment for vocal numbers.

One of the best sources of information about early theatre is the playbills published in newspapers to advertise performances. These contain information that is available nowhere else about genre, length, casting, added music, sources, and performance practices (figs. 1 and 2).

In many eighteenth- and nineteenth-century theatres, two statues stood above the entrance portico, in the lobby, or over the proscenium—one a representation of Melpomene, muse of tragedy, and the other of Thalia, the comic muse. To players and critics alike, these represented the two principal departments of the drama, hallowed by time and tradition.

Tragedy was undoubtedly considered the more important of the two, presenting timeless tales of larger-than-life figures and designed to inculcate elevated moral lessons. The typical tragedy was in five acts of poetry or blank verse, observing the unities of time, place, and action. The great model for tragedy was Shakespeare. Although the versions of Shakespeare's plays that appeared in eighteenth- and early nineteenth-century theatres had been considerably pruned, and were dressed up with music, processions, and other trappings to make them more palatable to the general public, they still represented a body of literature that offered wide range for the actor's finest talents, the critic's deepest consideration and analysis, and the aspiring playwright's sincerest imitation. The star players chose tragedy to exhibit their talents, and the chief tragedian was the most important player in the company.

Second in the theatrical hierarchy were the comedies, which "held the mirror up to nature" by means of wit and satire, exposing and punishing vice and rewarding virtue. Shakespeare was sometimes held up as the model for comedy, too, but such eighteenth-century masterpieces as Goldsmith's *She Stoops to Conquer,* Farquhar's *The Beaux' Stratagem,* and Sheridan's *The School for Scandal* were the real measuring sticks for later comedies. Their plots and characters were endlessly imitated, though some of the language in such early eighteenth-century comedies was considered too bawdy for the sensibilities of later audiences. Music was also an important part of most performances of comedy, either because it was written into the play or because it was added in representation.

Figure 1. Playbill, *Aurora. General Advertiser*, Philadelphia, March 1, 1811. Courtesy American Antiquarian Society.

Boston Theatre.

MR. DICKSON's BENEFIT.

This Evening, April 19th, 1813,
WILL BE PRESENTED,
for this night only, Pilon's much admired Comedy, in 5 acts, called,

He would be a Soldier.

Sir Oliver, Oldstock,	Mr. Dickson
Captain Crevelt,	Mr. Young
Count Pierpoint,	Mr. Spiller
Wilkins,	Mr. Allen
Caleb, (with a Song)	Mr. Entwisle
Mandeville,	Mr. Clarke
Johnson,	Mr. Johnson
Colonel Talbot,	Mr. Drake
Amber,	Mr. Powell
Charlotte,	Mrs. Young
Harriet,	Miss Dellinger
Lady Oldstock,	Mrs. Barnes
Mrs. Wilkins,	Mrs. Drake
Betty,	Mrs. Mills
Nancy,	Mrs. Wheatley

After the Play, will be presented, for the first time in Boston, a celebrated Serio, Comic, Burlesque Opera, in two acts, called,

HAMLET TRAVESTIE.

Altered, corrected and revised from the Original MS. precisely as it is acted at the Royalty Theatre, &c.

Hamlet, Prince of Denmark, Mr. Entwisle
[with a variety of Songs, Duets, &c.]
Claudius, King of Denmark, Mr. Drake
Polonius, { Chamberlain to the King, & a very good sort old gentleman, } Mr. Young
Horatio, Friend to Prince Hamlet, Mr. Spiller
[with a very serious Song, to the air of "Thimble's Scolding Wife."]
Laertes, Brother to Ophelia, Mr. Allen
Rosencrantz, { Courtiers, } Mr. Clarke
Guildenstern, Mr. Henry
Ostric, Bottle holder to Hamlet, Mr. A. Drake
Marcellus, Second to Laertes, Mr. Johnson
Ghost. of Hamlet's Father, Mr. Dickson
[with a very pathetic Song, to the tune of "Giles Scroggin's Ghost."]
Gertrude, Queen of Denmark, Mrs. Barnes
Ophelia, in love with Hamlet, Miss Dellinger
[with a serious Song; A Duo Amoroso, and a number of Mad Songs.]
IN SCENE LAST,
A Grand Sparring Match between Hamlet & Laertes.
and the Piece concludes with
The Death of Hamlet, Laertes, and their Royal Majesties of Denmark.

To which will be added, for the 2d time in Boston, a favorite Piece, in one act, called,

America, Commerce and Freedom !

Genius of Columbia, Mrs. Powell
Liberty, Miss Dellinger | Commerce, Mrs. Spiller
In the course of the Entertainment,
A New Patriotic Song, by Miss Dellinger.
A Sailors Hornpipe, by Miss Worrall.
Also, will be Exhibited,

Four Grand Transparent Paintings,
Representing the Engagement between the
Constitution & Guerriere, United States & Macedonian,
Wasp & Frolic, Constitution & Java.
SCENE LAST,
Nearly the whole extent of the Stage is laid under Real Water; the Scene will represent a Magnificent Temple; through which is seen CASCADES OF REAL WATER.—A Display of Brilliant Artificial Fire, representing, A shower of Golden Rain, which falls into the Water. The whole Scene backed by A Splendid Illuminated Temple.

⁎ Mr. & Miss WORRALL's Benefit will be on Wednesday next.—Places may be taken of Mr. Stevenson, This Day, at the usual hours at the Box Office of the Theatre.

Doors opened at 6, and Curtain rises at 7 precisely.

☞ Hamlet Travestie is for sale at GREENLEAF's Bookstore, 49, Cornhill.
April 19.

Figure 2. Playbill, *Boston Gazette*, April 19, 1813. Courtesy American Antiquarian Society.

The third line of the drama was opera, or "our English opera." This term was used to encompass anything that had music as its focus, with the plot frequently doing no more than providing an excuse for a series of musical numbers. "Opera" thus included everything from the old ballad operas to the unified works of such composers as Samuel Arnold, Stephen Storace, Thomas Attwood, Matthew Peter King, John Braham, Victor Pelissier, and Benjamin Carr. Though the term "comic opera" was used in a very general way to describe these works, their plots were sentimental as often as they were funny. They were also expected to communicate a moral lesson of some sort, with vice exposed and virtue rewarded. The lower place occupied by operas in the English eighteenth-century theatrical hierarchy was undoubtedly due to the word-centered nature of the theatrical tradition, and may also have been affected by the relative lack of tradition and precedence for English opera, by the shorter length of the operas, by their comparative lack of literary quality, and by their usual position as afterpieces to accompany the performance of a tragedy or comedy. The ability of music to relieve weariness, soothe the passions, and delight the heart added to the presumed moral value of opera.[1]

The typical theatrical critic would concentrate on the "main piece" of the evening's entertainment—tragedy, comedy, or an occasional full-length opera—reserving his best and longest-winded efforts for analysis of the text of the tragedy and every nuance of its performance. Any leftover space would be devoted to criticism of the afterpiece—the one- to three-act comedy or opera performed as the farce. Even lower in the hierarchy were the pantomimes and ballets, added generously to bills and loved by the masses but considered beneath the notice of "enlightened" audiences and critics. For the English censor these were not even considered genuine plays; to the literary-minded critic they were nothing at all.

By the end of the century this clear hierarchy had been obscured and the genres blurred by the development of sentimental comedy, dramatic romance, musical romance, and melodrama, which disdained to observe the boundaries of the traditional genres. English and American critics blamed this apparent deterioration of English drama on insidious foreign influences, such as the French *comédie larmoyante* (crying comedy) and the "immoral" German plays of Kotzebue and Schiller. These "modern comedies" were immensely popular with audiences, but the critics were scathing in their condemnation of "sentimental" plays that ignored all the rules of dramatic procedure: these works dealt with the misfortunes and foibles of common people instead of the tragic fate of heroes; they allowed sinners to be forgiven instead of punished; they ignored the unities and allowed rambling, complicated plots with multiple story lines; and they incorporated elements of tragedy, comedy, opera, and even the scorned ballet and pantomime into a thoughtless, sensuous hodgepodge. Music occupied an increasingly prominent place in these works, providing the ideal means of expressing the feelings and sentiments that were beyond the power of "mere words"—an idea that, if articulated, would have been even more outrageous to the contemporary critic. Perhaps another reason the critics were alarmed by these melodramas and romances was that they were increasingly found as the main piece of the evening instead of being relegated to the position of afterpiece. Thus they directly usurped the position of the tragedy or comedy in five acts that (at least for the critics) had formed the backbone of the English theatrical tradition.

The idea that theatre might aim simply to amuse or entertain was quite foreign to many a high-minded critic. It was stressed repeatedly that theatre was intended to educate, to introduce moral lessons, to serve as a mirror for society. Critics frequently found themselves at odds with audiences, and castigated them for a lack of idealism and taste, lamenting the fact that the public preferred spectacle, sentiment, and music to reason and nature. The term "musical entertainment" was frequently used by contemporary writers to describe all the various types of musical works presented at the playhouse, and may serve as the best guideline to what post-Revolutionary American or English audiences expected at the theatre.

English composers and historians have long apologized for the dearth of native music in the eighteenth and early nineteenth centuries. Joseph Addison complained in 1711 that "our English Musick is quite rooted out";[2] other writers expressed similar opinions. Dramatic music that could be considered "English Musick" was a product not of the opera house but of the playhouse. Richard Graves writes:

> The second half of the eighteenth century is a far from glorious period in the history of English music. Indeed, English music had almost ceased to exist. . . . It is only in the realm of light opera that any attempt at all seems to have been made to preserve something of an "English" style.[3]

During much of the eighteenth century, operatic life in England was dominated by Italian styles, first in performances at the opera house, then in borrowings for musical theatre. The Italian influence continued into the nineteenth century with the first grand opera performances in the United States. In the latter part of the eighteenth century, London composers came under the influence of the Viennese style: Haydn attended—and enjoyed—English opera at the playhouse, and members of the theatre orchestra played in his London concerts. One of England's finest composers of comic operas, Stephen Storace, studied with Mozart in Vienna. It is not surprising, then, to find many parallels in librettos, characterization, and musical techniques between late eighteenth-century English comic operas and the comic operas of the Viennese school. As the nineteenth century began, French and German influences became dominant, with English and American playwrights translating the plays of Pixérécourt, Schiller, and Kotzebue. All these trends were integrated into the predominantly English style that continued to mold standard shapes and genres.

One of the unchanging characteristics of the English style was the mixture of music with spoken dialogue. Since the genres produced in English playhouses were thus neither pure drama nor pure opera, they were condemned by contemporary critics from both camps. This dichotomy has persisted into the twentieth century, when musicologists and critics have often looked with skepticism on the music of the theatre. Donald Grout considered ballad opera an aberration, virtually ignoring all the genres that grew out of it simply because they were not "serious" but "popular":

> In a century which, to speak mildly, was not the Golden Age of British music, the ballad opera appeared as a vigorous but solitary gesture of revolt against foreign musical domination; but it lacked the principle of growth within itself, nor did external conditions favor the rise of an independent serious national opera on the basis of the popular comic-opera style.[4]

Critics still tend to draw the division between the opera house and its serious forms and the playhouse and its popular musical comedy; and musical theatre, with all its innovation, vigor, and contemporary relevance, is still considered to be a musical stepchild compromised by its theatrical parentage.

It is important, then, that we examine English and American theatre music at the turn of the nineteenth century for what it is, rather than criticizing it for what it is not. It is no more reasonable to criticize *Children in the Wood* for not being *Die Zauberflöte* than it is to criticize *West Side Story* for not being *Wozzeck*. Nor is it reasonable to expect *The Iron Chest* to "grow toward" an English *Tristan* or *Aida* (although it is not unreasonable to look for links to Gilbert and Sullivan).

Many different terms have been used to describe the dizzying variety of genres prevalent in English theatre at the turn of the nineteenth century. Thomas Holcroft included tragedy, comedy, mysteries, moralities, masques, intermèdes, interludes, comic operas, farces, speaking pantomimes, plays or serious dramas, ballets, dumb pantomimes, and spectacles in his list of genres.[5] John Durang divided his list of the repertory performed by his troupe in Pennsylvania and Maryland into the following categories: plays, operas, romance burlettas, farces, interludes of one act, ballettes, dances, pantomimes, transparencies, and "other entertainments consisting of scenery and machinery."[6]

In a general way, all the English operas and musical entertainments of the eighteenth and early nineteenth centuries may be said to share the following characteristics:

(*a*) The dialogue is spoken, usually in prose.

(*b*) The topics are familiar ones from everyday life; they are frequently romanticized, sentimentalized, or exaggerated, and often contain stereotyped situations and characters.

(*c*) The opera sometimes begins with a prologue, almost always includes an overture, and usually has several acts, with several scenes to an act. Its length depends upon its function, either as the evening's main piece or as the afterpiece.

(*d*) The solo song is the focal point of the vocal music, although choruses are occasionally used, and ensembles of soloists are frequently found.

(*e*) The songs vary widely in number, form, and style. An almost invariable element is the use of borrowed material (melodies or entire settings) from other sources such as traditional or popular tunes or other operas. The extent and type of this borrowed material helps to identify several distinct types of eighteenth-century comic opera and to trace the development of the genre.

BALLAD OPERA AND PASTICHE

The term "ballad opera," sometimes erroneously applied to all eighteenth-century English opera, actually refers to a specific form used for only a few years in the second quarter of the century. W. J. Lawrence provided a concise definition:

Broadly speaking, "ballad opera," together with its variant, "ballad-farce" (the term usually employed when the entertainment was in single-act form), signified a play of a humorous, satirical or pastoral order intermixed with simple song, the music for which was for the most part derived from popular ditties of the street-ballad type.[7]

In this context, the term "ballad" may be defined as "a simple popular song which can be given length only by strophic repetition and which owes nothing to orchestral elaboration."[8]

English opera's meteoric rise in popularity in the early eighteenth century owed much to the success of John Gay's *The Beggar's Opera* (1728), which, at least temporarily, threatened the dominance of foreign opera in London. Dialogue was spoken throughout in English. Its sixty-nine songs were set to well-known tunes of the day, the great majority of them ballad tunes, with the simplest of accompaniments provided by Dr. John Christopher Pepusch. Violins doubled the voice; viola and cello played the bass part, and the middle was probably filled only by a harpsichord. These short, familiar, strophic tunes and easily grasped words were in marked contrast to the complex arias of Italian opera.

The plot was a direct slap at Italian opera: it rejected royal or mythological personages, and substituted the lowest characters of the London gutters—pickpockets and highwaymen, fences, beggars, and whores. The two most famous sopranos of Italian opera (Faustina Bordoni and Francesca Cuzzoni) were satirized in the explicitly equal parts and bickering of the hero's two "wives." Even the ridiculously out-of-place happy ending parodied the equally absurd plot resolutions of Italian opera.

Ballad opera was a tremendous but short-lived success. "The active period of ballad opera lasted no more than nine or ten years (one might almost say five) . . ."[9] The seeds of its own destruction were contained in its reuse of common themes and settings and its repetition of familiar tunes, and it soon wore out its welcome. Roger Fiske has located forty-one ballad operas published with airs during the first eight seasons, and at least as many others that were published without music.[10] Thereafter new ballad operas were a rarity, though *The Beggar's Opera, Flora, or Hob in the Well* (1729), *The Devil to Pay* (1731), *The Mock Doctor* (1732), *The Virgin Unmask'd* (1735), and *The Honest Yorkshireman* (1735) continued to be performed in some form throughout the century. The works had obviously fallen out of style, however, and theatrical managers seemed at a loss to describe them. By the end of the century, the term "ballad opera" was no longer used. When *The Beggar's Opera* was performed by the Old American

Company at Philadelphia in 1794, it was "altered, revised, and corrected" and called a "musical satire."[11] In Boston in 1796, it was called a "satiric piece" and cut to an afterpiece of two acts.[12] When a new edition of *The Beggar's Opera* ("as performed at the Theatre-Royal, Drury-Lane") was published in London in 1791, the work was given the current nomenclature: "comic opera."

Beginning with Isaac Bickerstaffe's *Love in a Village* in 1762, English comic opera had evolved another clearly distinguishable type: the pastiche. Composers had tired of limiting their choice of music to strophic ballads, and increasingly used other sources as well, resulting in what has been called a "hodgepodge" or a "patchwork" of music and plot.[13] Thomas A. Arne provided the musical setting for Bickerstaffe's libretto; in his dedication he claimed that

the music is more pleasing that has hitherto appeared in compositions of this kind; and the words better adapted, considering the nature of the airs, which are not common ballads, than could be expected, supposing any degree of poetry to have been preserved in the versification.[14]

Pastiche opera differed from ballad opera in its use of a wider variety of music, usually by named English composers; in the way in which that music was selected; and in its use of the orchestra for a more elaborate accompaniment. Both *The Beggar's Opera* and *Love in a Village* are dramas interspersed with songs, and the songs are mostly borrowed. In ballad opera, however, new words were written to already popular tunes (and the associations with those tunes and the implications of their original texts were often important to the effectiveness of the song). In pastiche opera, tunes were selected because they suited the poetry of the libretto, both rhythmically and stylistically, and usually retained no reference to their original sources. For example, in *The Beggar's Opera* the tune most often associated with the ballad "Children in the Wood" is sung by Polly, whose opening words, "O ponder well," quote the opening words of the ballad—a fact her audience would immediately have recognized. When Arne borrowed tunes for *Love in a Village*, however, they retained no reference to their original text or context; six of the songs, in fact, were originally in Italian, and one was borrowed from a concerto grosso.

Of the forty-two musical numbers in *Love in a Village*, only five are based on traditional Irish or English ballads. All these ballads are sung by servants or introduced as "an old tune." The implication seems to be that these songs are out of style. Seven songs had new music, six of them by Arne. The remainder of the music was borrowed from a number of sources—twelve of the borrowed items were also by Arne; the others were from Handel, William Boyce, Samuel Howard, Joseph Baildon, Henry Carey, John Weldon, Girolamo Abos, Domenico Paradies, Baldassare Galuppi, Felice de Giardini and perhaps even one tune by King George III.[15]

Another important difference between ballad opera and pastiche can be seen in the surviving full score of *Love in a Village*. The ballads are scored for two violins and bass, a standard ballad opera scoring; the violins normally follow the vocal line. The first four bars usually serve as an introduction and the last two as a postlude. A much more elaborate orchestration, however, is used in some of the pieces borrowed from other operas and from oratorios, with considerably more independence in the strings. Of the forty-one songs in the manuscript full score, "six are for full orchestra of oboes (or flutes), bassoons, horns and strings, and fifteen others demand wind[s] as well as strings. Just under half are for strings alone."[16]

Even during the 1760s when pastiche operas were in vogue, there were several operas with music written by a single composer. One example from this decade is Arne's *The Guardian Outwitted* (1764).[17] With another one-composer comic opera, Charles Dibdin's *The Padlock* (1768), several important characteristics of late eighteenth-century comic opera appear: the songs usually contribute to plot advancement, and the finales offer opportunities for some action. This little afterpiece did not represent a trend, however. Dibdin himself returned to other techniques, and not until the 1790s did these characteristics become standard operatic practice.

Among the important pastiche operas of the 1760s were three with librettos by Isaac Bickerstaffe: Samuel Arnold provided music for *Maid of the Mill* (1765), and Charles Dibdin for *Love in the City* (1767) and *Lionel and Clarissa* (1768). These operas used no ballad tunes, and borrowed a higher percentage of the music from contemporary opera than had Arne. All featured an extended finale. Of the thirty-eight musical items in Arnold's *Maid of the Mill*, six were new; four were by Arnold. About two-thirds of the borrowings were from Italian opera. Arnold himself wrote the finales to acts 1 and 2, then borrowed the finale for act 3 from Philidor.[18]

THE ONE-COMPOSER COMIC OPERA

By the final decade of the eighteenth century, the one-composer opera was standard, with far more of the musical material created for the specific entertainment in which it is found. The turn-of-the-century comic operas had reversed the proportion of borrowed materials found in such mid-century works as *Love in a Village*. There were few traditional songs, though one or two, especially Scotch tunes, appeared in most English operas in the last quarter of the century. These were given a full orchestration in the light, clean-textured, consonant *galant* style. Although borrowing, acknowledged or not, was still common, only a small number of borrowed songs were likely to be found in any opera, and many of these came from other operas by the same composer. Increasingly, the music was used to advance the action of the opera, and the ensembles gained in weight and in their relationship to the plot.

Contemporary sources used a variety of designations for these mature English operas. The most widely used, by far, was the term "comic opera," though the same works were also called "musical entertainments," "musical farces," "musical dramas," "plays interspersed with songs," or simply "operas." They were never called "ballad operas" in contemporary scores or in playbills.[19]

Though the terminology applied to the form was loose, we can differentiate between two distinct types determined by function: the full-length opera and the afterpiece. The full-length opera served as an evening's main attraction. It was usually in three acts and had as many as thirty or forty songs. The afterpiece, a shorter play or musical work, followed the main theatrical fare of the evening. It was almost always light in plot and had only one or two acts, with correspondingly fewer musical numbers. The afterpiece was frequently called a "farce"; the term used in this sense had no plot implications. Sometimes full-length operas were shortened from three acts to two so they could be played as afterpieces, or from two acts to one for use as interludes. The term "musical farce" does not always indicate that changes were made to a work, but simply that the work was to be the second on the bill.

The diversity of nomenclature can be clearly illustrated by following two works, both with music by Samuel Arnold and first performed in 1793, through their various performances in the United States until 1810. Thomas Morton's *Children in the Wood* was written as a two-act afterpiece, and was published or advertised variously as a comic opera, a musical entertainment, an entertainment, a musical piece, a musical drama, a musical farce, and a farce. George Colman's *The Mountaineers* was sometimes performed with its original five acts and sometimes shortened to three. It was called a comic opera, a musical entertainment, a dramatic entertainment, a dramatic piece, a play interspersed with songs, an opera, and a drama. These designations tended to become more imaginative near the end of a season, as individual performers tried to dress up old favorites to attract crowds for their benefit nights.

Eighteenth-century English opera plots had a great deal in common with those of standard five-act comedies. Both dealt with light comic situations in a way perhaps comparable to the formulas of modern television situation comedies. Often a potentially disastrous situation was developed with wit and sophistication to a happy (if sometimes farfetched) ending. These stereotyped situations included the use of disguises and mistaken identities, romances foiled by misunderstanding, confrontations between villains and heroes, plot twists based on social position or custom, complications based on human foibles and frailties, and victories for the common people.

The artificial manners of eighteenth-century society were often reflected in the brittle, stylized reactions of the characters. In spite of the emphasis on nature that was a strong influence in the late eighteenth and early nineteenth centuries, the stock characters and situations of many of these comedies continued to reflect the attitudes of eighteenth-century society. Such artificial conventions as the perfectly obvious aside were an accepted part of the style.

The democratic tendencies of the eighteenth and early nineteenth centuries were also reflected in these comedies, not only in topical operas such as *The Launch; or Huzzah for the Constitution* (Boston, 1797) and pantomimes such as *Demolition of the Bastille* (New York, 1795) and *American Independence* (Charleston, 1795), but in the many situations in which the servants outwit their masters (as does the servant hero of *Children in the Wood*), and in the continual use of an idealized "common folk" in opera plots (i.e., in the many pastoral operas, including *Love in a Village* and William Shield's *Rosina*, 1782).

One important aspect of comedy and opera in this period reflected perhaps both the urgings to copy nature and of the general spirit of democracy and social consciousness: this was the growing sentimentalism that eventually replaced the biting satire and "careless aloofness from life"[20] which had been typical of English comedy since the Restoration. This tempering of wit with sentiment led to a more sympathetic treatment of stock characters. For example, the hero of *Children in the Wood* is a stereotypical clownish servant, but we feel sympathetic toward him as he fights to overcome his fear of his master and his own ineptitude in order to save the lives of the children. The character, in the hands of a capable actor, can be fleshed out with humanity and believability. Sentimentalism

invited the spectator to come up again on to the stage, and to recognize in the *dramatis personae* his brothers and sisters—people confronted by the same problems as himself, paralysed by the same weaknesses, redeemed by the same generosities . . . [21]

These sentimental operas were a hybrid, not really comedy and certainly not tragedy. They were often compared to the French *comédie larmoyante,* or crying comedy, which "presents us a Thalia, neither tittering, nor sneering, but 'Like Niobe—*all in tears.*' "[22] Nonetheless, the sentimental operas almost always found their way to a happy ending.

THE MUSICAL ROMANCE

As the nineteenth century began, the term "romance" was increasingly found in titles given to musical entertainments, clearly reflecting the romanticism that gained dominance as the eighteenth century ended and the nineteenth began. Speaking of the works of George Colman, Jr., George C. D. Odell wrote in 1927:

A special genre affected by this author, perhaps brought to perfection by him, consisted of a sort of Gothic-melodramatic main plot, with necessary comic relief, the whole interspersed with songs and choruses. Especially were the choristers likely to be bandits.[23]

Like Grétry's *Richard Coeur-de-Lion* (1784), Beethoven's *Fidelio* (1805), and other "rescue operas" of the European art music tradition, these grand dramatic romances frequently featured a principal character who was rescued from some sort of "durance vile" by other principal characters in the drama.[24] Emulating German dramatist August von Kotzebue, the librettists essayed a high moral tone and often included elements of social protest. Time after time, in such entertainments as *The Pirates* (1792), *The Cherokee* (1794), and *Blue Beard* (1798), the hero arrives to save his companions or the heroine from exotic and deviant situations.

Like the Gothic novels of Ann Radcliffe and the novels and plays of Matthew G. ("Monk") Lewis, these works included supernatural events and scenes of horror worthy of such later German works as Weber's *Der Freischütz* (1821). Gothic elements included the ghosts, dungeons, and dim, flickering lights found in *The Haunted Tower* (1789) and *The Castle Spectre* (1797), and the robbers featured in the American works *Edwin and Angelina; or the Banditti* (1796) and *Rudolph; or the Robbers of Calabria* (1807).

The characters and settings for these entertainments were often exotic, reflecting the current European interest in distant places and their importance in shaping events. The pirates of the Mediterranean offered continual grist for the plot mill, with sultans, "Mohametans," spahis, corsairs, and hapless heroines held in harems appearing continually in poetry, novels, and plays as well as in musical pieces. Interest in a poeticized medieval past led to portrayals of knights and ladies, castles and kings. Like the Italian composers of the early nineteenth century, English playwrights found inspiration in Sir Walter Scott; *The Lady of the Lake* found her way into myriad musical settings in both languages and styles.

Although musically these romances retained the forms and styles of the comic opera (with perhaps more Sturm und Drang in the use of sharp dynamic contrasts and expressive dissonances), the plots brought opera ever closer to the spirit of the contemporary melodrama (q.v.); in fact the boundary is so blurred that frequently a work described as a romance is actually a melodrama and vice versa. The following exegesis of romanticism could describe either the typical librettist at the turn of the nineteenth century, or his hero:

The clearest and most colorful traits of the romanticist are his loving and longing looks into the past and into the future, his delight in rosy recollections and fervid hopes, his easy and fanciful dreams of distant place and distant clime, and his preoccupation with the curious, the strange, and the mysterious. His revolutionary spirit prefers to act on faith, to trust the inner experiences of life, to follow the sentimental longings of his heart. He distrusts the strictures and painful rigidities of reasoned behavior. Inherited laws and customs, rules of conduct for life and art, and the barriers which would bind, encompass, and confine him to an earth-bound and prosaic existence fall before his insurgent protests. But vigorous as his insurgent rebellions may and do become, he remains a common man, tenderhearted and sentimental in his expansive love for his fellows and in his unshakable belief in a glorious future.[25]

Contemporary critics were scathing in their condemnation of romances as inferior to the works of the immortal Shakespeare. The plays of William Dimond were dismissed because there was "no distinction of character, the personages all speak the same language, which is neither poetry nor prose; and they all talk sentiment, whether princes, robbers, or clowns."[26] Dimond's *Foundling of the Forest* was, figuratively, a drug, "mixed up with a *quantum sufficit* of horror, and all the tenterhook interest, hairbreadth escapes, and incident so forced as to stagger belief, which make up the hotchpotch romances whether narrative or dramatic of the present day," and was recommended for "those who can be interested or affected by the marvellous and mysterious, and who love to step for amusement out of the precincts of nature, and the conduct of 'the folks of the world.'"[27] Stephen Cullen Carpenter articulated the feelings of many such critics when he wrote:

It were to be wished that, without violating the rights of the people, some legal power could be erected to prevent the representation of stupid plays. . . . The present year [1811] is likely to be more than ordinarily prolific of this TRASH, this murderer-drama trash.—Before us lies a list of plays—such trash! Were the bones of Shakspeare yet sticking together, his skeleton would turn in its coffin at the bare mention of them. . . . Of all plots there are none more vile than what may be called the *novel-plots,* the nature and manners of a circulating library. . . . Humour attaches to character; situation belongs properly to farce and caricature."[28]

Both musical romances and melodramas were condemned as "Anglo-German plays" regardless of their origin. Many, such as Dunlap's *Abaellino* and *Wild Goose Chase,* were translations of German plays; others simply shared many of their characteristics. These plays offended the critics because they refused to fit into the standard genres or follow the traditional rules. As Goldsmith had earlier railed against the introduction of sentimental comedy, so early nineteenth-century writers belittled the "play" as a bastard child, neither tragedy nor comedy, and not truly opera either. This resentment, perhaps exacerbated by suspicions engendered by Kotzebue's politics, led to the vilification of German plays, romances, and melodramas as immoral and licentious:

It has been considered a maxim in dramatic writing that every play should be written for some express moral purpose . . . The introduction of german plays on the English stage is a direct infringement of this principle; inasmuch as their stories are generally founded on some crime committed, which for the good of society ought never to be forgiven, but which the catastrophe seldom fails to extenuate.[29]

This opposition to "German plays" was summed up by George Colman the younger:

> To lull the soul by spurious strokes of art,
> To warp the genius and mislead the heart;
> To make mankind revere wives gone astray,
> Love pious sons, who rob on the highway;
> For this the FOREIGN MUSES trod our stage,
> Commanding *German schools* to be the *rage*,
> Hail to such schools! Oh fine *false feeling*, hail!
> Thou bad'st *Non Natural Nature* to prevail . . . [30]

Further suspicion was cast on the legitimacy of musical romances because of the centrality of the arts of the scene painter, the costumer, and the machinist. The words "spectacle" and "extravaganza" were frequently used in the bills describing their glories. In reading the librettos of such works today, it is impossible to judge the effect of these works upon early nineteenth-century audiences without considering the "magnificent scenery, the brilliant decorations, the music, the singing, the dancing, and the thousand other fascinations which that dialogue served to introduce."[31] Although generally opposed to German plays and melodramas, Carpenter believed that Matthew G. Lewis's *Timor the Tartar* was somewhat redeemed—even from its equestrian excesses—by the "interesting scenes, animated action, and magnificent decorations, heightened by genuine harmony" provided by the "beauty and grandeur" of Matthew P. King's music.[32]

Occasionally a writer came to the defense of the German plays. In 1810 "Dramaticus" wrote to Carpenter's *Mirror of Taste and Dramatic Censor* to defend plays translated from the German. He felt that the German plays had

Strong bold sentiment—incidents numerous and interesting—a dramatic personae of the boldest and most finished kind—and in fact every thing that can command the most marked and pointed attention of the reader or spectator. And all this notwithstanding the disadvantages of appearing in foreign dress; for it hardly need be stated how wretchedly many of the translations have been executed.[33]

In spite of all reservations, Carpenter grudgingly faced reality when he wrote:

All that can be said in favour of this whole class of compositions is that the authors write and make money by them; that the people are pleased to receive them; and that the critic must take them as they come, whether he will or no.[34]

PANTOMIME AND BALLET

Pantomimes were frequently used as afterpieces or as interval pieces in the late eighteenth and early nineteenth centuries. Often an evening's bill included not only a play or opera, and an afterpiece or farce, but a pantomime as well. Occasionally full-length pantomimes were presented, and fairy-tale pantomimes such as *Cinderella* and *Mother Goose* became popular early in the nineteenth century, particularly during the festive post-Christmas season.

The same composers wrote both operas and pantomimes, and both were presented by the same personnel. John Hodgkinson, for example, appeared in pantomimes as well as in tragedy, opera, and comedy throughout his distinguished career as actor and manager, performing all the leaps and magical transformations characteristic of the role of Harlequin.

John Weaver provided a description of an early pantomime in the preface to *The Loves of Mars and Venus* (1717):

these Mimes and Pantomimes were Dances that represented a Story or Fable in Motion and Measure: They were Imitators of all things, as the name of Pantomime imports, and perform'd all by Gesture and the Action of the Hands, Fingers, Legs, and Feet, without making use of the Tongue. The Face or Countenance had a large Share in this Performance, and they imitated the Manners, Passions, and Affections by the numerous Variety of Gesticulations . . . for Nature assigns each Motion of the Mind its proper Gesticulation and Countenance.[35]

Pantomimes were generally without spoken dialogue until about 1780; thereafter some speaking pantomimes appeared. The music was continuous, and often included songs, recitatives, and ensembles as well as the orchestral music used for the miming. Dramatically conceived music was important for the orchestral sections, since they helped to elaborate the plot; in fact, this orchestral music was far more dramatic than in most operas of the period.

Acrobatics and dance were important elements of the miming. By the turn of the century, dance was so vital a part of the pantomime that the terms "ballet" and "pantomime" were sometimes used interchangeably to describe the same works, or hyphenated as "ballet-pantomime" or "pantomime-ballet."

Pantomime plots were frequently mythological or supernatural. Many pantomimes were harlequinades as well; Harlequins filled every leading role from Apollo to Faust and appeared in every conceivable situation. (In Baltimore, a pantomime entertainment presented in 1783 was entitled *Columbus, or Discovery of America, with Harle-*

Figure 3. John Durang in the character of Harlequin. Historical Society of York County, Pennsylvania.

quin's Revels.)[36] Harlequin was a clown and a magician, and magical transformations and metamorphoses were an important part of every pantomime (fig. 3). At the end of the pantomime, Harlequin won the heart of the leading lady, Columbine. Other stock characters were her old father, Pantaloon, and his unnamed clownish servant.

Though French commedia dell'arte and its characters had some-

times been seen in London in the seventeenth century, English pantomime was not well established until the first quarter of the eighteenth
century. Both Lincoln's Inn Fields and Drury Lane added pantomimes
to their repertories in the 1710s, but no pantomime music survived
until 1723. Perhaps the most important pantomime of that year was
The Necromancer, or Harlequin Dr. Faustus, produced at Lincoln's
Inn Fields by John Rich, who played Harlequin.[37] The pantomimes
were essential at the minor theatres, which were limited by law to
musical and pantomimic shows.

Those who arranged the pantomimes—like Alexander Placide, J. K.
Labottierre, and William Francis—were given credit in the bills as
"composers" or "directors," or it was noted whom the ballet was "got
up by." Any term is inadequate to describe the labors of a man—or
occasionally woman or child—who chose or devised the "fable," selected the music, choreographed the movements and the dance, supervised the necessary costumes, scenery, and machinery, and usually performed a leading role. (The term "arranger" used in appendix A is
certainly deficient, but is, I hope, vague enough not to be limiting.)

In time, the "dancing, machinery, scenery and dresses" became
the most important elements of the pantomime.[38] Quick scene changes
were an important part of the transformations, as well as trick scenery
and costumes, acrobatics, and various mechanical devices such as
the seventeen-foot-long clockwork snake used in the pantomime of
Orpheus and Euridice.[39] The "magic wand of Harlequin" could
create the

sudden transformation of palaces and temples to huts and cottages; of men
and women into wheelbarrows and joint stools, of trees turned to houses;
colonades to beds of tulips; and mechanics' shops into serpents and
ostriches.[40]

Standard transformations and tricks found their way into pantomime
after pantomime. A study of all the works in appendix A that begin
with the words "Harlequin" or "Harlequin's" will reveal many ex-

amples with the same subtitles, revealing standard plot features used repeatedly. In other examples the title of one pantomime becomes the subtitle for another. Harlequin was born, died, and was reborn in countless permutations, always with a new title or a new twist to pique the curiosity of the audience and keep it coming back. A particularly unusual event occurred at Ricketts' Circus in Philadelphia on February 28, 1799, when a Mrs. J. Rowson performed the part of Harlequin in the new pantomime *Harlequin Everywhere* on her benefit night. The appearance was advertised as "the first attempt by any female in America."[41]

The production of *Don Juan* (London, 1787) became the standard for the "grand pantomime" that gradually replaced the harlequinades (designated "comic pantomimes") within the theatre. Bills for grand pantomimes tended to describe the elaborate scenery instead of the transformations and tricks of Harlequin. These pantomimes typically featured several acts of dialogue and dancing, and extensive music, both vocal and instrumental. In Boston, Samuel Arnold's *Obi, or Three Finger'd Jack* was performed during the Christmas season of 1801:

Entertainments of this class, are in general, calculated for the meridian of the holiday frequenters of the theatre only, but this is, by no means, the case with the piece under consideration. It is an interesting dramatic story, well told in action. . . . The interest of the story is increased by the songs and musical accompaniments, which are truly beautiful, and often highly appropriate. The scenery is in a style of superior excellence, and it was uniformly well performed.[42]

As the harlequinades disappeared gradually from the theatre after the turn of the century, they established themselves firmly in the repertory of the circus, where they were often combined with equestrian feats, tumbling, ropewalking, and other skills. Harlequin remained at the center of the pantomime, but the clown assumed increasing importance. It is sometimes hard to determine from newspaper bills the amount of music used in circus productions; it is fair to assume, however, that music of some kind, most often collected and arranged, was used for the typical circus pantomime. One indication of the presence of music at the circus was the benefits given at season's end for music directors such as Mr. Collet, leader of the band at Lailson's Circus in Philadelphia in 1797.[43]

Theatrical pantomimes were frequently attacked as an absurdity, but they were too profitable to consider abandoning them. A New York critic complained in 1785:

Instead of those energetic tragedies, abounding in excellent morals, with which our language abounds, and comedies replete with justest satire, where vice and folly meet perhaps the severest castigation, and the last of ridicule, we have the *Genii of the Rock,* the *Witches, Harlequin in the Moon,* with a thousand other pantomimical mummeries in which common sense stands aghast and idiots wonder.[44]

In Charleston, Carpenter lamented the presentation of the pantomime *Telemachus,* in two seemingly contradictory reviews. On March 12, 1804, he wrote:

Of the Pantomime of *Telemachus,* Thespis is unwilling to speak. Pantomimes are, critically speaking, indefensible. Certainly nothing can render them bearable but the capability of producing laughter, or by some extraordinary power exciting interest, in the way of *Don Juan* or *Perouse.* . . . To this kind of dumb spectacle we confess ourselves unfriendly; our taste as well as our judgment revolts from it. If Pantomimes must be, let them have the agility of Harlequin and the buffoonery of the Clown to put in balance against the absurdity of them.

On March 24 he continued:

Telemachus! great Heaven! that thinking beings should be gravely employed in playing and looking on upon such solemn nonsense! That such persons as Hodgkinson, Mrs. Whitlock, Mrs. Placide, and Mrs. Villiers, the ornaments of the American stage, should be working at such an owlish harlequinade![45]

When *Cinderella* was performed with great success in Boston in 1807, "The Drama" section of *The Emerald* grumbled:

> We cannot but regret, that the introduction of Cinderella on our boards should have excluded the regular entertainments of the drama. This little *cinder girl* must surely be a magician, since at the moment of her arrival, *Tragedy* is struck as dumb as if she had seen *Medusa's* head; and *Comedy* is turned out of doors, to make room for her half-sister, *Farce*.[46]

In spite of these criticisms, "From the days of *The Necromancer,* pantomimes never ceased to be the best trump card a manager could play."[47] Pantomimes also were significant because their use of descriptive orchestral music, dancers, and elaborate costumes, scenery, and machines influenced the staging and production of operas, melodramas, and musical romances.

MELODRAMA

When the melodrama *A Tale of Mystery* (London, 1802) was first performed in New York on March 16, 1803, the newspaper playbills carried a description of the new form:

> The Melo-Drame being new to the English and American Stage, it may be necesary [*sic*] to observe, that in this species of drama composition, instrumental music is introduced occasionally during the pauses in the dialogue, with a view of heightening the effect, and aiding the expression of those passions which occupy the scene; the present admirable piece may be considered as the first experiment to introduce a new species of Drama: on the English stage it has succeeded beyond calculation; and it is presented to the public of New-York, under the strongest impression, that it will contribute in an eminent degree to their rational pleasures.[48]

The essential element of melodrama was the music, which alternated with or accompanied the stage dialogue and action to heighten the emotional effect. Some scenes were carried on entirely in dumb show, using techniques borrowed from the pantomime. The stylized gestures may even, at times, have approached ballet; they certainly borrowed much from the "attitudes" of tragedy. The background music must have affected listeners in ways similar to that used in silent movies and in modern movie and television soundtracks.

The excerpts from Thomas Busby's music for *A Tale of Mystery* in example 1 accompanied such dramatic action. Victor Pelissier and James Hewitt provided music to accompany the American production; only two dances by Pelissier are extant.[49]

Example 1. Excerpts from Thomas Busby's melodrama, *A Tale of Mystery*, 1802.

Bonamo being about to examine Francisco, commands him to adhere to the truth.

Maestoso

Francisco with dignity points to Heaven and his Heart. Bonamo to Francisco, "your Family?"

Francisco in sorrow gives signs or "forbear," and writes "it must not be known."

By the end of the eighteenth century, the term "melodrama" was used throughout Europe. Melodrama had its roots in the French *mélodrame*, such as Jean-Jacques Rousseau's *Pygmalion* (1770) and Guilbert de Pixérécourt's *Coeline, ou L'enfant mystère* (1800, translated by Thomas Holcroft as *A Tale of Mystery*), which were essentially romantic plays with orchestral music added. Rousseau's *Pygmalion* was performed by a French troupe in Charleston in 1790, in New York in 1796, and again in Charleston in 1803. Appropriately, a French immigrant, Pelissier, was probably the first to compose a melodrama for performance in America; his *Ariadne Abandoned by Theseus in the Isle of Naxos* was performed in New York in 1797. Other early melodramas and their first American performance include *Pyrame and Thisbe* (1794); *Rudolph (The Robbers of Calabria)* (1804); *Lady of the Rock, Valentine and Orson* (1805); *Captain Smith and the Princess Pocahontas, The Pilgrims* (1806); *Black Castle (Spectre of the Forest), Tekeli* (1807); *The Blind Boy, Ella Rosenberg, The Fortress, The Indian Princess, The Magic Tower, The Wood Demon* (1808); *Forest of Hermanstadt* (1809); *The Exile, The Free Knights, Rugantino (The Bravo of Venice)* (1810); *Lady of the Lake, Twenty Years Ago* (1811); *The Bridal Ring, Marmion, Wandering Boys, Timor the Tartar* (1812); *Quadrupeds of Quedlinburgh* (1813); *The Faithful Wife, Lafitte and the Pirates of Barataria, The Miller and His Men* (1814), and *Aladdin, For Freedom Ho!, Zembuca*, and *The Magpie and the Maid* (1815). Earlier works such as *The Sicilian Romance* (1795), *The Stranger* (1798), and *Blue Beard* (1799), none true melodramas as written, were designated as melodramas in at least some performances. As the first decade of the century progressed, melodrama became more and more pervasive, until works of all genres were performed "after the manner of the Melo-Drame."[50]

A typical plot in an early nineteenth-century melodrama would concern a beautiful and virtuous young woman, motherless and in the clutches of some foppish or ogreish old man who coveted her hand in marriage, but loved hopelessly by a handsome, virtuous, yet socially unacceptable young man. Her long-lost father would typically appear at last to rescue her and reveal the true identity of the young suitor, to whom he would give her hand in marriage. One plot variation was that the young woman (or man) had been stolen at birth and forced to join a gang of robbers, pirates, or gypsies. Enchanted castles, gloomy caverns, dungeons, haunted towers, and mysterious strangers were frequent elements in these plots. There was always a moral—though it might be nothing more than to show the wages of sin and the poetry of justice.

Stephen Cullen Carpenter again represents the prevailing critical view of these plots:

> To write only to the passions, to expose human beings to circumstances that cannot in the natural course of life occur, and release them by means which outrage all probability, and to those ends to urge vice and virtue beyond all possible bounds, and fabricate extreme characters better than saints, or worse than devils, for the mere purpose of producing horror and astonishment, and hanging up the feelings of the multitude on the tenterhooks of fearful suspense and painful apprehension—to violate all the rules prescribed by nature and experience, and place heroes and heroines in situations so far out of the course of human conduct, that the poet cannot get them out again by rational, feasible means, but is compelled to leave their fate to the guess of the spectators by picturesque grouping and dropping the curtain.[51]

The most common spelling in American playbills was MeloDrame or Melo-Drame, though a number of variants appear. Grandiose combinations such as Grand Melodramatic Opera, Grand Melo-Dramatic Romance, or Grand Operatic Melodrame indicate the close relationship of these works to the musical romances. Other genre designations demonstrate the symbiosis between the melodrama and the techniques of pantomime. In the early years of the nineteenth century, hybrid forms combining elements of both, such as *Obi; or Three-Fingered Jack* (1800), became common. They were described by such nomenclature as Grand Serious Pantomimical MeloDrame, Grand Pantomimical Operatic Romance, or Grand Heroic Pantomimical Romance.

Melodramas typically joined "legendary romance with theatric spectacle, combining all the arts of dialogue, music, pantomime, and scenery." [52] The whole extravagant prospect was apparently too much for one New Yorker, who penned a three-act work titled *The Manhattan Stage; or Cupid in His Vagaries,* adapted the music himself, and offered it up for performance on April 11, 1806, as a "Grand, Local, Historical, Pantomimic Melo-Drame." The joke was taken even further in Boston, where the critic described the work as a "comick, pantomimick, historick, operatick, local melo-drama." [53]

Critics who complained of romances and pantomimes wrote even more bitterly of melodramas:

When the trash of modern compilation is substituted for solid intellect of ancient composition; we are presented not only with the custards and other trifles contained in previous productions, 'but the very egg shells from which our fare has been extracted.' . . . It is seriously to be wished that the more excellent species of dramatic composition, may be offered us, and we believe the Boston managers are willing to please the town with such productions, instead of the melo-dramas, the monstrous progeny of an union of pantomime and tragedy.[54]

When the American melodrama *Rudolph, or the Robbers of Calabria,* by John D. Turnbull, was performed in Boston for the benefit of the author, the critic for *The Polyanthos* was merciless in describing the evening's bill:

'A grand romantick melodrama, in three acts, interspersed with musick, chorus, combats, &c. called RUDOLPH, or the *Robbers of Calabria,* written by Mr. Turnbull.'—'A grand spectacle view of the burning of the frigate *Philadelphia,* in the harbour of Tripoli—a view of the Harbour, Town, and Fortifications of Tripoli.'—'A grand—[keep your temper, good reader]—A grand military heroick Pantomime, called THE MAID OF HUNGARY, or *The Rigid Father,* performed in London upwards of ninety nights, and at the theatres New-York, Charleston, &c. with unbounded applause; by Mr. Turnbull.' Patience, just Heaven! Is all this by Mr. Turnbull? and all for one evening's entertainment?

The critic supplied a few samples of the dialogue from *Rudolph;* one will probably suffice to demonstrate why the piece's first Boston performance was also its last:

Hark! some one descends from above! My Albert, resume the posture, and if possible the gestures of a man newly perished.[55]

OTHER GENRES

Various other genres were performed in the theatres of the turn of the nineteenth century. Masque and burletta were such forms, seldom newly composed but occasionally performed. Like most eighteenth-century theatrical nomenclature, the term "masque" or "mask" was used in a variety of ways. For the early part of the century, a masque was an

entertainment . . . all-sung but only half-length . . . In a masque classical deities played a major part and elaborate scenic effects were expected, usually with machines descending from the sky or ascending through traps.[56]

Later Thomas A. Arne wrote two masques, *Comus* and *Alfred,* with spoken dialogue. *Comus* continued to be performed in the United States, along with an American version of the same composer's *King Arthur,* sometimes performed as *Arthur and Emmeline; or the Promise of America's Future Glory.*[57] *Neptune and Amphitrite,* the masque from Shakespeare's *Tempest,* was also performed occasionally. The grandiose scale of these efforts was reflected in an American creation called *Americania and Elutheria,* performed in Charleston on February 9, 1798. In this masque the genie Americania presented an allegorical version of the American Revolution, culminating in a meeting of Americania with Elutheria, the goddess of liberty, while the two descended from the clouds on either side of the stage. Oscar Sonneck concluded that in America, "masque was merely a more learned and dignified term for pantomime."[58] In this case, that description may be justified, since the features of *Americania and Elutheria* were the scenery, the machines, and the dancing of Mr. and Mrs. Placide and various nymphs and satyrs.

In 1750, in Mrs. Clive's *The Rehearsal,* a burletta included in the play was described by one of the characters as "a kind of poor relation to an Opera."[59] The term "burletta" had a variety of applications. Fiske described it as "a skit on the masque . . . [which] mocked mythological personages,"[60] and Allardyce Nicoll wrote that

> Technically the term burletta ought to be confined to burlesque comic operas, to those for example which deal in a ludicrous way with classic legend or history, but there is no such sharp distinction in the eighteenth-century usage of the word.[61]

It is in the sense of a burlesque masque that the term describes Thomas Bridges' *Dido and Aeneas* (1771, music by James Hook) and Kane O'Hara's *Midas* (1762), a pastiche based on the legend in which Apollo loses a singing contest to Pan and gives asses' ears to the judge, Midas. Barthélémon's burletta of *Orpheus and Euridice* in David Garrick's *A Peep Behind the Curtain* (1767) is also of this type.

One circumstance that broadened the definition of the burletta was that it was permissible for performance in the minor theatres. Originally, a burletta was expected to have "the tinkling of the piano and the jingling of the rhyme," but eventually the interpretation was broadened, and "the Lord Chamberlain finally came to take the view that a three-act play—for five acts were always indicative of legitimacy—with not less than five songs could come within the burletta division."[62] This flexibility allowed many late eighteenth-century comic operas—including *The Battle of Hexham; No Song, No Supper;* and *My Grandmother*—to be performed under the classification of burletta.

The term "burletta" was quite loosely used in the United States. It was sometimes used to describe a ballad opera at the turn of the century, since those works obviously differed from the comic operas of the day and the term "ballad opera" was not commonly used. Durang's list of "romance burlettas" comprises a melodrama, *Forty Thieves,* a musical romance, *Blue Beard,* a burletta, *Tom Thumb the Great,* and a German piece, *Stoofel Rilps, or the SeuShwan Wedding.*

Operas in French were sometimes performed in America during the post-Revolutionary period, particularly in Charleston and New Orleans. No detailed study of these works is included here, in part because of the lack of sufficient information, but primarily because they represent an entirely different repertory best dealt with in another forum.[63]

Despite the enormously varied nomenclature for musical theatre works in English at the turn of the nineteenth century, and the frequent inconsistencies in its use, the characteristics of—and distinctions between—the principal genres emerge clearly. The comic opera, the musical romance, and the melodrama were the principal forms, and can be clearly delineated. The ballet and pantomime played major roles in the theatre, with changes reflecting the same tendencies found in contemporary operas. Works of other genres were often prepared as "additional entertainments," improvised, with little innovation or expectation of permanence, and used nomenclature freely, hastily, and expediently.

3

THE PARTS AND THE WHOLE

Relationships, Forms, and Revisions

The standard organization of late eighteenth- and early nine-teenth-century musical entertainments as plays with added music created dynamic tensions between the written word and its all-important musical complement. There were endless questions about which was more important, whether one could exist without or was dependent upon the other, and which should be written first.

All the period's musical genres shared many of the same vocal and instrumental forms. Most entertainments began with an overture, and included songs that took standard forms and fulfilled standard functions. Because of this uniformity, it was a simple matter to transfer music from one work to another, and composers, arrangers, and even performers did so without inhibition.

WORDS AND MUSIC

When credit was given for the creation of eighteenth- and early nineteenth-century English operas, the name of the librettist was always provided; the composer was mentioned as an afterthought, if at all. This provides a clear indication of the relative position of words and music in the minds of English critics and theatregoers. The play was normally written first; the music was either added as a unit (as when words and tunes were conceived together by the compilers of ballad operas) or written or compiled to fit previously written song texts (as in later pastiche and one-composer operas).

Debate concerning spoken dialogue versus recitative reveals widespread feeling among librettists that composers were taking too much upon themselves by writing excessive music. From these writings, it is possible to glean several specific references to the relative importance of words and music. An article in *The Euterpeiad: or Musical Intelligencer* (Boston, 1820), said:

The truth is, that the scenes and passions which occur most frequently in the English drama, are not of a kind that has much relation to music; and hence, the difficulty which an English audience feels in conceiving, that a speech, expressing the grave and profound affections of the mind, should be well declaimed to music.[1]

General John Burgoyne declared in 1780 in the preface of his libretto for *Lord of the Manor:*

In a representation which is to hold "a mirror up to nature," and which ought to draw its chief applause from reason, vocal music should be confined to express the feelings and the passions, but never to express the exercising of them. Song, in any action in which reason tells us it would be unnatural to sing, must be preposterous . . . it must not only be restrained from having part in the exercise or action of the passions; care must also be taken, that it does not interrupt or delay events for which the mind is become eager. It should always be the accessory, and not the principal subject of the drama.[2]

Even with this limitation on the extent to which music could take part in the dramatic action, librettos were often criticized for their preponderance of musical interest, particularly by critics interested principally in the spoken drama. A critic in the *Gentleman's Magazine* in 1764 said that with a libretto "little more is intended than to give a kind of vehicle to music"; and in the *European Magazine* in 1786 a comic opera libretto was still considered "the most monstrous of all dramatic absurdities."[3]

Not surprisingly, composers were sometimes reluctant to accept a view that minimized their role. One challenge to the supremacy of the librettist reportedly took place when David Garrick wrote to Thomas Arne: "'Tommy,' said he, 'you should consider, after all, that music is at best but pickle to my roast beef.'—'By ---, Davy,' rejoined Arne in the same strain, 'your beef shall be well pickled before I have done.'"[4]

Later in the century we find evidence that for at least one composer, Stephen Storace, a considerable influence over the librettist was considered a necessity. Not only does Storace's familiarity with the works of Mozart appear in the plots of his operas (as in a duet in *The Cherokee* in which two servants are continually interrupted by a bell summoning them to their master or mistress), but Mozart's philosophy concerning the relationship of words and music seems to have affected his pupil as well. Storace is quoted in the *Thespian Dictionary* of 1802:

It must, however, be remarked, that the words [of his librettos] were chiefly adapted to the music: indeed Mr. Storace openly declared in a music-seller's shop in Cheapside (then Longman and Broderip's) that it was impossible for any author to produce a good opera, without previously consulting his intended composer, for, added he, the songs must be introduced as he pleases, and the words (which are a secondary consideration) be written agreeably to his directions.[5]

Critics, however, continued to expect that the libretto should be the principal attraction of any theatre piece, and to denigrate those works that failed to meet this criterion. A Philadelphia critic described James Cobb's *The Siege of Belgrade* (music by Storace) in 1801:

Of this opera, the songs are remarkably well written, and the music is the delight of the amateurs. But, either from the hurry or incapacity of COBB, the author, the dialogue is very penurious of wit, and the attempts at gaiety, or smartness, are despicably impotent. Still this performance excites great interest, not only by its delectable songs, but by its striking scenery. The representation of the *siege* is terribly luminous, and the image of war and desolation is *before the eyes*.[6]

Englishman Thomas Dutton criticized the same opera because "the composer and the scene painter furnish the principal attractions." Far from being a desirable condition for an opera,

It affords a damning proof of the frivolity and vitiated taste of the age that such writers are tolerated; but music when carried to excess and made the object of primary, instead of secondary concern, has an infallible tendency to enervate and debauch the mind.[7]

A few writers recognized the possibility that opera might make special requirements on the librettists, but these were unusual:

Those specimens of the musical drama that are to be found upon our stage, are by no means calculated to give a favorable impression with regard to the capabilities of that species of composition. They are either slight comic pieces in prose, interspersed with songs, or they are vapid translations from Italian opera. . . . Still, however, . . . the profounder vein of poetry peculiar to this country, [need not] altogether vanish and forsake us if we were to compose pieces where the language were better adapted for musical purposes, and where there was a more continued flow of musical emotions throughout.[8]

The editor of an 1823 edition of the opera *Blue Beard* described the relative importance of the various elements of music and plot in that work; from a literary point of view he believed that *Blue Beard* was not in the highest degree interesting or instructive:

The poetry, we admit, is not of a very high order; the puns are vile, the sentiments stale, and the language in general bombastic. Yet, the author, who had little in view beyond manufacturing a convenient vehicle for the display of gorgeous scenery and shewy procession, has effected his intention with a cleverness, which many who may think meanly of the performance, would find some difficulty in equalling; and, what probably was to him but the pas-

time of an evening, has on numerous succeeding evenings imparted gratification to thousands. The reader, whilst he turns over the leaves, and smiles at
the trivial character of the language, should recollect that "Blue Beard" did
not owe its success to the charms of the dialogue, but to the magnificent
scenery, the brilliant decorations, the music, the singing, the dancing, and the
thousand other fascinations which that dialogue served to introduce.[9]

The writer recognized that though the libretto could not stand alone
as a work of literary art, it must be judged within the context of the
production as a whole—which was enormously successful and remained a favorite for decades. He recognized implicitly the fact that,
in this instance, music was preeminent to words in the creation of
the work.

A composer was typically hired by each playhouse to compose,
arrange, or adapt the music needed for each production, and often
supervise its performance as well. For this, the composer received a
regular weekly salary and some degree of security. The only other
genuine alternative for composers was to hire themselves out to librett-
tists. Since it was the libretto that was accepted by the manager, if it
was already provided with music, that was likely to be accepted also,
sight unseen. This method provided comparatively little security. The
play might sit on a manager's desk for months unread; if it were accepted, the manager would have no obligation to the composer. If the
play were produced and financially successful, the librettist would ordinarily give a portion of his profits to the composer.

By custom, the author was given the takings of the third, sixth, and ninth
nights, and out of them he usually had to pay the performers and orchestra
as well as his composer. If he was let off all or most of the house expenses, he
could hope for a clear profit of about £100 a night.[10]

When John O'Keeffe arranged with Thomas Harris of Covent Garden
to "write an opera for his house" in 1781, O'Keeffe provided the libretto for *The Banditti, or Love's Labyrinth* (later revised as *The Castle of Andalusia*). About this opera, O'Keeffe relates:

A few days after this interview, being in a room at the theatre with Mr. Harris and Dr. Arnold, the former said to me, "But Mr. O'Keeffe, what am I to give you for this opera; your nights, and copyright?" Dr. Arnold instantly said, "Six hundred guineas."—"Well, I will," was the prompt reply; and I stipulated to pay Dr. Arnold for composing it, 50 *l.* on the first night, 40 *l.* more on the sixth night, and an additional 30 *l.* should it go on nine nights, making 120 *l.* in the whole; he to have the sale of his music.[11]

A writer in *The Ramblers' Magazine* in New York in 1810 probably spoke from bitter experience when he summarized the fate of an American dramatist:

Much has been said about *want of talents,* in this country, for dramatic composition; but the last two or three years have proved beyond the possibility of denial that America contains jewels of no common lustre, which but require the fostering hand of patronage to lift their glories to the day. What is the fate amongst us of a poor *aspirant* after fame in the walks of the drama? His production is delivered into the hands of men capable perhaps of examining the correctness of a *leger,* but totally incompetent to the task of judging of literary merit. Admitting that a piece be put in rehearsal, that it be played, and that the public receive it favorably; the author receives an invitation to dinner, in company with a host of the manager's parasites, and is *be-praised* and *be-thanked* for the services he has rendered to the theatre until his head runs round, and then is dismissed with a general invitation to repeat his visit at every convenient opportunity.

Here then is the harvest the poor devil of an author reaps on this side the Atlantic, after four or six months' seclusion and labor. No *third night* dances before his eyes, to brighten his midnight lamp, and cheer the gloom of his dreary garret; no Maecenas is at hand to reward his toils; and his only compensation is the half-concealed sneer of the self-conceited critic, or the open abuse of envious and less successful candidates for praise.[12]

In other cases, the author did receive a benefit. When the opera *Tammany; or the Indian Chief* received its third performance in New York on March 8, 1794, it was a benefit for the author, Anne Julia Hatton;[13] and William Dunlap indicated in his diary that he "might bring forth a play each season & receive the full profit of a third night."[14] In other cases, the second night of a new piece was the author's night; H. Charnock of the New York theatre received the profits of the second night of the 1806 performance of *Tars from Tripoli,* his adaptation of Thomas Dibdin's *The Naval Pillar.*[15]

In spite of the fact that he did not receive a benefit in return for his efforts, the fate of the composer or musical arranger was perhaps a modicum better than that of the dramatist or librettist. The arranger was at least on the payroll of the theatre, and received additional compensation for his labors as part of his salary. Nonetheless, his position as a member of the theatrical staff, producing the necessities of the business, was clear. The American view was probably summed up by William Dunlap, playwright, librettist, manager of the New York theatre from 1796 to 1805, and theatre historian, when he said that Americans

write of the theatre as the home of Melpomene and Thalia, and view the sister, Euterpe, as a favored guest in the household where they preside. Let music have a temple of her own; but when in unison with the drama, music and painting are only to be considered as accessories.[16]

THE MUSICAL NUMBERS

Samuel Arnold's opera *Children in the Wood* (1793) is particularly useful in illustrating the instrumental and vocal styles and forms found in post-Revolutionary comic opera and related genres, not only because of its great popularity, but because its nine vocal numbers are representative of the major song types found in the genre. The piano-vocal score is readily accessible.

The Overture

The typical English opera overture at the turn of the nineteenth century used the Italian fast-slow-fast pattern, frequently with a slow introduction. The form used by Sir Henry Rowley Bishop (whose *Clari, the Maid of Milan* is the source of "Home, Sweet Home") in the early part of the nineteenth century is described disparagingly as follows:

Overtures. These are nearly all of the lowest type of Pot-pourri. They frequently begin with a Haydnesque introduction, often of considerable merit, then comes an Italian Allegro in the style of Spontini; halfway through, this gives way to a popular air for a solo instrument and this is followed by a trivial Rondo intended to keep on until the stage is ready. At the best, the subjects are devoid of interest, at the worst, there is no workmanship to compensate us for its absence.[17]

To this "catalogue of sins" we might add one other: Bishop's form was quite lacking in originality. This description might apply with similar accuracy to dozens of overtures by other English composers in the decades preceding, including that of *Children in the Wood.* Although contemporary sources sometimes speak of overtures of this type as having three movements, neither of the first two sections is tonally complete; it is therefore more accurate to speak of a single-movement overture with three tempi or sections—and in this case, with an introduction.

The key of D was by far the most common used for overtures, since trumpets and drums were almost always in that key. Roger Fiske claims that the overture to *Children in the Wood*

started a playhouse fashion for sombre D minor introductions, and though Arnold had been anticipated by Mozart's *Don Giovanni* overture and Kreutzer's *Lodoiska* he cannot have known either work. In the next two or three years at least six playhouse overtures started with a slow D minor introduction leading into a D Major Allegro.[18]

In *Children in the Wood,* although the D minor key is emphasized at the opening of the introduction by the octave announcement (ex. 2),

Example 2. Excerpt from overture, *Children in the Wood,* 1793.

midway in the section the dominant is reached, and the remainder is a strong preparation for the Allegro.

The Allegro begins with twenty-eight measures of D major tonic—enough to establish the key for a long first-movement form. There is a strong shift to the dominant in measures 29–40. Once established, however, the dominant elides quickly into F♯ minor, signaling a developmental section; this developmental nature is further emphasized by the sequential treatment. The Allegro ends with a strong dominant preparation, using the augmented-sixth chord to signal the return of the tonic that normally completes a first-movement form.

Instead there is an interruption in the form of a slow section in D major, using "a popular air for a solo instrument" (ex. 3). The harmonies here are far more complex than are dictated by the tune: especially rich is the V/IV to IV at measure 6. These romantic harmonies are quite appropriate in their associations, however. This was an era of interest in ballads and ballad tunes, and Arnold, especially interested in English traditional melodies, used them frequently. He obviously knew the tune traditionally used for the "Children in the Wood" ballad. The feelings evoked in those who knew the story would correspond well with this sentimental—even melodramatic—setting of the tune.

The point of arrival for this section—and for the entire overture—is

Example 3. Excerpt from overture, *Children in the Wood.*

the beginning of the Vivace. The theme of this final section duplicates the refrain melody of the opera's finale.

In the last quarter of the century English opera composers showed a marked liking for basing one movement of the overture, nearly always the last, on a tune that was later to be sung, nearly always in the finale. The trick was of French origin, for the earliest playhouse example of it occurs in *The Deserter* (1773), a rewriting by Dibdin of an opera by Monsigny. Dibdin himself tried the idea out in his *Poor Vulcan* and *Liberty Hall;* Shield and Arnold did so frequently. Besides being labor-saving, the trick helped to "plug" the tunes in a way audiences found agreeable, and it seems to have been commoner in England than anywhere else in Europe.[19]

The final Vivace is in ABA (first rondo) form. The theme is presented twice in D major in the opening A section; the B section is a "Turkish March" for a duet of "hautboy and small Flute" (probably flageolet or piccolo) with a drone bass (ex. 4).[20] There is an extended dominant preparation for the final arrival at the tonic, and the return of the rondo theme. Arnold reserves one more unusual touch for the last episode: the ballad tune from the second movement appears again complete in a duple version—*piano* and *staccato*. A brief coda ends the overture. A number of *galant* idioms are used, among them sudden dynamic contrasts, *sforzando* accents, the octave opening passage, and the rhythm ♪♩♪ used extensively in the introduction.

Example 4. Excerpt from overture, *Children in the Wood.*

Another popular form used for playhouse overtures was the medley. Sometimes medley overtures like Benjamin Carr's *Federal Overture* were part of the music preceding and in the intervals of the evening's entertainment. They also provided a practical way for a harried composer to compile a quick overture for an opera or other musical entertainment. When James Hewitt wrote a Naval Overture for *Tars from Tripoli* (1806), for example, he included "Black Ey'd Susan," "New Century Hornpipe," "Phillips Hornpipe," "Lullaby," "Polly Put the Kettle On," "Sailor Boy Capering Ashore," and "Yankee Doodle."[21]

Vocal Forms

Solo songs were the heart of English opera, far outnumbering any other type of musical number. Their popularity is also clear from the vast numbers that were published separately in England and America for the use of the amateur musician. Though *da capo* arias were seldom found, forms ranged from long bravura arias designed to show off a singer's technique to simple, strophic songs, either traditional or composed in ballad style. Comic patter songs were also common, and were particularly useful for performers who were more actor than singer.

Duets were often of the comic type, and usually given to comic characters, although love duets were also common. In concerted numbers—trios, quartets, ensembles—the actors often kept their individuality. Choruses seldom had much to do, and were often omitted entirely.[22]

Vocal items were selected not only for their musical value, but also for their appropriateness to a particular dramatic situation. Certain operatic conventions were followed, such as an entrance aria soon after the first appearance of each main character, and an ensemble finale sometimes at the end of each act, and almost always at the end of the last act.

Children in the Wood offers two examples of the comic song: "When Love Gets You Fast in Her Clutches" and "Dorothy Dump." Both are simple, strophic entrance songs with humorous texts. They enable Josephine and Walter, the female and male leads, to show their talents (and reveal a bit of their characters) at their first appearances.

Example 5. Score for "When Love Gets You Fast in Her Clutches," *Children in the Wood.* Music Division, Library of Congress.

Josephine's song (ex. 5) is subtly comic—and quite sentimental. Arnold takes advantage of the alternation of feminine and masculine endings in the text: the sixteenth-note "drawing back" on the first beat of "clutches" and "crutches," followed by the arpeggiated filigree, shows what a would-be-refined—and rather silly—little heroine Josephine really is. The exaggerated pathos of her reiterated "well-a-days" serves to strengthen this impression.

If Josephine is sensitive, Walter certainly is not. His broadly humorous text is sung to a stumbling jig—marked *moderato.* It is absolutely straightforward, and Walter immediately appears to be a bumbling peasant.

The accompaniments for these songs are no more elaborate than those of the older ballad operas. In "When Love Gets You Fast in Her Clutches," Arnold uses the opening motive from the vocal line to build an eight-measure introduction; the final four measures of the introduction serve also as an interlude between verses and as a postlude. The eight-measure introduction to "Dorothy Dump" is similarly based on the vocal melody; the postlude, however, is only two measures—minimal both in time and in music. Both songs use the typical repetition of the final text line: in Josephine's song it is extended and elaborated to provide an opportunity for a cadenza; in Walter's the repetition is much more straightforward.

If it were not already apparent from the number of songs written for each of the leading characters (four for Josephine, and one for Walter), it becomes more clear now: Josephine's role is written for a singer who also acts; Walter's is for an actor who also sings, but not necessarily very well. The text (and the accompanying prescribed clowning) are far more important in Walter's song.

The Italian opera prevalent in eighteenth-century London had a strong influence on playhouse style. Sometimes entire arias were borrowed and fitted with new English words; at other times composers wrote in familiar Italian styles when they were appropriate for particular situations. The singer slated to perform a given number might also influence its style.

Children in the Wood includes a variety of songs in more elaborate styles. In "Young Simon," Josephine gives the boy Simon a singing lesson. In order to do it properly, she uses a standard Italian operatic style and form: the *da capo* duet. The introduction is not borrowed from the opening vocal phrase, but both introduction and postlude are short and purely orchestral. The highly ornamented vocal line is distinctive: Josephine teaches the boy a song by having him echo her florid phrases. The meter change and the change to a simpler style for the contrasting B section are doubly appropriate, because the text reverts to a discussion between the two characters. At the end of the B section the boy sings the only bit of recitative in the entire opera, leading back to the return of the opening song, which is written out in its

Example 6. Crescendo from conclusion of "Young Simon," *Children in the Wood.*
Music Division, Library of Congress.

entirety. The dynamic indications in this duet are worth noting, particularly in the coda. The anacrusis on "For" is emphasized (*mf*) each time, with the word "love" sung *piano*. A crescendo is indicated seven measures from the end with stereotypical repeated eighth notes in the bass and an ascending line in the violins (ex. 6).[23]

"Great Sir, Consider," a comic parody of a serious style, is also in *da capo* form. The duet is sung by the maid and the butler, but the villainous uncle is indispensable: he silently pursues the maid, Josephine; she vocally defends her honor; and Apathy, the butler, just as relentlessly pursues his master, trying to obtain his dinner order. Although the actors remain seemingly unaware of the ridiculous non sequiturs produced by interspersing the two vocal parts, the audience is quite unable to miss them. The duet, closely linked with both plot and characterization, offers an excellent example of an ensemble that prescribes accompanying stage action. The action is built into the music in such a way that the actor knows when to move and what sort of movement is needed—one can see and hear Apathy panting to keep up with his master on every page. Almost the entire violin parts are notated on a separate staff, providing an excellent model of the sort of figuration expected in elaborate arias. The interchange between the two violin parts sounds particularly effective in performance, and demonstrates the importance of imaginative orchestration to the appreciation of a work that might otherwise sound quite simplistic (ex. 7). The final page of the duet, with its ever more frantic repetition of text, seems to demand a continual crescendo from the *mf* at the top of the page to the *f* at the bottom (ex. 8).

A contemporary style from grander opera is also used in "Mark the

Example 7. Violin figuration from "Great Sir, Consider," *Children in the Wood.* Music Division, Library of Congress.

Example 8. Conclusion of "Great Sir, Consider," *Children in the Wood*. Music Division, Library of Congress.

True Test of Passion." Here Lady Alford sings of her love for her husband in the dotted-note rhythms, stately pace, and E♭ major tonality of the heroic style. This entrance aria is not essential to the plot. Its introduction includes a clarinet solo that appears in its entirety in the score, along with at least part (if not all) of the violin parts. *Galant* snap rhythms are apparent here. Arnold has written out all the ornamentation for this aria (with the exception perhaps of some appoggiaturas, which would have been second nature to the singer anyway). The cadenzas (ex. 9) are of particular interest, since they may serve as a guide for other appropriate cadenzas indicated only by fermatas. The cadenzas also raise a question, however; if ornamentation was used to add variety, why are the written cadenzas identical in the two verses?

Example 9. Cadenza from "Mark the True Test of Passion," *Children in the Wood.*

"The Robin" is an aria with birdsong imitations, of a type common in the late eighteenth and early nineteenth centuries. In Dibdin's *The Padlock,* for example, the heroine sings an elaborately ornamented tune to her pet bird, represented by a flute;[24] and in Michael Kelly's "The Woodpecker," the rapping of the bird is played by the pianoforte.[25] The score of "The Robin" calls for a flageolet to play the birdsong. The scoring provided—for flageolet and three strings—is probably complete. The extended instrumental interludes suggest a need for action on the part of the singer, or perhaps for stage machinery such as a mechanical bird. The song was intended as a showpiece for a talented child, who was probably expected to carry the song with sheer charm and personality; many a young prodigy received rave notices for her performance of this song.

Other aria types from English operas of the period are similar in their naive, "sounds-like" approach, among them arias that imitate a musical instrument. Surely the most popular of these was "Tink-a-tink" from *Blue Beard,* which imitates the sound of the guitar.

One or two traditional tunes, especially Scotch tunes, appeared in most English operas in the last quarter of the eighteenth century. Such arrangements were enormously popular, and entire volumes of Scotch songs were published for the use of amateur singers. *Children in the Wood,* in addition to the ballad tune in the overture, uses two other traditional tunes as airs: one, "When First to Helen's Lute," is based on an old Scottish song, "Ay, wakin' oh";[26] the other, "The Ditty," is taken from an old English carol, "The Truth Sent from Above." Though both these arias are based on traditional songs, their function is entirely different: the first, an entrance aria for the father, is a generalized love song, unrelated to the plot; "The Ditty," however, is an indispensable part of the plot of the final scene. This variance in function is reflected in the different orchestrations used.

"When First to Helen's Lute" is given a rather simple setting, but the inclusion of both violin parts indicates that full strings, at least, were used for the accompaniment—probably a fairly standard turn-of-the-century aria setting. Both voice and instruments added the ornamentation generally associated with such "Scotch" airs; the singer may have added considerably more. The introduction is typical for strophic songs (eight measures based on the opening vocal line); the postlude is brief, and echoes the last phrase of the song. A showpiece for the father, this song stops the dramatic action for a standard but quite popular kind of vocal interlude.

"The Ditty," by contrast, occurs at the climactic moment of the final scene. Josephine says "I'll sing you what I bought of the old blind pedlar who passed by this morning—Its intitled and called, the Norfolk tragedy, shewing how the ghost of a murdered babe. . . ." The song, clearly introduced as a ballad, probably used the old-fashioned ballad opera scoring of violins doubling the voice plus basso. William Shield wrote that "You must not accompany a simple natural melody with an artful complicated harmony; so says one of our precepts"; he gives as an example a ballad that was performed with "no other accompaniment than what is here exhibited"—the melody and the bass line.[27] In the United States, the performers apparently took the next logical step: "Mrs. Marshall appeared as Josephine with her accustomed success . . . the ballad by Mrs. Marshall *without accompaniments* shewed the particular sweetness and expression of her voice to great advantage."[28]

Josephine sings the ballad, which tells of a murderer haunted by a "pretty babe" killed for its "large estate." Walter, already haunted by the knowledge that he has taken the children into the wood and "lost" them, is terrified; his panic is increased by noises at the window and door. With this building of suspense, a straightforward "telling" of the ballad, with no ornamentation or other musical distraction, is certainly appropriate. This is the only song in the opera interrupted by dialogue, although a similar example occurs in the final scene of Stephen Storace's *No Song, No Supper.*

Finales ordinarily required no action until late in the eighteenth century, when Storace, influenced by Mozart's concluding ensembles, wrote increasingly longer and more complex finales.[29] As a result, by the turn of the century many English and American operas and musical entertainments featured far more elaborate finales than that found in *Children in the Wood,* requiring action and characterization on the part of the singers. The conservative *Children in the Wood* finale is typical of works by Shield, Arnold, Thomas Linley, and other composers active in the 1780s. All the surviving characters assemble for a rousing strophic song, with each successive verse presenting the point of view of one of the four principals, while all join on the refrain. No action is called for or expected.

Musical unity for both this finale and the opera as a whole is provided by the return of the rondo theme from the overture, this time as the refrain. The eight-measure theme is simplicity itself; it is sung seven times, with only thirty-six measures of contrasting material in the verses. The bass line and second violin part are identical on each repetition, and the fact that four of the seven presentations use *fp* at the first of each phrase, and two use fermatas at the end of the third phrase, does little to relieve the sameness. The audience was doubtless indulgent by this point, however, and by singing at high speed the cast could carry off an impression of sparkling vitality.

THE TRADITION OF ALTERATION

During the eighteenth and early nineteenth centuries, the alteration of both plays and scores in various ways was almost universal; it was so thoroughly a part of theatrical life that its practice and extent were seldom questioned. New plays were altered during the preparations for the first production, more to meet technical or performance needs than to improve the work artistically. After the first production, still more cuts and alterations were made as a response to the audience and the critics.

The American Captive, written by James Ellison, a "gentleman of Boston," was presented at the Federal Street Theatre in Boston on December 13, 1811. *The Comet* reported that "Though the epilogue declares that the play has never yet felt 'the critick's pruning knife'; it is strongly suspected that some of its parts have undergone the operation of the *scalping knife,* by no very merciful hand." The second performance on the 16th was the author's benefit, after which the play "was withdrawn for the purpose of making some alterations." [30]

Even in works that were straight comedies, tragedies, or dramas, it was standard to add music of all kinds. Not only were songs and choruses added, but dance—from minuets to ballet—was included wherever permitted by the plot, as well as dirges, processions, special ethnic music (as, for example, bagpipes for *Macbeth* or *Oscar and Malvina*), and even full pieces of orchestral music. It was the practice in Philadelphia to include a concerto on the violin by George Gillingham as part of the gala in the Palace of Venice in act 5 of *Abaellino, the Great Bandit.* [31]

The procedure for preparing music for a new production grew largely from the practice of accepting a new play first, then expecting the composer to provide music as quickly as possible. Though music was considered secondary, it was still recognized that well-liked songs and ensembles could contribute to the success of the production. Composers, under the dual pressures of time and box office, not surprisingly turned to proven favorites and borrowed freely from their own works and those of others. There was nothing surreptitious about these borrowings; in fact, the composer was likely to receive suggestions for appropriate numbers from the librettist and for already-mastered airs from the performers—and he sometimes even included the source in the score.

Though major performances of new works sometimes produced elaborate orchestrations, composers frequently responded to the pressures of time by preparing as little as possible in the way of scores and parts. They used parts written for other operas; they borrowed overtures written by other composers or by members of the orchestra; they took shortcuts in notating instrumental parts. A composer could easily write only soprano and bass parts and, by giving verbal instructions to members of the orchestra and filling in the harmonies at the keyboard himself, squeak by in a pinch. Scores from the period for all kinds of orchestral music are plentifully sprinkled with such expedients as *simile, col voce,* and *col bassi.* It is possible that the entire orchestra would play at times from the same figured-bass or piano-vocal score.

When operas were revived or arranged for performance in a new city, the musical director/arranger at the theatre was responsible for supplying the music for the occasion. The more fortunate arrangers would obtain a copy of the piano-vocal score of the original musical numbers and then orchestrate to suit local conditions, including the size and instrumentation of the theatre orchestra and the ensemble of actor-singers. If no music were available, the arrangers found themselves in the role of composer and compiler as well.

Newspapers and playbills of the period suggest the fluidity of all these adaptations. Arnold's *Auld Robin Gray* (1794) was performed in Philadelphia in 1795 with "New music, with a Scottish Medley Overture" by Alexander Reinagle. Shield's *Robin Hood* (1784) was performed in Philadelphia in 1794 with "Original overture by Baumgarten, Additional airs by Alexander Reinagle," and in New York in 1800, "compressed into two acts" with music by James Hewitt.[32] At Baltimore in 1795, Dibdin's music for *The Quaker* was performed with accompaniments and an "Introductory Symphony" by Rayner Taylor;[33] when *The Sixty-Third Letter* premiered in New York in

1803, the credit for the overture and music went to Samuel Arnold, but the playbills added, "accompaniments by Pelissier."[34] For a production of the pantomime *Harlequin Shipwreck'd, or, the Grateful Lion* at Baltimore in 1795, a Mr. DeMarque compiled the music from "Pleyel, Giornowicki, Giordon, Shields, Reves [*sic*] Morehead, &c. &c. The New Music, and an Introductory overture by Mr. Reinagle."[35] Thomas Morton's play *Columbus* was performed as an opera in several American cities; in Philadelphia, Reinagle composed music in 1797; Hewitt provided music in New York the same year, and Peter Van Hagen for a Boston production in 1800. Even works outside the theatrical tradition received the same treatment: when Haydn's *Creation* was performed in Boston in 1815, "accompaniments" were provided by Frederick Granger and F. C. Shaffer of the theatre.[36]

The alterations found in American versions of *Children in the Wood* illustrate of the type and extent of modifications typically found in works of this period. All three American librettos contain the version prepared for the Old American Company, as performed in Philadelphia at the American premiere and afterward at New York, Boston, and other cities, "with accompaniments and additional songs by Benjamin Carr." Before the first Boston performance, the *Federal Orrery* prophesied:

> If we judge from a perusal of the work as now represented, having received some new touches from the pen of a master; and a number of justly celebrated Songs and Duets, it cannot fail to please *here*, uniting as it does every requisite, that is calculated to instruct, to enliven and to charm.[37]

Three of the ten musical numbers that appear in both London librettos and in the score were apparently never performed in the States. Two were replaced by American substitutes, and one was simply omitted; two further additions were made in nearly every American performance. The additions included borrowings from other contemporary works and newly composed works.

The nonessential nature of *Children in the Wood*'s entrance songs is apparent in these adaptations; of the four songs, two were replaced and one was omitted entirely. The New York librettos say that the father's entrance aria, "When First to Helen's Lute," was "sung in the original copy, but omitted in representation." [38] This omission permitted that role to be performed by someone with little musical ability; it is probable that the aria was sung by Carr during the brief time that he performed the part, and then dropped by his successors.

Carr provided Josephine with a new entrance song, "When Nights Were Cold," a typical eighteenth-century art song, comparable both to European *protolieder* and to the strophic songs of Francis Hopkinson and other early American composers. The song is frankly sentimental in tune and text; it is considerably less subtle than Arnold's "When Love Gets You Fast in Her Clutches." Carr's intention may have been to emphasize the sentimentality of the character; he may not have liked Arnold's song; or he may simply have wanted to use one of his own compositions. The song refers specifically to events and characters in the opera, so it seems to have been written especially for *Children in the Wood*.

In New York, Mrs. Melmoth wrote her own entrance song to replace "Mark the True Test of Passion" when she played the part of the mother. The melody of her "Mark My Alford All the Joys" is that eighteenth-century favorite, "Ah vous dirai-je, maman," with a particularly insipid strophic text. [39] One interesting measure of the popularity of *Children in the Wood* is the fact that two sets of variations on this tune exist in American versions, both named for the operatic song and not for the French tune. [40]

As opposed to the substitute songs, there were two American additions to the score. "The Jealous Man Won't You Assume When We Marry" is an almost literal borrowing of the popular duet "The Jealous Don" from Storace's *The Pirates*. It appeared widely on concert programs well into the nineteenth century, sometimes recurring week after week during the summer concerts at the various gardens in New York and Philadelphia. It was added simply because it was a crowd-pleaser and because the actors knew it. It also gave Walter an additional, more difficult, song. It was sung at the first New York performance and regularly thereafter.[41]

Another borrowing from contemporary opera was "When First I Slipped My Leading Strings," (also called "The Waxen Doll") from Shield's *The Woodman,* which was sung by the little girl.[42] It was probably added (or perhaps substituted for "The Robin" or "Young Simon") on the premise that once a child masters a song, you let her use it every chance she gets. The same premise probably governed the addition of a "dance in character" by the children in the Charleston performance, "Master Jones, and a Young Master of the City of Charleston."[43] It is likely that the songs delivered by the children at various performances varied widely, depending upon the ages of the children and the extent of their talents and repertory. The London 1825 libretto omits both of the songs originally intended by Arnold for the children.

Subsequent performances of a work, whether directed by the original composer or by others, followed this utilitarian path. Such factors as the success of particular numbers in earlier productions, the length of a work and the time available for performance, the abilities and preferences of new performers, the need to provide works suitable for specific occasions, change of taste and standards, and the availability of the original score were added to the considerations of the arranger. An opera was almost never performed exactly the same—in either text or music—in different cities, and alterations continued to be made as long as the work was performed. A Boston critic complained about such practices in 1811:

It has of late years become much in fashion *to cut plays* in representation. The manager applies, not the *pruning knife* merely, but the *saw* and *hatchet,* and lops off whole scenes with as little ceremony as a day labourer does the branches from the poplars in our streets, till little remains except the *stump.* After this, each character is suffered to undergo the excoriation of the performer, especially if he happen to have 'a bad study'; so that when the piece is brought upon the stage, the identity of the *acting* and *reading* editions is completely destroyed. Such was most lamentably the fate of *Pizarro* this eve ning. Four or five whole scenes were omitted, beside numberless speeches and sentences. Some of these may undoubtedly be spared; but the omission of others, disfigures the whole piece.[44]

Since the playbill for a single evening might include a full Shakespearean play, a pantomime, and a farce (plus various "additional entertainments"), in a time span of about four hours, it is clear that considerable cutting had to be done. In a *New York Magazine* review of *Love in a Village,* the critic points out that "the performance is much too long; and the inattention of the audience during the third act, is a strong hint for suppression of all those songs which may be omitted without injury to the opera."[45] Full-length works were also cut into afterpieces. A Boston critic in 1807 suggested: "We think the Finger Post might be cut down to a tolerable farce; it does not contain sufficient interest for a comedy of three acts."[46]

Promptbooks (both printed and manuscript) demonstrate the types of alterations made, and playbills, memoirs, and critical essays provide further information. Entire sections were cut for one performance and restored for another. The *Polyanthus* critic disagreed with the cuts made by the manager in an 1805 Boston performance of *The Iron Chest:*

Were all the superfluous characters abstracted from the piece, the representation would afford more pleasure; and there is much dialogue which could be better spared than any part of the last scene, which we apprehend the managers pruned with a liberal hand.[47]

The scarcity of actors able to sustain a difficult singing role often led to cuts of musical numbers. William Wood wrote that

as most of the operas had been composed with a view to the peculiar powers and voices of some original representative, it frequently happened that these pieces were not suited to the ability of later singers, and it became necessary to omit much of the composer's music, substituting such popular and approved airs as were most certain of obtaining applause.[48]

It is apparent from these critical commentaries that this sort of cutting was a continual process. Sometimes the music was simply omitted. In New York, 1794: "The Public are respectfully acquainted, that two of the songs [in the opera *Tammany*] will be omitted, as unnecessary to the conduct or interest of the piece."[49] In Philadelphia, 1806: *The Romp* "would have been very pleasing, if much of the music had not been omitted."[50] In New York, 1809: *Yes or No* "is interspersed with songs which were all omitted except corporal Barrel's; and that might as well have been omitted for it told not."[51] In Philadelphia, *Pizarro*, 1810: "the omission of Cora's exquisitely beautiful, wild, and pathetic song, was a great drawback from the effect of the part."[52] Boston, *The Forty Thieves*, 1811: "It is regretted that circumstances render the omission of many delightful airs and chorusses unavoidable."[53] Boston, 1812: "The Highland Reel was performed in a style not before seen in any theatre. Mr. Vaughan in Sandy very wisely declined any attempts to sing."[54]

Sometimes new songs were substituted for those in the original. In Philadelphia, 1805: *Paul and Virginia* "suffered by Mr. Woodham's omitting 'The wealth of the Cottage,' which, in this piece, is much more appropriate than 'Just like Love.'"[55] And in 1806, in *The Honey Moon*: "But why did she [Mrs. Darley as Juliana] substitute a song in the begining [*sic*] of the 5th act, instead of that furnished by the author? We always deem this an unwarrantable licence, unless there are very special reasons for it."[56]

On other occasions songs were simply added to the part. In Charleston, April 1805: John Hodgkinson introduced "Just Like Love, is yonder Rose" into the role of Count Almaviva in the comedy *The Follies of a Day; or, the Marriage of Figaro* (adapted by Holcroft).[57] In Boston, *Animal Magnetism*, 1811:

Miss Dellinger from the New York theatre made her first appearance on this stage. She played *Constance* in the farce, in which were introduced the songs of "Vive la bagatelle" and "The tuneful lark," for the purpose of displaying her musical talents.[58]

Operas were even altered for reasons of politics—international, national, or local. At the Boston Federal Street, the favorite opera *Poor Soldier* had a black valet, Domingo, instead of the original Bagatelle, a parody Frenchman, in an attempt to appease the Jacobins who patronized the theatre.[59] A masterpiece of political blandishment was presented by the Old American Company at Hartford on November 12, 1799. The evening began with a three-act drama, *Washington; or the year 1776,* adapted from the masque *Alfred the Great.* In act 1, Mary Harding, in the character of the Genius of Columbia, descended in an "Aerial Car" to deliver a Poetic Address to Washington. The afterpiece was a "Pantomime of Music, Dialogue and Song" called *Harlequin in Hartford, or, the Touchstone of Truth,* adapted by John Hodgkinson from Dibdin and Garrick. In the course of the pantomime, a view of the Hartford State House painted by Joseph Jefferson, and a view of the city "taken on the water near William's wharf," were exhibited."[60]

Hodgkinson was criticized in Boston in 1796 for his alteration of *The Purse; or Benevolent Tar* to *The Purse; or American Tar* "to flatter, as he thinks, the vanity of Americans."[61] When he took the piece with him to Charleston in 1804, with a new title, *The American Tar Returned from Tripoli,* to reflect current events, it was no better received:

The piece has so little in itself, that it would not have engaged a moment of critical notice, if it were not thought necessary to make a few remarks on the alterations in the name and in the piece; all of which we consider censurable for many reasons. In the first place, we think that there was nothing at all in the piece or its name so offensive as to justify the bold operations of the knife, or of the paste and scissors. Experiments of that kind are hazardous, and ought never to be attempted, but in an urgent and desperate case, which here was out of the question. . . . [The British tar is a] *species of character* wholly distinct, not only from the rest of the world, but from the rest of the very nation in which they were born, and for which they fight. . . . An attempt to tear him from his own home is ridiculous, for the moment he is taken from that he ceases to be. . . . The danger of these things may be perceived in the absurdity which followed close in its train into this alteration: For along with *Jack* we find a *Peer*, all at once Americanized.

No doubt the intention was good, but there was a mistake in the mode. If a compliment is to be paid, America affords abundant subjects of panegyric and honourable allusion, without going across the Atlantic and lugging over classes of character for the purpose of making them denizens of the United States.[62]

In 1813 the piece was still being performed in Boston, and *Polyanthos* reported:

This contemptible production of nobody-knows-who, has been several times repeated, as a trap to catch sailors. Such stage-loyalty may sound very well in England, coming from the mouths of 'his majesty's servants,' but here, it is really too much. The dialogue is more nauseous than a dose of ipecacuanha; and if repeated again, we hope the audience will be furnished by the managers with acids and astringents, gratis.[63]

Plays were also altered to meet the demands of contemporary morality. Nothing was exempt from censorship. *The Marriage of Figaro* was condemned in Philadelphia as "one of the most indecent productions of the last century."[64] That old warhorse of the eighteenth-century playhouse, *The Beaux' Stratagem,* was criticized in Boston in 1807 because of "the extreme licentiousness of its dialogue, and immorality of its tendency."[65] Even the grand old favorite *Love in a Village* fell out of favor in Boston:

The opera abounds with indelicacies of allusion and double entendres, which appear sometimes with only one meaning, and has only two excuses for being brought forward at this time, after twelve years quiet repose; the one is, that on the first night of a season, the managers could not justly anticipate the company of the ladies; and the other that it abounds with some fine songs . . ."[66]

The critics normally approved strongly "corrections" of offending dialogue: "All that is written should not be spoken. Cannot the manager erase? Why then must innocence blush, and modesty hide her face?"[67]

Censorship was not the only reason for changes in dialogue; actors were also rebuked when they failed to change words to reflect the realities of a particular performance:

Thus some years ago, when *mr. Crosby,* who was upwards of six feet high, and rotund in proportion, played *sir Oliver Surface,* he was invariably saluted as *"little Premium,"* and spoken of as "the *little* ill-looking fellow over on the settee." This night *mr. Collins,* who is not much shorter, though something less bulky, than *mr. Crosby,* was hailed as the *little* french tailor, from beginning to end.[68]

The practice of adaptation was not unique to English opera; straight drama and "grand" opera were similarly treated. Schiller's *The Robbers* was modified by Hodgkinson "to answer the requisitions of modern taste" and correctness.[69] Instead of having Charles de Moor kill his virtuous wife, he killed himself instead, and died "giving wholesome moral advice to the robbers, and extorting from them a promise of reformation."[70] Many of the Shakespeare plays performed in America were the adaptations made by David Garrick. When *Romeo and Juliet* was performed in Boston, it had "experienced many revisions and alterations . . . last by Garrick, whose judicious mind saw at once the most obvious points required for stage-effect, and who alone seems to have been successful in his improvement of the text."[71] *King Lear* was performed in the version by Nahum Tate, with further alterations by Garrick:

The moral is now more complete than before, for although Gonerill, Regen and Edmund were deservedly punished for their crimes, yet Lear and Cordelia, were killed without reason and without fault. But now they survive their enemies and their virtue is crowned with happiness.[72]

In *Macbeth,* the music of Matthew Locke was used along with "Scotch music between the Acts, adapted and compiled by Mr. Carr";[73] in *Coriolanus,* the entry of the hero was accompanied by a chorus singing Handel's "See the Conquering Hero Comes";[74] and in *Romeo and*

Juliet a main attraction was the procession of Juliet to the tomb of the Capulets, accompanied by a dirge.[75]

Nor was the practice of alteration unique to the States; the role of Lord Aimworth in *Maid of the Mill* was performed without the songs on the London stage by such actors as Barry, Mossop, and John Philip Kemble. This practice survived in England well into the nineteenth century; a German prince reported of a performance of *The Marriage of Figaro* late in the 1820s:

> You will hardly believe me when I tell you that neither the Count, the Countess nor Figaro sang; these parts were given to mere actors, and their principal songs, with some little alteration in the words, were sung by the other singers; to add to this, the gardener roared out some interpolated English songs, which suited Mozart just as a pitch-plaster would suit the face of the Venus de' Medici. The whole opera, was, moreover, "arranged" by a certain Mr. Bishop (a circumstance which I had seen noticed in the bill, but did not understand until now)—that is, adapted to English ears by means of the most tasteless and shocking alterations.[76]

Nor were the managers, arrangers, and performers of the late eighteenth- and early nineteenth-century unique in their urge to revise and adapt. Following the many permutations of *The Black Crook* through the latter part of the nineteenth century and the early part of the twentieth offers a similar lesson in opportunism and expediency. Anyone who has studied the checkered career of Leonard Bernstein's *Candide* on Broadway and in the opera house or seen the recent London revival of Stephen Sondheim's *Follies* knows that the urge to "improve" theatrical works remains nearly irresistible. What distinguishes the post-Revolutionary period, however, is the fact that music—or plays—once written ceased to be the intellectual or artistic property of the creator. Though usually still credited to the originator, the work became an independent entity, continually molded and remolded by countless individuals to meet the ever-changing demands of various repertory companies. Each performance created the work anew, and the whole was ever the sum of new and distinctive parts.

4
THE THEATRES

To fully appreciate the status and significance of theatrical enterprises in American cities, some statistics regarding their size
and number are in order. Three censuses taken at the turn of the nineteenth century show clearly the growth of the principal cities and their
size relative to other American towns of the day. The populations of
the six largest cities are shown in Table 1.[1]

In 1790 only twenty-four cities and towns in the country had populations of 2,500 or more. In 1800 only 390,000 Americans (about 7
percent of the population) lived in the "Western" states and territories
beyond the Appalachians. The remainder still lived in cities and towns
along the eastern seaboard. By 1810 western cities had grown dramatically. Providence had fallen to seventh in size and New Orleans
was sixth with 17,200 residents. Cincinnati was a thriving town of
2,500.

By the late 1790s the four largest American cities—New York, Boston, Philadelphia, and Charleston—had become major theatrical centers, each with one or more resident theatrical troupes and well-fitted
theatres in the English style. These theatres were often decorated with

Table 1   Populations of American Cities

	1790	1800	1810
New York	32,305	63,735	96,400
Philadelphia	28,522	68,200	91,900
Boston	18,038	35,248	33,300
Charleston	16,359	18,844	24,700
Baltimore	13,503	26,519	35,600
Providence	6,371	7,614	10,100
Total U.S. population	3,929,000	5,297,000	8,419,000

sufficient elegance to amaze and impress visitors from France and England. Many other American cities—Baltimore, Savannah, Hartford, Providence, and others—had theatres as well, often visited regularly by troupes from the four major centers and usually available to various smaller touring companies. As Americans moved west, so did the acting troupes, and increasing numbers of theatres were built as the nineteenth century began.

In the typical theatre the audience could choose from three areas of seating: the pit, the boxes, and the gallery. The pit lay well below the stage at the front and sloped upward toward the back; it was equipped with rows of backless benches that extended all the way across the theatre, leaving little knee room between, and the narrowest of aisles at the sides. Doors at the front, near the stage, provided access; corridors ran beside the pit, under the boxes, to the outside. A contemporary writer speaks of "groping our way through the dismal subterraneous passage that leads from the pit."[2] The pit dwellers generally reached their seats by walking on the benches; once there it was often necessary to remain standing—in order to see and hear what was occurring on the stage if one were near the front, to see over those standing in front, or simply to keep one's trousers clean. (The pit was traditionally occupied only by men; women sat in the boxes.)

I found, if I were near the orchestra, or within two or three seats of it, I could see nothing of what was going on above. It was like being in a well. I could hear, it is true; but the sounds came so confusedly to my ear from the mouths of the actors aloft, that I could not distinguish one word in five."[3]

The managers in New York complained that "the custom of standing on the seats in the pit is highly indecorous," and that "it is seen in no part of the world but in New-York. It in fact answers no other end to those who practise it, but to dirty the benches, and by that means to spoil their cloaths."[4]

The boxes encircled the sides and back of the auditorium in several tiers. The "front boxes" were actually located at the rear of the house, behind the pit and facing the stage; the "side boxes" faced inward toward each other on both sides of the house. Ordinarily protected to about waist height with railings, paneling, or curtains, they contained rows of benches or chairs, with little space for knees, elbows, or excess clothing. Each box had its own door with a key; though a boxkeeper was on duty to admit the patrons, there were still appeals in the newspapers for the return of the keys. In Royall Tyler's *The Contrast* (1787), Jonathan describes his visit to the John Street Theatre in New York: "And so I saw a power of topping folks, all sitting round in little cabbins, 'just like father's corn-cribs.'" In spite of the poor visibility in the side boxes (especially in the second or third rows of seats) the lower tiers were the accepted seats for persons of quality.

The "gallery gods" occupied the topmost balcony in the rear, above the front boxes and supported by pillars. The galleries had rows of benches or, in some cases, just standing room. Separate entrances and stairways protected the "better patrons" from the lower classes occupying these least expensive seats; gallery patrons were not allowed in the lobbies. Jonathan in *The Contrast* speaks of climbing "clean up to the garret, just like a meeting-house gallery."[5]

The stage extended twelve to fifteen feet beyond the proscenium arch, and most acting took place on this extension (what would today be called the apron). Exits and entrances could be made through the doorways in the sides of the proscenium arch, or between the wings. There were ordinarily stage boxes at either side of the stage apron, and when celebrities such as the President visited the theatre, they would sit in these highly visible boxes. Balconies were often located above the proscenium doors; they could be used for balcony scenes, or on occasion as additional stage boxes. The raked stage sloped upward from front to back, at the rate of $\frac{3}{8}$ inch to $\frac{1}{2}$ inch per foot.[6]

A traditional roller curtain of heavy green baize closed the opening of the proscenium arch until the beginning of the play. Once raised, it would remain open until the play was over. By the end of the eighteenth century a drop curtain was sometimes used to cover the stage at the end of each act; this was usually a decorative painted canvas curtain that fell just behind the position of the proscenium curtain.[7] Entertainments between acts, either before the curtain, on the apron in front of the scene for the previous act, or occasionally on an empty stage, were also used to mark off the sections of the play. The wall above the proscenium arch, called the frontispiece, was usually highly decorated, and contained an emblem and a motto of some sort.

The area called the orchestra lay below and between the pit and the stage, with access through a pair of doors below the stage, one at each side. Washington Irving describes how the "worthy gentlemen" of the orchestra "came crawling out of their holes" and began to tune their instruments, a process he believed could just as well have been done "in their cavern under the stage."[8] It was not only traditional but sometimes necessary to separate the orchestra from the pit by a rail surmounted with iron spikes.[9]

Much of the lighting for the stage served as house lighting, and vice versa. One of the reasons actors moved out onto the apron was to take advantage of the better lighting there, available from both the footlights and the houselights. A large chandelier hung above the center of the pit, and sometimes another was placed over the apron; it was a major refinement when these chandeliers could be raised before the performance began, but even so they would burn throughout the evening. Candle snuffers moved through the audience as needed, tending the candles, and the danger of hot candle grease dripping on one's head and clothes was one of the hazards of sitting in the pit. One gentleman who sat in the center of the pit in New York discovered a man near him "whose new dark coat had received a plentiful distillation of spermaceti, from the candles of the chandelier which hung over him, while his attention was wholly engrossed with gaping at what passed on the stage." Soon everyone in the vicinity "came in for a share of the same fate." [10]

Often other chandeliers hung near the proscenium doors, and there were frequently candelabra on the fronts of the boxes or on the columns between. In 1798 New York's Park Theatre was illuminated by seventy-six candles "exclusive of those . . . on the stage and in the orchestra." [11] Sometimes oil lamps with shades (called patent lamps) were also used; they eventually replaced the candles. The Charleston Theatre had oil lamps at its opening in 1793, the Philadelphia theatre converted to oil lighting in 1810 and the Boston Federal Street Theatre in 1811, while New York's Park Theatre possessed at least some patent lamps by 1807.

The heat and smoke in the upper parts of the theatre must have become nearly unbearable as performances progressed, especially in summer; in winter they partially compensated for the lack of other heating in many theatres. Such heat as there was came from a combination of radiation from the lighting, the fireplaces or stoves in the lobbies, and whatever heating devices the playgoers brought with them. Various efforts were made to warm the theatres, from installing flooring and advising theatregoers to bring their own stoves (New York, 1750),[12] to the provision of stoves in boxes (Albany, 1785).[13] In Boston's new theatre in 1794, the trustees required the managers to "provide sufficient fires in the several stoves to keep the house sufficiently warm." [14] The managers at Providence still found it necessary in 1801 to assure the public that "a large Stove will be fixed in the Lobby, and every Method taken to render the theatre warm and comfortable," [15] while in 1813, the managers at New York's Park Theatre "were at great expence in the erecting of RUSSIAN Stoves, to obviate the inconvenience hitherto experienced by the audience in cold and tempestuous weather, and thus feel warranted in assuring the public that the inside of the theatre will be perfectly warm and comfortable."[16] The bars found in the box lobbies of most theatres probably provided further warmth.

Numerous attempts were made to cool the theatres in summer. In Charleston these techniques included windows in the boxes, ventilators in the roof, and the installation of "an air-pump of such construction as to render the theatre pleasant and comfortable, even in cases of crowded audiences."[17] The managers made a colossal effort at the Southwark Theatre in Philadelphia in 1791, where "in addition to the wind sail, fire engines will, during the afternoon, be kept constantly playing on the roof and walls of the theatre."[18] A "new Front Cloth," the earliest act curtain at the Southwark, was used in 1802, not for dramatic ends but "in order to render the Theatre cool and pleasant" by shielding the audience from the heat of the stage lights between the acts![19]

The smoke of the lighting rapidly darkened the interiors of the playhouses, and the scene painters and carpenters were kept busy between seasons repainting and refurbishing. Repainting was an annual affair, and most houses seemed to need complete redecoration (new draperies, cushions, ornamental panels and columns, emblematic figures, and so on) after about five years. Audiences also contended with poor visibility and tainted air caused by the smoke. In 1810 the Philadelphia theatre had a new ceiling:

The interstices, which are all open for the purposes of ventilation, communicate with a large tube of no less than six feet in diameter, that ascends through the roof for the purpose of carrying off from the auditory, the smoke and foul air, which has hitherto, perceptibly to the eye, sojourned in it, like a thick fog.[20]

The Philadelphia theatre was altered for gas lighting in 1816, and other major cities followed suit within the next decade. While gas provided control of the amount and variation of lighting in both stage and auditorium, it generated additional heat; this problem continued to plague theatres through most of the nineteenth century.

The fire hazards were enormous: add to the open fires used for heating and lighting the fact that scenery, costumes, and the buildings themselves were extremely flammable. The buildings were always empty for a period of hours after every performance, and stray sparks or flames could easily gain a sure foothold. It is no surprise that many theatres burned to the ground not once, but several times.

THE CHARLESTON THEATRE

The Charleston Theatre, facing Broad Street on Savage's Green, was a particularly elegant structure seating 1,200. The architects were James Hoban, architect of the White House, and Captain Toomer.[21] Construction began in August 1792 under the supervision of Thomas Wade West, and it opened on February 11, 1793. A letter in the *New York Magazine* dated August 18, 1792, describes the plans for cornerstone laying two days later and gives details of the new theatre:

The dimensions, we are told, are as follows: 125 feet in length, the width 56 feet, the height 37 feet, with an handsome pediment, stone ornaments, a flight of stone steps, and a courtyard palisaded. The front will be in Broadstreet and the pit entrance in Middleton St. The different [ticket] offices will be calculated so as not to interfere with each other; the stage is to be 56 feet in length, the front circular, with three rows of patent [oil] lamps; the boxes will be constructed so that small parties may be accommodated with a single box; to every box there will be a window and a venetian blind; three tiers of boxes, decorated with 32 columns; to each column a glass chandelier, with five lights; the lower tier balustraded; the middle and upper tiers paneled; fancy paintings, the ground French white, the mouldings and projections silvered; in the ceiling there will be three ventilators. The frontispiece, balconies and stage doors, will be similar to those of the opera-house, London.[22]

A writer in the *City Gazette* applauded the "liberality and taste" of the managers "in the scenery, decorations and embellishments, which,

however they may be exceeded in gaudy glitter, can nowhere be surpassed in neatness and simple elegance."[23]

When the Charleston Theatre opened for the 1804–5 season, the
theatre had been "Elegantly Ornamented and Painted, by Mr. GRA-
HAM, from the Theatres of New-York and Boston."[24] In January
1805, the theatre's ceiling was altered to improve the acoustics:

The Managers respectfully acquaint the Public, that an alteration at very
considerable expense has been made in the form of this cieling [sic], which
they hope will not only prove an additional ornament of beauty to the eye of
the auditor, but add very much to the effect of the performances, by enabling
the weakest voice to be heard distinctly in any part of the house."[25]

Further improvements were made in 1812 to reassure the audience,
following a disastrous fire at Richmond in a theatre run by the same
management. To "facilitate the escape of the audience in case of
alarm," thirteen doors opened directly into the street, "by which the
House can be emptied, almost in an instant."[26]

A second Charleston theatre, known as the City Theatre or Church-
Street Theatre, was opened by a group of French actors in 1794. Located in the southern part of the city near the Battery, it was used
periodically until 1800, when it was remodeled as a concert hall. From
1800 until his death in 1812, Alexander Placide operated a summer
theatre at Vaux-Hall Gardens, which offered concerts, pantomimes,
ice cream, and cold baths.

PHILADELPHIA'S CHESTNUT STREET "NEW" THEATRE

Regular theatrical performances were originally brought to Philadelphia by the American Company at the wooden Society Hall Theatre,
built by David Douglass in 1759, and the brick and wood Southwark
Theatre, built in 1766. On February 17, 1794, Alexander Reinagle
and Thomas Wignell opened their new theatre on the north side of

Chestnut Street at Fourth Street, and thereafter Philadelphia had its own resident company, which soon eliminated all competition. The Old American Company performed at the Southwark once more in the fall of 1794; the playhouse was later used periodically by traveling companies or impromptu troupes, but never housed a regular season again. In 1813 it was used by the Theatrical Commonwealth for an unsuccessful season, and the actors complained that "vile and villainous prejudice" had made it unfashionable.[27]

The plans for the Chestnut Street theatre were brought from England by Wignell as "a true model of the new theatre," completely built in miniature.[28] The plans may well have been prepared by John Inigo Richards, Wignell's brother-in-law, who designed much of the scenery. The exterior of the New Theatre measured 90 feet across the front and 134 feet deep, with the center crowned by a pediment.[29]

As in most theatres of the period, lavish amounts of time and paint were expended in the decoration of the interior, while the exterior was nearly forgotten. Moreau de St. Méry said the building had "nothing on its brick facade to indicate that it is a public building. The entrance is shabby and differs in no wise from that of an ordinary house."[30] Indeed, an 1800 engraving shows a large, apparently wooden canopy where the entrance porch would eventually be placed. In 1801 the managers appropriated the receipts of one evening to "a fund for compleating the external decorations of the theatre,"[31] but the facade was not completed until 1805. An engraving made in 1804, and perhaps based on the plans for the new facade, shows the theatre nearly complete (fig. 4). The plans for completing the structure were prepared by Benjamin Henry Latrobe.[32] A flight of marble steps led up to the box lobby through a porch or entryway with ten Corinthian columns.[33] The facade included two fifteen-foot-wide marble wings at street level on either side of the portico, running back from the street on either side, and decorated with emblematical figures in tablets.[34] Entries to pit and gallery were through the wings.

Even after the completion of the facade, the condition of the theatre

Figure 4. Exterior of New Theatre, Philadelphia, from an aquatint by Gilbert Fox after the 1804 engracing by William Birch. Harvard Theatre Collection.

was not all that could be desired. In 1806 the *Theatrical Censor* commented that the theatre

deserves to be censured for its dirty appearance, and for its tasteless rose-coloured and clumsy columns. At a Theatre, every thing should be elegant. The eye should be exhilarated. We can mope at home, and at less expense. It must be long since this house was painted; and why is there not a little gilding?

In 1808 figures of Tragedy and Comedy by William Rush of Philadelphia were placed in niches on either side of the large central "Venetian" window, over which were emblematical insignia in two circular tablets.[35] The exterior walls of the house were given a fresh coat of paint in 1809, but *The Thespian Monitor* suggested that the managers should next tend to the glazing and painting of the broken windows in various parts of the front and sides.[36] Perhaps this was done; in 1811 James Mease described the exterior as "handsome."

The interior of the theatre, by contrast, was quite elegant from the time of its opening. At least three descriptions of the original interior survive: one in a letter written by Ezekiel Forman on March 25, 1794,[37] one in the account of *Moreau de Saint Méry's American Journey (1793–1798)*, and another in the *New York Magazine or Literary Repository* of April 1794. The same issue of the *New York Magazine* featured an engraving of the interior of the theatre (fig. 5).[38]

The auditorium was painted gray, with gilded scrolls and carvings.[39] "That part of the theatre *before* the curtain forms a semi-circle; having two rows of boxes extending from side to side, with another row above these, and on a line with the gallery in front."[40] Because of this semicircular construction, the box patron had "a full view from any part of them without having it obstructed by those near to the stage which was too generally the case in all the old theatres."[41] Each tier had fifteen boxes. Each of the five front boxes had seven rows of seats,

Figure 5. Interior of the New Theatre, Philadelphia, 1794. *New York Magazine; or Literary Repository* 4, no. 4 (April 1794), p 194. Harvard Theatre Collection.

rising one behind the other and accommodating a total of thirty-five people in each box. The side boxes had only two benches, with four persons per bench. The boxes could thus seat 755 in all.[42] The seats in the boxes were considered unusually comfortable because of the distance between them.[43]

Paneled at the front, the boxes were also "separated in the front by small columns which interfere with the view."[44] The pillars represented "bundles of reeds (gilt) bound with red fillets; between the pillars [across the top of each box], festoons of crimson curtains, with tassels intervening."[45] The *New York Magazine* reported that the boxes were lined with pink paper with small dark spots; St. Méry said the color was red and "in extremely bad taste." At the upper part of the rear of each box was a "little sash window" which opened into the surrounding box corridor so that air could be admitted without opening the doors.[46] Lighting was provided by

small four-branched chandeliers placed every second box, beginning at the middle of the second box on each side, starting at the stage. Thus there are seven of them on the upper exterior of each tier of boxes. They are supported by gilded iron S's.[47]

The *New York Magazine*'s commentator wrote that the "profusion of glass chandeliers form an assemblage that captivates the eye, and renders the whole a most pleasing spectacle."[48]

The boxes were separated from the gallery "by a partition and iron banister with sharp pointed spikes"; the front of the gallery had a "board wall" and "an iron railing of two bars so that a person is in very little risque of falling into the pit."[49] (The gallery is visible in both upper corners of fig. 5, but seems to lack these defensive details.) The pit itself contained thirteen rows of benches, seating thirty people each (about 400 persons) and "descended in amphitheatre style from the bottom tier of boxes to the orchestra."[50]

The ascent from the front to the back parts of both Pit and Gallery (but more particularly the latter) is very steep, which tho' it may appear a little inconvenient at the first entering of them still proves a great advantage to the persons in the hinder parts, as it renders their view of the Stage, unobstructed by those sitting in front of them.[51]

The entrances to the pit were near the front on either side.

The orchestra pit was rounded in front of the stage; it held "thirty musicians in two rows facing each other."[52] The stage apron was straight, and extended well in front of the proscenium, so that the actors could play directly to anyone in the stage boxes at the sides. The stage itself measured thirty-six feet wide and seventy-one feet deep.[53] Above each of the proscenium doors was a balcony. The stage was lighted by oil lamps. On the frontispiece,

Over the stage & in full view of the whole House two beautiful & descriptive figures are painted, one representing the Genius of Tragedy who sits in a mourning mellancholly [sic] attitude, & the other that of the Genius of Comedy, who stands a little to the left of where the other *sits* and in her hand she holds a scarf on which these words are inscribed in large legible characters: "The Eagle suffers little Birds to sing," & over the heads of these two figures the American Eagle with extended wings is displayed.[54]

St. Méry believed that the acoustics of the house were adequate and sight lines usually good; he described the corridors as roomy and comfortable.[55] A floor plan of the interior shows the location of the adjacent areas (fig. 6). Mease said the greenroom, dressing rooms, scene rooms, and so on were in the added wings.[56] There were numerous backstage dressing rooms, so only three or four persons dressed together. There were also two greenrooms, one used for "music rehearsals, dancing practices, &c., and it was a place where the juvenile members of the corps might indulge their freaks unrestrainedly. The principal greenroom was adjacent to the prompt side, in the west wing," and here actors waited their calls to go onstage.[57]

The theatre was refurbished in the summers of 1801 and 1805.[58] In the summers of 1809 and 1810 it was completely redecorated. In 1809:

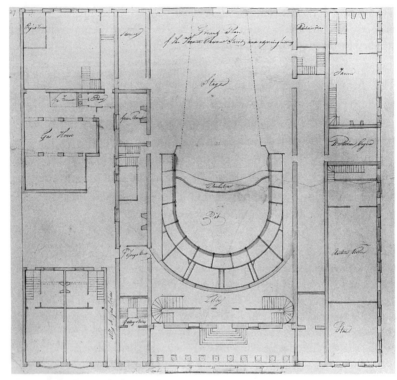

Figure 6. Floor plan of interior of Chestnut Street Theatre, Philadelphia, after 1805. Historical Society of Pennsylvania.

The audience-part is very tastily and superbly decorated with a variety of hues; the boxes have been newly painted, with a cluster of flowers in the resemblance of a wreath, upon the front of each, the ground of white, and the mouldings of a stone colour; the interior is composed of yellow, mingled with occasional white and blue; and the pillars or supporters, which before were of plain gilding, have been transformed into perfect white, with a burnished Corinthian capital to each, and the laurel entwined around the body; the leaf and berry of which forming a gaiety of contrast with a new suit of drapery, dispose the mind to cheerfulness and mirth.[59]

The stage area and ceiling were extensively reworked in 1810, with "allegorical designs and ornamental paintings" by Luke Robbins, the scene painter:

The cieling [*sic*] he has dedicated to Apollo. In the centre is a circle ornamented with the Apollonion lyre, entwined with laurel and fret work. . . . The radii from the circle are stone colour and divided by stiles, so as to form six large pannels, in which are basso relievo figures of boys, each holding an emblem of music. The oblong pannels are ornamented with musical trophies.

The stage area had been renewed as well, with fresh paint and some functional changes:

The frontispiece represents the tragic and comic Muses imploring protection from the genius of America. The motto is appropriate, and taken from Dr. Johnson's celebrated prologue on the opening of Drury Lane theatre.[60]

According to James Mease, this motto was "For useful mirth, and salutary woe."[61]

The whole is supported by imposts bearing fanciful pilasters of the composite order with sunk pannels on a verditer ground, embellished with ornaments of gold. The stage doors and balconies are displayed in the same way. The columns are bronze with varnished caps and bases. The ground of the dado is a rich yellowish stone colour, with sunk pannels of bright blue embellished with gold afagals and fret work. One improvement deserves to be here particularly noticed, as denoting not only a good taste in discerning a defect, but, as it could not be entirely removed, much ingenuity in diminishing it. The stage doors and balconies which opened too intimately upon the audience are now partially concealed by imposts and pilasters, and by that means apparently thrown back and separated from the proscenium.

The stage boxes, too, were remodeled, and refurbished with fresh paint, paper, cushions, and curtains.

The stage boxes, are thrown into an elliptical form, contain one seat more each than the other side boxes, and are so constructed as to have an equal view of the stage.

The draperies are scarlet and sky blue, with deep fringe and tassels. The cushions and seats blue, edged with scarlet and black fringe, with a small gold fillet all round. The interior of the boxes are lemon colour, with rich bordering, and terminates with two mock windows, the sashes of which are mirrors.[62]

New oil lighting was installed in the house and on the stage, as well, including Grecian globe lights around the circle of boxes (see chapter 5).

This theatre was destroyed by fire in 1820.

BOSTON'S FEDERAL STREET THEATRE

The Boston Theatre on Federal Street, designed by Charles Bulfinch, opened on February 3, 1794. It was destroyed by fire on January 26, 1798: "The entire inside of perhaps the most elegant building in the United States was totally destroyed—nothing being left unconsumed but the brick walls."[63] It was rebuilt within the year, however, using much of the original framework, and stood until 1852. William W. Clapp provided a description of this theatre:

The theatre in those days was considered a fine specimen of architecture and creditable to the architect, Mr. Bulfinch. It is alluded to as a lofty spacious edifice, substantially built of brick, with stone facias, imposts, &c. It was one hundred and forty feet long, sixty-one feet wide, and forty feet high. The entrances to the different parts of the house were distinct, and at the time the opponents of the theatre made strong use of this fact, alleging that by affording a special door to that portion of the house, usually the resort of the vile of both sexes, a premium on vice was offered. In front there was a projecting arcade, which enabled carriages to land company under cover.[64]

The original plan for the exterior (shown on a medal presented to Bulfinch in 1794), was far more elaborate than the facade that was rebuilt after the fire (fig. 7). The rebuilt exterior lacked many of the pillars, carvings, railings, and other decorative (and expensive) touches envisioned by the architect.[65]

The interior of the building was tastefully decorated. The stage opening was thirty-one feet wide, ornamented on each side by two columns, and between them a stage door and a projecting iron balcony. Over the columns a cornice and balustrade were carried across the opening; above was painted a flow of crimson drapery, and the arms of the Union and the State of Massachusetts,

Figure 7. Exterior of Boston Federal Street Theatre after the remodeling that followed the fire of 1798. Harvard Theatre Collection.

blended with emblems, tragic and comic. A ribbon depending from the arms, bore the motto, 'All the world's a stage.'[66]

The theatre was able to seat 1,060 people—350 in the thirty boxes arranged in two rows; 280 in the pit, 280 in the gallery, and 150 in the "slips" or side galleries. A third row of boxes was added—presumably in place of the slips—after the fire.[67]

The building also contained some of the nontheatrical amenities common to theatres of the time:

At the end of the building a noble and elegant dancing room was constructed. This was fifty-eight feet long, thirty-six wide, and twenty-six high, richly ornamented with Corinthian columns and pilasters. There were spacious card and tea rooms, and kitchens with proper conveniences.[68]

The chandeliers and free-standing girandoles used for lighting this assembly room were made by Robert Cribb of London on Bulfinch's order. The ground floor below the assembly room contained a restaurant and a room used for dancing classes.[69]

In the fall of 1813 *Polyanthos* reported that John Penniman had provided "two figures, representing the tragic muse standing on a pedestal on the right side of the stage, and her sister the comic muse, placed at the left. . . . The stage doors also, the pilastres, balconies, &c. have been newly painted and decorated."[70]

Two traveling Englishmen were impressed—and apparently surprised—by the Federal Street Theatre. Henry Wansey reported that the Boston Theatre in 1794 was "far superior in taste, elegance, and convenience to the Bath, or any other country theatre that I have yet seen in England."[71] After the rebuilding of the theatre in 1798, John Bernard reported that it "displayed a taste and completeness worthy of London."[72]

Bernard was also surprised to find a second playhouse in Boston: the Haymarket Theatre, a large and unpretentious wooden structure opened in 1796 at the corner of Boylston and Tremont streets. Boston was not yet able to support two theatres, but the two companies represented the opposing political views of the Federalists and Jacobins. The Haymarket stood until 1803.

NEW YORK'S PARK THEATRE

The Park Theatre in New York was in Park Row near Ann Street. It replaced the John Street Theatre, which had served New York from 1767 to 1798. The architect was Joseph Mangin, the designer of New York's City Hall, although some work may have been done by Marc Isambard Brunel, then a clerk in Mangin's office.[73] Plans were drawn in 1793, construction began in 1795, and the building was opened, unfinished, on January 19, 1798. It reopened for its second season on December 3, 1798, "after having undergone a total change in its appearance and being finished in the superb style, originally intended by its proprietors."[74]

The exterior dimensions of the Park Theatre were 80 feet wide and 165 feet deep, with an undecorated stone facade that apparently included little of the architect's original conception.[75] Mangin's design

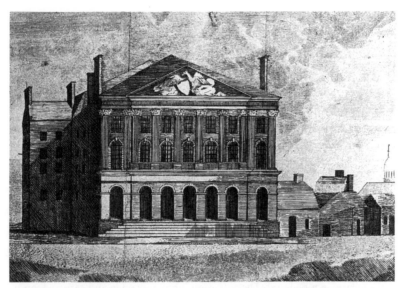

Figure 8. New York Park Theatre, engraving by Tisdale. *Longworth's American Almanack, New York Register, and City Directory,* 1797. Courtesy American Antiquarian Society.

had called for seven arched entries, each with an arched window above it on the second story and a square window on the third floor. The pediment above was to have featured a sculpted eagle and shield. These elements are all shown in an early engraving of the theatre by Tisdale (fig. 8), and although the architectural structure portrayed may be essentially correct, the decoration, including the coat-of-arms on the facade, was apparently never completed.[76] Ireland describes the theatre as "a plain, barn-like structure, devoid of any architectural pretensions . . ."[77] In 1807 the *Evening Post* disparaged the building as "a standing libel on the taste of the town,"[78] and in 1809 a writer described it in even less complimentary terms:

walking through the park, I was struck by the barbarous front of the theatre (the temple of the *muses*, the resort of *fashion*, the school of *morals*, the consolation of *rich* and *poor*, built by the most *spirited* men in town, managed by the most *liberal,* and supported by the *best* actors in the country) resembling a miserable barrack, stretching its vast crazy shoulders over a dead wall of brick, here and there interspersed with a few broken panes of glass, to illuminate the grog-shop up stairs, and the grand saloon below. Is this, thought I, the *grand* front of the *new* theatre of New-York? Do those bare joists and filthy walls bespeak wealthy proprietors? Do those copious streams of *indescribable distillation,* which run from its sides along the pavement, 'shedding their *sweets* around,' indicate the cleanliness or delicacy of *enlightened* managers?[79]

Access to the theatre was gained by ascending "about six steps up to the box entrance" and entering "three green baize doors from the outside lobby."

There was a box office on the right hand as you entered. In a niche in the centre of the building was, some time after the house was erected, a statue of Shakespeare on a pedestal. The extension lobby was wide and carpeted, and in cold weather two blazing fires were kept up at either end of the lobbies. There was a box door at each box of the first tier, and a box keeper ever ready to open to the audience.[80]

The interior of the house was commodious, with seats for 2,000. The *Daily Advertiser* praised it for its properties of sight and sound: "We do not remember to have been in any theatre where the view of the stage is so complete from all parts of the house, or where the actors are heard with such distinctness."[81] The *Commercial Advertiser* reported that spectators, even those in the front boxes, were "within a very convenient distance, both for seeing and hearing."[82] Dunlap says "there were no pillars as props to the upper boxes" in this house; "they were supported by timbers projecting from the walls, and appeared, with their tenons, self-balanced." This use of cantilevered boxes meant that there were no sight obstructions in the front of the boxes.[83]

"The interior was tastefully ornamented in light pink and gold,"[84] and was lighted by means of seventy-six candles on the fronts of the boxes.[85] The pit was "remarkably commodious,"[86] but it had to be approached by a "narrow, sandy and utterly dark passage." [87] "There were no chairs in either boxes or pit, but cushioned seats. The proscenium had stage doors and about four or five private boxes"; [88] the frontispiece was decorated with a gorgon head and the motto, "Know Thyself." The front curtain of blue mohair and gold fringe had a central lyre and the motto "To hold the Mirror up to Nature."

> The Boxes are disposed in three semi-circular rows, from one side to the other of the stage—and the Gallery is thrown back of the upper front boxes. The total omission of pillars as supports to the boxes, avoids a common and great obstacle (in Theatres) to the view—and when the house is filled, presents an unbroken line of spectators, which forms no uninteresting part of the *spectacle*. [89]

All the boxes were named for European playwrights. [90] A particularly large box occupied the second tier of front boxes; it was capable of holding 200 to 300 persons. This "Shakspeare Box," almost like a lower gallery, was where the critics sat. [91]

The art of the scene painters was used in the decoration of the house, as described by Washington Irving in 1802:

> Observe what a fine effect the dark colouring of the wall has upon the white faces of the audience, which glare like the stars in a dark night. And then what can be more pretty than the painting in the front of the boxes,—those little masters and misses sucking their thumbs, and making mouths at the audience? . . . [The chandelier was] to illumine the heavens, and set off to advantage the little periwigg'd Cupids, tumbling head over heels, with which the painter has decorated the dome. [92]

The dressing rooms at the Park Theatre were above the greenroom, and a passageway led from Theatre Alley at the rear directly to the greenroom, the stage, and the stairway to the dressing rooms. The second floor had three dressing rooms used by the principal performers, and the third floor also had three rooms, normally shared. Above this were other rooms, more crowded, for "the persons of lesser weight in this community, as in other places, rising nearer the clouds, as poets and painters mount to garrets." At the top of the house were the "tailors, supernumeraries and trumpery, all called *wardrobe*." Opposite the back door of the theatre, on Theatre Alley, was "a lofty wooden pile, erected for, and occupied by, the painters, machinists, and carpenters of the establishment."[93]

Major alterations were made to the theatre during the summer of 1807. The *New-York Evening Post* reported that, at least as far as the interior was concerned,

New-York may now boast of a Theatre which unites more of taste, grandeur, room, convenience and elegance than any one in the United States; several foreigners who have seen and examined it, have pronounced it superior to any one in Europe.[94]

The entire interior was taken apart, except for the walls and the stage, and rebuilt and elaborately redecorated under the direction of John J. Holland. The pit was widened and deepened, the gallery was reduced in size, and the angle of sight was improved in both. Instead of three tiers of boxes, the new house contained four, perhaps using some of the space formerly devoted to the gallery to construct boxes in the slips. Entrance to the boxes was through spacious, well-lighted lobbies. In case of fire, there were three passageways from the boxes to the street, and two large hallways from the pit. The boxes could accommodate more than 1,200 (392 in the lower tier, 360 each in the second and third tiers, and 160 in the slip tier), the pit 500, and the gallery about 600.

"The ceiling [was] painted as a dome, with panels of a light purple, and gold mouldings; the centre a balustrade and sky." The boxes were separated by "light, airy pillars of about five inches diameter, reeded and silver lackered, with gilt capitals and base." The box fronts "instead of being, as usual, perpendicular, fall in at top, and thus give room to the knees, which is considered an improvement upon the plan of all former theatres." The boxes were painted, papered, and ornamented in costly style: "The box-fronts (except the fourth row) are divided into panels, blue ground, with white and gold ornaments." The seats were covered with crimson, and a crimson festoon drapery separated each box from the next.

There were four private stage boxes, each with a "handsomely furnished" small retiring room attached. A large oval mirror was placed at the end of each stage box, to reflect "the whole of the audience on the first row." The massive columns on each side of the proscenium had been removed, and replaced by "two fluted pilastres of complete Corinthian order with an inscription of GNOTHI SEAUTON [Know thyself] on the architrave." This proscenium design was said to have been "modelled after the celebrated front of the temple of Jupiter, at Athens."

The lower boxes were lighted by ten glass chandeliers, projecting from the pillars at the front of every other box, and suspended from gilt iron brackets. The upper tiers were similarly lighted with patent lamps. The public rooms were also remodeled; the lower box lobby had a "handsome colonnade, with mirrors, and fireplaces at each end, the whole lighted by glass lamps between the columns." A bar room and supper room were annexed to the pit, and there were two large finished rooms, one over the other, adjacent to the box lobbies. The upper of these rooms was "a sort of bar room for gentlemen." The lower room was "fitted in an elegant style" and "intended as a tea, coffee, confectionary and fruit room for ladies." The furniture in this spacious room was "in the newest fashion," and it was "lighted by three elegant chandeliers suspended from the ceiling."[95]

The theatre received further refurbishment during the summer of 1809, once again employing the talents of the chief scene painter.

During the recess the interior of the house had undergone very material alterations, and had been embellished by the hand of mr. Holland in a style that reflects equal honor on his taste and judgment. 'The fronts of the boxes are in imitation of pannels of a beautiful fawn color, surrounded by a white border richly decorated with gold ornaments. The style is of french grey; and between it, and the border of the pannel, is a plain band of light purple. The cove, beneath the boxes, is also of purple with gold mouldings and ornaments. The columns, which were last year of silver, are now gold; and that which then formed their pedestal is translated into a small pannel, enriched with gold ornaments. The backs of the boxes are again painted in the fashion of pannels, and are changed from straw color to a light pink, with a border of white—the style purple and the doors mahogany.

'The lobbies have not been neglected. The walls are of light straw color, with white ceiling;—the colonnade in the first lobby corresponding with the others;—the shafts of the columns yellow, the caps and bases white as before.

'The patent lamps, by which the house was formerly lighted are intirely removed;—a large and brilliant chandelier, suspended from the dome, with two of corresponding richness on the right and left of the curtain, together with the smaller ones dispersed round the second and third tier of boxes, furnish a new and improved light to the audience part of the house.—Indeed, the alterations throughout are most judicious, and the *tout ensemble* airy and beautiful.'[96]

The boxes painted "in the fashion of panels," the pedestals which have been transformed to panels, and the ceiling "painted as a dome" raise interesting but probably unanswerable questions about the two- or three-dimensionality of much of the elaborate interior decoration of these theatres; after all, they were designed and executed by those master illusionists, the scene painters.

The Park Theatre burned in 1820, and reopened on the same site on September 1, 1821. It was rebuilt on the same foundation and using some of the walls, so it had the same dimensions,[97] with four tiers of boxes, each with fourteen boxes and fifteen pillars. This second theatre was destroyed by fire in 1848.

SMALL TOWN THEATRES

Many small towns had no theatre, and made do with whatever space was available, including taverns, assembly rooms, and public buildings. Other communities erected theatres for the use of major companies who visited on an annual basis to present legitimate drama and other forms of entertainment. Still other towns contrived theatres for the use of local semiprofessional companies and other entertainers, with the opportunity to host an occasional strolling company. The towns and cities discussed here are examples of these smaller centers.

When a group of actors from Boston presented the first dramatic performances in Portland, Maine, in October 1794, they used the assembly hall on King Street (later India Street).

The Assembly Room, on the second story, was about thirty-five feet by twenty-seven feet in floor dimensions, allowing for an audience of between seventy and a hundred, with a stage fifteen feet wide by seven deep. A six-foot fireplace at each end of the room kept the theatre warm.[98]

The first postwar theatrical performance in Providence took place at the courthouse in December 1792, where Joseph Harper, temporarily cast out of Boston because of the antitheatre laws, erected a temporary theatre for the performance of moral and entertaining "lectures." When Harper returned in December 1794, he performed at a temporary theatre behind Major McLane's Coffee House. This theatre was fitted with boxes, pit, and gallery. Gentlemen of the town met at the Coffee House on April 14, 1795, to raise a subscription to build a permanent theatre; a building committee was immediately appointed.[99]

When Mr. Ricketts' Equestrian Circus performed in Providence in the first week of August 1795, it performed in a structure located "On the Hill, near the Powder-House," which was complete with boxes and pit.[100] John Durang relates that Ricketts erected a new wooden circus in each town, and sold it for half price when the company moved on.[101]

On August 6, 1795, "the Workmen began to raise the New Theatre erecting in this Town.—The Building is to be 81 Feet by 50, and will be completed with all Expedition." This prediction apparently proved true; the "large and commodious" New Theatre was opened as "a Temple dedicated to Apollo and the Muses" on September 2, by a troupe of actors from Boston led by Harper. This theatre was complete with boxes (price, one dollar), pit (three-quarters of a dollar), and gallery (two and three pence).[102] The front of the theatre had three doors, with the center door leading to the boxes and separate doors to the pit and gallery on the sides. The proscenium measured sixteen feet high by twenty-four feet wide, and the frontispiece bore the motto "Pleasure the means, the end virtue." [103]

The Providence Theatre was remodeled with a patriotic and nautical theme in 1814 by Warrall of Boston:

Over the proscenium was an Ionic entablature, the frieze adorned with a gold scroll ornament. On the centre, resting on a tablet, were the sterns of three ships, viz.: the *Independence,* supported by the *United States* on the right, and the *Constitution* on the left. The motto on this tablet was: 'To hold the Mirror up to Nature.' From this hung a crimson curtain with gold fringe and tassels. The ceiling of the proscenium was divided into panels of purple and gold. The dados around the upper tier of boxes [were] adorned with three tablets; those on the right and left contained representations of vessels which had signalized themselves; the *Wasp,* the *Hornet,* the *Enterprise,* and the *Peacock;* that in the centre contained the *Lawrence,* the *Niagara,* and the *Caledonia.* Rostrated columns bore the names of Hull, Decatur, Bainbridge, Lawrence, Jones, Burrows, Washington, and Perry.

The stage was lighted by a new set of brass lamps with globe glasses, which gave brilliancy of effect, and were a security against accident. Many of the scenes were new, being the work of Mr. Warrall.[104]

In Albany, New York, Lewis Hallam's impromptu troupe of actors from the New York theatre performed at the Assembly-Room in Pearl-Street in August 1803.[105] Ten years later Albany had a new theatre, "a building which adds an ornament to this city, and reflects on all concerned in the establishment." [106] It was opened on January 13, 1813, under the management of John Bernard, late of the Boston Theatre.

In Augusta, Georgia, in 1805, "The temporary theatre erected in Reynold-street by Mr. Branthwaite" was opened with a course of entertainments called "Theatrical Varietes." The house had at least 300 seats with a good view, and several excellent scenes, including elegant chamber and street settings. The writer believed that with a small additional expense it would exceed "that of Savannah in size, beauty, and convenience." [107]

The first theatrical performance west of the Alleghenies was held at Transylvania Seminary in Lexington, Kentucky, on April 10, 1790, when a group of students presented a tragedy and a farce.[108] The town had grown to 2,400 persons and was the largest in the West when two theatrical performances were given in the space of a week in 1799. The students at Transylvania University (which had changed its status in 1798) presented *The Busy Body* and *Love a la Mode* on March 1, and a group of amateurs performed *He Would Be a Soldier* and *All the World's a Stage* at the courthouse on March 5. The amateurs performed at the courthouse again on November 21; the bill in the *Kentucky Gazette* announced that there would be "A considerable addition to the scenery." If the phrases "No admittance behind the scenes" and "the curtain to rise at six o'clock" are taken literally, they suggest that at least a few theatrical trappings had been incorporated, at least temporarily, into the room.[109]

In March 1807, the Thespian Society announced a performance at the Travellers' Hall. Bradley's Room at the Traveller's Inn was a fifty-four- by thirty-two-foot assembly room also used for musical performances, debates, and dancing schools.[110] The Thespian Society, a group of amateurs, donated their proceeds to various "laudable uses." When they performed again in December of that year, the bill included an opera, *The Review*.[111]

The first permanent theatre in the West opened at Lexington in October 1808. The *Kentucky Gazette* announced: "THE NEW THEATRE is now completed, in a very handsome style, and will be opened on Wednesday evening, the 13th [12th] October. . . . " The Thespian Society presented *The Sailor's Daughter* and *Ways and Means, or a Trip to Dover* for its first performance in the new theatre. Ticket prices (box, 75 cents; pit, 50 cents; and gallery, for servants, 37½ cents) indicate that the house had all the prescribed elements of a traditional playhouse.[112] The performance was reviewed in the *Kentucky Gazette*:

On Wednesday last, the new Theatre lately erected by Mr. [Luke] Usher in this town was opened. . . . The audience were gratified on their entrance of the Theatre, with a species of accommodation not heretofore known in this country—convenient and safe seats, separated as in Theatres in the atlantic cities. They were also pleased with the plan and decorations of the Theatre, which do much credit to the judgment of the proprietor, Mr. Usher, and with the scenery, which competent judges pronounce to equal what is seen to the eastward, and for which we are indebted to the taste of Mr. Beck. . . . We cannot quit this subject, without congratulating the lovers of the drama,— and the friends of morality, upon the success of the first attempt which has been made to introduce a Theatre in the western country.[113]

In succeeding years, theatre continued to flourish in Lexington, presented not only by various local groups but by touring companies as well. Noah Ludlow performed in the theatre with his touring company in 1816, and described it in uncomplimentary terms:

I was informed that the building had been a brewery, in which Mr. Luke Usher . . . had once conducted his business as a brewer of malt liquors. The second story of this building, a long and narrow one, had been fitted up for dramatic performances by an amateur society. It was probably seventy to eighty feet in length by about twenty-five to thirty feet in width. If I remember rightly, the seats were constructed upon the amphitheatre plan,—gradually rising from the floor, one above the other, to the back, these back seats being reached by a sloping platform at one side. They were simply covered with canvas and painted, without being stuffed or having any backs to them, and the surroundings were of the most simple and unpretending character. The stock of scenery was very limited, and not very well painted. The building stood on an abruptly rising piece of ground, and the audience entered from a street nearly on a level with the floor of the second story. Adjoining the end of the building was a room for the sale of beer and other equally refined refreshments. Underneath the stage were the dressing-rooms for the performers; into these they entered by a door that opened upon a cross-street. The dressing rooms were comfortable enough, and quite equal, in fact, I may say superior, to some theatres of greater pretensions.[114]

Ludlow was even less complimentary about the theatre in Pittsburgh in 1815:

It was the poorest apology for one I had then ever seen; I have, I confess, seen worse since. It was situated on the eastern outskirts of the city, and fronted, I think, on Fifth Street, not far from Wood street. It had been built, I think, by some amateur in theatricals. It contained a pit and one tier of boxes, as they were called. The form was after the old style,—two parallel elongations, with an elliptical curve at the entrance. The decorations, if such they might be termed, were of the plainest kind, and every portion bore the Pittsburgh stamp upon it—coal smut.[115]

John Durang toured in Pennsylvania and Maryland with a small troupe, mostly members of his family, in the summers of 1808 to 1816. In his *Memoir* he describes the theatres in some of the cities where they performed, providing glimpses of the ingenuity necessary for such small touring companies. At Lancaster, Durang performed in "Mr. Rohrer's ball room," and at Lebanon, he "erected a theatre in the unfinish'd third story of Esquire Steover's house, a spacious room over the whole house." He built a fully equipped theatre at Harrisburg:

I converted the store house of Colonel Brook near the ferry into a theatre. I constructed boxes and galery; my stage was compleatly theatrical, 12 foot front and fifteen deep, five wings of a side, with stage doors, frontispiece, and green curtain.

At Reading, Durang used "a large ball room at the principle inn, a sign of Gen'l Washington, keep by Mrs. Wood, an accomplished genteel lady." He performed "at a corner house" owned by a German baker in Carlisle, and at Hanover he used the ballroom at the stage house. At Chambersburg one year, Durang was able to benefit from an old friendship:

We performed in the brewhouse of Mr. George Barnetz, an old friend of mine or rather school fellow, who gave me the loan of the place through friendship. He had all the inside taken out to make alterations and stop'd the workmen to accommodate me till I was done, for which I made him a compliment of a sum, but he send [*sic*] me half of the money back again. Here we performed *The Forty Thieves*, and had a small horse on the stage.

Another year (1816), however, Durang had to make other arrangements in Chambersburg: "I converted a coachmaker's shope in to a

theatre, for which I paid $20 a week." At Hagerstown, he "erected
a theatre in the ball room at a hotel keep by Mr. Brown, a stage
house . . ."[116]

THE THEATRICAL CONTRACT

In 1794 John Hodgkinson and Lewis Hallam, then managers in New
York, resolved to build a new theatre in Hartford, Connecticut. Hodgkinson's ambition as a new manager is easily seen; he was also involved at the time in the planning and construction of the Park Theatre
in New York. The Harvard Theatre Collection has two letters in
Hodgkinson's hand, as well as the articles of agreement concerning the
establishment of the Hartford theatre; these provide insights into the
process of constructing and leasing a local theatre for the reception of
touring companies. The local architect, a Mr. Wadsworth, had apparently sent the plans for the building to Hodgkinson in 1794; Hodgkinson replied on December 14 saying that the shell could be built as
planned, but that he wished a New York architect, Mr. Wilson (perhaps one of the local architects associated with the Messrs. Mangin)
to study the plans before proceeding with the interior. On March 25,
1795, he wrote again to say that Mr. Wilson had been "too busily
employed" and that the plans had been delayed, but that it was im-
perative that the interior dimensions should be precisely observed:

One thing it may be necessary to mention: the plans of Mr. Wilson, are
drawn to the size of our present stage here, and as the scenery will be supplied *from* here, strict attention should be paid to that circumstance by forming the breadth and height exactly the same.[117]

Hodgkinson urged that the theatre be made ready hastily, since the
New York company planned to come to Hartford as soon as its New
York season closed in June.

The theatre was apparently not ready on time, however, because the
opening was not until August 3, 1795. The articles of agreement be-

tween the proprietors and the managers were signed on August 15. This agreement not only provides a brief description of the property, it also yields insights into the business operations of the house. The proprietors had, "by a subscription of Fifty Shares of Eighty dollars per share," raised $4,000, $1,000 of which had gone to purchase a parcel of land on Batchelor Street, the remaining $3,000 to be used in building and finishing the theatre itself. The theatre building was fifty-two feet wide and eighty-seven feet deep. If additional money was required, the managers were to "make up the deficiency"; if the managers should find it "nesecary" [sic] to erect some small buildings on the premises for the accommodation of the stage and performers, the proprietors would make reasonable compensation should the agreement be canceled. The managers would have "all the rents and proffits [sic] from said piece of Land and Building and that they shall have the privelidge [sic] of purchasing any number of shares from the proprietors at any time." In return, Hallam and Hodgkinson agreed to pay the proprietors an interest of 6 percent on the $4,000 on the last night of performance each year; to allow each shareholder one free box ticket every fifth night or every second week; and to perform in the theatre at least two months each year with "persons of both Sexes equal to any they can boast of, in point of ability and character."

In this typical kind of agreement, then, the subscribers provided all the capital for the construction of the building, and in return received free admissions to the theatre and a small return on their investment (if all went as planned and promised). The managers of the company, in turn, held total responsibility for the operation of the facility.

The Federal Street Theatre in Boston was financed in 1793 by the sale of 150 shares at $50 each (no more than two per shareholder) to raise $6,000.[118] The Park Theatre in New York cost $30,000 in 1798, raised by selling 80 shares at $375 each.[119] A similar agreement on a smaller scale was drawn in Savannah in January 1804 between Hodgkinson and Alexander Placide of the Charleston company and a group of twenty subscribers who agreed to collect $200 each to obtain $4,000 for the construction of a theatre. The articles of agreement appeared in the local newspaper.[120] Each subscriber was to receive a silver ticket that would entitle him to attend all performances in the regular season. While the ticket was not transferable, it could be left to an heir. In February there were still seven or eight subscribers needed, and a notice stressed the need for a theatre of brick, since "The barn used lately as a theatre is not only *dangerous in a very high degree,* but it is an improper place and really a reflection on us."[121] Apparently the plea went unanswered, and the company continued to perform in the old building.

Yet another scheme was used in Baltimore in 1814 in an attempt to complete the new theatre built for the Philadelphia Company there. Designed by Colonel Mosher and built by Long, the new brick building was to be "superior in comfort, convenience, and safety" to the old building built by Wignell and Reinagle in 1794.[122] The theatre was built by subscription, with the final installment on subscriptions due in April 1813 before the scheduled May opening.[123] Managers Warren and Wood announced on May 10, however, that the building was not complete. Further, as a consequence of the British naval blockade, some of the scenery prepared in Philadelphia had been destroyed by the enemy in transit, but the loss would "be supplied in the course of a few days."[124] The managers pledged to complete the decoration of the building at the conclusion of the short season.

When the theatre opened for its spring season in 1814, the gallery and third tier of boxes had been completed,[125] but the building was still not finished, so the proprietors devised a new plan to raise additional funds to "finish the front and remove the obstructions to the entrances." At the end of the season, stockholders in the Old Theatre were urged to exchange their stock plus $50 for stock in the new. In exchange they would receive a free ticket until $200 was repaid to them.[126] When the fall season began in September 1815 "the whole interior of the building" was at last "completed, and the Lobbies, Coffee Room, Passages, and discharging Doors fitted up in the best manner."[127]

This process of raising money to build theatres was repeated many times over in American cities. John Alden provides some details of the financial arrangements between proprietors and manager in *A Season in Federal Street; J. B. Williamson and the Boston Theatre, 1796–1797*. William Dunlap supplies a great deal of detail about the initial agreement governing the Park Theatre in his *History of the American Theatre* and in his *Diary*. Alden demonstrates that the arrangement was not profitable for the proprietors; Dunlap shows that managers could also lose a great deal of money.

American playhouses at the turn of the century, then, were constructed as a means of providing the necessary space for all the business of a theatre, both behind and before the curtain. As a business venture, they were risky for all concerned. They were expected to provide a feast for the eye and the ear, as well as reasonable comfort and the illusion of luxury for patrons. When successful, they reflected credit not only on the actors and managers who toiled within, but served as objects of civic pride, endlessly discussed, praised, criticized, compared, and imitated.

5
AND ALL THE TRIMMINGS

In the prologue to *Cymon* (Drury Lane, 1767), David Garrick indicated, humorously but realistically, the centrality of the "trimmings"—scenery, lighting, special effects, costumes, and makeup—in the theatre:

> As for the Plot, Wit, Humour, Language—I
> Beg you such Trifles kindly to pass by;
> The most essential part, which something means,
> Is Dresses, Dances, Sinkings, Flyings, Scenes,—
> They'll make you stare.[1]

The trimmings were not only the focal point of many wordless pantomimes and ballets, but they assumed major importance in operas and other genres as well.

Large companies had permanent stocks of costumes, scenery, and machinery, and employed regular staffs to build these necessities for the production of new pieces. The Boston Federal Street company included three men in the painting room, six men as machinists, two women in wardrobe, and three persons as dressers during the 1796–97 season.[2]

Even the smallest of companies traveled with a few pieces of stock scenery and some tired costumes in a wagon, and when a major company like the Old American Company toured, it carried along equipment that would make modern "roadies" feel at home. Theatres visited by large companies were sometimes constructed to the scale of the home theatre in order to accommodate the scenery carried, and extra outbuildings might be required to store the theatrical paraphernalia.[3]

SCENERY

Talented professional scene painters were employed in all major U.S. theatres by the 1790s. New York had Charles Ciceri, John Holland, Hugh Reinagle, and Charles Catten. Charleston enjoyed the talents of Belzons, Oliphant, Schultz, West, Holme, and the two Audins (or Odins), father and son. Philadelphia had Charles Milbourne, Joseph Jefferson, T. Reinagle, H. Warren, Evers, Megary, T[homas] Jefferson, Aikin, Paul, Strickland, McKenzie, Stewart, and Luke Robbins. Christian Gullager, George Graham, Thomas Codman, J. R. Penniman, West, and A. Worrall worked in Boston.[4] Many of these scene painters and designers were active in more than one theatrical center (and often doubled in other theatrical work as needed). In addition, each theatre had its "carpenters"—men who not only constructed the scenes but served as stagehands for the performance, moving scenery and operating machinery and lights. They were all popularly known as "John" or "Johnny."[5]

The scene painters worked throughout the season producing the scenery needed for new productions, traveled with the company to prepare additional scenery if it had a second season elsewhere, and often worked on decorations for the theatre itself when the building was closed. In the course of a year, a great deal of new scenery was prepared, comprising one of the era's major artistic resources. The scenery for the fall 1813 New York production of *Virgin of the Sun* consumed much of the time of Milbourne and Holland during the previous winter and spring; Robbins of Philadelphia assisted in completing it. One scene alone cost $2,000![6] In 1800 the New York theatre opened on the Fourth of July with a demonstration of the work of its scene painters, presented in the form of a pantomime, *Harlequin Traveller:*

One object of the exhibition will be to display in various and appropriate combinations, all (or at least the greatest part) of the scenery which has been executed during the time the present lessee has had possession of the building, an exhibition which it is hoped will be the most brilliant and satisfactory of any thing of that kind ever attempted in this country.

The scenery exhibited gave evidence of the industry and skill of the scene painters and machinists:

1. A cave scene
2. A Kamschadali Hut
3. A Snow Scene in Kamschatka
4. Harbor of Rolscheretsk, and the Icy Sea, with a ship ready for sailing
5. Scene of Incantation
6. Calm Sea—Steam arises and increases—the Ship appears and is wrecked—the people are seen as saved in their boat, which is afterward destroyed
7. Landscape—with the descent and ascent of the Enchanted Car
8. Sea Shore, with a Ship at anchor
9. A grand Scene in Peru, with a Sun Rising
10. Peruvian Landscape
11. House of Stars, with a Procession of Peruvian Priests
12. The Palace of the Inca
13. The Rock Scene, Cataract and Bridge
     To finish with the celebrated Scene of the
     Temple of the Sun.[7]

The materials used by the scene painters and machinists to create such marvels as these included lumber, canvas, colors, paper, paste, drapery, ironwork, tinwork, leatherwork, turnery, and ropes.[8] In the spring of 1797 J. B. Williamson, then manager of the Boston Federal Street Theatre, sold the entire stock of "sceenary, mesheanry, & deckorations" belonging to that theatre to the proprietors, and the inventory taken at that time provides endless information and interest for the modern theatre historian. Included in the contents of the painters' and carpenters' shop were the following:

    6 buckets with Collours
  19 paint potts. 1 oil bottle. 1 Varnish bottle
  31 do. [ditto] brushes
    1 pr. tin pans
    1 Glue pot
  10 books brass leafe [for gilding]
    1 pallet
    2 Ruf [rough] Tables. 1 bench
    4 fire tubs
    3 Wooden horses
    1 Iron vice
    1 Grind Stone & handle
    2 pr. Steps. 2 Ladders.

Various bits of hardware and spare parts (doors, windows) were also included. Over the flies were stored extra blocks and tackle, rollers, ropes, tracks, and other sceneshifting paraphernalia and "a quantity of lumber on bums."

Scenes could be painted either on canvas or on paper. Canvas was by far the most common; in 1811 the Richmond theatre had one paper scene in thirty-five.[9] Paper was probably used for scenes that were intended to be temporary; when the Boston company performed in Providence in 1807, painter West produced four new scenes on paper for a production of *Lodoiska*. Mr. West was complimented "especially for *effect* and *dispatch*."[10]

The paint used was a water-based paint, advantageous in that it was not highly flammable. It was water soluble, however, and therefore capable of being damaged by leaking roofs, rain during transport, or accidents. This paint was described by a correspondent in *The Port Folio:*

> The composition, with which they are painted, is mixed with a large quantity of whiting, the colours are earthy, and they are rendered fluid by a thin glue,* so that the canvass is covered, for the thickness of a quarter of an inch, with a composition, that is as uninflammable as a white limed wall. [*A very general, though mistaken opinion prevails, that the scenes are painted in oil. The glare of the lights would render scenes so painted, completely invisible.] [11]

Williamson's inventory of the Boston theatre included the following types of scenery: borders, flats, wings, rolling scenes either with rods or with barrels and windlasses, flies, ground pieces, set pieces, and transparencies. Three traditional types of scene pieces that were used to frame the stage throughout the eighteenth century were still considered basic at the beginning of the nineteenth: the back scene, the wings, and the borders. The back scene could be either a curtain or a tall, freestanding scene called a flat, constructed of canvas stretched over wooden frames. The flats were broken in the middle so that each panel—about sixteen feet wide and twenty-four to twenty-nine feet high [12]—could be moved to the right or left side of the stage; each of the eleven flat back scenes at the Boston Theatre was listed as "one pair." The flats and wings were held upright in overhead grooves; to move them, the stagehands laid down parallel pieces of wood on the floor for grooves and slid the scenes horizontally like shutters:

> The scene-shifters (or flat-hands, as they are dubbed) had to run out practicable grooves, by hand, on to the stage, from right and left sides at once, which nearly met, and, when thus down, fitted with the grooves in which the scenes rested, so that a flat could be drawn on and quickly fitted with its other half. [13]

The Boston inventory included six wing carriages, located in the loft over the flies. Figure 5 (an engraving of the Philadelphia theatre, appearing in chapter 4) shows a typical outdoor back scene painted with trees.

A series of flat scenes could be placed close together so the movement of one would reveal another immediately behind, or they could be used to open and close the stage at various depths. The instructions in librettos at the beginning of scenes often included such words as "Apathy discovered at a table . . . " or "Children discovered, seeming dead, folded in each other's arms"—indicating that these sliding scenes were to be pulled apart at the sound of the prompter's whistle to reveal the next part of the stage. They were useful, too, for removing portions of a scene, or for hiding dead bodies and other objects not reasonably moved in sight of the audience.

The rows of tall, narrow (not more than six feet wide), freestanding wings at the sides of the stage were often functional rather than representational.[14] Their purpose was to frame the stage and to screen the lights and backstage area; they also allowed space for entrances and exits to the stage between them. Since wings were as much functional as decorative or scenic, they did not always match the back scene. The New York *Daily Advertiser* reported in 1787: "Nor is it uncommon to see the back of the stage represent a street, while the side scenes represent a wood, as if two of the most opposite appearances must be put together to cause a natural effect."[15] More frequently, however, care was taken to maintain the illusion by matching wings with back scenes. Five pairs of wings, in the form of trees, may be seen in the engraving of the Philadelphia stage (fig. 5). The Boston inventory listed ten full sets of wings with four, six, or ten wings in each set (two, three, or five for each side), including a palace, an old palace, woods, small woods, "Gothick," a prison, a garden, a green chamber, a farmhouse, and street wings.

The borders were hung above the stage to complete the frame and screen provided by the wings. They sometimes took the form of clouds (the "skey borders" of the Boston inventory); just as often they were plain strips of cloth, as they are in figure 5. As much as the wings, the borders were functional rather than representational, hiding overhead lighting, scenery, and machinery.

By the end of the eighteenth century cloth drop scenes were increasingly replacing flats as back scenes. Drop scenes made it far easier to "discover" a new scene during the play, and to prepare and store scenery for a new production. It was necessary to use flats when usable doors or windows were needed in a scene; to some extent, drops were used for exterior scenes and flat scenes for interiors.[16]

The term "drop" well describes the workings of these hanging scenes. The earliest drops were rolled upward starting at the bottom, but cloth scenes were soon framed with wood for greater stability and lifted directly overhead into the loft. The scenes were reached by means of a carpenter's gallery. The inventory of the Boston theatre in 1796–97 reveals that most hanging scenes there were rolling scenes, each with its own rod or barrel and windlass, with only a few flies. In an account of the causes of the fire that destroyed the Richmond Theatre on December 26, 1811, the scene loft was said to contain thirty-five hanging scenes, not including "The flies or narrow borders which represent the skies, roofs, &c."[17]

Flat scenes were sometimes profiled or open. The open flat could be used when it was necessary to see through or around one scene to another. "It is framed exactly like the other, and the only difference consists in parts of the scene being left open to shew another behind, which terminates the view."[18] An open flat might enable a band of robbers to be concealed within a wood, or a procession to enter the gateway of a castle, for example. The Boston inventory included several caves, gateways, and arches that were probably open flats. Wings, too, could be cut out or profiled. The wings shown in figure 5 were cut out in the shape of trees.

A final type of scenery was the "set piece," which was variably sized and shaped, and often three-dimensional. The use of movable set pieces was actually a move toward the nineteenth-century box set. Rees said that set pieces were "scenes which may be occasionally placed and displaced, such as the fronts of cottages, cascades, rocks, or bridges and other appendages, requisite in the representation of particular dramas."[19]

American newspaper advertisements referred to waterfalls in the foreground, hills that were climbed, bridges that were crossed, castle turrets that were scaled, and a model (not a profile) of the frigate *Constitution*. Most of these were included in the Boston inventory. It is not clear, however, why the inventory distinguished between "ground pieces" and "set pieces," since the same types of items were included in both lists. In general, these items seem to have been listed by location within the theatre rather than by function, stage placement, materials used, or method of construction. The two categories included not only bridges, towers, shrubbery, seas, walls, cottages, barns, fireplaces, caves, ships, and the like (all of which seem to have been set pieces), but also a dragon, a mare, a bear, assorted statues, and various pantomime tricks.

Transparent scenery had been perfected by Philippe Jacques de Loutherbourg, chief scene painter at London's Drury Lane under Garrick, and was used to achieve "magical effects."[20] It consisted of an ordinary-looking scene painted on heavy gauze and coated with varnish, which became transparent when light passed through it. Transparent scenery was often used in cutout sections of flats for special effect; O'Keeffe wrote of the use of transparent scenery for "moonshine, sunshine, fire, volcanoes, &c."[21] A sky, a building, or a mountain could be painted on the scene and lighted from the front; when the scene was lighted from behind, the moon, sun, smoke, or flames on the back would suddenly become visible to replace or add to the scene on the front.

Such transparent scenery was used in America both before and soon after the Revolution. A performance of Garrick's *Cymon* at the John Street Theatre in New York in 1773 boasted a "new set of transparent scenes,"[22] and by 1785 performances of William Whitehead's *The Roman Father* in Charleston and Savannah were announced with "new transparent scenery."[23] Transparent scenery was also used for huge scenic paintings. When the New York theatre closed its season on July 1, 1801, for example, it was lighted by "500 variegated lamps" with "an appropriate transparency exhibited in front of the stage."[24] When the anniversary of the 1783 evacuation of the city by the British was celebrated in New York on November 25, 1809, "a grand transparent painting [was] exhibited, in allusion to the day, designed and executed by mr. Hugh Reinagle, a pupil of Holland's."[25] Luke Robbins prepared a "Grand Emblematic Transparency" of the "Genius of America,"containing 180 square feet of canvas, for the Philadelphia Theatre in 1811. "In the center is the *Genius of Liberty*, holding the bust of the *Immortal Washington*, beneath the *American Eagle* supporting the arms of the Union, with ancient and modern trophies of war. On the right she is supported by the *Goddess of Wisdom* bearing a spear and shield, on the left by *Justice* with her balance."[26]

The Boston theatre included only a few such transparencies in its 1796–97 inventory, but John Durang listed a relatively large number of them in the catalog of entertainments performed by his touring company in 1808–16, including "American Heroes at Tripoli," "Perry's Victory," "MacDonough Victory," and "Les Ombres chinoise."[27]

Though scenery was often elaborate, inadequacies were noted, too. There was no expectation or pretension of realism: a setting was only suggested, and two-dimensionality was accepted uncritically. Furniture, fireplaces, columns, balustrades, and drapes were all painted. Errors of perspective could be overlooked more easily when the actors were on the apron rather than back within the frame of the stage, but the use of accurate perspective was worthy of critical comment. In Philadelphia in 1806, Mr. Holland was praised for "the scene which is dropped between the acts, . . . a remarkably fine production of the art of perspective,"[28] and in Boston, Mr. Worrall's distant view of Timour's castle in *Timour the Tartar* "exemplifies in a surprising degree the deception of a painting in perspective."[29]

Colors were often garish and were little improved by the lighting. It was easier to forgive the poor coloring, two-dimensionality, and general lack of realism, however, as long as the lighting remained relatively dim and even wavering. It is surely no coincidence that the increasing use of set pieces and the development of the box set in the early nineteenth century coincided with the advent of stronger and better-placed stage lighting.

In small theatres, the same stock scenes were recycled repeatedly; the minimum scenery was one interior scene and one exterior scene. Traveling troupes could rely on merely two rolled drop scenes, easily packed in carts for transport from town to town. A well-stocked theatre soon after the American Revolution might have performed almost any play with a cottage interior (which doubled as a kitchen), a castle or parlor interior, a garden, a woods, and a street scene. These scenes were sometimes reused until they were ragged and dirty. Even in New York, there were complaints in 1787 that "where the author intended a handsome street or a beautiful landscape, we only see a dirty piece of canvas; what else can we call a scene in which the colours are defaced or obliterated?"[30] Dunlap observed of the New York theatre in 1794:

Heretofore the scenic decorations of the American theatre had been lamentably poor. Henry had not brought out with his recruits any artist to paint his scenes. Those of the old stock were originally of the lowest grade, and had become black with age. At this time, Charles Ciceri painted the scenes for Tammany [the opera by Hatton and Hewitt]. They were gaudy and unnatural, but had a brilliancy of colouring, reds and yellows being abundant. Ciceri afterwards made himself a better painter, and proved himself an excellent machinist.[31]

The larger stages of the new theatres of the 1790s provided inducements for new, larger, and better-proportioned scenery. In large theatres, scenery was imported, refurbished, or newly created for each major new production, and was sometimes described in detail in the bills. By the time the new theatres and their professional scene painters became the standard in the 1790s, local patrons and travelers alike considered American scenery as good as that of Europe. The *New York Magazine* reported that "the painting and scenery [of the Philadelphia

Theatre] are equal to the generality of the European," [32] while Henry
Wansey (speaking of the same theatre) reported that "to judge from
the dress and appearance of the company around me, and the actors
and scenery, I should have thought I had still been in England." [33]

John Hodgkinson took over the management of the Boston Federal
Street Theatre during its reconstruction after the fire of 1798. He sent
a list of the minimum necessary stock scenery to be supplied by the
proprietors. Scenery for new productions would be constructed at the
expense of the managers as needed, but this list represented the period's standard, reusable scenes for the most commonly performed
repertory.

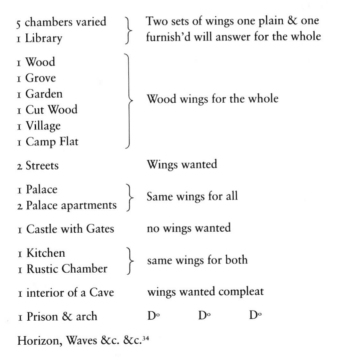

5 chambers varied 1 Library	} Two sets of wings one plain & one furnish'd will answer for the whole
1 Wood 1 Grove 1 Garden 1 Cut Wood 1 Village 1 Camp Flat	} Wood wings for the whole
2 Streets	Wings wanted
1 Palace 2 Palace apartments	} Same wings for all
1 Castle with Gates	no wings wanted
1 Kitchen 1 Rustic Chamber	} same wings for both
1 interior of a Cave	wings wanted compleat
1 Prison & arch	D° D° D°

Horizon, Waves &c. &c. [34]

Though the scene painters were responsible for the overall quality of
the scenic effects, scenery continued to be imported from Europe
throughout this period. When the Philadelphia Theatre opened in

1794, much of the scenery had been brought from England. William Wood reported that the "splendid English scenery" was "presented to Wignell in 1793 by Richards, Hodges, and Rooker, artists of the first reputation of the day." [35] John Inigo Richards, manager Wignell's brother-in-law, was scene painter at Covent Garden and secretary of the Royal Academy. Later, Wignell received manuscripts of new shows from England, along with models of the scenery and machinery. These were copied by the scene painters and carpenters in Philadelphia, including Joseph Jefferson; Wood noted "the taste and skill of Jefferson in the construction of intricate stage machinery, of which on many occasions, he proved himself a master, not infrequently improving materially on the English models sent out to us." [36]

Sometimes the scenery and machinery were constructed in England and shipped across the Atlantic. John Bernard imported from London, "at a great expense," the scenery and machinery for the "Grand Allegorical Pantomimical Spectacle" *Cinderella,* which opened in Boston on December 7, 1807." [37]

Sea scenes ranked as one of the most popular scenic effects, and often included such additional mechanical efforts as "an attack upon a Spanish Fort by the Algerine fleet; the arrival of the fleet of Spain, and a general engagement in which the Algerines are totally defeated by fireships, bombs from the fort, and blowing up their vessels." [38] In *The Shipwreck,* the scene is described as "Rocky Sea-Coast, on the English Channel—Sea in a violent Storm—A Ship appears tossing on the Waves, and is dash'd to pieces on the Rocks." [39]

The following anecdote describes a similar scene in a London theatre, and suggests how realistic such spectacles must have seemed to contemporary audiences:

On a London Theatre, a play was in representation, one scene of which discovered a violent storm on the ocean—two ships appeared in sight, their masts partly gone—their sails in tatters—they were hurried by the raging sea among the black clouds which obscured the sky, and anon sunk between the divided ocean and were for some moments invisible—To complete the horror of the scene, a seeshore [sic] was now in view, begirt with rocks, which offered the prospect of certain destruction to the unfortunate mariners. This sight was too much for Capt. F, an American, who had eagerly watched every motion of the vessels. He started from his seat in one of the boxes, and exclaimed with true nautical vehemence, "Helm's alee G-d d--n you, or all's lost by G-d!" and was with great difficulty composed to his seat again.[40]

The phrase "sunk between the divided ocean" indicates how simply these sea scenes could be achieved with parallel rows of waves crossing the stage. Sea effects were normally achieved by the use of a series of canvas profile scenes, "behind one another, their edges cut out after the conventional outline of waves." These scenes could then be rocked back and forth in a supposedly wavelike motion.[41] The ships were normally in profile, not models, and were moved mechanically between the waves. Further effects were painted on the back scene. The sound of waves was created by the use of a pebble box.[42] The 1797 inventory of the Boston theatre includes a rolling scene of the ocean, three "hanging seas," "5 Rooling Seas & 10 Bracketts," and various ships.

Other traditional ways of creating sea effects involved sea cloths and wave cylinders. In the oldest of these "a painted cloth is spread out over the stage, and a number of men and boys prone on their backs underneath, work feet and arms diligently."[43] With wave cylinders, spiral-like wave shapes would be placed on a series of cylinders, so the rotation of several rows of cylinders would create the effect of the rise and fall of waves.

Descriptions from playbills provide an indication of the complex scenery that could be compounded from flats of various types, hanging scenes, machinery, and special effects. When the pantomime *Don Juan* was performed in Charleston on November 19, 1803, "With all the Original Music, Accompanyments, Scenery, Machinery, Dresses, and Decorations," the scenery included

A STORM AT SEA, and SHIPWRECK. An EQUESTRIAN STATUE erected to the Memory of the Commandant slain by Don Juan. The HORSE and RIDER, as large as life, on a PEDESTAL—on which appears the dreadful

inscription in blood. A GRAND BANQUET, with the humours of Scaramouch; at which the animated statue appears, and gives the solemn invitation to Don Juan. A CHARNEL HOUSE. To conclude with a beautiful
TRANSPARENT VIEW of the INFERNAL REGIONS—with a tremendous
SHOWER OF FIRE, and Don Juan precipitated into the Flaming Gulph.[44]

One entertainment that always brought forth the best efforts of the
scene painters was *Blue Beard,* which was widely performed and immensely popular, probably as much for its scenery and special effects
as for its libretto by George Colman, Jr., or its music by Michael Kelly.
Advertisements for a New York performance in 1802 carried the following description of the scenery:

In Act I, Ibrahim's Cottage, with distant mountains, down which, first at a
great distance and afterwards nearer by degrees, Abomelique on his Elephant, and his train of guards, slaves, camels, &c. are seen descending.
    Act II, the illuminated Garden, a fountain playing in the middle, and other
decorations; Procession of Slaves and Dance.
    Act III, Scene 3, the BLUE APARTMENT, on one side a rich stair case; in
the centre a large door, over which is a picture of Abomelique at the feet of a
beautiful woman, on each side the door, a picture of a female. On Fatima's
putting the diamond key to the door the pictures all change to scenes of horror, the walls of the apartment are stained with blood, and the door sinking
discovers the internal of the sepulchre with its ghastly inhabitants; a moment
after, all resumes its former appearance.
    Scene 5, outside of Abomelique's Castle, Drawbridge, Turret, &c. the
Horsemen at a distance advancing to the attack.
    Last scene, the inside of the Sepulcre, the wall of which yielding to the fury
of the Spahis, falls and discovers the combatants without.[45]

Even making allowances for the fact that many of the effects described
above were painted and two-dimensional, this was certainly an ambi-
tious production! The *Evening Post* gives proof, moreover, that the
effects were not all painted. Describing the procession in act 1, the
Evening Post says:

All this is executed in artificial figures, corresponding in size to the trees
which crown the summits of the mountains; . . . Before the last soldiers have

disappeared the first part of the procession enters on the side opposite to that where it was first seen, and appears much nearer than before, winding down the hill . . . and the figures pass in the same order as before. This is performed by children, dressed as grown persons in the Turkish costumes—the camels, elephants, etc. by machinery. (In this pass, which seemed to be rugged, one of the camels, on Monday evening, unfortunately had his neck broke). The train having apparently crossed a second time, and reached the foot of the mountain, . . . the soldiers parade down the stage, and the *Bashaw* is brought on by an artificial elephant . . . [46]

In 1806 the same production was still being used, to judge from identical descriptions in the bills, but a spectacular new addition was made for the June 6 performance. An animal act had come to town, and the advance bills read: "Mr. Utt, for the gratification of the public, has engaged the *Elephant* and *Camels*—they will be introduced in the opera." [47] On the day of the performance, to clear up any doubts, the bill added "*Abomelique* on the LIVE ELEPHANT (lately arrived from the East Indies)." [48]

The transformation of Abomelique's blue apartment was achieved by the use of transparencies, with gauze inserts in a profiled canvas flat. In an 1813 Boston performance, "Some new transparencies, by Mr. J. R. Penniman, added to the *delightful horrors* of the blue chamber." [49] As Fatima inserted the key in the door of the forbidden chamber, the lights were uncovered behind the flat, allowing the paint on the back of the gauze sections to show through, transforming the paintings to "scenes of horror" and allowing a glimpse of the interior of the chamber through the doorway.

The exterior of Blue Beard's castle is pictured on the cover of the London piano-vocal score of the work (fig. 9). This set piece was constructed on three levels, so the servant could be in the garden (on the stage floor), while Fatima stood on a balcony on the second level and Irene was visible in the turret above. Painted on the back scene was the remainder of the castle, including the drawbridge, and distant horsemen. The set was so complex that an extra song was added to the New York production to help fill time during the scene change to the next, equally complicated set of the forbidden chamber.

Figure 9. Cover of piano-vocal score for *Blue Beard,* showing the London set for the exterior of the castle. Music Division, Library of Congress.

The final scene—the inside of the "Sepulcre" or forbidden chamber—used a set piece, with a profiled flat at the rear that afforded a glimpse of the Spahis without and allowed access for the hero, Selim, through the back wall. This final scene may also have included a trapdoor for the demise of Blue Beard, as was used in the London production.

Most theatres had at least a "grave trap," and in the early nineteenth century many theatres also had a "star trap" to provide access for Harlequin in magic scenes. Many traps worked by means of a system of counterweights located below the stage, which had to be properly adjusted to allow objects to be raised or lowered on the trap like an elevator. The trapdoor at the Norfolk Theatre malfunctioned in 1801:

It is recommended to the manager to have a regular examination of the machinery below the stage; for on Tuesday evening, owing to the ponderosity of

Mrs. Rowson, the springs of a trap door gave way, and not only the leading lady disappeared, but she carried little Mrs. Stuart down also. A sailor in the pit observed, that it put him in mind of the Royal George, which when she went down, sucked a sloop of war into the vortex with her, that was at anchor at a little distance.[50]

During most of the eighteenth century, the curtain did not close between acts, and the changing of scenes was intended to be visible. When it became customary to use an act curtain at the end of the century, the scenery may have remained unchanged until the curtain was raised for the beginning of the next act; for the audience, the change was still an accustomed part of the show.[51] Even when the act curtain masked scene changes between acts, it was not necessarily used for changes within acts. A portion of the stage might be masked by means of flat scenes, however, to allow for continuous action while carpenters prepared the next scene behind the flat.

By the turn of the century it was so fashionable to have an "act drop" that if none were available the green curtain was often used in its place. In the Providence theatre in 1795, "The few scenes that were prepared were tolerably good; but as no act drop was painted, the traditional green curtain was obliged to serve a double purpose."[52] Washington Irving's Jonathan Oldstyle complained of the New York theatre:

I wish the manager would use a drop-scene at the close of the acts; we might then always ascertain the termination of the piece by the green curtain. On this occasion, I was indebted to the polite bows of the actors for this pleasing information.[53]

The movement of the scenery was sometimes poorly performed. When *Cinderella* was performed in Philadelphia in 1806, *The Theatrical Censor* accepted this as a matter of course: "The first evening's performance of a piece which requires so much precision in the management of scenery, &c., is sure to be attended with mistakes and delays."[54] In Norfolk, a critic complained:

If the sound of the hammer, in the change of scenery, could either be avoided or lowered, it would be a great improvement; and although voices cannot be particularly ascertained, yet more discretion ought to be observed between the acts, behind the scenes. It is very grating, even at the most extreme part of the house, to hear vociferated, "d-mn your eyes," and "You blood of a b----." [55]

In 1810 a critic complimented the Baltimore company because

the management of the scenery is as correct and subject to as few interruptions as possible; and the expedition with which one act succeeds another, can only be appreciated by those who have witnessed the tedious delay so often experienced in other places. [56]

When scenery was changed efficiently, it must have been impressive indeed to see the wings and back scene slide away simultaneously to reveal the next scene already in place behind, and perhaps coordinated with the changing of the borders overhead.

Stage properties were sparingly used, especially in opera, at least in part because so much of the acting took place on the apron. These consisted mostly of hand properties; furniture in any number of indoor scenes was summed up as "table and chairs." At the Baltimore Theatre in 1782, manager Thomas Wall was required "on or before Twelve o' Clock on the Day after Performance [to] write or cause to be wrote a Dress List, and Bill of Properties for the next Play or Farce and deliver them to Adam Lindsay; and for every neglect to forfeit five Shillings." If his partner, Lindsay, as property man, "being possess'd of said Dress List, and Bill of Properties," failed to "provide them against the time they are wanted" he would be fined five shillings for every deficient article. [57]

The property man was responsible for acquiring all the items on the "bill of properties" supplied by the manager or the prompter—which consisted of "every imaginable thing," including "Arms and ammunition, loaded pistols for sham mischief, and decanters of liquor for real:—(for though the actors could dispense with the bullets, they required the alcohol)—love letters and challenges—beds, bed-linen, and babies."[58]

Several methods were used to get properties on and off stage when needed. They could be carried on—in full sight of the audience—by one of the stagehands, and they were sometimes carried on and off by the actors at their entrances and exits. The final scene of *Children in the Wood* begins with the instructions: "Enter Josephine, Winifred and a female Servant. Winifred and Servant bring in a Table, on which is placed three wooden Trenchers, a roast Fowl, knives, forks, &c."[59] A third possibility is mentioned by Percy Fitzgerald, when in 1881 he refers to the "old" method of pulling the props (tables, chairs, sofas, etc.) off the stage with a cord at the sound of the prompter's whistle.[60] One unusual prop was a rug spread on the stage floor to protect the clothing of the chief tragedian when he died; when the stagehands brought out the rug, the audience immediately guessed the ending of the play.[61]

Many stage properties are listed in the 1796–97 inventory of the Boston theatre, including sixteen Indian clubs, a large tambourine, a wooden leg, six parrots, two pistols, four fruit baskets, a small boat with four wheels, four sets of iron chains, and twenty-nine long lances. Only a very limited amount of furniture is listed.

STAGE LIGHTING

In addition to the house lights discussed earlier, there were three main types of lighting used on the stage at the turn of the century: chandeliers, sidelights, and footlights. Most theatres still used wax (spermaceti) or tallow candles, although oil lamps were increasingly common both in England and in the United States. The earliest oil lamps were pans filled with oil or tallow, each with several wicks, easily spilled and quite dangerous—likely to cause burns, fires, and stains. "The stench and smoke was very disturbing, especially to the singers, and particularly in hot weather."[62] The stage in Philadelphia's Southwark Theatre was lighted by such "plain oil lamps without glasses."[63]

Oil lamps with single wicks and chimneys—called English lamps or patent lamps—were introduced in the 1790s. They were safer and brighter than candles or the older open pan lamps, and were soon adopted in American theatres. Although the house was lighted with candles until 1810, the stage of Philadelphia's Chestnut Street theatre was lighted by oil lamps at its opening in 1794: "These can be changed from high to low for night scenes and those that require dimness."[64] *The Mirror of Taste and Dramatic Censor* reported in 1810 that the auditorium of the remodeled theatre was

to be lighted with patent lamps. The area of the circle with Grecian globe lamps. The stage with seven large brass vases, each containing eight patent globe lamps, and the whole of the wings with patent globe lights also.[65]

The "large brass vases" on the stage cannot have been a great improvement over the chandelier as far as realism of outdoor scenes is concerned!

In Boston, the Federal Street Theatre built an entire new stage for the 1811–12 season, lighted with "new constructed LAMPS of AMERICAN MANUFACTURE."[66] When the theatre began the 1814–15 season, the lighting had once again been improved: "The front, round the Boxes will be brilliantly lighted by *Twelve Elegant GRECIAN LAMPS of American manufacture*."[67] "Brass lamps with globe glasses" gave "brilliancy of effect" in Providence in 1814,[68] and the new Park Theatre in 1821 was lighted with three oil-burning chandeliers, each with thirty-five lights, and patent oil lamps.[69]

In 1816 the New Theatre in Philadelphia pioneered in the use of gas to light the stage; most major theatres converted to gas for stage lighting within the next decade. Gas was more easily controlled from a central location, but it was expensive to install and just as dangerous as oil lamps. Candles and oil were still used on the American frontier in the 1880s.

Theatre lighting was a major worry not only because of the continual danger of fire, but because of its cost:

To minimize the expense of wax and tallow the house was allowed to remain in semi-darkness until the time of "second music," when all the candles were lit. . . . Wax, on account of its extra cost, was only used on special occasions, such as benefit nights, and tallow was apt to gutter and scatter its hot grease on the dresses of the ladies.[70]

The Federal Street Theatre in Boston, which used a combination of fuels as a money-saving measure, listed the costs of lighting the theatre for each night of performance as:

23 lb. Spermaceti	$12.50
33 lb. Tallow Candles	8.75
6 Gallons Oil	7.50
15 lb. Hoggs Lard	2.25
	$31.--

The inventory of equipment necessary to light a major theatre was extensive as well. At the Federal Street Theatre, the assembly room contained three glass chandeliers, four large girandoles with four arms each, ten single girandoles, and twenty tin hanging candlesticks. Two brass-armed chandeliers lit the gallery, and ten lit the boxes. The storage cellar, devoted almost entirely to heating and lighting equipment, included nineteen tin float lamps, fifty-four patent wing lamps, forty-three wing lamps, eighteen large glass street lamps with tops, twenty round chain lamps, eight reservoir patent lamps, one large tin fountain lamp, four each oil pans, dippers, funnels, and oil pots, nearly two hundred varied tin candlesticks with sockets, five large tin candle stands, four pairs of candle snuffers, and fifteen dozen lamp glasses. Other rooms contained additional lighting fixtures and equipment, and there were a number of lighting-related properties in the storage closet.

The chandeliers were generally located over the apron and either suspended or ensconced over the proscenium doors. The early theatres used "barrel hoops" with candles stuck on spikes around the rims; as theatres became more elaborate the chandeliers gained correspondingly in elegance and efficiency, while candles were often replaced by oil lamps. The continual presence of these chandeliers, even in outdoor or "dark scenes," became objectionable, and mechanisms were developed to make it possible to raise and lower them to adjust the lighting. The chandeliers above the apron were eventually replaced by indirect lighting from the front or sides of the stage or by overhead lighting that could be drawn above the borders out of sight of the audience.

The report of the causes of the 1811 Richmond fire gives a description of the oil-burning chandelier that had been used for overhead lighting in that theatre:

> In the first Act, amongst other scenes, was the scene of the Cottage of Baptist the Robber, which was illuminated by a chandelier apparently hanging from the ceiling. When the curtain fell on the first Act and before it rose on the second, this chandelier was lifted from its position among the scenery above. It was fixed with two wicks to it; one only of them had been lit; yet when it was lifted above, *this fatal lamp was not extinguished.* . . . The chandelier above was moved by two cords which worked over two pulleys, inserted in a collar-beam of the roof; . . .[71]

Placement of overhead lighting behind the proscenium, along with the improvement of perspective in stage scenery and the brighter illumination provided by the conversion to oil lighting, contributed to the movement of the playing area from the apron to the framed stage and finally to the box set.

The sidelights were vertical wooden battens with candles or simple oil lamps one above the other, located behind the proscenium and wings (sometimes on the prompter's side only). "These battens could be pulled up a few inches by means of a thin rope so that each candle-flame became hidden behind a small metal shield; this was another dimming device."[72] It was also possible to dim the stage in some theatres by pivoting the wing lights away from the stage.[73]

Footlights were of several types. John Bernard described a simple footlight system used in a theatre in Mallow, Ireland, in 1782; he speaks of "the stage, being divided from the pit by a board bored with holes, as the sockets for so many candles, or footlights."[74] Oil-burning footlights comprised a narrow metal trough filled with oil, with a row of floating wicks (the entire apparatus called a float). A board hid the glare from the audience, and the entire box could be lowered beneath the stage "by cords and counterweights" to trim the lights or to darken the stage. "The Prompter in the wing rang a bell to the stage hand in the cellar and the thing was done. Another bell and the float ascended to its old place."[75]

In the London libretto for *Children in the Wood* (1794), act 2, scene 5 begins with the instruction "Moonlight, lamps down." The lamps that were to be lowered were apparently the footlights. At the beginning of scene 6 the indication is "Lamps up." Modern playwrights have continued to use this terminology even though the process is no longer literally carried out.

Because of the apron, the footlights were an indispensable lighting source, supplementing the light of the chandelier overhead.

This light from below the singers' faces was a boon to the older players, erasing many a wrinkle and sagging jowl; it was a veritable fountain of youth. Features of actors were 'washed out' by them and a fresh physiognomy could be erected by the use of paints, in place of a faulty original.[76]

SPECIAL EFFECTS

Special effects were common in early American theatre—indeed, in many pantomimes and spectacles they were central. Among the most important effects used were the "natural effects" such as thunder, rain, and moonlight. The sound of rain could be imitated by a cylinder filled with small pebbles or dried peas, rotated by a belt run by the prompter.[77] Theatres without a rain machine resorted to such expedients as heavy brown paper rubbed briskly against the wall.[78] The appearance of rain could be created by the use of transparencies. Thunder and lightning could add to the effect. In his recollections Henry Phillips tells of singing "Bay of Biscay" in Harrogate, Yorkshire, as a boy (in 1809); he

strutted on in the midst of a flash of lightning—which electric effect was produced by a candle and a large pepper box, filled with dangerous elements,
while somebody shook something behind the scenes with the intention of in-
ducing weak-minded people to believe it was thunder.[79]

The "dangerous elements" were probably "three parts of magnesium
powder and one part of potassium chlorate."[80] Another method of
producing lightning was "by a *flare,* a sort of torch, which, when
shaken, flared up."[81] A bolt of lightning could be represented onstage
by "an explosive of a harmless kind, prepared especially for the stage,
and which flew down a sort of invisible wire, descending at an
angle."[82] When *The Banditti* was produced in 1781, O'Keeffe attributed its failure partly to the fact that "The audience seemed to take
offence at lightning flashing outside of the house through the windows
of a dark room."[83] Fitzgerald said that

the old thunder was invariably produced by a huge sheet of suspended metal,
which, when shaken, produced a strange sound, quite unlike what it was
supposed to imitate, but which from convention was accepted. Another
method, found only in foreign theatres, is an apparatus like an enormous
venetian blind, which is pulled by two men, and then allowed to rattle down
violently.[84]

Other time-honored methods, used as early as the Renaissance, were
the rolling of rocks or shot, or the sound of a drum. It was common
practice to have wooden troughs built overhead next to the roof, so
that cannonballs could be rolled over the heads of the audience to
create the sound of thunder. English theatres in Lancaster and Bristol
still possess the remains of such mechanisms. William Dunlap speaks
of "the crackling of tin sheets, or rolling of iron cannon-balls" for
thunder.[85]

Dunlap also tells the tale of an adventure of George Frederick
Cooke as a stagestruck young man in Edinburgh. Cooke stole backstage before a performance of *Macbeth* and hid himself in a barrel.

Cooke soon perceived that he had, as companions, two twenty-four pound cannon balls; but not yet being initiated into the mysteries of the scene, he did not suspect that cannon balls assisted in making thunder in a barrel, as well as in a twenty-four pounder; poor George Frederick was in the thunder barrel of the theatre. . . . the property man approached and seized the barrel. . . . His tormentor proceeded to cover the open end of the barrel with a piece of old carpet, and tie it carefully to prevent the thunder from being spilt. . . . the machine was lifted by the Herculean property man; and carried carefully to the side-scene, lest in rolling the thunder should rumble before its *cue*. . . . the witches entered amid flames of rosin, the thunder bell rang, the barrel received its impetus, and away rolled George Frederick and his ponderous companions. . . . he roared most manfully, to the surprise of the thunderer, who neglecting to stop the rolling machine, it entered on the stage, and George Frederick bursting off the carpet head of the barrel, appeared before the audience, just as the witches had agreed to meet again, when 'the hurly-burly's done.'[86]

In a performance of the musical entertainment *The Captive of Spilburgh* at the New York theatre on Wednesday, March 25, 1801, the final scene displayed a "ruinous part of the castle in which Eugenia is confined; the upper part open to the Sky—*SNOW DESCENDING*."[87] Snow could be created on stage by showering down baskets of confetti-like paper from above the stage. On the clothing of actors it could be created with flour, or in order to allow melting, with soapsuds.[88] The sound of whistling wind was made by revolving a cylinder against a piece of ribbed silk.[89] Mist was produced by placing lamps behind gauzes.[90]

In the same production of *The Captive of Spilburgh* mentioned above, the first scene had "Snow Scene, Mountains, Castle, Cloudy Sky; The Clouds afterward clear away, and disclose the *MOON IN FULL SPLENDOR*." Green was apparently the accepted color for moonlight. It could be achieved by the use of "different colored silks in the flies or side scenes, which turned on a pivot, and with lights behind."[91] Oil lamps could be "furnished with chimneys of white and green glass, which, by an ingenious system of levers commanded by the prompter, ascend or descend as required and produce moonlight or other optical effects."[92] Moonlight could also be portrayed by use of a transparency. If the moon itself were to be seen, the attempts were

rather lame, . . . not reaching beyond the elemental principle of cutting a hole in the canvas and covering it with a transparent material. Sometimes, indeed, a ragged cloud is suffered to trail across, but the edges are so hard that they betray that they are of stouter material than vapor.[93]

The 1796–97 inventory of the Boston theatre included various items used to achieve "natural effects": a rolling scene of moonlight, two "roals" for moonlight, one thunder box, six transparent shades, one hail box, four lightning pipes, six star lights, one "Windmishean for Storm," and two "peaces black silk for wind mishean."

The Federal Street Theatre developed a special effect in 1812 that enabled it to flood the stage with real water. Two scenes in *The Caravan* used cascades of water—one "A Rude Natural Bridge over A CASCADE OF REAL WATER" and the other a distant view of Barcelona, "In front of which, a great part of the stage is laid under REAL WATER: representing *Cascades of Waterfalls dashing from the Rocks, &c.*"[94] This new effect could also be used for sea scenes, as in the depiction of naval battles during the war of 1812.[95]

One further effect essential for the theatre was fire. For example, *The 14th of July, 1789, or the Destruction of the Bastille*, performed in Charleston in 1794, used "the flare and glare of stage fire,"[96] and in New York, in February 1805, the "town in flames" in *The Africans* was "managed with fine effect."[97] The use of "flames of rosin" is mentioned above; a chemical preparation known as "red fire" was also burned in pans to give the desired effect.[98] Fitzgerald, in 1881, pointed out that "so lately as thirty or forty years ago, a stage fire was symbolized rather than represented, some blazing cressets being waved to and fro inside the building that was being consumed."[99] Red painted transparencies could also be used to represent larger fires, encompassing the entire stage.

A tragedy called *Bunker's Hill* was presented at the Haymarket in Boston in 1796; its author, John Burk, wrote to John Hodgkinson of the New York Theatre offering the use of the work, and describing the means by which the special effects were achieved:

A square piece about nine feet high and five wide, having some houses and a meeting-house painted on fire, with flame and smoke issuing from it, should be raised two feet distance from the horizon scene at the back of your stage, the windows and doors cut out for transparencies—in a word, it should have the appearance of a town on fire. We had painted smoke suspended. . . . The fire should be played skilfully behind this burning town, and the smoke to evaporate.[100]

William Dunlap considered this an "odd production," but it proved quite popular in Boston.

Spectacular effects using gunfire, explosives, and bombs were also popular. The *Charleston Courier* reported on March 19, 1805, that the conclusion of the evening's entertainment would be a new interlude, *The Bombardment of Tripoli, by the American Fleet:*

The Naval Engagement got up under the direction of Mr. Rosinville, one of the first artists in the fire-work line. . . . The Public are respectfully informed that the Bombardment will be represented in a manner that cannot fail to astonish the spectators . . . The Fire and the Report of the Cannon and Musquetry—the Gun-Boats throwing Shells into the Town—and the enemy's Fort and Batteries firing red hot Balls, &c. The whole to conclude with The Town of Tripoli on Fire.[101]

For spectacles like this, representing entire battles, fireworks were sometimes used within the theatre. Real guns were sometimes used for single shots, but in scenes requiring volleys they apparently sometimes frightened the audience,[102] and "the smoke of gunpowder proved objectionable, as it obscured the scene and choked the audience." Frequently, therefore, "a blow on a bass drum represented the discharge of a cannon, and rapid strokes with rattans on a dried calf-skin, a volley of rifles."[103]

All these effects were combined for the first performance of *Columbus* in Philadelphia on January 30, 1797. It included a procession of
Indians, the landing of Columbus, a representation of a storm and
earthquake, a grand eruption from a volcano, a sacrifice, and a grand
pageant. The volcano was designed by John Inigo Richards, principal scene painter at Covent Garden Theatre, and the remainder by
Charles Milbourne of Philadelphia, who supervised its execution. The
machinist was Mr. Lunthall. The *Aurora and General Advertiser* reported that

The brilliancy of spectacle and decoration produced universal pleasure; till
the representation of an earthquake and the eruption from a volcano really
inspired those feelings which a real representation could only encrease. The
horrid subterraneous sounds, the rocking of trees, the violent destruction of
[houses], the sight of falling ruins, presented perhaps, as true a delineation of
such an awful scene as description can afford.—Persons, who have often witnessed exhibitions of this kind in Europe, declare the volcano not to be surpassed by any representation they ever saw.[104]

MACHINERY AND TRANSFORMATIONS

Some of the special effects achieved on the early American stage were
the result of simple materials and procedures plus a bit of acting ingenuity. Other required special properties or machinery. One of the important contributions of the pantomimes was that their elaborate scenery and machinery were available for other productions; they helped
to create the demand for full-time professional scene painters.

Acrobatic tricks and transformations were central to the harlequinades performed by actors like John Durang. Durang became a stage
dancer and acrobat in 1783, at the age of fifteen, and joined the Hallam troupe in 1785. In the course of his *Memoirs* he tells, often in
passing, the secrets of some of the tricks he performed. He describes
"contriving a trample [trampoline]" behind the scenes to enable him
to reach the center of the stage in a single spring.[105] When an actor
needed to leap off the stage, several men stood behind the scenes with

a blanket to catch him when he landed.[106] Far more machinery was required for the performance of some of the pantomimic tricks. At the Southwark in Philadelphia, for example, Mr. West's benefit concluded with "a FLY, by Mr. West: NECK OR NOTHING: or, HARLE-QUIN's Flight to and from the GODS; He rises, from the back of the Stage and ascends into the Gallery and returns head foremost back again over the Pitt."[107]

One of Durang's simple transformations was a dwarf who changed to a woman (fig. 10):

The body and the head of the Dwarf where tied above my hip, and the uper-pard of my body and head where covered by a coloured paticoat gathered with my hands at the top of my head. In this concealed manner I could make my entrance.

Figure 10. John Durang's metamorphosis from a dwarf to a woman. Historical Society of York County, Philadelphia.

While dancing in Philadelphia one night, Durang mistook the footlights for the wing lights and made his exit over the spikes of the orchestra pit; the resulting injury to his leg prevented his dancing for three months. As a result, he altered the dance to improve the visibility during his exit. He simply dropped the petticoat, revealing the upper half of his body costumed as a woman—completing the metamorphosis from a man of three feet tall to a woman of six feet tall.[108]

In the pantomime *Cinderella*, a number of transformations and machines were required. *The Theatrical Censor* ridiculed various elements of an 1806 Philadelphia performance. Flying cupids were featured at the beginning:

I felt myself very uncomfortable, on seeing several poor infants suspended by ropes, in attitudes which made me suppose they had been placed there as a punishment: in a few minutes, however, I was convinced this was not the case, as they were let down to assist in a rigadon with the rest of the celestials.[109]

The same sets of wires, ropes, pulleys, cages, harnesses, and winches that enabled Mr. West to fly over the pit may have been reconfigured by the machinists to raise and lower cupids, to allow chariots to descend from or ascend into the heavens, and to draw carriages across the stage. A Boston 1807 production included "*Cinderella's Kitchen*, which changes to an *elegant Apartment*. . . . the *Dresser* to a *Toilet* [table] . . . a *Pumpkin* to a *rich Carriage*, and four *White Mice* to *Horses*." Later a rosebush changed to a car (carriage) for the ascent of Cupid.[110] The *Censor* grumbled about the transformation of the pumpkin in the Philadelphia production; it hoped that "the *pumpkin* will undergo its metamorphosis [into a carriage] with less difficulty, and *Cinderella* part with her humble garments more expeditiously."[111] The mice that changed into horses for the coach apparently involved costumes worn by boys. "Nicholas Bottom" gave "the boys who play the horses, a hint not to peep at the audience under the trappings, which should conceal them. Tom Urchin was recognized by one of his playfellows in the gallery."[112] When the same pantomime was performed in Boston in 1812, mechanical horses drew the coach. "The machinery, in some instances, was clumsily managed. The horses might be improved in appearance, as well as in motion, which is too slow and heavy to produce a pleasing effect." [113]

When *Harlequin's Invasion; or the Taylor without a Head* was performed in Baltimore in 1795, the following transformations were included:

A Farm House, which changes to the Wood and Cave, in which is discovered THE FAIRY GROUP [all children] . . . The Magic Bush, changes to a Tailor without a Head. The Transforming Chairs, and (by particular desire) the much admired Dying and Skeleton Scenes, from the Pantomime of HARLE-QUIN SKELETON. [114]

In an advertisement for a performance of *Vulcan's Gift, or Harlequin Humourist,* the *Charleston Courier* for May 17, 1804, listed the following "machines, tricks, leaps, and changes":

The Enchanted Grove, which changes to the Forge of Vulcan and the Cyclops at Work.
The Transforming Clock, a Leap over Columbine's head, or the Lover Defeated.
The Magic Toilette Table, or Harlequin's escape, assisted by his aid-de-camp. The Necromantic Grove and Convent, which changes to a Company of grenadiers.
Harlequin's Admission to the Convent, by a Leap twelve feet high.
The whimsical Change of a Dog Kennel to a Dove House, or Harlequin among the Pigeons.
A Serenading party, with Magic Guitars, which changes to Nuns.
The whole to conclude with a Grand Change from the Bower of Vulcan to the Temple of Flora, forming Festoons of Roses and Flying Cupids.

The scenery for this pantomime was designed and executed by Mr. Stuart, and the machinery by Mr. Irons; Harlequin was performed by Matthew Sully, with Alexander Placide as the clown. The same two performers presented the pantomime *Care and Mirth, or Harlequin Skeleton* on April 25, 1805, with the Magic Tree, which is changed to a Pedestal, and Harlequin discovered on it.—The celebrated Gladiator Scene.—The escape of Harlequin, with the Clown, on the Prongs of a Pitch-Fork.—The Death of Harlequin; with the laughable scene between the Clown and the Animated Skeleton.[115]

These instant transformations might be achieved in several ways. One was to use some sort of hinged set piece that would fold or turn into a new shape, revealing a different scene painted on the other side. Another method was to "reveal" the new scene by separating and removing the two halves of a flat or by raising a fly. It is even possible that some theatres were able to use the "rise-and-sink" method, where the upper part of a scene rose into the flies at the same time that the lower part sank into a cut or slot in the stage floor.[116]

The 1797 Boston inventory includes a number of properties, set pieces, and machines for use in the pantomimes. These include a forge for Vulcan, a clock chamber flat with a "Lion's head for jump," a "Pantamime trick from Bower to Church," a trick desk and a trick chest, a bones dress (skeleton costume), and a miraculous mill for the pantomime of that name.[117]

COSTUMES

Actors in most companies were responsible for procuring their own costumes for most of their roles; Hodgkinson reported in 1797 that he "found principally my own Wardrobe" for the many roles he performed;[118] he and his wife Frances were each allowed $5 a week for "extra wardrobe."[119] Actors were frequently given a small allowance to aid in the purchase of costumes; at the turn of the century, the New York theatre budgeted $15 per week for costumes[120] and Philadelphia actors received a small costume allowance.[121] This practice probably worked well as long as the roles to be performed were the stock characters of eighteenth-century drama, with no special requirements of place or time.

The theatre or the managers normally owned a group of stock costumes of various types, which could be used to supplement those

owned by the actors. Wood reported that the New Theatre at Philadelphia owned "the whole of the dresses from Lord Barrymore's theatre, as well as those from a French establishment recently purchased"
when that theatre burned in 1820.[122] (The term "dresses" refers to
costumes of any kind, for either men or women.) When the proprietors of Boston's Federal Street Theatre purchased the twelve trunks
and boxes of costumes owned by manager J. B. Williamson in 1797,
the inventory was extensive. It included entire costumes (coat, vest,
smallclothes or trousers, cloak, and hat, for example) as well as many
stock items suitable for entire choruses of supernumeraries (such as
thirty-three pairs of blue and white cotton "trowsers," twenty-four
red soldier cloaks, eleven green and orange soldier suits, twenty-two
yellow-baize Indian dresses, twenty-four blue paper breastplates, and
fourteen pairs of coarse stockings).[123]

Several of the "Articles to be strictly observ'd by the Managers and
Performers belonging to the Maryland Company of Comedians"
(1782) reveal procedures used in handling the costumes of a company.
The dress list for the next play and farce was to be prepared by noon
on the day after a performance, so that Adam Lindsay might procure
all the needed articles, "That the Gentlemen's Dresser shall have every
Article according to the Dress List, laid in their respective Places by
One o'Clock on the Day of Performance or forfeit One Shilling for
every Neglect." Further, "every Performer who is wanted in the first
or Second Act of any Play, shall be compleatly dressed by Six o'Clock,
or Fined Ten Shillings." After the performance,

every Performer shall undress as soon as possible, after they have done their
Part, the gentlemen to leave their Cloaths and other Articles in the Boxes ap-
pointed in their Dressing Room, and the Ladies, shall deliver theirs to the
Dresser appointed to receive them, and for every Neglect to forfeit Five Shill-
ings. Or if any of the Cloaths, or other Articles shall be carried out of the
Theatre, and damaged, the person so transgressing shall be obliged to pay
Prime Cost for such Articles.

The day following a performance, the dressers were to be at the theatre
by noon to "regularly Brush, Fold, and lay carefully by, all Dresses,"

or pay a fine of five shillings. That done, the dresser would be just in time to pick up the dress list for the next performance and start the process again.

Large theatres kept a staff of tailors, wardrobe mistresses, and dressers to assist with the work of costuming. As the new century began, musical romances increasingly demanded lavish, exotic, and occasionally even realistic costuming. Bills reflected this in the claims for "scenery, costumes, and decorations entirely new" that invariably accompanied the premiere or revival of such a show. For elaborate "costume epics," new costumes were frequently constructed, and costume designers and sometimes tailors were increasingly recognized by name in the opening-night bills. For example, a Mr. Shapter constructed costumes for the 1802 New York production and a Mr. McCubbin for the 1808 Philadelphia production of *Blue Beard,* a show that required special ethnic costuming for all participants.[124] When *Lady of the Lake* was performed at the Chestnut Street Theatre, it included a "Morrice Dance" with costumes "exactly copied" from "Mr. Tollet's description of an antique painted window."[125] Dresses and decorations for the 1813 production of *Marmion* in Philadelphia were directed by Joseph Jefferson, and executed by a Mr. Harburg "precisely after the poem."[126] In 1814 Russian costuming for *The Exile* was "copied from original and recent drawings," and directed by Joseph and Thomas Jefferson, father and son.[127]

In other shows that mixed street dress with ethnic or historical dress, there was a mixture of old and new, stock and personally owned costumes. Economy on the part of the actors, as well as a lack of overall planning, naturally led to a number of abuses. Judging from critical complaints, little progress had been made since the second quarter of the eighteenth century, when English actor James Quin reportedly wore the same costume for all his roles.[128] In 1807 a Boston critic suggested that Elizabeth Poe "attend a little more to costume, and not dress *every character alike.*"[129]

Most actresses wore the current fashions, and were sometimes considered models for the costumes of other women. Shortly after the

Revolutionary War, Mrs. Henry wore hoopskirts so wide that she had to be brought by carriage to the theatre, where her husband slid her out sideways and carried her to the stage door.[130] When costume colors and styles clashed—or matched too closely—arguments could take place between the players.

Sometimes actresses were criticized when their costumes, though in fashion, were out of step with local sensibilities. Sleeveless dresses were popular for evening wear in England early in the nineteenth century. In January 1813, Agnes Holman's acting was considered gratifying, but one gentleman wondered aloud during the play "*what kept her gown from falling off.* Our nerves instantly took the alarm, and we could not again look upon her without trembling lest we should behold the fatal consequences of wearing a gown without sleeves."[131] Three months later, a letter from a "young lady" declaimed: "I was gratified by the talents some of the actresses exhibited, but wished they had exhibited less of their persons. More covering and less skin would have suited my taste in dress quite as well."[132]

Historical or ethnic authenticity—and even consistency—were accorded little attention. Dunlap reported that, in the days of the American Company, John Henry played Othello in "the uniform of a British general officer, his face black, and hair woolly." Dunlap pointed out, however, that his contemporaries in England, including John Philip Kemble in 1786–87, did the same.[133] When James Fennell made his debut as Othello in Edinburgh in 1787, he "had no dress," so the manager loaned him

the customary costume: a coat, waistcoat, and lower garment of white cloth, cut in the old fashioned style; the coat and waistcoat ornamented, or rather loaded, with broad silver lace; to which was superadded a black wig, with long hair, and to which was suspended a ramillies of about three feet in length. . . . This, with the addition of a pair of white silk stockings, and my dancing pumps, made up my equipment.[134]

English actor Charles Macklin was credited with starting a trend toward ethnic costuming when he appeared as Macbeth in 1773, in

"Scottish kilt, hose, and plaid" instead of the powdered wig, three-cocked hat, and gold-laced scarlet coat previously worn for such roles.[135] John Durang wore Scottish dress when he danced a highland reel in the pantomime *Auld Robin Gray,* as did John Martin when he played Charley in the opera *The Highland Reel* in 1785 (fig. 11). John Hodgkinson, too, wore Scottish dress for Macbeth when he played in Providence in 1805, "and thus the character has always been played in America."[136] The inventory of the Boston company listed fourteen "Plad Pettecoats," one of them with gold laces, and fourteen "Plad Cloaks."[137]

Though Macbeth may have been played in Scottish dress, other costumes for the same production did not necessarily correspond. Lady Macbeth may have worn modern dress, while Duncan sported a wig, neckcloth, and breeches. By the end of the century, complaints about such practices were increasing: in 1798 Wood reported of a performance of *Every One Has His Fault* by the Wignell-Reinagle company in Annapolis that

the ill-dressing of the old John Street Company never equalled the absurd variety exhibited on this occasion. Lord Norland was well enough in a court suit—Morris looked like the wearer of the first cut of coat and vest, when the earliest approach to modern dress was attempted. Mr. Placid[e] walked about the streets in a black silk stockinet, full suit, trimmed and sparkling with black bugles [one of his dancing costumes]. Captain Irwin looked like the latest edition of a modern disbanded officer, as he should. Warren as Harmony, was properly equipped, while the servants revelled in every age and variety of livery. The ladies were appropriately habited, as was the boy Edward, delightfully acted by Mrs. Marshall. . . . Bernard (the worst dresser on the stage), was as usual in the rearward of fashion at least half a century, but acted Sir Robert so well that his dress was wholly overlooked, or pardoned.[138]

The New York theatre received its share of criticism in 1802, when Washington Irving's Jonathan Oldstyle complained that

Figure 11. Mr. Martin as Charley from *The Highland Reel*. By permission of the
Houghton Library, Harvard University.

another fault that prevails among our performers . . . [is] of dressing for the same piece in the fashions of different ages and countries, so that while one actor is strutting about the stage in the cuirass and helmet of Alexander, another, dressed up in a gold-laced coat and bag wig, with a *chapeau de bras* under his arm, is taking snuff in the fashion of one or two centuries back, and perhaps a third figures in Suwarrow boots, in the true style of modern buckism.[139]

Another critic played the same tune in 1808:

But the American stage, we presume, claims an exemption from historical correctness, by the right of prescription, by a sort of *quodlibet vivendi* by whose agency the incongruously diversified dresses of all ages and nations are crowded into one play, like wild beasts of the field into the ark, and a feather from all the birds in the air is added by way of codicil to grace them![140]

Sometimes the same costumes were brought out of the wardrobe year after year and play after play. In 1809 the critics complained about the reuse of stock costumes for a performance of *Soldier's Daughter:*

One word to governor Heartall—if the coat in which his *excellency* appeared, is not entailed upon the character, we would advise him without delay to provide one more *befitting* his rank. Against its quality we can certainly say nothing; for it must be an excellent piece of stuff to have stood, for twenty years, the chops and changes to which it has been subject. There has not been a governor under the present or any former reign as far as we recollect, no matter what his size, whom this self same coat did not fit. It is but putting in or letting out a tack or two and it suits every body: to day it is turned down to the standard of *five feet three* in captain Doyle, and tomorrow raised up, by a double tack, to *three feet six* in mr. Twaits. It has covered the broad shoulders of fat Jack, and by the same necromantic power, if necessity required, would be adapted to the slender forms of Robertson or Collins. But it begins now to be a little soil'd, and as the governor has doubtless brought home a few pagodas, it would perhaps be not uncharacteristic that his wardrobe should testify to his *faithful* administration.[141]

The same critic thought he recognized a uniform from about a quarter-century earlier:

Mr. Tyler . . . was badly dressed—his coat wanted the wardrobe tack in it, to make it fit; it seemed as though it had been let down to the standard of mr. Fennel [who was very tall], . . . and had never since been taken up again; or is it the old staff uniform in which *Henry* used to play *Othello* just after the war?[142]

Certain types of roles were given pseudohistorical or pseudoethnic costuming, with little regard for accuracy; these styles were particularly associated with tragedy. When not wearing modern military uniform, Othello and other eastern heroes wore a "peculiar furred dressing-gown-like overcoat, broad sash, curved sword and plumed head-gear,"[143] or wore turbans like Muslims.[144] When the New York theatre presented Burke's *Female Patriotism* in 1798, Joan of Arc led her army "habited in the Grecian dress, and armed *cap a pe,* like the figure of Minerva."[145] In *The Africans,* performed at New York on January 1, 1810, "The mandingo king looked as if he had borrowed his dress from the grand turk, and *Farulho* [the priest] might have very well passed for the high priest of the greek church."[146]

   The Comet objected to the Russian costumes in an 1811 Boston production of *The Exile:*

Dr. Clarke, who has lately published a volume of *Travels in Russia,* speaking of the dresses and figures of the priests, says, 'Their long, dark hair, without powder, fell down in ringlets, or straight and thick, far over their rich robes and shoulders. Their dark, thick beards, also, entirely covered their breasts. On the heads of the archbishop and bishops were high caps covered with gems, and adorned by miniature paintings, set in jewels, of the crucifixion, the virgin, and the saints. Their robes of various coloured satin, were of the most costly embroidery; and even on these were miniature pictures set with precious stones.'

   What would a Russian think to see the empress Elizabeth's coronation, now exhibiting at the Boston theatre, in which the grand Patriarch is bare headed, and dressed in a robe of *pink coloured shallon,* without ornament; and the attendant priests, (only two in number) in gowns of *India cotton* that once was white, but which from too frequent use, and the scarcity of soap and water, are now of '*no colour* at all!' and as to a beard, there is no such thing to be seen in the whole procession.[147]

One can only speculate on the results when, in a 1799 production of *Count Benyowski,* "the costumes of Russia and Siberia were strictly conformed to."[148]

On other occasions costumes were simply incongruous within the context of the play. Mrs. Young was criticized for her costume when she performed in *The Belle's Stratagem* in New York in December 1809:

Mrs. Young was not guided by her author when dressing for the earlier scenes of the play. A court dress for the morning is absurd. Her costume should have been adapted to walking; for *mrs. Racket* is made to say to her, 'you will have time enough to dress for dinner when we return.'[149]

When Mrs. Young played Alexina in *The Exile* at Boston in 1813, "A bonnet no bigger than a nut-shell, and arms with no covering but their 'whiter skin than alabaster,' during a journey on foot from Tobolsk to Moscow, would be but a sorry defence against the Siberian winter, which could destroy the 'invincible army' of Napoleon."[150] When Jefferson played the role of a servant in *Deaf and Dumb,* instead of appearing in livery, he was "the most fashionably dressed man on the boards."[151] In *Castle Spectre,* "it appeared to us rather singular that *Osmond* should start from his bed, after awaking from a frightful dream, and appear in full dress. Perhaps, Mr. Fennell conceived it indecent to wear a night-gown."[152]

An English writer on the theatre in 1791 recommended the following symbolic colors for costumes:

Blue	signifies	Constancy
Yellow	————	Jealousy

Green	——	Being forsaken
Pink	——	Innocence
White	——	Modesty
Black	——	Sorrow
	and	
Red	——	Defiance.[153]

The costumes used for an early nineteenth-century English production of *Children in the Wood* are described in the 1827 libretto as follows. These are probably standard "Old English" costumes of unspecific date, of a style easy to find in any troupe accustomed to performing Shakespeare regularly. The opera is based on a Renaissance ballad, but has no more specificity in time than most fairy tales.

SIR ROWLAND [of noble blood, but villainous]—Old English crimson puffed dress, cloak, sword and chain, russet boots, point-lace ruff, black velvet hat and feather—black gown and mask for second act.

LORD ALFORD [brother and victim of Sir Rowland]—Purple-coloured tunic, handsomely trimmed with silver leather and spangles, white pantaloons, point ruff, russet boots, black hat and feathers.

APATHY [the tutor]—Dark gray old English dress, trimmed with black binding and puffs, point ruff, black stockings, black shoes, and russets.

WALTER [a carpenter and the hero]—A dark green doublet and waistcoat, leather apron, belt and buckle, short trunks, russet shoes, shirt collar open.

OLIVER [the villain; servant]—Old English black dress, trimmed with red puffs and red binding, plain blue hose, russet boots, belt, buckle and sword, old English hat and one black feather hung drooping.

SIR ROWLAND'S SERVANTS—Ibid. no hats.

RUFFIANS—Brown coarse cloth tunics, with red worsted trimming, black cross-belts, and swords, hats and black feathers.

LADY HELEN [wife of Lord Alford]—Old English white satin puffed dress.

GABRIEL [a servant]—Salmon coloured old English doublet and tabs, trunks, little cloak, and hat trimmed with blue worsted binding.

Figure 12. Frontispiece from *Children in the Wood*, New York, Columbian Press, 1795, showing costumes worn by Walter, Oliver, and the boy and girl. Courtesy American Antiquarian Society.

JOSEPHINE [the chambermaid]—Blue petticoat, dark body and tabs, petticoat trimmed with dark points or point lace, old English hat, and point-lace
apron.

WINIFRED [old woman, peasant]—Dark brown old English petticoat and
gown, lace apron, cap tied under the chin.[154]

In an American edition of the same play, published in New York in
1795, the frontispiece gives some idea of the costumes worn by actors
of the Old American Company (fig. 12).[155] John Hodgkinson, in the
part of Walter, wears a dark coat with high collar and split lapels of
contrasting fabric, cut away just above the waist to short tails. His
neckcloth is high on his throat, and his white waistcoat is cut straight
across just below the waist, with the top hidden under the neckcloth.
He wears light-colored knee breeches, white hose, and black low-cut
shoes. His hair is shoulder length, probably pulled into a queue at
the back. Mr. Lee as Oliver is costumed similarly, with an added
hat—square-crowned, with a narrow brim, folded upward in front.

The children can be seen in the background. The boy has long, loose
pants of light color, and a loose, long-sleeved jacket with a short pep-
lum around the waist and an open collar. His hat is tall with a wide
brim, gently turned up all around. The girl's back is turned, but she
has elbow-length sleeves with tight, scalloped cuffs, a long skirt, and a
fitted waist. Her hat has a tall, conical crown, a wide, drooping brim,
and a ribbon tied in front. Her long hair falls loosely down her back.

These are all generalized late eighteenth-century costumes, identical
with the street clothes worn by these actors; the men might easily have
worn the same costumes throughout the evening while playing several
different roles. Note that Hodgkinson wears almost exactly the same
coat in the role of Robin in *No Song, No Supper;* only the sleeves seem
altered (fig. 13). The look, however, is changed from the gentlemanly-
appearing Walter the carpenter by the addition of the hat, and by the
substitutions of a kerchief for the neatly tied cravat and of a sailor's
wide-legged trousers for the knee breeches. Knee breeches were standard for gentlemen during the eighteenth century; loose trousers like

Figure 13. John Hodgkinson as Robin, from *No Song, No Supper*. New York, 1793. Courtesy American Antiquarian Society.

those worn by the boy would have classified a man as a farmer or servant.[156] As the nineteenth century began, trousers gradually became standard wear for men of all classes, but actors continued to wear knee breeches for many theatrical roles. The 1797 Boston inventory included seventy-six pairs of breeches (often called "small clothes"), sixteen pairs of pantaloons, forty-eight pairs of trousers (thirty-three of which were of blue and white cotton and probably part of a sailor's costume), nine puffs (used in old English costuming), and seven pairs of trunks (short pants used for old-fashioned servant or farmer costumes).[157]

MAKEUP AND HAIRSTYLING

The fact that actors—both male and female—wore makeup was taken for granted in the eighteenth and nineteenth centuries; painting was considered "an indispensable art on the stage, in which great skill and delicacy, derived from experience or instruction, are necessary."[158] Among conservative religious groups who opposed the establishment of theatres, it was felt that "the playhouse was the devil's drawing-room, and that actors paint their faces, and deserve the fate of Jezebel."[159] The actors used liquid makeup to highlight features under the glare of the lights, to create effects of youth or age, and to produce special effects. Details of the method of applying makeup or the actual substances used are hard to find. The 1797 inventory of the Boston theatre included no mention of makeup or wigs, probably because the actors supplied their own.

Actors colored their faces in various base makeup shades to represent various ethnic groups, including "white" Caucasians, "red" Indians, and "black" Africans. The color used to represent a Caucasian tone was no longer the stark white zinc oxide used during the Restoration, but was not always more realistic. When an 1806 visitor to New York took a seat in a stage box, he objected that "the nearness of the performers" spoiled "the illusion of the scene" and "the complexion of the handsomest actress, by rendering too apparent the *artificial white and red*." [160]

Actors wore rouge to provide highlights as well as to brighten the general color of their makeup. Sometimes they overdid it. When William Warren played Sir Peter Teazle in *The School for Scandal*, the critic for *The Theatrical Censor* saw no reason why "Sir Peter, although a choleric man, should have a face like the well-known Red-Lion of Brentford. Mr. W. had used the *rouge* a little too freely." [161] Similarly,

Mr. [Hopkins] robinson . . . was coloured so highly, that we could not help conjecturing Mr. R. had some good reason to suppose that his lordship was a little addicted to the bottle. As this over colouring seems to be the fashion of the house, we shall say nothing against it, although the ladies in the boxes should complain of their pink bonnets being put out of countenance. [162]

Mrs. Stanley was criticized when she performed the part of Lady Townley in *The Provoked Husband* because both the color of the dress and "the colour of her face were too glaring." [163] Even the supernumeraries wore rouge; in 1809 a New York critic complained of two male supernumeraries fighting for a rouge pot in their dressing area under the stage. [164]

Although black actors were not a part of established American companies of this era, many roles were traditionally played in blackface. The part of Mungo in *The Padlock* was black; it had been created in London by the author, Charles Dibdin, himself. *Inkle and Yarico* supposedly took place "on the American main" on the way to Barbados, but the roles of the natives were played in blackface. [165] The black page boy, Juba, in *The Prize* was normally played by a young woman in blackface. [166] Eleven of the fifteen principal actors, including all three women, in *The Africans* (New York, 1810) played their roles in blackface. [167]

It is often reported that minstrel performers used burnt cork to blacken their faces, and that may have been used by theatre actors in this period as well. Others used lampblack, which must have been readily available. "Dan Dilly played *Amos* [in *To Marry or Not to Marry*] and in spite of the coat of lampblack that covered his muffin face, there was no difficulty in penetrating the veil and discovering the worthy [David Poe]."[168]

The best-known of all blackface roles was Othello. Actors—and critics—apparently had different ideas of what constituted an appropriate Moorish hue. When James Fennell performed the role in Philadelphia in 1806, the critic took a "decided exception" to his color, which was that of "a hale, sun-burnt soldier":

He was rather a *Red-man* than a *Moor;* and this inconsistency was the less pardonable, on account of the references so frequently made to the black complexion of *Othello;* references which ought to overrule all arguments founded on the unfavourableness of a black skin to the display of the passions.[169]

When John Duff played it in Boston in 1812, he seemed to take this advice to heart, yet his color was censured for the opposite effect: "the Moors we believe were only tawney; Mr. Duff's face and hands might vie in *blackness* with the natives of Guinea."[170] Fennell wore black gloves instead of makeup on his hands.

In spite of such criticisms, the makeup was good enough to fool a variety of observers. When Wansey reported in his *Journal* in 1794 that "one of the dramatis personae was a negro, and he filled his character with great propriety," he was apparently taken in by one of these blackface actors.[171] When Lewis Hallam played Mungo in *The Padlock,* his makeup was sufficiently convincing that an African from the slave coast who saw him and heard his dialect identified him as from Ibo, an area near his native country.[172] Fennell reported that when he played Othello in Annapolis in 1794,

a country gentleman in the boxes, having paid great attention to the play, which he had never seen performed before, started suddenly from a state of wrapt attention and observed, with an oath, to his neighbor, that he had never thought a negro could have been possessed of so much intelligence, and that if my master would sell me, he would give five hundred dollars for me that moment.

Being directed to the stage door after the performance, the gentleman was astonished to discover that the actor "possessed the additional accomplishment of being able to wash himself white."[173]

Through the eighteenth century, spectacles were used in costuming as an indication of age. In the early nineteenth century, spectacles became an affectation of the Bond Street beau in London, and young men everywhere began to wear them (sometimes because of nearsightedness). Spectacles in the eighteenth century were pince-nez or lorgnettes; spectacles with temples became popular in the early nineteenth century.[174]

Actors also used wigs and false beards and mustaches as part of their costuming. Dunlap reports that in 1811, actors "found their own wigs and beards, but then *property-beards* and *wigs* were supplied to the supernumeraries."[175] Gentlemen characters at the time were invariably clean-shaven. Eastern Europeans wore mustaches, and beards were used as part of the costume for old men and certain ethnic groups. John Bernard was praised for his performance of Sheva in *The Jew*, in which all traces of his identity were concealed under a long coat and beard.[176] Noble Usher, however, was condemned because his appearance lacked "venerableness" when he failed to wear a beard in the role of Evander in *The Grecian Daughter*. "It is natural, an old man confined so long, should have a long beard."[177] Mustaches were frequently a sign of a rustic or an eccentric. In 1809 Captain Doyle began the New York season with a luxuriant mustache of his own: "Captain Doyle who has opened the campaign with a tremendous pair of whiskers, played the king [in *The Africans*] most majestically."[178]

Before and during the American Revolution, it was the fashion for gentlemen to wear powdered and curled wigs at all times. After the Revolution, men began to wear their own hair, although powder, either white or brown, was often used on the hair as it had been on wigs. Hair powdering was a messy business. In Baltimore in 1782, performers could be fined five shillings for having their hair powdered in the dressing rooms; the barber could be fined an equal amount "if he Powders any Person, without putting on them, one of the Wrappers, provided for that purpose."[179]

Men's hair was pulled smoothly back from the forehead, with or without a part, the sidelocks were "frizzled" or curled, and the back was normally plaited and queued or "clubbed," or put into a black silk sack or bag with a ribbon at the top. If nature was unkind, men used their long side hair to form toupees on top; if the queue were too short, they added a splice. Only an extremely unfashionable or rustic man would let his long hair hang straight down to his shoulders. In the early nineteenth century, men began gradually to leave off the powder and eventually to "crop" the hair "à la Brutus" in the manner of the ancient Romans. The hair was clipped to follow the contour of the head in the back, with enough hair left on top to set ringlets or for a carefully contrived "windblown" look. Sideburns were sometimes added, or the side hair might be brushed forward across the cheeks.[180]

Eighteenth-century women might sit for four hours getting their hair properly crimped and frizzled for some special occasion.[181] Sarah Siddons (1755–1831) was one of the first English actresses to stop wearing elaborate "heads"—the "monstrous inventions of the hairdresser and the milliner" in which the hair was piled to great heights atop the head.[182] Siddons wore her

hair without powder, which at that time was used in great profusion, with a reddish-brown tint, and a great quantity of pomatum, which, well kneaded together, modelled the fair ladies' tresses into large curls like demi-cannon.

Siddons simply braided her hair and wrapped it around her head.[183] Generally women wore their hair loosely about the face and on the shoulders, with a profusion of "natural" curls; the hair was sometimes wide at the sides with a few long curls emerging below. By the early nineteenth century the hair was curled by combing it back from the forehead and placing it on rollers, with a series of tight curls on the sides and back of the head. On special occasions additional dressed hair was sometimes added.[184] After 1800 women sometimes cut their hair, and coaxed locks forward onto the cheeks and forehead in "studied confusion." They sometimes adopted a "Grecian" look, with longer hair in a topknot and shorter locks curled about the face.[185] They always covered their heads when outdoors.

Ladies' and gentlemen's hairdressing fashions for 1800 can be seen in an illustration taken from John Fanning Watson's *Annals of Philadelphia* (fig. 14).[186] These heads are similar to those found as illustrations for men's or women's hairdressers in early nineteenth-century newspapers. Actors and actresses often wore wigs onstage as part of their costuming, either to save the time of hairdressing or to add comedy or character. Mr. Dykes, for example, chose a comic wig "with carroty locks and a tortuosity of tail" for the role of Old Grovely in *Maid of the Oaks*.[187] When a man wished to appear with a bald head, a piece of bladder could be applied to the head with gum.[188]

When all the arts of makeup were correctly applied, the results at the turn of the nineteenth century were as effective as any actor could wish today. John Hodgkinson was not only one of the finest actors of his day, but a master of all the theatrical arts as well; he marshaled these talents when he performed in Kotzebue's *Fraternal Discord* in Charleston in December 1804:

The play was in general very well performed—but all of it vanished before old *Captain Bertram*, which, taking character and actor together, surpassed any thing of the kind we have seen. The Proteus-like powers of HODGKIN-SON appeared in a new, an extraordinary, and an improved light. When he came on in the hoary old veteran of the sea, he was so little like HODGKIN-SON, that whispers could be heard—"Who is that?—Who is he?"—Till his voice discovered him, he was as much unknown as any stranger could be. His head appeared utterly bereft of hair, except a little tuft on either side, near the ears and temples, and on his broad bald head scars and deep cuts were visibly and naturally marked. His little hair and beard were quite white, and he had all the appearance of the age of seventy. Take him altogether, we have never seen on the stage so perfect a transformation of person, or an

Figure 14. "Head-Dress Fashions for 1800," from John Fanning Watson, *Annals of Philadelphia,* 1842. Courtesy American Antiquarian Society.

appearance more correct and characteristic, and his acting did indeed keep pace with his appearance.[189]

The value of all the "trimmings" used in early American theatre is difficult to estimate. Williamson in Boston put a value of $5,000 on all his scenery, properties, and costumes in 1797 (approximately $35,000 in present-day terms). The value of the knowledge, skill, and experience of the designers and technicians is even more difficult to assess. The nine painters and machinists from Boston received a total of $120.50 in salary each week, perhaps 10 percent of the theatre's expected weekly income.[190]

In spite of the maxim that "The play must be made *attractive,* before it can be *profitable,*"[191] the real value of the scenery, special effects, costumes, and makeup used in a theatre can never be figured in dollars. Illusion has always been vital to the success of any playhouse, and it was nowhere more important than in the elaborate musical entertainments of the turn of the nineteenth century, which provided fascination for the eye while delighting the ear.

6

THE ACTING COMPANY

The typical American actor at the turn of the nineteenth century was a family man, whose wife and children took their turns upon the boards along with him. He had emigrated from England to improve his fortune, and made the most of every opportunity. He was settled in a large city for perhaps half the year, and was more often than not a responsible citizen. He performed from three to six nights each week during the season, often acting in more than one piece each night, with a different bill each evening. He was expected to have a full range of varied abilities, both as an actor and as a singer.

In addition to his rehearsals and preparations for the theatre and his family responsibilities, he supplemented his irregular and unpredictable income by giving concerts and recitations and teaching various aspects of his craft. When the season closed, he often took to the road, either with his own company or with a smaller group, performing whatever and whenever he could. If he became a star, life became more difficult, because he traveled more often and had fewer hours of rehearsal; if he organized his own troupe, he could easily be ruined financially while appearing to be quite successful.

Critics were merciless in pointing out his faults, and audiences were impatient with ineptitude or forgetfulness and skeptical about illness. Persons outside the theatre often questioned his morality, and in some places his means of livelihood were illegal. If he performed well he was described as "useful," "respectable," or even "eminent." When he was assigned a good role, he held it for as many years as he could, because as he grew older new roles usually went to younger men. He continued to appear on the stage as long as he was able, and passed on his craft to his children and even his grandchildren.

The actress usually came from a theatrical family. Her career was directed by her closest male relative—father, brother, or husband—who signed all contracts and collected her salary. As a child she could play either boys' or girls' roles, and as a young woman she could play "singing chambermaids," "hoydens," or other youthful roles, or become a dancer. She sometimes played trouser roles, although this was not always approved by the moralists.

As she grew older, she probably married a member of the company (or at least used the name of the actor with whom she resided). If she remained single, she eventually used the designation "Mrs." anyway as a mark of maturity and respect. Even if her role was the most important in the play, her name always appeared at the end of the bill, after all the male roles had been listed.

Critics felt free to comment on her personal life, her morals, her features and complexion, and her figure (particularly if she tended toward rotundity). In questions of manners, behavior, and morals, she was never given the benefit of the doubt.

She was expected to continue on the stage as long as possible during her pregnancies, and to resume her career as soon as possible after the birth—or the death—of her babies. If she belonged to a traveling troupe, her entire family life was contained in the boxes and cases that traveled with the troupe from town to town. Even in the largest troupes, she could expect to be on the road during some portion of each year.

She played as many roles as her husband but, unless she was a leading actress, she was expected to share his benefit night. Aging before her time, she was often expected to move into character and old woman parts while her husband continued to play leading roles. In spite of all this, if she had grace and character as well as talent, she could gain the admiration and honor of the community in which she lived and worked.

THE COMPANY

The stock companies of players attached to theatres in major U.S. cities at the end of the eighteenth century were for the most part English-born, though an occasional American-born actor—the second generation of a theatrical family or a stagestruck amateur—could become a part of the troupe. They played a full season (sometimes divided between two cities), usually beginning in the fall and lasting throughout the spring, performing a different full-length play plus one or more afterpieces or pantomimes each play night. The same actors were expected to perform in all types of dramatic production, musical or nonmusical, often taking more than one role during the evening. A typical evening's entertainment might include a five-act tragedy such as *Macbeth*, plus a two-act musical afterpiece such as *Children in the Wood* (two English works performed at Charleston, March 17, 1796); or perhaps an opera in three acts such as *The Archers*, plus a "dramatic tale in two acts" such as *Edgar and Emmeline* (two American works performed at New York, April 18, 1796); or a comedy such as *The Provoked Husband*, a pantomimical ballet dance such as *Two Misers*, and a two-act serious melodrama such as *Black Castle* (March 20, 1807, Philadelphia).

When the theatre closed for the season, normally in June, the actors usually took to the road to continue earning a living. Sometimes the entire troupe established a circuit to nearby cities; often small groups established temporary companies. Depending on such factors as the weather, the health of the community, or the gathering of a crowd for some special event such as annual races or the Fourth of July, the company might reopen its principal theatre for a summer season. In Boston, for example, it was traditional to reopen during state election week at the end of May and beginning of June. Even though some of the members of the regular company were out of town, the theatre would be crowded with "our country friends, who then visit the metropolis, [and who] would return with ungratified curiosity, without having seen a play." [1]

Sometimes a pleasure garden, such as New York's Mount Vernon Gardens or Charleston's Vauxhall Gardens, would hire some actors between regular seasons for a series of concerts and light musical entertainments. Here the actors would share the spotlight with such attractions as fireworks, ice cream, and liquor. Since the stages in such establishments were at least partially open to the weather, performances were frequently postponed, and seasons sometimes ended abruptly when fall rains or cooler weather began.

If nothing materialized for the company as a whole, individuals would strike out on their own:

if an actor were unemployed, want and shame were not before him: he had merely to visit some town in the interior where no theatre existed, but "readings" were permitted; and giving a few recitations from Shakespeare and Sterne, his pockets in a night or two were amply replenished. [2]

On one such trip, John Bernard and Thomas Caulfield of the Boston Theatre spent the summer of 1807 touring in the eastern parts of Massachusetts and New Hampshire with an entertainment of *"Recitation, Song, and Imitation."* At Salem, Massachusetts, they applied for permission to perform, but it was not granted. [3]

Actors were normally engaged for an entire season of a specified length, at a previously agreed weekly salary, paid only during the season. A large troupe would have at least fifty members including the players, the musicians of the orchestra, the scene painters, carpenters, and machinists, the dancers and pantomimists, as well as such supernumeraries as candlesnuffers, constables to guard the galleries, box salesmen and attendants, dressers, and the prompter. When John Durang listed the personnel of the Philadelphia company, he included a treasurer, a property man, a housekeeper, a mistress of the ladies' wardrobe and her assistant, a master tailor, a master carpenter, and a master painter.[4] The Boston Company during the 1796–97 season included sixteen actors, twelve actresses, a secretary, fifteen orchestra members, twelve doorkeepers, three painters, six machinists, two stage-door attendants, two wardrobe mistresses, two men to tend the lights and three to tend the fires, a callboy, three dressers, four members of the corps de ballet, a master of ceremonies, and various supernumeraries for the stage and as servants—a total of eighty-three people, not counting the supernumeraries.[5]

Many of the performers were European emigrants—English actors, French and German orchestra members, and French dancers. Since the emergence of native-born actors was slow in coming, American managers regularly traveled to England to recruit reinforcements. When John Bernard returned to England in the summer of 1806, he discovered that English stages, too, were talent-hunting in England, Scotland, Ireland, and even in America.[6] A little later, Alfred Bunn lamented that Stephen Price had become,

since his secession from Drury Lane theatre, one of the most formidable enemies that the due cultivation of the drama in England has had to contend with. In his capacity of proprietor of the Park Theatre, New York [he purchased a share of the theatre in 1808 and became sole manager in 1816], he has lured away to the shores of America every performer of any distinction (and what is of greater importance—utility), whom gold could tempt, or speculation seduce.[7]

The gold that tempted actors to play in American theatres varied greatly. Until the 1790s the custom was for members of the company to share in its profits; if the company failed, the losses fell on both actors and managers. In 1791 the Old American Company converted to salaries, and other companies followed suit.

Some idea of the salary scale may be derived from a comparison with other occupations. Moreau de St. Méry reported that, between 1792 and 1794, a workman's pay rose from $1 to $1.25 per day ($6 to $7.50 a week for a six-day week, working each day from six in the morning to eight, from nine to noon, and from two to six.) A sailor was paid $1.75 a day ($10.50 a week for a six-day week). A week's "pension and lodging" could be purchased for $2.50 to $9.[8]

Salaries were paid by the week during the regular season, normally for three performances in the week; the salary remained fixed even if the play nights varied from two to four.[9] When the Wignell-Reinagle company opened at Philadelphia in 1794, weekly salaries for actors ranged from $10 to $37 each; since the opening was delayed by an epidemic of yellow fever, the managers owed $20,000 in salaries before the season began.[10] In Boston actors received $10 to $27 a week during the 1796–97 season at the Federal Street Theatre.[11] In 1798–99 the actors of the Old American Company received from $4 to $25 per week during the season; the following year, with the Hodgkinsons in the company, the range was from $4 to $50.[12] The $50 given to Mr. and Mrs. Hodgkinson was reportedly the highest salary received by American actors to that time. The salaries received by women whose husbands were in the company seemed to reflect—at least to some extent—the relative usefulness to the company of the persons involved. Mrs. Seymour received $16, her husband only $9; Mrs. Johnson received $25 and her husband $20. The fact that Mrs. Hodgkinson received the same $50 a week as her husband may have reflected her husband's bargaining power!

Actors were subject to various fines if they failed to meet their contractual obligations. Hodgkinson, for example, offered Dunlap a contract in which he would pay a £5 fine for every first-line role he declined to play.[13] At Baltimore, where an orderly system of fines enforced all sorts of acting conventions and behavior, fines were "collected out of the Salaries, every Six Months, and Expended as a Majority of the Company shall propose." Fines were "in full force, unless such an excuse is made, as a Majority of the Company shall think sufficient."[14]

In addition to their salaries, the actors were ordinarily guaranteed a benefit or a half-benefit each season, and time for these was allotted at the end of the season. The "BENEFIT was to the actor, what HARVEST is to the Farmer." [15] After paying expenses, a typical performer might earn about $100,[16] or about one-third of his salary if he managed two benefits a year,[17] and some performers earned much more. John Harwood reportedly cleared $800 or $900 at Philadelphia in 1806,[18] and Mr. Duff cleared $719 there in 1812.[19] John Hodgkinson had $920 "in the house" at his benefit in 1798—with $448 profit after the $380 house expenses and 10 percent for the proprietors were deducted.[20] The popular songstress Mrs. Burke received $985.50 at her Theatrical Commonwealth benefit in Philadelphia in 1814.[21]

A benefit was considered a measure of the performer's popularity, and young performers worked hard to sell tickets for their night. When benefits failed—for whatever reason—it could mean severe hardship for the performer:

Most people look upon the benefit given to a performer as a mere gratuity; a something allowed to him over and above the emoluments, to which his labours fairly intitle him; but, this is to view the thing in an erroneous and, we must say it, not very generous light. The benefit is a sort of test of the opinion entertained by the public of the performer's merit; and is, in fact, a portion of his compensation, made wholly distinct from his fixt salary, in order that so much of it at least may be measured by the general estimate of his services, and the value set upon his acting by the public. This is the true reason, why actors feel so much about their benefit; for, upon an average, very little profit accrues to them after paying the expenses, even when the house is what they call a middling one.[22]

Two sets of rules governing benefits shed some light on the procedures followed. The "Rules to be Observ'd in the Baltimore Theatre respecting Benefits" (1782) contrast in several particulars with those posted in the greenroom of the New York theatre by Dunlap and Hodgkinson in March 1797.[23] In Baltimore benefit nights alternated with regular play nights beginning in May. Each of the fourteen actors had his name put into a bag, with fourteen numbers placed in another; "Two Boys shall be blind-folded, the one shall draw a Number, and the other a Name." The benefits were to fall in the order given. (Since there were only two nights of performance each week, the benefits ran well into the summer, when the heat forced the theatre to close, and the performers who had not yet had a benefit would divide the meager proceeds of the last few performances.) In New York, once the benefits began they normally continued uninterrupted three nights each week, unless they were disrupted by the arrival of a visiting star or some other unusual occurrence.

In New York a performer who wished to "get up" a new piece for his or her benefit could get "prior right" to it by notifying the acting manager. At Baltimore a player could choose either a new play and an old farce, or an old play and a new farce for his or her night. Baltimore actors had "the Priviledge of casting their Benefit Plays, and Farces as they please. And it is hoped that no one Performer will refuse their cast for the benefit of another if they expect to be obliged themselves." This golden rule of casting had less effect in New York, where jealousies over ownership and hierarchy of parts were much more prevalent; there, "No piece shall be performed in any other manner than as cast by the acting manager for the time being, that cast to be obtained previous to advertising the piece."

In Baltimore the actors were to be charged £17 as the "real Expences" of the benefit, plus the cost of any new dresses or scenery required. In the 1798 season in New York, most actors were required to pay a standard charge of $380 for the costs of the house.[24] New York actors were also required to curb the number of new pieces in their benefits by a limitation on the total length of new parts other actors could be required to prepare. In Baltimore the temptation to "cut and run" with the profits of the benefit was lessened by the requirement that "Each Performer shall three Days before their respective Benefit give a Bond to the Manager, to perform the Remaining part of a Year from their first appearance on the Stage."

This standard organization of a company as a group of salaried actors awarded great power to the manager, who not only determined who should be hired and how much they should be paid, but assigned roles, allotted benefit nights (timing could be crucial), approved their repertory, and determined the costs that must be paid by the actor. From the actor's point of view the manager had all the power, and whatever profits were to be made besides! Occasionally there was a rebellion by actors determined to return to the good old days of share and share alike; the Theatrical Commonwealth was formed in this spirit in 1813, aiming to be free of the tyranny of "managerial despots"[25] (apparently principally Thomas Cooper in New York). This company included William Twaits, Leigh Waring, Thomas Burke, William Clark, Thomas Caulfield, William Anderson, George H. Hathwell, J. Jacobs, A. C. Fisher, and James Fennell, Jr.[26] along with Mesdames Twaits, Goldson, Burke, and Clark and Miss Clark. (Equality in the company seems to have extended only to the men involved.) Some of the company were from the Charleston Theatre, closed by the War of 1812, but others, like Twaits, had seceded from established companies or, like Waring, had newly arrived in the United States. The company rented circus buildings in Philadelphia and New York, and shared all expenses and all profits from the venture. A poem entitled "New-York," extracted in the *National Advocate* (December 1, 1813), contained the following:

The Rival Theatres

> Thus when oppress'd by Britain's iron band,
> Her sons migrated to this happy land,
> They formed a *Commonwealth*, and grew in might
> Till *haughty* Britain owned them lords in fight;
> The same event these rival chiefs await,
> Like Britain, Cooper—like Columbia, Twaits.

Twaits explained in a letter to the *National Advocate* that the company had been formed by actors who had been invited to American theatres but found themselves "imposed on, rejected, and absolutely out of employ, with a prospect little short of real want," and who associated "with the theatrical Commonwealth for the purpose of establishing an asylum from the ill usage and persecution of managers."[27] Even so, Twaits had assumed one role often associated with managers when he bestowed his own property and talents freely to insure the success of the enterprise.

Though the Theatrical Commonwealth was initially quite successful, it suffered from internal dissension and inadequate facilities. It finally dissolved after the death of Twaits (August 23, 1814) deprived it of his leadership and property, and the ending of the war allowed the reopening of the Charleston Theatre.

THE MANAGER

All responsibility for the company of actors in early American theatres fell to the manager, who was usually an actor himself. He leased the theatre from the proprietors, procured any necessary licenses and paid taxes in accordance with local law,[28] hired the actors, arranged for all necessary equipment (scenery, costumes, properties), chose the repertory, supervised the preparation of scores and acting copies, directed the plays, enforced the decorum of the performances, and attempted to balance the books. In a description that would win the sympathy of many college and community theatre directors today, John Hodgkinson described his duties in 1797 as manager of the Old American Company in New York:

I had to cast and arrange the Business [staging] of every Play brought forward. I had the various Tempers, Rivalships and Ambitions of thirty and forty people to encounter and please. I kept all the accounts; I made all Disbursements, and was made, in all Money Transactions, solely responsible. My Professional Labours were extreme, and I never finished them for the Evening that I did not attend to take the State of each Night's Receipts. Nay, instead of enjoying my comfortable Hour of social Intercourse with my Family, on my Arrival Home, I had a Check Account to take, and to make the regular Entries in my Books. I wrote and corrected every Play-Bill for the Printer. I planned and copied every Scene-Plot for the Carpenter. I attended every Rehearsal, to give Directions. I went through a varied and extensive Line of Characters on the Stage. I found principally my own Wardrobe for them; and my Salary, for all this was twenty Dollars per Week, paid only when we performed![29]

Hodgkinson played a leading role in nearly every production, and was an accomplished violinist who "could if necessary jump into the orchestra and take the lead."[30] Hodgkinson's comanager, William Dunlap, describes Hodgkinson's arrangement with the Park Theatre's proprietors in somewhat different terms. Hodgkinson received $20 a week as an actor, $5 as a wardrobe allowance, and $30 a week for superintending the stage, rehearsals, etc., thus making $55 a week.[31]

The manager had to select a repertory that balanced the preferences of a varied audience. He had to include an occasional Shakespeare play for the gratification of the all-powerful critic—although attendance would probably be light unless some visiting star were present. He had to pander to the tastes of the multitude for pantomime and melodrama, while risking the condemnation of the critics. He had to introduce new works as quickly as possible after their success in London, balancing the enormous cost of mounting elaborate new productions with the potential for increased income. He had to repeat favorite old works with sufficient frequency to satisfy the conservative, yet avoid such frequent repetition as to cause boredom. He had to consider the total length of the evening's entertainment, and the demands on actors who must learn new roles while performing regularly. No matter what his choice of repertory, there were inevitable complaints and suggestions from actors, critics, and the public.

Some of the most popular musical entertainments were performed repeatedly throughout the season. *The Port Folio* complained in Philadelphia that *The Poor Soldier* had been "worn to rags, to very tatters,"[32] and in Boston, *No Song, No Supper* had "been so often and so badly done, that its very name creates dislike."[33] Between 1808 and 1812, forty-four new productions were mounted in New York, most of them melodramas or spectacles.[34] In spite of this continual variety, a critic for *The Ramblers' Magazine* complained that the same after-pieces had been performed repeatedly again until "they perfectly sicken the taste and pall the stomach." He protested against "riding a free horse to death" with *The Agreeable Surprise, The Wags of Windsor, Rosina, The Forty Thieves, The Spoiled Child,* and perhaps even *Children in the Wood.*[35]

The Theatrical Censor made the public's view of the position of the manager quite clear:

For the beneficial direction of these advantages on whom must he [the public] depend? On the manager. On him devolves the responsibility, the credit, or the discredit. His is the satisfaction in the just and careful discharge of his duty; of the enviable consciousness that his private views are accomplished with public advantage, and that while he enriches himself, he is bestowing an invaluable treasure on his fellow-citizens, on the state. . . . A manager, however, is seldom in a situation to make his will his sole guide. . . . The public, in the final resort, govern the stage. First, the public forms the stage; then the stage forms the public; and again the public directs the stage. The manager must produce what the public will sit to hear.[36]

Managing a company was no guarantee of financial success. Charles Janson reported in 1807, after a thirteen-year stay in the States, that most theatre managers were in financial trouble or, in his words, "all the American managers are losers." In Philadelphia Wignell and Reinagle "were ever involved in debt, and finally availed themselves of the bankrupt laws, thus giving up the theatre to their creditors." Other American cities fared no better:

At Boston, Powell, with great encouragement, made nothing—Harper could barely keep his ground, and was often much reduced—West, of the Virginia Company, is greatly in debt, so as to prevent the opening of the theatre at Alexandria for several years; and Placide, at Charleston, says, that he can barely support himself by his theatre.[37]

During one season under the managership of J. B. Williamson in 1796–97, the Boston Theatre lost $7,904.90![38]

Hodgkinson and Dunlap paid the following costs for leasing the newly built Park Theatre in 1798: 5 percent on a nightly receipt of $450–500; 10 percent on $500–600; 12½ percent on $600–700, 15 percent on $700–800; 17 percent from $800–1,200, and 20 percent above $1,200, with a flat fee of 10 percent on benefit nights. Later, when they discovered that the proprietors expected to receive 113 free tickets for the season, the managers negotiated a reduction in which they paid no fees on nights that grossed less than $500, and paid 7½ percent on $500–600, with the percentages remaining the same on higher amounts.[39] Even the rent of the Olympic Theatre in Philadelphia—a converted circus—was considerable. When it was advertised for sale in 1814, it was said to rent "at the rate of 6000 dollars per annum."[40]

Another cost borne by the management was that of advertising. When the Charleston Comedians prepared to open their theatre for a spring season in 1798, manager Charles Edward Whitlock wrote ahead to the *South-Carolina State Gazette and Timothy's Daily Advertiser* with the text of a notice to be inserted. It was the practice of the printer to write the number of insertions and the amount paid for the ad in pen in his own copy (now at the Library of Congress). Beside the notice on April 2 is the penned note, "Whitlock—Gratis as it has not been paid." The printer soon got back his own, however, as the cost for the daily insertion of playbills throughout the season ranged from £6 to £18, depending on the length and the number of repetitions.

When John Bernard arrived from England in 1797, it seemed to him that a manager had "little other trouble than to attend to his treasury"; it appeared that

he had nothing to do at the opening of a season but to put up a cast of the common stock plays. . . . The actors were all studied, hardly a rehearsal was needed, and if the fever kept off, the house filled and closed without one jar to his nerves. And his social existence was hardly less enviable. Hodgkinson, for instance, possessed every luxury; he had his town and country house, drove his curricle or tandem, and gave dinners to all the leading people of the city, . . . [41]

A few years later, however, everything had changed, and the lot of managers had suddenly worsened a great deal:

After nine years' pleasant experience in America as a successful actor I had determined to try my fate as a manager, and agreed to take a third share of the Boston Theatre, in conjunction with Powell and Dickenson. But to lease a theatre was but a small part of the business; we needed actors and actresses, scenery, dresses, etc., such as could not be found on this side of the Atlantic, and it was therefore, resolved that I should proceed to England to obtain all that was required; . . . [42]

The situation had not improved a few years later, and Bernard lamented:

The season of 1809–10 commenced with very inauspicious prospects, and verified our worst apprehensions as it proceeded. . . . From the losses I had hitherto sustained, and the gloomy prospects before me, I began now bitterly to reproach myself for having meddled with management. [43]

The management of an "irregular" company could be even more disastrous. A company of actors opened the Olympic Theatre (formerly the circus) on January 1, 1812, with a company of respectable but principally "second-line" actors from various American theatres under the directions of McKenzie and Dwyer. They performed till the middle of May—apparently with some success—and then reopened at the end of June for six nights (to take advantage of the July 4 celebrations). On July 10 manager Donald McKenzie wrote a letter to the public that was published in the Philadelphia *Aurora:*

On Saturday last, 4th July, the OLYMPIC THEATRE was fashionably and numerously attended . . . Sunday the 5th, Mr. McKenzie passed with some friends in West Jersey, on his return to the city, he found that Mr. Wilmot, Mr. Fisher, and a person by the name of Brown, who had previously been dismissed the employ, had in conjunction with another . . . absconded with the greatest part of the money taken on Saturday, leaving Mr. McKenzie in the dreadful situation of responsibility for the debts accrued during the performances, and depriving Messrs. Hogg, Allen, Cross, Mrs. Morris, Miss

Ellis (a young lady under Mr. McKenzie's protection), Mr. and Mrs. Mc-Kenzie, the musicians, carpenters, tradesmen, and servants of their respective shares of the emoluments which might have accrued on that night.

McKenzie pursued the runaways and overtook them at Holmesberg, where a magistrate committed the three miscreants to state prison on a charge of robbery. Wilmot, Brown, and Fisher were then brought back to Philadelphia, where a "patient hearing" before the mayor "sanctioned and confirmed" the judgment.

Unfortunately, Mr. McKenzie could not recover the money found in this possession, as he could not possible swear to the identity of the notes and dollars, amounting nearly (by confession) to the sum stolen. . . . Wilmot, Fisher and Brown, have obtained bail, and have proceeded, as it is understood, to New York, on their way to Canada.

McKenzie announced that he would offer a benefit performance on July 17 (using the services of "gentlemen amateurs" to supplement his now meager company), and would "make his last appearance on any stage."[44] McKenzie apparently felt himself impelled to return to the stage to support his family, and in October 1814 joined the company of the Federal Street Theatre in Boston. On April 25, 1815, his body was found in the Charles River—he had been missing seven or eight weeks and was presumed to have drowned himself.[45] This story probably represents the extreme among all the sad stories told of the fates of managers.

In some theatres the duties of the manager were shared in some way. When Anne Wignell and Alexander Reinagle opened the Philadelphia Theatre in 1803, they were billed as "directors" with William Warren and William Wood as "acting managers"—what would today be called a "stage director," in charge of actors, acting, and staging.[46] The directors, Wignell and Reinagle, acted as business managers, although the relationship was actually far more subtle and complex, since Wignell was a leading actress and Reinagle led the orchestra and supposedly helped in preparing other aspects of musical performances. Alexander Placide was manager at Charleston for many years, but since he was himself primarily a dancer, he employed a number of "acting managers," including J. Brown Williamson, Giles Barrett, and John Hodgkinson. At New York, William Dunlap served as comanager with Hodgkinson for the 1797–98 season; Dunlap had "a voice in the selection of pieces," acted as "Treasurer & accomptant" and examined, corrected, and revised new pieces, while Hodgkinson was responsible for "the direction of the stage, rehearsals &c." The two were jointly responsible for the engagement of performers and "other arrangements for the Theatre."[47] Dunlap's *History of the American Theatre* makes it clear that the two managers disagreed in many ways over procedures and responsibilities.

The following year Hodgkinson formed a company and went to Boston; Dunlap served as acting manager at New York, directing the business and choosing the plays and casts. He hired John Martin to "superintend the stage and prompter; take charge of the Taylors and Wardrobe, armoury, &c &c, make ornaments, armour &c."[48]

The Federal Street Theatre in Boston evolved an unusual arrangement aimed to keep order within the theatre. Its "master of ceremonies" position was created by the proprietors and was separate from the theatrical management, though it was paid from the receipts ($28.66 per week in the 1796–97 season).[49] The position was first announced in the regulations published by the trustees in the *Columbian Centinel* on January 29, 1794:

To preserve the order and decorum of the house, a gentleman shall be appointed to superintend the Boxes, Pit and Galleries, and shall be called, *Master of Ceremonies,* whose business it shall be to take care, that the ladies and gentlemen are seated in the places, to which they are entitled by their Tickets, to direct the disposition of the carriages in coming to and going from the Theatre, and generally to arrange the whole etiquette of the auditory, and to prevent or suppress all kind of disorder and indecorum; and for these purposes shall call to his aid, when occasion requires, all the Constables and other attendants upon the Theatre; and he shall have authority, if need be, to turn any refractory persons out of the Theatre, returning to every such person the cost of his Ticket; and the Trustees pledge themselves in behalf of all the Proprietors, that the Master of Ceremonies, whenever it may become necessary, shall cheerfully receive their aid and countenance in the discharge of his duty.

Colonel John S. Tyler was appointed as master of ceremonies and immediately began his duties by asking women seated in the boxes to "attend without hats, bonnets, feathers, or any other high head-dress that the sight of the Gentlemen, who are seated behind them, may not be obstructed." He also barred unauthorized persons from behind the scenes, established a set order of music for each evening, and devised traffic rules to control carriages in front of the theatre.[50]

Col. Tyler served as master of ceremonies until 1812, and when the position became vacant, a facetious ad in *Polyanthos* provided an inkling of some of the additional duties of the position:

WANTED—A gentleman to act as *Master of Ceremonies* at the Boston Theatre. The business will be to keep silence in the box lobbies during the performance, to preserve, if possible, decorum among the *bucks* in the boxes, to keep *gentlemen* from wiping the mud of their boots upon the drapery of ladies who happen to be on the seat before them, to confine the *grog-sellers* to their *north room*, and to assist those *young blades* to find the outside of the theatre that have drank too much to stay within. Any one disposed to undertake this employment, will receive the sincere thanks of those who go to be amused with the performances, and ought to receive a prompt engagement and a good salary from the PROPRIETORS and MANAGERS.[51]

In most cities, all these duties undertaken by the master of ceremonies in Boston remained the responsibility of the manager.

The same set of regulations that described the duties of Boston's master of ceremonies listed several other responsibilities of the manager. It set maximum prices that the manager could charge for the various seats (one dollar per seat[52] in the first range of boxes, five-eighths of a dollar for the pit, and one-fourth of a dollar for the galleries), and it set forth the rights of the proprietors for free tickets to the regular season (but not the benefits). It declared that the manager should "provide sufficient fires in the several stoves to keep the house comfortably warm," and insisted that the curtain be raised "precisely at the time appointed." Near the top of the list was the manager's responsibility for the company, especially the members of the orchestra:

3d. If, in the opinion of the Trustees, there shall be a deficiency in the Music, the Manager, at their request, shall be held to enlarge the band; and if any of the performers on the Stage, or in the Orchestra, shall be guilty of gross misconduct, the Manager shall dismiss the delinquents at the request of the Trustees.[53]

In the 1782 "Articles to be strictly observed, by the Managers and Performers belonging to the Maryland Company of Comedians," Thomas Wall and Adam Lindsay as managers were not only subject to fines for failure to prepare proper costume and properties lists, but were subject to double fines if they broke any rules governing the troupe as a whole.

Women occasionally managed troupes. Mrs. Arnold's troupe performed in New England in 1796, but before the season ended the troupe was, at least nominally, managed by her new husband, Mr. Tubbs. When Thomas Wignell died in February 1803, his wife, the former Anne Brunton Merry, joined with Alexander Reinagle to reopen the Philadelphia theatre. In spite of Mrs. Wignell's skill and prestige as an actress, the actors refused to cooperate, and William Wood and William Warren were hired as acting managers. Three and a half years later, Anne Wignell married William Warren, who took over the property and management of the company. John Durang says: "I was sorry to see her in the situation, harass'd by some of the performers as she was. Mr. Warren relieved her of that anxiety by marriage and took on himself the management, in whose reign the well-meaning actors are happy. . . . "[54] Durang himself showed a similar prejudice against women as managers. He performed two summers at Layman's Gardens in Baltimore, constructing a stage and circus ring, but "Mrs. Layman assumed the rein of management so I quit the garden."[55] After the death of Charleston manager Alexander Placide in the summer of 1812, his wife Charlotte attempted to resume operations. In spite of pleas in the local newspapers for support for the "widow with a young and numerous family," the theatre could not muster enough support for a season. In February 1813 Mrs. Placide turned to concertizing for support, then traveled north to perform with various companies included the Theatrical Commonwealth (1814) and the Philadelphia and Baltimore theatres (1815).[56]

THE PROMPTER

One indispensable part of any troupe was its prompter. The primary duty of the prompter, of course, was to give actors their lines when needed, which was sometimes quite frequently. In practice, though, the entire management of actual performance fell to this busy gentleman, who filled the role of the modern stage manager. He not only supervised the workings of the scenery, lights, special effects, and properties during the performance, he also sent the callboy to summon the orchestra to its seats and the actors for their entrances, rang or whistled up the curtain, saw to the training of young actors when needed,[57] and even filled in on the stage when necessary:

How often do we see that second Proteus, the little prompter with his *parenthetical* legs, rolled on in five or six different parts on the same evening. Gentleman, jailer, footman, king, and beggar are to him equally indifferent; and next to Mr. Hallam we conceive him to be the very best murderer on the boards.[58]

Mr. L'Estrange (d. 1804), the prompter at the Chestnut Street Theatre in Philadelphia, was described by Charles Durang:

While sitting in his official prompter's box, at the side wing, or on the stage at the prompt-table at rehearsal, he looked like a senior manager or umpire in full dress, presiding over an assemblage of ladies and gentlemen to settle some controverted literary point, his appearance forming a good counterpart to his musical manager, Mr. A. Reinagle. Mr. L'Estrange occasionally acted, if necessity required it, in a piece where an aged, dignified gentleman was wanted. In the capacity of prompter (although supplied with an efficient deputy) he was seldom called upon to act. That official, in the well-regulated corps at the Chesnut, was never allowed to leave his book and station for an instant, the under-prompter attending to the necessary "cues" for knocking or other actions which take place behind or off the stage.

Durang complained that when the prompter filled in on the stage to save the manager six dollars, the whole cast could stand like statues for want of a word.[59] Perhaps the New York prompter was less missed in the wings when he appeared on stage in the 1809–10 season:

That well-known character, Mr. Oliff, appears frequently in the bills this season; he had before been on the stage—never heard—at least, never understood. He held the promptbook at the P.S. entrance, and rung the bells for up and down curtain—up and down lamps—thunder, lightning, and fiddlers—gave the signals for the carpenters to storm with the crackling of tin sheets, or rolling of cannon balls—and served for performers to storm at when they had neglected to be perfect in their parts: but for the purpose which gives name to the office, viz. prompting,—Mr. Oliff being prompter—for *giving the word,* the pillar behind which he was ensconced was just as efficient as Mr. Oliff.[60]

The importance of the prompter in this era can be inferred from the fact that the sides of the stage were designated by his traditional location. Prompt side (P.S.) was stage right (the right side, assuming the actor to be onstage facing the audience) and O.P. (opposite prompt) was used for stage left. In Boston as well as in New York, mention was occasionally made of the pillar behind which the prompter stood;[61] this was apparently part of the decoration of the proscenium, since wings would be altered from one set to another.

The copies held by these versatile gentlemen are invaluable today in preparing works for modern performance. They note the cuts made in the text, musical numbers added or omitted, lists of properties, cues for scene changes and mechanical instructions (i.e., "woods set in three [third groove]"), and descriptions of incidental and background music. They are frequently available in American libraries, either with manuscript additions or in less valuable printed prompt versions.

THE TOURING COMPANY

At the end of the regular season, major companies often moved on to a secondary season at other theatres on a regular circuit. For example, the New York company might travel to Hartford; the Boston company to Providence, Portsmouth, or Newport; the Philadelphia company to Baltimore, Annapolis, Alexandria, or Washington; and the Charleston company to Richmond, Norfolk, Savannah, or Augusta. It took two days to journey from New York to Hartford by stagecoach in 1805; Dunlap indicates that the scenery and costumes were sent to Hartford by sea.[62] The financial prospects of such trips were never secure, and weather, local prejudices, illness, and epidemic frequently complicated schedules.

Sometimes a large urban company would split into two smaller touring companies, each taking a necessary portion of the costumes, scenery, and properties and embarking on an impromptu expedition. John Bernard described this process in 1798:

Wignell, having to go to Philadelphia on business, placed me at the helm of his affairs, and as our season had now exceeded its limit, and it was necessary we should fill up our time until the fever should have left Baltimore, I thought it best to divide the company and make lecturing excursions to the smaller towns, an experiment which had been often tried before under similar circumstances. Accordingly, to my friend Warren I committed one division, . . . Allotting him the North of Maryland and Virginia, I took the conduct of the remainder . . . and resolved upon a trip to the Delaware.[63]

Individual actors or small groups of actors filled gaps in the season by delivering scenes from plays or giving recitations of poetry. In the fall of 1799, Bernard was faced with such a situation:

As the autumn advanced I received a summons from Wignell to prepare for a visit to Baltimore; but meeting Cooper at Richmond, I proposed to him to fill up a month's interim by a lecturing excursion through this state and the western part of Maryland, which he consented to, as a more agreeable mode of combining profit with pleasure than playing in small theatres with the thermometer at eighty degrees.[64]

In addition to the major regular companies, there were many traveling troupes not associated with the large cities. These groups were often called strollers, ranging from large companies such as Bignall and West, who established regular circuits and even built theatres at times, to small anonymous troupes, moving from town to town for a day or so at a time, carrying their costumes, scenery, properties, and green curtain in a wagon or two, and eking a precarious existence from engagement to engagement. Fifteen years after their performances at Baltimore at the end of the Revolution, Mr. and Mrs. Thomas Wall were performing at Edenton, North Carolina, with a company that included Mr. and Mrs. Douglass. The townspeople were audibly summoned to witness a repertory that included the opera *Inkle and Yarico;* "Days of performance [were] . . . announced by the beating of a drum."[65]

Carpenter wrote that "traveling actors are considered as having a strong propensity to wandering, to novelty of situation and change of place, which they indulge often to the great detriment of their professional character and pecuniary interest."[66] "Irregular" companies were also criticized in the *New York Magazine* in 1794:

There needs no stronger argument in favour of a well regulated stage, than that it tends to suppress those paltry exhibitions with which every city is infested which has not a regular Theatre, or during the seasons that the Theatres are closed. The very refuse of society, those whom ignorance, idleness and vice have cast from other men, and associated together, undertake to exercise a profession which requires the utmost powers of humanity, and ought (as every liberal profession ought) to be adorned with its highest virtues. Their exhibitions are in every light contemptible and immoral; they chuse from the worst farces those scenes which are most congenial to their

own disposition, and represent them with stupidity and the lowest buffoonery. Their audiences are composed of people like themselves, or of idle unthinking youth, who here receive the poison of the mind, which is to blast all
their future exertions, and every hope of the anxious parents; oaths are received as jokes, and the grossest absurdity excites the loudest laughter and
the warmest applause.[67]

Not every irregular company was a danger to communities' artistic
sensibilities and moral welfare, however. John Durang toured in Pennsylvania and Maryland for many years (1808–16) with a small
troupe and limited means, yet received a warm welcome in nearly every city. His troupe played in Lancaster, Harrisburg, Lebanon, Reading, Carlisle, Hanover, Yorktown, Chambersburg, and Gettysburg in
Pennsylvania, and at Fredericktown, Hagerstown, and Petersburg in
Maryland. Their performances included plays in German, dancing,
pantomimes, feats on the rope and wire, transparencies, and mechanical exhibitions:

I allways studied the taste and manners of the people before whome I intended to perform, and gain their patronage. My great attraction was to gain
the attention of the leading people of the place to visit me and that secured
the other classes of people to follow, and assured me success. Accordingly I
selected and arranged my bill affair to suit their taste, and I never failed in
my object. The whole fabric of my scheme was build on the foundation of
my own private conduct, to make myself to be respected by the rich and
poor. I observed a reserve of industry and sobriety, a compliant address conformed with the manners and rules of the family I lived with and inhabitants,
found no fault tho' it sometimes was not so good as I had been accustomed
too. I pay'd my way, I secured the love and commerce of the people who
where allways glad to see me again with a cheering welcome; no man need to
risk'd on a country scheme unless he will keep within the strict bounds of my
plan.[68]

Durang made adaptations of "tragedys, comedys, farces, and operas,"
curtailing them so they could be performed by one woman and three
men or two women and five men, but still preserving "as much as
possible the plot and incidents."[69] The repertory included such favor-

ite musical entertainments as *The Mountaineers, Rosina, Poor Soldier, The Farmer, Highland Reel, Forty Thieves, Blue Beard, The Sultan, The Purse, The Prize, Tale of Mystery,* and *No Song, No Supper,* all curtailed and with the dialogue spoken in German.[70]

Durang's troupe included the members of his family and various others needed to fill up the numbers. On his second excursion into Pennsylvania, he took along Mr. Loaft, an Englishman and a good musician, but a problem nonetheless: "it was with difficulty that I could keep him sober enough to play. At night he had a black suit of clothes and never undress'd himself, but lay in bed all day, so that when he got up he look'd like a wild bird, feathered."[71]

Seven or eight nights of entertainment were typically planned, with different pieces each night; the sequence would be repeated in each town. Durang insisted that the actors learn all their parts before the first stop; he had learned that once they received their first pay they had less motivation to study their lines.

Durang described his travel arrangements:

> I set out on my fourth summer tour with my own carriage and two horses for my family, my wagon compleat with a canvas top and two horses for the baggage and scenery, and I travelled on horseback. I keep'd the horse, Cornplanter, for that express purpose to accompany the family and baggage wagon, who I would allways send off a day before, over take it on the road, and then ride on before to make the arrangements in the lodgeings for my family and the company.[72]

One summer the wagon turned over in a large brook near Frederick-town, drenching about a third of the clothes and scenery. The troupe had to return to Hanover to make repairs and dry the clothes and scenery.[73] At Carlisle in 1815, the wagons were sabotaged in an attempt to prevent their departure.[74]

Durang went about the normal business of raising a family during the years of his touring. His wife died during the tour in 1812. In 1814 his two sons left the troupe at Harrisburg to march off to war as volunteers; Durang himself assisted in making cartridges.[75]

The company usually made a tidy profit during the summer; in 1808 it took in $1,967.95 and cleared $486.66. At the end of the season, Durang would leave the wagon and all his equipment with someone in the last city on the itinerary, ready for the next year's tour.[76]

Travel was never easy: the roads were unpaved and sometimes hardly more than a track; wet weather compounded the problems considerably. When Wignell and Reinagle decided to establish a theatre in Washington, D.C., in 1800, Wignell had the scenery painted in Philadelphia.

On the way to Washington a furious storm of rain invaded the wagons, and drenched the tasteful labors of the painters so seriously as to make it necessary to repaint nearly the whole, besides occasioning a considerable delay in opening the house.[77]

Although carts (or, for the more fortunate, carriages) were relied upon for transportation in the interior, the rivers and other waterways also were used. Bernard tells of hiring a sloop on the Chester River in Maryland to convey his group of actors and actresses in 1798;[78] most actors arrived in Charleston, South Carolina, by sea. When Durang brought his family from Boston to New York in the winter of 1795, he traveled overland by sleigh. He arrived in New York well before the remainder of the Old American Company, which had spent nearly two weeks frozen in the ice while attempting the trip by sea.[79]

By 1808 John Bernard was in Boston, and his description of a tour he took with that company gives an idea of the difficult performing conditions and unpredictable receptions faced by many traveling companies:

My partners, Powell and Dickinson, now proposed to me an excursion through Vermont, with a small company and a limited wardrobe, to give an entertainment of play and farce. As this promised to be a successful trip I agreed to go, [and] purchased a light little traveling carriage for my wife and self, . . . Our party, consisting of [Charles S.] Powell, Dickinson, and their wives, [Francis] Mallet, Morgan, myself, and Mrs. [Catherine] Graupner, set off from Boston in three travelling-carriages and in the best spirits and expectations. Mallet merely played—his instrument—and Mrs. Graupner was only a singer. The remaining six, therefore, had need to have had each the versatility of a Garrick in order to assume the variety and number of characters our little plays afforded, even cut down, to the strength of our miniature corps. Dickinson, for instance, in "The Jew," played Frederick Bertram, Jubal, and a fiddle in the orchestra; but, to his praise be it spoken, he played them all very well. This is a sufficient specimen of the shifts and devices we were put to.[80]

At Concord the troupe tried to perform at the inn, but a large crowd gathered below the windows, screaming and threatening. "Monsieur Mallet, who was a better politician than a fiddle-player, came to the rescue." He put down his fiddle and ran to the window; when he discovered that the noise was due to the fear of the townspeople that the players were "reg'lar British spies and mountebanks," he cried: "Yes, I vas von Frenchman, sare, and I glory in the name of Frenchman, sare; I vas serve vid Napoleon in de battle of Marengo; and I vas know vat it vas to put one rascal to death that makes a noise outside of de vindow." Either Mallet's nationality or his implied threat quieted the Vermonters, and the performance continued.[81]

The attitude of rural audiences toward actors was often contempt, either for their profession or for their morals, real or imagined. Musician William Priest arrived in the States in 1793 with a group of players bound for the Philadelphia theatre. He soon discovered it was unsafe to go into the city, where a plague had killed 4,000 people (a tenth of the population). On a reconnoitering expedition, he met a farmer who explained that the plague was

a judgment on the inhabitants for their sins, insomuch that they sent to England for a number of play-actors, singers, and *musicians,* who were actually arrived; and as a just judgment on the Philadelphians for encouraging these children of iniquity, they were now afflicted with the yellow fever.[82]

Joseph Harper, touring in Virginia with the Old American Company, described his arrival in Richmond:

the people were assembled when the performers arrived; at first they were
stared at as though they were so many wild beasts; but at length the gaping
croud [*sic*] discovered them "to be men and women, formed and dressed like
other folks!" [83]

The fickleness of rural audiences also added to traveling troupes' financial woes, as Bernard relates of his 1798 tour. Arriving in Chester-
town, Maryland,

we delivered our entertainment of songs and recitations, in the Assembly
Room, to about twenty persons (at a dollar each), more than double that
number standing outside and contenting themselves with reading the bill,
catching fragments of the songs, and imagining the rest. At night, therefore,
some of the company resolved on going round the town to give all the pretty
girls a serenade, flattering themselves that if the women—the most influential
part of all communities—once heard their voices, the next evening our room
would be as packed as the "Black Hole." The compliment was so novel in
the quiet streets of this secluded place that every window flew up and some
score of female faces popped out, which was considered a favorable omen.
But the Delaware maidens were better calculators; the next night we performed to only ten dollars; and I learned that "they could not think of *paying* to hear what they had already heard for nothing." This was a hint, so
next day I obtained conveyances and we visited Dover, Lewiston, and some
other places, varying in size, but agreeing so much in spirit that the pleasure
of the trip soon began to over-balance its profit, and like more eminent com-
manders, I was compelled with chagrin, to give the signal for retreat.[84]

Their financial problems were only beginning, however. Bernard
rented a sloop for the company and a horse for himself, and left the
members of the troupe to fend for themselves, providing, he thought,
enough money to see them home. The sloop took two extra days to
leave port, however, the wind then did not rise, and the company ran
out of money before it was halfway to Annapolis. Facing starvation,
the actors put on an impromptu performance of a different sort. Spot-
ting a prosperous plantation on the bank with unmistakable signs of
merriment and, more important, feasting, they delved into their costume trunks and presented themselves as a party of foreign ambassa-
dors on the way to General Washington's home on the Potomac:

Tempting as was the bait—a Delaware supper, a very encyclopaedia of meals—they were at first staggered by the proposition, until a due consideration convincing them that its performance was not too difficult, left them no room to perceive that it was too criminal. Accordingly Bates took out of his box a kind of Lord Ogleby's dress, for the English ambassador; Marshall selected a sparkling, spangled affair for the Spaniard; Fox spruced himself in the costume of Lord Trinket, as minister of France; while Gillingham and Francis, as Austria and Russia, put on plain brown coats and black-silk breeches; all of them agreeing in certain "properties" which were no doubt mistaken for official insignia—bagwigs, ruffles, hangers, and snuff-boxes.[85]

The planter, his family, and his guests were completely taken in by the costumes and by the performance (as other audiences had undoubtedly been as well). The players had a good meal and soft beds, "and in the morning, after being provided with a sumptuous breakfast, the distinguished party were waited upon with the utmost politeness to the sloop which, before a better wind, speedily conveyed them home."[86]

The touring troupe, then, was an important part of the American theatrical scene at the turn of the century. Acting skills ranged from total ineptitude to the art of some of the era's most respected actors. The theatres were usually crude; casts, scenery, costumes, and orchestra were makeshift; and profits were doubtful. Nonetheless the touring companies provided an element that must be considered, along with the established theatres of the cities, in a complete picture of early American theatrical practice.

THE ADVENT OF THE STAR

By about 1800 emphasis began to shift from self-contained stock companies to traveling stars with support from resident companies. The star became "the sun of the drama, around which the great and little planets and their satellites were to revolve."[87] Such actors would write ahead to report that they were coming and what they would perform. Stars usually specialized in either tragedy or comedy, and had a few special plays that they performed repeatedly. The resident manager would cast the plays and, often with only one rehearsal, the stock company and the visiting stars would perform.

William Wood reported that the first instance of the star system in America was "at Baltimore in 1795, when [James] Fennell received $30 per night for two weeks."[88] John B. Williamson inaugurated the star system at Boston in the 1796–97 season, when he engaged James Chalmers for two nights a week at $50 per night; that same season he hired Elizabeth Kemble Whitlock for twelve nights at a fee of $275.[89] Thomas Brown reports that the star system reached New York in 1801, when tragedienne Ann Merry arrived from Philadelphia for an engagement. Her terms were $100 per week, with "a clear half benefit."[90] The visit of Thomas Cooper marked the advent of the star system at Charleston in April 1806.

During the 1808–9 season, Stephen Price inaugurated "a sort of trust with the managers of other cities, by which he was to supply them with notable imported stars."[91] He hired well-known English stars to perform at the Park Theatre, then arranged for them to appear with the Boston and Philadelphia companies, too—often at a considerable profit for himself. In 1810 Price hired George Frederick Cooke for $1,400 and leased his services to other theatres.[92]

Most American stars booked their own itineraries, and tried to visit each major city at least once each season. They might stay for a few days or a few weeks, with the length of the engagement agreed upon and usually announced in the papers in advance.

Thomas Apthorpe Cooper was a typical early star—versatile, popular, and an asset to any company with which he played. William Wood describes him as

in truth a star, but his starring was so regular, so dependable, and so long continued, that it was reduced to all the advantages of stock acting. He was in truth in many aspects of the case a stock actor; a stock actor attached to several companies; permanently, in fact, to all of them, though not in form and in their structure to any. His relation with all was . . . absolutely beneficial and almost indispensable, by enriching the season with variety.[93]

Cooper was perhaps not so typical in his traveling habits. For many years he traveled night and day up and down the East Coast and eventually as far as New Orleans, driving his own small carriage:

By a skillful distribution of his time and exertions, he takes care never to stay so long in one place as to satiate the public appetite. Regardless of the fatigue of travelling, and always supplied with the best cattle, he flies from city to city over this extended union, like a comet; one day he is seen at New-York, the very next he performs in Philadelphia. A few days after, we have an account of his playing at Boston, and perhaps before a month elapses we again have intelligence of his acting at Charleston, (S.C) in each of which places he receives an enormous salary, and always has a full benefit.[94]

Janson reported in 1807 that

after acting his limited number of nights last season at Philadelphia, he [Cooper] set off in his phaeton on a Saturday morning, and arrived at Baltimore on Monday, where he performed on that stage the same evening. . . . Having performed three nights at Baltimore, for the trifling consideration of a free benefit, he proceeded on his route to Richmond in Virginia, where he performed the same number of nights, and on the same terms. He arrived in Charleston in ten days, a distance of between five and six hundred miles; and after skimming the theatrical cream there, he returned with equal expedition to the north, ready for the opening of the Boston theatre.[95]

Benefits could be highly profitable indeed. When Cooper received a "free benefit," the normal house expenses of the evening were not deducted from his profits. In 1807 he received more than $2,000 as his share of the profits after nine performances in Boston.[96]

Many abuses followed the advent of the star system. William Wood lists a number of these, and his discussion forms the basis for the following summary:

(a) It was nearly impossible to plan an orderly season of plays selected for the strength of the resident troupe when each star "has his own times, his own pieces, his own plan of business [staging], and his own preferences of every sort."[97] Some stars brought actors with them, thus leaving additional stock actors displaced; most traveled alone. Sometimes a star decided to perform a play that had already been performed that season by the regular troupe, or was already in rehearsal with another cast.

(b) Rehearsal was difficult, sometimes impossible; actors sometimes arrived on the day of performance, bringing a new piece with them:

There are perhaps no plays exhibited under more disadvantageous circum-stances, than those which are brought forward to display the abilities of a celebrated performer. However brilliant may be the talents which support the principal character, the play goes off heavily when the subordinate parts are studied at short notice, (or rather not studied at all for want of time). It would be injustice to examine with the eye of criticism, the efforts of an ac-tor, who in order that the public may be gratified with the exhibition of a star, undertakes a part, which perhaps he had never before read, which he never expects to play again, and which he is sometimes compelled to appear in without the customary advantage of a rehearsal. Thus the members of the regular company appear only as reflectors to make the talents of an itinerant shine with redoubled splendor.[98]

First performances were often disastrous; even seasoned actors could not perform well under those circumstances. Wood claimed that he had heard actors ask each other during a performance: "What is this play about?"[99]

(c) Not only was it sometimes impossible to obtain appropriate scenery, but the stagehands did not have time to learn the changes properly, and thus delayed the play.

(d) The star market was soon glutted with both English and Ameri-can actors of mediocre talents, leading yet others to decide that it was pointless for them to "act as subsidiaries, or, perhaps as foils to some foreign adventurer, who possessed no merit half so great as their own; while he took away in one night twice as much as they could earn as their whole weekly wages."[100] Eventually, in some communi-ties, nearly the entire dramatic corps was converted into "stars," and there was no stock company left. Such a situation existed in New York in 1810:

Our company, weak and bad in the extreme, is by bad management rendered much worse. To the annoyance of the public; when one actor, as a *star*, is thought to have sufficient attraction to make a good house of himself, the best performers of the company (and heaven knows bad enough is the best) are left out; prompter, scene-shifters, supernumeraries, and candle-snuffers being dragged in by the ears, as occasion may require, to *complete* the *Dramatis Personae*.[101]

(*e*) The audience soon demanded the presence of stars. Since the best players were out touring, the regular company was lackluster; stars from other companies who happened by for a few days were no substitute for the engagement of the favorites. *The Emerald* made the attitude of the public very clear:

One word however to the managers. *What are in fact the novelties of the season?* If, as has been intimated, they consist of occasional recruits, picked up by chance for 'three evenings,' at a time, let us tell you that it will not be sufficient to satisfy the expectations, or command the patronage of the public. . . . Is its only return an occasional song singer, or a single hero in buskin, whose exertions however great, can never be an equivalent for the ennui and disgust attending the lifeless misshapen personations of frivolity and ignorance?[102]

Since audiences tended to wait for the arrival of the next star, attendance would suffer during the rest of the season.

(*f*) Since each star had to have a benefit, it meant that increasingly benefits were scattered throughout the season. The manager and regular company found that their profits were considerably diminished by the time their own benefits arrived at season's end. The problem was compounded by the natural tendency of stars to save their best efforts for their benefits, when they received all the profits, thus further decreasing the manager's income.

(*g*) Actors vied to outdo each other with praise for their own efforts. The use of "orderly Clappermen [hired clappers] and hir'd Puffers" had long been an abuse; it was referred to in England at the middle of the eighteenth century.[103] Soon every evening presented a "tremendous attraction," an instance of the manager's "unparalleled success," with a star who was "the greatest performer of this or any age," or "the wonder of two hemispheres." [104] Tickets were given away "that it may be reported that the house was full." [105] Various "underlings of the press" were bribed to include superlatives; letters to the editor were even written by the actors themselves. These paid "puffs" became so extravagant that they were eventually discounted.

In Boston, when Mrs. Beaumont "of Liverpool, Dublin, and Philadelphia" made a star appearance in 1811, she was extravagantly praised. *The Comet* reported that

such contemptible *puffs direct* as usually appear in the newspapers respecting new performers are highly reprehensible; they are disgusting as the recommendations which attend the nostrums of a quack doctor, and probably contain about as much trust.

The editor quoted a notice about Mrs. Beaumont's performance from the *Columbian Centinel* of November 2, which had itself quoted *The Mirror of Taste and Dramatic Censor* for the previous year. *The Comet* believed that Mrs. Beaumont's talents fully merited the praise,

yet to show what degree of credit is due to these newspaper *puffs,* we declare, without fear of contradiction, that the *whole* of the above quotation, was in type at the office of the Centinel *two hours before Mrs. B. performed the part!* [106]

Contrived tributes reached their extreme with the tradition of presenting wreaths, bouquets, and other tokens; Wood reported that

in the career of . . . [some] performers, these marks of a grateful and admiring public were made use of on several different nights, when the ambition of the performer outran his means; and not only so, but that the identical vases, goblets and cups, have travelled with the performer from theatre to theatre, and been presented and accepted at every place with new "emotions of the deepest sensibility." [107]

The entire star system developed so many abuses so quickly that by
1811 *The Cynick* carried the following satirical advertisement:

Blatherum Bombast & Co. have the honour to inform the publick, and more
particularly the managers of the theatres throughout the continent, that they
intend opening a histrionick school for the purpose of furnishing the theatres of America, with actors of all descriptions, who shall be perfect masters of gesticulation, articulation, emphasis, intonation, and all the bodily
exercises—. . . they have on hand, at present, and ready to be disposed of,
one Garrick, two Cookes, and fifty Coopers, seventy-five Woods, and Paines,
&c. &c. in any number required; . . . they also undertake to furnish theatrical criticisms, in the most lavish and artful style of puff: and to aid those
theatrical gentlemen, who employ them, they will occasionally undertake
to puff themselves, in order to ensure to their employers a more undoubted
success . . . [108]

SOME ACTOR-SINGERS

Many of the finest actors and actresses in the United States at the turn
of the century were known for their musical ability. An introduction
to some of these actors can provide insights into the era's general abilities, standards, versatility, and limitations. Some of those discussed
here were fine singers; others were better known for other accomplishments. Some met with considerable acclaim and even fortune, while
others were barely tolerated and worked hard at survival.

Actors frequently toured as families, with husband and wife and
often several children involved in some aspect of theatrical production.
One intrepid woman, Mrs. Arnold,[109] formed her own troupe to tour
New England. Formerly a vocalist at London's Covent Garden theatre,
Mrs. Arnold came to the States late in 1795 [110] with her eight-year-old
daughter, Elizabeth (1787–1811), and made her American debut at
Boston in the 1795–96 season. In August 1796 she traveled to Portsmouth, New Hampshire, where she performed a pair of concerts before opening a theatrical season on September 5. Using a combination
of amateurs and professional performers, she presented a series of operas that included *The Spoil'd Child, The Mountaineers, Lethe, The*

Devil to Pay, and *Rosina,* all standard fare, before the season ended on October 31. She was so pleased with the prospects that she proposed raising $1,500 to build a theatre, but this ambition came to nothing.[111]

Mrs. Arnold sang once more in Portsmouth on November 9, but when she next performed in Portland, Maine, on November 22, she had become Mrs. Tubbs, and her troupe was suddenly managed (at least in name) by her husband. Mr. Tubbs was described as "late of London, but for the moment connected with the Boston Theatre."[112] Such moments of connection were fleeting, as Mr. Tubbs spent most of his career in the hamlets of America. The *Eastern Herald and Gazette of Maine* reported:

Mrs. Tubbs always does well. Her vocal powers we believe are equal to any of her sex who have appeared in this country. But the powers of her daughter, Miss Arnold, astonish us. Add to these her youth, her beauty, her innocence, and a character is composed which has not, and perhaps will not again be found in any theatre.—Lovely child![113]

The same newspaper which praised his wife and her daughter reported that Mr. Tubbs was to provide the accompaniment for "the whole of the music of 'Rosina'" on the pianoforte, and lamented: "Mr. Tubbs performs well on the pianoforte, but he cannot sing. Why does he not oftener introduce that instrument? and why does he attempt to sing at all?"[114] During their stay in Portland, the company performed a number of musical pieces, including *The Padlock, The Waterman, Harlequin Skeleton, The Devil to Pay, Rosina, The Spoil'd Child, The Mountaineers, Children in the Wood,* and *The Deserter.*[115]

The company closed in Portland on January 13, 1797, and returned to Portsmouth, with Mr. Tubbs and Mr. Harper of the Boston theatre sharing managerial responsibilities. After performing for four nights in Portsmouth, the company moved on to Providence. By April 1798 the company arrived in Charleston from Wilmington, North Carolina.[116] The family continued to tour as far south as Charleston and as

Figure 15. Elizabeth Arnold Poe. Harvard Theatre Collection.

far north as Maine for a decade. Dunlap says that Mrs. Tubbs died somewhere in Virginia many years later.[117]

As a teenager, her daughter, Elizabeth Arnold (fig. 15), played at Philadelphia from 1800 to 1802. In March 1801 she was highly praised for her vocal powers

at her benefit on Saturday evening last, where a thin but indulging audience, expressed their satisfaction of the talents of this amiable young lady; each syllable was uttered with such enchanting sweetness and harmony, each look adorned with so much innocence, and each sentence so perfect, that the writer of this is induced to believe, that in a short time none will be able to excel her in her vocal merits.[118]

She continued to play leading musical roles as an adult, although she never fulfilled her youthful promise. She married David Poe, an actor of no great ability, about 1806; their son, Edgar Allen Poe, was born in Boston in 1809. They were performing in the southern theatres at the time of their marriage, and later performed in Boston and New York. Elizabeth Poe performed in Charleston again in the 1810–11 season, just before her death.

When the Poes played at Boston in the 1806–7 season, *Polyanthos* lamented that "the publick were compelled to listen night after night to the 'childish treble' of Mrs. Poe, who has never before ranked higher than a third or fourth rate singer."[119] Stephen Cullen Carpenter wrote that she was "a pleasing actress, with many striking defects. She should never attempt to sing."[120]

Mr. and Mrs. Chambers provide excellent examples of the peripatetic routine of many American actors at the turn of the nineteenth century. Chambers had appeared in light comedy and singing parts at the Royalty Theatre in London in the summers of 1787 and 1788, and at the Haymarket in 1789. His first American appearance was at the Southwark in Philadelphia in December 1792. He then traveled southward to join the West-Bignall Company in Charleston in February 1793; in June of that year he married Charlotte Sully, an actress in the company. In the fall of 1794 the couple were at Savannah, and in the summer of 1795 they appeared with the Old American Company in Hartford. In November 1795 they were at Boston, where the *Federal Orrery* reported that Chambers "was engaged chiefly for the operas."[121] In July 1796 Chambers made his first Baltimore appearance; the couple sang and danced at Ricketts' Amphitheatre in New York in 1797. They returned to the South for a time, appearing at Charleston at the end of the century. Chambers was back in New York by 1807, performing as a singer in concerts and between the acts of plays until he disappeared from records of the American stage in 1811. Despite the difficulties of traveling in the early days of American independence, many actors and actresses compiled similar travel records.

Thomas Apthorpe Cooper (1777–1849; fig. 16) has already been mentioned as one of America's earliest traveling stars. He was born in London in 1777, received dramatic training from Thomas Holcroft, and made his London debuts in *Hamlet* and *Macbeth* at the age of eighteen.[122] According to Dunlap, he decided at sixteen to become a

Figure 16. Thomas Apthorpe Cooper. Harvard Theatre Collection.

chorus singer at the theatre, but Holcroft, on hearing him sing, suggested that he become an actor instead.[123] Refusing a contract to play
second-line roles at Covent Garden, he signed instead to play for
Thomas Wignell in Philadelphia, sailing to America in 1796. His
"many careless and some dissipated habits" made him less than an
immediate favorite, and only four seats were taken for his first benefit.
(He then filled the house by hiring an elephant.) When the Philadelphia company traveled to New York, however, he was received so enthusiastically that he broke his Philadelphia contract and joined the
New York company. With the exception of one successful season in
Philadelphia, Cooper remained in New York until January 1803. He
then traveled to London, where he had modest success, and to Liverpool, where he was well received,[124] before returning to the United
States in the fall of 1804.

Cooper took over as manager of the New York theatre in 1806, and shortly afterward began his tours throughout the country; in spite of his inaccuracies and his lapses of memory, he remained a great favorite. A correspondent to *The Port Folio* described him thus in 1807:

Mr. C. is in figure extremely graceful, slender, and inclining to tall; his face is peculiarly handsome, and his features uncommonly expressive; his voice is strong, clear, and capable of infinite modulation. Mr. Cooper is undoubtedly the best tragedian on the American continent.[125]

Bernard qualified his praise: "Endowed with great genius, and highest qualifications in face, voice and person, he had little or no art, which he never strove to acquire, being content to cover its want by his impulse and freshness."[126] Cooper was not known as a singer but, during his years as a member of stock companies, played regularly in opera and melodrama, in both character and serious roles.

Two generations of the Darley family acted on the American stage. The elder Mr. Darley (d. 1819; fig. 17) was from Birmingham and had appeared as principal bass singer at Covent Garden, where he was

Mr. DARLEY, *as performing in* the Orchestra at VAUXHALL.

Figure 17. The elder Darley. Harvard Theatre Collection.

received "with great applause" in such roles as Farmer Blackberry in *The Farmer*. Thomas Wignell recruited him for Philadelphia in 1793. He played in the "operatic corps" at Annapolis, Philadelphia, Baltimore, Charleston, and New York. William Dunlap said that he was "a stout, perhaps we might say, a fat man, and his appearance was not suited to any great variety of character." [127] The *Euterpeiad* reported that he "possessed a very fine and mellow bass voice, with a truly brilliant falsetto." [128] About 1801 he returned to England and reappeared briefly at Covent Garden before retiring to become the proprietor of a public house in London.

His son John Darley (c. 1775–1853) made his debut on the Philadelphia stage in 1794. He joined the Marine Corps (1799–1800), then resigned his commission to return to the stage as a vocalist in the 1800–1801 season. He married Ellen Westray in Philadelphia on December 4, 1800. Ellen Westray Darley (1780–1848; fig. 18) was one of the three musical daughters of Mrs. Simpson of Bath; they had come with their mother to Boston in 1796. [129] Ellen made her debut in musical roles there and then performed three years in New York. In 1798 she and her older sister Juliana shared a benefit that received $559. [130] After their marriage, Ellen and John Darley spent the next season in Charleston, then appeared at Mt. Vernon Gardens in New York in August 1801. They appeared in Boston in 1802, where the *Boston Gazette* reported that

Frequent and universal applause was excited by the fullness and harmony of his voice, and the exquisite science he discovered in the conduct and exertion of it. . . . We are the more gratified in this as the long desired, and long-lost opera will be restored to us. [131]

The *Gazette* reported succinctly that Mrs. Darley was "very correct, characteristic, lovely and fascinating." [132] Blake called her "beautiful and accomplished" and one of the "most fascinating beings who ever graced the stage." [133] *Polyanthos* said she was best in "characters of sentimental young ladies." [134]

The couple joined the New York company in 1804, and Dunlap

Figure 18. Ellen Westray Darley. Harvard Theatre Collection.

found Darley "the first and best the New-York theatre had known" in opera, and Mrs. Darley "resumed her station with undiminished charms" and "was much improved in opera."[135] They were back in Boston in 1805–6, and in New York in 1806–7, before playing in Charleston in the spring of 1807 and in Providence with the Boston company in the summer of that year.[136] They returned to Boston for two seasons from 1809 to 1811, and to New York again for the 1811–12 season.

A correspondent to *The Port Folio* wrote that John Darley was an excellent bass singer, but an indifferent theatrical performer.[137] The critics seemed to agree that he was successful as long as he stuck to the things he did best. Ireland said that he

had a manly, well proportioned person, and a handsome face, and though not warmly attached to his profession, had great merit as a singer, and in a French character, or a light walking gentleman, played with ease and vivacity.[138]

At the end of the 1805–6 season in Boston, however, the theatrical reviewer in *Polyanthos* summarized Darley's abilities thus:

> To DARLEY, sure, those potent strains belong,
> That mighty master of the powers of song:
> Manly, though soft; mellifluous, though clear;
> Correct, yet wild, he charms the enchanted ear.
> "Let Fame sound the trumpet," and Candour proclaim,
> That DARLEY's unrivall'd in song-singing Fame.
> The favour'd lover pleasing DARLEY plays
> In style as happy as his favourite lays.
> 'Tis false ambition thy desire awaits,
> To copy COOPER or to mimick TWAITS;
> Believe me, DARLEY, that I tell you true,
> To sing and love is all that you can do.[139]

The Darleys had a large family; the opening of the New York theatre was delayed in the fall of 1806 for the birth of their fourth child.[140] The family moved to Philadelphia in 1819, where she continued to play until 1832 and he until about 1840.

An engraver or engineer by profession, Gilbert Fox made his theatrical debut in July 1796 at Baltimore. He appeared in Philadelphia in 1797, and Dunlap says that while "yet a youth, he added to talents as an actor a voice for, and some knowledge of, music."[141] He had "less melody in singing" than Darley, but "more spirit in acting."[142] He played in theatres from Boston to Charleston until 1810. His principal claim to fame may be his introduction of Joseph Hopkinson's "Hail Columbia" text; Hopkinson wrote the words to accompany Philip Phile's *President's March* in order to attract a crowd to Fox's benefit night.

Catherine Comerford Graupner (1769– or 1772–1821) made her American debut as Mrs. Hillier (Hellyer) on December 15, 1794, in Boston and played there until the following June. Her reviews were mildly favorable at first: her "elegant voice wants only professional experience to make it captivating—study and a little stage *degagee* will render her highly agreeable."[143] Only a week later, the reviews had changed in tune:

Mrs. HELLYER really appears ignorant of every principle of music, her voice is generally upon one key, while the instruments are leading another; greatly deficient in both *time* and *tune;* she has neither melody, pathos, power, nor expression. . . . we are informed [she] has never trod the *Boards,* till her appearance in *Boston,* but was retained at *Drury Lane* theatre, merely to fill up Groups, and join Chorusses behind the Scenes!!![144]

Apparently Mrs. Hellyer's generous figure contributed to her problems onstage. She left Boston at the end of the season and traveled to Charleston with Sollee's company; she married Gottlieb Graupner (1767–1836) there in April 1796. Graupner was a fine oboist who played with a Hanoverian regiment and in Haydn's London concerts before coming to the United States in 1795. After several months of touring in the southern theatres, the Graupners settled permanently in Boston in January 1797 and joined the Federal Street company. Graupner became a teacher on a variety of musical instruments; in 1800 he became leader of the orchestra at the Federal Street Theatre, and he continued to appear with the orchestra until 1832. He also established the American Conservatorio, a highly successful music store and music publishing firm, in 1801. He was the founder of the PhiloHarmonic Orchestra and helped to organize the Handel and Haydn Society; he was reported to have "done more to improve the musical taste of this town, than any other person of his profession."[145]

Perhaps additional experience and her husband's tutelage improved Mrs. Graupner's singing. For the most part she was considered a useful performer, and for many years was called upon at intervals when a singer was needed by the company. The critics were usually at least kind: "She sings a fine song, and she plays generally very well, she is an useful actress, and we are happy to see her again on the stage."[146] She gradually appeared less in the theatre but continued to perform

Figure 19. Frances Brett Hodgkinson. Harvard Theatre Collection.

regularly in concerts; unlike many actresses, she was a highly respected member of the community. She retired from singing in 1818.

Frances Brett Hodgkinson (1771–1803; fig. 19) was the daughter
of William Brett, a singer at Covent Garden and the Haymarket in
London. She made her London debut in 1784 at the Haymarket in the
part of a dwarf. She accompanied John Hodgkinson from Bath in
1792; they were reportedly married in America shortly afterward. A
sister who traveled with them became Mrs. King early in 1793. The
family first appeared at Philadelphia in 1792 and at New York in January 1793. The family was expanded by the arrival of Frances's mother,
Hannah, and her sister, Arabella, and by the birth of daughters Fanny
and Rosina in 1793 and 1795. The whole entourage plus Hodgkinson's ward and pupil, Mary Harding, traveled together from theatre
to theatre, where all eventually appeared on stage.

Primarily a singer, Frances Hodgkinson was a tiny, blue-eyed blonde. She was recruited to play young lovers, chambermaids, and romps, but proved nearly as versatile as her husband. The *New York Magazine* reported in 1794 that

with voice and power of expression equal to her taste, she never fails to fascinate both ear and eye. Mrs. Hodgkinson adds a propriety of speaking and playing, both serious and comic, with her delightful singing, so as to render her undoubtedly the most generally useful female performer on the stage.[147]

In 1802 she was reported to have sung Arne's "Sweet Passions of Love" with "a delicacy of tone, a distinctness of articulation, a force of emphasis, and a degree of impassioned tenderness, which reached every heart."[148] Judging from the music sung by Frances and Arabella, both were sopranos, with considerable coloratura flexibility and an extensive range (their songs range from about $e\flat'$ to $c\sharp'''$). Both sisters died of consumption in September 1803.

John Hodgkinson (c. 1765–1805; fig. 20) was born near Manchester, England, and played in most of the important English provincial theatres (including York, Newcastle, Chester, Brighton, Bath, and Bristol) as a young man. He was recruited for the Old American Company in 1792, and soon became active in the management of the company. Dunlap believed he was motivated by greed and personal ambition, but found his services indispensable; Clapp said that although "his ability . . . as a financier was wanting," a "better stage manager never existed."[149] Hodgkinson left the New York company after the death of his wife and managed the company at Charleston; he was preparing to resume management of the Park Theatre when he died.

Hodgkinson was credited with an "exquisite voice and a fine taste for music";[150] it was said that he could perform

very respectably, both on the violin and the flute; sufficiently to take a part on either in a quartette or overture. He was peculiarly fond of music, and to participate in its performance was to him at all times the highest of his gratifications. His knowledge of solfeggio likewise enabled him to take part at sight in any glee, catch or duett.[151]

Figure 20. John Hodgkinson. Harvard Theatre Collection.

Hodgkinson often performed in concerts, with a voice that was "powerful, melodious, variable, and of immense compass;" [152] he was the president of the Columbian Anacreontic Society in New York in 1802. [153]

Hodgkinson's critics sometimes disliked his pronunciations and accused him of ranting in tragedy; Jonathan Oldstyle described him as a "portly gentleman, who . . . fumed his hour out, after he had slapped his breast and drawn his sword half-a-dozen times." [154] His "person and face," though very fine, were "by no means faultless." He was tall (about five feet ten inches), strong, and erect, with muscular chest and shoulders. His legs, however, were "ill fashioned and clumsy" and appeared best "in drapery that concealed his limbs, or in black." Though "his features taken together composed a physiognomy eminently comely," his eyes suffered from a "disparity in their size," which Hodgkinson tried to overcome by squinting—hoping, no doubt, that the audience would notice instead "the finest eye lashes in the world."[155]

Hodgkinson was universally praised for his versatility: "Those who spoke most reluctantly in his praise being forced to confess this at least, that as a general actor he was the greatest in America."[156] He was "always correct, always perfect in his part, and master of himself and of his character," able "to constantly prompt any character that played with him," and with a mind so vigorous that

he had ready at his call all the criticisms and commentaries upon the dramatic poets, and on any dubious point could instantly repeat the opinions of every great annotator on Shakespeare, and even turn at once to the page.[157]

Hodgkinson died while still in his prime as an actor. He left New York to escape a yellow fever epidemic, but died of the disease while en route to Washington, D.C., where his daughters were in school, and where he was to play at the opening of a new theatre. Newspapers throughout the nation carried notices of his death, even though dozens of casualties from the epidemic were announced in every issue. Many carried eulogies or poetic epitaphs in his honor; the news of his death was even reported in London. All the major American theatres held benefit performances for his orphans, Fanny and Rosina, and a trust fund was established for their education. The *Columbian Centinel* summarized the general feeling:

Few men, in his profession, possessed such general talents as an actor, united with so clear a head, and such a fund of literary knowledge. . . . As a comedian, we can say in the language of his favorite author—*"Take him for all in all, we ne'er shall look upon his like again."*[158]

Joseph Jefferson (1774–1832; fig. 21) grew up in the theatrical profession, starting as a boy in his father's company in England. He made his American debut with the Old American Company in Boston in 1796 as one of the witches in *Macbeth;* he played with the company at the John Street and Park theatres in New York until 1803. He then

Figure 21. Joseph Jefferson. Harvard Theatre Collection.

joined the Philadelphia company, where he remained for nearly thirty years, though he toured regularly to other cities. He married in 1801.

He was "of a small and light figure, well formed, with a singular physiognomy, a nose perfectly Grecian, and blue eyes full of laughter."[159] Jefferson's talents as a scene painter and machinist were enough to make him welcome in any American company; his son Joseph was even more talented in this line. As an actor, Jefferson was particularly known for his low comedy and old men's roles; "he had the faculty of exciting mirth to as great a degree by power of feature, although handsome, as any ugly-featured low comedian ever seen."[160] Wood said he had "an excellent ear for music;"[161] he also danced in the pantomimes on occasion.

Jefferson's old men's roles were so convincing that while he was still quite a young man, a sympathetic lady who had seen him "bent and tottering" on the stage attempted to raise a subscription to enable him to retire in comfort; all his life he was known as "Old Jefferson."[162]

Jefferson was the first of an American dynasty of actors. His gravestone in Harrisburg, Pennsylvania, reads:

Joseph Jefferson, An actor whose unrivalled powers took in the whole range of comic character, from Pathos to soul-shaking Mirth. His colouring of the part was that of nature, warm, pure, and fresh; but of nature enriched with the finest conceptions of genius.[163]

Mrs. Jones (d. 1806) of the Boston and New York theatres had the distinction of being admired equally as an actress and as a singer. She was one of three daughters of a London physician named Granger, whose death when she was young left her in the care of her grandmother, Mrs. Booth, of Drury Lane, where she was introduced as a singer at an early age. She is said to have played several musical parts with success. About 1800 she married a comedian, Mr. Jones, and having been engaged by Mr. Whitlock to perform in Boston, they embarked for the States. She made her American debut on October 19, 1800, as Miss Blandford in Thomas Morton's comedy, *Speed the Plough,* and "was the principal favourite of the audience during the whole season."[164]

She then joined the Wignell-Reinagle company and played three seasons in Philadelphia, where she was approved as a singer and respected as a wife and mother, but "did not receive sufficient success at her benefits."[165] At the time of her Philadelphia debut, *The Port Folio* commented that "In singing, her voice is plaintive and expressive, and possesses one excellence, which cannot be too highly commended: a distinct and perfectly articulate pronunciation." A month later, the same writer reported that "Mrs. Jones's voice improves upon us by repetition; but her action is susceptive of great improvement."[166]

Powell invited her to return to Boston; there "her talents first began to expand,"[167] and her petite figure and pleasing face[168] contributed to her enthusiastic reception as chambermaids, hoydens, and such breeches roles as that of Little Pickle in *The Spoil'd Child*.

"Domestick disquiet entered her dwelling,"[169] and her husband left her in 1805 to play in Charleston, where he was highly praised as Hamlet and Macbeth. By spring, however, Jones was "abandoned to ebriety [*sic*]; so much so, that as no dependance [*sic*] can be placed on his services, he is not permitted to perform,"[170] and he died on August 7, 1806.[171]

Mrs. Jones played in New York in the 1805–6 season, and again criticism "spoke goldenly":[172] "Mrs. Jones is as great a favorite as ever; her Little Pickle has been acted for the *twelfth time!* She is on the stage every night, play and farce, and often comes forward with a song, by way of interlude."[173] William Coleman described her voice: "The characteristics of her singing are not so much strength and volume as sweetness, compass and a great neatness in running divisions."[174] When she performed in Sheridan's *The Duenna* on January 24, 1806, the *Thespian Mirror* raved:

Of Mrs. JONES' *Clara* too much cannot be said, in the way of encomium. This lady certainly possesses the strongest claims to public approbation and support. Her voice has melody, sweetness and expression—her manner ease, sportiveness, and interest. In the song of *"Adieu thou dreary pile!"* she almost surpassed herself. Her trills were given with the utmost delicacy; and such was the delight which this song imparted, that applause could scarcely continue silent to its termination.[175]

The opening of the New York theatre was postponed from September 22 to October 13 in 1806, "owing to the *accouchement* of Mrs. Darley, and the illness of Mrs. Jones."[176] During the fall, other actresses began to take the roles Mrs. Jones had performed, and she died in New York on November 11. Although some confusion about the time apparently prevented the theatrical corps from attending her funeral,[177] the company volunteered its services for a benefit for the Jones children (three girls and a boy, the oldest five years of age).[178] Mr. Cooper had "taken the little daughter Mrs. Jones had with her, at the time of her death, and, from a regard to the memory of the mother, intends to give it the best and most careful education that can be procured in this country."[179] The benefit, held on December 19, raised $765 for the orphans.[180] In writing of her life and death, *Polyanthos* summarized:

All, who have witnessed the charming exhibitions of this favorite of Thalia, will acknowledge the justice of the opinion, that, in her death, the New-York theatre has lost its principal female attraction and ornament. . . . and when we consider, that, to her comick talents, she added . . . extraordinary powers in opera, it may be doubted whether even the London stage can boast of her superior. In the ballad and pathetick style of Musick, she was unrivalled. Her voice had a heart-felt sweetness peculiar to herself, and its flexibility was wonderful. She could
     Dwell on the note, and die along the strain,
without the appearance of labour to herself, or giving uneasiness on her account to the auditor. Her cantabiles were executed with a neatness, a taste and a grace, never before heard on our boards.[181]

The finest tragic actress in the United States at the turn of the nineteenth century was Anne Brunton Merry (1770–1808; fig. 22), daughter of an actor and theatre manager in England. She made her debut at Bristol in the winter of 1786–87, and later that same season performed at London's Covent Garden, playing leading tragic roles. At the end of the season she married Robert Merry (1755–98), a poet, occasional playwright, and *bon vivant,* and retired from the stage. By 1796 Merry's fortune was sufficiently reduced that he consented for his wife to appear on the stage again, though not in England. Wignell engaged her for the Philadelphia company, and the Merrys arrived in New York in October 1796, along with Thomas Cooper, William Warren, and other actors for the company. Mrs. Merry made her first American appearance as Juliet in *Romeo and Juliet* in December 1796.

Robert Merry died at Baltimore in December 1798. Dunlap immediately offered Anne Merry a New York engagement at the unheard-of figure of $60 a week for a guaranteed season of thirty-four or forty weeks, and a minimum benefit of $600. She responded that she was

Figure 22. Anne Brunton Merry Wignell Warren. Harvard Theatre Collection.

"every day in expectation of receiving letters from my connexions in England, and before I know what their wishes are, it will be improper for me to enter into any new engagement."[182] Apparently Mrs. Merry's relatives approved of her continuance in America, because she remained based in Philadelphia for the duration of her career.

In 1801 she visited New York during the summer for $100 a week plus a benefit (which netted $884); this occasion represented the first "star" engagement for the New York company. Thereafter Mrs. Merry traveled regularly while the Philadelphia theatre was closed, making guest appearances on all the major American stages.

In January 1803 Mrs. Merry married Thomas Wignell, manager of the Philadelphia theatre. Seven weeks later he was dead, "in consequence of injury received from a spring-lancet in blood-letting."[183] In due course his widow became the mother of a daughter. Although Mrs. Wignell signed a four-year contract to operate the Philadelphia theatre (along with her husband's original partner, Alexander Reinagle), the day-to-day management of the company was handled by William Warren and William Wood. Mrs. Wignell became Mrs. Warren on August 15, 1806, and Warren took over the "property and management" of the theatre and the guardianship of Wignell's child. Although Mrs. Warren's figure was now "inclining to corpulency"[184] (at thirty-six), she remained the most popular tragic actress in the States and, in the opinion of many, second only to Sarah Siddons. She died in childbirth on June 28, 1808, at Alexandria, Virginia, "having, contrary to the advice of her physicians, accompanied her husband on the southern tour required by his duties as actor and manager."[185]

It was unusual for tragediennes such as Anne Merry Wignell Warren to be considered singers, but reviewers regularly commented on the quality of her singing. In *Edwy and Elgiva*, "Mrs. Merry personated the persecuted queen with wonted excellence, and sang with such '*pleasing sorcery*,' that many a bright eye, in the boxes, glistened with sensibility." In *The Secret*, Mrs. Merry's song was "sweetly sung. Even in speaking, this inimitable actress always 'discourses most eloquent music.' No wonder, then, when she modulates her voice, in a song, the chaste simplicity of her strains, at once claims the admiration of the unskilful and the connoisseur."[186]

Mrs. Oldmixon (c. 1762–1836) had been a favorite in London theatres (Haymarket and Drury Lane) as Miss George (fig. 23), having made her London debut in 1783. She married Sir John Oldmixon and retired from the London stage in 1789. She later performed in Ireland, then came to Philadelphia in May 1794 as the performer of "chambermaids and country girls" for the new Wignell-Reinagle company. Her unrealistic expectations of America as a place where the

streets are paved with dollars, and our houses covered with doubloons, that ready-roasted pigs run about our streets with knives and forks sticking in their backs, inviting people to eat them, and that fricaseed chickens hop through the public walks, with the most delicious sauces in their bills, humbly requesting to be devoured

were poetically lampooned by a wag in *The Ramblers' Magazine* in 1809:

Figure 23. Miss George (later Mrs. Oldmixon). Harvard Theatre Collection.

> Mrs. Oldmixon sings like a lark,
> And frisks like a colt in high clover;
> 'Tis said she was much in the dark,
> When she, hapless, from England came over.[187]

According to Dunlap, Sir John became a gentleman farmer at German-town, bringing his vegetables to market as he delivered his wife to the theatre each day.[188]

When Dunlap contacted Mrs. Oldmixon in 1798 concerning an engagement with the New York company, she agreed to play "the first line of opera or the best old women in comedy, the comic singing characters, and occasionally a serious one, and the best chamber-maids—and referred the manager to Sir John." Dunlap traveled out to Germantown, walked the mile and a half to the Oldmixon cottage, and negotiated the contract—which included a stipulation that Mrs. Oldmixon was not required to sing in choruses unless she herself chose to do so. The contract was signed not by the lady, but by her husband, whose signature was "in very gentlemanly illegible letters." [189]

Mrs. Oldmixon played in New York in the 1798–99 season, then rejoined the Philadelphia company until 1805; after a season in Charleston (1805–6) she became a regular member of the New York company in the fall of 1806. When she gave a benefit concert in 1809, it was noted that she was "a widow with seven children dependent on a mother's professional talents for support;" [190] her widowhood may have been of the "grass" variety, however, since Dunlap reports that Sir John was still living in obscurity at Sag Harbour, Long Island, in 1816. [191] After her retirement from the stage in 1814, she managed a seminary for young ladies in Philadelphia.

Ireland contended that she was "indisputably the finest vocalist ever heard in this country at this time, though the personal appearance of Mrs. Hodgkinson made her more pleasing to the multitude." [192] When Mrs. Oldmixon performed in Charleston at a benefit for the Hodgkinson children in 1805,

The taste with which she sung, and the expression she threw into the tender passages of the beautiful music of GIARDINI, the command she possessed over a voice of uncommon compass, and modulated with nicest accuracy, and the height to which she ascended, making a double octave from G, can only be credited by those who have had the delight of listening to the necromancy of her notes. [193]

Critics often complimented her "scientifick music" and compared her voice with a flute. The *Euterpeiad* reported:

Mrs. Oldmixon's voice is of uncommon extent, being from B below the staff, to A in altissimo: that is A upon the additional keys of the pianoforte [a'''].
Her tones are remarkably sweet and fluty, if I may use the expression, and her upper notes resemble staccato passages upon the flageolet. Her taste is exquisite—her ornaments are highly polished,—and nothing can be more sweet and touching than her cantabiles. . . . She possessed a peculiarly happy

gift of dressing up a little rondo or ballad in a manner altogether enchanting, and entirely her own.[194]

Though she had "neither youth nor personal beauty to recommend her,"[195] she maintained her appeal as a singer as long as she remained on the stage. She was also admired as an actress, especially when playing old women and other comic roles.

Only a month after the arrival of the Hodgkinsons, the Old American Company welcomed another "singing chambermaid," Mary Ann Pownall (c. 1756–96). As Mrs. James Wrighten (fig. 24), she had made her debut at Drury Lane while still quite young, and became a great favorite both on the stage and as a concert singer, said to be surpassed as a singer only by Mrs. Billington and Mrs. Oldmixon. In 1786 Mrs. Wrighten disappeared from the stage, and was not seen publicly again until she appeared in Philadelphia late in 1792. She had her two daughters, Charlotte and Mary Wrighten, with her—and also a new husband, Mr. Pownall. Mary Ann Pownall was perhaps the

Figure 24. Mary Ann Wrighten Pownall. Harvard Theatre Collection.

most eminent English actress on the American stage, but "the skill of the veteran will not always compensate for the charms which belong alone to the freshness of youth,"[196] and she had to share her lines of acting with the younger Mrs. Hodgkinson. "Her voice was round, full and deliciously sweet, and her manner grand and impressive."[197]

In August 1796 Mrs. Pownall fell victim to the fever in Charleston, South Carolina, along with her daughter Mary and a young son. Her daughter Charlotte, also a fine singer, became the wife of Alexander Placide, the pantomimist and manager; together they launched an American theatrical dynasty.

One typical itinerant family of actors, the Solomons, played in many small American cities in the last decade of the eighteenth century and the early years of the nineteenth. When they played in Newburyport, Massachusetts, in April 1794, they were billed as "Vocal performers from the Southward, having performed their concerts in South Carolina, Georgia, Virginia, Boston, Portsmouth, and Salem, with great applause."[198] Although Mrs. Solomon was a better actress than her husband was an actor, when she performed in New York in the winter of 1794–95 she "soon disappeared."[199] When she performed in Philadelphia later that season, a reviewer for a local newspaper was not enthusiastic:

Of Mrs. Solomon's acting much cannot be said. It is at least *mediocre*. As a singer she possesses not much merit. Her voice is neither strong, sweet, nor is it correct. She may however be very useful in the Theatre by filling those parts, which first rate talent even, cannot render prominent.[200]

Several children from the family also took small roles. Miss M. Solomon was praised in the same review: "Her manner is easy and natural; her voice is strong and articulate, and in her singing remarkably clear." When the couple and their oldest daughter performed at the Federal Street theatre in Boston in the 1796–97 season, together they received $28 a week, the lowest salaries in the company.[201]

William Twaits (c. 1781–1814; fig. 25) was an English orphan who had haunted the backstage area of Drury Lane, determined to be an

Figure 25. William Twaits as Sir Adam Contest in *The Wedding Day*. Harvard Theatre Collection.

actor. He took parts at various provincial theatres and was acting at Birmingham and Sheffield when William Wood recruited him for the Philadelphia company in 1803. He "was considered one of the best burletta singers in England," and was best in comic and musical roles.[202] Twaits came to New York in 1806 and performed there until 1811. He became a close friend of Cooper and Harwood, and sometimes traveled with them for guest appearances at other theatres; the three went to Boston in January 1808 to attempt to help the financially pressed Barnard.

Twaits was barely over five feet in height, and had "a large head, with stiff, stubborn, carroty hair; long colourless face, prominent hooked nose, projecting large hazel eyes, thin lips, and large mouth, which could be twisted into a variety of expression." [203] In spite of his appearance, Twaits wanted to be a tragedian; critics objected strenuously when he attempted to play a gentleman or a hero. When Cooper was indisposed in 1809, Twaits volunteered to fill the Shakespearean role of Richard III:

Mr. Twaits's peculiar physiognomy, his awkward gait, nasal twang, and *petite* form, all disqualify him for those parts where dignity of person, and gracefulness of carriage are essential concomitants. This was strikingly palpable in the love scene with *lady Anne,* where the most insinuating manners and persuasive address are necessary to reconcile us to its otherwise unaccountable conclusion;—but here we saw *Dicky Gossip* rather than *Dicky the third.* The bowing and scraping was borrowed from *Lingo's* scene with the *princess Rusty-Fusty,* and when he knelt, we fancied it was *Jobson* the cobler going to take measure for a pair of shoes. All was burlesque and whimsey. The audience kept their countenances because the actor himself was grave: but it was a seriousness imposed by respect for the man, not by admiration of the performance. In a word, we would advise mr. Twaits never again to wander from his natural path:—it is so strongly marked that none but a man wilfully blind would ever deviate.[204]

Twaits's voice had "an extraordinary compass and sweetness" and an elegance that contrasted strongly with "the inelegance of his character and the buffoonery of his action." [205] In spite of his limitations, Twaits was highly respected as an individual and extremely knowledgeable in his craft: "behind the scenes his judgment and genius are often resorted to in the most refined departments of the drama; and at home his hours are so spent as to render him eminently qualified for rendering this species of service." [206]

Twaits married Elizabeth A. Westray Villiers, youngest sister of Mrs. Darley, in 1808; she died five years later at the age of twenty-seven.[207] In 1811 he joined Placide and Greene in the management of the theatres at Norfolk, Richmond, and Charleston, and was associated with them at the time of the disastrous fire at Richmond in December of that year.[208] He was manager of the Olympic Theatre in Philadelphia in the fall of 1812 and director of the Theatrical Commonwealth in Philadelphia and New York during the 1813–14 season. With scene painter John Holland he opened a new theatre on Anthony Street, New York, in April 1814. Twaits had reportedly been so badly afflicted with asthma since 1806 that he was unable to sleep in a bed,[209] and although he continued to manage a company and even to sing and act occasionally until the end, his death on August 23, 1814, at the age of thirty-three, was due to the ravages of the disease.

Originally a barber, Joseph Tyler (1751–1823) had played in English provincial theatres before coming to the States to join the Old American Company. He made his debut in Boston in 1795, and in New York in 1796. He played regularly with the New York company thereafter, occasionally making guest appearances in other cities. With "some natural qualifications and much industry," he was for many years considered by New Yorkers "the most useful actor on our boards."[210] Dunlap described him as "always perfect in the words of his author, and respectable in the delineation of his characters."[211] He "possessed a voice of rare excellence," and "was entrusted with many important singing parts";[212] he continued to sing occasionally until he was sixty.

In 1798 Tyler opened a public house and tea garden called Washington Gardens, which was a gathering place for actors and musicians.[213] He was highly respected in private life and by his peers; when Dunlap went bankrupt in the spring of 1805, the other actors chose Tyler and his friend Johnson as comanagers for the remainder of that season and the next. After the death of John Hodgkinson, Tyler became the guardian of his young daughters.[214]

Tyler was considered exceptionally effective in portraying aristocratic old gentlemen, and in later life his resemblance to George Washington "made it good policy to array him in powder and small-clothes as often as possible."[215] He played the role of Washington at the theatre the night before he died at the age of seventy-two.

Contemporary reviews also give us a glimpse of the sorts of actors—and performances—to be expected in minor roles. Such performers regularly appeared without fanfare and quickly vanished. Mr. Ashton, a cockney, made his New York debut in 1791, was later associated with the Federal Street company in Boston, and departed thence in January 1797 for Charleston. Dunlap reported he was "without any powers except those of voice";[216] in Boston the *Federal Orrery* said "his performance was such, as pronounced him useful in still life."[217] Mr. Lee was said by Dunlap to be "a heavy, stupid, vulgar fellow, with no requisite for the stage but a bass voice and some knowledge of music."[218] He appeared in concerts and with the Old American Company from 1794 to 1802; in addition to acting, he sang in the chorus, danced in the pantomimes, and helped with the properties. Even a scene painter could be recruited as a singer on occasion, if needed; John Luke Robbins (or Robins) began working for the Park Theatre in 1792, worked for a time in Philadelphia and Baltimore, and was head scene painter in New York by 1813. A tall young man, he was hired to "be scene-painter, occasionally to sing a song, and join in the choruses."[219]

Still lower than these bit players were the supernumeraries, often nameless in cast lists and even in account books, and frequently recruited from the technical personnel, the families of the actors, and other theatrical hangers-on. *Polyanthos* asked in 1807: "Where, in the name of wonder, could our managers find so many stupid supernumeraries? From what wild flock of cream-faced loons with goose looks, could they catch all the lily-liver patches, which fill up the *bleeding captains, messengers,* &c."[220]

This question is answered by the following advertisement in the *Boston Gazette:* "Wanted—a number of steady, respectable men, to attend the theatre occasionally, as Supernumeraries.—Apply at the Theatre, *this* evening, Thursday, at 1/2 past 6 o'clock precisely."[221] Perhaps the supernumeraries were put to work immediately in that evening's production of Stephen Storace's operatic drama *Lodoiska.* A similar ad in the *New York Evening Post* at the opening of the 1815–16 season read: "A number of respectable YOUNG MEN are wanted in the PARK THEATRE, as supernumeraries. Apply at 44 Leonard street, between the hours of 12 and 2."[222]

These English and American actor-singers established the traditions, and sometimes the dynasties, of American musical theatre. They were "at least mediocre" and often possessed considerable musical and theatrical ability. Conditions and attitudes demanded that they be versatile, creative, resourceful, and indefatigable. They were often the principal performers of the musical mainstream in American communities, and as such merit consideration not only as an aspect of American theatre but as important contributors to the art of music—and its popularity—in the early days of the republic.[223]

7
MELPOMENE, MIRTH, AND MELODY

Acting Traditions

The term "comedian" was used at the turn of the nineteenth century to include any actor; a good general comedian was expected to perform not only in comedy, but also in tragedy, melodrama, comic opera, and perhaps even in pantomime. Many conventions and traditions governed the way in which actors learned their trade, how they were assigned parts, how they prepared their roles, and how they portrayed their characters onstage.

TRAINING THE ACTOR

There were no formal training programs for actors in the eighteenth or early nineteenth centuries.

It has often been regretted by those who think that the theatre ought to be restored to its ancient and natural dignity, that society furnishes no establishments for a regular scheme of theatrical education. . . . The actor is left to explore his way in the dark, exposed to all the errors of his own taste, and to the dangerous contagion of bad examples. . . . If such institutions actually existed, they would be of very little use. The wretched remuneration received by the bulk of the profession, and the rank it holds in public estimation, must prevent any gentleman of birth and education from embracing it as a means of subsistence. It is commonly the resource of necessity or of indolence, sometimes of a visionary weakness, or an ill placed enthusiasm for the arts. In all these cases, there is neither the will nor the power to go through a course of preparatory study.[1]

Many young actors served a sort of apprenticeship within the family business, appearing in minor roles while still children, sometimes singing or dancing when their talents merited it, and gradually taking larger roles as they grew older. The inclusion of such names as Miss Hodgkinson, Miss Arnold, or Master Barrett in the bills indicated the first steps in training the offspring of some well-known thespian.

Sometimes one of the members of an acting company would accept pupils in the art of acting or singing. John Durang took a young student with him in his touring company:

I had in company with me my own family, Miss Mullin, who was put apprentice to me by her own will and her mother's wish and entreaties. I watched with a father's care over her and taught her dancing, singing, and in a short time she became a usefull actress.[2]

John Hodgkinson supervised the training of his ward, Mary Harding (later Mrs. G. Marshall), who also studied singing with his wife, Frances. The young son of Giles L. Barrett was also submitted to Hodgkinson's "tender and laudable care" as tutor when he began performing as a child prodigy.[3]

When Thomas Apthorpe Cooper became stagestruck while a youth in England, his guardian, William Godwin, took him to actor and playwright Thomas Holcroft for some preparatory lessons:

Mr. Holcroft . . . took him in hand; read Shakspeare with him, and accompanied their reading with practical commentaries upon the force of that author's meaning, marked out to him those parts where the character was to depend for its interest and impression, on the actor's exertions; heard him over and over again repeat the most difficult speeches, and instructed him how to adapt his action, looks, and utterance to the passion which the author designed to exhibit, so as to excite appropriate feelings in the auditor.[4]

Later Cooper himself undertook the training of other young actors.[5]

Other actors received their training at the hands of a prompter. According to Stephen Cullen Carpenter, young John Hodgkinson was turned over to the prompter in Bristol, England, for training in about 1780.[6] Young Master William Betty, a child prodigy, was first taught to "recite passages from the best authors" to help him "pronounce the language with propriety," then was given further training by Mr. Hough, prompter at the Belfast theatre, where he made his debut in 1803 at the age of eleven. Hough then traveled with the boy on tour as a permanent acting coach.[7]

Sometimes young amateurs approached the stage through a study of the classics. Young John Howard Payne fancied himself a critic at the age of thirteen and began his own periodical, *The Thespian Mirror*, to criticize the actors of his day. After a few months, he announced his resignation as a critic and his intention to devote himself to the study of the law, but he eventually ended up on the stage after all. His success as a tragic actor was no doubt due at least partly to his own careful study of the plays, and his interpretation of their significance.

Amateurs also honed their craft through imitation. Many an aspiring thespian must have stalked and ranted, simpered and coquetted, in front of the mirror in his or her closet, aping the mannerisms of a favorite actor or actress:

[Mr. Robertson] has apparently taken mr. Cooper for his model, and almost all that he exhibits of excellence is the result of a close imitation of that distinguished actor. The voice, the attitude, the gesture, the enunciation, &c. are all copies, more or less successful;—now, though we would be much better pleased to see mr. Robertson acting in a style of originality, yet as he has, perhaps judiciously chosen to rely more upon his talents of mimicry than invention, we are anxious that he should at least confine himself to the excellencies of his model, and not, in his indiscriminate eagerness to imitate, fall into an adoption of his faults. . . . We are sick of these phlegmatic, half-finished copies of mr. Cooper—these tedious tardy enunciations—these la-borings after grace—these rowings of the arms—twistings of the head—sawings of the air—these pauses without signification, and all the other fan-tastic grimaces, by which a set of unmeaning creatures weary us to death, and really seem to imagine that they are successful imitators of mr. Cooper, because they have not suffered one of his faults to escape them.[8]

"Tragedy airs" were more easily imitated than was natural acting, and every would-be Shakespearean hero could imitate them; "even our old acquaintance *John, who seems to 'flourish in immortal youth'* can hardly carry off a chair or snuff a candle without a grace or an attitude."[9]

No matter how young players received their initial training, once they began their public careers the critics assumed the role of instruc-tor, schooling the actors in the proper modulation of the voice, pacing, gesture, byplay, and other aspects of their craft. In the fall of 1811 James Fennell introduced two of his students to the stage in Philadel-phia. Mary White had been "for some time under the tuition of Mr. Fennell, who undertook the office under the impression that she had talents which only wanted judicious instruction to obtain her in due time a respectable rank in the theatre." Stephen Cullen Carpenter of the *Mirror of Taste* concluded, however, that

the direction given to her action is radically bad, and ought to be got rid of as soon as possible . . . the too great elevation, expansion and winding about of her arms, as general action, is unbecoming in any character of either sex; but is peculiarly unfit for a female . . .

When Miss Brobston made her debut about two months later, she had the same problem: "he has taught her also to use that monotonous *sweeping* gesture, which is a great blemish of his own; and which re-sembles nothing in nature but that exertion of the arms made in the act of swimming."[10]

DECLAMATORY AND NATURAL TRADITIONS

Two distinct styles of acting prevailed at the turn of the century: the declamatory and the natural styles. These styles can be considered as chronological, following the succession of the finest English actors of the day. James Quin (1693–1766) had been associated with the slow, impressive, declamatory style; when David Garrick (1717–1779) succeeded him, he established a more natural approach. Yet these styles remained coexistent: John Philip Kemble (1757–1823) returned to a more formal, measured style, which was contrasted to the more natural delivery of his contemporary George Frederick Cooke (1755–1812).

At any time between 1785 and 1815 both schools of acting could be found among the various performers on the English and American stage, sometimes used by the same actor in different roles. Tragedians tended to favor the older, oratorical style, partly because its dignity suited these roles and a careful, deliberate "attitude" could suggest deep feeling, and partly because the language of the plays was highly stylized and poetic. This rhetorical style was decried as extravagant, stilted, and pompous by critics who emphasized the need for "copying nature." One reviewer characterized the declamatory style as "noise, ranting, and grimaces," and contrasted it with the more natural comic style: "nervous, simple and easy."[11] The comic actor was generally more spontaneous in both speech and action, responding more quickly to the audience's reactions, and speaking in tones more approaching normal speech. The declamatory style might seem to have been more at home in *opera serie* and the natural style in comic opera, but in practice the delivery depended on the actor and the role as well as the genre.

Tragedians emphasized rules for declamation, gesture, and intonation:

Many, not long dead, could not only recollect the principal actors who preceded Garrick, but were able to convey a strong idea, and afford a concep-

tion of the ancient declamation, and mode of repeating verse; their enunciation was more sonorous, lofty, and what we should term bombastic.[12]

America's earliest actors favored this conservative dramatic style. William Wood reported that Lewis Hallam's

manner was of that peculiar kind that in my youth I always heard called
"the Old School," and which Garrick effectually exploded. In tragedy he
"spouted," by which I mean declaimed without passion. . . . In comedy, . . .
Mr. Hallam always struck me as extravagant . . . [13]

That this style was still present at the turn of the century is apparent
from the many comments in contemporary newspapers, such as that
contained in a long letter to the New York *Daily Advertiser* in 1801.
The first ground for criticism was the strutting gait of the actor:

Even the walk of the actors offends against propriety here. It is a formal measured step, not a free, easy, natural one, such as is used in common life; a
graceful and dignified carriage requires nothing of the pomp and rule which
they have adopted.[14]

The "formal, measured step" was an essential part of the rule of tragic
acting, condemned as unnatural on the one hand, yet expected as part
of the tradition:

Of the measured step and affected strut of tragedy of old, there exists not
one more hearty contemner than ourselves. Yet the elevation of the tragic
scene demands something in air, attitude, deportment and movement of every kind, a little raised above the usage of life—even of high life. Nothing
can be more unsuitable to Melpomene than a short, patting step, and a celerity of motion.[15]

In a technique related both to the old doctrine of the affections and to
the more modern techniques of rhetoric, the tragic actor used standard
formulas or "attitudes" for the expression of emotion. The *Daily Advertiser* critic continues:

In their gesture, looks and tone of voice—also, there is just foundation for criticism. In the first place, there is great uniformity in them—and in the next place, they frequently and greatly "overstep the modesty of nature." In expressing rage, terror, pity, grief, love, or any violent emotion, there is in all the performers a great similarity of manner. It is true the passions have each a general characteristic feature which must always appear. But every judicious spectator knows that they have an infinite variety of modifications, from different circumstances. When he sees, therefore, that the performers seem, as it were, to have agreed among themselves what shall be the precise manner of expressing every emotion, that each sentiment and action has always one uniform complexion in opposition to experience which has taught him that they are varied in their appearance according to the proportions of those numberless motives which are ever mingling themselves with and giving a colouring to our conduct. When grief, for instance, is always displayed and by every actor, by turning away the body, retiring a few steps, then inclining forward, covering the eyes and face with a handkerchief and heaving the breath with violence like a bellows, when he observes I say such a studied sameness of manner, it is impossible for him to be interested or to catch any of the emotions which are thus dully acted, or indeed to have any emotion but of disgust.

> "The modes of grief are not included all,
> In the white handkerchief or mournful drawl;
> A single look more marks the internal woe,
> Than all the windings of the lengthen'd Oh!" [16]

The manners mentioned here—rage, terror, pity, grief, love—and many others, along with the attitudes used by the tragedian in expressing specific passions, are discussed by Henry Siddons in his *Practical Illustrations of Rhetorical Gesture and Action*, which includes sixty-nine engravings.[17]

The attitude assumed by John Hodgkinson in the title role of *Pizarro* was described in the *New-York Evening Post* in 1801:

when he hears *Cora* accuse him of sacrificing *Alonzo*, the attitude in which he places himself—overwhelmed with astonishment and looking to heaven as in appeal from such unjust suspicion, commands our approbation. But it is unworthy of him to dwell upon this attitude till a plaudit is drawn from the house. We dislike these *Clap-traps;* and we abhor to be reminded by a performer in an interesting situation, that he is merely *enacting* a part.[18]

Tragedians slipped easily into a sing-song rant because of the language's measured cadences. A Philadelphia critic deplored the excessive "tragedy-airs" of Mr. Cone:

Who can refrain from laughter at his sing-song? He has an utterance peculiar to himself, and which he must have learned in China. There, they say, ordinary conversation has its gamut; and this has certainly been the study of Mr. Cone. He not only drops his sentences and his arms; but, in every dissyllable, he drops the final syllable; as, per'fect, cott'age, i'dle; resting immoderately on the first, and jumping over the second.[19]

Stephen Cullen Carpenter, a recent immigrant from England, also disapproved of this "tuneful" technique of versification, but knew from experience that it was not unique to the United States:

The monotonous sing-song of verse offends taste, and is disapproved by common sense. . . . There are players in London, men of no mean note too, who in level recitation, and long declamatory speeches, may be followed as precisely as tenor and counter-tenor run in musical harmony, with
TI TITUM TITUM, TITUM TITUM TE.[20]

In addition to this "sing-song ditty-drawl speechification"[21] actors were frequently chastised because their tone of voice was elevated to a roar or descended to a whine. Thomas Caulfield was criticized for his fustian and rant when he whined while declaiming in verse; "If he would speak poetry *naturally,* that is without the least *whine,* the improvement would make his performance a thousand times better.[22] Ranting could also take the form of shouting:

Vociferation is a common fault. In order to touch the passions most persons imagine that it is necessary to make a great deal of noise. Thus the vagrant preachers of a certain sect think to perform all the wonders of true eloquence

and real pathos, by straining their lungs. But nothing betrays more ignorance
of human nature.[23]

A Boston critic made the same point more colorfully:

We have often observed one general fault in the declamation of Mr. Fox;—
he is too *flatulent*. And it may be added, that where this vice in speaking
exists, the soul of all acting or reading, *discrimination* itself, is lost in a hurri-
cane of *sound*.[24]

Actors were also criticized for drawling, or stretching the syllables of
words to unnatural lengths. Carpenter asked: "Does it give real force,
interest or dignity to the lines of a speech to take up twice or thrice as
much time in speaking them as the most formal, deliberate, or pompous prig of an orator would employ upon them?"[25]

  When Cooper performed in Richmond in 1806, the local critic observed that Cooper's voice would sometimes "drawl and spin itself
into a long hissing accent: 'Like a wounded snake dragging his slow
length along'"; when Cooper said "face" the critic wished for a stop-
watch to number the seconds it consumed.[26] A review of a Philadelphia performance of the melodrama *The Africans* in 1810 documents
further instances of drawling:

mr. Robertson seems to have said to himself, in the words of *Nick Bottom*,
'here will be salt tears shed, or I'm mistaken'; and at it he goes, in a manner that made our hearts ache;—not for poor *Selico* and his starved mother
and half burnt wife, but for the unhappy english language, thus barbarously
tortured. There were such m-m-mothers, and bl-l-l-lesseds, and mur-r-r-
der-r-r-ed l-l-loves, that we dreaded, what between the mumbling and rum-
bling, scarcely a word would get away in its natural form. It seems as if these
mannerists never know when to let an M escape from their lips, and as to an
unlucky R, they never happen upon one, but they are sure to r-r-ride it to
death. The preceding was accompanied with indescribable writhings and
stretches, in which *mr. Robertson*, through an over zeal to be graceful and
affecting, continually indulges. . . . Indeed, we are sorry to see him so partial
to these straddle-bag attitudes, wherein the body is shown at full length,

from the point of one finger, to the extremity of the opposite toe. And since such is his ambition, it is a pity it should not be gratified, and we here put his heart at rest by assuring him that both in enunciation, and gesture, and attitude he is, to use a yankee phrase, "a very *lengthy* actor—by *lengthy* meaning *tedious*."[27]

Lest it be assumed that only men used the old style, let it be said that women, too, had the same faults, although critics were usually more gentle in their strictures:

Mrs. Barrett's *Elvira,* with all its majesty of strut, and upright deportment, was drawled with too lingering an emphasis to be either natural or pleasing, though some of the attitudes which the different situations of *Elvira* required, were extremely fine.[28]

The traditional style of acting, then, as it was still associated with tragedy at the turn of the century, was stilted and monotonous in its intonation, stylized and repetitive in its gesture, and slow and measured but not necessarily clear in its declamation. It was criticized as "without heart and soul" at the same time it was described as extravagant.

While both styles were artificial, the style associated with comedy placed more emphasis on facial expression, natural word rhythms, and an easy spontaneous manner. The English actor most associated with the development of the "natural" style was David Garrick, who made his debut in 1741. Garrick was a versatile actor who acted in both tragedy and comedy; he is credited with developing "character acting":

From the first his success was assured; accustomed to the cold and stilted declamation, without heart, soul, or impulse, of the time, the effect of his fire and passion upon the audience was electrical. . . . The press declared his reception to have been the greatest and most extraordinary ever known on such an occasion.[29]

Richard Cumberland (1732–1811) wrote of this debut:

Heavens, what a transition!—it seemed as if a whole century had been stepped over in the transition of a single scene; old things were done away, and a new order at once brought forward, bright and luminous, and clearly destined to dispel the barbarisms and bigotry of a tasteless age, too long superstitiously devoted to the illusions of imposing declamation.[30]

When Irish actor James Quin appeared with Garrick at Covent Garden, Garrick's acclaim was such that Quin is reported to have said: "If this young fellow is right, we are all wrong."[31]

The *Daily Advertiser* advised even the most acclaimed actors to reflect their setting: "Like Proteus, an actor should be able to transform himself into a thousand shapes, and cameleon like, take his hue from every varying circumstance that surrounds him."[32] Joseph Jefferson seems to have approached this "chameleon" ideal:

He always understands the character he personates and catches it with a peculiar felicity; he never utters a sentence the scope and spirit of which he does not comprehend; while his voice, action and eyes, and even every limb and muscle gives it the liveliest impression on the audience.[33]

Joseph Tyler was praised for his operatic performance because "he had no affectation or grimace whatever," and Mrs. Johnson because "the various passions, which she represented, were seen to *undulate* in her countenance, with a translucency that was little short of enchantment."[34] This stress on facial expression instead of sweeping gesture played an important part in American acting technique. Mrs. Young was cautioned that

Passion and feeling are not to be expressed by a *twinkling* of the eyes, or waving about of the hands; a tyrolese doll could do all that; the muscles of the face must move, or all action is mummery, and the most impassioned language completely lost.[35]

John Bernard, too, stressed facial expression as he described the Boston Haymarket Theatre in the summer of 1797:

Its smaller size as compared with the London ones was a great advantage to the actors. It was not necessary to take the ear by storm, and whereas, in London, the players were so far from the audience that I often thought the old Greek custom of wearing masks might well have been revived, here the naked eye could thoroughly discern the play of countenance, and the face—that living, burning comment on voice and gesture, that flash to their detonation—had its full effect. Especially was this a gain to the ruling favorite of the States, Hodgkinson, whose well-defined features showed every minutest change of thought or throe of feeling; while his voice could be compared to nothing but a many-stringed instrument which his passion played upon at pleasure. While such were his endowments, his method was to work himself up to a certain pitch of excitement which rendered everything he said or did the direct prompting of impulse.[36]

Time after time the critics emphasized the imitation of nature as the most important criterion for the actor. A letter in the Philadelphia *Aurora. General Advertiser* in 1795 complained of the acting style at the New Theatre:

In tragedy the company does not appear as strong as in comedy. In one and the other I have seen misplaced buffoonery and antic tricks applauded, more than real good and chaste acting. The effect of this is, that actors whose abilities are promising are spoiled and attend much more to caricature than to nature. It must follow, of course, that if an actor is applauded only in proportion to the unintelligibility of his delivery, the extravagance of his action, and the obscurity of his enunciation, now retrenching, then repeating several times a syllable of some words, he will study very little to be true, chaste, and distinct,—he will attend very little to copying nature. If this practice of misapplying applause should long prevail, it would not astonish me to see one of the performers, whom I shall not name, change his nervous, simple, easy and truly comic manner which is not applauded, for the noise, ranting and grimaces which alone obtain the plaudits of the house.[37]

By the turn of the century, John Philip Kemble had become the most prominent tragedian on the London stage and, like his sisters Sarah Siddons and Elizabeth Kemble Whitlock (sometimes called the American Siddons), had returned to a more formal style than that of Garrick.

Carpenter believed that Kemble had "new-read and new-fangled him-self out of a large share of his natural excellence." Kemble, however, was still a "great and dignified actor" who had produced a "servile herd of imitators."[38] The natural style had its ablest representative at the time in the acting of George Frederick Cooke, who took America by storm in 1810:

After the tedious, monotonous syllabizing, dead march speechifying to which this country has hitherto been so much accustomed, the natural acting, and familiar colloquial speech of Cooke, seemed at first strange and new; but be-ing conformable to nature, it stood its ground, and has carried away the crown of laurel.[39]

Critic Stephen Cullen Carpenter was one of the ablest proponents of the natural style. He described his observations of Cooke:

There is this difference between Cooke and almost all other actors. He re-sorts to no stage trick and uses no unnatural gesticulations, or mechanical dispositions of his limbs; practices no grimace; has no affected pauses, starts, attitudes or intonations; but acts 'e'en like the folks of this world.' He nei-ther frisks about the stage nor whirls his arms, nor does, in a word, as most players do, every thing that nobody does in common life.[40]

Excesses and affectations of all kinds were decried, yet the actor and the critic continued to seek compromises between naturalism and the traditions of the theatre. Traditions endured governing pronunciation, stage position and movement, characterization, and stage business. Actors were expected to apply these traditions according to genre, role, and even local practice; this was as true in musical entertain-ments as in other genres.

As we have discussed, the actors who played in tragedy were, more often than not, the same actors who played in comedy and sang in operas. The popularity of the musical romance and, even more, the melodrama provided rich opportunities for tragic-style strutting and bombast. In many cases the same criteria—such as the degree of naturalism—were applied to all performance; at other times, however, the actors were expected to be able to modulate their delivery. When Frances Hodgkinson played the title role of William Shield's opera *Rosina* in 1795, the critic for the *Federal Orrery* expected her to differentiate between her comic and her tragic acting:

But could it not be said, that she wanted that simplicity of articulation, which so naturally flows from the lips of rural innocence?—"Do not the whole village love you," should surely be spoken in a tone, very different from the "Out damned spot" of Lady Macbeth.[41]

Thirteen-year-old John Howard Payne stated it succinctly: "tragedy may sometimes be allowed to declaim, but comedy never."[42] Carpenter noted the contrast of the two styles in the performances of several well-known actors:

The comedy of Cooke is as completely distinct from his tragedy, as if they were the workings of two separate men: And this was certainly one of Mr. Garrick's excellencies. We have heretofore made the same remark upon Hodgkinson, who, inferior though he was to either of those great men in tragic exhibition, had not only more generality and diversity than any other person, but marked his comedy and tragedy with expressions so very distinct that no one could have imagined them to be the offspring of the same parent.[43]

Even child actors playing children's roles were expected to adopt the natural manner appropriate to comic opera; in a 1795 review of the Wignell-Reinagle company's presentation of *Children in the Wood*, it was reported that

Miss SOLOMONS personated the little girl with singular propriety and grace. Her manner is easy and natural; her voice strong and articulate, and in her singing remarkably clear. Master PARKER in the boy, merited a great share of praise; he was however less at his ease than the little Miss. He appeared overtaught in his manner and attitudes. A little more boyish awkwardness would fit the character better. The boy has every natural requisite, even to equal the little girl; it rests with his instructors not to mistake the part he ought to personate.[44]

It is apparent from the study of specific librettos that within a single work the various characters were expected to adopt the particular acting styles appropriate to their roles. Actors portrayed stock tragic characters (often nonmusical) in opera, sentimental plays, musical romances, and melodramas with the same ponderousness found in Shakespearean tragedy. In the opera *Children in the Wood*, for example, the members of the nobility—Sir Rowland and Lord and Lady Alford—make deliberately stilted, pompous, and often unnecessarily verbose speeches, in what might be described as blank verse. Sir Rowland speaks of the children: "Soon, their silence shall be eternal; my brother being concluded dead—that 'lustrious orb being set in night, shall these pigmy satellites eclipse me?" Lord Alford addresses his wife: "Here rest a while; this place is most dear to my remembrance. When my good falcon urged on his quarry to this forest's verge, reclined beneath this aged oak, I first saw thee, my Helen." These roles are completely devoid of comedy and seem to require the traditional tragic style, as well as the deliberate use of outdated and poetic pronunciation (reclined in three syllables and aged in two).

Other roles in the same operas and plays were played using the natural, comic style. The roles of the servants in *Children in the Wood*— including the hero and heroine—are all comic. The language, while occasionally containing words and constructions no longer in use today, was perfectly natural in its own day. The hero, Walter, is quite candid when he re-emerges after killing the ruffian, Oliver, to exclaim: "Damme, I didn't think I had so much pluck in me!" and the language descends to cliché when the children ask, "Have you killed Oliver?" and Walter replies, "Dead as a door nail!" The boy responds, "Go kill him again! Such a rascal as he cannot be *too* dead!"

The writer in the *Daily Advertiser* speaks for dozens of critics in his summary of the strengths and weaknesses of acting at the turn of the century:

True eloquence is a sublime and fascinating art—it must be founded in good sense, animated by a vigorous fancy and an ardent sensibility, and guided by a correct judgment. Supported by these, and by all graces and energies of voice and action, the actor can delight, transport, and seduce us at pleasure—provided he is sincere and in earnest—or persuades us that he is. But here alas! is the misfortune of the theatre. I never once forgot that they were actors. I never lost sight of the mask. The deception therefore being incomplete, just in proportion to the greatness of the attempt, was my disappointment. Nor is this to be wondered at when you recollect the tone of voice so universal to the stage—it is affected, pompous, and turgid—ever swelling into what is usually denominated the theatrical rant. As this is so contrary to nature, the only guide to the heart and standard of what is true—failure is inevitable—because nothing can give pleasure but justness of imitation. To attain this most successfully, in my opinion, an actor ought to study with care the part that is assigned to him—the meaning of every sentence and force of every word—commit it well to memory—and then in the performance enter into it with his whole soul—discarding everything from the mind that has a tendency to cool its fervor—or prevent him from imagining that he is a *real* actor in the scene.[45]

Young John Howard Payne once again managed to get to the root of the matter with his pithy comment: "It is an observation as current as it is just, that *the height of acting* IS NOT TO ACT."[46]

THE LINES OF ACTING

A variety of traditions and patterns governed the casting—and even the writing—of plays and operas in the eighteenth and early nineteenth centuries. Actor and manager John Bernard (1756–1828) provided a justification for this specialization:

Nature being full of rule, being a law as it were in action, is of course a great classifier, a worker on models, fond of species and types, and thus the old man and the young, the hero and the rogue of tragedy and comedy, being distinct types or models, actors usually come into the world with their own special aptitude . . . [47]

Once actors established their own lines of business—based on the stereotypical role classifications that governed casting—they accepted roles outside their normal sphere reluctantly, and almost never accepted roles in a line "below" their own. There was a definite pecking order in the assignment of roles, dependent upon several factors, including genre. Tragedy (and therefore tragedians) occupied the top of the list in terms of prestige. Next came comedy, then opera, and finally pantomime. The position of opera in the theatrical hierarchy is suggested by the comment in the *New York Magazine* that John Hodgkinson's singing "ranks him as a musical performer almost as high as he stands in the higher lines of his profession."[48] Actors were occasionally hired specifically for a single genre, and many specialized in only one; Hodgkinson was unusual in his ability to play leading roles in every genre.

There was also a hierarchy of skill and importance among actors. An actor might be hired specifically for the "first line of characters" in tragedy or comedy, or as "first singer," or for the "second line" in tragedy, comedy, or opera. Frances Hodgkinson, for example, signed a contract in 1792 that guaranteed her a share of the first line of opera characters. This meant figuratively that she would perform a "line" or group of characters that were accepted as being the leading parts in each of the stock plays within the genre, and also literally that her name would appear on the first line or second line among the women's roles listed on the playbill for those days' performances.

Roles were further classified by sex, gentility or social class, and age. Women's roles were always listed separately in the bills, following the roles performed by men. Even female stars of considerable magnitude, such as Anne Merry Wignell Warren, were listed at the head of the women's roles, not at the head of the bill. The one exception occurred when a young woman assumed a boy's part; then she might be listed among the men.

An even more important division was that of social class. Actors strove to "rise in class" in their profession as in society, by acquiring grace in movement, correctness in dress and deportment, and elegance in speech. The "first line" of actors in both tragedy and comedy required at least the unceasing appearance of gentility. Actors and actresses customarily addressed each other with refined speech, manners, and forms of address in the greenroom, which thus served as a training ground in gentility. There were always roles for characters of middle and lower classes, but in tragedies and genteel comedies they were more likely to be filled by lesser actors and supernumeraries. Even fine actors like Hodgkinson, Cooper, Cooke, and Bernard played first-line low comedy roles on occasion, however, adapting their carriage, dress, and speech to suit the parts.

Other actors specialized in roles of a particular age. Old women and old men were common lines, played by actors of all ages. These were often character parts, and could be either genteel or low comedy in nature. An actor's chronological age and appearance were often ignored; youthful leading roles such as Juliet in *Romeo and Juliet,* Priscilla Tomboy in *The Romp,* or Fatima in *Blue Beard* were regularly assigned to the first actress or first singer of the company, regardless of age or figure. When twenty-seven-year-old John Hodgkinson was hired for the Old American Company in 1792, his contract stated that he would divide the "young heroes of tragedy and gentlemen in first comedy" with Lewis Hallam, then fifty-seven years old.

It was an actor of rare skill and ability (or, in Hallam's case, of considerable rank and power) who was able to maintain the first line of characters throughout a career. Usually actors rose from supernumerary to minor roles to second line to first line in an orderly progression; as they grew older and their skills declined, they would descend down the professional ranks again. When an actor retired, resigned a role, or left the company, there were always successors waiting to move upward in the hierarchy and assume his or her roles. When a first- or second-line actor was involved, such moves often involved a chain reaction, with several actors moving up to better roles.

In addition to all these classifications, roles were also grouped according to the stereotyped characters prevalent in eighteenth-century drama, with actors and actresses specializing in all the roles similar to those characters. *Polyanthos* reported that Mrs. Whitlock was playing "the *Rosalinda* and *Beatrice* line" in Charleston, for example, and John Durang described Mrs. Francis as "the Mrs. Malaprop and Mrs. Quickly" of the Philadelphia company, and William Warren as the "Falstaff and Benevolent Merchant."[49]

Thomas Holcroft described these lines of acting in "The Art of Acting, No. 1," quoted in *The Thespian Mirror* in 1806. He pointed out that although the "classes might be multiplied almost at pleasure," most others could be encompassed in these: *"Heroes, lovers, gentlemen, tradesmen, clowns; heroines, fine ladies, hoydens, chambermaids; characters of middle and old age, male and female."* Holcroft cautioned that in all classes and characters, both actions and words were necessary to complete the character, and that both insipidity and exaggeration should be avoided. The qualities he deemed necessary for each of these lines or classes form the basis for the following general discussion.[50]

Heroes. No performer can personate a hero truly unless, did events favour him he be capable of actually becoming a hero; . . . Let him be possessed by this magnetic power of mind, and his defects of voice and person must be excessive, if they are unconquerable. Give him that mighty power, and a distinct articulation, clearness, compass, and strength of voice, an athletic and correct symmetry of person, with pliant yet pleasing features, capable of all the varieties and the full force of expressing the various passions, and this *imaginary actor* will be one who has never yet been behind.

Holcroft's hero, then, was the first line in tragedy, and was found in melodrama and sentimental comedy. He also served as the larger-than-life hero of opera or musical romance, but normally only if the role used the language and acting style appropriate for the tragic hero; it was frequently a nonmusical role. The hero could be of any age (casting could consider whether the role required an older or younger man), but was always of a genteel style. Many of the fathers in melodrama fit this pattern. Roles in the hero line included Hamlet and

Macbeth, Penruddock in Cumberland's *Wheel of Fortune,* Sir Edward Mortimer in Colman's *The Iron Chest,* Sir William Blandford in Morton's *Speed the Plow,* and William Tell in *The Archers.* This line also included characters who were heroes in the tragic sense of flawed greatness; they could be tyrants or even murderers, but they were always persons of great power and strength of character.

John Bernard said that two contrasting characters—the hero and the villain—normally "occupy the foreground" in tragedy. As heroes he named Othello, Alexander, and Brutus; he said these characters demand "a commanding figure, a fine-toned voice, and a dignified action." His villains included Richard III, Shylock, and Iago; he said they required "a strongly marked and flexible set of features; for the peculiarity of this character lies greatly in soliloquy, through the medium of which the villain conveys to the audience, in a series of opinions, reasonings, and resolutions, his own character and his connection with the fable." He further divided villains into two classes: "The majestic or heroic, such as the tyrants Barbarossa, Dionysius, Zanga or Pierre, and the specious and designing, such as Richard, Iago, and Stukely."[51]

Among the actors in the hero line at this period were John Hodgkinson, George Frederick Cooke, and Thomas Cooper, who was for many years the first tragedian at all the principal American theatres. The critic in *Polyanthos* said that "as a tragedian, he is without a rival in our country: and we regret the necessity of his ever appearing in comedy."[52]

Lovers. In the lover all the exterior charms, which can steal upon and enslave the female heart, should be combined: a smiling, prepossessing, yet anxious face, beauty of form, elegance of manners, sweetness of voice, passionate eyes, and susceptibility of heart, should all enrapture his mistress. Add to these the feminine beauties, graces, and accomplishments, and the description will be suitable to the other sex.

The first line of actors and actresses in comedy were often the lovers. Young first lines in tragedy, such as Romeo and Juliet, Desdemona, and Ophelia, were also lovers. Usually the roles were written for young actors, and almost always they were intended to be genteel. There were innumerable lovers in opera as well. John Darley was classified as "a lover," and in 1805 a local critic opined that "as a singer, he is undoubtedly the first in America."[53] It was at the close of this season, however, that the poetic epilogue quoted in the previous chapter (ending "To Sing and love is all that you can do") made clear that Darley's capabilities ran no further than these lines.

Gentlemen. The requisites to *personate this character completely* are many, and difficult to attain: they are, perfect ease of deportment, even under the most embarrassing circumstances; manners that conciliate, and gain universal esteem; good breeding so disciplined as never to be thrown from its guard, or, except on the most extraordinary occasions, betrayed to the discovery of passion; a smooth and flowing enunciation; a bland gaiety of heart, that no trifles can disturb; a flattering, yet not officious, attention to every person present; and all those charms of address and demeanor which cannot fail to win our affections. There have been almost *as few gentlemen* on the Stage *as heroes.*

The gentleman was often the first- or second-line actor in comedy, opera, or tragedy. John Durang described actors who were classified as "genteel first line" (John Pollard Moreton), "the genteel sprightly line" (James Chalmers), and "genteel steady old gentlemen" (Charles Whitlock).[54] "Fops" and "genteel walking gentlemen" were also common nomenclatures.

In 1806 the *Theatrical Censor* in Philadelphia classified William Wood as "best in the lively walks of genteel comedy," and Mr. Cain as adept in "sentimental comedy."[55] In 1811 the *Comet* in Boston declared that John Duff "will always be admired in modern comedy; no actor that ever appeared on our boards can better hit off the eccentrick and fashionable rakes of Colman, Morton, and Reynolds."[56]

Stephen Cullen Carpenter described the physical characteristics needed for genteel comedy; Mr. Rutherford was small, but

very well formed, and . . . proportioned with strict symmetry. It will not fill up an idea of the hero or the tyrant, but it is well suited for genteel comedy, and for characters rather of elegance than of weight. . . . his figure is admirably calculated for the sprightly gentleman in comedy."[57]

Many times more gentleman and fine ladies were required for genteel comedy and opera than were available, and critics complained about the recruitment of actors from other lines who were unable to sustain the illusion. Critics were merciless to those who failed to meet the standards for gentlemen. Joseph Jefferson was much-loved and respected in low comedy and as old men, but he failed as a gentleman:

> Mr. Jefferson is a good actor in many characters, and in some almost inimitable; but his *forte* is certainly not in genteel comedy. There is nothing more vulgar than the constant display of a white handkerchief dangling out of the pocket, or flourishing in the hand. This is, however, not peculiar to Mr. Jefferson.[58]

When Mr. Doyle played the role of an Irishman in *The Mountaineers,* the critic approved only his brogue:

> The gentility of the part, however, was wanting:—this was not unexpected, for no one, we presume, will ever do captain *Doyle* the injustice to suppose, that in any thing, except wearing white top boots, with a full suit of black, he can play the gentleman.[59]

The critic suggested a remedy, however; the actor should observe gentlemen as models

> in which he might learn something of that ease of gesture, gracefulness of carriage, and polished conversation, which mark the difference between that society which he is generally accustomed to, and that which it is his endeavor to exhibit for imitation.[60]

This division between roles that demanded gentility and the actors who could create at least the illusion of it, and roles and actors that did not, was a mirror of the division of Anglo-American society into those of the upper classes who were gentlemen and ladies, and those of the middle and lower classes who were not. All male roles might be divided generally into these two broad categories, with heroes, lovers, and gentlemen on one side and all those parts that fell to the "low comedians" on the other.

Low comedians performed in all genres and played some of the favorite roles in comedy and opera, including tradesmen, servants, farmers, rustics, and various ethnic roles. These parts were central to many operas, and included such prominent roles as Darby in the *Poor Soldier* and *Darby's Return*, Ruttekin in *Robin Hood*, Shacabac in *Blue Beard*, and Walter in *Children in the Wood*. To play low comedy was not synonymous with broad or vulgar comedy: these roles could include depth of character and demand considerable acting skill and sensitivity.

A few actors—such as John Hodgkinson—were capable of playing roles throughout the entire spectrum from the hero to the clown. Other actors chose low comedy because they possessed natural comic talents, along with the necessary mobility of feature, flexibility of voice, agility of body, and split-second timing. Yet others played low comedy because they lacked aristocratic manners and style, because they were too short, too fat, too ugly, or in other ways physically unsuited for the role of gentleman, or because their voices were coarse or inappropriately accented. Some of America's finest actors—among them Joseph Jefferson, Joseph Tyler, and William Twaits—were low comedians, and even tragedians like Cooper occasionally let their hair down to play Ruttekin or Walter.

The degree of realism or of caricature was one distinction found within the line of the low comedian. Actors were often cautioned not to make their humor too broad; thus when Twaits played the role of Varbel in *Lodoiska* in Philadelphia in 1806, the critic gave "unqualified admiration":

With an abundant store of *comick salt*, he never sprinkles it without discretion; and though no man alive knows better *when* and *how* to sharpen the sting of a jest, he seems always aware, that
> A cobweb partition but thinly divides
> Those efforts, a critick applauds or derides.[61]

Holman discusses only two lines, tradesmen and clowns, within the broad spectrum of low comedy, but these may serve as a starting point for consideration of additional lines:

Tradesmen. In a certain sense, all the characters of middle life are affiliated to this class: but, as it is not here intended to individualize them, this subdivision will be deferred. The qualities of a tradesman are such as most performers, who have abilities for the dramatic art, may easily personate. Habit induces the mere tradesman to be subservient in his manner, especially to the wealthy, and on extraordinary occasions servile: he renders contradiction smooth, listens to it patiently, intends to flatter but does it aukwardly [*sic*], complies with any request if his interest be not compromised, is always ready with the tradesman's bow, not only at meeting and parting, but wherever it can be intruded, and his eye, attitudes, and slightest actions, wherever his interest is concerned, are all anxiously intent on and subservient to that eager desire of gain which habit has rendered a predominant passion. By the nature and extent of this, his deportment is regulated. His propensities appear on all occasions; but they appear slightly, earnestly, or extravagantly, in proportion to supposed loss or gain. It is not by this intended to depreciate a class of men, but to describe habits, which are inevitably fostered by barter and sale, unless counteracted by superiority of mind, or extraneous circumstances; and to give a picture such as an actor, who literally personates a tradesman, ought to have in contemplation.

The term "tradesman" should not be taken too literally in describing this wide-ranging comic repertoire. When John Durang defined William Warren's specialty by naming the roles "Falstaff and Benevolent Merchant," he was placing him in this line. Francis Blissett also played tradesman roles; Durang says he was the "Doctor Caious, Sheepface, Jerry Sneck" of the Philadelphia company.[62] Those who pretended gentility but failed in the attempt also fell into this line. When William Wood played Dick Dowlas in Philadelphia in 1806,

He personified admirably the awkward gait of a freshly-made beau; and, by constant grinning, peeping through his glass, playing with his watch-chain, and flourishing every moment an enormous white handkerchief, marked the difference between the behavior of a well-bred man and a mushroom buck.[63]

Many servants' roles fit this tradesman category, among them the tutor and general factotum Apathy in *Children in the Wood;* perhaps the best-known role of this type was the Spanish barber, Figaro. Although he was in every sense a tradesman, Figaro was also the epitome of what might be considered the comic servant line—which also included Robert in *The Haunted Tower,* Shacabac in *Blue Beard,* the servant lover Walter in *Children in the Wood,* and countless others.[64]

Another broad line was that of the "bluff, hearty farmer," the "dignified rustic," or the "simple country lad"—roles "where rusticity is to be depicted, blended with honest feeling, and where there is no occasion for broad farce or comic caricature."[65] John Bray was approved by the critics in his portrayal of "*Yorkshire lads,* where chaste simplicity is intended."[66] John Hogg "made his mark in the line of honest, blunt, bluff old countrymen."[67] Joseph Jefferson was admonished not to play the character of Farmer Ashfield in *Speed the Plow* as a scaramouch or buffoon, but to portray him with "traits of the highest respectability . . . set off . . . by the contrast of a certain ungainness. . . . simplicity that approaches the sublime . . . should shine through its unpolished envelope."[68]

Clowns. Rustic appearance, vacant or gazing eyes, an open mouth, arms dangling yet the shoulders raised, the toes turned inward, a shambling gait with a heavy step, great slowness of conception, and apparent stupidity of mind and manner, characterize the absolute clown. The varieties of the class, like the last, are interesting subjects of study for the stage; but are too frequently misunderstood. Vary the portrait by red ribbands, yellow petticoats, timidity, and maudlin freaks, and his counterpart is seen.

The clown was a nearly invariable participant in the old-fashioned stock pantomimes. At the turn of the nineteenth century, Harlequin and the Clown were the central characters in many harlequinades. Tradesmen, servants, farmers could all become clowns with the proper broad-brushed portrayal. Joseph Jefferson was probably the best all-around low comedian on the boards; "in *burletta,* and in very broad farce he is inimitable. As a pantomimic clown he surpasses most others."[69]

One special line of low comedy was the "provincial," which could include Irishmen (such as Darby), Scotsmen, Welshmen, Jews, Frenchmen, Yorkshiremen, and other country characters, including Yankees such as Jonathan in *The Contrast*. A convincing accent was essential for these roles, although not all roles that required accents were provincial or low comedy parts.

Low comedy lines often overlapped in a single character, and the successful low comedian had to be a master of all:

Mr. Blissett, as Herbert, an affectionate domestic, with the dialect of a clown, but with the honest feelings of unsophisticated nature, excited pleasurable emotion, throughout the house. The fidelity of a good servant, and the simplicity of the rustic character were very accurately displayed by Mr. Blissett.[70]

Mr. Entwisle displayed versatility as a low comedian at Boston in 1813:

Although his powers are competent to a respectable personation of a great variety of character, yet it is in the country louts, both serious and comic, that he is really and truly excellent. In Yorkshire *sharpers* he is better than the best, and, in *Farmer Ashfield,* is utterly unapproachable by any one of the American stage.[71]

In many ways the women's roles paralleled those of the men, with a similar division into genteel and low comedy roles, and corresponding lines of acting.

Heroines. Give feminine dignity of person, and all the qualities described under the title *heroes,* with that pervading force of sensibility which shall never vanquish though it shall often endanger heroism, and the heroine will be nearly perfect.

The heroines were the first female line in tragedy. There was seldom a counterpart in opera or melodrama. Heroines could be played by women of any age, and tragediennes such as Ann Merry and Elizabeth Whitlock often performed the same roles throughout their careers.

Fine Ladies. The fine lady is, or should be, even a more fascinating character on the stage, than that which has been pictured under the head *gentlemen;* for, to the almost unattainable graces of the gentleman, she should add a continued playfulness, a visible coquetry, which, though perfectly at her command, should appear spontaneous, and an ample mixture of delightful caprice, which she evidently indulges only to make herself more captivating. Should the actress suffer the least vulgarity to appear, in either walk, attitude, dress, or enunciation, the fine lady instantly vanishes. Her *dress* is of so much consequence, that the moment she appears, her character should be visible; and this *art of dress* is only to be attained by the study of that which is almost simplicity itself; or would be, were she but to take away a very few ornaments, tastefully selected and admirably placed, by which she intends to be distinguished.

"Walk, attitude, dress, and enunciation"—this is what distinguished the fine lady from other female lines, both higher and lower. She lacked the dignity and force of the tragic heroine, yet if she could create the illusion of gentility she was vital to fill the first and second line of ladies in comedy and opera, and often second lines in tragedy as well. Fine ladies' roles included Lady Townley in *The Provoked Husband*, Lady Teazle in *The School for Scandal*, Beatrice in *Much Ado about Nothing*, and Lady Alford in *Children in the Wood*. Mrs. Johnson, brought from England in 1795 to perform "the elegant Characters in Comedy"[72] at the New York theatre, "particularly excelled in the delineation of the fashionable high bred lady."[73] Mrs. Hughes, on the other hand, "never appears to equal advantage in *genteel* comedy; she does not know how to *wear* her fine cloaths, and is apparently more intent upon her dress than upon her part"; the critic recommended that she stick with "village girls and humble simplicity."[74]

Hoydens. A hoyden exhibits herself by an impatient readiness to romp, eagerness to contradict, fretfulness if contradicted, vehement wishes to enjoy, dress that is ridiculous by exceeding the fashion, and while absurd in manner, loud of voice, and a total stranger to good breeding, by an air of excessive self-satisfaction.

The epitome of the hoyden was Priscilla Tomboy in *The Romp,* and the term "romp" was used to describe this line more often than "hoyden." The hoyden was generally of the upper class, and was portrayed as a pert child or adolescent. Because of her youth, the hoyden could get by with things not permitted to "fine ladies" (although she was expected to grow up to become one). Mature ladies could play romps, although they were also played by young women. A refined accent was necessary to play hoydens, as well as a girlish figure. When thirteen-year-old Elizabeth Arnold played the role of Priscilla Tomboy in 1800, "Simon" described her in the *Philadelphia Repository and Weekly Register:*

> Thou art a little Romp, the point's agreed,
> A wicked, roguish, playful romp indeed.
> So full of saucy pranks—vagaries wild,
> A very baggage—nature's vivid child![75]

Six years later, when Miss Arnold had become Mrs. Poe, *Polyanthos* believed that the hoyden was still her forte.[76]

One standard variation on the romp was the "breeches role"—either a part that had a young woman dressed in man's clothing as a disguise, or a boy's role like Little Pickle in *The Spoil'd Child,* played by the same actress who usually played hoydens, and using many of the same movements and manners. Sometimes roles written for a man were performed by a woman as a breeches role; Mrs. Williamson played the part of Patrick in *The Poor Soldier* in Boston in 1796; Mrs. Woodham played the same character there in 1808.[77] Actresses of all ages and sizes assumed breeches for one role or another (even "heroines" played Portia in *The Merchant of Venice*), and critics commented freely on their clothing and their figures. When Mrs. Poe played Little Pickle at Boston in 1807, one reviewer grumped:

Little Pickle, by Mrs. Poe, if we may be allowed the use of a pun, was a very green *Little Pickle.* We never knew before that the *Spoiled Child* belonged to that class of beings termed *hermaphroditical,* as the uncouthness of his costume seemed to indicate.[78]

A Philadelphia critic in 1805 described Mrs. Woodham's performance in the same role:

Those who delight in a woman's asumption of that appendage to manhood, vulgarly yclep'd breeches, must have been highly gratified by the metamorphosis of Mrs. Woodham. To a good figure she adds the graces of action peculiar to our sex. In her songs, although her voice is not of the first order, she exhibited much taste, and was deservedly applauded. Dibdin's "Flowing Can" was introduced by her with great effect; and we remarked with pleasure that Mrs. W. was judiciously restrained by the most scrupulous delicacy through the whole of this part, where it frequently happens that the eye of decency is offended, in order to engage the attention of the grosser part of the audience.[79]

William Wood complained that the inappropriate costume worn by Mrs. Whitlock as the peasant boy Fidele in *Cymbeline* was:

a tight vest, and pantaloons of a sky blue satin, fitting closely, and scarcely the apology for a very short cloak. This was the dress of one of the largest female performers ever seen on our stage, and excited no disapprobation or remark. Mrs. Marshall too degraded the stage on her benefit night, by the performance of Marplot, in a fashionable male habit of the day, but little calculated for a character which was to undergo numerous shakings, beatings, tumblings, and other personal assaults.[80]

Often, particularly in small companies, the same actresses played both romps and chambermaids. Mary Harding, for example, was said by Ireland to play "boys and second-rate chambermaids."[81]

Chambermaids. Volubility, pertness, a prevailing sense of self-importance, irksome curiosity, uncommon acuteness in all that relates to family secrets, extreme ignorance of every thing beyond her sphere, impatience to prattle, timidity when overawed, and a pleasure in being rude when she dare, are most of them what the chambermaid supposes to be her peculiar airs and graces.

The chambermaid was in many ways the female counterpart of the tradesman. She did not need—indeed, she needed to avoid—the gentility of carriage, voice, manners, and accent characteristic of the "fine lady." Many of the young servant lovers, such as Walter's sweetheart Josephine in *Children in the Wood*, were chambermaids. The chambermaid was generally a young woman's role, and was found in opera and melodrama as often as in comedy. Occasionally these roles could be played by older actresses; Ireland described Mrs. Brett as "a valuable actress of old women and coarse chambermaids."[82]

Middle and old age. In the various stages of declining life, though the passions are less strong, many of the evil habits of youth become rooted, and should appear mingled with the propensities which prevail in age. Among these propensities are, anxiety concerning trifles, increasing avarice, obstinacy, a petulant inclination to contradict, a gradual disregard of good breeding, ceremony, and dress, uncontrollable peevishness, and change of voice, walk, and carriage; all which qualities are to be regulated partly by age, but still more by the mental strength or debility of the character supposed.

Although old men and women were found in all theatrical genres, the characters described by Holcroft were not the dignified figures of tragedy or melodrama, but what today might be called character roles, often with considerable color and weight. Such roles were sometimes played by general low comedians of any age, like Jefferson, but there were also specialists who played them by choice or because of their age or physiognomy. Joseph Ireland described Ann Hogg as "the best actress of old women ever seen in New York."[83]

Critics emphasized the necessity for playing old characters—in either comedy or tragedy—with the entire voice and body. Hodgkinson was complimented for his assumption of "the voice of tremulous age" in the role of Old Norval, but was occasionally forgetful and allowed "his natural accents" to appear.[84] A Philadelphia critic complained after a performance of *The Hunter of the Alps* that the appearance and manner of Mr. Taylor, a young man, "were more like those of a London undertaker soliciting a job" than "a good old steward, bending beneath the weight of years."[85] Joshua Collins fared no better with a Boston critic who complained that his acting lacked uniformity when Collins played Gaspard in *Foundling of the Forest*. "The *old* man was at some times, entirely forsaken . . . the capers he cut bore too strong a resemblance to *three and twenty*—the stiff and feeble figuring of sixty five were not to be seen."[86]

The best players were praised for their ability to play characters in all genres and lines, old and young, from gentlemen to clowns, or from heroines to chambermaids. A Philadelphia critic said that "Mr. Francis is the best general performer we ever saw. He is an invaluable treasure to the stage."[87] John Bernard played an extensive range of comedy roles "from the most polished gentlemen to the most awkward clown, through the intermediate families of fops, humourists, and instinctive characters of various kinds."[88] Bernard in turn said that Hodgkinson "was a wonder. In the whole range of the living drama there was no variety of character he could not perceive and embody, from a Richard [III] or a Hamlet down to a Shelty or a Sharp . . . he was also a singer, and could charm you in a burletta, after thrilling you in a play."[89] Mrs. Hodgkinson surpassed "all her contemporaries in rustic comedy and singing parts, in chambermaids and *soubrettes*," and equaled "most of them in pathetic tragedy and the general range of the drama."[90] Mrs. Oldmixon's "line in opera, were the lively characters. . . . The antiquated dame or lively romp—the lack-a-daisical lady of quality or awkward gawky—the pert chambermaid or simple rural lass—the Irish peasant or French governante, were alike within the scope of her powers."[91]

It was this stereotyping of roles—rather than the genre or whether or not the role required singing—that ultimately determined the assignment of parts in any production. The types of characters found within a genre, rather than the genre itself, determined the actors who appeared; the fact that more singers took major roles in comedies than in tragedies was a reflection of the types of characters in common between comedy and comic opera. There were also correspondences between the characters in English opera and the comic operas of the rest of Europe in the same period; Mozart's Figaro and Susanna were classics of the tradesman and chambermaid lines, Don Giovanni was a flawed hero, Leporello a comic servant, and Donna Elvira and Donna Anna fine ladies.

TRADITIONS OF CASTING

One of the most important aspects of casting in both England and the United States was the custom of "ownership of parts." James Fennell explained "that parts having been once played, and therefore possessed . . . by one, cannot be taken away by the manager and given to another, without a breech of the fundamental laws of the theatre."[92] In other words, once an actor "owned" a role, he could play it forever, no matter his age or infirmity, unless he voluntarily resigned the role, retired from the theatre, or died. Often an actor

continued to figure as a youthful hero or lover long after all nature's qualifications for the parts had become the very prey of time, the despoiler, and the wrinkles of age, and the cracked voice changed to "childish treble," should have consigned him to the representation of the lean and slippered pantaloon.[93]

Giles Leonard Barrett (1744–1809) was a mature man when he "retired" from the British stage to come to the States in 1796, but he retained his first-line roles in genteel comedy. When he performed in *Which Is the Man?* and *Love in a Village* in Charleston in 1805, Carpenter noted:

If Mr. BARRET's time of life and size were not a little beyond the mark, he would have rendered the parts of *Beauchamp* in the play and *Young Mea-*

dows, in the opera respectable; but both were rather against the necessary illusion.[94]

Lewis Hallam (1735–1808), though past sixty, quarreled with John Hodgkinson because he was not allowed to "perform many of the young, First Rate Characters, which he said he had supplied since his first Arrival in America, and that he had not resigned them, nor ever would."[95]

The problem was even worse with Mrs. Hallam, whose increasing drunkenness had made her unfit for the stage. Hodgkinson hired Mrs. Johnson in 1795 to replace Mrs. Hallam, but Mrs. Hallam refused to relinquish her roles. Mrs. Johnson reluctantly agreed to allow Mrs. Hallam to retain all the roles she had played, but insisted that she be given all the new roles in those lines of business.[96]

The number of roles claimed by a seasoned actor could be enormous. When Hodgkinson negotiated with William Dunlap to rejoin the Park Theatre company in New York for the 1799–1800 season, he enclosed a list of 146 roles he claimed for himself, and nearly as many for his wife.[97]

If more than one actor in a company claimed the same role by having played it in other companies or through having played it in different seasons in the absence of the other, the manager had to arbitrate between them to decide who got to play it. In the case of first-line roles, such situations could create any number of tantrums in the greenroom and a commensurate number of headaches for the manager. When the opera *Agreeable Surprise* was given in Boston in 1795,

Mrs. Jones and Mrs. Hughes both laid claim to the part of *Cowslip,* both prepared to play the character, and both came on the stage at the same time, each offering her bowl of cream to *Lingo.* As Mr. Jones was playing *Lingo,* he at once settled the dispute by accepting his wife's offering.[98]

Furthermore, if an actor had played a leading role (even in a minor theatre), he could not be asked to play a lesser role in the same play (even in a major theatre). Thus an actor might "decline" an offered role because it was not of the first line (or even the second line). In one season at Edinburgh, there were six Hamlets in the troupe, but not enough performers to stage the play.[99] The situation was just as bad in Philadelphia in 1806.

Mr. Harwood, an actor of uncommon merit, is almost excluded from the boards, because the other gentlemen will not *give up* their parts to him. What is the duty of a manager, if every actor, like Bottom in 'Midsummer Night's Dream,' is to chuse his own part, in defiance of justice and common sense? Mr. Harwood's not appearing oftener is, no doubt, occasioned by the *prior* claims of others; and the city must therefore be deprived of this gentleman's talents till these claims shall cease!"[100]

The critic does not suggest to Harwood that *he* consider the alternative of accepting second line roles rather than not appearing at all. At Boston, later the same year, the performers were

so fastidious and such resolute adherents of the etiquette of the Greenroom, that we seldom see a play supported by the whole strength of the company. There are *two* or *three* who lay claim to the first character in every piece, and as only *one* can appear in it, the others, who will not abate one jot or tittle of their imaginary consequence, are left out, and the play is *damned,* for want of suitable actors to fill the parts of secondary importance. This is a vice common to all theatres, but in ours has arisen to a degree ridiculous and unparalleled, and calls loudly for a remedy.[101]

When Hodgkinson negotiated with Dunlap in the spring of 1799, he offered a contract that read: "Mr. Hodgkinson *shall not* have the *power* of objecting to any character appointed by the manager, provided such character be in tragedy the first character, *also in genteel comedy;* and if Mr. Hodgkinson *should* object, he shall pay for every such objection a forfeit of five pounds sterling."[102] In other words Hodgkinson was willing to play as many roles as requested by the manager, as long as he was never asked to play other than a first-line role—which meant that he would have to resign nothing, and would never have to accept a secondary role. The star system made the situation considerably worse, because each time a visiting star arrived, he or she took the leading role in each play, and most of the principal actors would then decline to play any other parts.

Strange miscastings resulted from the necessity of assigning roles by rule instead of reason. The father in Miller's *Mahomet* was taken by a new actor much younger than his children, Hodgkinson and Mrs. Melmoth, at New York in 1795. Hodgkinson was five feet ten and becoming portly; Mrs. Melmoth was "the largest and most matronly figure on the stage."[103] Mrs. Simpson, a mature actress, played the Queen in *Richard III* in Charleston, while Miss Field, the age of her daughters, played the Queen Mother.[104] James Fennell, who was six and one half feet tall, played Romeo to the Juliet of Mrs. Marshall, who measured barely five feet.[105] When Fennell played Macbeth, Noble Usher was Banquo:

To see him and Fennel together reminded us of the fable, where the ox and the frog! But comparisons are odious. Mr. Usher's puny dimension, however, unfits him for such a character as Banquo, for though he *may swell and swell and swell,* yet the edge of Fennel's shoulder, is the *"ne plus ultra,"* of his attainment.[106]

When companies were short of actors for whatever reason, players and managers were sometimes forced to unreasonable extremes to fill parts. This included the use of unqualified supernumeraries, amateurs, and children, the use of actors who were ill or otherwise incapacitated, and the doubling and tripling of roles.

Because their services were needed, Elizabeth Arnold and Mary Harding started playing romps and chambermaids while in their middle teens. Young women also played pages, young princes, and other similar boys' roles when no other suitable representative was available. When there was a shortage of children available to play roles actually written for children, little boys were given girls' roles (and marked thus in the bill) and vice versa.

Early in the nineteenth century it even became fashionable for children to play parts written for adults, especially the heroes of serious drama or tragedy such as *Macbeth, Alexander the Great,* or *The Roman Father.* Following the model of England's "Master Betty," such children apparently learned the standard formulas of the tragedian and imitated them, much as child evangelists today learn the intonation, pacing, cant, and mannerisms of their elders. These precocious children were invariably billed as "the infant Roscius," and budding talents like Master Payne and Master Barrett followed the same star circuit—and played the same roles—as adult actors like Thomas A. Cooper and James Fennell. The effect must have been similar to that experienced today by operagoers who see middle-aged women portraying the romantic young heroes and generals of Baroque opera.

Another unusual custom was the practice of using "a young gentleman" or "a lady" for various roles, usually commenting in the bills that it was a "first appearance on the stage." This practice was particularly resorted to by small companies short of actors, but it was also a way for managers of larger companies to save money on salaries while attracting an audience composed of friends of the aspirant to stardom. One speculates that the star-struck amateur himself might have contributed an extra subsidy for the manager, as well. The anonymity would have protected the gentility of the amateur from the contamination of theatrical association. Occasionally such recruits became regular members of the company, and their names began to appear on the bills; more often they disappeared as quickly as they came.

When publisher and composer Benjamin Carr performed with the Old American Company in Philadelphia and New York in 1794, he was a novice. He played several roles for a few weeks, but the reviewers noted that he was a better musician than he was an actor, and he soon left the stage and devoted himself to his various musical enterprises.

A young man named Morrell acted the leading role of Rolla in *Pizarro* at the New York theatre in 1809, to the disgust of the *Ramblers'*

Magazine critic: "His person is diminutive, his face inexpressive, his actions ungraceful, his conception erroneous, and his pronunciation vulgar." In spite of his total unsuitability, he was greeted with uproarious good cheer by his friends from the "noted row of Broadway": "not a shop but poured forth its *noblesse*—young and old—masters and apprentices—small fry and large fry, all were assembled." These partisans provided a "complete tempest, torrent, and whirlwind of applause" throughout the piece.[107]

The stigma usually attached to a gentleman who performed in the theatre is demonstrated by the letters exchanged by William Charles White (1777–1818) and his father when the younger man joined the Boston theatrical corps in 1796. After it became clear that the stage-struck youth would go onstage despite all advice to the contrary, his father urged him *not* to accept any remuneration and to make it clear that he played occasionally only for his own amusement. He was urged to accept only "first rate characters" in tragedy, and never a role in any comedy where "Dancing and Singing and Kissing may be thought amusement Enough for a Dollar."[108]

The show-must-go-on tradition, though not articulated in those terms, was as strong two centuries ago as it is today. Actors often performed even when illness made them unable to meet a role's demands competently. When Mr. Morse returned to the stage in 1811 after an absence of several weeks, he was welcomed heartily, although he "yet evidently labours under the effects of his rheumatism; his left arm being confined in a sling."[109] Actors arriving by ship from Europe often performed within hours of debarkation.

Women continued to perform long after their pregnancies were visible, and resumed their careers as quickly as possible after the births of their children. One critic admonished:

Respect for the audience ought to restrain ladies from appearing on the stage in *certain* situations, and in certain characters. We hope the lady who played the *Hostess* will take the hint. If she was compelled by the managers, she is entitled to pity; if it was her own choice, she should be rewarded with the frowns of modesty and propriety.[110]

Charlotte Placide was pregnant in 1803, and Carpenter could not resist alluding to it in his reviews in the *Charleston Courier*. On December 10 he criticized her appearance in a ballet:

Of Jupiter and Europa we have nothing to say, but that whatever pleasure the unthinking part of the audience might have received from it, was more than counterbalanced by their dislike to see Mrs. Placide in the hazardous, or at least apparently hazardous process of going up in the cloud.

Two days later he objected to her assumption of the role of the chambermaid in the opera *Children in the Wood*: "Mrs. Placide was as always pleasing in Josephine, though she laboured under one disadvantage. There were *visible* reasons for thinking that she did not exactly *look* the *Maiden Josephine*."

The doubling of small roles was a continual problem. Most audiences did not object to the supernumeraries in the chorus or in the crowd scenes appearing in a variety of parts, but disliked obvious doublings of other roles. A small touring company might have only four members, and many did well to muster a dozen actors; a large company might have thirty-five. (A London company typically had twice that many.) When the ranks were further thinned by illness or by declining of roles, a manager might be hard-pressed to fill roles without doubling. A performance of *The Merchant of Venice* at Boston's Haymarket Theatre in 1797 had five characters doubled. The critic from the *Columbian Centinel* sniped that "Such a cast would have disgraced even a *barn*."[111] In 1812 the opera *Battle of Hexham* was presented at the Federal Street Theatre during the benefits, and *Polyanthos* complained, "For want of numbers, the company were inadequate to its representation. We are so accustomed to *doubles*, that they are expected as things of course; but here we had *trebles, quadruples, and quintuples*."[112] Mr. Shapter played three roles in *Mac-*

beth at Philadelphia in 1806: King Duncan, Hecate, and the Apothecary! "Though he was *Shapter* in all, he acquitted himself quite well."[113]

ACTING SKILLS AND CONVENTIONS

In mastering their craft, actors at the turn of the nineteenth century had to develop a wide variety of skills, from singing and dancing to fencing. Their work was also governed by a number of theatrical conventions, some of which are still practiced.

Most large companies hired specialists to play the leading roles in opera or ballet. These singers and dancers were expected to be convincing in speaking roles in opera and pantomime, and to fill in as necessity and their abilities dictated in all the works performed. In turn, all members of the troupe were expected to be able to sing and dance a little, at least enough to fill up the choruses if they were unable to sing alone. A surprising number of them apparently met these requirements; others failed in the attempt. In Boston in 1811, "the grace of Mrs. B[eaumont]'s minuet, was heightened by contrasting it with the insufferable stupidity of her partner."[114] The dancing in *Cinderella* was so poor in 1812 that a Boston critic advised the managers to "*see a dancing master, and bespeak him a fortnight beforehand,* before they bring forward a piece which depends so materially on the *grace* and *agility* of the performers."[115]

Critics also suggested dancing as a means of increasing ease of movement. When a young amateur made his first appearance in Philadelphia, "the novelty of his situation weighted heavily upon his spirits, and fettered his action." The critic recommended "Industry, . . . the aid of a good dancing master, and the practice of a season or two" to complete his preparation for the stage.[116]

The Baltimore Theatre may actually have had a dancing master attend rehearsals regularly. The Articles of Agreement for the 1782 season single out the dancing master, George James L'Argeau, for a fine of ten shillings for failure to attend rehearsals; actors were fined only one shilling. L'Argeau was also a fencing instructor, so he may have been paid to stage the fight scenes.[117] His name does not appear on the bills as a performer during the 1782 season, which may indicate that he attended rehearsals only as an instructor—or perhaps that he was so offended by the company's new rules that he never came back!

Individual and massed combat scenes, using weapons of the day and of earlier times, were commonplace crowd-pleasers, used frequently in the dramas of Shakespeare, in melodrama, and in opera. The men of the company therefore trained in fencing, wrestling, and other combat skills. When *Inkle and Yarico,* for example, was presented as a pantomime in Newport, Rhode Island, the bills touted the "COMBAT, with the SWORD and the CLUB, by Messrs. Dubois, Francisquy, and Hallam."[118] The libretto of *Children in the Wood* calls for two scenes involving swordplay, and the libretto provides some description of the action. In act 1, scene 4, Walter and the ruffian Oliver

fight, Oliver gains ground upon Walter, and strikes his sword out of his hand—the girl runs and picks up Walter's sword, gives it to him, just as Oliver is aiming to run him through the body—Walter renews the fight, and kills Oliver—off.

In act 2, scene 2, a group combat scene occurs when Walter rescues Lord Alford and his servant from a lopsided battle with Sir Rowland and two ruffians.

Real weapons were used in stage combat, and they sometimes inflicted injuries. One actor was accidentally run through by a sword used in the ballet *The Death of Captain Cook* in London in 1789. He was helped off the stage while the audience applauded what they considered a "fine piece of realism," but he later died.[119] In the fall of 1798 John Hodgkinson received "a severe wound on the cheek with a sword in playing William Tell" in the second Boston performance of *The Archers.*[120] Another accident occurred in Philadelphia in 1801 during the final combat scene between Richard and Richmond in *Richard III;* it "excited considerable alarm and anxiety in the audience," but no one was seriously injured.[121]

Audiences expected skill in theatrical combat. When *Much Ado about Nothing* was performed in Boston in 1813, a critic complained that "The style in which the wrestling was conducted in the first act was supremely farcical. The scene had better be omitted than be thus exposed to ridicule." The women were also required to display combat skills on occasion. When Mrs. Jones performed in *The Farm House* in Philadelphia in 1806, she was "enthusiastically applauded—particularly toward the conclusion where she appears in a military disguise. The fall in the duel, was so natural that many of the auditors imagined her really hurt."[122]

Advertisements in Boston in 1803 and in Providence and Charleston in 1804 touted "The elegant art of fencing, taught by G. L. Barret, of the Theatre,"[123] and Giles Barrett and his young son gave fencing demonstrations at various theatres on their benefit nights. Barrett probably also served as instructor for other members of the company. Practice at arms was one method of maintaining the physical fitness required of any of the actors who performed in combat scenes or who needed to perform the leaps and tumbling tricks of the pantomimes.

The skills of combat, like those of dancing, were probably also helpful in acquiring ease and control of movement onstage. Dignity of carriage and deliberation in movement were required for the hero or heroine, and grace and elegance for the lovers, gentlemen, and fine ladies:

To tragedians and the performers of gentlemen, a short step is peculiarly destructive of dignity; while in characters of low breeding but of animation, it is no less a true mark of such persons. To step with measured affectation, like an opera dancer to a march, is no less laughable; it destroys reality: for a spectator cannot but imagine he sees a foolish actor, instead of the character he ought to personify.[124]

Too much dignity and attitude led to what Carpenter called "the perspective and statuary school of action."[125] Comedians, on the other hand, needed agility—to a degree:

Honest Joe had nearly made *Ali Baba* into a dancing-bear—he hopped and skipped about, not as was remarked by some one near us, 'like a flea in a tar barrel,' but to use a more appropriate and no less refined comparison, 'like a parched pea on a hot shovel.'[126]

In a Boston production of *The School of Reform* in 1806, excessive movement brought comments from two critics. The first said:

Mr. Fox exhibited *Ferment* in a terrible state of fermentation. A little less dancing and a little more moderation in speaking, would have added a little to the dignity even of *Ferment*.[127]

The other added: "If he could exchange a little of his *fire*, with Mr. Downie, for a small quantity of *frigidity*, neither of the gentlemen would lose by the bargain."[128]

One of the standard rules quoted to actors was *"Learn to stand still."*[129] Stephen Cullen Carpenter stressed the point in his advice to a young actor:

Where action is imperfect, it should be called upon as little as possible. Nothing but length of time, and long, laborious practice can ever impart the kind of action that is adapted to the stage; and which is by no means the same that is considered elegant deportment in private life. . . . This, therefore, is one of the qualifications which an actor must learn after he has gone upon the stage—being entirely out of his habits before. We, therefore, strenuously recommend it to all young actors . . . to be as sparing as possible of action till they have acquired that smoothness which practice only can impart.[130]

Many of the acting practices and conventions used in both tragedy and comedy would seem "contrary to nature" to later audiences. The perfectly obvious "aside" was an accepted theatrical convention, enabling the actor to confide in his or her audience out of the hearing of the other actors on the stage. Critics complained, however, when actors shouted their asides from the back of the stage, making it all too obvious that the actors in between could hear everything very well indeed.[131]

During much of the eighteenth century, it was not considered strictly necessary to stay in character between speeches. Actors even carried on conversations at times with those seated in the stage boxes (although the earlier practice of seating part of the audience onstage was virtually eliminated by the last decade of the century), and they frequently nodded or smiled at friends in the audience.

By the end of the century, critics were insisting that actors should stay in character at all times. "Too often," said John Howard Payne, "we are compelled to hear our actors recite their parts, as school-boys do their *lessons,* and when they finish speaking they are *themselves* again." [132] During a Philadelphia performance of *The Soldier's Daughter,* three of the company "had placed themselves like statues, in a retired part of the stage, *expressively* gaping at the audience in the gallery." Mr. Wood, like "the generality of our actors and actresses" was guilty of constantly "glancing at the boxes, to such a degree, that the conversation seems rather addressed to some individual in that part of the house than to the person on the stage;" [133] even worse, Mr. Barrett twinkled his eyes toward the side boxes "to see what consequences his acting produces there on the ladies." [134] Mr. Harwood was praised, however, because he "has the very commendable practice of attending closely to the business of the scene in which he is engaged. His eyes never wander in vacant gaze from the objects which alone should engage his attention." [135] Mrs. Johnson, too, was admired because "she does not, like so many of her sister actresses, cease to *personate,* when she ceases to *speak;* whether speaking or addressed, she is always in character." [136]

When James Fennell performed the role of Othello, during his address to the Duke in Council he addressed the audience instead of the Duke. He was reminded that he should behave "as if he were really 'in such a presence' as he appears, and not merely standing before a brother-player, whom, perhaps, he treats with little ceremony behind the scenes." In the same play, one actor had his arms folded, forgetting he was in the presence of a "Magnifico of Venice," and gave Desdemona a familiar nod instead of a bow as he left the stage. ("We are glad *Iago* did not see it," said a critic.) Yet another actor forgot to remove his hat in the presence of the Venetian general and the Cyprian governor.[137] When *Julius Caesar* was performed in Boston, one spectator found it difficult to conceive "how some nine or ten people, (all but *two* of whom were mutes,) standing in a semi-circle to hear Antony's oration, could have 'ought the least similitude' to a Roman rabble."[138]

It was generally accepted that actors should look at the audience during the performance instead of at each other, partly, of course, to avoid losing audibility and facial expression by facing upstage. Thomas Holcroft believed that "there scarcely can be an occasion when an actor ought to speak with his profile, much less with half his back, turned to the audience." He termed it an "unpardonable fault" to continue throughout a scene with the profile toward the audience:

If possible, the face should front the stage, yet the eye remain totally unconscious of the presence of an audience; and when, the nature of the scene absolutely requires the actor to look directly at the person with whom he is speaking, he still should keep a three-quarter face to the audience.[139]

Mrs. Wheatley apparently tried to follow these instructions, but to no avail.

Mrs. Wheatly's face and figure are very pretty, . . . but we wish she could be cured of the habit of continually turning her face up to the ceiling over the pit. She seems to have a settled determination to look *straight forward*.[140]

The "business" that accompanied a role was a necessary part of stage effect. When John Hodgkinson first performed in New York, the extent and realism of his stage business startled the critics:

Mr. Hodgkinson introduced a kind of practical wit, which we have been totally unused to. He several times greatly excited our concern for some of our old acquaintance of the company whom he handled without mercy. Mr. Ryan was in the utmost danger of suffocation; for when Mr. Hodgkinson would enjoin his taciturnity, he so effectually stopped his mouth with his hand that the poor man was in agonies for want of breath.[141]

Tragedians had their "attitudes," while comedians had their "tricks" or effects. Although some of the tricks used by actors before Garrick—"stamping before he made his appearance, crossing at every period, protruding the elbow, slapping the thigh, pointing the toe" [142]—came to be ridiculed as provincial and absurd, plenty of tricks were left to replace them. Standard tricks included thumping the breast, squeezing the hat, tapping, "pawing and hawling" other characters about, stalking back and forth between the other characters and the audience (usually during the other character's speech), stepping forward at the beginning of a speech and back at the end of it, clenching or shaking the fist, folding the arms, extending the right arm with the left folded across the chest, heaving the chest, thumping the stage at the ends of sentences with a cane, stick, or weapon, and sawing the air with the hands. [143]

Actors were occasionally praised for their stage tricks, but were much more often condemned. Carpenter believed that Cooper's dying scene in *Richard III* was particularly effective because it was natural: "There was a fine practical imitation of the anguish of a wounded man; and in the writhing of his body when he received the wound, and in his manner of falling, there was much stage effect." [144] Too often, however, the actor might be "heaving his chest, distorting his countenance, and 'sawing the air' with his hands" while "the other parts of his body are in profound apathy." [145] A New York spectator thought

The gentleman performers seemed to have entered into a sort of agreement to see if they could not raise a laugh and obtain applause by substituting noise and bustle, and running about the stage, in place of giving the words or the meaning of the author. [146]

The women, too, were berated for various exaggerations. Mrs. Mason was rebuked for "an excess of grief," but she was by no means alone:

There is no fault in a good actress, that is not more readily pardoned by a New-York audience than a superabundance of tears. Mrs. Melmoth was remarkable for this, but she possessed a skill in the management, that enabled her to resist the popular disapprobation: mrs. Whitlock is another and less fortunate instance; she absolutely cried herself to death, and was near drowning the whole *dramatis personae* by the copiousness of her inundations. At all events, they floated her away at the end of one season, never to return.[147]

Mrs. Barnes of the Boston Theatre possessed another talent

in a higher degree than any other lady on the boards—*videlicit,* the knack of screaming. In some plays, where a sudden shriek is so necessary to *stage effect,* to be able to scream with propriety is no mean accomplishment.[148]

One critic recommended that actors might well devote their spare time "to the study of the effects of passions on the human frame."[149] Carpenter pointed out that "our best actors have always found *stage-trick* a necessary practice," but complained that they too often seemed to copy other actors, and that "every imitator . . . has been ridiculous in the attempt."[150] He advised that "the best skill of an actor is often shown, not so much in what he does, as in what he abstains from doing."[151]

Critics often wrote of the byplay necessary to maintain the illusion of a scene. "Open" play was business performed during one's own lines; byplay was done by a character who was not speaking.[152] Some of the traveling stars seem to have used byplay as a means of keeping all eyes on them throughout the play, which relieved the audience "from the tedium of bad passages and bad performers."[153]

Mr. Cooke never gives the spectator a chance to look at the other characters long enough to break the illusion of the scene. Whether speaking or not, he claims undivided attention; and with such wonderful art does he draw our senses within his own magick circle, that every thing without it might be annihilated and the loss not be felt.[154]

Cooke had come directly from the London theatres, and the amount of byplay he used caused comment wherever he went, increasing awareness of the importance of byplay for all actors in all situations. Sometimes critics noted specific examples of Cooke's byplay, such as tapping the hilt of his sword with his left thumb, clawing with his fingers, the quivering of his lips, jaw, or "whole frame" in the throes of passion, and biting his lips.[155] Carpenter praised Cooke, but recommended that young performers use byplay sparingly, as "it is a dangerous experiment and one which, if unluckily executed, does more to detract from other excellence than any occasional success in it can do good."[156] Carpenter "begged leave to give a hint" that

to be too droll is not fair play. If by unnecessary action while other characters are speaking, they raise laughter which prevents them from being heard, they obstruct the progress of the play, and it is wrong, no matter how comical it is, or rather its being comical is the mischief of the thing.[157]

One further skill that had to be acquired by actors was a proper speaking voice. They were cautioned against speaking too slowly or too precipitately, urged to articulate strongly and distinctly, and encouraged to modulate their voices to a proper pitch yet to avoid monotony. Above all, they needed to acquire a proper tone: round and mellifluous. Poor Kenny in Boston was endowed with a voice that filled none of the requirements, and he received sardonic attention in the poetic epilogue to the Boston season of 1806:

> But zounds! what different sounds confound the ear!
> Is this indeed a human voice I hear?
> Or rusty hinge of some old creeking gate?
> Or some knife scratching on an earthen plate?
> Or Indian pappoose yell? or scolding squaw?
> Or smoking Dutchman, whetting cross-cut saw?
> Or those fam'd mousers, twin-tied by the tail,
> Which show'd where BILLINGS' musick was for sale?
> Is this the voice of that stout man of size?
> Lend me thy handkerchief to rub my eyes.
> I beg thy pardon, Muse, I had forgot it—

You're in the fashion, girl, and have no pocket.
Is this the voice of that stout reverend youth?
It seems the echo of his hollow tooth.
O KENNY, KENNY! didst thou know thy powers,
Thou'dst rival GARRICK on this stage of ours:
Play apparitions, witches, spectres, hosts,
Hobgoblins, furies, and enchanted posts,
Whose dismal screams and horrid shrieks foretel
The deadly voices come from lowest hell:
Here you *must shine*, since 'tis by all confest,
Who speaks most horrid's sure to speak the best.[158]

PROBLEMS OF PRONUNCIATION

Critics were much concerned with the pronunciations used in early American theatres. They repeatedly stressed the need for actors to serve as models of correct pronunciation for the public. Endless lists were compiled of mispronounced words, or "offenses of orthoepy," sometimes contradicting each other on the proper pronunciation. The standard reference, to which actors were repeatedly referred, was John Walker's *A Critical Pronouncing Dictionary and Expositor of the English Language,* first published in England in 1791, with the first American imprint in Philadelphia in 1803. Charles Durang said, "Walker's Dictionary, at that day, was the acknowledged guide to the stage, and was always to be found on the prompter's table at rehearsal."[159] Walker (1732–1807) was an actor turned elocution teacher, who had published his first dictionary in 1775. Walker's 1791 dictionary obviously aimed to preserve the lingual *status quo,* providing a model of "good English" rather than "good American."

From a distance of two centuries—and with no training as a linguist—it is not simple to sort out the reasons for the mispronunciation of a particular word. In general, however, these problems of pronunciation can be divided into six types. First, there was the intentional assumption of an accent deemed necessary for a particular role—Irish, Scottish, Welsh, Yorkshire, French, and "Jewish" accents were common. Although some actors were highly praised for their abilities with accents, still more were maligned. Francis Blissett's Yorkshireman "seemed to have acquired his knowledge of rustic manners and language in Somersetshire,"[160] but Mr. Entwisle was "unrivalled in Yorkshiremen, and speaks the dialect as if it were his mother tongue." The *Polyanthos* critic could not understand, however, why Mrs. Young, in character, "could not speak the Yorkshire dialect as well as her brother."[161] Actors were also faulted for lack of consistency; when Mrs. Woodham played in the opera *The Shipwreck*, "we were long before we discovered that she intended to use the Irish accent."[162] Some operas, such as *Inkle and Yarico,* required a never-never-land accent of the playwright's own invention; Inkle used a sort of baby talk with "iss" for yes, omitting connectives and most adjectives.

Second was the unintentional use of a regional accent as a part of an actor's normal speech. In Charleston, Mr. Hardinge sounded like an Irish gentleman (his forte) even when he wasn't playing one.[163] A Philadelphia critic termed Donald McKenzie's pronunciation "vicious," but added that "The Scottish accent, we conceive, may be overcome by strict attention."[164] Many actors had the dual problem of eliminating a natural accent while attempting to portray another. When two gardeners conversed in the opera *The Mountaineers*, "one of them would willingly have been thought an *Irishman*," said the critic, "but I was not to be duped in that way; I could have sworn the *blockhead* had been born in Kentucky."[165]

Third, actors frequently attempted to acquire artificial gentility through stilted, unnatural pronunciations. The drawl of the tragedian further complicated this problem. Some of these mispronunciations had become traditional—such as the pronunciation of *i* as *ee′i* when singers sang "one keeind kiss before we part." Another such pronunciation was the use of *the* for *thy*, in imitation of John Philip Kemble. This affectation could change the entire meaning of a phrase, making the listener wonder, for instance, when a tragedian said, "Thy arts have done this," whether the sciences had joined in producing the effect.[166] Carpenter complained repeatedly of the pronunciation of *true* to rhyme with *few* instead of *do*, or *rule* to rhyme with *mule* instead of *fool*.[167] *Polyanthos* quibbled, however, and held that when *u* preceded *t* or *d*, the correction pronunciation was *ew*, as in *tewtor* (not the vulgar *tootor* or Sheridan's theatrical *tschootur*).[168]

A fourth problem was unintentional mispronunciation, even of familiar words. John Hodgkinson, for example, pronounced *sigh* as *scythe*, *sacrifice* with a long *a*, and *put* to rhyme with *gun* instead of *foot;* apparently he allowed or encouraged his entire troupe to imitate him. He also added an extra syllable to some words, as in *to-ward* or *per forum*, thus "unversifying" Shakespeare.[169] He extended the common practice of substituting a *ch* for a *t* in such words as *misfortune* (which was not universally approved by the critics) to other words such as *critical*, which became *critchical*.[170]

Fifth was the occasional speech impediment that made pronunciation a problem, such as Mrs. Melmoth's inability, "from a natural deficiency of the organs of speech," to pronounce the letter *r*.[171]

Finally, tensions and snobberies were caused by the development of various regional dialects from the rich polyglot of Irish and English dialects and other languages spoken in various American communities. John Howard Payne was criticized for provincialisms like *good boy* for *goodbye* and *taown* for *town*,[172] and Mrs. Jefferson was censured for the "American" pronunciation of *man* as *mai-an*.[173] In Boston, the omission of an *r* in words like *misfochtune* could be forgiven, but adding them in words like *Uthellur (Othello)* was unacceptable.[174] When Mr. Morse, a young man from "a provincial town in Massachusetts" who had studied law at Harvard, appeared in New York in 1806, the New York correspondent for *Polyanthos* wrote that, after three weeks training with Cooper, "his pronunciation is nearly cleared of those provincialisms, which are so immediately apparent, and so offensive, to an inhabitant of the metropolis."[175]

Many mispronunciations were wittily summarized in a poem written by a young man of Boston immediately after the close of the season in 1806. He spelled the words "as they were pronounced on the boards" and provided a glossary for those unable to translate.

Love Varses to the bucheous Daffodel.

Alas! my *schweet* Daffodel's eyes
   Ave made a *greet ole* in my *art:*
With *rapchure* my *art* almost dies,
   When I see my *adjored* depart.

She's as *bucheous* as morning in May;
   No wonder to love I'm *injuc'd;*
She's the *schweetest* of *creachures* I say,
   That *nachure* has ever *projuc'd.*

Not *Harculus* boast of more force;
   Not *Dougle-as* shows more desire;
Not *Caato* more *virchus* resource;
Nor *Uthellur* e'er rag'd with more fire—

Than I for *schweet* Daffodel feel,
   When *jest* by the woodlands we meet:
She's the *emblum* of all that's genteel;
   She's *parfect* in all that is *schweet.*

I made her a *promus* of love;
   To *ajore* her was ever my *juty;*
I was *onest* and true as a dove,
For who could be false to such *beauche!*

I never my *promus* will *breek,*
Though the *whirld* should in *phalanx* [short *a*] oppose.
Her *virchue* will bind me to keep
What her *radiunt* [short *a*] eyes did impose.

My *art haches* to think on her charms,
   Lest *forchune* her aspect should *churn;*—
Was the beauche but once in my *harms,*
   She from me should never *rechurn.*

Shet out from her presence, I mope;
   The shepherd's all call me quite *schupid:*
Would *forchune* then lend me a rope,
   I'd soon bid *ajue* to *schweet* Cupid.

If I lose her I'll mount on my *orse,*
   To bid her *ajue* then inclin'd;

And to cheer my *art* under her loss,
I'll drink off a bottle of *wind*. [176]

PREPARATION AND REHEARSAL

Rehearsals were typically informal, interrupted, noisy, and poorly attended. The manager supervised the "getting up" of the play, but had
no real authority over the way actors—especially popular leading actors or stars—performed their roles. When Giles L. Barrett contracted
with William Dunlap for the 1798–99 season in New York, he said,
"I hope you will have no objection to my regulating the stage Business
of Mrs. Bs and my own, which liberty I have ever had in all the theatres
I have been in." Dunlap replied tactfully:

In regulating stage business, I shall pay just deference to your opinion, and I
think it not improbable but your knowledge may be rendered serviceable to
me . . . notwithstanding this I would wish clearly to be understood, that
while I direct the stage my opinion must be paramount to any, or all other. [177]

Rehearsals were not truly "acting" rehearsals, but simply run-
throughs to determine the evening's business. Charles Durang remembered rehearsals at the Chestnut Street Theatre in the late 1790s as
being run with great formality, but what he describes is principally a
technical rehearsal:

The stage was set—that is, the flats were in their grooves agreeably to the
requirements of the scene plot, the properties were ready for use, as called
for by the property plot, before the rehearsal commenced. The time of the
rehearsals was as promptly attended to as the ringing up of the curtain at
night. The scene-shifters were at their respective stations to answer the
prompter's whistle by changing the scenes. The property-man and stage-
clearers were at the proper entrances, with the tables and chairs, to place
them in their appropriate situations, as the business of the scene required; so
that all the details of the performances, bating the costume, were *minutely,*
we may say ceremoniously and decorously, gone through with. [178]

The performers gathered in the greenroom to await the summons of the callboy as they would at a performance, and the prompter sat at his table onstage to check and provide cues for both actors and scene-shifters, and to read the lines of those actors who did not attend the rehearsal.[179] The actors did not fully play their roles at these rehearsals, but simply got through the essential business.

Absenteeism was a serious problem. While John Hodgkinson was acting manager in New York, he complained to Dunlap "that Cooper attends no rehearsals regularly." During the benefits in June 1798 Hodgkinson left the stage, threatening not to perform again when actors missed rehearsal. As a result, an extra rehearsal was called for Sunday, to Dunlap's dismay.[180] On the other hand, John Bernard reported that Hodgkinson himself was irregular in his attendance at rehearsals: "being well-studied in every character of the 'Stock Drama,' new pieces, which were not more than two in a season, were the only chances that dragged him to a rehearsal."[181]

In spite of this seeming laxness, the demands made on the performers were heavy:

Let it, for example, be remembered, that an actor passes his hours for months together in the following routine, and it will require some ingenuity to find *time* for either idleness or dissipation. His rehearsal begins at 10 o'clock, and usually occupies till 1, or more frequently till 2 o'clock. Between this hour is his time for *study*, which in long or new parts is often most severe, and which must be constant even with short or old parts. Costume, and mechanical or personal arrangements for the stage, require much attention always; and by 7 o'clock in the evening he must be at the theatre, for the important labors of the night, frequently protracted to the very hour of morning. The hours, therefore, devoted to study are limited to a short term after rehearsal, and what can be snatched after midnight, or after rising early in the morning. I say nothing of course of those cares of a family, or of interests not professional but yet common to an actor, along with other men, nor of those which, though not connected with the *immediate* and daily or nightly duties of his profession, yet spring more or less directly from that source. How absurd then to talk of the idle life of an actor![182]

William Wood drew from a long career in outlining this schedule; in the early part of that career, the evening's entertainment would have begun earlier and ended well before midnight; the actor would usually have had several evenings a week free from acting. Many actor-singers filled some of these nights with concerts; others were occupied by rehearsals.

At Baltimore in 1782, actors were typically told following one evening's performance what would be performed on the next play night, the cast, and the time the rehearsals would be held the next day. The morning rehearsals began at ten, music rehearsals at four, and evening rehearsals at five. It was particularly difficult for actors, accustomed to a rigorous schedule of nighttime activities (with a normal winding-down period to follow), to appear promptly at morning rehearsals. The Articles[183] that governed the company took due note of this natural tendency; the rules concerning rehearsal attendance were as follows:

That when a Morning Rehearsal is Order'd, The Prompter shall at the hour of Ten, call over on the Stage, all the Performer's Names belonging to the said Rehearsal, and every absentee to be fined One Shilling.

That as soon as the Names are called over, the Prompter shall order the Rehearsal to begin and the Absentees to be fined One Shilling, for every Act.

Since an actor was expected to perform a different bill each night, including both a play and an afterpiece, and the theatres were open from three to six nights a week, it was not unusual for a troupe to play 150 different works in the course of a season. In New York, no performer could be "required to study more than four lengths [a length is forty lines] from play night to play night, and in the same proportion for a longer time."[184] William Wood reported that actors in Philadelphia were "not bound to study more than eighty-four lines of tragedy, or one hundred and sixty-eight of comedy within twenty-four hours, then acting only three or four times a week."[185] He complained, however, that with the advent of the star system, an actor was sometimes expected to learn from 300 to 500 lines in a single day while appearing in the current play.

Some actors were capable of doing much more than this minimal requirement: John Hodgkinson, for example, could

read over a new part of twenty lengths, and lay it aside until the night before he was going to play it, attending the rehearsals meantime, then sit up pretty late to *study* it, and the next morning, at rehearsal, repeat every word, and prompt others.[186]

In the 1803–4 season at Charleston, Hodgkinson played eighty-nine different roles![187]

Other actors, even highly celebrated stars, had difficulty memorizing their parts, and complaints were often voiced about lapses in memory. Thomas Apthorpe Cooper was one of the worst offenders. When Cooper played in *Pizarro* in Philadelphia early in 1801, a reviewer complained, "In a few instances we detected his attention wandering, and the occasional whisper of the prompter admonished us, not of the actor's want of genius and memory, but of his being above, or below the drudgery of application.[188] Things were even worse the following month when Cooper played in *The Grecian Daughter:* "It was mortifying, to behold Mr. Warren, following the tyrant round the stage, to supply him with words, appropriate to those forcible gestures and expressions of countenance, of which he is so complete a master."[189] Dunlap reported that in his play *Andre*, Cooper completely forgot his lines, and

after repeating "Oh Andre!—oh, Andre!" . . . [Cooper] approached the unfortunate Andre, who in vain waited for *his* cue, and falling in a burst of sorrow on his neck, cried, loud enough to be heard at the side scene, "Oh, Andre!—damn the prompter!—Oh Andre! What's next, Hodgkinson?" and sunk in unutterable sorrow on the breast of his overwhelmed friend.[190]

On another occasion Cooper was so unprepared for the part of Ford in *The Merry Wives of Windsor* that he "resorted to the artifice of slyly placing his written part on the table at which they were seated, and actually read his whole portion of the dialogue."[191] One of the singers of the Philadelphia company showed more ingenuity:

Either from bad memory or carelessness, or both, she never, by any chance, learned the words of her songs; but it was a secret she carefully concealed from the audience by writing on the palm of her kid glove the first words or more of each line. This was her invariable practice. This glove manoeuvre, however, was not always available, and her ignorance of the text frequently led her into the most ludicrous blunders. In Laura, (in the "Agreeable Surprise,") instead of saying, "Eugene's virtues have made me a proselyte," she actually substituted, unconsciously, "Eugene's virtues have made me a prostitute."[192]

Stephen Cullen Carpenter recommended that when managers failed to gain proper cooperation from the players in memorizing a new part or attending rehearsals, they should be honest with the audience and deliver the following speech:

Ladies and Gentleman, you will acquit us of the mistakes and blunders of the evening, when we tell you that we cannot get Mr. Z. or Mr. Y. or whatever the persons name may be, to get his part, or to come prepared, according to the rules of all theatres, to rehearsal. We hope too you will have the goodness to observe that in the mistakes which have happened Mr. A. or Mrs. B. have no share, having been put out, lost their cue, and confounded by the unpardonable neglect of Mr. Z. or Mr. Y.

Carpenter believed that the fear created by this speech would get far better results than politeness and indulgence.[193]

Forgetful actors sometimes received their lines from another actor; sometimes they waited for the prompter. When William Charles White joined the New York company in 1801, he received this tongue-in-cheek recommendation:

There is a certain knack in this thing of *theatrical memory*, which Mr. W. must make himself acquainted with. It consists in acquiring not so much a perfect recollection of every word so as to go on with a part without assistance, but such a kind of recollection of it as to catch up a line or a sentence by hearing the first word from the prompter. There are actors whom we have many times seen come on without knowing two sentences together, yet, speaking very slow and possessing themselves perfectly, will take up the lines from the prompter and repeat them to the house, who never suspect this, and see nothing but uncommonly bad playing.[194]

Since understudies were not provided, if an actor became ill, another actor would go on in the part, attempting to make the best of the situation. In New York Joseph Tyler "blundered" through a part assigned to Harwood "in a style ridiculous and unnatural: scarcely a word that he uttered was the word of his author, and not unfrequently was his stage companion obliged to carry on the dialogue, by speaking his part for him."[195] It was more common for substitute actors to take their lines from the prompter or read them from the book; that neither expedient was successful is shown by contradictory reviews in the *New York Magazine*. In December 1794,

owing to the indisposition of Mr. Prigmore, Mr. Richards read the part of Sir Luke Tremor. It would certainly add much to the pleasure of the audience, if those gentlemen who cannot, or will not study even the words of those characters they undertake to represent, would appear with the book in their hands. Surely it is easier to take the words from the book than from the prompter; it would cause less embarrassment, and the performer would be more at his ease.

Just two months later, when the occasion again arose to replace an ailing actor, the advice of the reviewer was followed; on February 23, 1795, the reviewer opined:

Mr. King being ill, the manager informed the house, that Mr. Fawcet would read the part of the Marquis de Montalt. This circumstance threw a damp upon the feelings of the audience. . . . the effect of the two finest scenes in the piece was lost by half the dialogue being read, (though well read).[196]

Of course, reading a part could result in ridiculous situations on stage. In New York, Mr. Twaits, who was just over five feet, stepped in for Captain Doyle, who was a foot taller; he kept his own role, as well, and doubled the parts. Like a "modern Proteus" or David and Goliath in one, Twaits tried to fool the audience by "cunningly" slipping on Doyle's gigantic surcoat whenever he played the captain's role. The *Ramblers' Magazine* critic suggested that Twaits might complete the deception if "instead of speaking through his nose," he would speak "from the bottom of his belly." [197] On another night, when an actor read for one who was ill,

It was droll enough to see Sigismunda on her knees, distractedly grasping the right hand of her father, tearfully supplicating a fair parental indulgence, and old Siffredi, holding the book in the left, with eye averted, and with a philosophy and indifference perfectly stoic, taking no notice of her, but coolly perusing the pages he had opened.[198]

When Thomas Caulfield apologized for reading a part in New York, the public accepted his excuses of illness grudgingly, since "he was observed among the choir at Trinity Church on Sunday morning, to the neglect of his professional duties." Even without the excuse of illness, opening night often found actors unprepared for a new work. A critic for *The Port Folio* was pleasantly surprised when he attended the new production of *Alexander the Great* in Philadelphia in 1801: "Although a first night's representation can scarcely be considered in any other light, than that of a last rehearsal, the business of the piece was conducted with great regularity." [199]

The situation was worse during benefits and star appearances, when the plays were "studied from one night to the next." [200] The theatre was sometimes open every night for these performances (except Sunday), an actor might have to prepare two new roles for each evening, regular company members might not be performing, the star had his or her own business, and seldom was more than a single rehearsal possible.

Due to the length of the typical evening's entertainment, many works were routinely curtailed by the manager, who would cut various scenes. Harried actors sometimes made further cuts in their own speeches; when Usher and Dickenson stepped into unfamiliar roles "at very short notice" in Boston, "much of the dialogue was of course necessarily cut out."[201] Actors often resorted to the expedient of extemporizing text when they could not remember their lines. On occasion they alternated between the poetry of the author and their own bad prose. Sometimes in the heat of the moment, they even recalled lines from the wrong play:

We recollect a performer, once the favourite of the Boston publick, who when imperfect in one part supplied the deficiency from another. Thus it became common to hear *Rover* speaking the language of *Charles Surface, Lord Hastings* addressing his mistress in that of *Lothario,* &c.[202]

They also let improper language slip into their roles. In Boston, the *Polyanthos* critic commented that "Mrs. Downie ought to have credit for so often and so elegantly introducing into the part of the housekeeper, 'a fiddlestick's end,' which the author unluckily forgot."[203] In Philadelphia, Mr. Wood,

when he tries to exhibit an extra portion of animation in his comic scenes, interlards the dialogue with a comfortable variety of *energetic* phrases, such as 'by the lord,' 'damme,' &c. It has been customary latterly for a good actor to expunge such words as are forbidden by the decalogue, instead of adding to their number; and if this were the case with us, the stage might become less obnoxious to many branches of society.[204]

One of the manager's responsibilities was to organize the business of the night's performance—to copy out the scene plot and decide where entrances were to take place. There were "customary, regular blunders in stage business."[205] Actors frequently forgot and used the wrong door, or came in where there wasn't supposed to be a door at all. In Charleston it was worth noting when the entrances were all correct—a player sometimes said "'Oh, here he comes,' looking to the left wing for some minutes without any body appearing, when behold, in popped the person supposed to be seen, on the right, taking my gentleman by surprise in the rear."[206] A New York critic observed that the fines paid by actors "for losing or forgetting black lead pencils, presented by the managers to the performers, to mark O.P. and P.S." would provide sufficient funds to decorate the outside of the theatre.[207]

Without sufficient opportunity to develop a feel for the timing of an unfamiliar play, actors could miss entrance cues, and a gap in the performance would ensue while the audience waited for them to appear:

Where were the managers during the representation of the play? There was a shameful neglect somewhere; the scene was kept waiting to an unpardonable length of time for Mr. Duff, and afterwards for Mrs. Mills. These things ought not so to be.[208]

In New York, when Fennell missed his entrance one of the performers onstage was "obliged repeatedly to *cry aloud* to the Prompter, in the hearing of the audience," to send for him.[209] At Baltimore there was a substantial fine for missed entrances: "every Performer who does not attend when regularly warned by the Call-Boy, but suffer the Stage to Stand, shall for every such Neglect forfeit Thirty Shillings."[210] There was no regular season in Baltimore in 1811 because of plans to build a new theatre. A group of players organized an impromptu performance of *The Revenge* and *Rosina* that turned out to be a disaster. *Rosina* was farcical in every sense:

I sat at one corner of the second row of boxes, and could see both before and behind the scenes!—Webster was manager, and for his exertions (fruitless as they were) to manage well, he deserves great credit. . . . One would enter at one wing, and one at another, and looking round, find that they were wrong, then *both* retiring, a sort of *interregnum* of five or six minutes would succeed. Webster, in the mean time, was behind, wringing his hands, stamping his feet, (a *manager in distress!*) and every minute or two vociferating, "Come off,"—"You're on in the wrong scene;"—and, to crown the whole, he appeared a moment afterwards in the wrong scene himself!—but shaking his head three times, and lifting up both hands, he slowly retired with all the dignity and importance, of a second BURLEIGH [in Sheridan's *Critic*].
At length, however, they made out to muster a chorus. The audience joined in the finale, . . . and the green curtain dropped amid reiterated shouts and applauses.

The critic then left the theatre, but came back at the sound of cheering to discover that Webster was onstage, trying to get the attention of the crowd to tell them that "the entertainment is not over—this is only the end of the first act—the scene shifters have made a mistake—they let down the green curtain instead of the drop—have a little patience, and you shall hear another act." The audience returned to its seats and waited to be entertained by more blunders.[211]

Actors were responsible for their own properties, and sometimes they forgot to bring them on or take them off. One night in Boston Mr. Downie reached into his pocket for a letter that was not there.[212] This problem was not unique to the States; Holcroft complained that English actors would bring a letter, hat, or sword onstage and walk off without it, so a stagehand would have to come on "in the face of the audience and take it away."[213]

Stagehands often had insufficient time or instruction to master changes, and there were long delays between scenes. In a performance of *Abaellino* at Boston in 1811, "The stage business in general was badly conducted, and much of its effect lost by unlucky mistakes in the *property man*."[214]

These thoroughly human actors, then, seem to have had just as many problems as a modern company would have, given the same pressures and limitations. All in all, they learned to do whatever was necessary to cope with the vicissitudes of stock playing. No matter what pressures and passions were entailed in preparation and presentation, the performance itself was approached with a veneer of formal professionalism. As the actors waited in the greenroom for their call to go onstage, "the perfect etiquette of the polished drawing-room was always preserved."[215]

THE ACTOR AND THE AUDIENCE

Since the design of American playhouses gave some members of the audience intimate contact with the actors onstage, and all the audience easy access to them, there was much interchange. The actors were never allowed to forget that they were supported by the indulgence of the public. The audience determined whether a new work, often mounted at great expense, would be brought forward again the next night. They stopped performances to cheer the entrances, speeches, and songs of their favorites, and were acknowledged with nods, smiles, and bows. They hissed individual performers, too, either because of real or assumed inadequacies or because of personal animosities. They demanded encores from singers during the performance, and popular tunes from the orchestra between the acts. When a performer was ill or unprepared, a new production was not ready, or a star did not arrive on time, the manager or someone else from the company had to go onstage to explain the situation, apologize, and request the public's indulgence.

Certain rules were established by the management "for the benefit of the public," and these conventions governed audience procedures at most theatres. The only reserved seats were normally in the boxes; tickets for these places could be purchased from the boxkeeper at the theatre before the performance. Even so, patrons were advised to send their servants well before the performance to save their seats. Late-comers often found that their seats had been taken, and the performance would be disrupted while the dispute was settled. Even after a performance had begun, extra persons crowded into the backs—or even the fronts—of the boxes:

the sight is intercepted and all comfort destroyed by the unmannerly and un-just conduct of intruders in the boxes and pit, who think they have a right to push in and even stand up before another who has been previously seated, provided they have bodily strength to make good their violence.[216]

Theatres periodically resorted to locking all the boxes before the per-formance, so patrons had to wait for the boxkeeper to admit them, creating additional confusion at the beginning of the evening. Though such an arrangement had been in use at the John Street Theatre in 1795, Charleston still had no box keys in 1803, and box doors stood open during performances, allowing unwanted persons to wander in and causing drafts. Carpenter recommended that the manager procure latches similar to those in London, with a handle to turn within, and one Master key for all to be kept by the Box keeper, whose duty it will be to be ready when called upon to open any particular box. The boxes too ought to be numbered and the numbers painted on the doors.[217]

Such arrangements were usually short-lived, and the same complaints about crowded boxes and lost seats were soon heard again.

When a guest star like Thomas Cooper appeared there was enormous demand for tickets. In Philadelphia, people sat all night in the portico of the theatre the night before box tickets for George Frederick Cooke's appearance went on sale, and finally forced the doors in an attempt to get seats. When benefits were held at the end of seasons, popular actors sold as many tickets as possible, apparently willing to gamble that people would be moved enough by their apology and not ask for a return of their money if there were more tickets sold than seats available.

The pit was usually used exclusively by men. St. Méry commented in 1794 that in Philadelphia, "Women go into the pit like men; but these are not women of any social standing."[218] Merchants took their wives and families into the pit on special occasions, but complained bitterly of the behavior of those around and above them. Periodic attempts were made to get "the ladies" to sit there, but usually to no avail. In Hartford in 1795 and in Charleston in 1804, part of the pit was railed off "in boxes" for "the ladies."[219] In Hartford in 1799, managers Hallam and Hodgkinson created a furor by suggesting that the pit was appropriate for "tradesmen and their wives," unintentionally implying "nice distinctions in society" that offended a portion of their audience.[220] In Philadelphia, it was reported in 1811 that

During the crowded houses of the last winter, several ladies, urged by the longings of curiosity, ventured into the pit, after finding it impossible to get seats in the boxes. For weeks afterwards, their indiscretion, or what was called, their boldness, was bandied about from tea-table to the breakfast, and from the breakfast to the tea-table, till it had completely run the rounds of scandal.[221]

There was, however, a gradual trend toward the seating of women in the pit during the nineteenth century. When the Charleston Theatre reopened on November 1, 1815, after a cessation of performances during the war, "the *first* Boxes, together with the Pit," were "appropriated to the reception of Ladies of respectability exclusively." [222]

Children also attended the theatre as part of a family or school group. Families attended performances together on special occasions and at holidays, particularly during the Christmas–New Year season, when a special pantomime with lavish scenery, costumes, and effects was often presented especially for families with children. Throughout the year, particularly lavish productions of new shows or old favorites were often advertised as being presented early in the evening for the benefit of "the juvenile members of the audience." The theatre was often referred to as a school for manners and morality; George Lillo's tragedy *George Barnwell, or the London Merchant* (1731) was given annually in most theatres for the moral education of children and apprentices, and early nineteenth-century American theatres adopted the London practice of admitting them at half-price for that night. When the Richmond Theatre burned on December 26, 1811, there were probably more children than usual because of the holiday; there were 518 dollar tickets reported sold for boxes and pit, plus eighty children. [223] Notices in bills for the 1782 Baltimore season repeatedly warned playgoers that "Children in Laps will not be admitted." This notice probably served to eliminate both crying babies and attempts to bring older children into the theatre without charge.

The galleries provided inexpensive seating for servants, sailors, boys, street urchins, and rowdies. St. Méry noted that the gallery in Philadelphia also held "women and colored people who can't sit anywhere else." [224] At Richmond black theatregoers were apparently seated in the gallery, with "No persons of colour admitted to the pit or boxes," [225] and in Charleston, "No People of Colour [were] to be admitted in any part of the House." [226] The "gallery gods" were typically noisy and unruly, and were the source of varied liquid and solid debris tossed into the pit. Unruly boys and hangers-on who were unwilling or unable to pay the price of admission even to the gallery sometimes waited outside the theatre, begging for the pass checks of departing playgoers.[227]

Somehow it had become the practice in urban theatres for women to stay home on the opening night of the season, and the theatre was generally crowded on such evenings with boisterous men:

if the most sagacious man in America were asked, why it was considered a violation of the laws of fashion for a lady to attend the theatre on the open-ing night of a season, he would be puzzled for any other reply than that it was permanently fashionable, because it was prodigiously absurd. . . . The audience presented one dark tissue of drab and brown, and black and blue woolen drapery, with here and there a solitary exception of cheering female attire.[228]

On opening nights, as each returning member of the company entered a scene for the first time, the action was interrupted by welcoming applause in proportion to his or her popularity and merit. Newcomers were welcomed, too, but with politeness and curiosity rather than en-thusiasm until their capabilities could be judged.

Theatrical proprietors offered both food and drink to their patrons for a price. At Philadelphia, there was "a store in a pretty little shop in the lobby behind the first boxes," where the refreshments "cost fifty per cent more than in the city, which is the natural result of the rental cost of the shop." The shop was one of the first places in Philadelphia to offer ice cream to the public.[229] Patrons looking for a bargain brought their own food or dashed out into the streets between the acts to buy nuts, fruit, or liquor. Food and drink could be carried into any part of the theatre for consumption during the performance.

Audiences at the turn of the nineteenth century were never known for their good behavior; no class of patrons, least of all the gallery gods, hesitated to let the actors know its desires and opinions. Public opinion was made clear not only by clapping and hissing, but by mak-ing all manner of noises, shouting, and throwing various objects onto the stage or into the orchestra pit. When Sheridan's ever-popular opera

The Duenna was presented in Philadelphia in 1806, the ears of the audience "were repeatedly exhilirated [*sic*] by the applause of the boxes; the *encore* of the pit; and the *thunders* of the gallery." A quiet audience was a high compliment to the performer, and a rarity worth comment:

It may not be amiss here to notice the style of applause, peculiar to a New-York audience. When they are diverted with comic exhibitions, or when their eyes or ears are tickled with splendid pageantry, striking attitudes, tinsel sentiments, or noisy passion (which their judgment considers appropriate) they express their approbation with their hands. But when their feelings are *deeply* interested, they hang in mute and motionless attention on every word, look, and gesture of the actor, or express their delight in confused and half suppressed murmurs.[230]

At the Southwark in Philadelphia, the *"boys of the gallery"* demanded that each man who entered the pit "*doff* his hat to those *respectable blades* in token of his *inferiority"*; if he refused to do so he became the target of apples, pears, sticks, stones, and verbal abuse. During the remainder of the evening he was the object of *"spitting* and emptying *beer bottles* on him, tho' very frequently the innocent suffer equally with the guilty."[231] Jonathan Oldstyle described similar behavior in the New York theatre as the audience waited for the play to begin:

I was much amused with the waggery and humour of the gallery, which, by-the-way, is kept in excellent order by the constables who are stationed there. The noise in this part of the house is somewhat similar to that which prevailed in Noah's ark; for we have an imitation of the whistles and yells of every kind of animal. . . . Somehow or another, the anger of the gods seemed to be aroused all of a sudden, and they commenced a discharge of apples, nuts, and gingerbread, on the heads of the honest folks in the pit, who had no possibility of retreating from this new kind of thunderbolts.[232]

The appearance of the orchestra was the signal for further disturbance:

I observed that every part of the house has its different department. The good folks of the gallery have all the trouble of ordering the music (their directions, however, are not more frequently followed than they deserve). The mode by which they issue their mandates is stamping, hissing, roaring, whistling, and when the musicians are refractory, groaning in cadence. They also have the privilege of demanding a bow from John, (by which name they designate every servant at the theatre who enters to move a table or snuff a candle), and of detecting those cunning dogs who peep from behind the curtain.[233]

In Philadelphia one night, a boy "stood up at the front corner of the gallery, roaring out and speaking as loud as he could to some one on the opposite side."[234]

The gallery did not contain all the offenders, however; those in the boxes were particularly likely to offend "from a habit of talking loud," so their neighbors suffered from "not hearing half of the play."[235] A theatregoer complained in Philadelphia in 1810 that

it was but a few nights ago, a company (of perhaps ten,) converted the boxes into a grog shop—brought jug and bottle, and glass, and tumbler into the front seats, and there caroused, laughing, talking aloud, and swearing aloud, even during the performance.[236]

One offense usually confined to the boxes was "the indecent traffic of impures" who came "not to the play, but to a market."[237] At the John Street Theatre in New York, a measure of correction was provided in 1795 when the management promised that henceforth "no persons of notorious ill-fame will be suffered to occupy any seat in a box where places are already taken."[238] When the Park Theatre opened, "No lady was admitted to the first or second tier unless accompanied by a gentleman."[239] The theatres thus followed the English custom of relegating the "impure sisterhood" to the upper tier of boxes, which were referred to as the "green boxes."[240] Critics frequently demanded banishing the "women of the town" altogether, but nothing seemed to alter the toleration of the custom.

In Boston in 1806, a man fell from the third tier of boxes into the pit; he was uninjured, but the man he landed on suffered a broken arm.[241] In 1814 two constables were stationed in the green boxes, and one in the lower part of the house, to take into custody any person making an improper noise or otherwise disturbing the peace.[242] In Philadelphia a spectator complained that

The titter of the impure, and the dull chatter of her stupid wooer, are not infrequently louder than the words of the actor. The stentorian lungs of Warren himself are no more than sufficient to drown the clack of these abominables.[243]

In New York the third tier was so "noisy and riotous" that it "bid fair soon to rival even the *gods*."[244]

These complaints and others similar were echoed repeatedly in the newspapers and magazines of the day, as well as in the writings of actors and managers. The "Journal of a Philadelphia Lounger" contains this entry, which describes the behavior of a man assumed to be a "gentleman":

Half past six. Went up Chestnut-street. People going into the theatre—went in myself—peeped into the lower front boxes—scarce a soul that I knew in the house.—Went up stairs.—One of Shakspear's plays performing—cursed heavy things, so did not go into a box.—No fun going forward—nobody drunk, and every one attending to the play.—Practised new steps in walking the lobby—new pair of boots on—creaked famously—some queer fellow called out silence.—Never minded him, but walked on. . . .

Seven.—Went to the bar and took a glass of punch—lighted a segar, fumigated the lobby a little, and then walked down stairs—warmed myself at the stove—box-keeper came up, and begged me not to smoke—damned his impertinence—fellow was savage—said his orders were peremptory—smoked on—fellow talked of going for a constable, and went out—segar was finished, so I went out too.—N.B. There's no dealing with savages.[245]

If those of the "higher orders" behaved so, it is not surprising that behavior in the gallery was intolerable. One patron in 1794 wrote concerning the gallery of the Southwark Theatre at Philadelphia in a long letter to the managers, Hallam and Hodgkinson:

> I was not displeased last evening to find these *Bucks* and *Bloods* had carried their excesses to so great a height as to drive the greater part of the band from the orchestra and break some of the instruments, since it must have opened your eyes to the abominable and shameful deprivation of those rights which every person ought to enjoy who pays his entrance here.[246]

Managers (and in Boston, the master of ceremonies) did try to control audience behavior: in addition to the constables stationed in the gallery, they offered a $50 reward for the discovery of a person who threw a bottle into the orchestra;[247] they prohibited the use of liquor in the house until the end of the first piece;[248] and they frequently appealed to patrons to modify their behavior in various ways, such as the elimination of cigar smoking and large hats, which today seem like modest requests for common courtesy. One of the factors that led to problems was the need to attract people from all walks of life in order to fill the theatre and balance the books; at the same time managers strove to produce entertainment that would satisfy the increasingly discriminating critics.

Actors reciprocated the audience's attentions with an easy informality. They often addressed the audience directly, or inserted improvised lines in the drama in answer to the situation of the moment. They responded with gratitude to applause and with indignation to hisses. Sometimes they solicited applause by waiting for an encore or by holding an attitude until the audience responded. The critics took note of Giles Barrett's "old habit of hanging on the wing, and supplicating an *encore* with a piteous look."[249]

When John Hodgkinson arrived at the theatre late in 1793, he was hissed at his first entrance. "Putting on an air of authority, Hodgkinson demanded the cause of the dissatisfaction, and he then went on to tell how Mrs. Hodgkinson had been insulted on the way to the theatre, and how he had beaten the ruffian."[250]

If Hodgkinson sometimes offended his audience while seeking to placate them, Thomas Cleveland developed his public relations to a high art. William Clapp related the manner in which Cleveland addressed his audience while acting with the Boston company in the 1795 season:

He was the apologist of the theatre. If an actor was sick, no one could state to the public the substitution of another with so much grace; if a play was not ready on the night announced, no one could lay the case before the audience with such a certainty of having the piece proposed in its place so warmly applauded—in fact, he had a peculiar knack for making apologies, and rarely did he retire from the execution of this, to him agreeable task, without receiving a round of applause. On one evening he was performing "Romeo." The play had reached the fifth act, and the noble Montague lay dead, the fair Juliet weeping over him. At this point the Old South bell began to toll out alarming peals, and with such vehemence did the bell-puller do his work, that the audience began to fear that even the theatre was in flames, and movement occurred in the dress circle. Poor Cleveland, dead as Romeo, but still alive as the Apologist, could not resist the ruling passion. He immediately, in the midst of Juliet's lamentations, sat up and said: *"Ladies and Gentlemen, I beg you not to be alarmed. It is only the Old South bell, I assure you,"* and before the fair Capulet had time to recover from her astonishment, Romeo again lay dead before her.[251]

Occasionally the actors responded to the impositions of the audience in kind. On one occasion, another Romeo managed to give the audience exactly what it asked for in a way that must have been gratifying to his fellow victims on the stage. It was a story actors must have loved to tell, and it probably grew in the telling. John Bernard says it took place "somewhere in Virginia, some years ago." At the conclusion of *Romeo and Juliet,* the audience set up a howl for a national song that had been announced as the conclusion of the evening's entertainment:

Obedient to their summons Romeo forthwith ran forward and bowed, to the great surprise and severe disappointment of the damsels, at least, who had given him credit for being really dead, but whose smiling appearance gave proof that his ten minutes' nap on the floor had rather tended to the invigoration of his faculties than their dissolution. The band striking up briskly with the tune, he began his ditty, sang twenty verses through without stopping (repeating every second verse again), then drawing his breath went on for another fifteen, but with rather less spirit; halted again to take in a fresh atmospheric supply, then, but with difficulty, added another ten, making in all forty-five. Here he appeared perfectly exhausted, in memory as well as windpipe, and it was only after making two or three pantomimical gesticulations that he found sufficient air in his bellows (as Voltaire vulgarly calls it) and sufficient words in his cranium to acquaint the audience that that was all he knew of the song, but that if they would like to have any more, his wife (the dead Juliet behind the scenes) would come on with pleasure and favor them with seventy-three verses more.

This information had an electrical effect upon the whole body spectatorial. Love of country and love of song alike fled before it. If a dead lover could get through forty-five verses with so much spirit, thought they, a resuscitated woman with seventy-three more was beyond what mortal patience could endure. Romeo could not have given them a better hint to *"avaunt,"* for, hardly staying to say, "No, thank you," they clapped their hats on their heads and their damsels under their arms, and departed from the room with the utmost expedition.[252]

To some extent theatrical attendance depended on quality, but bad weather, other scheduled activities, and various public caprices could result in skimpy audiences. Attendance also tended to fall off at the ends of seasons and after the departure of guest performers. Managers tried various novelties—elaborate pantomimes, ballets, tumblers, revivals of old favorites, even live elephants or horses—to regain their audiences. Regular play nights were Monday, Wednesday, and Friday in most cities, and a change of date could also shrink the crowd. When the play *The Wonder* and the farce *Raising the Wind* were performed in New York in 1809, it "was a Saturday night's performance, attended by a Saturday night's audience. If it *raised the wind,* it certainly was a *wonder.*"[253]

Even a good house got smaller after the main work of the evening, since many patrons departed without waiting for the afterpiece, particularly if the first piece were long. In Boston, John Duff "walked through the three Singles" in the opera *Three and the Deuce* "with as little *concernment,* as he would put on his night-cap; and in truth we cannot reprove him for his carelessness" since the entire audience consisted of "some dozen or twenty boys in the pit and as many holders of season tickets in the boxes."[254]

Managers and individual performers had to walk a careful line to avoid being associated with one side or another in the vituperative political battles waged in every city. When Anne Julia Hatton's opera *Tammany* was performed in New York in 1794, Mrs. Melmoth "refused to speak the *Epilogue . . .* because of the *patriotic* sentiments contained in it!!!" A correspondent to the *New-York Journal and Patriotic Register* hoped that when she performed next she would be "*convinced,* by the *absence* of republicans when she appears, that *the people* resent her impertinence." He continued, "I think that she ought not to be suffered to go on the New-York stage again."[255]

With the example of the Boston season of 1796–97 before them, managers were well aware that political associations could destroy their profits. Still reeling that season from the fight with the antitheatre laws and the $40,000 expense of constructing the theatre, the proprietors of the Federal Street Theatre had faced competition from the new Haymarket Theatre. Somehow the Federal Street Theatre became involved in the controversy between the Jacobin or Republican cause and the Federalists, further reducing its audience. Both companies lost money on the season, and the Federal Street proprietors lost more than $15,000.

No matter how dangerous politics could be, patriotism would never be taken amiss by the audience. A performance was sometimes interrupted for announcements of events of great public interest. The frigate *Constitution* sailed out of Boston, and her activities were of great interest to the populace, particularly after she captured and destroyed the British frigate *Guerriere* on August 20, 1812. On October 2 "Constitution and Guerriere" was performed as a new afterpiece; it was popular enough to be repeated on the 5th and the 9th.[256]

The *Constitution,* commanded by Commodore Bainbridge, captured and destroyed the British frigate *Java* on December 29, 1812.

The news reached Boston on February 15, and the play was stopped in the midst of the second act to announce the victory, which brought "reiterated shouts from the audience." On the 24th, as the interlude between the play and afterpiece,

a naval spectacle was exhibited, in honor of the anniversary of the birth of GENERAL WASHINGTON, and of the late brilliant naval victory of Commodore Bainbridge. At the close of the spectacle, Mr. Spiller introduced a song, called *Yankee Chronology*, being a recapitulation of some of the leading events during our revolutionary and present war.[257]

When a military review was held in Boston on October 14, 1813, an extra performance was given at the theatre, with several officers in full uniform in attendance:

The audience, which was numerous and fashionable, testified their satisfaction by repeated plaudits on Mrs. Power's recitation of "The Standard of Liberty" and Mr. M'Farland's song, "Arouse, arouse, Columbia's sons, arouse."[258]

All over the States similar observances were held; patriotic songs were among the most popular interlude pieces throughout the year.

Theatre audiences at the turn of the nineteenth century may be said, then, to have had—in addition to the attentive anticipation of a theatrical audience today—the energy, enthusiasm, boisterousness, and patriotism of a crowd at a modern baseball game, the lawlessness and apathy found at a punk rock concert, and the high expectations and discrimination of a symphony or opera audience. Theatre was truly the entertainment of the early American masses.

8

THE SINGER AND THE SONG

Singers were often the most popular performers in the day-to-day operation of early American theatre. Though tragedians were theoretically at the top of the hierarchy, actors who could respond to the insatiable thirst of the audience for the popular songs of the day, who could sing them "in character," and who had mastered the vocal techniques of tone, enunciation, and ornamentation were virtually assured a hearty welcome and a profitable benefit.

THE ACTOR AS SINGER

It was taken for granted that every English or American theatrical company would include musical entertainments in its repertory, and that its actors could perform them. Though it was certainly the goal of theatrical companies to make all actors singers and all singers actors, the reality was not always so convenient. In the English theatre, George Hogarth complained: "It has been all along an impediment to the improvement of our English opera, that our singers have not been actors, nor our actors singers. . . . Our vocalists, however, are improving as actors."[1] Most actors specialized in a particular line of acting, and singers were often hired particularly for the opera productions. Many tragedians took no operatic roles; other actors could sing only a little. Most singers could act a bit, but not always well enough to carry a major acting role.

There were outraged cries from the critics when there were not enough singers in the company to present an opera respectably. During the 1805–6 season in Philadelphia there were continual complaints, and the *Theatrical Censor's* critic begged: "In the name of Harmony let them procure a good female singer!"[2] So desperate was the situation that the role of Zamora in *The Honey Moon* was assigned to Mrs. Dykes, who could not sing at all. The critic protested: "Why was not *Zamora* cast for a lady that sings? The *reading* of a song, when the audience have been accustomed to hear it *sung,* is not satisfactory."[3]

At Boston in 1811, Mr. Lindsley omitted the songs entirely when he played the role of Count Calmar in *The Exile:*

"The gale of Love," set to a delightful air by Mazzinghi, which ought to be sung by the *Count,* is omitted for want of a suitable representative. Is it not passing strange that the managers have not an actor in their company, that can play the genteel lover in an opera? Seeing there [*sic*] parts filled by Mr. Lindsley, makes us regret the absence of *little* Vining, who if he could not *speak,* could *sing;* and a man who possesses one of those qualifications is certainly preferable to him who has neither.[4]

The Comet's critic was subsequently taken to task in a letter from "Leander," who felt that "if the songs are omitted, which was done because Mr. L. is no singer—[it was] not his fault but nature's."[5]

Opera may have ranked below tragedy and comedy in the theatrical hierarchy, but the importance of music in all genres remained critical: "Music furnishes more than half the charms of the drama; and where *sense* is so often violated, we should at least be compensated by *sound.*"[6] Singing ability alone could not compensate for lack of dramatic talent, however, and singers were as frequently criticized for their thespian shortcomings as actors were criticized for their vocal flaws. In Philadelphia the *Theatrical Censor*'s critic noted that "Mr. Woodham is the most scientific singer on the American boards; but, like the generality of good singers, he is a very indifferent actor."[7]

This natural disparity between acting and singing was reflected in the parts written for specific performers in opera. Not only was the style and ability of the singer reflected in the music, but there were also cases where the principal singing parts and principal acting parts were not the same:

One point emerges from an examination of *The Duenna:* the principal singing parts in this opera (Don Carlos and Donna Clara) are the least important from the dramatic point of view. These were performed by professional singers, while the other main characters were represented by actors and actresses, who were not professed vocalists. This divorce between singers and actors became symptomatic of the English opera stage at the end of the eighteenth and the beginning of the nineteenth centuries.[8]

The difference in the roles in *Children in the Wood* has been discussed in chapter 3. The role of the chambermaid, Josephine, was written for a vocalist, and she sings two of the six solo songs and both duets, as well as the most complex music in the work. Both children's roles were written to display the abilities of young prodigies, and each sings challenging music (the girl an aria, the boy a duet with Josephine). The role of the tutor and general factotum, Apathy, is relatively minor except for his comic duet with Josephine, while the servant hero, Walter, plays a major role but sings only one comic song; both of these parts could be played by a character actor who could, in modern jargon, "put across" a song. Each of the parents sing one characteristic song at their entrance.

Most operas had roles that included no music at all. Sir Rowland, the servant Winifred, and various ruffians in *Children in the Wood* do not sing, for example, and Blue Beard in Michael Kelly's opera sings only a little. Of course actors adapted roles to their own abilities, adding, substituting, and eliminating songs as desired.

In American theatres, the actor who could play a variety of roles and sing effectively evoked considerable comment. John Hodgkinson was praised as "a very useful general actor" who even as a youth "played any thing and every thing the managers thought it their interest to appoint him to, whether tragedy, comedy, opera, or farce." [9] He was considered "at once a great actor and a great singer; so that if, of the three departments of tragedy, comedy, and opera, he had been restricted from performing in any two, he would have been greatly eminent in the third." [10]

When Hodgkinson performed the title role in the masque *Comus* on April 22, 1805, "with all the original Songs," recent immigrant Stephen Cullen Carpenter was amazed that the part could be sung and spoken by the same person:

The union of singer and excellent speaker is so little found, that the same man has never, that we know of, spoke the speeches and sung the songs of COMUS. Quin, Sheridan, Mossop, Henderson, Cooke and Kemble, and, in a word, all the first speakers of the stage, have played the character, but the songs have been given to *mere* singers. *Hodgkinson* alone does both—and we have great doubts whether COMUS has altogether been ever so well performed in Europe as it will be this evening in Charleston. [11]

Though Carpenter was surprised to see the role performed thus, it had been done so in the United States for at least a decade. On September 9, 1805, Mr. Marshall had performed the role of Comus *"with the songs,"* according to the playbill, while acting with the Wignell-Reinagle Company at Baltimore. [12]

Such versatility was rare, however, and many a "company of respectability" found itself without enough actor-singers. In 1810, five years after the death of Hodgkinson, Joseph Tyler was reported to be "the only man in the [Old American] company, with the exception of Mr. Twaits, capable of singing." Mrs. Oldmixon (then twenty-seven years past her London debut) was "the only female singer among us!" [13] The situation in Philadelphia and Baltimore was perhaps a little better; it was reported from Baltimore in the same year that "Although our dramatis personae do not afford much strength as to their vocal abilities; some of [them] . . . form a group sufficient to render a musical piece very entertaining." [14]

When roles requiring solo singing were filled from the ranks of the chorus, it became necessary to find choral substitutes. As a result, property men, scene painters, and other supernumeraries reportedly swelled the ranks of the vocalists. Vocal training, costuming, and staging for the chorus were often haphazard, and clearly not considered a high priority. Choral finales were often written—and apparently frequently performed—in unison. Minimal ornamentation was probably used by choruses, although ensemble singers were probably accustomed to adding an occasional appoggiatura in the melody part. [15]

Trille LaBarre served not only as leader of the band during the Boston season of 1796–97, but also undertook the training of the ensembles and the chorus, with notable effect.

The attention and industry of Mons. LABARRE in perfecting the supernumerary vocal performers in their respective chorusses, also deserve much credit.—It has heretofore been invariably the attendant fatality of all operas, produced on our stage, that from the inability of the performers, either in the *science* or *number,* to execute compound music, they never have supported with success a musical dialogue, in which more than three voices were concerned. This imputation, however, was entirely removed by the performance of [*Richard Coeur de Lion* on] Monday evening; for the chorusses, with which the Opera abounds, and all of them difficult and intricate music, were fitted throughout with an ample power of voice, and given with a pleasing accuracy of execution. [16]

In keeping with the idea of "plays with music added," the music of an opera or play was normally rehearsed separately from the stage business. At Baltimore in 1782, stage rehearsals were at 10 A.M. or 5 P.M. daily, with a separate musical rehearsal at 4 P.M. Apparently attendance at these rehearsals was a problem; the Baltimore "Articles to be strictly observ'd" includes this rule: "That Notice shall be given to every Performer concern'd in Musical Rehearsals, the Day before, and should they not attend at the hour appointed, they shall be fined One

Shilling for every Ten Minute's Absence." When John Hodgkinson indicated to William Dunlap that he no longer wished to be involved in the management of the New York company, Dunlap offered him a contract for 1798–99 (declined by Hodgkinson) in which his only responsibility other than acting would be to supervise the music department—presumably to supervise rehearsals with singers and orchestra as well as to oversee the band.[17]

Two problems common to singers everywhere—intonation and enunciation—were especially bothersome to actors with minimal musical training. In Philadelphia Mrs. Seymour sang frequently, and just as frequently the critics protested: "Mrs. Seymour, with the usual exception (out of tune), was spirited and pleasant." [18] The same critic complained, "DON JUAN this evening was a very flat exhibition. The delightful duet, "Thus for Men the Women fair," &c. was sung in all the sublimity of discord." [19] At Boston in 1811 *The Comet*'s critic wrote that "Mrs. Mills's voice is not unpleasant, if she would contrive to get it in *unison* with Mr. Hewitt's violin instead of running parallel to it at the distance of a *semitone* above." [20]

Various references to modifications of intonation occur in the literature. It was a standard rule to treat ascending naturals as sharps and descending naturals as flats. A treatise on singing by Giacomo Ferrari (1818), in a section dealing with intonation, said:

> It will also be a proof of taste and judgement to strengthen the voice on notes elevated by an accidental sharp, and to soften it on those which are depressed by a flat. The natural ought to be reinforced when it elevates a flat note [thus acting as a sharp], and mollified when it depresses a sharp one.[21]

Though Ferrari uses the terminology of dynamics, it can be assumed that he is referring to the traditional practice of string players and vocalists of making sharps sharper and flats flatter.

One well-known American singer at the turn of the century was Miss Broadhurst; the *Euterpeiad* remembered in 1822 that her intonation was "correct, rather inclining to sharp without being positively so, a quality said by some late critics to give great brilliancy of effect."[22] Miss Brent, on the other hand, seemed to possess the art "of flattening those notes, which upon the voice and every natural instrument, as the trumpet and horn, are naturally too sharp."[23]

An amateur performer at the Boston Theatre in 1813 was advised "to endeavor to attain to a clear and distinct articulation, an accomplishment above all things desirable in a vocal performer."[24] When Miss Dellinger of New York, a pupil of James Hewitt, appeared in Boston in 1811, she received advice from another critic about her enunciation:

when we say that the *ear* is pleased with her performance, but that the *intellect* has no share in the enjoyment, it is believed that we do but echo the general sentiment. She certainly has a fine voice, and we doubt not her scientifick knowledge of musick, but the mind receives no more gratification from her performance, than if the same sounds were produced from a *hand organ*. It is the sentiment of the poet that must be heard, to give intellectual pleasure, and until she can give distinct utterance to *that*, as well as the notes of the composer, her exertions are fruitless.[25]

Singers followed the conventions practiced by all actors, including the custom of facing forward and speaking or singing to the audience, regardless of its effect on the credibility of the drama. A Boston critic complained that if Mrs. Hodgkinson "has *any* fault (and the Sun itself has spots) it is the operatical error of addressing the audience, even in speeches where the second personal pronoun is used."[26] The "operatical error" of facing the audience (and the footlights) and singing as in a concert was still prevalent in the 1790s; no fewer than three of the nine vocal numbers (including the finale) in the London score of *Children in the Wood*[27] are clearly addressed to no one but the audience, and most of the others were probably performed in this manner as well.

The point at which the actor or actress dropped out of character and faced forward was the introduction to a song:

In modern *opera* the Song is announced by some studied phrase which drops from the lips of the performers, and which is well understood to be preparatory to the exercise of the lungs. The Orchestra then opens upon us, and the singer in dumb suspense, awaits the termination of the symphony. This interval is on every occasion a *mighty melancholy* one. From the sadness into which the visage of the performer settles, the moment that he has uttered the preparatory sentence, one would suppose it had been his *sentence of death;* and from the doleful manner in which he paces the stage, during the interval of the symphony one would imagine he was listening to his *requiem.* In an instant the Hoyden of sixteen, has become the heartbroken widow of thirty; and the careless spark, assumes a visage and deportment, like that which immortalized the *"Knight of the rueful countenance."* For this departure from the uniform personation of character, we can see no plausible excuse; and perhaps the *apparently dreaded* interval, which is to introduce us to *"Dorothy Dump,"* or *"Amo Amas"* would be better filled up by an easy deportment on the part of the performer than by the long-visaged sadness, which would seem to predict nothing less, than the *torture* of *lungs and ears.* [28]

When Ellen Westray Darley sang the role of Rosamunda in *Abaellino* at the Boston Theatre in 1806, she simply faced forward and folded her hands, bringing a poetic reaction from the *Polyanthos* critic:

> With folded hands see Rosamunda stands:
> Ah me! how pretty are her folded hands!
> Enchanting attitude, which Nature draws—
> Pit, boxes, gallery, bellow out applause.
> With varied voice, which can all hearts control,
> With various movements to entrap the soul,
> With air, face, person, shape and blooming age,
> With powers to grace with novelty the stage,
> Do not, lov'd actress, while each heart expands,
> Forever bore us with your folded hands.
> But if this gentle hint won't make you screen 'em,
> Oh, take the gentle poet in between 'em. [29]

There was considerable movement on the stage during dialogue and between speeches, so this "operatical error" was perhaps in part due to the fact that operas were still considered "plays with music added." The "play" literally stopped when the music was added and began again when it was concluded. At the turn of the nineteenth century, as the music assumed greater importance in carrying forward the action and became more essential to the plot, so too did actors tend to stay in character while singing, and even to include movement in their musical numbers. Stage action during musical sequences was introduced to London by Nancy Storace and Michael Kelly after their return from Vienna in the 1790s:

> The foreign habits of these accomplished singers enabled them to sing steadily while moving about the stage (a difficulty of no mean rank) and infused a life, and a bustle into our opera, which before had hardly trusted itself with action.[30]

In Philadelphia in 1809, the songs of Maria in *Of Age To-morrow* were "given with considerable effect, much force, and characteristick gesture," which was met with "universal approbation."[31] In "The Ditty" in *Children in the Wood*, Josephine's ballad of a "murdered babe" includes references to "knocking at the window" and the ghost which "bursts ope the door." These lines not only elicit spoken response from the other characters at the ends of verses, but also demand byplay from those characters during the song.

The texts of ensembles—duets, trios, and larger—began to prescribe specific action as well. In the duet "Great Sir, Consider" in *Children in the Wood*, Apathy follows his master around in an effort to obtain his dinner order, while Sir Rowland silently pursues the chambermaid Josephine with lecherous intent, and she vocally and with "characteristick gesture" defends her honor. None of the staging for this number is spelled out in the score or libretto, but it is so strongly implied that it is difficult to imagine any troupe performing the duet without it. The turret scene in *Blue Beard*, too, demands action from all the participants. It was originally performed on an elaborate three-level set, with sister Irene in the tower watching for the Spahis to ride to the rescue, Fatima locked into her room but visible on the balcony, and a servant in the garden below. Action must have been added when Fatima cried "Look out again!" or responded to Blue Beard's cry of "Beware" with "Succour or my existence ends!" When Irene sang "I see them gallopping!" at the first London performance, "She gave it such irresistible force of expression, as to call from the audience loud and continued shouts of applause."[32]

In 1802 the chorus in the New York theatre still "arranged themselves very orderly on each side of the stage, and sung something, doubtless very affecting, for they all looked pitiful enough."[33] It was increasingly less acceptable, however, for a chorus of supernumeraries to sing without appropriate movement, facial expression, and characterization.

One additional demand on singers who were predominantly actors resulted in misuse of the voice. Like all actors, singers were expected to follow the tradition of going onstage despite illness and fatigue. Frequently actors sang major roles in an afterpiece after speaking strenuous roles in the evening's principal work. Reviews sometimes refer to actors performing while hoarse, and occasionally mention singers who had omitted their songs because of hoarseness but who continued to play the speaking portion of the role. The *Charleston Courier* reported on March 27, 1804, that "Hodgkinson was so hoarse that he got with difficulty through his part in the play. It became necessary therefore, to substitute West in his place in the character of Patrick" in the afterpiece, *The Poor Soldier.* On April 5, the *Courier* reported that Hodgkinson "laboured under such a depression of spirits from indisposition, and still retained so much of his hoarseness, that he was not himself."[34] Singers apparently sang out of their proper range on occasion because of the need to fill a part on short notice. In Philadelphia in 1806, for example, in *The Farmer,* "The song of 'Bonny Bet' was evidently pitched too high for Mr. Woodham, who felt uncomfortable under it."[35]

When all went well, the audience showed its appreciation for a song with "unbounded applause," and the singer frequently responded by repeating it (demonstrating once again that the play was simply a vehicle for the songs and could wait as long as necessary before resuming). When Mr. Hardinge appeared at Philadelphia in 1810 for the first time in four years in *The Review; or Wags of Windsor*, "His return to this stage was hailed with thunders of applause; and all his songs were *encored*."[36] In Boston Mr. M'Farland was particularly successful in his 1813 debut as an actor, and all three of his songs were encored.[37] At Charleston Hodgkinson sang "a very curious song. It is needless to remark that he sung it to full effect. As usual he was encored. And had it not been that it would have been unreasonable to expect a second repetition it would have been encored again."[38] When John Durang's older sister Catherine sang in the play *The Roman Father*, her song was encored one night, and "She was obliged to sing three times before the house could be passive reconciled."[39] This may seem an excessive demand for encores, but the performers may not have required much encouragement. In Boston *Polyanthos* reprinted Jonathan Swift's *Directions to Players*, which includes the instruction:

After you've very indifferently sung a very indifferent song, do not quit the side scenes; but if, amidst a hundred hisses, you hear a little boy in the gallery cry *encore*, come on and sing it again. That's the *sense* of the house. Nothing like respect.[40]

THE VOCAL INSTRUMENT

A great deal was written about the voices of the singers in English and American theatres. Often, however, these observations are of a very general nature, and detailed descriptions of tone and vocal production are rare.

One area with plenty of available data is the range of the various voices. The great majority of arias for women lie in the soprano range. The majority of arias for men—especially those written for singers as opposed to actors—appear to be for tenors, because of the abundant high notes; the predominant use of falsetto by all male singers obscures this apparent distinction in range, however. In 1825 Thomas Busby placed the ranges of English singers as shown in Table 2.[41]

During the latter part of the eighteenth century, soprano range rose

Table 2   Thomas Busby's Ranges of English Singers, 1825

Treble	$c'-c'''$
Mezzo	$b-a''$
Counter Tenor	$f-g''$
Tenor	$d-b'$
Tenor Bass	$B-a'$
Bass	$F-f'$

The Helmholtz method of pitch classification is used: c' indicates middle C, c the octave below, C two octaves below, C' three octaves below, c'' the octave above, c''' two octaves above, and so on. Notes upward within an octave are given the same designation.

steadily higher, reaching a high of about a''' in the early nineteenth century. The *Euterpeiad* reported that Miss Broadhurst had a range from "B below the staff, to C in alto," $(b-c''')$[42] and that Mrs. Old-mixon's range was "of uncommon extent, being from B below the staff, to A in altissimo" $(b-a''')$.[43] William Parke reported that Miss George (later Mrs. Oldmixon) "sang up to B in alto $[b''']$ perfectly clear, and in tune; this being three notes higher than any singer I ever heard."[44] Mrs. Oldmixon's English rival, Elizabeth Billington, encompassed three full octaves—"from A to A in altissimo" $(a-a''')$.[45] In arias, Mary Ann Wrighten (Pownall) sang to d''' in the 1770s, and Mrs. Billington and Anna Maria Crouch to f''' or g'''.

Arias were almost never written higher than e''' or f''', and they reached that height only when composed for specific, highly trained singers. Sopranos probably showed off their highest notes in their cadenzas. It should also be noted that concert pitch in 1800 was up to a semitone lower than it is today.

As late as 1825, the term "countertenor" was used to describe the contralto range. Very few contralto parts are found in early English or American opera, and not many more for baritones. Tenor range often extended into the countertenor range, since the use of falsetto for high notes was accepted throughout the eighteenth century. Male contraltos, even in falsetto, were frowned on by late in the century, however, because of their association with the castrati, and writers became in-

creasingly critical about the uses of falsetto early in the nineteenth
century.

In the late eighteenth century, however, both tenors and baritones
ordinarily sang their high notes in falsetto, switching at about d′ or e′;
tenors could sometimes go an octave higher. James Nares, in his *Treatise on Singing* (1785), writes that the singing master should make the
student

acquainted with the Compass of his Voice, shewing him where his Voce di
petto [chest voice] ends, and where to cultivate the falsetto, or Voce di Testa
[head voice], and instruct him how they should be joined, so as to be imperceptible, without which the pleasing Variety will be lost.[46]

The great English tenors at the turn of the century were Charles Incledon, John Johnstone, Michael Kelly, and John Braham. Incledon
(1763–1826) was engaged at Covent Garden in 1790; he made his
American debut at New York in 1817. *The Musical Quarterly* reported in 1818 that

he had a voice of uncommon power, both in the natural and the falsetto. The
former was from A to G [A–g′], a compass of about fourteen notes; the latter he could use from D to E or F [d′–e″ or f″] or about ten notes. . . . His
falsetto was rich, sweet and brilliant, but totally unlike the other. He took it
without preparation, according to circumstances, either about D, E, or F, or
ascending an octave, which was his most frequent custom.[47]

When Franz Joseph Haydn heard Shield's *The Woodman* performed
at Covent Garden in 1791, he wrote in his diary:

The first tenor [Incledon] has a good voice and a fairly good style, but he
uses the falsetto to excess. He sang a trill on high C and ran up to G. The
second tenor tried to imitate him but could not make the change from the
natural voice to the falsetto; besides he is very unmusical.[48]

In spite of a generally favorable reception, Incledon's use of falsetto
was considered excessive in the States, too. When he made his debut,
the New York *Post* reported that he had a

mellow, full-toned voice, of great compass, under the guidance of much taste and science. But it was soon evident, that . . . the more sweet and delicate touches . . . were almost lost to the audience. . . . But his greatest and his most successful effort was in Stevens . . . *The Storm.* Mr. Incledon immediately by his manner and the tones of his powerful voice, made the most forcible impression on every part of the house. But, with great deference . . . we would beg permission to 'hesitate dislike' to the trill and falsetto which he introduced into a song meant to be descriptive of the utmost distress and despair.[49]

The second tenor referred to by Haydn was John Johnstone (1759–1828), who sang at Covent Garden from 1783 until the end of the century. *The Euterpeiad* provides further information on his singing:

At Covent Garden, Johnstone was a principal tenor singer—a very sweet falsetto; in tone resembling a flute, of which he made ample use, and all his songs composed purposely for him, were written with high notes. He was, probably the first who introduced falsetto embellishments, which have been so liberally followed up by a host of imitators. His natural voice was harsh, and formed an unpleasant contrast to his falsetto. Instead of blending he frequently came with a kind of crack from the falsetto to his natural tone, which induced Anthony Pasquin in his Poem of the children of Thespis to say,

> "One half's Robinelli, the other Paddy Whack."[50]

The Irishman Michael Kelly (1762–1826) studied in Italy and (sometimes as "Ochelly") sang extensively there, in Vienna, and in other parts of Europe, before signing on at Drury Lane in 1787. He created the part of Don Basilio in Mozart's *Le Nozze di Figaro.* According to Roger Fiske, "His vocal quality was unremarkable, but he had style, and he was the first playhouse tenor who never sang falsetto."[51] He was able to sing to a' with full voice, even leaping up a fifth to reach it. Boaden described Kelly in his *Life of Kemble:* "His compass was extraordinary. In vigorous passages he never cheated the ear with feeble wailings of falsetto, but sprung upon the ascending fifth with a sustained energy that electrified the audience."[52]

John Braham (1774–1856) made a triumphant London debut at

Drury Lane in 1796, then sang in Europe for five years before returning to London. Leigh Hunt criticized him for "that nasal tone which has been observed in Jews . . . and in Americans,"[53] but *The Musical Quarterly* reported in 1818 that he was

gifted with the most extraordinary genius and aptitude for the exercise of his profession that was ever implanted in a human being. . . . The whole compass of Mr. Braham's voice is 19 notes, and if not all of equal strength, they yet differ so little in power perceptibly to the auditor, that it seems as if the singer could at pleasure produce any given quantity of tone from pianissimo to fortissimo upon any one of them. Mr. Braham can take his falsetto upon any note from D to A at pleasure and the juncture is so nicely managed that in an experiment to which this gentleman had the kindness to submit, of ascending and descending by semitones, it was impossible to distinguish at what point he substituted the falsetto for the natural tone.[54]

Braham came to the United States in 1840, at the age of sixty-eight, and toured for two years, singing in concerts and opera.

Baritones (called "tenor basses" by Busby) were normally called basses in contemporary sources and thus not distinguished from them. These lower voices also cultivated the falsetto range. John Bannister (1760–1836) made his debut at the Little Theatre in 1778 as an actor; after 1783 he turned increasingly to operatic roles at both the Little Theatre and Drury Lane. Parke reported that he "never sang out of time or out of tune, but did not know one note of music;"[55] he learned all his parts by rote. *The Thespian Dictionary* reported that "His voice united in extraordinary perfection the extremes of deep bass and high-toned falsetto."[56] In the States, John Darley (ca. 1775–1853) was said to rank "high in the first class of vocal performers, uniting science with power, flexibility, and sweetness of tone, and perhaps surpassing in the 'feigned voice' every other musical competitor now in this country."[57]

Some of the elements of vocal tone produced by these singers may be inferred from such comments. Others may be deduced from the writings of contemporary teachers of singers. James Nares emphasized the importance of a relaxed and open throat to gain the flexibility needed for ornamentation and figuration (divisions). Nares warned that the head should be held up, with the neck stretched rather than bent forward:

Division depends entirely on the flexibility of the Throat, which being composed of many Annular and Muscular parts that have great power of dilation and Contraction, whoever would practice this with success, must seperate [sic] those little rings one from another by such a position of the Head, that the Throat may receive the Pulsation necessary in Division, with the greatest ease.[58]

Experts in the Italian method of singing recommended that the mouth not be opened too far—just sufficient to introduce the tip of a finger—and the lips be pulled back to a relaxed, smile-like position.[59] Nares wrote:

The formation of the Mouth in singing is a thing carefully to be attended to and a gracefull Delivery by no means to be neglected, for all *Grimaces* should be avoided, as only proper in Burlettas and things of *Mimickry*. Some Masters a few Years since were very sanguine in having the Mouth (in general) opened rather beyond the bounds of Decency; but this is a good deal laid aside, and I would only recommend forming the Mouth so hollow as to seperate [sic] the Teeth, which will open the upper part of the Larinx [sic] (or wind pipe) and give a free Delivery to the Voice, but many who very properly learn this formation of the Mouth at first, carry it to such a Height, as not to recollect that some Words, and Sense require it much more than others: Solemnity and Grandeur require the hollow Mouth; but Vivacity, Love, and Peace, require it no more than to deliver the voice freely and easily.[60]

In contrast, the American Benjamin Carr emphasized the openness of the mouth:

In practicing . . . any . . . Exercise, or in singing any Song &c. let it be strictly observed that the Mouth must be Open: this is always the first and the most useful advice given in Singing, and of all things avoid Singing through the Teeth or the Nose, as it always disgusts the hearers—the first of these habits is always difficult to be overcome, and the last except in a very few instances, has been found to be absolutely invincible.[61]

Nares cautioned that the singing master should "attend strictly to the delivery of the Voice, whether di petto or di testa, that it be not checked by contracting the Throat, nor forced thro' the Nose in a disagreeable manner, both which Faults are unpardonable in a Singer."[62]

In their quest to deliver crowd-pleasing high notes, singers may have distorted the tone of the entire voice; William Jackson complained in 1791 that "instead of developing their voices so as to be soft at the top and full at the bottom, singers were achieving the opposite effect."[63] It was reported that

the mechanical operation by which Mr. Braham increases his power is a very peculiar alteration in the parts adjacent to the upper region of the throat and the back of the mouth, so that the voice proceeds more from the head than the chest, by which the tone is swelled in its passage, but at the same time, it becomes very disagreeably reedy, and takes a near resemblance to the clarinet, or to that known effect which in trumpet playing is called "over-broke."[64]

A reader's letter to the Philadelphia *Aurora. General Advertiser* concerning the singers at the New Theatre contended that several excellent voices were being misused:

But it must be said, that they shew more science than expression in their singing, and appear emulous rather of exciting admiration than of pleasing; that they have been too often applauded for having rivalled the treble string of the violin, and are too seldom noticed when they develope a full sonorous voice, and an expression truly musical. They appear to stoop to the taste of the gallery, as the actors also do, and can no longer execute an arietta, without departing from the spirit of their part, and imitating a metallic string, which more and more shortened, ceases to vibrate. These ladies are certainly too well informed, to believe that these efforts of the throat can be called singing; sounds produced in this way are classed as noise. . . . The singer cannot possibly express this sentiment or passion, or rather cannot feel it when occupied in painfully drawing, in the interval of a quintal, sounds which require considerable efforts of the frame, and a fixed attention to give them with truth and precision.[65]

A contemporary anatomical description of the vocal apparatus from a "Gentleman of the Faculty" was quoted by Nares:

The LUNGS perform, with respect to the human Voice, what the Bellows do in the Organ, they supply the Air, but have little else to do in Singing.

The Reflections of the Voice, and all the Variety of musical Tones, depend on the Larynx, and other Parts which are added to the Lungs, by means of a Tube called the Trachea, or Air Pipe. Within the Larynx, between a number of moveable Cartilages, there is an oblong aperture called the Glottis. This aperture is bordered by Ligaments which vibrate as the Air passes through the Trachea from the Lungs. The Trachea is a flexible Tube, and therefore capable of being shortened, or lengthened, contracted or dilated, so as to admit a larger or smaller Column of Air. The Aperture in the Larynx can also be varied in such a manner as not only to admit a certain Stream of Air to pass through it with a given Celerity, but also to increase or diminish the Vibration of that Air in its Passage on which depends in a great measure the whole variety of musical Tones in Singing, which Tones indeed can never be doubled.

To the Trachea and Larynx are fixed a number of Muscles, these might be (and not unjustly) compared to the Fingers acting upon a Common Flute. What the Fingers do by opening and stopping the Holes of the Flute, these little Muscles do, by lengthening or shortening the Trachea, by opening or closing the Glottis, or Aperture in the Larynx: so that as we play upon a Flute with the Fingers, it may be said, we play upon the Trachea and Larynx with these Muscles.[66]

Nares introduced the problem of breathing in his treatise as follows:

As the Art of managing the Breath is an essential point in Singing and might make a Treatise of itself, I shall give but one general rule about it, which from Experience has seldom failed to give a strong Idea of it to the Singer. I would propose to the Scholar to take Breath as if it were to call to some Person at a Distance. He would then put his Mouth, Throat, Lungs and Chest into such a position as to give strength and firmness to his Voice. But then in singing, this Action must be retained, and not suffered to be relaxed immediately, as if a Person made a Sigh; which young beginners are very apt to do. In healthy high braced Constitutions, this position of the Breast is almost natural, or easy to be acquired; which in relaxed Habits is more difficult to be gained and must be done by Care and Practice.[67]

In his book *The Singing of John Braham,* John M. Levien quotes a treatise by George G. Cathcart, M.D. (fl. 1895), that discussed the old Italian method of voice production. Cathcart contended that singers were traditionally taught to use the upper chest in breathing, not the abdomen and diaphragm. Not until the middle of the nineteenth century did some voice teachers advocate using the lower chest, and this technique remained controversial at the beginning of the twentieth century. To prove that Braham could not have used his diaphragm in breathing, Levien quotes Joseph Heywood of Manchester (from the *Cornhill Magazine,* December 1865):

Braham got up to sing one single line of recitative; he stood with his head well on one side, held his music also on one side, and far out before him gave a funny little stamp with his foot [stamping was a practice of the old tragedians] and then proceeded to lay in his breath with such a tremendous shrug of his shoulders and swelling of his chest that I very nearly burst out laughing.[68]

This practice of breathing with the upper chest only may have resulted in additional sound during inhalation. Mrs. Hodgkinson was criticized for "a disagreeable aspiration at every pause."[69] In Boston *The Comet*'s critic complained of the sound of Mrs. Mills's breathing: "Her singing is also rendered harsh and discordant to musical ears, by the sudden drawing in of her breath; which produces a noise that continually reminds one of the heaving of a bellows."[70]

Nares's "Gentleman of the Faculty" makes no mention of the diaphragm; indeed, his instructions seem to imply a lifting of the chest, and folding the arms across the chest to strengthen the muscles and force air out slowly. He suggests that the flow of air from the lungs must be controlled by the throat, not the diaphragm, which seems a sure recipe for a tight throat and a "clear and brilliant"—or perhaps harsh—tone.

I apprehend that in Singing; in order to produce a clear, brilliant, and lasting Tone, it must be absolutely necessary always to fill the Lungs compleatly; and then to husband the collected Air as much as possible, by the management of the Throat, when the Lungs are thus distended; another advantage is

gained, the Chest is fixed, many of the Muscles of the Throat which are connected with the Chest, will now have a firm Point to act from, and will certainly exert themselves with more Advantage.

Compressing the Breast gently, by laying the Arms across it, must therefore assist a weak Voice; as this Attitude will also steady the Chest, and
strengthen the Muscular Power.

The Mouth, Tongue, Lips, and cavities of the Nostrils, are all secondary
Agents. Any considerable defect in these Parts will not only render the Voice
very unmusical, but may destroy it entirely.[71]

Levien reports that the glottal explosion—as recommended by Ma-
nuel García—was Braham's method of tonal attack. The breath was
raised to the vocal cords before the sound began, so that tone emerged
when the valve opened. Later teachers advocated "simultaneous onset
of breath force and approximation of the membranes."[72]

VOCAL TRAINING

In his *Memoirs,* Richard Brinsley Sheridan reported that "Everyone
sings according to their own ideas and what chance instruction they
can come by."[73] Indeed, some successful performers remained un-
trained "natural singers." *Polyanthos* commented that Mr. Garner,
who had been engaged to sing between acts at the Boston theatre in
1813, was "what is called a *natural singer,* by which we understand
one who sings by rote, without knowledge of music as a science, or
the power of reading it in notes." The critic recommended that if Mr.
Garner intended to remain on the stage, he should pursue the study of
music.[74]

Beginning singers were sometimes apprenticed for a period of four
or five years, much as young persons entered other trades or profes-
sions. Theatre singers often received their training, not surprisingly,
from the man responsible for all aspects of theatre music: the company
composer. In Philadelphia Benjamin Carr studied and taught the vocal
art, while in New York James Hewitt offered such instruction. When
Miss Dellinger made her first appearance at the Boston Federal Street

Theatre in 1811, it was noted that she was a student of composer James Hewitt, then in charge of the theatre orchestra.[75] Students also obtained instruction from older singers, as did Mary Harding (known as Mrs. G. Marshall) when she lived and studied with Frances Hodgkinson. When the opera *Shipwreck* was performed in Charleston in May 1804, the *Courier* reported:

Mrs. Marshall in the boy Dick gave evident proofs of a natural genius for certain departments of acting and singing, and of their being assiduously cultivated. It will not appear surprising that she should, even at her early time of life, be so capable and skilfull, when it is known that she was trained under the tuition of the accomplished Mrs. Hodgkinson, deceased. Her singing shews her to be a considerable adept in music.[76]

John Bannister was by some reports a "natural singer," but William Oxberry reported that "All the merit he possesses as a singer, is to be attributed to the instruction of Mrs. Bannister," who was the singer Elizabeth Harper.[77]

Teachers received a proportion of students' earnings during the apprenticeship period, so it was to their advantage to place their protégés onstage as quickly as possible. Young singers typically made their debuts while in their teens; Nancy Storace was singing leading Mozart roles in Vienna at eighteen. One of Samuel Arnold's pupils, Miss Leake, made her Drury Lane debut at fourteen as Rosetta in *Love in a Village;* her voice was gone before she was out of her teens.[78] Mary Harding made her debut in singing roles while still a child, and was a teenager when she sang major roles in Charleston as Mrs. G. Marshall.

Since the theatre composer frequently was not himself a singer, vocal training usually focused on the technical aspects of music rather than on vocal tone or production. When Charles Dibdin taught English singers like Mrs. Bland, Mrs. Mountain, and Miss DeCamp, he wrote: "I took care that they should be taught nothing more than correct expression, and an unaffected pronunciation of the words; the infallible and only way to perfect a singer."[79] Nonetheless, some composers had notable successes in voice cultivation. Thomas Busby reported on one of Arnold's pupils:

Among all the numerous instances of extraordinary advancement in vocal excellence, no one, perhaps, ever exceeded that of Mr. Phillips, some time since of Covent Garden Theatre. This gentleman, when he first intended to make music his profession, applied to the late Dr. Arnold, from whom he received some instructions. He soon afterwards was engaged at the Norwich Theatre, where his performance was distinguished by its very florid and ornamental style. His voice, which, when he commenced his musical studies, was a mere thread, and without a particle of what may be called tone, speedily became so mellifluous, rich and round, that those who had heard him when he was ignorant of the art which now rendered him so fine a singer, could scarcely persuade themselves that he was the same individual to whom they had formerly listened with so little comparative gratification.[80]

Various surviving textbooks from the period—both on general music and on vocal development—and collections of the era's vocal music give an idea of the techniques then used in teaching singing and matters that were considered essential knowledge for singers. Nares's *Treatise on Singing* summarized his recommended steps in teaching singing:

The first step in Singing should be to endeavour with an easy good Delivery, and steady Voice, to sing slow Notes rising or falling, well in Tune, a good Intonation of the Voice being the first perfection in Singing, and without which all others are useless. The next step is to add the messa di Voce or swelling of the Voice, then the Scholar may proceed to moving Notes of all sorts mixed with Rests and Specks [dotted notes], from thence advance to Skips ascending and descending, then study the Use of the Flats and Sharps, and from thence proceed to Duetts and Music in several Parts.

In the Interim the Master should give the Scholar proper Lessons for acquiring a Volubility of Throat, and gaining a Shake; (the most beautifull Grace in Music.)[81]

Benjamin Carr's *Lessons and Exercises in Vocal Music*, an American source, follows a similar plan. Carr gave "Some Concise Rules for Singing," using solfeggio techniques,[82] and a variety of exercises to be used in mastering "Singing by Note." After a student had mastered all the major and minor intervals, he or she was given various "little Songs" and duets to learn, first with solfeggio, then with poetry added, and some "passages"—more difficult vocalises—to practice. Finally, having mastered these rudiments, the student was ready for voice cultivation. Carr recommended "a constant practice" of a very slow scale ascending two octaves from written c′ to c‴, then descending to g before returning to c′. Practice, "especially in the Morning before Breakfast, will be found of great utility in strengthening and equalizing the voice."[83] If the endeavor to reach the extreme notes was found to "strain the breast," they could be omitted, though it was possible through practice to acquire additional notes in the voice.

Among the bad habits that Carr considered incurable except in cases of unusual perseverance were the determination "to keep the mouth and teeth immovably closed"; "singing with a nasal tone"; and "a provincial accent, a psalmodic twang, or a sleepy drawling manner." He advised students to "take a good breath every two Bars," and to "Open the mouth—Sing them in an equally strong tone of Voice and seem to throw out the Voice from you."

Having thus disposed of vocal development, Carr dealt with the problems of pronunciation as follows:

In Recapitulating the absolute necessity of keeping the mouth open and teeth apart, throwing out the Voice, sustaining the Tones, the avoidance of Gutteral, Nasal and Dental sounds, (all of which cannot be too often impressed upon the Memory,) it is necessary to mention Pronunciation, every syllable to be sung full and distinctly: When two or more sounds occur to one syllable, do not dwell on the Consonant supposing the word to begin with one, but let the passage be on the Vowel, and if concluding with a Consonant do not let it be heard 'till the very last. Let all the Labial and Dental consonants be as quickly passed over as possible, so as to come upon the sound of the Vowel, Let this advice be strictly observed. In respect to the M's and N's & S's to prevent the humms, unns and hisses that will otherwise occur, the broad A and the soft O will be preferable where those Vowels occur, and they are the vowels most in use for divisions, but in that case the latter must have a more open sound. Also avoid harshness in pronouncing the K, and widen when more notes than one are to a syllable, the pronunciation of the E and I; two words must be sung differently to what they are spoken, this must be invariably attended to, as for instance, Tha for the Article The, and something between Me and Ma for the Pronoun My.[84]

Carr's rules for breathing included:

1st always take your breath when a rest occurs whether or not you may seem to want it; when you have not the advantage of a rest for that purpose, then catch it as quickly as possible in a manner imperceptible, at the same places as you would in reading. 2d Avoid taking breath in the middle of a word, or in any way that may destroy the sense of the Poetry, except before a holding note, a division, a shake or cadence in which instance it is allowable.[85]

Carr concluded with two versions of "The vi'let nurs'd in woodland wild." The first was for voice and bass, with plentiful advice to the singer, including ornamentation written out as it was to be performed, the proper positions for breath to be taken, and the correct pronunciation and placement of vowels and consonants. The second version contained complete accompaniments and "symphonies" for pianoforte, and included the voice part as it would appear in a typical printed version. The two are compiled in ex. 10, with the written out ornamentation occupying the top staff and the second version on the lower three staves.

Carr gave the following advice to the accompanist:

it is proper to impress upon the minds of all, the absolute necessity of the Accompaniments to a Song being played perfect, and the Symphonies not to be hurried over—the manner in which Songs are too often accompanied is very reprehensible; . . . let it be recollected, that a song, no matter how sweet the voice or how exquisite the taste, that is accompanied with false notes PARTICULARLY in the bass, blundering passages, hurried and imperfect symphonies &c will most assuredly make the good natured Critic pity and the ill natured one ridicule the performer, and even those who have never studied Music, but are possessed of correct ears will be disgusted, at the same time the most simple ditty, sung in time and tune and correctly played will give satisfaction.[86]

Example 10. "The Vi'let Nurs'd in Woodland Wild," by Benjamin Carr, with written-out ornamentation and instructions to vocalists as provided by Carr (line 1) and melody and ornament signs as normally found in printed version (line 2).

Example 10. (*continued*)

Example 10. (*continued*)

*Be careful of a disagreeable hum upon this syllable

Example 10. (*continued*)

* Sing this vowel with a more open pronunciation than in reading.
** Play the small notes to support the voice.

Example 10. (*continued*)

Example 10. (*continued*)

Example 10. (*continued*)

Example 10. (*continued*)

Example 10. (*continued*)

Phi- lo- mel a- wakes tha plain a- wakes tha plain a-

Phi- lomel a- wakes the plain a- wakes the plain a-

28 Portamento, gradually swell the voice to loud
then diminish the tone

wa--kes a-

wakes-- a-

tr   tr   tr

29 a succession of prepared turns

wa---

wakes---

Example 10. (*continued*)

* The syllable is here not completed, merely to show that in staccato passages on notes *in alt* or high notes to words concluding with consonants it is allowable to finish with the vowel, omitting the consonants at the end. The above are given merely as an example, as it is to be observed that staccato notes or the omittance of a conclusive vowel usually occur upon notes higher in the scale than these—but as the wish was to make this song useful, care has been taken not to extend its compass beyond the general run of voices.

Thus were American singers trained at the turn of the century: a bit of realistic advice, Dibdin's "correct expression and unaffected pronunciation," some assistance with ornamentation, and the student was ready to face the critics. The entire art of singing was summarized by Giusto Ferdinando Tenducci (ca. 1734–90), a castrato who arranged, composed, and sang in English operas, in twenty-one "Necessary Rules for Students and Dilettanti of Vocal Music":

> I. The first and most necessary Rule in singing, is to keep the Voice steady.
> II. To form the Voice in as pleasing a Tone, as is in the Power of the Scholar.
> III. To be exactly in Tune; as without a perfect intonation, it is needless to attempt singing.
> IV. To vocalize correctly; that is, to give as open and clear a Sound to the Vowels, as the Nature of the Language in which the Student sings, will admit.
> V. To articulate perfectly each Syllable.
> VI. To sing the Scale, or Gamut, frequently; allowing to each sound one BREVE, or two SEMIBREVES, which must be sung in the same Breath; and this must be done, in both, A MESSI DI VOCE: that is, by swelling the Voice, beginning Pianissimo, and encreasing [*sic*] gradually to Forte, in the first part of the Time; and so diminishing gradually to the end of each Note, which will be expressed in this way [see ex. 11],

Example 11. Illustration of *messa di voce* for Giusto Ferdinando's "Necessary Rules for Students and Dilettanti of Vocal Music," [1785]. Music Division, Library of Congress.

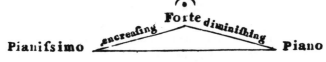

> VII. To exercise the Voice in SOLFEGIO every Day, with the Monosyllables Do, Re, Mi, &c.
> VIII. To copy a little Music every Day, in order to accustom the Eye to divide the Time into all its Proportions.

IX. Never to force the Voice, in order to extend its Compass in the VOCE DI PETTO upwards; but rather to cultivate the VOCE DI TESTA in what is called FALSETTO, in order to join it well and imperceptibly, to the VOCE DI PETTO for fear of incurring the disagreeable Habit of singing in the Throat, or through the Nose;—unpardonable Faults in a Singer.

X. In the Exercise of singing, never to discover any Pain or Difficulty, by Distortion of the Mouth, or Grimace of any Kind; which will be best avoided by examining the Countenance in a Looking glass, during the most difficult Passages.

XI. It is recommended to sing a little at a Time, and often; and, if standing, so much the better for the Chest.

XII. That Scholars should appear at the Harpsichord and to their Friends with a calm and chearful [sic] Countenance.

XIII. To rest or take breath between the Passages, and in proper Time; that is to say, to take it only when the Periods, or members of the Melody, are ended; which Periods, or Portions of the Air, generally terminate on the accented Parts of a Bar. And this Rule is the more necessary, as by dwelling too long upon the last Note of a musical Period, the Singer loses the Oppertunity [sic] it affords of taking Breath, without breaking the Passages, or even being perceived by the Audience.

XIV. That without the most urgent necessity, of either a long Passage, or of an affecting Expression, Words must never be broken, or divided.

XV. That a good MESSA DI VOCE, or Swell of the Voice, must always precede the AD LIBITUM Pause ⌒ and CADENZA.

XVI. That in pronouncing the Words, Care must be taken to accord with the Sentiment that was intended by the Poet.

XVII. That the acute and super acute Sounds must never be so forced as to render them similar to Shrieks.

XVIII. That in singing, the Tones of the Voice must be united, except in the case of Staccato Notes.

XIX. That in pronouncing the Words, double Consonants in the Italian Language, must be particularly enforced, and Care taken not to make those that are single seem double.

XX. To practice the Shake with the greatest Care and Attention, which must generally commence with the highest of the two Notes, and finish with the lowest.

XXI. That the Ornaments and Embellishments of Songs should be derived from the Character of the Air, and Passion of the Words.[87]

In 1820 Tenducci's techniques were still being used, and the *Euterpeiad* lamented that there was still no science of teaching singing in English, and that the Italians alone possessed the necessary knowledge for the teaching of singing:

Singing, though, as an art, it has reached perhaps as high perfection as it is capable of attaining, yet, strange to say, is very imperfectly understood as a science in England. If we are asked how or why this is so, we shall reply, because literature has yet lent but small help to music; because its higher principles have never been analysed, examined, and demonstrated; because the technical parts of the education of vocalists, and their necessary acquaintance with language, their cultivation of personal grace, and study of the usages of the stage, occupy so much time, and imperatively demand such vast labour;—lastly, because the English, having no musical school of their own, are compelled to erect the superstructure of their national performances upon foreign foundations. The Italians—(we may almost say the Italians alone)—possess the entrances and passages to organic perfections in singing; yet so soon as the elements of instruction which we borrow from them terminate; so soon as our students attain to the production of pure tone—the *messa da voce,* as they term it, or that power which practice gives the singer of modifying the quantity of tone at will, by the most gradual increase or diminution—so soon as the shake, execution, and general facility are attained—the practical application of these several powers and graces to the purposes of expression, differs as widely as the feelings, the habits, the manners of Italy differ from those of England.[88]

ORNAMENTATION

One thing always present in published tutors and song collections at the turn of the nineteenth century was a table of ornaments. Various collections and tutors also included examples of ornamented songs, such as that presented by Carr and those in the various volumes of songs published by Domenico Corri (1746–1825), showing the place of "proper Graces and Ornaments peculiar to their character" in the melody.[89] Many of the English, Scottish, and Irish songs in these collections were taken from contemporary operas, and their main attraction was that the ornaments ordinarily added by the professional singer were indicated in the score for the amateur.

The application of such tables and examples of ornamentation to performance practice today is considerably complicated by several factors.

(a) Ornamentation is a means of expression. It enhances the emotive power of a melody in an intensely personal way. It should be a direct and spontaneous result of a particular singer's involvement with the music.

(b) The techniques of ornamentation are no longer natural to modern singers in the way they would have been to singers who heard them day after day. Even moderate ornamentation now risks sounding ostentatious to both singers and listeners. (A perfectly crafted and performed cadenza, appearing suddenly in the middle of an otherwise straightforward song, is likely to draw a laugh in modern performance.)

(c) Many of the subtleties of ornamentation are best understood by hearing them performed well. Slight stresses on a dissonance, small distortions of rhythm, and minute variations in tempo are impossible to notate but essential for expressive effect.

Despite these difficulties in understanding and applying characteristic ornamentation, however, it is vital to the tradition, and essential to the successful performance of the early American vocal repertory. It was taken for granted that some degree of "gracing" would be added in songs of all types. The amount of ornamentation, however, varied widely, depending on the style of the song and even more on the habits of the individual performer. The majority of singers probably contented themselves with the addition of an occasional appoggiatura and a brief cadence (cadenza) at the pause mark (fermata). Other singers varied from little or no ornamentation (ballad style) to profuse, Italianate figuration. The *Euterpeiad* contrasted the "great" and the "ornamented" styles: the elements of the "great" style were "power, pure tone, and a varied expression;—an entire command of manner, correct taste and perfect simplicity"; while the ornamented style "consists in the substitution of light, graceful, florid, and surprising passages of execution." The writer showed his preference for the expressive power of the "great" style over the technical display of the ornamented style. The "most difficult *graces*" were attained, he said, "by mere repetition, by a vast number of acts, and imply no mental exertion whatever"; while the "great" style was the result of "reasoning and imagination."[90]

Many English singers favored the "great" style. Maria Theresa Bland (1769–1838) was praised by Henry Phillips:

Such pure and silvery tones surely never issued from a human throat before; this, added to the extreme simplicity of her style, threw a charm and magic round all she did, that was perfectly entrancing. Her singing of "Little Tafline with her silken sash," . . . without an ornament of any kind, threw her audience into raptures."[91]

Elizabeth Harper Bannister (ca. 1757–1849) was also conservative in style. Oxberry said that she "scarcely ever used any ornament whatever, her style being purely that of ballad singing"; O'Keeffe said that "She sung the notes, all the notes, and nothing but the notes"; and *The Thespian Dictionary* complained that she "lacked ingenuity in her cadences," and was deficient in Mrs. Billington's "beautiful exuberance of fancy."[92] Anna Maria Crouch (1763–1805) was said by Oxberry to use few ornaments, and those were "more correct than brilliant."[93] Although the *Euterpeiad* referred to the "falsetto embellishments" of John Johnstone, Boaden wrote that he had a "plain and pleasing style, without the slightest affectation or mixture of the foreign graces."[94]

American singers used the "great" style as well, and usually gained praise from the critics. When Mrs. Merry performed the role of Ophelia in *Hamlet* at Philadelphia, her "'snatches of old tune' were 'chaunted' with the most exquisite and touching simplicity." [95] *The Emerald* commended Mr. Vining for his "clear and melodious voice" and "chaste stile," which "does not pain the ear with unnatural trills or affected and ridiculous quavers." [96] When the nonsinging Mr. Lindsley at Boston was at last replaced in the role of Count Calmar in *The Exile* by Mr. M'Farland, the Count was "restored to his *musical honors*." The *Polyanthos* critic wrote that

if a clear and distinct utterance of the *words* and *sentiments* of a song be of any worth, (and to those, who wish for the gratification of the *mind* as the *ear,* it will outweigh all the chromatics, and cadences, and bravuras even of Catalani herself) he may put in his claim to the approbation of "the judicious." [97]

The "lightly graced" songs in the Corri collections are probably typical of the style of these performers; in spite of the references to the complete absence of ornaments, the appoggiaturas and five- or six-note cadences included by Corri were so much a part of the style as to be accepted by listeners as part of the work.

The other extreme of ornamentation was represented in America by Mrs. Oldmixon, Mrs. Jones, Frances Hodgkinson, and Arabella Brett, and in England by Elizabeth Billington and John Braham. The lack of appreciation of some Americans for the ornamented style was shown when the first New York performance of *The Africans* was given on January 1, 1810, with a record house:

The audience, as was to be expected, was riotous and noisy, but excepting the throwing a fork at mrs. Oldmixon, when singing the bravura song, was not guilty of any very striking indecorum. We thought it injudicious to expose her to insult, on an occasion such as this; for it is well known that our taste is not yet sufficiently refined, to enjoy this style of singing; and a New-York audience, in their *soberest* moments, will only listen to it from respect for the performer. [98]

Oxberry said that Braham "so revelled in his powers of variety that an accurate ear could scarcely follow the air through his multifarious modulations."[99] The *Euterpeiad* opined that Braham,

though certainly gifted with the most various and powerful expression of any singer within recollection, has nevertheless, most unaccountably lowered the effects of his singing by an overwhelming exuberance of florid ornamentation.[100]

Much of Braham's ornamentation was apparently added to appease his audience, though Braham might have sung quite differently to please other musical tastes. Reverend Julian Young discussed this contrast in style:

No man understood better, or more thoroughly appreciated in others, purity of style, yet no man oftener violated the canons of good taste by florid interpolations when singing before a miscellaneous audience. I have heard him sing the best sacred music at the house of friends whom he knew to be refined and fastidious musicians, and then his rendering of Handel has been glorious and worthy of his theme. I have heard him, at an oratorio at the theatre the very next night, sing the same air to a miscellaneous audience and so overlay the composition with florid interpolations as entirely to distract the listener's attention from the simplicity and solemnity of his theme. This violation of propriety was attributable to the fact of his having observed that a display of flexible vocalization always brought down thunder from the gods in the gallery; and therefore he was tempted by the greed of clap-trap applause to sacrifice his own convictions of propriety to the demands of the vulgar and unenlightened.[101]

Elizabeth Billington's ornamented style was "caviare [*sic*] to the million":

Though the pit yawned, and the galleries gaped in amazement, the musical world were enraptured; and the effect produced in the orchestra, by her performance, is said to have been magnetic;—though, during one of her beautiful cadences, every musician (and especially the leader) was so wrapt, that he neglected to give his chord at the close of it, and proceed with the air, until the cessation of sound woke him to his senses.[102]

In 1801 Thomas Busby published the songs from *Artaxerxes, Love in a Village,* and *The Duenna,* ornamented as Mrs. Billington sang them. Fiske includes several examples from this collection in his *English Theatre Music in the Eighteenth Century,*[103] comparing them with the same passages as ornamented by Corri. Like Braham, Mrs. Billington obviously understood the difference between the Italian style and the ballad style, and was capable of using either for expressive purposes. William Parke saw her perform the part of Eliza in *The Flitch of Bacon* in 1790:

It had been considered by many that she was merely a bravura singer, and therefore perhaps she selected this character to prove that she could sing with effect in simple and plaintive melodies. If this was her object, she attained it completely, by singing the natural and plaintive music of the part in the most chaste and beautiful style imaginable.[104]

Composers and teachers often advocated simplicity and suitability. A song in Samuel Arnold's *The Son-in-Law* began "I like the plain song without fine repetitions, soft cadences, graces, or running divisions"—though other songs in the same opera are highly florid. William Shield wrote "ornamented and difficult parts . . . far beyond the style of common bravura," but his great characteristic, according to John Rowe Parker, was simplicity—"a style of writing pure, chaste and original."[105] Shield wrote that plain, folklike airs "want no foreign ornament; but performers are so often applauded for embellishments, that simplicity seldom appears in its native dress." He continued, "I once was silly enough to write a fine flourishing double cadence to a pathetic air: which so destroyed the passion, rendered both the singer and myself so ridiculous, that I hope never to be importuned to repeat such an absurdity."[106] Benjamin Carr advised that one rule is always observed: "to *slow Songs slow Graces* and Vice Versa, always making *your embellishments partake* of the character of the piece in which they occur.[107]

There is much evidence that songs were composed to suit the abilities of the specific singer performing a role. Although improvised ornamentation was the ideal, and "a singer was largely judged by the variety and originality of his or her 'improvised embellishments,'"[108] many ornaments and cadenzas were notated in advance, either by the composers or by the singers themselves. Thus songs written for Mrs. Billington were predictably Italianate in style, while those written for Mrs. Bland or Mr. Bannister were usually light or moderate in their ornamentation. In the United States, songs sold with the notation "as sung by Mrs. Hodgkinson," or "Mrs. Jones," or "Miss Brett" frequently included extensive ornamentation.[109] There is also evidence that composers considered individual singers' abilities and preferences for adding their own ornamentation. Sometimes, for instance, the arias written for Elizabeth Harper, who was known for the simplicity of her style, appear more elaborate than those written for such bravura singers as John Braham; the composer apparently realized that he would have to indicate any required ornamentation in the score in order for Miss Harper to sing it. Such parts (see, for example, Miss Harper's parts in *The Son-in-Law*) make it clear that she *could* sing highly ornamented music, demanding in range, flexibility, and breath control.

Because Mrs. Billington had a poor memory and no talent for extemporizing, she needed to write out all her graces and learn them laboriously (these provided, of course, the sources for Busby's collection of her arias). Busby recounts her method in Naples in 1794:

She was immediately engaged at the theatre *San Carlo;* and, on her account, Signor Bianchi was instructed to set to music the opera of *Ines di Castro;* into which, in consequence of her defective memory, she requested him to introduce a favorite song, composed by Salieri, which for years, she had been in the habit of singing in London. Bianchi added to the melody a few bars and three cadenzas, in order that she might change them in course of the opera; Cimarosa also wrote three; the German composer, Hermil, added three more; while Marescalche, one of the orchestra, likewise contributed three. It will scarcely be credited, that, of these twelve cadenzas, this charming singer could only retain one, with which she graced every song she sung in the Carnival.[110]

When professional jealousy arose between Braham and Mrs. Billington at Milan, he listened to her carefully written embellishments at rehearsal, and

having a quick ear, learnt them. His first aria in the opera preceded that of the lady, and unto it he introduced every one of these embellishments. Not unnaturally furious at the infringement of her vocal copyright, Mrs. Billington refused to sing with him in the next opera, but later they made up their quarrel and became good partners.[111]

Most tutors included some instruction for learning and practicing ornaments. Nares also provided information on the appropriate placement of ornaments on various vowels. Nares recommended that divisions

at first should be practiced soft, on the Vowel A, only, and afterwards louder and on the rest of the Vowels, in order to apply them to all sorts of words, tho' long Divisions should be confined to the 1st, 3d, & 4th Vowel, the 2d and 5th according to the English pronunciation being not sonorous enough.[112]

It was vital that the ornamentation added should not distort the steady beat of the orchestra. With no conductor, a singer who took unreasonable liberties with the rhythm could easily create chaos in the orchestra. Galliard's translation of Tosi's *Observations on the Florid Song* (1743), still used at the turn of the century, advised that

Good taste does not consist in the continual Velocity of the Voice, which goes thus rambling on, without a Guide, and without Foundation; but rather . . . in the true Notion of Graces, going from one Note to another with Singular and unexpected Surprizes, and stealing the Time exactly on the true Motion of the Bass.[113]

Even at the pause marks, where the orchestra broke its momentum and waited for the singer, there were limitations. Mount-Edgcumbe complained in his *Musical Reminiscences* (1834) of singers who spin "out their cadences to an unreasonable length," sometimes to the length of four breaths. "When cadenzas ad libitum invariably closed every song," he remembered, "it was a positive rule to confine them, shake included, to one breath."[114]

Many songs are available in various collections, including those of Corri, with ornamentation provided for the singer. Corri's ornamentation of "Now Ponder Well" from *The Beggar's Opera* (ex. 12) offers a representative example of simple ornamentation using appoggiaturas

Example 12. Domenico Corri's ornamentation of "Oh! Ponder Well" from *The Beggar's Opera*, from *A Select Collection of the Most Admired Songs, Duetts, &c. . . .*, [1779]. Music Division, Library of Congress.

Example 13. Cadenza from "On the Rock Where Hangs the Willow," by James Hewitt.

and "after notes." It can be compared with other versions of this song found as ex. 3 and ex. 51. A more elaborate example "as sung by Mrs. Jones" is "On the Rock Where Hangs the Willow," by James Hewitt, which begins with a simple ballad, moderately graced throughout. The cadenza supplied at the first pause mark (at the end of the first stanza) is typical of those added in such situations (ex. 13). The second verse begins as simply as the first, but is soon varied and plunges into an elaborate allegro that seems to have little relationship to the foregoing ballad. Long vocalises, trills, and leaps (b♭" to d' to e' to g") lead to a forceful, majestic ending.[115] The song from Benjamin Carr's *Lessons and Exercises in Vocal Music* reproduced as ex. 10 provides an example of moderate ornamentation.

Among the many ornamentation tables available from the turn of the nineteenth century, several were particularly appropriate for English and American opera. These included several by opera composers: a brief table in Samuel Arnold's harpsichord and pianoforte tutor, published about 1777,[116] and the tables in Benjamin Carr's instructor for pianoforte[117] and in his *Lessons and Exercises in Vocal Music.* Nares included a table in his treatise; Corri included a table in each of his collections and applied its principles to the many English opera songs therein.

The most important ornaments were the appoggiaturas, the turns, and the shakes, though many others were mentioned in various sources; most authors also discussed cadences or closes (which may include some of the above). Perhaps the most complete table was that included by Benjamin Carr in his *Analytical Instructor for the Pianoforte,* titled "A Compendium of the graces and embellishments of music as exemplified by Dr. Callcott";[118] examples from this table are used in the following discussion.[119] Further examples of most of these ornaments may be seen in the ornamented song from Carr's vocal treatise (ex. 10).

The Appoggiatura

Carr listed the single appoggiatura as both long and short; he stated plainly, "whenever you can by an appoggiatura equalize the notes do it" (ex. 14; also see ornaments 1, 2, 4, 6, and 18 in Carr's song, ex. 10).

On dotted notes, the ornamental note received the first third of the note value (ex. 10, ornaments 23 and 24). In a series of notes of the same length, Carr divided the first note equally and placed the appoggiatura on the beat, even though he recognized the inelegant jerk that often caused an appoggiatura in this position to be performed before the beat (ex. 15).

Appoggiaturas before chords were also placed on the beat and equalized, with the remaining notes of the chord performed with the ornamental note (ex. 16). Carr gave "ascending grace notes" (moving

Example 14. Appoggiaturas from Benjamin Carr's *Lessons and Exercises in Vocal Music,* ca. 1811. This example and examples 15–42 were notated for the treble staff.

Example 15. Appoggiaturas from Carr's *Lessons and Exercises in Vocal Music.*

Example 16. Appoggiaturas before chords, from Carr's *Lessons and Exercises in Vocal Music.*

Example 17. "Ascending grace notes" from Carr's *Lessons and Exercises in Vocal Music.*

Example 18. "Half beats" from Carr's *Lessons and Exercises in Vocal Music.*

both by step and by leap) with the added note apparently on the beat, but performed as a short note (ex. 17); and "half beats" with the appoggiatura crushed into a series of eighth notes, still on the beat or half beat. Even when the ornament filled in a series of rising thirds, it was placed on, rather than before, the beat (ex. 18). Unfortunately, neither Carr's notation nor that of a majority of his contemporaries gave a clear indication of when the grace note was to be substituted for the preferred appoggiatura. Nor was he consistent in using the term "appoggiatura" to indicate an ornamental dissonance *on* the beat and the term "grace note" to indicate a short decoration placed before the beat.

In his vocal method, Carr said that

The Appoggiatura or Grace Note should be sung as if you laid a stress thereon—it is too common a method 'tho placed before long notes, to play it or sing it quickly, which is not only inelegant but contrary to the meaning of the word, which is derived from appoggiatura, to lean, therefore it some-times is called the leaning note.[120]

Carr gave three types of double appoggiaturas: the simultaneous double appoggiatura, performed like two single appoggiaturas (ex. 19); the conjunct double appoggiatura, or slide, performed on the beat and rapidly (ex. 20); and the disjunct double appoggiatura, called skips, also performed rapidly on the beat (ex. 21).

Since appoggiaturas were used to add tension, they were particu-

Example 19. "Double and treble appoggiaturas" from Carr's *Lessons and Exercises in Vocal Music.*

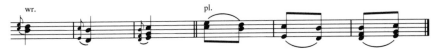

Example 20. "Slide" from Carr's *Lessons and Exercises in Vocal Music.*

Example 21. "Skips" from Carr's *Lessons and Exercises in Vocal Music.*

Example 22. Appoggiatura (as written).

Example 23. Appoggiatura (as performed).

larly common on long notes, at strong points in the rhythm, and at points of textual emphasis. One figure that frequently indicated an appoggiatura was ex. 22, which was performed as ex. 23.

Corri gave the following instructions for expressive singing of various types of appoggiaturas:

The Ascending Grace of one interval [ex. 24], is expressed softly, and its strength encreased [*sic*] gradually up to the Note.

The Descending Grace of one interval [ex. 25], is a degree stronger than the note and gradually softened into it.

The Grace of successive intervals [slide, ex. 26], is rather of a rapid execution and encreases its strength as it rises. . . . [If it descends, it decreases to the note.]

Example 24. "Ascending grace" from Domenico Corri's *Select Collection* and *New and Complete Collection.*

Example 25. "Descending grace" from Domenico Corri's *Select Collection* and *New and Complete Collection.*

Example 26. "Grace of successive intervals" from Domenico Corri's *Select Collection* and *New and Complete Collection.*

Example 27. "Leaping grace" from Domenico Corri's *Select Collection* and *New and Complete Collection.*

Example 28. "Turn grace" from Domenico Corri's *Select Collection* and *New and Complete Collection.*

The Grace of more intervals [leaping grace, ex. 27] always ascends. It is to be taken softly, and to leap into the note rapidly.

The Turn Grace [ex. 28] is to be taken strong, and melted into the note.[121]

Corri's preference for a crescendo on ascending appoggiaturas seems directly counter to Carr's instruction to "lay a stress" on the "leaning note," though some of that stress may have been rhythmic rather than dynamic.

Turns

Carr provided several types of turns in his compendium, including the unprepared (four-note) turn, beginning on the note above the principal note, and the prepared (five-note) turn, beginning on the given note (ex. 29; see prepared turns in ex. 10, ornaments 8 and 14.) Carr gave the turn itself in triplets in every case, implying that the earlier equal-note turn had validity; Samuel Arnold, however, wrote all his turns with equal notes. Carr pointed out that the lower auxiliary of the turn was usually a semitone below the principal note, but the designation was not clear (i.e., the sharp might be placed above, rather than below the turn symbol; see ex. 30). In his turns on dotted notes (Arnold's "turn on the speck") the turn sign was placed to the right of the principal note, and the prepared turn was used (ex. 31; see ex. 10, ornaments 19, 20, 29). He placed the turn sign on end to indicate a

Example 29. Turns from from Carr's *Lessons and Exercises in Vocal Music.*

Example 30. "Sharp turn" from Carr's *Lessons and Exercises in Vocal Music.*

The meaning of a Sharp Turn is that you must play the last note, but one only a half tone below the note written — therefore it falls on a white key as well as on a black key.

Example 31. "Turns on dotted notes" from Carr's *Lessons and Exercises in Vocal Music.*

On dotted note the prepared Turn is generally used.

Example 32. Inverted turn from Carr's *Lessons and Exercises in Vocal Music.*

four-note inverted turn (ex. 32; see ex. 10, ornaments 3, 12, 13, 26, 27); in his vocal treatise, he also used a prepared inverted turn (ornament 15).

Corri wrote that "The Ascending Turn inverted, prepared or unprepared, begins softly, and encreases its strength as it rises, then gently again sinks into the note," while "The Descending unprepared or prepared Turn, begins strong, and decreases its strength as it falls, then rises into the note strong again."[122]

The Shake or Trill

Carr wrote that trills might begin either on the given note or the upper auxiliary; most of his examples begin on the principal note. They might or might not use the note below the principal note as an ending formula or turned shake (ex. 33; see ex. 10, ornaments 5, 22, 30 for plain shakes beginning on the principal note). Carr's "chain shake" rhythmically emphasized the beginning of each new unit by repetition of the principal note (ex. 34). In a trill on a note tied across the bar line, the trill continued for the full value of the tie (ex. 35).

Carr's "Passing shake or Mordente" showed clearly how much the trill had lost its appoggiatura function; though the origin of the name "passing shake" was evident when the full ornament was notated, Carr began and ended his three-note trill on the given note (presumably for use in fast tempos), losing the accented dissonance (ex. 36). The shape of this trill was like an inverted mordent, but the rhythm was opposite (see the "spring" below, ex. 42).

Arnold's passing shake was much clearer in its function. By beginning on the upper auxiliary, his four-note trill retained its appoggiatura function (ex. 37).[123] Carr's "beat" was yet another trill (ex. 38). In his vocal treatise, Carr wrote that

Example 33. "Shake" (trill) from Carr's *Lessons and Exercises in Vocal Music.*

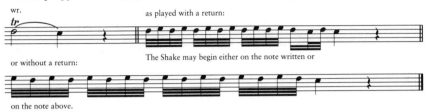

Example 34. "Chain shake" from Carr's *Lessons and Exercises in Vocal Music.*

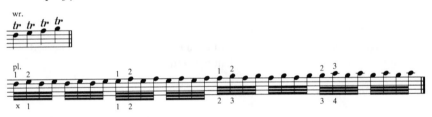

Example 35. "Continued shake" from Carr's *Lessons and Exercises in Vocal Music.*

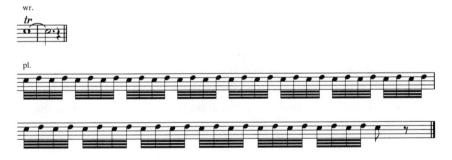

Example 36. "Passing shakes or mordentes" from Carr's *Lessons and Exercises in Vocal Music.*

Example 37. Trill from Samuel Arnold's *A Set of Progressive Lessons*, ca. 1777.

Example 38. "Beat" from Carr's *Lessons and Exercises in Vocal Music*.

A good Shake or Trill is reckoned so necessary an acquirement, that no one is thought a perfect Singer who has not acquired it—yet it must be observed, that it is now more sparingly used than formerly.[124]

Other Ornaments

Carr's "after note" was similar to the *nachschlag* of German music. These small notes might look like appoggiaturas (creating another confusion, since they were performed *before* the beat like later grace notes) or, as in Carr's treatise, might be tied to the preceding note to clarify their function. The "short appoggiatura" that appeared in Carr's ornamented song (ex. 10, ornament 11) was written and performed as an after note, as was the "transient shake" (ex. 39; ornament 7). One of the most common after notes was equal to the modern anticipation; Corri called this a "Swelling Grace."[125] He described the after note as follows:

This Grace close after a note is to show that the time necessary for its execution is to be deducted from the last part of that note. . . . As this has the peculiar quality of uniting two notes of any intervals, in executing it, it is necessary to swell the note into the Grace, and the Grace must melt itself again into the note following.[126]

The closes and half-closes Carr gave for use at pause marks were actually trills plus three after notes "sung rather slowly . . . to make an elegant termination" (ex. 40; see ex. 10, ornaments 10, 17, 25). If

Example 39. "After notes" from Carr's *Lessons and Exercises in Vocal Music.*

Example 40. Close from Carr's *Lessons and Exercises in Vocal Music.*

Example 41. Close from Carr's *Lessons and Exercises in Vocal Music.*

Example 42. "Spring" from Carr's *Lessons and Exercises in Vocal Music.*

there were no pause mark, the ending was as in ex. 41, "as usual."[127] This was apparently *so* usual that Shield called it a "worn out close."[128] (A similar formula occurred in Carr's song in ornament 32.)

Although Carr's "mordente" had no relationship to the usual ornament of that name (see above), his "spring" (ex. 42) was an inverted mordant. (The term "springer" usually indicated a type of *nachschlag*.)

Carr's "portamento" was equivalent to the Italian *messa di voce*, which was illustrated in Tenducci's rule VI above. It was a technique used in training the voice, but it was also used as an ornament:

PORTAMENTO or a good method of sustaining, swelling and diminishing the Voice, is a very desirable attainment in a singer . . . draw in as great a volume of breath as possible; in sounding the note let it come forth by regularly increasing degrees, and towards the middle sing the strongest, so as to make a gradual swell of the Voice—the natural decrease of the breath will assist in diminishing the tone. . . . a gradual swell and decrease, is one of the greatest beauties in singing.[129]

(This swelling and diminishing occurs in ex. 10, ornaments 21 and 27.) Another description of the same effect was found in a comparison of Miss Brent and Mrs. Vincent:

Both have faults . . . one among the rest is in the execution of those holding notes of which they both seem so fond. They seem to think that all the art in this respect lies, in beginning one of those tedious notes very soft, and then swelling it as loud as possible in the middle, then falling off, and so forth.[130]

The Italians used the term portamento to mean passing smoothly and firmly from one note to another on a vowel. In Ferrari's *A Concise Treatise on Italian Singing* the two terms were used together, and Ferrari distinguished between the two much as musicians do today:

To produce what the Italians call *Messa di voce*, the singer must attack the note readily and sustain it firmly. *Portamento* means the carriage of the voice with dignified expression. In carrying the voice from one note to another, the second must receive a slight intonation, previously to its being articulated. When ascending, the second note must receive the most strength; but in descending, more stress should be laid on the first, taking care however not to produce harsh shrieks instead of mellifluous tones.[131]

Many of the vocal techniques used by singers at the turn of the nineteenth century are of historical interest only. No modern singer would seriously consider breathing only in the upper chest, for example. The art of ornamentation, however—in spite of the difficulties involved in understanding and execution—should not be neglected. It is essential to the style, and the music of this period can never be fully realized or appreciated without the application of appropriate ornamentation.

9

THE ORCHESTRA IN
THE THEATRE

The theatre orchestra, normally called "the band" or "the band of music,"[1] had three principal functions: it provided music to entertain the audience before the performance began, it played the music needed for the productions themselves, and it provided "interval music" between the acts of the evening's production and between the main entertainment and the afterpiece.

At the sound of the prompter's bell, the members of the band would enter the orchestra pit from beneath the stage, seat themselves in two long rows facing each other, tune their instruments, and play about half an hour of music.[2] The English custom of "first, second, and third music" may have been followed; in that event three overtures, symphonies, or concertos would have filled the allotted time.[3] Often at least part of the time was used to perform popular tunes requested (or demanded) by the audience.

The music for the production itself typically included an overture, plus marches, dances, processionals, accompaniments for melodrama or mime, or other types of music called for in the script, and, of course, the accompaniments to the songs and ensembles. As plays were expanded with additional "business," appropriate music was added as well. In *Richard III*, for example, it was suggested that the manager add "some skirmishes" between the contending armies to the representation of the Battle of Bosworth Field, or "at least the clashing of their weapons behind the scenes, and a little more of warlike music."[4]

"Interval music" could include further overtures, symphonies, and concertos, and frequently included vocal numbers and dances as well; this segment, particularly, was the time when the gallery "ordered the music." Since requests by gallery patrons were often crude, repetitive, tasteless, and politically, morally, and socially offensive, managers and orchestra leaders regularly tried to reassert control over the type of music to be played. When Thomas Wall's Baltimore Company of Comedians performed in 1782, the bills regularly carried this notice: "Some tunes having been called for by Persons in the Gallery, which have given Offence to Others, the Managers have resolved, that no Music will be played, but such as they shall order the Day before the Representation."

The following program of orchestral music was published for use in Boston's Federal Street Theatre on February 3, 1794, and was designed to "give what we conceive to be the most harmonic to the soul, and congenial to the sentiments of our brethren of the land we live in." It lists three works to be performed before the commencement of the play, plus sufficient interval music to fill the time between the acts of a five-act tragedy or comedy. Before "the drawing up of the Curtain" the band was to play

YANKEE DOODLE
Grand Battle Overture in HENRY IV*th* [Martini].
General WASHINGTON'S *March*

Between the acts of the tragedy *Gustavus Vasa*, the band performed

A Grand Symphony by Sig. *Charles Stamitz;*
Grand Overture by Sig. *Vanhall;*
Grand Symphony by Sig. *Haydn;* do. by *Carlos Ditters.*[5]

Additional selections, quite possibly vocal music, would have been used between the acts of the farce *Modern Antiques*.

The attitude of the audience toward the orchestra was certainly proprietary; while the methods of the gallery might be deplored, the right of the audience to demand that their favorites be performed was seldom questioned. Managers were aware that to ignore the wishes of their customers was dangerous to the company's financial well-being, and tried various methods of appeasing them. The ideal program of music had to include something for every political faction (particularly the Jacobins and the Federalists in the last decade of the century), as well as a few general patriotic songs and some popular airs. The managers would announce the evening's music in advance, at least in part so the audience could not legitimately complain of having been disappointed in their expectations.

On successive nights there would be considerable repetition of the music performed, and less detail would be announced in advance. On February 5, 1794, the music for a performance of the same play and farce at the Federal Street Theatre included "The Boston March, Grand Symphony by Sig. Hadyn [*sic*], General Washington's favorite March; Grand Overture;—SONG, The Greenwich Pensioner—Grand Symphony by Sig. Ditters—SONG, The Lass of Richmond Hill—Grand Overture; Yankee Doodle, a favourite tune; Grand Symphony by Sig. Vanhall."[6] On February 10 the music included "Grand Symphony by Sig. Haydn, favourite Air, Yankee Doodle, General Washington's favourite March; Grand Overture; Air, Machere amie; Grand Symphony; Air, The Mulberry Tree; Grand Overture."[7]

Subsequent newspaper bills no longer listed the music, but a letter dated February 20 contained an appeal from the musicians themselves:

The Musicians that perform in the Orchestra of the Boston Theatre, assure the public, that it is not more their duty than it is their wish to oblige in playing such tunes as are called for, but at the same time they wish them to consider the peculiar poignancy of insult to men not accustomed to it. Thus situated they entreat a generous people so far to compassionate their feelings as to prevent the thoughtless, or ill disposed from throwing Apples, Stones,

&c. into the Orchestra, that while they eat the bread of industry in a free country, it may not be tinctured with the poison of humiliation.[8]

The same season saw trouble in New York, at a March 3 performance of the opera *Tammany,* when the "republicans" crowded the house and demanded favorite patriotic tunes. They attacked James Hewitt, "the leader of the band, and a very respectable, inoffensive character," because "as a foreigner, he did not know the tune which was called for." The audience refused to wait until Hewitt could find someone else in the band who knew the tune, and a considerable altercation ensued.[9] The solution was to create a medley overture of enough popular and patriotic tunes to placate most listeners.

In December 1794 the New York manager, John Hodgkinson, made a speech "previous to the commencement of the opera" in which he explained that "popular tunes and favorite overtures will be performed at stated times . . . and Mr. Carr's Overture was composed for this purpose." The overture referred to was Benjamin Carr's *Federal Overture,* first performed by the Old American Company at Philadelphia on September 22, 1794.[10] It included "Yankee Doodle," the French favorites "Ça ira," "Carmagnole," and the "Marseilles Hymn," the popular tunes "Irish Washerwoman," "The Rose Tree," and "Oh Dear, What Can the Matter Be," and ended up with the "President's March." Carr's overture became the model for other such medleys composed for the same purpose, using the same politically expedient title but not always containing the same music. On September 21, 1795, a "new Federal Overture" composed by Mr. Leaumont of the Boston company was performed at Providence, Rhode Island.[11] When Hodgkinson took the Old American Company to Boston that year, Carr's overture had been adapted to meet current needs; it included the first four pieces listed above plus "Knox's March," "Richmond Hill," and "The President's March."[12] In 1798 Peter Van Hagen wrote his own new *Federal Overture* for use at the Boston Theatre,[13] and James Hewitt wrote a *New Federal Overture* for use in New York early in the nineteenth century.[14] Hewitt's overture included yet another set of popular, politically acceptable, or patriotic pieces: "Yankey Doodle, French Air, President's March, Air in *Rosina* [Lads and Lasses All Advance], Allemand, French Air, Oui' noir mais pas si diable, Ça ira, Pauvre Madelon [from Arnold's *The Surrender of Calais*], Airiette, and Washington's New March." [15]

Reports of disturbances caused by demands upon the orchestra continued well into the nineteenth century. One such occurrence in Philadelphia in 1796 was deplored in a Boston newspaper:

> Disturbance at the Theatre
> Philadelphia, Jan. 13
> Audience, versus Orchestre [*sic*]
>
> Last evening an affair happened at the theatre, which excited a high degree of surprise in the mind of every man who reflects on the attention due to an audience, from the manager, company and orchestre of all theatres. The gallery, availing itself of its long established, altho' unwritten privileges, called for the President's March. The band with a most culpable pertinacity, obstinately refused compliance—the gallery as resolutely persisted to their demands. At length, the musicians, to end the strife, threw down their instruments, with all the indignation that offended dignity can inspire.
>
> When their indignation had a little subsided, they returned to their stations—but with the same unalterable determination to refuse to gratify the audience. The latter were as resolute as at the first, and by their vociferations totally drowned the "concerts of sweet sounds" proceeding from the orchestre. The audience now in earnest felt exasperated with the indifference, not to say contempt, with which they were treated; and many gentlemen in the pit and boxes united with the gallery, against the band. This formidable alliance brought the enemy to a parley; they played the desired tune, and all was hushed. However, two of the most active persons in the gallery were seized, and hurried away by the constables; this was the more irritating, as the tumult had, by that time, almost wholly subsided.—Various reflections crowd on the mind, from this apparently trivial circumstance. While every man of liberality must sincerely wish the managers success, and must be alive to preserve them, the players, and the orchestre, from insult; or illiberal treatment; the public have an unquestionable right to a high degree of attention from these gentlemen, in their respective walks, not only to gratify every innocent and harmless desire, but even to anticipate their wishes. What then are we to think of an orchestre which almost invariably refuses to comply with the requisitions of the audience, however general the demand, however easy an acquiescence may be? Which hardly ever plays those song tunes that

are calculated to give universal satisfaction, but confides [*sic*] itself to set pieces of music, from the chief part of which it is requisite to be a connoisseur to derive any pleasure? Surely these things require reformation.—Surely there is a fault or an error in judgment somewhere—and as surely the Philadelphia audience will apply a remedy.[16]

It is apparent that the author of this piece had no sympathy at all for the rights of the orchestra, which was probably making a valiant attempt to raise the standard of music performed in the theatre, as well as to eliminate the confusion and clamor that destroyed the mood of the play between the acts. The sympathies of the writer were all with the "long established, altho' unwritten privileges" and "unquestionable right" of the gallery. The opinions expressed were too much for one reader, however, who penned a long reply, ending:

It is, I own, the duty as well as the interest of managers to anticipate the reasonable desires of the audience, and according here, and I believe in Philadelphia, the Orchestra never omits playing the Federal Overture, in which are introduced all the popular airs and marches. Perhaps the managers would do well to advertise in the bills the music to be performed, and thereby preclude all pretext of discontent.

The "Gods" have ever assumed the privilege of insulting the Orchestra. If this insult is continued with impunity, in a short time there will not be a man of talent and respectability in any Orchestra in the United States.[17]

This was certainly not an isolated incident. Durang reported of the gallery gods in Philadelphia in the late 1790s:

As soon as the curtain was down, they would throw apples, nuts, sometimes bottles, on the stage and in the orchestra from the gallery which was allways crowded, and call out for "Carlisle March," "Cherry Charlott's Jigg," "Mother Brown's Retreat," and the names of many noted characters [i.e., prostitutes]."[18]

Such incidents occurred in all the principal American theatres. Lest it be assumed that such attitudes and incidents were due to "provincialism," we note an incident that occurred at Drury Lane in London in

November 1796. After the play, *God Save the King* was "called for" but ignored. After the first act of the farce the call was renewed:

The Band, on this occasion evinced the most *indecent* reluctance; and when obliged to comply with the almost unanimous demand of the House, they played this *Constitutional Air* in a manner so spiritless, as to excite the indignation of all who observed their conduct.—It is worthy to remark, that only eight Performers appeared in the orchestra.

The audience then demanded the words, but the "performers" were as reluctant as the "band," and "the same want of spirit and *good will* was evident." The writer warned the musicians and actors that "it is their *duty* to comply with the wishes of the Audience, by whom they are ultimately paid," and that if not heeded, the audience could be expected "to wreak their vengeance on the theatre."[19]

Despite such dire threats, orchestras continued to try to improve the quality of music played in the theatre—and the public continued to appreciate it more when the prevailing tastes were accommodated. In Philadelphia things had not improved after a decade. A letter to Mr. CENSOR in December 1805 complained:

I CANNOT help thinking that the Musicians at the theatre appear to pay more attention to their own gratification than to that of a great part of the audience, in their continual repetition of the sonatas, and other airs, which they usually play. . . . it surely would . . . conduce more . . . if some of our patriotic airs, or other popular tunes, were oftener introduced. . . . I have observed very few people in the theatre pleased with the music generally given. No person could help being interested at the sudden and pleasing effect produced yesterday evening by the playing of one of our favorite marches, after being *entertained,* in the interludes, between the first three acts, with the usual tunes. The gentlemen in the orchestra may act from the best motives, and they do not now appear to be inattentive to their duty; but they should pay more attention to popular opinion in this instance.[20]

The *New-York Evening Post* complained in 1805 that the orchestra not only played the same tunes, but played them badly. It recommended that

If the gentlemen musicians cannot read at sight we wish they would employ their leisure time in committing to memory a few easy and popular airs. . . . And while they are engaged in this much to be desired employment, it will increase the obligation if they will add to their stock of country dances; we never having, during the last seven years, been treated to any music of this sort excepting the single air of *La Belle Catherine*.[21]

At the beginning of the next season neither the orchestra nor the reviewers had changed their tune. James Hewitt was condemned for his use of the "same old symphonies" he had played since he became leader of the orchestra; the *Theatrical Censor's* critic complained that for seven years he had "never failed to recognize the same, same tiresome, disgusting sounds."[22] In 1811 Hewitt may have changed his habits; he had at least changed audiences. He was complimented for his "judicious and popular arrangements" for the orchestra at the Boston Theatre; the *Comet's* critic believed that "his selection of well known and favourite pieces for interludes, in preference to the 'sinfonia' and 'sonata,'" were "highly deserving of approbation."[23] A letter in *Polyanthos* in 1812 also spoke of the change in musical style:

Speaking of the Theatre,—it is more entertaining than when you *was* here, because they play *pantomines,* and the *musicianers* of the *ortchestra* play marches and song tunes, instead of *them* horrid pieces, that nobody *can't* understand, and that *sounds* like tuning a million of fiddles at once.[24]

In Charleston in 1803, Stephen Cullen Carpenter had more refined tastes, and his criticism was more to the point. He suggested that "The music introduced between the acts, if it cannot be made to increase and enliven the feelings excited by the piece, ought at least to be so contrived as not to break their continuity."[25]

On occasion, the behavior of the musicians brought legitimate objection. In Richmond the audience retaliated against one member of the orchestra who played badly:

Epigram to a musician of the theatre, occasioned by oranges, apples, &c. being thrown at him.

Fam'd Orpheus played with so much skill,
The very *trees* he mov'd 'tis said;
But you, my friend, perform so ill,
You bring the *fruit* about your head.[26]

In 1787 the orchestra at the John Street Theatre neglected its duty; instead of providing music between the play and farce they "are suffered to leave the orchestra to pay a visit to the tippling houses," and the ladies (presumably deserted by their escorts for the same reason) were left to "amuse themselves by looking at the candles and empty benches."[27] In Philadelphia nearly two decades later, the members of the orchestra wandered in and out of the pit whenever there was a break in the musical performance, and sometimes even when there was not. *The Theatrical Censor* complained in 1805 that "the musicians have an uphappy [*sic*] knack of being out of the way when their assistance is wanted. . . . Poor Mr. Gillingham is frequently seen *fiddling* almost by himself for half an hour together."[28] In 1811 *The Cynick* suggested that in future the musicians

should not be suffered, to twang the fiddle strings, to strike their harpsichords, or to remove their stools and benches, whilst an actor is delivering his soliloquy; or to bustle through the orchestre, occasionally throwing down their instruments, with violence, and continually popping up their heads, before the spectator, whilst an interesting scene attracts his attention.[29]

A month later, however, the musicians were still "interrupting the performance by coming prematurely, at the end of each act, into the orchestra."[30]

THE BAND OF MUSIC

Orchestras in both England and America varied widely in size and quality, depending on time, place, and circumstance. If we assume that London orchestras set the standard, then it may be useful to consider the size and instrumentation of some of London's theatre orchestras

Table 3   Instrumentation in English and American Orchestras

	1783 Charleston Concert	1790 King's Theatre London	1791 Pantheon, London	1794 Philadelphia Theatre	1795 Charleston Concert	1798 New York Theatre	1809 Covent Garden Theatre	1810 Philadelphia Concert
Flutes	2	2	2	2	2	—	2	6
Oboes	} 2*	2	2	2	2	—	2	—
Clarinets		—	2	—	2	2	2	4
Bassoons	2	2	2	2	1	1	2	3
Horns	2	2	2	2	2	2	2	[2]
Trumpets	—	—	2	2	—	—	1	2
Trombones	—	—	—	—	—	—	1	—
Violins	7	9	16	12–16	12	4	12–16	21
Violas	2	2	4	2–4	5	1	2	6
Cellos	2	3	4	2–3	} 3**	2	2	3
Double Bass	—	1	4	2–3		1	3–4	3
Drums	—	—	1	1	2	—	1	2
Keyboard	1	1	1	2	1	1	1	—
Total	20	24	42	30	32	14	33–38	57

* Two performers doubled on these instruments as needed.
** Designated simply as "basses" with no differentiation between instruments.

during this period. (A summary of instrumentation in several English and American orchestras during the period is shown in Table 3.)

The principal London theatres for the performance of English opera were the Drury Lane and Covent Garden theatres and the Little Theatre in the Haymarket. The tiny orchestra pit at the Little Theatre had room for only six wind players at one time.[31] A variety of woodwind parts could be written only if the players were able to double on various instruments. The orchestra at Drury Lane had as few as eight players at a time, and at Covent Garden, where Handel's operas were produced, the orchestra held only fifteen to twenty musicians.[32]

In 1790 at the King's Theatre in the Haymarket, which was the home for Italian opera, the band included a harpsichord, two flutes, two oboes, two bassoons, two horns, nine violins, two tenors (violas), three violoncellos, and one double bass—a total of twenty-four players. When the company was forced by patent problems to move to the Pantheon, it enlarged its orchestra so that it included a harpsichord, two flutes, two oboes, two clarinets, two bassoons, two horns, two trumpets, drums, sixteen violins, four tenors, four cellos, and four double basses (forty-two players),[33] but this alteration may have been forced by acoustical necessity. The *Morning Chronicle* of February 19, 1791, commented that "the orchestra of the Pantheon is composed of the Professional Band; but never was the execution of that admirable band so stifled and drowned as in the well into which they have been thrust."[34] Even after the orchestra returned to its home theatre, it apparently left much to be desired. Haydn commented after a visit to the King's Theatre in the 1794–95 season: "The orchestra is larger this year than before but just as mechanical and indiscreet in accompanying, and just as badly placed."[35]

Orchestras tended to become larger in the early nineteenth century. The new Covent Garden theatre in 1809 had the following ensemble: six or eight first violins, six or eight second violins, two tenors, two violoncellos, three or four double basses, oboe and flageolet, two flutes, two "clarionets," two horns, two bassoons, trombone, trumpet and bugle, pianoforte, bells, carillons or small bells, and kettledrums (thirty-five to forty players).[36]

In its early days the American Company may have occasionally performed with an orchestra composed of "the 'one Mr. Pelham,' and his harpsichord, or the single fiddle of Mr. Hewlett."[37] By the 1790s, however, in spite of what must be considered poor working conditions, the major theatres of the United States had begun to attract competent musicians, some of whom could even boast, like Gottlieb Graupner and Mr. Menel, of having played under Haydn. A number of refugees from the French Revolution, many of them noblemen, found themselves compelled to earn a living by their former artistic avocations, and another group of French refugees arrived after the uprising in Saint-Domingue (Haiti) in the early 1790s. When Moreau de St. Méry visited Philadelphia in 1794, he reported that "most of the musicians of the orchestra are Frenchmen, enabled to exist by this means." One member of the orchestra was M. Collot, son of the former president of the high council of Cap François. "Like so many other colonists, he has been reduced to earning his living by his labors. His talent for the violin, which he studied for his own amusement, has made him first violinist at the Philadelphia theatre." [38] In Charleston the *Courier* appealed for support for Robert Leaumont, the leader of the orchestra, in 1803:

pecuniary help cannot be supposed a matter of indifference to a gentleman who once luxuriated in honourable rank and affluence, but by the sad reverses of an unpropitious fate, has been driven to the mortifying, but we maintain honourable expedient, of making provision for a numerous family, by practising as a profession that which was originally acquired as an elegant accomplishment, and exercised only as an amusement. [39]

These French players remained a significant part of most American theatre orchestras. England and Germany continued to supply musical emigrants, too, with a smattering of players from other European countries. All frequently combined theatre music with private teaching, instrument repair and tuning, church music, recitals, and music printing and sales in order to earn a living.

American orchestras at this period, like European orchestras, consisted entirely of men. Since the names of orchestra members did not ordinarily appear on the playbills or in the advertisements, however, it is not easy to be certain of the precise membership of early American orchestras, or even to find many references to them as individuals. The mobility and rapid turnover among musicians made any listing transitory, and the same players turned up in various cities and orchestras in the course of several seasons.

The pantomimist John Durang reported about 1785 that the orchestra for the American Company included "[Philip] Phile, leader; [John] Bentley, harpsicoard [*sic*]; Woolf, principle clarinate [*sic*];

Trimner, Decker and Son, Curtsrock; five or six more whose names I do not remember, all Germans [twelve or thirteen players]."[40] When John Hodgkinson arrived in New York in September 1792, he reported that "the orchestra was composed of about six musicians, some of whom were incapable of their business."[41] The competition provided by the Wignell-Reinagle company may have stimulated the improvement of this orchestra, however, because when the John Street theatre opened on December 15, 1794, it was reported that "The orchestra was a pleasing spectacle; but when the band struck up, it excited in us as delightful sensations as ever we remember to have experienced on a similar occasion."[42]

The orchestra was still small, however. William Dunlap listed fourteen members for the 1798–99 season at the Park Theatre. In his diary he recorded the instruments played by thirteen of them.[43] The orchestration thus was a bottom-heavy four violins (James Everdell and James Hewitt on first and Nicolai, Sr., and Sammo on second); one viola, identified on the list as a tenor (George Gilfert); two violoncellos, identified on the list as basses (Adet and Nicolai, Jr.); double bass (Dangle); two clarinets (Henri, first, and Libeschesky, second); two horns (Victor Pelissier, first, and Lewis Depuy [Depuis], second); and one bassoon (James H. Hoffman). Many players were able to perform on both wind and stringed instruments, and almost all high wind players could double on flute, oboe, and clarinet if needed. It is surprising that the only two high woodwinds included in this ensemble were clarinets, then the least common of the orchestral winds, but this doubling ability doubtless provided considerably more versatility than Dunlap's list suggests at first. Dunlap listed no keyboard performer for this orchestra, but Hewitt was well able to double in that position, perhaps leaving George Ulschoeffer (the musician whose instrument is not listed) to assist Everdell with the first violin; Ulschoeffer was also a keyboard player and builder.

Although I have found no further lists of complete orchestras, it is possible to discover likely members in the listings for various concerts throughout a given season. Members of the theatre orchestra regularly earned extra income in this manner. During 1814, for example, various New York concert notices list Gautier, Moffatt, and Curphiew as clarinetists, Smith as a cellist, Charles Gilfert in various capacities, and Perossier and Lafolle as leaders.

Although a French visitor to New York in 1801 reported an orchestra of twenty-five members at the Park Theatre,[44] this was probably not the usual ensemble there. Victor Pelissier wrote for a minimum of five winds and four-part strings in 1803,[45] about the size of the 1798 orchestra, but with flute and oboe instead of clarinet. In a painting of the Park Theatre in 1822 no more than ten orchestra members are visible in the pit,[46] and when the García troupe brought Italian opera to New York in 1825–26, the orchestra—"a large one for the period"—consisted of "seven violins, two violas, three violoncellos, two contrabasses, two flutes, two clarinets, [no oboe], one bassoon, two horns, two trumpets, and one pair of kettledrums" (twenty-four players).[47]

When the new Philadelphia Theatre opened in 1794, Ezekiel Forman wrote: "The orchestra may justly boast of having a band of Music and Musicians superior to what any other theatre in America ever did or does now possess."[48] John Durang joined this company and reported that Mr. [George] Gillingham was leader of a "band of 20";[49] later, the *Euterpeiad* remembered that the orchestra included "thirty instrumental performers, with Gillingham as leader, Henry as first clarionette, Mavell [Menel] first violoncello [*sic*], Demarque principal Double Bass, Reinagle at the Grand piano forte and organ, &c, &c."[50] The full band included

several violins—two each of flutes, oboes, horns, and bassoons, with trumpets and kettledrums, together with a grand piano forte and organ.—This collection gave for the first time, a full and complete orchestra to the American public.[51]

Robert Gerson's *Music in Philadelphia* provides the nucleus for a list of instrumentalists active in Philadelphia in the last decade of the eighteenth century who probably constituted the members of this orchestra: Berenger,* viola; Bouchony,* violin; Louis Boullay, violin; William Brown,* flute; Henry Capron,* cello; Benjamin Carr, leader; Daugel,* violin; Demarque,* double bass, cello; Dubois, clarinet; Jean Gehot, violin; George Gillingham,* leader and first violin; Gray,* horn; Henry, clarinet; Homman,* horn, viola; Alexander Juhan,* violin; Menell,* cello; Philip Phile, violin; William Priest,* bassoon, trumpet; Alexander Reinagle,* keyboard and director; George Schetky,* cello, violin, double bass; Robert Shaw,* oboe, bassoon; Stewart,* violin; Rayner Taylor,* leader; A. Wolff, clarinet; and William Young, flute, bassoon.[52]

During the 1800–1801 season the Philadelphia orchestra was described as "numerous, and scientific."[53] The afterpiece, *A Wedding in Wales,* by Philadelphian Thomas Stock, which requires the sound of the harp as an essential part of the plot, was performed in December 1801; perhaps the harp was part of the orchestra.[54] By 1810 Carr, Taylor, and Schetky assembled a fifty-three-piece orchestra, including "gentlemen amateurs," for a concert of excerpts from *The Creation* and *Messiah,* including twenty-one violins, six violas, five violoncellos, three string basses, six flutes, four clarinets, three bassoons, four trumpets (apparently horns and trumpets), drums, and kettle drums.[55] The Philadelphia *Aurora* reported the following principals: leader, George Gillingham; principal violins, Nenninger, of Baltimore, LeFolle, Hupfeldt, and C. Hupfeldt; principal clarinet, Thibault; Principal tenor, Homman; principal violoncello, George Schetky; principal horns and trumpets, Victor Pelissier and G. Hupfeldt.[56]

In January 1810 Stephen Cullen Carpenter complained that the "neglect of the band" of the Philadelphia Theatre had spoiled a song by Hardinge, and their "conduct deserved reprehension for the manager."[57] Perhaps some correction was made, because the following month Carpenter reported that the orchestra (performing in Baltimore with Gillingham and Niniger) "will assuredly bear the strictest scrutiny," and that the accompaniments were played in a manner that was "very respectable."[58] By the fall of 1811, however, there were more troubles, and *The Cynick* complained that the number of musicians in the orchestra had been divided in half.[59]

During the 1813–14 season various newspaper sources list the following performers at Philadelphia: Blondeau, flute; Carusi, clarinet; DiLuce, leader; Gallagher, clarinet; George Gillingham, leader; Charles F. Hupfeldt, violinist, leader; Lefolle, violin; and Rayner Taylor, organ, flute, and pianoforte.

For a concert in Boston in 1796, Mrs. Arnold assembled an orchestra of about fifteen that included Messrs. F. C. Shaffer, Francis Mallet, Stone, Trille LaBarre, Frederick Granger, Anderson, Bonnemort, Sweeney, Vakner, Austin, Muck, Henry L'Espouse, and Calligan.[60] J. B. Williamson listed seventeen members in the Boston orchestra in the 1796–97 season.[61] Robert Leaumont led the orchestra at the Federal Street Theatre during the 1795–97 seasons;[62] Trille LaBarre then led the group until his death in 1798. Gottlieb Graupner, Peter A. Van Hagen, and James Hewitt were also associated with the Boston theatre at a later time; when he arrived in New York in 1789, Van Hagen's advertisement had indicated his willingness to teach "violin, harpsichord, tenor, violoncello, German flute, Hautboy, clarinet, bassoon, singing."[63] The following list of players was active in Boston, ca. 1800 (members of the 1796–97 Federal Street Theatre orchestra are marked with asterisks): Anderson,* clarinet; Augier; Austin;* Barbotheau;* Bonnemort; Boquet; Louis Boullay,* violin; Brook;* Calligan; Colet [Collet], violin; Drake; Drake, Jr.; James Everdell, violin, leader; Feckner (or Vakner); Fries; Gayetano; George Gillingham, violin, leader; B. Glaan;* Frederick Granger,* clarinet; Frederick Granger, Jr.; Thomas Granger, violin; Gottlieb Graupner,* contrabass, piano, clarinet, oboe, leader; Hart; Henrief (or Henri), clarinet; James Hewitt, violin, pianoforte, leader; Trille LaBarre,* violin, leader; Layerne;* Henry L'Espouse;* Robert Leaumont,* clarinet, violin, leader; Francis Linley, pianoforte; Francis Mallet,* pianoforte, violin, contrabass; Mallet, Jr.; McIntire; Menel, violoncello; Muck,* trumpet; Frederick Mumler, violin, violoncello; Ostinelli, violin, leader; H. W. Pilkington, flute; William Priest,* bassoon; Relain, harp; Sçavoye;* George Schetky, violoncello; F. C. Shaffer, leader; Shaffer, Jr., violin; Stockwell; Stone,* oboe, clarinet, flute; Sweeney; Filippo Trajetta, violin; Turner; Peter A. Van Hagen, strings and winds, leader; and Wood.

The Charleston Theatre was able to depend upon "gentlemen amateurs" to help its orchestra on occasion; the local St. Cecilia Society provided a continual source of good music. In 1783 it was reported that Charleston had two concerts a month with the following orchestra: four first violins, three second violins, two violas, two violoncellos, two bassoons, one harpsichord, two clarinets or oboes, two flutes, and two horns (twenty players).[64] When a French troupe first played in Charleston in 1793, it was able to raise an orchestra of volunteers to accompany its pantomimes.[65] A letter to Messrs. Bignall and West in 1794 indicated that there were "thirteen performers who compose the orchestra of the Charleston Theatre."[66] During the 1795–96 season, while Gottlieb Graupner was engaged as leader of the orchestra at the Charleston Theatre, the *City Gazette* reported the arrival of a troupe from Boston under the management of John Sollee, which was to perform at the City Theatre; it listed among them "Mr. Bergman, formerly the leader of the Philadelphia orchestra."[67] During the same season, Mary Ann Pownall assembled more than thirty musicians for a performance of Haydn's *Stabat Mater,* including "one organ, twelve violins, three basses, 5 tenors, six oboes, flutes and clarinets, two horns, one bassoon and two pair kettledrums."[68]

Even circuses had orchestras, but few ensembles at either circus or theatre met the standards claimed by the Pepin and Breschard Circus in 1811, when it stated that "The BAND of music will be composed of several perfect musicians, who will execute choice and very agreeable tunes."[69]

During the 1803–4 Charleston season, Stephen Cullen Carpenter complained that the music of the pantomime *Care and Mirth* was "intirely spoiled by the orchestra. In the flute and hautboy we thought that we could discern masterly hands, but what could they avail in the discordant *strepor* of the violins, some of which scarcely played a bar in tune."[70] Carpenter believed that Alexander Placide had the inclination to engage a suitable band of musicians, but had not yet had the good fortune to do so. When the "wonderful little sprite" Fanny Hodgkinson danced at the theatre, the critic noted "the anxiety displayed by her master, Mr. *Fayal* [Fayolle], who stood playing the violin in the orchestra, and expressed his enthusiastic admiration of his little scholar by motions so animated and expressive as to strike all the beholders."[71] Later that season the benefit of Mr. Labotierre included a "GRAND CONCERT (the Orchestre placed on the Stage) by the principal musicians and gentlemen amateurs."[72]

The orchestra had been improved when the theatre opened for the following season on November 15:

Considering that it was the opening night of the season, the house was respectably full, and we were happy on entering to perceive that the Orchestra had been considerably enlarged, as it indicated an improvement in the Music, which was much wanting, the band having been last season extremely deficient; and gave promise of operas which by diversifying the performances will afford more amusement and satisfaction to the public.[73]

Other Charleston musicians included Robert Leaumont, mentioned above as leader of the orchestra in 1803, Mr. Bellinger, Mr. Muck (trumpet), Mr. Foucard (clarinet), and Mr. Decker, who led the orchestra in 1807 while the troupe was at Richmond.

By 1786 Savannah, Georgia, could muster an orchestra that included violins, German flutes, clarinets, French horns, bassoons, a violoncello, and a pianoforte. John Mack Patrick reports that the theatre orchestra usually numbered about nine.[74] When the Thespian Society performed in Lexington, Kentucky, in 1807, they enjoyed the assistance of the Musical Society, which gave regular concerts of vocal and instrumental music.[75]

Most small cities did not fare so well in their theatrical music; they often relied on makeshift expedients of one type or another. For example, when a group from the Boston Theatre visited New England communities including Portsmouth, New Hampshire, and Portland,

Maine, in 1796 and 1797, "the whole of the music of 'Rosina' was to be accompanied on the pianoforte by Mr. Tubbs."[76] On April 19, 1798, a troupe managed by Mr. Hamilton played in Alexandria, Virginia, and with unintentional humor announced that "several gentlemen of the town, Amateurs, have politely offered, as on similar occasions, to assist the music, which will add much to the entertainment of the audience."[77]

A group from New York led by Lewis Hallam performed at the Assembly Room in Albany, New York, in August and September 1803. Their musical numbers were accompanied by some local gentlemen, but a critic complained:

The Highland Reel did not make our *hearts as light and merry* as could justly have been expected from so celebrated a performance. . . . The music of Mrs. Seymour and Mrs. Villiers was so lost in the notes of the piano forte, that we cannot pretend to hazard an opinion of what we could not hear. The musicians should have remembered that his province was to *accompany* and *assist,* not to *drown* the vocal in the instrumental music.[78]

When John Bernard took a contingent from Boston to Vermont in 1808, the entire company numbered just eight persons. Francis Mallet, a violinist of sorts, was in charge of the music, but the actor Dickenson sometimes played along on his fiddle when he was not engaged onstage.[79] Even in Boston, a Haydn overture could be played by just three players: Mallet at the pianoforte, accompanied by Graupner and Trajetta on bass and violin (May 19, 1801).[80]

In general, then, American theatre orchestras at the turn of the nineteenth century were composed of not more than thirty members, and often less than half that number. The proportion of winds to strings was about one to two. The orchestra was strongly weighted on upper and lower parts, with middle parts considerably weaker. Winds were in pairs; of the normal orchestral winds, only the horns seemed indispensable. All others could be and often were doubled; particularly the upper winds (flutes, oboes, clarinets) were considered interchangeable. Since bassoons, violoncellos, violas, and double basses all doubled on the bass line, one or more of these instruments could be omitted as well. Because the term "bass" was often used to indicate not only either of the lower strings, but sometimes any of the instruments doubling that voice, it is often unclear precisely what instruments were used on this part. Perhaps the "ideal" small orchestra consisted of two oboes (doubling on flute or clarinet as needed), a bassoon, two horns, two first violins, two second violins, viola, violoncello, double bass, and pianoforte.

Orchestra members were generally valued less than any actors in the company, with the exception of children and supernumeraries. Salaries were paid only when the troupe was actually performing. The management supplied at least a portion of the musical instruments (the inventory of the Boston Theatre in June 1797 listed among the "inventerry of best furniture in privit rooms" one large "Base Voyal & Case"; an inventory of additional equipment acquired listed a trumpet, a double bass, and a pianoforte[81]). Most instruments were owned by the players themselves, however, in spite of the risk of breakage. The players were responsible for all their personal expenses, including travel to out-of-town engagements.

When William Dunlap listed his expenses for the 1798–99 season at the New York theatre, the entire fourteen-man orchestra was paid $140 per week, including the leader, Mr. Hewitt—an average of $10 per person. Actors' salaries at the same time were as high as $25 per player ($50 for a couple) per week.[82] Dunlap recorded in his *Diary* for June 3, 1798: "Pelissier & Dupuy call'd on me, the last wished and I promised his present situation in y^e Orchestra, the former proposes an augmentation of salary from 15 (the present) to 18. I did not agree to it."[83]

The fifteen members of the Boston orchestra received a total of $175 per week in the 1796–97 season. Trille LaBarre, as composer, was paid $16 per week. Louis Boullay, a French violinist, received $15 (perhaps for assistance in copying parts). The leader, Robert Leaumont, received $14, as did a Mr. Sçavoye. Mr. Brook and Mr. Muck each were paid $12, and the remaining eight members each received

$10 per week. This range compares with actors' salaries from $10 to $27. Gottlieb Graupner is listed with his wife among the actors; together they received $30 a week.[84]

An event at the Park Theatre in New York in the spring of 1808 illustrates the low position of the orchestra within the theatrical hierarchy. A new pantomime, *Cinderella,* directed by Holland and Twaits, was in preparation, with elaborate costumes, scenery, machinery, and great expense. According to advertisements in the New York papers, the theatre was closed on March 21 to allow for preparations for the piece, which was to open on the 30th. The musicians would not be paid, of course, while the theatre was closed, even though they were expected to attend rehearsals. Dunlap wrote that "In rehearsing the piece, the duty required of the band was so great, that they rebelled; but all difficulties yielded to the determination of the manager."[85] William Wood tells a different version of the story: the manager (Wood misremembers him as Thomas Cooper, who was a member of the company) instituted a system of fines because the band demonstrated "the most insolent neglect of rehearsals." The manager recognized that the pantomime's success would depend on its music:

Cooper placed a notice in the music-room to the effect, that all absentees from rehearsal would in future suffer such fines and forfeits as were designated by the orchestra rules and their several contracts. The notice was in vain; the fines were extracted, and a conspiracy determined on.

When a full house had assembled for the opening of *Cinderella,* and the bell rang for the orchestra, the "ringleader" disclosed the "plot" to the orchestra leader, Mr. Hewitt: the entire orchestra would refuse to play until the fines were refunded. Cooper appeared before the audience with two alternatives: they could receive a full refund, or, if they refused to be "deprived of their amusement by the freaks of underlings," the pantomime could proceed, with the music played by Mr. Hewitt on a single violin. The performance went on, the entire orchestra was dismissed, and after two or three days the pantomime reopened "with a splendid band."[86]

This colorful version of the story, which has Mr. Hewitt playing alone for the first performance, is probably not entirely accurate. On March 21, the same day that the theatre closed, Mr. Dunlap placed an advertisement in *L'Oracle and Daily Advertiser* in both French and English asking for eight or ten musicians to apply to him as manager. The opening of the piece was postponed two days until Friday, April 1, without explanation, but then opened on time and ran until the 20th without cessation (nine performances), playing on Monday, Wednesday, and Friday evenings. On Saturday, April 2, Mr. Bork, a violinist, announced a concert at the City Hall for the following Wednesday, April 6 (directly against the third performance of *Cinderella*), by "the first Musical talents in this city." Tickets were sold at Hewitt's Musical Repository, and the following Wednesday the *Oracle* announced that Hewitt himself would direct the orchestra. In the meantime, the theatre manager announced, on the 4th (after the first performance on the 1st) "that the MUSICAL DEPARTMENT of the *Theatre,* is nearly completed, that *Mr. Everdale* [James Everdell?] has arrived, & will take his place, as leader of the band. Several other performers are engaged . . . "[87] In spite of these conflicting details, what emerges is that fact that when the orchestra and the management disagreed over the terms of their contract, virtually the entire ensemble, including the leader, was dismissed and a new group hired to replace them.

In the spring of 1798 John Hodgkinson supervised the musicians at the Park Theatre as part of his management responsibilities. He quarreled with the wind players after a performance one evening, then tried (in vain) to get Dunlap "to join with him in a declaration that the musicians who had quitted the orchestra in consequence of his message to them t'other night should never play in it again."[88]

In Charleston, when the French theatre opened in 1794, it was announced that the gentlemen in the orchestra were offering their services "without any wish of payment."[89] This situation apparently changed rapidly, however, and the salaries offered were enough to tempt players already under contract elsewhere. In April 1794 the

Charleston *Gazette* published a letter from three disgruntled members of the Charleston Theatre orchestra, addressed to "Messrs. West and Bignall, Managers of the South Carolina and Virginia Company of Comedians." Though their regular salary was apparently $10 per week, the musicians had toured with West and Bignall's troupe, receiving as salary "seven or eight dollars a week: with such a salary we were obliged to defray all expenses, though we do not receive money from you but from the drawing of the curtain to its fall, in every town or place where your interest may call you." The musicians then enumerated their expenses for the preceding weeks, and the weeks in which they had received no salaries at all (two weeks from Norfolk to Richmond with no salary but $20 in travel and other expenses; five weeks from Norfolk to Richmond and Charleston, $60 lost; and a $10 loss for Passion Week, when theatres traditionally remained closed). They asked that they be allowed to earn extra money by playing for Mr. Placide at the French theatre, so long as their first duty lay with their original troupe at the Charleston Theatre.

West and Bignall replied in the next day's *Gazette*, apologizing that the public should be troubled by so trifling a matter, and complaining that the musicians' demands were "improper, unreasonable, and indeed not quite grateful." The managers had "thrown in their mite" to relieve the extreme indigence of the French refugees, though "our occasion for their services by no means equalled our desire to relieve them from distress." After further self-justification, the managers fired the three recalcitrant musicians and sent them off to see if their interests would be better served in the employ of the French company.[90]

One other little-noted hazard of being a member of theatrical orchestras in the early nineteenth century related to the popular circus productions. Prominently featured in such shows were equestrian processions. At the Olympic Theatre in Philadelphia, the orchestra pit was located midway between the stage and the ring used for equestrian exhibitions. When the melodrama *Marmion* was performed there in 1812, the pageantry included "a flourish of trumpets; a grand procession of Marmion's suite; they proceed down the stage, cross a bridge over the Orchestra into the ring, march round and exit to martial music."[91] It seems doubtful that the horses were invariably well-behaved on such occasions.

In general, then, orchestral musicians in early American theatre were faced with job conditions and status worse even than the other performers, were subject to the whims and violence of the audience, and were poorly and irregularly paid. It is not surprising that players routinely sought other employment to supplement or replace what they found in the theatre. Dunlap told of one fellow who "eked out his income by making ice-creams,"[92] and Moreau de St. Méry wrote of M. Collot, a member of the theatre orchestra in Philadelphia, who did the same. Mr. Dangel, the double bass player of the New York theatre, taught French to Dunlap's son John.[93] Many musicians advertised for private students and offered to repair and tune instruments. They found some opportunities to earn extra income within the theatre by copying parts for the orchestra, arranging music for new pieces, or writing piano accompaniments for "popular favorites" that were to be published. Dunlap related a grim story of an exiled French nobleman, M. Gardie, who attempted to support his wife and child by working as a musician; for a time he copied parts for John Hodgkinson, but when Hodgkinson left town Gardie became so desperate that he killed his wife and himself.[94] Most musicians found less dramatic solutions to their problems, but even the most faithful orchestra member, copyist, and arranger could find himself like Frederick Granger, "who, having outlived his abilities, is now descending the vale, and may be denominated a *decayed musician*."[95]

THE LEADER AND DIRECTOR

The theatre orchestra operated under a system of dual control at the turn of the nineteenth century. Though the harpsichordist was no longer as essential to provide harmonic "filler" in symphonic music, in most operas the keyboard-director was still needed not only to supply the harmonies but to supervise the musical aspects of the performance as a whole and give cues to the singers, playing their parts if necessary. He set the tempi for the performance, playing regular chords until the appropriate tempo was established for each song or section. If necessary he could also accentuate the beat with movements of head or body. If the composer or arranger were present, he was expected to be at the keyboard supervising the performance. J. B. Williamson differentiated between the two roles in his 1796–97 list of salaries at the Boston theatre, describing Robert Leaumont as leader of the orchestra and Trille LaBarre as composer.[96]

Contemporary accounts refer to Alexander Reinagle, who "presided" at his pianoforte at the Philadelphia theatre. Though Reinagle's position as keyboard-director is quite clear, the *Euterpeiad* reported that he was adept also in a number of other areas: "his talents on the violin, though not equal to" those at the keyboard, "were nevertheless of the same nature. He could also take part in a band on the flute, the trumpet or violoncello."[97]

Next to the keyboard-director sat the violinist-leader.[98] In symphonic music the leader often took precedence over the keyboard-director, but in opera he tended to supervise the instrumentalists and, assisted by the leading bass player, transmit the tempi set by the keyboard-director to the other members of the orchestra. He led the orchestra by means of strongly accentuated playing, exaggerated body movements (particularly those of the bow arm), and occasionally by movements of the bow in the air. The relationship between keyboard-director and violinist leader was in a state of change at the turn of the century. Gradually the violinist-leader assumed the dominant position, and the keyboard-director took a less prominent role or was even omitted.

George Gillingham was the leader of the Philadelphia orchestra when that theatre opened (he later played at the New York and Boston theatres). The *Euterpeiad* reported that "his superiority of talent lies in leading a band, in which perhaps, he is inferior to no one living as well as to time, as to understanding every style of music."[99] *The Theatrical Censor* added:

In this place, it would be unjust not to mention Mr. Gillingham, leader of the orchestra; the excellence of whose execution on the violin often compensates for the ear-rending discords occasioned particularly by the female singers. The importance of a good leader is easily conceived; and his services cannot be too highly appreciated.[100]

James Hewitt was prominent as leader of the New York orchestra; he, too, later appeared in other cities, including Boston. Hewitt was described as a "Violinist, Organist, Composer and Instructor; he is eminent in science and a gentleman of great experience and versatility of talent."[101] It is not clear whether Hewitt always functioned as violinist-leader or if he sometimes served as keyboard-director; he was apparently capable of filling either role. It is certainly possible that he alternated in the two positions, filling the keyboard-director role when he was the composer or arranger of the music performed, or when extra strength was needed in the harmonies. The emphasis on Hewitt's role may indicate that the violinist-leader had already assumed a dominant position in New York in opera as well as in symphonic music.

When Gottlieb Graupner directed orchestras in Charleston and Boston he may have directed from the keyboard; it is also possible that he led the orchestra from his position as "leading bass player." John Dwight remembered that as a boy he had seen Graupner "lead the little orchestra in the old Federal St. Theatre, with his double bass. He was a famous 'timist.'"[102]

As long as orchestras remained small, the problems of ensemble caused by the lack of a clearly visible beat were probably not serious; orchestra members could easily see and hear most other players. It may have taken a few measures to establish the tempo clearly, but as long as all performers (including the singers) maintained a steady beat until the pause marks, the system must have worked fairly well.[103]

THE INSTRUMENTS

Since the great majority of early English and American operas have no surviving orchestral scores, it is necessary to understand the capabilities and uses of the various instruments in the era's theatre orchestras in order to reconstruct full scores for modern performance. Mechanical differences in the instruments themselves as well as various matters of playing technique differentiate the style of orchestral writing of today from that at the turn of the nineteenth century.

Several sources are particularly valuable in determining authentic performance practices. While works dealing with the orchestra in general, particularly those of Adam Carse for the eighteenth century, are invaluable, it is also necessary to consider the ways in which instruments were used specifically in opera and theatre in England and America.

Of primary importance are the surviving scores themselves. Though the minimum published piano-vocal score included two staves which carried the melody and the bass line, additional information was added in various ways. First, the name of the instrument that played a particular melody might be written into the score, as, for example, the indication that the original ballad tune in the overture to *Children in the Wood* was played first by the horns (ex. 43).[104] Second, important instrumental lines were occasionally "cued" in small notes on the staff with the vocal part (ex. 44). Third, one or more additional staves might be added. Since the first violin ordinarily doubled the voice, when a third staff was added—even though it was normally at the top of the score—it usually carried the second violin part (ex. 45).

Duet scores sometimes required three staves, and publishers would take advantage of the rests in the vocal parts to provide additional instrumental parts. Occasionally a nearly complete score can be reconstructed from such added lines. An unusually generous example was

Example 43. Horn passage from overture, *Children in the Wood*, 1793. Music Division, Library of Congress.

Example 44. Instrumental cues from "When Love Gets You Fast in Her Clutches," *Children in the Wood.* Music Division, Library of Congress.

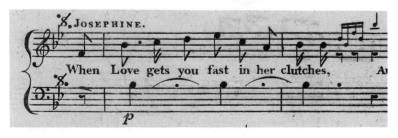

Example 45. Violin parts from "Young Simon," *Children in the Wood.* Music Division, Library of Congress.

"The Robin" from *Children in the Wood,* which provided a full score including the flageolet part, both violin parts, and the bass (ex. 46).

The "symphonies" at the beginning and end of vocal numbers may be particularly useful in providing cues to the type of string figuration appropriate for use throughout the piece. When it was necessary to provide complete vocal melodies, there was little space for other material on the staff, but more elaboration may be found in the purely instrumental sections.

Example 46. Excerpt from full score of "The Robin," *Children in the Wood.* Music Division, Library of Congress.

A particularly valuable score for the reconstruction of orchestral parts is Stephen Storace's *No Song, No Supper* (Drury Lane, 1790), the only English opera from 1790–1800 that survives in full score. Roger Fiske, in the preface to his edition of the opera, presents convincing evidence that this score was prepared for the Little Theatre in the Haymarket in the 1793–94 season; *No Song, No Supper* was performed fourteen times that season, since it could be adapted for the tiny pit and stage. "Though there are parts for flutes, oboes, clarinets and bassoons, the score is so arranged that there are never more than six woodwind[s] playing at once." [105] Thus this score provides direct clues to the musical capabilities of the Little Theatre's orchestra and the scoring used to overcome its limitations of space and size.

Also of particular interest are the manuscript piano-vocal score and complete parts for Victor Pelissier's incidental music for *The Voice of*

Nature (archived at the New York Public Library). Pelissier wrote for only two high winds (with the upper part indicating doubling on flute and oboe and the lower part for oboe alone), a bassoon, two horns, and four-part strings for this New York production in 1803. The upper wind line could be played by one performer who alternated between the two instruments as needed. Though it is possible that extra winds were added when occasion demanded, it is also probable that five winds made a perfectly acceptable group.

Treatises by composers and theatre observers at the turn of the century provide other sources of information. Although I am aware of no treatise dealing generally and comprehensively with writing for the theatre orchestra, several treatises deal with specific areas of performance or problems of orchestration.

William Shield (1748–1829) is described in John Sainsbury's *Dictionary of Musicians* (1824) as leader of the theatre orchestra at Scarborough, violinist and principal violist for the Italian opera in London, and musical director at Covent Garden, where he was the composer of more than twenty English operas, including *Rosina* (1782), which survives in parts. Sainsbury described Shield's journey from London to Taplow with Haydn, where he "gained more important information by four days' communion with that founder of a style which has given fame to so many imitators, than he ever did by the best directed studies in any four years of any part of his life." [106]

Shield's *Introduction to Harmony* was published in 1800; Busby reported that its "principal object . . . was to facilitate the acquisition of the harmonic art, by simplifying its laws, and divesting the science of the forbidding complexity which deters so many from venturing into its labyrinths." [107] Shield's knowledge of theatre music was particularly used in the third part of this work, where he included advice for accompanists and discussed the problems of writing for specific instruments (particularly horns and clarinets) with charts and examples.

Information can be gleaned in small bits from throughout Shield's volume. The representative page shown here (ex. 47) suggests the type

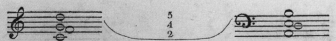

Either the fifth or the fourth must be prepared *, and it becomes the chord of the fifth and sixth at the resolution of the second by the bass.

This chord may be drawn into passages for different instruments in the following manner.

(A)   For the piano-forte.

For the violoncello.

In the second position (B)   A similar passage for the Violin.

(A) The notes of each chord may be inverted into various divisions, and genius will be the best director how to make the arrangement. The first four bars in the treble of the example for the piano-forte would imitate the bass to the remainder better thus :

&c.

(B) When a passage requires the first finger to be removed to the second fingers original place, it is said to be in the second position.

* The fourth is not prepared in any of the above examples, but these few notes will serve as a model.

Example 47. How to "draw a chord into passages," from William Shield's *Introduction to Harmony*, 1800. Music Division, Library of Congress.

Table 4   Range of Orchestral Instruments in the Early Nineteenth Century

Woodwinds:	
Oboe	c′ and all semitones from d′ to d‴, occasionally extended to g‴
Flute	Lowest note c′, usable range d′ to d‴
Small Flute	d″ to d‴ (an octave above the flute) (piccolo, recorder, flageolet; also called octave flute)
Clarinet	e (written) to about three octaves higher; lower range seldom used
Bassoon	B♭′ up 2½ octaves; extremes of range seldom used
Brass:	
Trumpets	Crooked into various keys; most often in D
Horns	Crooked into various keys; generally use only the open notes between written g and g″ in orchestral playing
Strings:	
Violins	Seldom went above third position in orchestra, but occasionally up to f‴ or g‴; Busby gives a range of g to c‴
Violas	c to e″
Violoncello	C to e′
Double Bass	G′ to e

All pitch indications use the Helmholtz system, designating middle C as c′, the octave below as c, two octaves below as C, three octaves below as C′; the octave above c′ is c″, and so on. Notes upward within the octave use the same designation.

of information to be gained for the contemporary orchestrator. In showing how to "draw a chord into passages" on various instruments, Shield not only indicates types of figuration usable in reconstructions, but incidentally indicates ways to interpret figuration in piano-vocal scores as cues to probable instrumentation.

The summaries that follow of the music written for the various instruments of the theatre orchestra are based on all the sources referred to above. The ranges of all the instruments commonly used in orchestras at the turn of the nineteenth century are summarized in Table 4.[108]

Woodwinds

Woodwinds in the soprano register were largely interchangeable in terms of pitch and performance style. The most important woodwinds in the eighteenth-century orchestra were the double reeds, and a small orchestra could get by quite well with a pair of oboists who could double on clarinet and flute when needed. In a pinch the woodwind parts could be replaced by strings, but by the 1790s there was considerable distinction made between timbres, even within the upper winds. In general, woodwind timbre at the turn of the nineteenth century tended to be more strident than that of today's descendants; double reeds were especially so. With small string sections, therefore, a woodwind melody could be heard quite clearly over the remainder of the orchestra. The high woodwinds were also used frequently to double and strengthen melodies played by the softer strings.

Oboe (Hautboy). A normal orchestral score contained parts for two oboes, though they were sometimes doubled by other high winds if the orchestra were large. The oboes often doubled the two violin parts, and the first oboe was occasionally given a solo line. At the turn of the century, there was an increasing tendency to use oboes and bassoons (and sometimes other winds) as a choir to provide contrast to the timbre and figuration of the strings. The basic job of the oboist was to double harmonies in tutti sections (with complex figuration omitted). The double-reed parts tended to be more sustained, in contrast to the repeated-note patterns of the strings.

Flute. The flute was still considered more a solo instrument than an orchestral instrument at the end of the eighteenth century; many orchestral scores called indiscriminately for "hautboys and flutes." The most common flute was the transverse flute, called the "German" flute in the United States. Most American concert programs, advertisements for lessons, and music specified the "German flute," indicating the possibility that the use of the term "flute" alone might imply either the transverse flute or the recorder. When flute parts were included in opera scores, they frequently replaced the oboe parts for a portion of the work.

Small Flute. The indications "small flute" or "octave flute" may have meant any of several instruments capable of playing the octave above the flute range: fife, piccolo, recorder, or flageolet. Sometimes one of these instruments was specified (*Children in the Wood* specifies a flageolet, for example, in "The Robin"; Shield's *Fontainbleau* calls for both fife and flageolet). The designation "small flute," however, which indicated flexibility in orchestration, was most common. The "Turkish March" in the final section of the *Children in the Wood* overture called for "Hautboy and small Flute," indicating only that the two should be an octave apart.

The second number in *The Voice of Nature* called for "small flute" in the individual part provided for the player doubling on first oboe and flute. The piano-vocal score of the same selection specified that the part be played by a flageolet.

The flageolet was similar to a recorder, but with a different mouthpiece,[109] and a softer, slightly reedier tone. One type had a recorder mouthpiece inside the flageolet mouthpiece.[110] Flageolets were imported into the States by 1716;[111] they figured on concert programs for more than a century. About 1800 these instruments were particularly popular. In April 1796 Rayner Taylor conducted a program in Philadelphia that included his own cantata, *The Nightingale*, sung by Miss Huntley with a "Bird accompaniment on the flageolet" by Robert Shaw, the principal oboist.[112] An 1805 concert program in Boston included an "Andante—with Variation and Rondo on the new patent Flageolet, lately introduced in all the Theatres and Musical Societies in London," played by Messrs. Augier, Everdell, Shaffer, and Mallet.[113]

Clarinet. The last of the high winds to be added to the orchestra, the clarinet was occasionally used in place of the oboe. At first composers linked it with the horns at times, playing with and sometimes even doubling the horns (as in Arne's *Thomas and Sally*, 1760), and Shield in his treatise still spoke of clarinets and horns in the same breath. Although vocal scores do not indicate the key of the instrument, Shield showed examples written for clarinets in both B♭ and C (examples marked in B, the common German marking, are actually in B♭). Storace used instruments in these same keys in *No Song, No Supper*. Because of their penetrating tone, clarinets were associated with outdoor music and with military bands; perhaps this was why Arnold chose a clarinet for the mother's "heroic" aria in *Children in the Wood*. In Air No. 5 of *No Song, No Supper*, the indication "clarinet solo" is given, but the first oboe doubles the part throughout, probably as an insurance against the unavailability of a clarinet. A second part is written only for oboe, but could of course be doubled on a clarinet in C if a second instrument were available. Air No. 12 opens with a two-measure unaccompanied clarinet duet.

Bassoon. The bassoons almost always played in unison and usually doubled the bass, simplifying it if necessary. Even if there was no indication in the score for bassoons, they were still expected; even small orchestras had a single bassoon. By 1800 the bassoon was recognized both as a solo instrument and as the logical bass instrument for the woodwinds. Bassoon solos, which could be quite difficult, were sometimes found in operas: see, for example, the opening of act 1, scene 1, of *No Song, No Supper*. At the opening of Air No. 8 (the finale of act 1), an unusual dialogue takes place between flute and bassoon (in octaves) and oboe. At the Andantino in that air, two bassoons and two clarinets double the voices in the closing ensemble, with flutes and horns added later. Strings are tacet until the repetition. "In Scotch songs," Fiske writes, "both real and imitated, the two bassoons were often asked to hold bass octaves in imitation of a bagpipe drone";[114] the bassoon most likely provided the drone bass for the hautboy and small flute duet in the overture to *Children in the Wood*.

Brasses

Brass instruments still maintained traces of their original orchestral use at the turn of the nineteenth century. They were used whenever the score referred to battle or hunting scenes, or any time the quantity of sound needed to be increased. By far the most important of the brass instruments was the horn, which was nearly indispensable in an orchestra in which "one might drive a coach and four between the bass and first violin,"[115] because of its ability to fill in the middle register.

A Boston critic in 1806 spoke of Noble Usher's asides, "With mouth, like French horn, sounding o'er one shoulder," suggesting that horn players there still used the common eighteenth-century playing position.[116] These instruments were valveless hand horns, which could be played in many keys by use of interchangeable crooks, but which were limited to the notes of the harmonic series. Orchestra parts made little use of stopped sounds, which could fill in the harmonic series and give a complete chromatic scale, but differed in timbre from the open tones. Shield provided a transposition chart for those who wished to write for horns or to read horn parts at the keyboard; he believed that the "best masters prefer any part of the scale to the 4th & 6th of the key for holding notes . . . but when they pass over quickly . . . their imperfection is not offensive."[117]

Horn players were sometimes asked to change crooks in the middle of a number, though the results were probably not always satisfactory due to the difficulties of retuning with a new crook. Though it is conceivable that horns in different keys could have been used simultaneously to provide greater harmonic and melodic versatility within a selection, I know of no example demonstrating that this was done. An excellent example of the type of writing found in late eighteenth-century horn parts is the opening of the slow section of the *Children in the Wood* overture, in the passage marked *corni* where two consecutive "horn fifths" are indicated (see ex. 43). Another example may be seen in "The Twins of Latona," in Shield's *The Poor Soldier*.[118]

The natural (unvalved) trumpet could also be crooked into a number of keys, though it was used most often in the key of D. It usually played parts similar to those of the horn, with little melodic movement; if trumpets were unavailable, their parts could easily be played on horns. Trumpets were generally reserved for the loudest moments; it was simply impossible to play them softly. In *Children in the Wood* they were called for at the end of the overture, and probably used on the same melody in the finale. The trumpet player was generally expected to play all the notes in the upper octave in the key of D—at least as high as g″—but only the fifth in the octave below.

Trumpet and drum parts were often added when the instruments were available; their absence in a full score is no indication that they were not present in performance. Trombones were used only rarely. Fiske reports that Kelly's use of them in *Blue Beard* in 1798 was their earliest appearance in eighteenth-century English musical theatre.[119] The grouping together of "trombone, trumpet, and bugle" in the listing of the orchestra at Covent Garden in 1809, after all the listings of pairs of other winds, may imply that those instruments were doubled by the same player or players.[120]

Percussion

A variety of percussion instruments were called for in English opera scores,[121] but the most important percussion instruments were timpani, which, like trumpets, were usually tuned in the key of D. Improvised percussion parts were added when appropriate, as in the finale of *No Song, No Supper,* where the text indicates that a tabor (or other available drum) should emphasize the rhythm, at least beginning with Margaret's verse (p. 104) where the cued carillon part begins.

Strings

The stringed instruments used in late eighteenth- and early nineteenth-century theatre orchestras had low bridges, short necks, and gut strings. Since vibrato was used only as an "ornament," the tone was not only softer, but had less carrying power than that of today's instruments. Since woodwinds tended to be louder, it is not surprising that they reinforced the melody on loud passages. A small orchestra might contain two or three first violins, two or three second violins, one viola (tenor), one or two violoncellos (basses), and one double bass—no more than could read from one copy of each part.

Violin. In opera the first violins most frequently doubled the vocal line, but could also play various types of passage work and harmonically conceived material. Shield gave several examples of chords "drawn into passages" for the violin (see ex. 47); repeated-note patterns were also frequent. The first and second violins were usually equal in num-

Example 48. Violin figuration in "Great Sir, Consider," *Children in the Wood*. Music Division, Library of Congress.

ber, though not necessarily in ability; they often played either in unison or in duet style, with frequent use of parallel thirds and sixths. In "Great Sir, Consider" from *Children in the Wood,* a great deal of the violin part is given, and it is clear that at various times the violins play in unison (A), in duet style (B), or even in alternation (C); some of the types of figuration used in a typical violin part also appear (ex. 48).

The varying use of violins to double or accompany the vocal line can also be seen in the first and second airs of *No Song, No Supper*. The first, an elaborate Italianate aria, has important solo lines for the winds, with strings maintaining a subordinate position throughout much of the piece, doubling neither the wind nor the vocal melodies, but playing repeated notes and other figuration. The violins are used "pictorially" at measures 20–24 to portray the ocean's billows, and at measures 25–26 to add further drama to the text. In the second, a "French air" is set strophically, with the first violin playing the melody of both the introduction and the verse except for a brief section at measures 30–37. The second violin plays figuration throughout.

Viola. The viola usually filled in the harmony or simply duplicated the bass at the octave. When they had a separate part the violas, like the violins, played figuration of various types and repeated notes, but the violists must have felt that they received more than their share of this type of writing. Even when they played the melody, it was usually doubled elsewhere. It was expected that the viola should not go above the top voice (melody), even when the composer or arranger made mistakes. Although the viola was invaluable for filling in harmonies in the middle range, the opinion expressed by Johann Joachim Quantz at the middle of the eighteenth century still applied at the end:

The viola is commonly regarded as a thing of little consequence in music. This may be because the instrument is generally played either by beginners or by those who have no particular talent for playing the violin, or perhaps because it is unprofitable to the player; therefore, able musicians are not at all anxious to play it.[122]

Stephen Storace wrote a better-than-average but still typical viola part for the overture of *No Song, No Supper*. The violist doubles either bass or violins much of the time, occasionally there is an independent part for a few measures, and twice the violas play divisi—once with the violins, once with the basses (measures 51–54, 111–14). At the opening of the first air the violas seem momentarily to receive a solo line; it is, however, simply doubling the opening of the bassoon solo. At the beginning of the finale the violas have a moment of glory: for four measures they play the bass line alone in trio with the two flutes.

Bass. The bass part, whether separately written or not, was always taken for granted. The terms "bass" and "basso" could mean both violoncello and double bass or could be used to differentiate the cello ("bass") from the double bass. If no separate parts were available, both or either instruments played the lower line of the reduced score provided for the keyboard. Separate parts, when provided, did not always double the keyboard bass, nor did the string part necessarily duplicate that of the bassoon. In *The Voice of Nature* score, however, the separate basso part for low strings almost always follows the keyboard bass. Though the rule of thumb for English orchestras was that double basses and violoncellos should be equal in number, in the States there is evidence—particularly from lists of performers—that violoncellos were more widely used. In 1800 a communication to the *Commercial Advertiser* concerning the entertainments at New York's Mount Vernon Gardens suggested "We should take it as a favor if Mr. Hewitt would add to the band a double bass, as it is very much wanted in an open garden." [123]

Keyboard Instruments

The pianoforte, harpsichord, or organ was used in early American theatre orchestras to provide harmonic background, to set the tempo, to fill in missing parts, and to provide cues for soloists. Even though the performer was expected to fill in the harmonies from the skeleton score, little figuring was ever provided.

Pianofortes began being imported into America in the 1770s, at about the same time they began to be used in England. [124] By the end of the century the pianoforte was in almost universal use in the American theatre. There is evidence that by 1794 both Philadelphia theatres had two pianofortes in the orchestra: the advertisement for the premiere of *Children in the Wood* (at the Southwark) announced: "Between the Play and Entertainment, a Concertante Duett, for two grand Piano Fortes, by Messrs. Guenin and Carr"; [125] and William Wood reports there were "two grand pianos and a noble organ" at the New Theatre. [126]

In Boston J. B. Williamson listed the purchase of a pianoforte (for $186.66) in the spring of 1797. [127] Benjamin Crehorne, a stage carpenter at the Federal Street Theatre in 1794, was a builder of pianofortes; Peter Van Hagen advertised Crehorne's instruments for sale at his store in 1801, and Mr. Mallet of the theatre orchestra was selling pianofortes by 1805.[128] Circumstantial evidence abounds for the use of pianofortes rather than harpsichords in other theatres. Charleston, too, had a pianoforte builder in the 1790s,[129] and a "grand piano forte" was used in concerts there by 1793.[130]

In New York a cabinetmaker and actor named Tremaine made a harpsichord of "a most agreeable and melodious volume and tone character" for the John Street Theatre in 1759—the first known to be made in New York.[131] During the Revolution, however, the British soldiers brought a pianoforte into the theatre for at least one play.[132] In 1785 George Ulschoeffer (later in the theatre orchestra) "exhibited a pianoforte of his own make in the coffee room of the City Tavern," claiming to "have made every part of the instrument himself."[133] When Mount Vernon Gardens opened in 1791 a pianoforte was in use there,[134] and Benjamin Carr sold a variety of pianofortes in his Musical Magazine Repository in 1795.[135] Many theatre musicians appeared in concerts during the 1790s, and invariably the keyboard instrument listed in the programs was the pianoforte.

Though the evidence for the dominance of the pianoforte in the pit is overwhelming, the presence of an organ at the Philadelphia theatre offered additional possibilities. It may have been used as a solo instrument, or simply to fill in harmonies in the orchestration. It is tempting to conjecture that the presence of the organ may have had some bearing on the fact that the number of players in the Philadelphia orchestra was cut in half in 1811.

PROBLEMS OF ORCHESTRAL ACCOMPANIMENT

Contemporary writers frequently mentioned the problems inherent in using an orchestra to accompany the solo voice. The problems of balancing voices with an overenthusiastic pianist in Albany have already been mentioned; in other cases voices had difficulty being heard over the orchestra. In general, orchestral arrangers working with this music today will be well advised to favor light scoring and clean, predominantly homophonic textures, to use simple, repetitive figuration and standard chord progressions, and to avoid dissonances except when indicated by the piano-vocal score or when clearly demanded for expressive purposes.

In addition to the problems of balance and related textural considerations, the questions of orchestral figuration in general and, more specifically, of ornamentation in instrumental solo lines were frequently discussed by late eighteenth-century critics and commentators. William Shield gave several bits of advice to the composer or arranger, with examples that are reproduced here. After setting down the general precept that "You must not accompany a simple melody with an artful complicated harmony,"[136] he continued with a discussion of the accompaniment for a cantabile melody:

As the person who performs the principal part in a Cantabile movement is expected to ornament the melody (but more with feeling than flourishes) the accompaniment cannot be too simple, and the best masters generally avoid extraneous modulations in this graceful part of musical composition.[137]

He provided two examples of string figuration used in such cases (ex. 49), then continued, "Inexperienced composers too frequently accompany Divisions with a Violin in unison, or with a crouded harmony." He also presented examples "to shew how the best masters support the Voice without rendering it inaudible"[138] (ex. 50).

According to Fiske, orchestral musicians played little ornamentation not written in the part.[139] The potential for interference with each other and with the vocalist was obvious. Corri instructed that an accompanist when doubling the voice should not play any "grace or variation" other than appoggiaturas ("the ascending and descending graces of one interval").[140] Further support for Fiske's conclusion is given by the fact that appoggiaturas are sometimes included in orchestra parts, but omitted in the vocal parts being doubled. The implication is that vocalists were expected to know when to add ornamentation, but instrumentalists had to be told.[141] In a solo part, either in an aria or in an overture or other instrumental piece, instrumentalists

Example 49. "Of the cantabile," from William Shield's *Introduction to Harmony.* Music Division, Library of Congress.

Example 50. Figuration example from Shield's *Introduction to Harmony.* Music Division, Library of Congress.

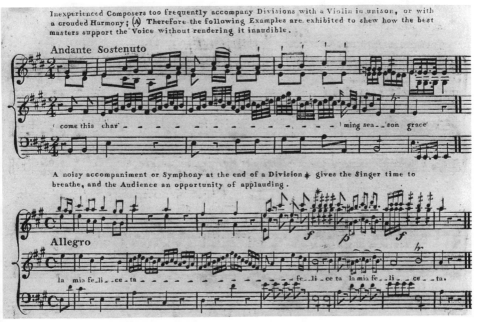

(A) Which may be proper enough when they do not wish the Singer to be heard.

Example 51. Writing for horns and clarinets: "Oh! Ponder Well" from *The Beggar's Opera*, in Shield's *Introduction to Harmony*. Music Division, Library of Congress.

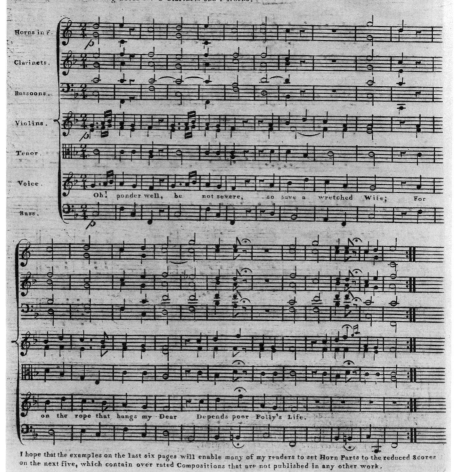

The best **Historians** may sometimes be mistaken when they become **Prognosticators**. The truth of this assertion may be made evident by a quotation from a **Work** which I ever read with pleasure and the following **Example** which I ever hear with rapture.

"D.ᵣ **Pepush** furnished the wild rude and often vulgar melodies in the **Beggars Opera** with basses so excellent that no sound **Contrapuntist** will ever attempt to alter them". But since that Paragraph was written the Public has been highly delighted with the effect of ingenious accompaniments to the whole of that Opera set by a **Dramatic Composer** whose Death was an irreparable loss to the English stage, for he not only supplied it with charming compositions, but with excellent singers. Here I'm obliged to pause and drop a heart felt tear, while my mind is filled with the remembrance of the Prodigies which he produced in his own family. Prodigies! Angels! who were called to the heavenly **Choir** long before their divine **Instructor**, which caused a stream of melancholly to flow through his latest compositions.

The following is the **Example** to refute the foregoing quotation, and may assist the **Learner** who is desirous of setting effective holding notes for C Clarinets and F Horns.

I hope that the examples on the last six pages will enable many of my readers to set **Horn Parts** to the reduced Scores on the next five, which contain over rated **Compositions** that are not published in any other work.

could ornament more freely, although even then the ornamentation was often notated in to a large extent.[142]

When there was a pause mark, particularly at the final cadence of an introduction, the soloist was expected to add a cadenza. The violinist-leader could easily add a cadenza at a place like the end of the slow section in the overture to *Children in the Wood;* he has just had an ornamented solo, and at the end of the tutti the pause mark would give him the freedom to stretch the cadence before directing the downbeat to the Vivace. The oboist was given a similar opportunity for a cadenza at the end of the introduction to the overture of *No Song, No Supper*.

A setting of "O Ponder Well," as it appears in Thomas Linley's setting of *The Beggar's Opera,* was given by Shield as an example for "the Learner who is desirous of setting effective holding notes for C clarinets and F horns"[143] (ex. 51). Several general characteristics of the types of orchestral settings frequently used in simple strophic airs may be seen in this example, and it may serve as a summary of the orchestral practice of the theatre:

(a) Only one pair of high winds is used. The clarinet part is often similar to that of the horn, though the use of thirds and sixths is more characteristic.

(b) The horns use sustained notes, with the fifths characteristic of the natural horn.

(c) The bassoons atypically have two separate parts here (making a rather thick texture), but much of the part is a simplification of the continuo bass.

(d) The first violin doubles the voice part, while the second violin plays an accompanying line, frequently in thirds. The first violin has an opportunity for a cadenza at measure 21.

(e) The viola supports the vocal rhythm; centered about middle C, it never moves above d" or below e.

(f) The position of the vocal part at the bottom of the score is, of course, for the convenience of the harpsichordist, who plays the melody and the bass and fills in the harmonies. Low strings are taken for granted on the bass part.

10

THE MODERN PERFORMANCE

Many of the American musical entertainments from the decades around the turn of the nineteenth century offer significant potential for modern performers. Though in the past these works have frequently been considered scarcely more than footnotes in the study of opera and drama, in recent years they have begun to receive the fuller attention they merit from both performers and scholars. The humor and pathos that made many of these works popular for decades after their introduction can still attract a modern audience, and some of the wit has ripened with age. The music is pleasant and melodious; despite its seeming simplicity, it has a sure theatrical touch.

Musicians who prepare a modern performance of one of these musical entertainments must deal with several problems. After selecting a work that will be musically and dramatically satisfying to modern audiences, the arranger must locate the available sources, prepare a performing edition using relevant contemporary practices, and present a historically accurate or at least adequate performance. Any work that exists both in libretto and in piano-vocal score versions is a possibility for modern revival. Performance scores based on these sources should be prepared according to the best standards of modern editing, and in light of late eighteenth- and early nineteenth-century practice.

THE STATE OF PUBLICATION

At the turn of the nineteenth century most operas were disseminated in three forms: the published libretto, the published piano-vocal score, and the manuscript orchestral parts used in the theatres. Many librettos were published within a few days or weeks of the opening of the production. Following the London procedure, the song texts of major new shows were available from the first night; for example, when *Tammany; or the Indian Chief* was first performed in New York in 1794, "Books, with the words of the Songs" were sold at the door for one shilling.[1] Full texts of the play or complete descriptions of the pantomimes were available shortly thereafter, so the audience could follow along during the performance. Hundreds of copies "as performed by the Old American Company" or by the Boston or Philadelphia companies were sold for this purpose. When *Cinderella; or the Little Glass Slipper* was performed in New York in 1808, a book containing the songs and a prospectus of the pantomime was published by A. Ming and sold at the theatre. When D. Longworth published a competing prospectus, the theatre announced that the Ming version was "the ONLY edition which can describe the pantomime as it is done in the New-York Theatre."[2] Longworth retorted in another advertisement that his book contained "The description of the *Grand Pantomimic* Spectacle, as it was originally performed in *London* and repeated in *Philadelphia,* and as it will be represented in the *New-York* Theatre, with the *exception of some difficult passages.*"[3]

Longworth obviously took his copy of *Cinderella* directly from the London publication and simply reset it in new type. Since such London publications not only allowed other publishers to take a slice of the manager's profits, but also allowed rival producers to acquire copies of plays or operas for their own use, Richard Brinsley Sheridan, while manager of Drury Lane, began withholding plays and librettos, including his own play *The School for Scandal* and the operas *The Duenna* and *The Pirates*. This practice seldom delayed other performances unduly, since there are several reports of "pirates" who sat in the audience night after night writing librettos for use in other theatres.[4] It was effective in the case of both of these operas, however; *The Duenna* was not performed in the States for eleven years, and *The Pirates,* one of Stephen Storace's best operas, was never performed in America. Although George Colman refused to allow the manuscript of his translation of Beaumarchais's *The Spanish Barber* to be taken from London's Little Theatre in the Haymarket, J. B. Williamson was able to remember (or copy) enough to prepare a text for performance at Boston with the original English music, "chiefly compiled by Dr. Arnold."[5]

Since the censor had to approve all plays or operas staged at London playhouses,[6] a complete copy of the words of new productions had to be submitted several days before opening night. These copies survive as the Larpent Collection, now located at the Huntington Library at San Marino, California. These copies do not always coincide with the published librettos.

During the nineteenth century various publishers and individuals prepared bound collections of similar-sized librettos. One example is the English collection, *Cumberland's Plays,* edited by George Daniels and published by G. H. Davidson from 1825 to 1855, which contains English plays originally published before 1800. An important private collection is that made by Francis Longe, Spixworth Park, Norfolk, in the nineteenth century, which was acquired by the Library of Congress about 1844; it includes about 375 plays. The J. P. Kemble–Duke of Devonshire Collection of about 4,000 printed English plays is at the Huntington Library.

The music was generally published only in piano-vocal scores. Although these included all the principal numbers (overture, solo songs, choruses), they contained only a skeletal outline of the music as it was performed. The minimum supplied was the melody and the bass line, though other parts were sometimes added in various ways (see chapter

9). These scores were usually available within a few weeks after a successful production opened, and were, like the librettos, sometimes published by the thousands. They were intended for use at home, but they also made their way to other playhouses.

Between 1763 and 1800 only two full scores of English operas were published,[7] though there were dozens of piano-vocal scores. One reason may have been the problem of piracy; another was the added engraving expense involved in the increased orchestration of the later operas. Neither do many manuscript full scores survive after 1763; Storace's *No Song, No Supper* (1790) survives in manuscript full score, and a set of orchestral parts survives for Shield's *Rosina* (1785). The overture for Mazzinghi's *Ramah Droog* (1798) survives in parts as printed in 1800, and the overture to Reeve-Mazzinghi's *The Turnpike Gate* (1799) survives in parts printed in the first year of the nineteenth century. Thomas Shaw's 1791 overture for Michael Arne's *Cymon* was printed but apparently has no surviving sets of parts. The New York Public Library has a manuscript piano-vocal score and complete manuscript parts for Victor Pelissier's incidental music for *The Voice of Nature*, first performed in New York in 1803. Multitudinous contemporary references to other parts and scores make it evident that they did exist, though they were probably copied and even arranged anew for each theatre.

All the remainder of this music was apparently destroyed by the fires that consumed nearly every theatre of note which existed in England or America during this period.[8] When the Philadelphia theatre burned in 1820, manager William Wood reported that the loss of the orchestral music was felt keenly, since "after the destruction of Covent Garden and Drury Lane theatres, the complete orchestra parts of many operas were only to be found in this theatre."[9] Because the Philadelphia theatre received many production materials directly from London, it may have had complete *original* orchestrations. Most American theatres had only the orchestrations prepared by local arrangers.

Whether these scores were English and American in origin, the impact of their loss cannot be overstated. While orchestral scores in general were lost, perhaps the greatest loss was to the instrumental music of the ballets, pantomimes, and melodramas. These works were not published in piano-vocal scores for home use, and thus depended entirely upon the lost orchestral parts and scores. Had this music survived, it might have rewritten the book concerning English influences on early American theatre music, since most of the arrangers of the pantomimes and ballets were French. Surely those lost scores included a great deal of music from French sources. And who knows whether another Wolf Glen scene—or something with similar impact—has been lost along with the other instrumental music of the early theatre? Even if the arrangements made for English provincial or American theatres escaped fire, they apparently did not survive nineteenth-century housecleaning; nevertheless, additional copies may yet be discovered in local or private theatre collections in the United States or in England.

The most straightforward method of obtaining new plays for use in early American theatres was simply to purchase, or have an agent purchase, copies of all new scores and librettos as they became available in London. Managers used several additional methods, among them the traditional "beg, borrow, or steal." In 1782 Thomas Wall placed a notice on his Baltimore playbills that "Any Gentleman possessed of good Farces, and will lend or dispose of them to the Managers, will greatly oblige them." Thomas Wignell of the Philadelphia theatre brought back a "library of dramatic and musical books" [10] when he recruited his company in England in 1793. Thereafter he received new plays directly from the London theatres by special arrangement:

Wignell's friendly relations with the London managers and authors, gave him the advantage of an early manuscript of each new piece, on the condition of its use being confined to his own theatre. Being yet unpublished, such was the public curiosity to read the piece of which I have spoken [*John Bull; or an Englishman's Fireside*, by George Colman], that a person of less delicacy than enterprise obtained a loan of our manuscripts from a careless prompter, and took an unworthy opportunity to copy the play and publish it, with a copyright announcement. Some of the copies found their way to England, where a deep indignation was expressed, both by the manager and author. Every effort was made to prove the fraudulent manner in which the copy had been obtained. The case, however, operated unfavorably on other new pieces, and nearly destroyed a monopoly so important to our house. The faithless prompter suffered the penalty of dismission [sic] for his fault.[11]

Sometimes the players owned copies of plays or music that they had used at other theatres, and were willing to loan them. In 1798 the Charleston Theatre granted a "free benefit" to J. B. Williamson for "furnishing his own wardrobe and music."[12] John Hodgkinson copied orchestral music in New York and carried it to Boston with him in 1798; he took "borrowed manuscript plays" to Charleston in 1803.[13] William Dunlap reported that Hodgkinson wrote to him from Boston in May 1799 to request "the loan of the plays of *Benyowski* and *The Italian Father*. The manuscripts were sent to him."[14] This type of borrowing may have caused the disappearance of many plays. James Nelson Barker's play, *The Embargo, or What News?*, was produced in Philadelphia at the time of the Embargo Bills in 1803; Barker wrote: "I know not what became of the manuscript: Blissett took the piece to Baltimore, where it was performed, and whence it was sent, at the request of Bernard, to Boston. It was never printed."[15]

PREPARING A PERFORMANCE SCORE

The first problem facing a modern music director is the choice of a work. Some works' librettos lack sufficient interest or merit, though appealing music often helps to redeem a mediocre story line. Other works contain little or nothing of genuine musical interest, or part or all of the music has disappeared. (Appendix A contains a complete listing of the musical entertainments performed in the United States between 1785 and 1815.)

One indicator of the probable success of a revised work is its popularity and longevity when it was originally performed. Although popularity and quality do not always go together, certainly a work that continued to please audience after audience at the turn of the nineteenth century is more likely to please now than one that closed after only a few performances and was never heard again. According to my records, the works most performed in the five principal American theatrical centers between 1785 and 1815 are:

1. *The Poor Soldier* (first performance, 1783; 233 performances, 1785–1815)
2. *Highland Reel* (1786; 175)
3. *The Mountaineers* (1793; 173)
4. *The Romp* (1778; 167)
5. *Rosina* (1782; 166)
6. *Blue Beard* (1798; 163)
7. *The Purse* (1794; 159)
8. *No Song, No Supper* (1790; 154)
9. *Children in the Wood* (1793; 153)
10. *The Agreeable Surprise* (1781; 147)
11. *The Padlock* (1790; 119)

Tempting as it is to look for a "completely American" work to perform, the sad truth is that there were no hits among works written and composed by Americans. Not one of the works on this "most popular" list is American in origin. There are, however, many good possibilities among American adaptations of English works.

Lists of performances in American theatres before 1800 are available in Sonneck's *Early Opera in America*. Though these lists are not always complete and are occasionally misleading, they are still of enormous value. Appendix B of this book continues the list of performances in four American cities—New York, Boston, Philadelphia, and Baltimore—for the first fifteen years of the nineteenth century.

If a piano-vocal score exists, the lack of a full score should be no deterrent to modern arrangers, who after all face exactly the same problems of reconstruction as did their forerunners. The work must be adapted to a specific set of performance requirements, and the piano-vocal score must be expanded to match the number and skills of the available orchestral forces.

Most afterpieces run only about an hour in length, with full-length works correspondingly longer; the length of any work can be adapted by adding and deleting musical numbers in the best authentic tradition. Even if only the options offered by various known versions of a work are considered, the arranger may encounter an embarrassment of riches. In choosing the numbers to be used for a particular performance, the function of each piece must be examined, and several questions addressed: What is essential? What can be omitted or replaced without disruption of the work? What are the strengths and limitations of the cast that will perform this version?

Having selected the musical numbers, the arranger turns to the problems of orchestration. The clues given in the piano-vocal score—either by direct allusion to the instruments used or by the type of figuration given—and a general knowledge of turn-of-the-century practice (as discussed in chapter 9) should be considered.

Although it is certainly a mistake to underestimate the skills of such theatre orchestrators as Pelissier, Reinagle, Taylor, Hewitt, and Carr, it is probably wise to err on the side of simplicity in reconstructing these scores. It is particularly tempting to fill in the middle of the texture, but the result may be surprisingly heavy and thick. The arranger should notate all parts originally improvised, the keyboard realization in particular, and also any necessary percussion parts.

A basic theatre orchestra—strings, horns, bassoon, one pair of high winds, and perhaps a piano or organ—is certainly sufficient, but it may be expanded or contracted according to the demands of the score and the resources available. A chamber ensemble of keyboard, violin, and violoncello was a standard expedient in performing early American music of all types—symphonies and concertos as well as opera. Since the violin almost always doubles the vocal line and the cello can play the given bass line, the only demand on the arranger is to fill in the missing harmonies at the keyboard. A second violin can supply many of those harmonies with a minimum of preparation or arrangement; sometimes the second violin part can be taken directly from the piano-vocal score.

The thirteen-member orchestra found in the New York theatre in 1798—two first violins, two second violins, one viola, two violoncellos, one double bass, two clarinets, one bassoon, and two horns (with perhaps a keyboard player added)—should prove well-suited to most modern performances. The Philadelphia orchestra, which was about twice as large, had complete winds in pairs and considerably more weight on the lower strings. Such a configuration would be the ideal for those few works with fairly complex orchestrations.

The arranger may wish to add desirable ornamentation, both instrumental and vocal, rather than rely on the limited improvisational abilities of most twentieth-century performers. Proper ornamentation should be supplied for songs of all types, though the degree of gracing appropriate will vary widely with the song, the role, and the performer. Minimum ornamentation of the vocal line should include an occasional appoggiatura at points of tension and a five- or six-note cadence at each pause mark. Some singers may wish to add further ornamentation, particularly in Italian-style arias. No matter how extensive the ornamentation, however, it must never interfere with the steady, underlying beat except at the pause marks. Even though all ornamentation may be written out and memorized in advance, the aim should be to make it sound relaxed and spontaneous.

One of the most vexing problems facing the arranger is the simple matter of key. Several factors were and are important in the choice of key for the numbers in comic opera. The first, and most obvious, is the pitch involved. Pitch was not standardized, even within a single country, and the common pitch levels used for voices and for instruments differed as well. In general, though, most English songs were probably performed about a semitone lower than we would read them today.[16]

A second factor is the problem of the range of singers. Although sopranos and tenors were the most widely used voices, baritones or basses were sometimes used to provide a contrast in vocal color, and the abilities and ranges of specific singers were sometimes taken into consideration. Since baritones as well as tenors sang their high notes in falsetto, the upper ranges of these parts may cause problems for modern singers. Though these baritone roles may be assigned to tenors, such an expedient sacrifices the color contrast appropriate to the characterization. It may be a better choice in many cases to preserve the timbre by transposing the songs to a more comfortable range. After all, alteration of these operas to meet the needs of individual singers was standard practice. Though we know that eighteenth-century composers frequently rewrote their own compositions entirely, placing them in new keys for new performing situations, I have not found specific references to transposition for the convenience of singers. Perhaps it was so common that performers did not consider it worth mentioning, and reviewers—our other principal source of performance information—were probably unaware of it.

The third factor is the practical one of considering the capabilities of the instruments in the ensemble. Any number using trumpets or drums was likely to be in D, because instruments were sure to be available in that most common key. Wind instruments in general were more easily played in standard keys, and in orchestras where rehearsal time was limited and players were commonly required to master several different instruments, it was important to avoid intricate fingerings and extra technical problems.

The fourth factor is the practice of associating specific moods or passions with various keys. Since equal temperament was by no means universal in England or in the United States at the turn of the century, there was some basis for differentiating between the "flavor" of the various keys. The association of the key of E♭ major with the heroic is well known. As late as 1824 John R. Parker wrote, "Every practitioner in the art must have noticed the various complexions, so to speak, by which they [keys] are characterized."[17] He listed several keys and their characteristics: F major, with its relative, D minor, was the "key of nature," rich, mild, sober, and contemplative. C major was bold, vigorous, and commanding, suited to the expression of war and enterprise. A minor was plaintive but not feeble. C minor was complaining and whining. D♭ major was dark, and so forth. Parker's specific descriptions are not so important; other lists offer quite different associations. What is important is that composers thought of keys not merely in terms of practicality but in terms of symbolism.

The question of dynamics must also be considered by modern arrangers. Piano-vocal scores were quite sparing in their use of dynamic markings; those markings given were generally in the instrumental sections. There might be a cautionary *p* marked in the accompaniment when the singer entered after the introduction to a vocal number, and sometimes a postlude was marked *f*. William Shield described the practice of using "a noisy accompaniment or Symphony at the end of a Division," which "gives the singer time to breathe, and the Audience an opportunity of applauding." He later remarked that "Composers are very fond of finishing Compositions with noisy Accompaniments, which my master used to mark con Strepito."[18]

In the same example Shield demonstrated the contrasts of dynamic level from *piano* to *forte* at the one-, two-, or four-measure intervals *galant* composers were so fond of using. This technique might produce an echo effect (as in measures 70–77 of the overture to *Children in the Wood*), or two different melodies might add to the contrast (as in measures 47–54 of the overture). A single note might also be marked *forte* in a soft section for a *sforzando* effect (measures 14–16, overture, and in the prelude and postlude to the first vocal number, reproduced in chapter 3 as ex. 5). Crescendos were frequently either implied, as at the end of "Great Sir, Consider" (ex. 8), or specifically indicated, as in "Young Simon" (ex. 6) or in measures 7–9 of "The Fearless Tar" from *The American Captive* (Boston, 1808) (ex. 52).

None of these dynamic effects was unusual in post-Revolutionary music in general, and a search of comic opera scores will discover other similar examples. More important, all these examples represent formulas that can be applied to other scores that contain similar passages but few or no dynamic markings. It would certainly be a mistake to assume that the lack of specific markings in a score is an indication that dynamic variations were not used as an expressive device.

While hand-copying scores and parts for operas and scenes from

Example 52. Crescendo, mm. 7–9, "The Fearless Tar," *The American Captive*,
Boston, 1808. Courtesy American Antiquarian Society.

this period, I've often thought of William Shield's cryptic remark:
"Composers and copyists furnish a theatre with the score and parts of
an opera very expeditiously since the invention of a musical short-
hand." [19] Perhaps he meant only that they had begun to use signs for
repeated measures and terms like *col voce, col bassi,* and *simile;* if he
had other secrets I can only hope that they are someday rediscovered!

CHOICES FOR MODERN PERFORMANCE

After the completion of the musical score, problems of interpretation
and of historical authenticity must still be solved before an opera or

other musical entertainment can be restored to life. Based on the wealth of information available in contemporary diaries, newspapers, periodicals, books, scores, and other sources, some guidelines for modern performance options may be summarized.

One sure way to guarantee the failure of a modern performance is to treat the work as something esoteric, of great historical value but understandable only by scholars and the cultural elite. On the contrary, these works were intended for mass audiences. They were primarily aimed at literate and socially prominent members of middle- and upper-class society, but they also pleased the sailors and other uneducated working-class men who occupied the galleries. Though a careful examination of the works themselves and the performance practices of the time is essential for the director's full understanding and adequate interpretation, a dogmatic approach can quickly raise barriers between the audience and the play. Imagine, for example, the confused reaction of a modern audience to the mishmash of costume styles found in many turn-of-the-nineteenth-century productions.

The original authors provided humor and sentiment of many types—most of which can still be understood today. Though a modern audience may miss some topical allusions and laugh at some things not originally considered humorous, the great majority of the humor can be mutually appreciated. Most of the musical works are light-hearted; the afterpieces in particular are little more than confections to provide the last course of an evening's entertainment. Even the terrors and tribulations of the sentimental dramas and melodramas cannot be taken too seriously. Though it is wrong to broaden lines, gestures, and characterizations to create a raucous, condescending parody of the original work, it is equally mistaken for the modern performer to be afraid of a little honest sentiment.

There have always been many different options available in every area of musical and theatrical performance practice, permitting ample opportunity to consider available performers, facilities, and budget. It is possible, too, to find many areas of reasonable compromise that should allow these works to be performed successfully under a wide range of modern conditions. The final criterion for a dramatic work must always be the response of the audience, and whatever can make the work accessible—both as entertainment and as an artistic unity—must be considered valuable.

Not many modern directors are fortunate enough to possess a historically authentic theatre in which to work, or to have the funds necessary to construct a replica of such a theatre. It is possible, however, to consider a wide range of options. A fully authentic production might feature a raked stage with an apron, proscenium doors with balconies above, a green curtain to signal the start of the production, and a second curtain to use between acts. The house would remain dimly lighted throughout the performance, while footlights and sidelights provided most of the stage lighting. All stage lighting could be shaded for dark scenes. Appropriate traps would allow needed access. Borders and drop scenes could be lifted into the loft above, but grooves could be laid down to move wings and flat scenes when needed. Each scene would have an appropriate setting, with scene changes accomplished in full view of the audience as part of the theatrical effect.

An equally authentic performance might take place on an open platform, with a single curtain. Scenery could include as few as two scenes—one interior and one exterior. Lighting could be from any available source—room lighting or a row of candles along the front of the stage. Such a production would lean heavily on the ability of its actors to create an appropriate atmosphere, but countless barns, taverns, and meeting rooms have been filled with such magic for an evening.

Many musical entertainments that require minimal scenery and properties can be produced successfully as theatre-in-the-round, and some even work well in concert halls with no scenery except what can be described verbally at the beginning of each scene. Other productions may necessitate more elaborate scenery or effects, but the principle of "symbol rather than representation" may be followed. *Poor Soldier* can readily be performed with only two scenes (interior and exterior), and *Children in the Wood* and *The Voice of Nature* require only three (a palace interior, a cottage interior, and an exterior). Other works such as *Blue Beard* require special scenery and effects that are essential to the plot; many of the more romantic operas such as *The Haunted Tower* require special lighting, spectral forms, and traps to create their Gothic atmosphere.

The burden of the production of early American musical theatre rested squarely on the shoulders of its actors. They were projected into the theatre by the stage apron, and the relatively small sizes of the theatres gave them intimate contact with their audience, with actors sometimes addressing the audience directly or fielding comments from the crowd. Away from the support of scenery and properties, actors were compelled to create their own illusions. Most operatic roles of this era are suited to the relatively spontaneous, straightforward, unexaggerated style used in comedy, with its stress on facial expression, nuance of gesture, and natural pronunciation. Though a few roles, particularly in dramatic romances and melodrama, call for the magisterial, rule-bound, formal style of the tragedian, this must never be allowed to degenerate into laugh-seeking, hiss-the-villain posing. These works represent the articulation of a popular system of moral and ethical behavior. What may seem to us today to be parody or exaggeration was actually total sincerity. It is therefore not appropriate to use broadened gestures, over-effusive speech, or a knowing smirk. Even though the conventions of eighteenth-century tragic acting may have led to exaggerated, bombastic portrayals on occasion (particularly in father or guardian roles, which often spout moral precepts), these would not have been perceived by contemporary viewers as humorous or parodistic. Tempting as it may be to modern performers to make the heroine languish, the villain leer and drool, and the hero strut and posture, such "attitudes" belie the early nineteenth-century conception of these characters.

Although historic performance practice included insufficient rehearsal, improvised speeches, forgotten lines, and last-minute substitutions—and these contingencies certainly justify modifications and additions to fit a specific situation (such as the need for verbal stage-setting)—it cannot be taken as an excuse for inadequate preparation.

To clarify outdated usages, complex plots, and plays on words, it is vital that modern actors thoroughly understand their lines and deliver them with absolute clarity.

The matter of costuming also allows flexibility. Turn-of-the-nineteenth-century troupes could be dressed in stylized costumes representing the time and place of the play's setting; they could be clothed in their own contemporary style; or, as often happened, they could wear a mixture of recent, outdated, and stylized costumes. Though a modern production should at least strive for consistency, there are at least two authentic choices for most operas: costumes of the period of the setting and costumes of the period of its first production. Following the line of reasoning represented by the actual practice of the original actors—that the authenticity of the costuming is not essential to the work's success—a modern troupe could just as easily justify the production of many works in twentieth-century dress. For productions set in indefinite "long ago and far away" periods, the standard "Old English" costumes used in Shakespearean plays are as useful now as they were at the turn of the nineteenth century.

Staging may involve appropriate business or tricks, and should certainly take into account the acting conventions of the day. Musical numbers should be examined carefully to determine whether specific movements or gestures are prescribed by either text or music. Some numbers may be totally ineffectual without stage action or greatly enhanced by it; others may be just as effective when performed concert style, with no action or physical characterization. Ensembles, too, may vary from vigorous action finales in the style of Mozart to those in which the chorus and principals simply line up at the front of the stage.

In spite of critics' periodic complaints that orchestras were unskilled or amateurish, many members of those groups were accomplished solo performers, composers, and teachers. No matter how large the orchestra used for any performance, sensitive and competent musicianship must be considered essential.

One option to be considered in modern performance is the possibility of using historic instruments—hand horns, pre-Boehm clarinets, pianofortes—in performance. This can be a fascinating experience for both performers and audiences, particularly if good quality original instruments or reproductions are available; such a presentation carries a special touch of authenticity. The intonation problems can be formidable, however. One frustrated clarinetist concluded while trying to play an early-nineteenth-century clarinet that "The only old instruments still around are the ones that weren't worth playing at the time. All the good ones were worn out long ago." With some compromise, however, at least the sound of many old instruments may be copied with exciting results.

One especially knotty problem is keyboard timbre. Even if the decision has been made to use modern instruments in the orchestra, the modern piano's strength and timbre is so far from that of the early nineteenth-century pianoforte that it seems ludicrously out of place in a small orchestra. I prefer a strong harpsichord sound to a piano trying to be unobtrusive. Since later works may have been performed without keyboard, it may be preferable to omit the keyboard part entirely rather than use a modern piano. The use of a pipe organ, which offers alluring tonal and expressive possibilities for melodramas and musical romances, may also be considered, although the total lack of information on historic performance practice makes this a risky business.

Although it is certainly possible for an experienced keyboard-director to direct a performance, perhaps assisted by a violinist-leader, the habits of modern performers must be considered. Modern players are, alas, trained to watch the stick, and an orchestra stretched out along the pit may not be sensitive to subtle cues offered from the keyboard or even from the first violin. Solutions may depend on the size of the orchestra, the competence and experience of the players, and the length of time available for rehearsal, but this is one point of authenticity that must usually be sacrificed when the ease and accuracy of the performance demand a more visible conductor.

Early American musical entertainments offer a fine opportunity for cooperation between musical and dramatic organizations of various types, and are particularly suited for college and community theatre groups. A small number of accomplished singers can carry most productions, while many of the roles can be filled by actors with little or no singing ability. Doubling of parts is frequently possible, and the number of servants, ruffians, and other supernumeraries can be increased or decreased as needed.

With proper preparation and the right amount of ingenuity, the best of these works might even become an occasional part of the permanent theatrical repertory. The flexibility of performance practice at the turn of the nineteenth century, as well as the attitude of composers and arrangers toward the adaptability of the score itself, provide a situation ideal for modern reconstruction. These works were written as pure entertainment, and they can still provide it in large measure. When versatile performers, able and willing to act and sing in the manner appropriate to the period, may be found, and when their enthusiasm is communicated to their hearers, the entertainments of post-Revolutionary America can still move and delight a modern audience.

APPENDIX A

A Preliminary Checklist of Musical Entertainments Performed in the United States, 1785–1815

When evaluating early American theatrical works for possible modern performance, it is often difficult to find concise yet comprehensive information in a single source. This checklist provides basic facts concerning titles, composers, librettists, genres, and premieres of musical entertainments performed in American cities between 1785 and 1815, and may serve as a starting point for study of individual works. Although every attempt has been made to be comprehensive and accurate, the listing is not definitive; it remains for future researchers, no doubt with a computerized data base, to identify and survey all possible sources, sort out murky relationships, resolve contradictions and inconsistencies, and fill in gaps.

It is important to recognize that versions performed in different cities may have varied widely in both text and music. Separate versions are indicated where possible, but there is often insufficient information in contemporary sources to differentiate accurately which of several versions was given at a specific performance.

Material for American performances 1801–1815 is compiled from contemporary newspapers, periodicals, scores, and librettos by the author, with Charleston information supplemented from Hoole's *The Ante-Bellum Charleston Theatre*. Information on eighteenth-century performances is compiled from newspapers, periodicals, scores, and librettos and from Sonneck, *Early Opera in America*; Odell, *Annals of the New York Stage*; and Pollock, *The*

Philadelphia Theatre in the Eighteenth Century. Additional information on English performances is taken from Fiske, *English Theatre Music in the Eighteenth Century* and from Nicoll, *History of the English Drama.*

Information on musical excerpts printed in America may be obtained from the standard bibliographies by Sonneck and Upton (eighteenth century) and Richard Wolfe (early nineteenth century).

Title: Works are listed alphabetically by the most-used title of the work with alternate titles following in parentheses. When works are widely known by alternate titles, those titles are cross-referenced.

Frequency of performance: The asterisks preceding some titles provide a rough indication of popularity by indicating the frequency of performance in the five most populous American cities in the years 1785–1815. * indicates 25 or more performances; ** indicates 50 or more performances; *** indicates 100 or more performances. For works which premiered after 1800, a more accurate record of performances can be found in Appendix B.

Subtitle(s): All subtitles used for various performances are given, in an order not necessarily indicating frequency of use or correlation with the order of titles given. The usual way of printing title and subtitle was, for example, *Abroad and at Home; or, The King's Bench.*

Libretto: The principal author or authors of each work are listed first. Following are the sources for the libretto—a novel or earlier opera, for example—and the names of others who translated or adapted the original work. When possible, differentiation is made between various adaptations; when this is done, the letter "a" in this classification corresponds with the letter "a" in the next category, and so forth.

In the case of pantomimes, the person in charge is indicated here as the "arranger," although contemporary sources often used the terms "composer" or "director." There is no implication that such a person wrote the music, however. Although the full responsibilities of the arranger are almost never clear in any individual case, they may have included writing or devising a scenario, selecting the music, choreographing dances or movements, supervising the preparation of scenery, machinery, and costumes, and performing a principal role.

Composer: The principal composer or composers are listed first. If a later composer is given credit for "music entirely new," or is otherwise known to have written new music, his name is separated from the first composer by a semicolon. "Add. by" indicates later additions (songs, overtures, miming music) that were added in some performances while retaining much of the original music. "Arr. by" indicates that the person designated is known to have written orchestral parts for some performance of the work. It must be clearly understood that music used for one performance was not necessarily used for another.

Genre: A contemporary genre designation is provided for each work, along with the length in acts when available. (Some works were altered and acts were combined or omitted.)

It is difficult to draw fine distinctions in genre, partly because the works themselves are not always available for study, and partly because contemporary designations are often misleading and contradictory. Works were sometimes altered for different performances, perhaps even changed from one genre to another. Operas became pantomimes, for example, and many Shakespearean plays had enough music added at some performances that by any other name they would be considered an opera. Many works of all genres were performed "in the manner of a melodrama." The terms "pantomime" and "ballet" were often used interchangeably, and when speaking parts and arias were added, the line between pantomime and comic opera was very thin. Wherever possible, I have used contemporary designations, preferring those from librettos or scores (which do not always agree) and relying on contemporary periodical sources as necessary.

I have included all works in English designated as operas (either all-sung or with spoken dialogue), masques, burlettas, musical plays, melodramas, musical farces, interludes, and similar works using both drama and music in some combination. I have included all works described as pantomimes (unless I have a clear indication that no music was included) and ballets that are for more than one performer. I have included some works performed in French (although I have omitted the all-sung operas performed in New Orleans in the early years of the nineteenth century).

I have also included works classified as tragedies, comedies, or other theatrical genres that contemporary sources indicate were performed with added music, if some of the added music survives, if the composer or arranger is known, or if the titles of added music are given.

First Performance(s): The date and location of the first performance is given here, as far as it is known. A superscript 2 following the date indicates a second performance, with the date of the premiere unknown. When two dates are given, the first is a performance elsewhere that preceded the American premiere. Unless otherwise noted, performances in Boston took place at the

Federal Street Theatre; performances in Charleston at the Charleston Theatre; in New York at the John Street Theatre until January 13, 1798, and the Park after January 19, 1798; and in Philadelphia at the Southwark until December 1793, and at the Chestnut Street Theatre after February 17, 1794.

***Abaellino, The Great Bandit; **Libretto:** Heinrich Zschokke, *Abaellino der grosse Bandit;* tr. by William Dunlap; **Genre:** Grand Dramatic Romance; 5 acts; **First Performance:** 1801/2/11, New York

Abroad and at Home; **Subtitle(s):** The King's Bench; **Libretto:** Joseph G. Holman; **Music:** William Shield (Pastiche); **Genre:** Comic Opera; 3 acts; **First Performance, London:** 1796/11/19, Covent Garden; **First Performance, America:** 1797/1/27, Philadelphia

*Adelgitha; **Subtitle(s):** The Fruits of a Single Error; **Libretto:** Matthew G. Lewis; **Music:** Michael Kelly; add. by Victor Pelissier; **Genre:** Tragedy, Incidental Music; 5 acts; **First Performance, London:** 1807/4/30, Drury Lane; **First Performance, America:** 1808/11/14, New York

Adelina—See *The Escape of Adelina*

*Adelmorn, the Outlaw; **Libretto:** Matthew G. Lewis; **Music:** Michael Kelly; add. by Victor Pelissier, arr. by Frederick Granger; **Genre:** Dramatic Romance; 3 acts; **First Performance, London:** 1801/5/4, Drury Lane; **First Performance, America:** 1802/2/25, New York

***Adopted Child, The; **Subtitle(s):** Milford Castle; The Baron of Milford Castle; The Fatherless Protected; **Libretto:** Samuel Birch; **Music:** Thomas Attwood; Peter van Hagen; **Genre:** Musical Drama; 2 acts; **First Performance, London:** 1795/5/1, Drury Lane; **First Performance, America:** 1796/5/23, New York

*Adrian and Orrila; **Subtitle(s):** A Mother's Vengeance; **Libretto:** William Dimond; **Music:** Thomas Attwood, Michael Kelly; arr. by James Hewitt; Victor Pelissier; **Genre:** Drama, Incidental Music; **First Performance, London:** 1806/11/15, Covent Garden; **First Performance, America:** 1807/9/2, New York, Vauxhall

Aesop in the Shades (See also *Lethe*); **Genre:** Farce, with music; **First Performance:** 1787/2/1, Philadelphia

*Aethiop, The; **Subtitle(s):** The Child of the Desert; **Libretto:** William Dimond; **Music:** (a) James Perrosier; (b) Rayner Taylor; acc. by John Bray in Boston; **Genre:** Drama interpersed with Music; **First Performance, London:** 1812/10/6, Covent Garden; **First Performance, America:** (a) 1813/4/5, New York; (b) 1814/1/1, Philadelphia

Africans, The; **Subtitle(s):** War, Love, and Duty; **Libretto:** George Colman, jr.; **Music:** Michael Kelly; **Genre:** Play, interspersed with songs, duets, and choruses; 3 acts; **First Performance, London:** 1808/7/29, Little Theatre, Haymarket; **First Performance, America:** 1810/1/1, New York

***Agreeable Surprise, The; **Libretto:** John O'Keeffe (originally produced in Dublin as *The Secret Enlarged*); **Music:** Samuel Arnold; **Genre:** Comic Opera; 2 acts; **First Performance, London:** 1781/9/4, Little Theatre, Haymarket; **First Performance, America:** 1787/1/27, Philadelphia, Southwark

Aladdin; **Subtitle(s):** The Wonderful Lamp; **Libretto:** John O'Keeffe; **Music:** William Shield; **Genre:** Pantomimical Entertainment; **First Performance, London:** 1788/12/26, Covent Garden; **First Performance, America:** 1801/3/14, Philadelphia

Aladdin; **Subtitle(s):** The Wonderful Lamp; **Libretto:** Charles Farley; **Genre:** Melodrama (Grand Romantic Spectacle); **First Performance, London:** 1813/4/19, Covent Garden; **First Performance, America:** 1815/11/25, New York

Alberto Albertini; **Subtitle(s):** The Robber King; **Libretto:** William Dunlap; **Music:** John Bray; **Genre:** Dramatic Romance; 5 acts; **First Performance:** 1811/1/25, New York

Alcesta; **Libretto:** "Taken from the story of Admetus"; **Genre:** Pantomime; **First Performance:** 1797/3/23, Charleston, City Theatre

Alexis and Justine; **Libretto:** J. M. Boutet de Monvel; **Music:** Nicolas Dezède; **Genre:** Comic Opera; 2 acts; **First Performance:** 1785/1/14, Versailles; **First Performance, America:** 1795/7/10, Charleston

Algerine Pirates, The; **Subtitle(s):** The Spanish Lovers; **Genre:** Serious Pantomimic Ballad [*sic*]; 1 act; **First Performance:** 1807/5/1, Boston

Alonzo and Imogen; **Subtitle(s):** The Bridal Spectre; **Libretto:** One of several English and American ballets and pantomimes based on M. G. Lewis's ballad, "Alonzo the Brave and the Fair Imogene"; **Music:** James Byrne, arranger; **Genre:** Pantomime; **First Performance:** 1797/4/17, Philadelphia

Alzuma (acted in America as *Peru Avenged*); **Subtitle(s):** The Death of Pizarro; **Libretto:** Altered from A. F. F. Kotzebue by Arthur Murphy; **Music:** Victor Pelissier; Alexander Reinagle; **Genre:** Tragedy, Incidental Music; 5 acts; **First Performance, London:** 1773/2/19, Covent Garden; **First Performance, America:** 1801/3/2, Philadelphia

Amant statue, L'; **Libretto:** Desfontaines; **Music:** Nicholas Dalayrac; **Genre:** Comedy with songs; 1 act; **First Performance:** 1785/8/4, Paris; **First Performance, America:** 1794/8/12, Charleston

Ambrosia and Matilda; **Libretto:** Taken from M. G. Lewis, *The Monk*; **Genre:** Pantomime; **First Performance:** 1811/4/22, Charleston

Amelia and Valcour; **Subtitle(s):** Banditti of the Black Forest; **Music:** Carusi; **Genre:** Pantomime; 3 acts; **First Performance:** Olympian Circus, Paris; **First Performance, America:** 1811/7/10, New York, Pepin and Breschard Circus

America, Commerce, and Freedom; **Subtitle(s):** More Laurels for Gallant Tars; **Music:** Includes songs, "America, Commerce, and Freedom," "Yankee Chronology," "Yankee Frolics"; **Genre:** Patriotic Sketch; 1 act; **First Performance:** 1812/12/18, New York

America Discovered—See *Tammany*

Americain, L'; **Genre:** Pantomime; **First Performance:** 1794/7/2, Philadelphia

American Camp, The; **Subtitle(s):** Female Volunteer; **Genre:** Interlude with patriotic song and chorus; 1 act; **First Performance:** 1812/10/8, Boston

American Captive; **Subtitle(s):** Siege of Tripoli; **Libretto:** James Ellison; **Music:** Includes "The fearless tar," set to music by John Braham, and "a new Turkish song" by Miss Dellinger; **Genre:** Drama, Incidental Music; 5 acts; **First Performance:** 1811/12/11, Boston

American Captive; **Libretto:** altered from *The Sultan* (cf) by John Hodgkinson; **First Performance:** 1796/2/29, New York

American Farmer, The; **Subtitle(s):** Sailors in the Country; **Genre:** Comic Pantomime; **First Performance:** 1808/9/5, New York, Vauxhall Gardens

American Generosity (American Liberality); **Subtitle(s):** Moorish Ingratitude; **Genre:** Pantomime; **First Performance:** 1810/10/24, Boston

American Heroine; **Subtitle(s):** The Cruel Return; **Libretto:** Based on *Inkle and Yarico* (cf); several English pantomimes and entertainments with this name; **Genre:** Grand History and Military Pantomime; 3 acts (also play by Dunlap, 1790); **First Performance:** 1796/5/3, New York

American Heroine; **Subtitle(s):** Harlequin Neptune; **Genre:** Pantomime Entertainment; **First Performance:** 1801/3/30, Philadelphia

American in London, The; **Subtitle(s):** Love at First Sight; The American Merchant in London; **Music:** Benjamin Carr; **Genre:** Musical Entertainment; **First Performance:** 1798/3/28, Philadelphia

American Independence—The 4th of July, 1776; **Genre:** Grand Patriotic Pantomime; 3 acts; **First Performance:** 1795/6/30, Charleston

American Naval Pillar—See *Tars From Tripoli*

American Tar—See *The Purse*

American Tar; **Subtitle(s):** The Press Gang Defeated; **Libretto:** "Founded on a recent fact at Liverpool"; William Francis, arranger; **Music:** Rayner Taylor; **Genre:** Ballet; **First Performance:** 1796/6/17, Philadelphia

American Tars; **Subtitle(s):** Huzzah for the Navy; **Genre:** Patriotic Effusion (with songs); 2 acts; **First Performance:** 1812/12/16, Boston

American Tars; **Subtitle(s):** Preparations for Privateering; **Genre:** Musical Interlude; **First Performance:** 1812/4/8, Charleston

American True Blues; **Subtitle(s):** The Naval Volunteers; **Genre:** Musical Interlude; **First Performance:** 1799/4/3, Philadelphia

American Volunteer, The; **Subtitle(s):** A Scene on the Frontier; **Genre:** Pantomimical Ballet; **First Performance:** 1813/4/3, Philadelphia

American Volunteers; **Genre:** Pantomime; **First Performance:** 1800/3/5, Boston

American Volunteers; **Subtitle(s):** Who's Afraid; **Genre:** Pantomimical Spectacle, interspersed with singing and dancing; **First Performance:** 1813/5/12, Philadelphia, Commonwealth

Americana and Elutheria; **Subtitle(s):** A New Tale of the Genii; **Libretto:** James Tobine; **Genre:** Masque; 5 acts; **First Performance:** 1798/2/9, Charleston, City Theatre

America's Independence; **Subtitle(s):** The Fourth of July (cf); **Genre:** Prelude; **First Performance:** 1793/7/5, Baltimore, Maryland company

Amour dans les Rose, L'; **Subtitle(s):** Cupid's Frolic; **Libretto:** Master Whale, arranger; **Genre:** Pantomime ballet; **First Performance:** 1812/6/5, New York, Olympic Theatre

Amour et la Marriage; **Genre:** Pas de deux; **First Performance:** 1815/4/17, Philadelphia

Amour trouve les moyens, L'; **Subtitle(s):** Fruitless Precaution; **Genre:** Comic Ballet; **First Performance:** 1794/5/16, Philadelphia

Amour vient a bout de tour, L'; **Subtitle(s):** La precaution inutile; **Libretto:** William Francis, arranger; **Genre:** Pastoral ballet; **First Performance:** "As performed in Paris"; **First Performance, America:** 1813/2/24, Philadelphia

Animated Statue; **Libretto:** Based on *L'Amant statue* (cf); **Genre:** Ballet; Pantomime; **First Performance:** 1797/10/9, New York, Wignell-Reinagle

Animation and Death of Harlequin; **Genre:** Pantomime; **First Performance:** 1786/11/24, Charleston

Annette et Lubin; **Libretto:** M. J. B. and C. S. Favart (apparently not Charles Dibdin's English adaptation); **Music:** Adolphe Blaise; **Genre:** Comic Opera; 1 act; **First Performance:** 1762/2/15, Paris; **First Performance, America:** 1794/7/16, Charleston

Anniversary of Shelah, The; **Genre:** "A piece consisting of scenery, song, and dancing"; **First Performance:** 1808/3/18, Philadelphia

Anonymous Disguises (*The Lover Disguised,* 1804); **Subtitle(s):** The Useless Resolution; **Genre:** Comic Opera; **First Performance:** 1794/4/26, Charleston

Any Thing New?; **Libretto:** Isaac Pocock; **Music:** Charles Smith; **Genre:** Musical Farce; 2 acts; **First Performance, London:** 1811/7/1, Lyceum; **First Performance, America:** 1814/4/11, Boston

Apotheosis of Franklin; **Subtitle(s):** His Reception in the Elysian Fields; **Libretto:** Audin, arranger; **Genre:** "Grand allegorical finale" (Pantomime); **First Performance:** 1796/4/16, Charleston, City Theatre

Arabs of the Desert; **Subtitle(s):** Harlequin's Flight from Egypt; **Music:** Alexander Reinagle; **Genre:** Pantomime Olio; **First Performance:** 1799/4/13, Philadelphia

Arbitration—See *Love for Love I Promise Him*

Arbitration; **Subtitle(s):** Free and Easy; **Libretto:** Frederick Reynolds; **Music:** Gesualdo Lanza; **Genre:** Operatic Farce; 2 acts; **First Performance, London:** 1806/12/11, Covent Garden; **First Performance, America:** 1808/3/14, Charleston

Archers, The; **Subtitle(s):** Mountaineers of Switzerland; **Libretto:** William Dunlap; **Music:** Benjamin Carr; add. by Victor Pelissier; **Genre:** Opera; 3 acts; **First Performance:** 1796/4/18, New York

Ariadne Abandoned by Theseus in the Isle of Naxos; **Libretto:** from J. J. C. Brandes *Ariadne auf Naxos* (1775)?; **Music:** Victor Pelissier; **Genre:** Melodrama; **First Performance:** 1797/4/26, New York

Arianne abandonnée in the Island of Naxos; **Libretto:** From P. L. Moline, *Ariane dans l'Isle de Naxos;* **Music:** Johann Friedrich Edelmann; **Genre:** Opera; 1 act; **First Performance:** 1782/9/24, Paris; **First Performance, America:** 1791/3/28, New York, Corri's Hotel

Armans d'Arcade, Les; **Libretto:** William Francis, arranger; **Genre:** Pantomime Divertissement; **First Performance:** 1795/6/11, Philadelphia

Arthur and Emmeline—See *King Arthur*

Astrologer's Cave, The; **Subtitle(s):** The Child of Fancy; **Genre:** Pantomime; **First Performance:** 1799/3/12, New York, Pantheon, Greenwich St.

Asylum, The; **Subtitle(s):** Female Orphans; **Genre:** Pantomimical Interlude; **First Performance:** 1804/4/16, Boston

At Home; **Libretto:** Henry Bate Dudley; **Genre:** Operatic Farce; **First Performance, London:** 1813/2/25, Covent Garden; **First Performance, America:** 1814/2/23, New York

Auld Robin Gray; **Subtitle(s):** Jemmy's Return; **Genre:** Scotch Ballet Dance; **First Performance:** 1796/8/10, Newport, R. I., Old American

Auld Robin Gray; **Libretto:** Samuel J. Arnold; **Music:** Samuel Arnold (Pastiche); arr. by Alexander Reinagle; **Genre:** Pastoral Entertainment; 2 acts; **First Performance, London:** 1794/7/29, Little Theatre, Haymarket; **First Performance, America:** 1795/5/4, Philadelphia

Aurelio and Miranda; **Libretto:** James Boaden; based on M. G. Lewis, *The Monk;* **Music:** Michael Kelly; **Genre:** Drama with music; 5 acts; **First Performance, London:** 1798/12/29, Drury Lane; **First Performance, America:** 1800/12/1, Boston

Ballet des Provencaux; **Subtitle(s):** Sailor of Marseillois; **Genre:** Pantomime; **First Performance:** 1794/12/17, Charleston

Banditti (became *Castle of Andalusia* (cf) in 1782); **Subtitle(s):** Love's Labyrinth; **Libretto:** John O'Keeffe; **Music:** Samuel Arnold; **Genre:** Comic Opera; 2 acts; **First Performance, London:** 1781/11/28, Covent Garden; **First Performance, America:** 1788/4/21, New York

Bastile, The; **Subtitle(s):** Liberty Triumphant; **Genre:** Pantomime; **First Performance, London:** 1789/10/19, Royal Circus; **First Performance, America:** 1795/6/25, New York

Battle of Eutaw Springs and Evacuation of Charleston; **Subtitle(s):** The Glorious 14th of December, 1782; **Libretto:** William Ioor; **Genre:** Grand National Drama with music; 5 acts (1813/6/9, Philadelphia Commonwealth); **First Performance:** 1807/1/10, Charleston

*Battle of Hexham; **Subtitle(s):** Days of Old; **Libretto:** George Colman, jr.; altered by John Hodgkinson as "Days of Old"; **Music:** Samuel Arnold; arr. by P. A. van Hagen, sr.; **Genre:** Comedy with songs and choruses; 3 acts; **First Performance, London:** 1789/8/11, Little Theatre, Haymarket; **First Performance, America:** 1794/3/20, New York

Battle of Lodi, The; **Subtitle(s):** Osway and Lilla; **Libretto:** Allen, arranger; **Music:** Maline; **Genre:** Pantomime; **First Performance:** 1812/4/18, Philadelphia, Olympic

Battle of Savanna; **Genre:** Pantomime; **First Performance:** 1808/11/25, New York, Pepin and Breschard Circus

Battle of Trenton; **Subtitle(s):** The Death of General Warren; **Genre:** Grand Historical Pantomime; **First Performance:** 1799/4/8, Philadelphia

Battle of York *(The Capture of York; The Fall of York);* **Subtitle(s):** The Death of General Pike; **Libretto:** Joseph Hutton; **Genre:** Pantomime Afterpiece; 1 act; **First Performance:** 1813/11/17, Philadelphia, Pepin and Breschard Circus

Bear Hunters (See also *The Merry Hunters; Two Hunters and the Milkmaid*); **Genre:** Pantomime; **First Performance:** 1792/11/26, Boston, Joseph Harper, under Blue Laws

Bee Hive (Bee-Hive); **Subtitle(s):** Industry Must Prosper; A Soldier's Love; **Libretto:** John G. Millingen; based on Pigault-Lebrun's *Le rivaux d'eux mêmes;* **Music:** Charles E. Horn; Charles Gilfert (Charleston); **Genre:**

Comic Opera; 2 acts; **First Performance, London:** 1811/1/19, Lyceum; **First Performance, America:** 1811/10/23, New York

Beggar's Opera; **Libretto:** John Gay; **Music:** John Christopher Pepusch, compiler; **Genre:** Ballad Opera; 3 acts; **First Performance, London:** 1728/1/29, Lincoln's Inn Fields; **First Performance, America:** 1750/12/3, New York, Kean and Murray

Belle Dorothée; **Subtitle(s):** Maternal Affection; **Genre:** Heroic Pantomime; **First Performance:** 1792/2/17, New York

Benevolent Friend—See *The Quaker*

Benyowsky—See *Count Benyowsky*

Billy the Oysterman, Coachman, and Chimney Sweeper; **Subtitle(s):** The Lover Disguised; **Libretto:** L. Gleise, arranger; **Genre:** Pantomime; **First Performance:** 1798/6/8, Philadelphia, Lailson's Circus

Bird Catcher(s); **Subtitle(s):** The Hunters; **Libretto:** Based on *Les Oiseleurs;* not Reeve's burletta (1799); **Genre:** Pantomime-Ballet; **First Performance, London:** 1750/11/27, Drury Lane; **First Performance, America:** 1792/1/25, New York

Birth, Death, and Animation of Harlequin; **Genre:** Pantomime; **First Performance:** 1793/1/1, Providence, R. I., Harper Co.

Birth, Death, and Renovation of Harlequin; **Subtitle(s):** The Enchanted Cavern; **Libretto:** Alexander Placide, arranger; **Genre:** Pantomime; **First Performance:** 1805/5/9, Charleston

Birth of Harlequin; **Subtitle(s):** The Witches Frolic; The Witches at their Night Works; **Genre:** Pantomime; Entertainment; 2 acts; **First Performance, London:** Sadler's Wells; **First Performance, America:** 1791/7/7, Philadelphia, Southwark

Birthday; **Subtitle(s):** Rural Fete; **Libretto:** Legé, arranger; **Music:** Rayner Taylor; **Genre:** Ballet; **First Performance:** 1797/2/22, Boston

Black Beard (orig. *The Genoese Pirate*); **Subtitle(s):** The Captive Princess; The Pirate; Genoese Pirate; The Outlawed Pirates (Blackbeard); **Libretto:** John C. Cross; **Music:** James Sanderson; add. by James Hewitt; **Genre:** Full-length Pantomime; **First Performance, London:** 1798/4/0, Royal Circus; 1798/10/15, Covent Garden; **First Performance, America:** 1804/4/2, Philadelphia

Black Castle; **Subtitle(s):** Spectre of the Forest; **Libretto:** M. G. Lewis; based on C. F. Barrett's Gothic Romance (or on J. H. Amherst, *Black Castle*, 1801/2/16, Royalty); **Music:** James Hewitt; Alexander Reinagle; **Genre:** Melodrama; 2 acts; **First Performance:** 1807/3/20, Philadelphia

Black Forest (See also *Le Foret Noire);* **Subtitle(s):** The Natural Son; Maternal

Affection; **Libretto:** Legé, arranger; **Genre:** Serious Pantomime; 3 acts; **First Performance:** 1797/3/17, Boston

Blacksmith, The; **Subtitle(s):** Le Maréchal ferrant; **Libretto:** A. F. Quétant; **Music:** F. A. D. Philidor; **Genre:** Opera; 1 act; **First Performance:** 1761/8/22, Paris; **First Performance, America:** 1793/3/25, Boston, Alexander Placide troupe

Blaise et Babet; **Subtitle(s):** Les Suite des Trois fermiers; **Libretto:** J. M. Boutet de Monvel; **Music:** Nicolas Dezède; **Genre:** Comic Opera; 2 acts; **First Performance:** 1783/4/4, Versailles; **First Performance, America:** 1794/7/23, Charleston

Blind Bargain, The; **Subtitle(s):** Hear It Out; Hear Him Out; **Libretto:** Frederick Reynolds; **Music:** Michael Kelly; add. by James Hewitt; **Genre:** Comedy, Incidental Music; 5 acts; **First Performance, London:** 1804/10/24, Covent Garden; **First Performance, America:** 1805/5/13, New York

*Blind Boy, The; **Subtitle(s):** Sarmatia's Heir; **Libretto:** James Kenney or William B. Hewetson; adapted from L. C. Caignez's *L'illustre aveugle;* **Music:** John Davy; add. by Victor Pelissier; **Genre:** Melodrama; 2 acts; **First Performance, London:** 1807/12/1, Covent Garden; **First Performance, America:** 1808/12/7, New York

Blind Cupid; **Music:** Selected by a gentleman of New York; **Genre:** Pantomime; 1 act; **First Performance:** 1809/1/24, New York, Lyceum

Blind Girl, The; **Subtitle(s):** A Receipt for Beauty; A Recipe for Beauty; **Libretto:** Thomas Morton; **Music:** Joseph Mazzinghi, William Reeve; **Genre:** Comic Opera; 3 acts; **First Performance, London:** 1801/4/22, Covent Garden; **First Performance, America:** 1802/3/10, Philadelphia

***Blue Beard; **Subtitle(s):** Female Curiosity; The Fatal Effects of Female Curiosity; **Libretto:** George Colman, jr.; based on Grétry's opera *Barbe Bleue;* altered by William Dunlap for New York theatre; **Music:** Michael Kelly (overture and finale from Grétry); add. by Victor Pelissier; **Genre:** Dramatic Romance; 2 acts; **First Performance, London:** 1798/1/16, Drury Lane; **First Performance, America:** 1799/5/24, Philadelphia

Bluebeard; **Subtitle(s):** The Flight of Harlequin; **Libretto:** James Byrne, arranger; **Music:** Carl Baumgarten; **Genre:** Pantomime; **First Performance, London:** 1791/12/21, Covent Garden; **First Performance, America:** 1797/5/3, Philadelphia

Boarding House, The; **Subtitle(s):** Five Hours at Brighton; **Libretto:** Samuel Beazley, jr. (John Bray's interpolations in the part of Simon in American edition); **Music:** Charles E. Horn; **Genre:** Musical Farce; 2 acts; **First Performance, London:** 1811/8/26, Lyceum; **First Performance, America:** 1812/6/5, New York

Boiteuse, La; **Subtitle(s):** The Country Tricks; **Libretto:** Legé, arranger; **Music:** Horace Coignet and Simon; **Genre:** Pantomime-Ballet; **First Performance:** 1795/12/14, Philadelphia

Bondocani, Il; **Subtitle(s):** The Caliph Robber; **Libretto:** Thomas Dibdin, from *Arabian Nights Entertainment;* **Music:** John Moorehead and Thomas Attwood; add. by Alexander Reinagle, arr. by James Hewitt; **Genre:** Dramatic Romance; 3 acts; **First Performance, London:** 1800/11/15, Covent Garden; **First Performance, America:** 1801/12/11, Philadelphia

Bonne Fille, La; **Subtitle(s):** The Perfidious Cottager; The Bandit of the Forest; The Banditti; **Genre:** Pantomime; 1 act; **First Performance:** 1804/5/3, Charleston

Boston Sailors; **Subtitle(s):** Generous Tar; **Genre:** Musical Interlude; **First Performance:** 1807/5/4, Boston

Bouquet; **Genre:** Ballet; **First Performance:** 1797/4/19, Philadelphia

Bourville Castle; **Subtitle(s):** The Gallic Orphan; **Libretto:** John Blair Linn; **Music:** Benjamin Carr, Victor Pelissier (pastiche); **Genre:** Comic Opera; **First Performance:** 1797/1/16, New York

Braconnier; **Subtitle(s):** The Game Laws; **Libretto:** Based on Raymont's opera, Paris, c. 1785; **Genre:** Pantomime; **First Performance:** 1794/11/19, Charleston

Brave Soldier and the Two Robbers—See *The Valiant Soldier*

Bravo of Spain, The; **Subtitle(s):** Woane the Tyger; **Libretto:** Joseph Hutton ("founded on facts of the 14th century"); **Genre:** Heroic Pantomime; **First Performance:** 1814/3/24, Baltimore, Pepin & Breschard Circus

*Brazen Mask, The; **Subtitle(s):** Alberto and Rosabella; **Libretto:** Thomas John Dibdin; **Music:** John Davy, John Mountain; **Genre:** Grand Serious Pantomime interspersed with songs, choruses, and dances; 2 acts; **First Performance, London:** 1802/4/5, Covent Garden; **First Performance, America:** 1806/3/1, Philadelphia

Bridal Ring; **Libretto:** Frederick Reynolds; William Francis, arranger; **Music:** Henry Condell; Victor Pelissier; **Genre:** Melodrama; 2 acts; **First Performance, London:** 1810/10/16, Covent Garden; **First Performance, America:** 1812/2/10, Philadelphia

Brother Quakers; **Genre:** Comic Ballet; **First Performance:** 1796/2/16, Charleston

Buxom Joan; **Subtitle(s):** A Sailor's the Lad; **Libretto:** Thomas Willet; **Music:** Rayner Taylor; **Genre:** All-Sung, Burletta Comedy; 1 act; **First Performance, London:** 1778/6/25, Little Theatre, Haymarket; **First Performance, America:** 1801/1/30, Philadelphia

Cabinet, The; **Libretto:** Thomas John Dibdin; founded on an ancient ballad called "The Golden Bull"; **Music:** Pastiche: John Braham, William Reeve, Domenico Corri, John Davy, John Moorehead; **Genre:** Comic Opera; 3 acts; **First Performance, London:** 1802/2/9, Covent Garden; **First Performance, America:** 1807/3/28, Philadelphia

Caledonian Frolic; **Libretto:** William Francis, arranger; **Music:** Benjamin Carr; **Genre:** Ballet; **First Performance:** 1793/11/2, Boston

Caledonian Lasses (Caledonian Girls); **Genre:** Pantomime; **First Performance:** 1810/4/27, Charleston

Caledonian Lovers, The; **Subtitle(s):** The Awkward Recruits; **Genre:** Pantomimic Ballet; **First Performance:** 1808/8/22, New York, Vauxhall Gardens

Camp, The; **Subtitle(s):** Soldier's Festival; **Libretto:** Richard Tickell; rev. by R. B. Sheridan; **Music:** Thomas Linley, sr., borrowed in part from his *The Royal Merchant;* **Genre:** Musical Entertainment; 2 acts; **First Performance, London:** 1778/10/15, Drury Lane; **First Performance, America:** 1806/12/15, Charleston

Capocchio and Dorinna; **Subtitle(s):** The Happy Captive; The Temple of Dullness; **Libretto:** Rayner Taylor, "mock Italian opera" (based on Colley Cibber's *The Temple of Dullness,* with music by Thomas Arne); **Music:** Rayner Taylor; **Genre:** All-Sung, Musical Interlude; 2 acts; **First Performance, London:** 1745/1/17, Drury Lane; 1768/7/28, Marylebone Gardens (Arne); **First Performance, America:** 1793/1/20, Annapolis

Captain Cook—See *The Death of Captain Cook*

Captain Smith and the Princess Pocahontas; **Libretto:** Based on John Davis's "Indian Tale" of that name, London, 1803; **Music:** G. Woodham (pastiche); **Genre:** Melodrama; **First Performance:** 1806/3/5, Philadelphia

Captive of Spilberg, The; **Libretto:** Prince Hoare; based on B. J. Marsollier, *Camille, ou, Le Souterrain;* **Music:** Jan L. Dussek; add. by Michael Kelly; arr. by Victor Pelissier; **Genre:** Comic Opera; 2 acts; **First Performance, London:** 1798/11/14, Drury Lane; **First Performance, America:** 1801/3/25, New York

Capture of York—See *The Battle of York*

Caravan, The; **Subtitle(s):** The Driver and His Dog; **Libretto:** Frederick Reynolds; **Music:** William Reeve; arr. by Victor Pelissier; **Genre:** Grand Serio-comic Romance; 2 acts; **First Performance, London:** 1803/12/5, Drury Lane; **First Performance, America:** 1810/3/23, Philadelphia

Caravan of Cairo (Caravane du Caire); **Libretto:** E. Morel de Chédeville; **Music:** André E. M. Grétry; **Genre:** Opera; 3 acts; **First Performance:** 1783/10/30, Fontainebleau, France; **First Performance, America:** 1795/8/3, Charleston (in French)

Care and Mirth; **Subtitle(s):** Harlequin Restored (cf); Harlequin's Animation

(cf); Harlequin Skeleton (cf); Harlequin Gladiator; **Genre:** Pantomime; 1
act; **First Performance:** 1801/9/7, New York, Mount Vernon Gardens

Castle Besieged; **Subtitle(s):** The Return of the Laborers (cf); **Genre:** Pantomime; **First Performance:** 1797/10/7, Fredericksburg, Va., West-Bignall
company

Castle of Andalusia; **Subtitle(s):** The Banditti; **Libretto:** John O'Keeffe; based
on his *The Banditti* (cf); **Music:** Samuel Arnold (Pastiche); **Genre:** Comic
Opera; 3 acts; **First Performance, London:** 1782/11/2, Covent Garden; **First
Performance, America:** 1794/2/17, Philadelphia

Castle of Otranto; **Libretto:** Altered from Henry Siddons's *Sicilian Romance*
(cf); based on Horace Walpole's novel, *The Castle of Otranto;* **Music:**
Victor Pelissier; **Genre:** Comic Opera; **First Performance:** 1800/11/7, New
York

Castle of Sorrento; **Subtitle(s):** The Prisoner of Rochelle; Which is He?; **Libretto:** George Colman and Henry Heartwell; based on Alexandre Duval's
opera, *Le Prisonnier, ou la Resemblance;* **Music:** Dominique Della Maria;
Thomas Attwood; **Genre:** Comic Opera; 2 acts; **First Performance, London:** 1799/7/3, Little Theatre, Haymarket; **First Performance, America:**
1801/4/13, Boston

***Castle Spectre; **Subtitle(s):** The Secrets of Conway Castle; **Libretto:** Matthew G. Lewis; **Music:** Michael Kelly (pastiche); add. by Alexander Reinagle; Francis Linley; **Genre:** Drama, Incidental Music; 5 acts; **First Performance, London:** 1797/12/14, Drury Lane; **First Performance, America:**
1798/6/1, New York

Catch Club, The; **Subtitle(s):** Feast of Anacreon; Sons of Apollo; Sons of
Anacreon (These four names were used interchangeably); **Genre:** Musical
Interlude (Olio); **First Performance, London:** 1788/8/22, Little Theatre,
Haymarket; 1789/5/14, Covent Garden; **First Performance, America:** 1799/
4/24, Philadelphia

Catch Him Who Can; **Libretto:** Theodore E. Hook; **Music:** James Hook; arr.
by Victor Pelissier; **Genre:** Musical Farce; 2 acts; **First Performance, London:** 1806/6/12, Little Theatre, Haymarket; **First Performance, America:**
1809/3/8, Philadelphia

Cave of Enchantment; **Subtitle(s):** The Stockwell Wonder; **Music:** John Bentley (selected and composed); **Genre:** Pantomime; **First Performance:** 1785/
8/26, New York

Celebrated London Shoemaker, The; **Genre:** Pantomime; **First Performance:**
1808/5/7, New York, Pearl St. Theatre

Chains of the Heart; **Subtitle(s):** The Slave By Choice; **Libretto:** Prince Hoare;

Music: Joseph Mazzinghi, William Reeve; add. by Victor Pelissier; **Genre:** Comic Opera; 3 acts; **First Performance, London:** 1801/12/9, Covent Garden; **First Performance, America:** 1804/2/1, New York

Champlain and Plattsburgh; **Subtitle(s):** The Army and Navy; **Genre:** Patriotic Spectacle; **First Performance:** New York, 1814/11/18

Cherokee, The; **Libretto:** James Cobb; **Music:** Stephen Storace (revived in 1802 with music by Michael Kelly as *Algonah*); **Genre:** Opera; 3 acts; **First Performance, London:** 1794/12/20, Drury Lane; **First Performance, America:** 1799/6/24, Boston, Haymarket

***Children in the Wood, The; **Libretto:** Thomas Morton; **Music:** Samuel Arnold; add. by Benjamin Carr; Mrs. Melmoth; **Genre:** Comic Opera; 2 acts; **First Performance, London:** 1793/10/1, Little Theatre, Haymarket; **First Performance, America:** 1794/11/24, Philadelphia, Southwark

Chinese in Boston, The; **Subtitle(s):** Frolics at a Fair; **Genre:** Comic Ballet; **First Performance:** 1808/2/22, Boston

Christmas Box; **Subtitle(s):** Harlequin in Philadelphia (cf); **Libretto:** Abercrombie, arranger; **Genre:** Grand Comic Pantomime; **First Performance:** 1812/12/24, Philadelphia, Southwark

Christmas Frolick; **Subtitle(s):** Harlequin's Gambols; **Genre:** Pantomime; Divertissement; **First Performance:** 1797/12/26, Philadelphia

Christmas Gambols; **Subtitle(s):** Harlequin in the Moon (cf); Harlequin Mariner (cf); **Music:** Selected from the most approved compositions; **Genre:** Pantomime; **First Performance:** 1801/1/2, Philadelphia

Chrononhotonthologos; **Libretto:** Henry Carey; **Music:** Henry Carey, compiler; **Genre:** Burlesque tragedy; 1 act; **First Performance, London:** 1734/2/22, Little Theatre, Haymarket; **First Performance, America:** 1777/3/20, New York

***Cinderella; **Subtitle(s):** The Little Glass Slipper; **Music:** Michael Kelly; acc. by James Hewitt; **Genre:** Grand Allegorical Pantomimical Spectacle interspersed with song, recitative, and dancing; 2 acts; **First Performance, London:** 1804/1/14, Drury Lane; **First Performance, America:** 1806/1/1, Philadelphia

Cinque Savoyards (See also *Trois Savoyards*); **Subtitle(s):** The Magic Lanthern; **Libretto:** J. K. Labottierre, arranger; **Genre:** Ballet; **First Performance:** 1811/10/25, New York

City of Philadelphia, The; **Subtitle(s):** The Ship Launch; **Genre:** Occasional Pantomime; **First Performance:** 1799/11/28, Philadelphia, Rickett's Circus

Clemency of Charlemagne—See *Four Valiant Brothers*

Clown's Triumph, The (The Clown Triumphant); **Subtitle(s):** Sportsman Outwitted (cf); The Sportsman Deceived; The Brave Soldier; **Genre:** Pantomime; **First Performance:** 1801/6/8, New York

Coal Man of the Jura Mountains; **Subtitle(s):** Unfortunate Family (cf); **Genre:** Pantomime; **First Performance:** 1808/12/8, New York, Pepin and Breschard Circus

Cobler's Frolic; **Genre:** Speaking Pantomime; **First Performance:** 1811/3/1, Baltimore, Pepin and Breschard Circus

Columbine Invisible; **Subtitle(s):** Harlequin Junior (cf); **Genre:** Pantomime; **First Performance:** 1792/2/24, New York

Columbine Statue; **Genre:** Pantomime Entertainment; **First Performance:** 1796/8/10, Newport, Rhode Island, Old American

Columbine's Choice; **Subtitle(s):** Harlequin Statue (cf); **Libretto:** Alexander Placide, arranger; **Genre:** Pantomime; **First Performance:** 1808/4/18, Charleston

Columbus; **Subtitle(s): A World Discovered; America Discovered; The Discovery of America; **Libretto:** Thomas Morton; **Music:** Alexander Reinagle; James Hewitt; Peter A. van Hagen; **Genre:** Historical Play, Incidental Music; 5 acts shortened to 3; **First Performance, London:** 1792/12/1, Covent Garden; **First Performance, America:** 1797/1/30, Philadelphia

Comet, The; **Subtitle(s):** New Philosophy; He Would Be an Astronomer; He Would Be a Philosopher; **Libretto:** William Milns; **Music:** James Hewitt; **Genre:** Comedy, Incidental Music; 5 (3, 2) acts; **First Performance, London:** 1789/8/5, Little Theatre, Haymarket; **First Performance, America:** 1797/2/1, New York

Comus; **Subtitle(s):** The Sorcerer; The Enchanted Wood; **Libretto:** (a) John Milton; (b) John Dalton; (c) adapted by George Colman, sr.; **Music:** (a) Henry Lawes; (b) Thomas Arne; **Genre:** Masque; 3 acts; **First Performance, London:** (a) 1634; (b) 1738/3/4, Drury Lane; (c) 1773/10/16, Covent Garden; **First Performance, America:** (b) 1770/3/9, Philadelphia, Southwark

Confusion; **Genre:** Prelude with dialogue, song, and recitation; 1 act; **First Performance:** 1807/9/9, New York

Constellation (See also *Enterprize*); **Subtitle(s):** A Wreath for American Tars; American Triumph; **Genre:** Pantomime; Dramatic sketch, incidental music; **First Performance:** 1799/3/20, Philadelphia

Constitution, The (See also *Constitution and Wasp*); **Subtitle(s):** American Tars Triumphant; **Music:** New music includes "The Pride of Columbia," "American Chronology"; **Genre:** Patriotic Opera; 2 acts; **First Performance:** 1812/9/28, Philadelphia

Constitution Again, The; **Subtitle(s):** More Naval Laurels; **Genre:** Piece consisting of songs, dances, and illuminations; **First Performance:** 1813/2/22, Philadelphia

Constitution and Guerriere (altered 1813/3/5 to *Constitution and Java*); **Subtitle(s):** A Tribute to the Brave; **Music:** Includes songs "Huzza for the Constitution!," "A Cruising we will Go," Duet, "Conquer or Die," Song and Chorus, "The Good Ship Columbia!"; *Constitution and Java* concludes with "Yankee Chronology"; **Genre:** Patriotic Effusion; 2 acts; **First Performance:** 1812/10/2, Boston

Constitution and Wasp, The; **Subtitle(s):** American Tars Triumphant; **Music:** New music; **Genre:** Patriotic Opera; **First Performance:** 1813/5/12, Baltimore

Contrivances, The; **Libretto:** Henry Carey; based on a 1715 work; **Music:** Henry Carey; **Genre:** Ballad Opera; **First Performance, London:** 1729/6/20, Drury Lane; **First Performance, America:** 1767/4/20, Philadelphia

Cooper, The; **Libretto:** Thomas Arne; based on Nicolas Audinot's *Le Tonnelier* (cf); **Music:** Thomas Arne; **Genre:** Musical Entertainment; 2 acts; **First Performance, London:** 1772/6/12, Little Theatre, Haymarket; **First Performance, America:** 1793/4/3, Boston, Alexander Placide troupe

Cooper, The (The Cooper Outwitted); **Subtitle(s):** The Guardian Outwitted; Love in a Tub; The Old Man Outwitted; The Guardian in Love with his Pupil; The Tutor Outwitted; Amorous Guardian; **Libretto:** Based on Audinot's *Le Tonnelier* (cf), Francisquy, arranger; **Genre:** Pantomime Ballet; **First Performance:** 1796/3/3, New York

Coronation of Napoleon Bonaparte, Emperor of the Gauls; **Music:** James Hewitt; **Genre:** Historical Drama interspersed with songs, choruses, processions, &c.; 2 acts; **First Performance:** 1805/5/31, New York

Corsair, The; **Subtitle(s):** The Tripolitan Robbers; The Egyptian Robbers; The Naval Sons of America; **Libretto:** Based on *Obi* (cf); William Francis and Harris, arrangers; **Genre:** Pantomimic Drama, interspersed with songs, duets, choruses; 2 acts; **First Performance:** 1802/6/8, Baltimore

Cottagers, The; **Libretto:** May be based on one of several English works by this title; **Music:** James Hewitt; **Genre:** Comic Opera; 2 acts; **First Performance:** 1801/5/6, New York

*Count Benyowsky; **Subtitle(s):** The Conspiracy of Kamschatka; Freedom to the Oppressed; **Libretto:** A. F. F. Kotzebue; altered by (a) William Dunlap; (b) William Render, 1798; **Music:** (a) Victor Pelissier; **Genre:** Play, interspersed with songs, duets, and choruses; 5 acts; **First Performance:** (a) 1799/4/1, New York; (b) 1804/3/23, Philadelphia

Country Mad-cap, The (The Country Mad-cap in London); **Libretto:** Adapted from Henry Fielding, *Miss Lucy in Town;* **Genre:** Musical Farce; 1 act; **First Performance, London:** 1770/12/12, Covent Garden; **First Performance, America:** 1803/4/1, Philadelphia

Country Wake (See also *The Jovial Crew*); **Subtitle(s):** The Frolicsome Crew; **Genre:** Ballet Dance (probably not the "Musical Interlude" by M. P. Andrews and James Hook performed at Sadler's Wells before 1784); **First Performance:** 1797/4/1, New York, Ricketts Circus

Cripples, The; **Genre:** Comic Pantomime Ballet; **First Performance:** 1797/3/6, Boston

Cupid's Revenge; **Libretto:** Francis Gentleman; **Music:** James Hook; **Genre:** Ballet, based on all-sung "Arcadian pastoral"; **First Performance, London:** 1772/7/27, Little Theatre, Haymarket; **First Performance, America:** 1795/4/15, Charleston

Cure for the Heart Ache (not Morton's comedy of this title); **Subtitle(s):** The Magic Cauldron; **Libretto:** Legé, arranger; **Genre:** Ballet Pantomime; **First Performance:** 1797/5/1, Boston

Curfew, The; **Subtitle(s):** The Norman Barons; The Danish Banditti; Vision of the Dead; **Libretto:** John Tobin; **Music:** Thomas Attwood; **Genre:** Comedy, Incidental Music; 5 acts; **First Performance, London:** 1805/1/31, Drury Lane; **First Performance, America:** 1807/5/6, Boston

*Cymon (Cymon and Sylvia); **Subtitle(s):** The Enchantress; Love Triumphant (cf); Love and Magic (cf); The Power of Enchantment; **Libretto:** David Garrick; **Music:** Michael Arne; **Genre:** Dramatic Romance; Musical Romance; 2 acts; **First Performance, London:** 1767/1/2, Drury Lane; **First Performance, America:** 1773/3/3, Philadelphia

Damon and Phillida; **Libretto:** (a) Henry Carey (1729); (b) rev. by Colley Cibber (1768); **Music:** (a) Selected by Henry Carey; (b) new music by Charles Dibdin; **Genre:** (a) Ballad Opera; 1 act; (b) Comic Opera; **First Performance, London:** (a) 1729/8/16, Little Theatre, Haymarket; (b) 1768; **First Performance, America:** 1751/2/18, New York, Kean and Murray

Danaides; **Subtitle(s):** Vice Punished; **Libretto:** Quenet, arranger; **Music:** Victor Pelissier; **Genre:** Pantomime; **First Performance:** 1794/10/8, Philadelphia, Southwark

Daphne and Amintor; **Subtitle(s):** The Fairies; **Libretto:** Isaac Bickerstaffe; based on St. Foix *L'Oracle;* **Music:** John Shalon, Matteo Vento, etc. (Pastiche); **Genre:** Comic Opera; 1 act; **First Performance, London:** 1765/10/8, Drury Lane; **First Performance, America:** 1786/5/29, New York

Darby and Patrick—See *Poor Soldier*

Darby's Return *(Darby's Return to his own Potato Ground);* **Libretto:** William Dunlap; sequel to *Poor Soldier* (cf); **Genre:** Comic sketch; 1 act; **First Performance:** 1789/11/24, New York

Day in Turkey, A; **Subtitle(s):** The Russian Slaves; **Libretto:** Based on Hannah Cowley's comic opera, 1791; **Music:** Joseph Mazzinghi; **Genre:** Pantomime; **First Performance, London:** 1791/3/12, Covent Garden; **First Performance, America:** 1794/5/23, Charleston

Days of Old—See *Battle of Hexham*

De Montfort; **Subtitle(s):** The Force of Hatred; **Libretto:** Joanna Baillie; **Music:** Michael Kelly; Victor Pelissier; **Genre:** Tragedy, Incidental Music; 5 acts; **First Performance, London:** 1800/4/29, Drury Lane; **First Performance, America:** 1801/4/13, New York

Dead Alive, The; **Subtitle(s):** The Double Funeral; **Libretto:** John O'Keeffe; **Music:** Samuel Arnold; **Genre:** Comic Opera; 2 acts; **First Performance, London:** 1781/6/16, Little Theatre, Haymarket; **First Performance, America:** 1789/9/24, New York

Deaf and Dumb; **Subtitle(s):** The Orphan Protected; L'Abbé de l'Epée; **Libretto:** William Dunlap; from J. N. Bouilly, *L'Abbé de l'Epée;* also tr. by Thomas Holcroft, 1801; **Music:** Michael Kelly; **Genre:** Historical Drama, Incidental Music; 5 acts; **First Performance, London:** 1801/2/24, Drury Lane (Holcroft); **First Performance, America:** 1802/1/23, Charleston

*Deaf Lover, The; **Libretto:** Louis Carrogis Carmontelle, *Le Poulet;* tr. by Frederick Pilon; **Music:** William Shield; Victor Pelissier; **Genre:** Musical Interlude; 2 acts; **First Performance, London:** 1780/2/2, Covent Garden; **First Performance, America:** 1780/11/20, New York, British army

Deaf Lover; **Music:** May be based on Shield's incidental music to Pilon's 1780 play; **Genre:** Pantomime; **First Performance:** 1795/5/9, New York

Death and Renovation of Harlequin; **Genre:** Pantomime; **First Performnce** 1796/9/21, New York, Rickett's Amphitheatre

Death of Captain Cook; **Libretto: Jean François Arnould; John C. Cross, arranger; **Music:** Rochefort; song "America, Commerce, and Freedom" added, Boston, 1797; **Genre:** Grand Historic Pantomime; 2 acts; **First Performance, London:** 1789/9/21, Covent Garden; **First Performance, America:** 1793/5/31, New York

Death of General Wolfe—See *Siege of Quebec*

Death of Harlequin; **Genre:** Pantomimic Interlude; **First Performance, London:** 1716; **First Performance, America:** 1791/5/19, Philadelphia, Southwark

Death of Major Andre; **Subtitle(s):** West Point Preserved; **Libretto:** Alexander Placide, arranger; **Genre:** Grand Pantomime; 3 acts; **First Performance:** 1796/5/11, Charleston

Delays and Blunders; **Subtitle(s):** The Vestil Buried Alive; **Libretto:** Frederick Reynolds; **Genre:** Comedy, Incidental Music; 5 acts; **First Performance, London:** 1802/10/30, Covent Garden; **First Performance, America:** 1803/4/25, Charleston

Demolition of the Bastille; **Subtitle(s):** Liberty Triumphant; **Libretto:** Performed to John L. Berkenhead's harpsichord work of that title (Boston, 1795); **Genre:** Pantomime; 2 acts; **First Performance:** 1795/6/8, New York

Dermot and Kathleen; **Subtitle(s):** The Irish Wedding; **Libretto:** James Byrne, arranger; based on Shield's *Poor Soldier* (cf); **Music:** William Shield; **Genre:** Pantomime-Ballet; **First Performance, London:** 1793/10/18, Covent Garden; **First Performance, America:** 1795/8/22, Baltimore

*Deserter, The; **Libretto:** Charles Dibdin; based on M. J. Sedaine, *Le Déserteur;* **Music:** Charles Dibdin (pastiche, partially from Monsigny); arr. by Victor Pelissier and Benjamin Carr; **Genre:** Comic Opera; 2 acts; **First Performance, London:** 1773/11/2, Drury Lane; **First Performance, America:** 1787/6/8, New York

Deserter, The; **Libretto:** Based on Sedaine/Monsigny; **Genre:** Grand Serious Pantomime; 3 acts; **First Performance, London:** 1789/11/13, Covent Garden; **First Performance, America:** 1797/1/13, Boston

Deserter of Naples (Le Deserteur de Naples); **Libretto:** Carlo Delpini; **Music:** May use some music from Sedaine/Monsigny's *Le Deserteur;* **Genre:** Serio-Comic Military Pantomime; **First Performance, London:** Royalty Theatre, 1788/6/16; **First Performance, America:** 1796/5/9, Philadelphia

Deserteur Francais, Le; **Subtitle(s):** The Supposed Marriage; **Libretto:** Based on Monsigny; **Genre:** Pantomime; **First Performance:** 1794/12/12, Charleston

Destruction of the Bastille—See *The Fourteenth of July, 1789*

Dettes, Les; **Subtitle(s):** The Way to Pay Debts; **Libretto:** N. J. Forgeot; **Music:** Stanislas Champein; **Genre:** Comic Opera; 2 acts; **First Performance:** 1787/1/11, Paris; **First Performance, America:** 1795/7/21, Charleston

Deux Chasseurs (ballet)—See *Two Huntsmen and the Milkmaid*

Deux Chasseurs et la Laitière; **Libretto:** Louis Anseaume; **Music:** Egidio Duni; arr. DeMarque; **Genre:** Comic Opera; 1 act; **First Performance:** 1763/7/21, Paris; **First Performance, America:** 1790/11/9, New York, City Tavern

Deux Petits Savoyards, Les; **Libretto:** B. J. Marsollier; **Music:** Nicholas Dalayrac; **Genre:** Comic Opera; 1 act; **First Performance:** 1789/1/14, Paris; **First Performance, America:** 1797/1/16, Philadelphia

Deux Soeurs, Les; **Genre:** Pantomime; **First Performance:** 1796/6/15, Philadelphia

Devil to Pay, The; **Subtitle(s): The Wives Metamorphosed; **Libretto:** Charles Coffey, John Mottley; reduced to 1 act by Colley Cibber; based on Thomas Jevon's *The Devil of a Wife*, 1783; **Music:** Seedo; **Genre:** Ballad Opera; 3, 2 acts; **First Performance, London:** 1731/8/6, Drury Lane; **First Performance, America:** 1736/3/16, Charleston

Devil Upon Two Sticks; **Subtitle(s):** Columbine Invisible (cf); **Libretto:** From LeSage's *Diable Boiteaux;* Legé, arranger, Boston; **Genre:** Comic Pantomime; **First Performance:** 1783/7/5, New York, Dennis Ryan Company

Devil's Bridge; **Subtitle(s):** The Piedmontese Alps; **Libretto:** Samuel James Arnold; **Music:** Charles E. Horn, John Braham, Henry R. Bishop; **Genre:** Operatic Melodramatic Romance; 3 acts; **First Performance, London:** 1812/5/6, Lyceum; **First Performance, America:** 1815/7/4, New York

Devin du Village; **Libretto:** J. J. Rousseau; **Music:** J. J. Rousseau; **Genre:** Opera (Intermezzo); 1 act; **First Performance:** 1752/10/18, Fontainebleau, France; **First Performance, America:** 1790/10/21, New York, City Tavern

Diana and Actaeon; **Libretto:** James Byrne, arranger; **Genre:** Pantomime-Ballet; **First Performance, London:** 1730; **First Performance, America:** 1799/2/18, Philadelphia

Doctor and (the) Apothecary, The; **Libretto:** James Cobb; **Music:** Karl Ditters von Dittersdorf (Pastiche); add. by Stephen Storace; arr. by B. Bergmann; **Genre:** Comic Opera; 2 acts; **First Performance, London:** 1788/10/25, Drury Lane; **First Performance, America:** 1796/4/26, Charleston, City Theatre

Dominion of Fancy, The; **Subtitle(s):** Harlequin Rambler; **Libretto:** As *Harlequin's Tour; or The Dominion of Fancy*, London; **Music:** John Moorehead; **Genre:** Pantomime; **First Performance, London:** 1800, Covent Garden; **First Performance, America:** 1807/3/30, Charleston

***Don Juan; **Subtitle(s):** The Libertine Destroyed; **Libretto:** Carlo Delpini; **Music:** Songs by William Reeve, Instrumental music by C. W. Gluck; Alexander Reinagle (Philadelphia); **Genre:** Tragical Pantomimical Entertainment; 2 acts; **First Performance, London:** 1787, Royalty Theatre; 1790/10/26, Drury Lane; **First Performance, America:** 1792/12/20, Philadelphia

Don Quixote de la Mancha; **Libretto:** D. J. Piguenit; **Music:** Samuel Arnold; **Genre:** Pantomime, performed on foot and horseback; **First Performance, London:** 1774, Marylebone Gardens; **First Performance, America:** 1811/2/20, Baltimore, Pepin and Breschard Circus

*Double Disguise, The; **Subtitle(s):** The Irish Chambermaid; **Libretto:** Harriet Hornscastle Hook; **Music:** James Hook; arr. by R. Chateaudun; Victor Pelissier; **Genre:** Comic Opera; 2 acts; **First Performance, London:** 1784/3/

8, Drury Lane; **First Performance, America:** 1794/11/10, Charleston, City Theatre

Douglas; **Subtitle(s): The Noble Shepherd; **Libretto:** John Home; **Music:** Overture and incidental music by James Hewitt; **Genre:** Tragedy, Incidental Music; 5 acts; **First Performance:** 1756/12/0, Edinburgh; **First Performance, America:** 1759/1/24, New York

*Dramatist, The; **Subtitle(s):** Stop Him Who Can!; **Libretto:** Frederick Reynolds; **Music:** James Hook; **Genre:** Comedy, Incidental Music; 5 acts; **First Performance, London:** 1789/5/15, Covent Garden; **First Performance, America:** 1791/5/16, Philadelphia, Southwark

Drunken German, The; **Subtitle(s):** The Landlord in Danger; **Genre:** Comic Dance; **First Performance:** 1807/4/22, Boston

Drunken Peasant (Drunken Provençal); **Subtitle(s):** The Sailor's Return (cf); **Libretto:** James Byrne, arranger; **Genre:** Pantomime-Ballet; **First Performance:** 1797/2/3, Philadelphia

Duel; **Subtitle(s):** Midnight Elopement; **Libretto:** Roberts (of Boston Theatre); **Genre:** Drama interspersed with songs; 3 acts; **First Performance:** 1812/4/27, Boston

*Duenna, The; **Subtitle(s):** The Double Elopement; **Libretto:** Richard B. Sheridan; **Music:** Thomas Linley, sr., Thomas Linley, jr.; arr. Bradford; **Genre:** Comic Opera; 3 acts; **First Performance, London:** 1775/11/21, Covent Garden; **First Performance, America:** 1786/7/10, New York

The Dutch Wake; **Subtitle(s):** The Sailor's Return from Algiers; **Genre:** Comic Ballet; **First Performance:** 1797/2/11, Philadelphia, Pantheon

Dutchman, The; **Subtitle(s):** The Merry Girl; **Libretto:** Based on Thomas Bridges, "The Dutch-Man" (1775)?; **Genre:** Ballet; **First Performance:** 1792/6/7, Philadelphia, Southwark

Easter Frolics; **Subtitle(s):** Harlequin Hurry-Scurry (cf); **Genre:** Pantomime; **First Performance:** 1805/4/15, Charleston

Easter Gambols; **Genre:** Pantomimical Dance; **First Performance:** 1807/3/30, Philadelphia

Easter Gift; **Genre:** Pantomime; **First Performance:** 1796/3/28, Philadelphia

Echo and Narcissus; **Subtitle(s):** The Levee of Cupid; **Libretto:** Charlotte Placide, arranger; **Genre:** Pastoral Dialogue Pantomime; 3 acts; **First Performance:** 1796/5/9, Charleston, City Theatre

Edgar and Emmeline; **Subtitle(s):** The Fairy Favor; **Libretto:** John Hawkesworth; **Music:** Michael Arne; **Genre:** "A fairy tale in a dramatic entertainment"; 2 acts; **First Performance, London:** 1761/1/31, Drury Lane; **First Performance, America:** 1770/3/9, Philadelphia, Southwark

Edwin and Angelina; **Subtitle(s):** The Banditti; **Libretto:** Elihu H. Smith; based on ballad by Oliver Goldsmith; **Music:** Victor Pelissier; **Genre:** Comic Opera; 3 acts; **First Performance:** 1796/12/19, New York

Edwy and Elgiva; **Libretto:** Charles Jared Ingersoll, jr.; **Music:** Alexander Reinagle; **Genre:** Tragedy, Incidental Music; 5 acts; **First Performance:** 1801/4/2, Philadelphia

Egyptian Festival; **Libretto:** Legé, arranger; **Genre:** Divertissement; **First Performance:** 1796/3/7, Philadelphia

Election, The—See *Theatrical Candidates*

Ella Rosenberg; **Libretto: James Kenney; **Music:** Michael Kelly, M. P. King; arr. by Victor Pelissier (first Boston perf. with orig. music, 1814/4/20); **Genre:** Melodrama; 2 acts; **First Performance, London:** 1807/11/19, Drury Lane; **First Performance, America:** 1808/4/18, Boston

Elopement, The; **Subtitle(s):** Harlequin's Tour through the continent of North America; **Music:** Arr. by DeMarque; **Genre:** Pantomime; **First Performance:** 1787/5/31, New York

Elopement, The; **Subtitle(s):** The Triumph of Genius; **Music:** Pastiche; overture by Giordani; **Genre:** Pantomime; **First Performance, London:** 1767/12/26, Drury Lane; **First Performance, America:** 1785/9/30, New York

Elopement, The; **Libretto:** Cut from *The Duenna* (cf); **Music:** "A full band of Music"; **First Performance:** 1792/5/11, Philadelphia, Kenna Company, Northern Liberties

Embarassments of Harlequin, The; **Subtitle(s):** The Roman Mausoleum; **Genre:** Pantomime; **First Performance:** 1803/6/6, New York

Embargo, The; **Subtitle(s):** What News?; Sailors on Shore; The Honest Countryman; **Libretto:** James Nelson Barker; **Genre:** Musical Interlude; **First Performance:** 1808/3/16, Philadelphia

Enchanted Island; **Subtitle(s):** Calypso's Grotto; **Genre:** Pantomime; **First Performance:** 1799/9/30, Hartford, Conn.; Old American

Enchanted Nosegay, The—See *Harlequin Protected by Cupid*

Enraged Musician, The; **Subtitle(s):** Ut pictura poesis!; **Libretto:** George Colman, sr.; based on Hogarth's picture; **Music:** Samuel Arnold; **Genre:** Musical Farce (All-Sung); **First Performance, London:** 1789/5/18, Little Theatre, Haymarket; **First Performance, America:** 1802/3/20, Philadelphia

Enterprize, The (See also *Constellation*); **Subtitle(s):** A Wreath for American Tars; **Genre:** Entertainment of dialogue, singing, and spectacle; **First Performance:** 1803/3/14, Philadelphia

Erl King, The; **Subtitle(s):** Harlequin's Vagaries (cf); **Genre:** Pantomimical Sketch; **First Performance:** Baltimore, 1807/11/28

Escape of Adelina; **Subtitle(s):** The Robbers of The Pyrenees; **Music:** "With the original music from Paris"; **Genre:** Equestrian Pantomime; **First Performance:** OlympicTheatre, Paris; **First Performance, America:** 1811/3/4, Baltimore, Pepin and Breschard Circus

Ethiop—See *The Aethiop*

Exile, The (Exiles; Exile of Siberia); **Subtitle(s): The Russian Daughter; The Deserts of Siberia; **Libretto:** Frederick Reynolds; based on novel *Elisabeth, ou Les Exilés de Sibérie* by Sophie Cottin; **Music:** Joseph Mazzinghi; acc. by Frederick Granger, Boston; "Music entirely new" in Philadelphia; **Genre:** Melodramatic Opera; 3 acts; **First Performance, London:** 1808/11/10, Covent Garden; **First Performance, America:** 1810/4/27, New York

Fairies, The—See *Daphne and Amyntor*

Fairies Rivals, The; **Genre:** Ballet Pantomime; **First Performance, America:** 1805/6/19, New York

Fairy Favor, The—See *Edgar and Emmeline*

Fairy Gambols; **Subtitle(s):** Harlequin's Restoration (cf); **Genre:** Pantomime; **First Performance:** 1794/5/23, Charleston

Faithful Wife, The; **Subtitle(s):** Cozaks on the Road to Paris; **Music:** National Russian Music selected and arranged by James Hewitt; **Genre:** Melodrama; 3 acts; **First Performance:** 1814/4/13, Boston

Fall of York and the Death of General Pike—See *The Battle of York*

False Alarms; **Subtitle(s):** My Cousin; **Libretto:** James Kenney; **Music:** John Braham, Matthew Peter King; **Genre:** Comic Opera; 3, 2 acts; **First Performance, London:** 1807/1/12, Drury Lane; **First Performance, America:** 1809/2/6, Boston

False and True; **Subtitle(s):** The Irishman in Italy; A Trip to Naples; The Irishman in Naples; The Irishman's Medley; The Warrior Triumphant; **Libretto:** George Moultru; **Music:** Samuel Arnold; **Genre:** Play, interspersed with songs; 3 acts; **First Performance, London:** 1798/8/11, Little Theatre, Haymarket; **First Performance, America:** 1799/4/13, Philadelphia

Family Harlequin; **Genre:** Pantomime; **First Performance:** 1799/4/10, Charleston, City Theatre

Farmer, The; **Libretto: John O'Keeffe (Orig. title, *The Plague of Riches*); **Music:** William Shield (Pastiche); **Genre:** Comic Opera; 2 acts; **First Performance, London:** 1787/10/31, Covent Garden; **First Performance, America:** 1790/10/18, Richmond, Va., West-Bignall

Farmer's Wife; **Libretto:** Charles Dibdin, jr.; **Music:** Henry R. Bishop, William Reeve (Pastiche); **Genre:** Comic Opera; 3 acts; **First Performance, London:** 1814/2/1, Covent Garden; **First Performance, America:** 1814/9/26, New York

Fashionable Barber; **Subtitle(s):** The Humors of Harlequin; **Genre:** Pantomime; **First Performance:** 1803/8/1, New York, Mount Vernon Gardens

Fausse Magie (False Magic); **Libretto:** J. F. Marmontel; **Music:** André E. M. Grétry; **Genre:** Comic Opera; 2 acts; **First Performance:** 1775/2/1, Paris; **First Performance, America:** 1795/6/3, Charleston

Feast of Anacreon, The—See *Catch Club*

Federal Oath, The; **Subtitle(s):** Americans Strike Home; The Independence of 1776; **Libretto:** John Williams (Anthony Pasquin, pseud.); **Genre:** Masque; pantomimical sketch; **First Performance:** 1798/6/27, New York

Female Heroism; **Subtitle(s):** The Siege of Orleans; **Genre:** Pantomime; **First Performance:** 1794/6/27, Philadelphia

Female Hussar—See *La Fille Hussar*

Festival of Peace; **Subtitle(s):** Commerce Restored; **Genre:** Patriotic Spectacle (Patriotic Allegory); **First Performance:** 1815/2/20, New York

Fete des Vendanges, La; **Subtitle(s):** Love's Contrivances; **Genre:** Ballet-Pantomime; **First Performance:** 1802/4/12, Philadelphia

Feudal Times; **Subtitle(s):** The Banquet Gallery; **Libretto:** George Colman; **Music:** Michael Kelly; arr. by Frederick Granger; **Genre:** Musical Drama; 2 acts; **First Performance, London:** 1799/1/19, Drury Lane; **First Performance, America:** 1809/3/20, Boston

Fille d'Hungerie, La; **Subtitle(s):** La Pere Riged; **Libretto:** John Turnbull; **Music:** James Hewitt (music entirely new); **Genre:** Grand Military, Heroic Pantomime; 3 acts; **First Performance:** Paris; **First Performance, America:** 1805/5/24, New York

Fille Hussar, La (The Female Hussar); **Libretto:** James Sanderson; **Music:** Victor Pelissier; **Genre:** Heroic Pantomime (with horses); **First Performance:** 1813/6/13, New York

Finger Post, The; **Subtitle(s):** Five Miles Off; **Libretto:** Thomas Dibdin; William Reeve; **Music:** John Bray; James Hewitt; **Genre:** Comedy, Incidental Music; 3, 2 acts; **First Performance, London:** 1806/7/9, Little Theatre, Haymarket; **First Performance, America:** 1806/11/26, New York

Fire King, The; **Subtitle(s):** Albert and Rosalie; **Libretto:** John C. Cross; **Music:** William Reeve; **Genre:** Serious Pantomime; **First Performance, London:** 1801/6/20, Royal Circus; **First Performance, America:** 1806/3/17, Boston

Five Miles Off—See *The Finger Post*

Flash in the Pan; **Libretto:** William Milns; **Music:** James Hewitt; **Genre:** Musical Farce; **First Performance:** 1798/4/20, New York

*Flitch of Bacon; **Subtitle(s):** The Custom of Dunmow Priory; Dunmow Priory; **Libretto:** Henry Bate Dudley; **Music:** William Shield (Pastiche); arr. by Victor Pelissier; **Genre:** Comic Opera; 2 acts; **First Performance, London:**

1778/8/17, Little Theatre, Haymarket; **First Performance, America:** 1780/ 10/30, New York, Burgoyne's Thespians (British soldiers)

Flora; **Subtitle(s):** Hob in the Well; The Frolics of a Country Wake; The Humors of a Country Wake; **Libretto:** John Hippisley or Colley Cibber; based on Dogget's *The Country Wake;* **Music:** arr. by William Bates; **Genre:** Ballad Opera; 2 acts; **First Performance, London:** 1729/4/17, Lincoln's Inn Fields; **First Performance, America:** 1735/2/18, Charleston

Folie, Une; **Libretto:** J. N. Bouilly; **Music:** Étienne Méhul; **Genre:** Opera; 2 acts; **First Performance:** 1802/4/5, Paris; **First Performance, America:** 1808/ 1/30, New Orleans

Follies of a Day; **Subtitle(s):** The Marriage of Figaro; **Libretto:** P. A. C. Beaumarchais; tr. by Thomas Holcroft; **Music:** William Shield; **Genre:** Comedy, Incidental Music; 3, later 2 acts; **First Performance, London:** 1784/12/14, Covent Garden; **First Performance, America:** 1795/6/15, Philadelphia

Fontainbleau; **Subtitle(s):** Our Way in France; A Trip to Fontainbleau; Fontainbleau Races; John Bull in France; **Libretto:** John O'Keeffe; **Music:** William Shield (Pastiche); **Genre:** Comic Opera; 3 acts; **First Performance, London:** 1784/11/16, Covent Garden; **First Performance, America:** 1795/3/ 9, Charleston

For Freedom Ho (Orig. title *For England Ho*); **Libretto:** Isaac Pocock; **Music:** Henry Rowley Bishop; Charles Gilfert (publ. as *Freedom Ho*); **Genre:** Melodramatic Opera; 2 acts; **First Performance, London:** 1813/12/15, Covent Garden; **First Performance, America:** 1815/4/5, New York

Forest of Hermanstadt; **Subtitle(s):** Princess and No Princess; **Libretto:** Louis Charles Caignez, tr. by W. B. Hewetson; arr. as melodrama by Thomas J. Dibdin; **Music:** "with new music"; **Genre:** Melodrama; 2 acts; **First Performance, London:** 1808/10/7, Covent Garden; **First Performance, America:** 1809/9/29, New York

Forêt Noire, Le (See also *Black Forest*); **Subtitle(s): The Robbers' Cave; The Natural Son; The Robbers of the Black Forest; Maternal Affection; **Libretto:** Jean François Arnould; William Francis, arranger; **Music:** Alexander Reinagle; Victor Pelissier; **Genre:** Heroic, Serious Pantomime; 3 acts; **First Performance, London:** 1792/8/27, Sadlers Wells (originally performed in Paris); **First Performance, America:** 1794/4/26, Philadelphia

*Fortress, The; **Libretto:** Theodore Hook; adapted from Pixerécourt, *La forteresse du Danube* (Paris, 1805); **Music:** James Hook; arr. by Victor Pelissier; **Genre:** Melodrama; 3 acts; **First Performance, London:** 1807/7/16, Little Theatre, Haymarket; **First Performance, America:** 1808/2/26, Philadelphia

Fortunatus; **Subtitle(s):** Harlequin's Wishing Cup (cf); **Genre:** Pantomime; **First Performance:** 1798/5/2, Philadelphia

***Forty Thieves, The; **Subtitle(s):** Female Duelist; **Libretto:** George Colman, jr.; based on R. B. Sheridan's *Arabian Night's Entertainment;* **Music:** Michael Kelly; arr. by Victor Pelissier; **Genre:** Grand Operatic Romance; 2 acts; **First Performance, London:** 1806/4/8, Drury Lane; **First Performance, America:** 1807/12/18, Charleston

Foundling of the Forest; **Subtitle(s): The Unknown Female; **Libretto:** William Dimond; **Music:** Michael Kelly; arr. by Victor Pelissier; **Genre:** Drama, interspersed with songs; 3 acts; **First Performance, London:** 1809/7/9, Little Theatre, Haymarket; **First Performance, America:** 1809/11/20, Boston

Four Seasons, The; **Subtitle(s):** Harlequin in Boston; Harlequin's Vagaries (cf); **Genre:** Pantomime; **First Performance:** 1806/3/19, Boston

Four Valiant Brothers (Four Sons of Aymond; Les Quatre Fils Aymond); **Subtitle(s):** Clemency of Charlemagne; **Libretto:** From *Les Quatre Fils d'Hemons;* Jaymond, arranger at Philadelphia Circus; Francesquy, arranger at Boston Haymarket; **Genre:** Pantomime; 3 acts; **First Performance, London:** 1788/6/2, Sadler's Wells; **First Performance, America:** 1794/11/5, Charleston

Fourteenth of July, 1789; **Subtitle(s):** The Destruction of the Bastille; **Genre:** Pantomime; **First Performance:** 1794/11/14, Charleston

Fourth of July; **Subtitle(s):** America, Commerce, and Freedom (cf); **Genre:** Patriotic Spectacle; **First Performance:** 1815/7/4, New York

Fourth of July; **Subtitle(s):** American Glory; **Genre:** "Civic prelude"; Pantomime; **First Performance:** 1796/7/4, Alexandria, McGrath's Strollers

Fourth of July; **Subtitle(s):** Columbian Masquerade; **Genre:** Fete; **First Performance:** 1803/3/9, Philadelphia

Fourth of July; **Subtitle(s):** The Sailor's Festival (cf); **Genre:** Opera; 1 act; **First Performance:** 1788/7/4, Philadelphia

Fourth of July; **Subtitle(s):** Temple of American Independence (cf); **Music:** Victor Pelissier; **Genre:** Allegorical Musical Drama; **First Performance:** 1799/7/4, New York

Free and Easy—See *Arbitration*

Free Knights, The; **Subtitle(s):** The Edict of Charlemagne; **Libretto:** Frederick Reynolds; **Music:** Joseph Mazzinghi; **Genre:** Drama interspersed with music; 3 acts; **First Performance, London:** 1810/2/8, Covent Garden; **First Performance, America:** 1810/6/13, New York

Freedom Ho—See *For Freedom Ho*

Freemen in Arms; **Subtitle(s):** A Tribute to the Memory of the Brave; **Music:**

John Bray (pastiche); **Genre:** Patriotic entertainment with music; **First Performance:** 1813/5/24, Baltimore

French Vauxhall Gardens; **Subtitle(s):** The Amusements of the Day; **Genre:** Ballet; **First Performance:** 1796/5/2, Charleston

Friar Metamorphosed; **Genre:** Pantomime; **First Performance:** 1792/5/4, Portsmouth, New Hampshire

Frolics in the Moon; **Subtitle(s):** Harlequin's Medley (cf); **Genre:** Pantomimic Entertainment; 1 act; **First Performance:** 1807/5/15, Boston

Fruitless Precaution—See *L'amour trouve les moyens, Padlock,* or *Spanish Barber*

Fusilier; **Subtitle(s):** The Clown Outwitted; **Libretto:** Dibdin; **Genre:** Pantomime Interlude; 1 act; **First Performance:** 1794/7/21, Charleston

Gallitea (Galatea, La); **Subtitle(s):** The Garden of Love (cf); **Libretto:** Based on Bruni's melodrama?; **Genre:** Pantomime; **First Performance:** 1797/4/10, Boston, Haymarket

Garden of Love, The; **Subtitle(s):** The Wounds of Cupid Healed by Hymen; The Fountain of Youth; The Old Man Young; **Libretto:** L. Gleise, arranger; **Music:** Pasticcio; **Genre:** Pantomime-Ballet; **First Performance:** 1797/3/312, Boston Haymarket

Generous Farmers, The; **Subtitle(s):** Ched Melah, Faultheroth; A Chead, Meelch, Faultha; **Libretto:** Mrs. Melmoth; **Genre:** Dramatic Pastoral with songs; 1 act; **First Performance:** 1803/3/28, Charleston

Generous Tars, The; **Libretto:** James Byrne, arranger; **Genre:** Pantomime-Ballet; **First Performance:** 1798/3/7, Philadelphia, Lailson's Circus

Genevieve of Brabant; **Subtitle(s):** Virtue triumphant; **Genre:** Pantomime; **First Performance:** 1794/8/12, Charleston

Genii; **Subtitle(s):** Harlequin's Vagaries (cf); Harlequin Fisherman (cf); **Libretto:** John Durang, arranger; taken from Henry Woodward, *The Genie; or, The Arabian Nights Entertainment;* **Genre:** Pantomime; **First Performance, London:** 1752/12/26, Drury Lane; **First Performance, America:** 1788/2/22, New York

Genii of the Rock; **Music:** John Bentley; **Genre:** Pantomime; **First Performance:** 1785/8/20, New York

Genius of America, The; **Genre:** Grand Allegorial Entertainment; 1 act; **First Performance:** 1814/6/6, Boston

Genoese Pirate—See *Blackbeard*

Gentle Shepherd, The; **Subtitle(s):** Patie and Roger; **Libretto:** (a) Allan Ramsay; (b) altered from Ramsay by Richard Tickell; **Music:** (a) compiled by Allan Ramsay; (b) arr. by Thomas Linley; (c) Benjamin Carr, arranger (New York, 1795); **Genre:** (a) Ballad Opera; 5 acts; (b) Scots Pastoral Comedy; 1

act; **First Performance:** (a) 1729/2/9, Edinburgh; (b) 1781/10/29, London, Drury Lane; **First Performance, America:** 1786/6/7, New York

Gentle Shepherd; **Music:** Alexander Reinagle; **Genre:** Pantomime; **First Performance:** 1798/4/16, Philadelphia

Gil Blas; **Subtitle(s):** The Cave of the Robbers; The Fool of Fortune; The Cavern; **Libretto:** Bates, arranger; **Music:** William Reeve; Victor Pelissier; **Genre:** Serio-Comic Pantomime; **First Performance, London:** 1788, Royalty Theatre; **First Performance, America:** 1796/5/16, Philadelphia

*Glory of Columbia: Her Yeomanry, The; **Subtitle(s):** What We Have Done, We Can Do (added during War of 1812); **Libretto:** William Dunlap, based on his tragedy, *Andre*, 1798; **Music:** Victor Pelissier (pastiche); **Genre:** Historical Play interspersed with songs, duets, and choruses; 5, 3 acts; **First Performance, America:** 1803/7/4, New York

Good Neighbor, The; **Libretto:** William Dunlap; based on a scene by August W. Iffland; **Music:** Victor Pelissier; **Genre:** Musical Interlude; 1 act; **First Performance:** 1803/2/28, New York

Grateful Lion, The; **Subtitle(s):** The Liliputian's Power; Harlequin Shipwrecked (cf); **Music:** Compiled from the most favorite composers; overture by Alexander Reinagle; **Genre:** Comic Pantomime; **First Performance, London:** 1793; **First Performance, America:** 1793/6/7, New York

Gray Mare's the Best Horse; **Subtitle(s):** Welsh Opera; **Libretto:** Henry Fielding; **Music:** arr. by Rayner Taylor; **Genre:** Burletta; 3 acts; **First Performance, London:** 1731/7/0, King's Theatre, Haymarket; **First Performance, America:** 1793/1/24, Annapolis

Great Battle of Marengo; **Subtitle(s):** Apotheosis of General Dessaix; **Music:** James Hewitt; **Genre:** Heroic Pantomime; **First Performance:** 1805/5/15, New York

Great Devil; **Subtitle(s):** The Robber of Genoa (cf); **Libretto:** Charles Dibdin, jr.; **Genre:** Pantomime; 2 acts; **First Performance, London:** 1801/8/7, Sadler's Wells; **First Performance, America:** 1811/9/14, New York, Pepin and Breschard Circus

Gretna Green; **Subtitle(s):** Matrimony in Scotland; **Libretto:** Charles Stuart; lyrics by John O'Keeffe; **Music:** Samuel Arnold (pastiche based on Scots tunes); **Genre:** Comic Opera; 2 acts; **First Performance, London:** 1783/8/28, Little Theatre, Haymarket; **First Performance, America:** 1803/3/11, Philadelphia

Gustavus Vasa—See *The Hero of the North*

Hamlet Travestie; **Libretto:** John Poole; **Music:** Pastiche; opening soliloquy sung to tune "Derry down, down, down, derry down"; orig. music arr. by John Bray; **Genre:** Tragic-Comic Burlesque Opera; 2 acts; **First Perfor-**

mance, London: 1811/1/24, New Theatre; 1813/6/17, Covent Garden; **First Performance, America:** 1812/3/7, *Philadelphia*

Harlequin; **Subtitle(s):** The Clown Outwitted by the Milkmaid; **Genre:** Pantomime; **First Performance:** 1814/10/28, Philadelphia, Villalave at Olympic Theatre

Harlequin a Supposed Nobleman; **Genre:** Pantomime; **First Performance:** 1794/8/10, Charleston

Harlequin and the Moon; **Genre:** Pantomime; **First Performance:** 1787/1/22, Philadelphia, Southwark

Harlequin Apprentice; **Genre:** Pantomime; **First Performance:** 1813/11/5, Philadelphia, Pepin and Breschard Circus

Harlequin Balloonist; **Subtitle(s):** Pierrot in the Clouds; **Genre:** Pantomime; **First Performance:** 1792/5/3, New York

Harlequin Barber; **Genre:** Pantomime; **First Performance:** 1791/11/29, Philadelphia, Kenna company

Harlequin Collector; **Genre:** Pantomime; **First Performance:** 1794/6/2, New York

Harlequin Conqueror—See *Magician of the Enchanted Castle*

Harlequin Cook; **Subtitle(s):** The Enchanted Pye; **Genre:** Pantomime; 1 act; **First Performance:** 1790/7/1, Philadelphia, Southwark

Harlequin Dead and Alive; **Genre:** Pantomime; **First Performance:** 1791/12/3, Philadelphia, Kenna company, Northern Liberties

Harlequin Doctor; **Subtitle(s):** The Power of Magic (cf); The Metamorphosis of Pierrot; The Apprentice Magician; The Magician's Power; **Genre:** Pantomime; **First Performance:** 1791/9/15, New York, City Tavern

Harlequin Dr. Faustus; **Subtitle(s):** The Punishment of Profligacy; The Magician Tricked; **Libretto:** Henry Woodward; William Francis, arranger; **Music:** Samuel Arnold; **Genre:** Pantomime; 2 acts; **First Performance, London:** 1766, Covent Garden; **First Performance, America:** 1796/6/3, Philadelphia

Harlequin Everywhere; **Subtitle(s):** What Does it Signify; **Genre:** Pantomime; **First Performance:** 1796/10/26, Philadelphia, Pantheon

Harlequin Fisherman; **Genre:** Pantomime; **First Performance:** 1793/5/17, New York

Harlequin Foundling; **Libretto:** Sully, arranger; **Genre:** Pantomime; **First Performance:** 1798/2/1, New York, Lailson's Amphitheatre

Harlequin Freemason; **Libretto:** Scenario by Charles Dibdin; Messink, arranger; **Music:** Charles Dibdin; **Genre:** Pantomime; 2 acts; **First Performance, London:** 1780/12/29, Covent Garden; **First Performance, America:** 1800/4/21, Philadelphia

Harlequin Gardener; **Subtitle(s):** Columbine Statue (cf.); **Genre:** Pantomime; **First Performance:** 1795/10/2, Hartford, Conn., Old American

Harlequin Gentleman; **Genre:** Pantomime; **First Performance:** 1798/2/15, Charleston, City Theatre

Harlequin Highlander; **Subtitle(s):** Sawney Beane, the Antrophophagos; **Genre:** Pantomime; **First Performance:** 1812/4/24, Philadelphia, Olympic Theatre

Harlequin Hostler; **Genre:** Pantomime; 2 acts; **First Performance:** 1803/1/10, New York

Harlequin Hurry-Scurry (based on cast lists, this title was used for a variety of pantomimes); **Subtitle(s):** The Rural Rumpus; The Village in an Uproar; Christmas Gambols (cf); **Libretto:** William Francis, Philadelphia; **Genre:** Pantomime; **First Performance:** 1795/5/25, Philadelphia

Harlequin in Despair; **Genre:** Pantomime; **First Performance:** 1808/5/3, New York, Pearl Street Theatre

Harlequin in Hartford; **Libretto:** adapted by John Hodgkinson; **Genre:** Pantomime; **First Performance:** 1799/11/11, Hartford, Conn., Old American

Harlequin in Hell; **Genre:** Pantomime; **First Performance:** 1784/1/16, Baltimore

Harlequin in Philadelphia; **Subtitle(s):** The Triumph of Virtue (cf); **Genre:** Pantomime; **First Performance** 1796/2/6, Philadelphia, Pantheon

Harlequin in the Moon *(Arlequin dans la Lune);* **Subtitle(s):** The Village in an Uproar; The Fourth of July (cf); Half an Hour's Laugh; Whitsuntide Vagaries; The Clown in the Suds; La Fette du Village; **Libretto:** William Francis, arranger; **Genre:** Comic Pantomime; **First Performance, London:** 1799; **First Performance, America:** 1804/3/28, Philadelphia

Harlequin in the Sun; **Genre:** Pantomime; **First Performance:** 1796/4/12, Philadelphia, Pantheon

Harlequin Indian—See *Nootka Sound; The Pilgrims*

Harlequin Junior; **Subtitle(s):** The Magic Cestus; **Genre:** Pantomime; **First Performance, London:** 1784/1/7, Drury Lane; **First Performance, America:** 1798/5/4, Philadelphia

Harlequin Magician; **Subtitle(s):** The Miser Outwitted; **Genre:** Pantomime; **First Performance:** 1791/12/1, Philadelphia, Kenna company

Harlequin Magician Apprentice; **Subtitle(s):** Harlequin Protected by a Lion (cf); **Genre:** Pantomime; **First Performance:** 1811/3/29, Baltimore, Pepin and Breschard

Harlequin Mariner; **Genre:** Pantomime; **First Performance, London:** 1797/5/18, Royal Circus; **First Performance, America:** 1797/1/28, Philadelphia, Pantheon

Harlequin Panattahah; **Subtitle(s):** The Genii of the Algonquins; **Genre:** Pantomime; **First Performance:** 1809/1/4, New York

Harlequin Pastry Cook; **Music:** Victor Pelissier; **Genre:** Pantomime; **First Performance:** "As performed at Paris"; **First Performance, America:** 1794/11/21, Philadelphia, Southwark

Harlequin Patriot; **Subtitle(s):** Brooklyn Heights; **Genre:** Pantomime; **First Performance:** 1814/8/26, New York Circus

Harlequin Pluto; **Subtitle(s):** A Friend in Need is a Friend Indeed; **Genre:** Comic Pantomime; **First Performance:** 1815/1/2, New York

Harlequin Prisoner; **Subtitle(s):** The Genii of the Rocks (cf); The Enchantress of the Rocks; **Genre:** Pigmy Pantomime (performed by children); **First Performance:** 1803/10/22, Baltimore

Harlequin Prodigal; **Subtitle(s):** The Father's Legacy; **Genre:** Pantomime; **First Performance:** 1814/1/3, New York, Commonwealth

Harlequin Protected by a Lion; **Genre:** Pantomime; **First Performance:** 1805/8/28, New York, Italian theatre

Harlequin Protected by Cupid; **Subtitle(s):** The Enchanted Nosegay; **Genre:** Pantomime; **First Performance:** 1792/6/5, Philadelphia, Southwark

Harlequin Ranger; **Subtitle(s):** The Power of Magic (cf); **Libretto:** Henry Woodward; **Genre:** Grand Pantomime; **First Performance, London:** 1751/12/26, Drury Lane; **First Performance, America:** 1803/3/7, Boston

Harlequin Recruit; **Subtitle(s):** Columbine's Resurrection; **Genre:** Comic Pantomime; **First Performance:** 1801/7/4, New York

Harlequin Restored; **Subtitle(s):** Taste a la Mode; **Genre:** Pantomime; **First Performance, London:** 1732/12/14, Drury Lane; 1767/7/10, Sadler's Wells; **First Performance, America:** 1795/8/31, Hartford, Conn., Old American

Harlequin Restored; **Subtitle(s):** The Gift of the Seasons; **Libretto:** Altered from *Harlequin's Almanac* (cf); **Music:** Alexander Reinagle; **Genre:** Pantomime; **First Performance:** 1803/12/26, Philadelphia

Harlequin Sailor; **Genre:** Pantomime Entertainment; **First Performance:** 1807/5/11, Boston

Harlequin Salamander; **Subtitle(s):** Humours of the Clown; **Genre:** Pantomime; 1 act; **First Performance, London:** 1766; **First Performance, America:** 1812/4/29, Boston

Harlequin Shipwrecked; **Subtitle(s):** The Power of Enchantment; The Grateful Lion (cf); A New Year's Gift (cf); **Libretto:** James Byrne, arranger; **Music:** DeMarque (pastiche from Pleyel, Grétry, Reinagle, etc.); **Genre:** Pantomimical Interlude; **First Performance:** 1791/6/13, Philadelphia, Southwark

Harlequin Skeleton; **Subtitle(s):** Magic and Mirth; The Clown Metamorphosed; **Libretto:** Based on *The Royal Chace, or Merlin's Cave;* **Genre:** Pantomime; **First Performance, London:** 1736/1/23, Covent Garden; **First Performance, America:** 1754/2/18, New York, Hallam, American

Harlequin Statue; **Subtitle(s):** The Spirit of Fancy; **Genre:** Pantomime; 2 acts; **First Performance, London:** 1763/4/7, Covent Garden; **First Performance, America:** 1795/12/24, Philadelphia, Pantheon

Harlequin Supposed Conjurer; **Genre:** Pantomime; **First Performance:** 1794/5/1, Charleston

Harlequin Supposed Gentleman; **Genre:** Pantomime; **First Performance:** 1792/8/29, Boston, Joseph Harper, under Blue Laws

Harlequin Tammany; **Subtitle(s):** The Birth of Independence; **Music:** Song and chorus by Michael Fortune; **Genre:** Pantomime Entertainment; **First Performance:** 1801/7/4, Philadelphia

Harlequin the English Dog; **Genre:** Pantomime; **First Performance:** 1805/11/28, New York, Italian theatre

Harlequin the Magician's Apprentice; **Genre:** Pantomime; **First Performance:** 1805/5/10, New York, Italian theatre

Harlequin Transformed Into a Dog; **Genre:** Pantomime; **First Performance:** 1813/7/13, Philadelphia, Columbian Gardens

Harlequin Triumphant; **Genre:** Pantomime; **First Performance:** 1797/6/10, Philadelphia, Pantheon

Harlequin Traveler; **Genre:** Pantomime; **First Performance:** 1800/7/4, New York

Harlequin Turned Barber; **Subtitle(s):** The Clown in the Suds; **Genre:** Pantomime; **First Performance:** 1804/5/28, New York

Harlequin Turned Doctor; **Genre:** Pantomime; **First Performance:** 1791/12/13, Philadelphia, Kenna company, Northern Liberties

Harlequin Turn'd Washerwoman; **Subtitle(s):** The Clown in the Suds; **Genre:** Pantomimical Interlude; **First Performance:** 1802/4/9, Philadelphia

Harlequin Valetudinarian; **Genre:** Pantomime; **First Performance:** 1805/8/2, New York, Italian theatre

Harlequin Veteran; **Genre:** Pantomime; **First Performance:** 1798/3/16, Charleston, City Theatre

Harlequin Volunteer; **Subtitle(s):** Valor Rewarded; **Genre:** Pantomimical Interlude; **First Performance:** 1804/5/23, New York

Harlequin Woodcutter; **Subtitle(s):** The Magic Garden; **Libretto:** Allport, arranger; **Genre:** Pantomime; **First Performance:** 1814/7/25, New York Circus

Harlequin's Almanac; **Subtitle(s):** The Four Seasons (cf); **Libretto:** Thomas

Dibdin; **Music:** William Reeve and William Henry Ware; Alexander Reinagle; **Genre:** Pantomime; **First Performance, London:** 1801/12/28, Covent Garden; **First Performance, America:** 1803/4/2, Philadelphia

Harlequin's Animation; **Subtitle(s):** The Triumph of Mirth (cf); The Witches Frolic; **Libretto:** Partly compiled and partly new; **Genre:** Pantomime; **First Performance:** 1795/1/1, New York

Harlequin's Choice (Pleasure and Virtue); **Music:** Mati?; **Genre:** Pantomime; 2 acts; **First Performance:** 1808/3/25, Boston

Harlequin's Club; **Libretto:** William Francis, arranger; **Genre:** Pantomime-Ballet; **First Performance:** 1796/5/30, Philadelphia

Harlequin's Cook; **Genre:** Pantomime; **First Performance:** 1794/9/8, Hartford, Conn., Old American

Harlequin's Frolic(s); **Subtitle(s):** Devil to Pay in the Village; The Wedding Day; The Village in an Uproar; **Genre:** Pantomime; 1 act; **First Performance, London:** 1757/6/16, Little Theatre, Haymarket; 1776/12/26, Covent Carden; **First Performance, America:** 1787/1/19, Philadelphia, Southwark

Harlequin's Invasion of the Realms of Shakespeare (The Medley (cf); Harlequin's Invasion); **Subtitle(s):** A Christmas Gambol; The Tailor without a Head; **Libretto:** David Garrick; **Music:** William Boyce; **Genre:** Speaking Pantomime; **First Performance, London:** 1759/12/31, Drury Lane; **First Performance, America:** 1786/6/5, New York

Harlequin's Ireland; **Subtitle(s):** St. Patrick's Day; **Genre:** Pantomime; **First Performance:** 1799/2/21, New York, Lailson's Circus

Harlequin's Jubilee; **Subtitle(s):** The Triumph of Virtue (cf); **Libretto:** Henry Woodward; **Genre:** Pantomime; 2 acts; **First Performance, London:** 1770/1/27, Covent Garden; **First Performance, America:** 1809/3/6, Boston

Harlequin's Medley; **Genre:** Pantomime Interlude; 1 act; **First Performance, London:** 1793/5/6, Royal Saloon; **First Performance, America:** 1797/1/5, Philadelphia, Pantheon

Harlequin's Olio; **Genre:** Pantomime; **First Performance:** 1796/4/5, Philadelphia, Pantheon

Harlequin's Ramble(s); **Subtitle(s):** The Fortune Teller; The Absurdities of Mankind; **Libretto:** Based on O'Keeffe/Shield *Harlequin Rambler* (1784)?; **Genre:** Pantomime; **First Performance:** 1796/7/14, Newport, R. I., Old American

Harlequin's Release; **Subtitle(s):** Liberty Triumphant; **Genre:** Pantomime interspersed with singing, dancing, &c.; **First Performance:** 1804/4/13, Boston

Harlequin's Renovations; **Genre:** Pantomime; **Libretto:** John William Ricketts, Sully, Spinacuta, arrangers; **First Performance:** 1796/3/28, Philadelphia, Pantheon

Harlequin's Restoration; **Genre:** Pantomime; **First Performance:** 1797/3/1, New York

Harlequin's Revenge; **Genre:** Pantomime; **First Performance:** 1797/2/9, Lailson's Circus

Harlequin's Statue; **Subtitle(s):** The Witches of the Lakes; **Genre:** Pantomime; **First Performance:** 1804/4/25, New York

Harlequin's Triumph in War and Love; **Libretto:** Philip Traetta; **Music:** Philip Traetta; **Genre:** Musical Farce; 2 acts; **First Performance:** 1810/1/22, New York, City Tavern

Harlequin's Vagaries; **Subtitle(s):** The Village in an Uproar; Hurley Burley; All in a Bustle; **Music:** James Hewitt; **Genre:** Pantomime; **First Performance, London:** 1792/5/24, Royal Saloon; **First Performance, America:** 1794/5/14, New York

Harlequin's Whim; **Subtitle(s):** The Doctor Outwitted; **Genre:** Pantomime; **First Performance:** 1797/5/23, Philadelphia, Lailson's Circus

Harlequin's Wishing Cup; **Genre:** Pantomime; **First Performance:** 1800/1/13, Boston

Hartford Bridge; **Subtitle(s):** The Skirts of the Camp; **Libretto:** William Pearce; **Music:** William Shield (pastiche); **Genre:** Musical Entertainment; 2 acts; **First Performance, London:** 1792/11/3, Covent Garden; **First Performance, America:** 1794/5/30, Philadelphia

Harvest Home; **Subtitle(s):** Rustic Merriment; The Reaper's Frolick; **Libretto:** May be based on Charles Dibdin's Comic Opera, 1787; **Genre:** Pantomime Ballet; **First Performance:** 1797/6/8, New York, Ricketts Circus

*Haunted Tower, The; **Libretto:** James Cobb; **Music:** Stephen Storace (pastiche); arr. by Victor Pelissier; **Genre:** Comic Opera; 3 acts; **First Performance, London:** 1789/11/24, Drury Lane; **First Performance, America:** 1793/4/24, Charleston

Hear Both Sides; **Libretto:** Thomas Holcroft; **Music:** add. by Satoly von Rosenberg; **Genre:** Comedy, Incidental Music; 5 acts; **First Performance, London:** 1803/1/29, Drury Lane; **First Performance, America:** 1803/5/2, New York

Heiress, The; **Libretto:** John Burgoyne; **Music:** Giovanni Paisiello; **Genre:** Comedy, Incidental Music; **First Performance, London:** 1786/1/14, Drury Lane; **First Performance, America:** 1788/2/25, New York

Hercules and Omphale; **Libretto:** William Francis, arranger; **Music:** William

Shield (pastiche); **Genre:** Grand Heroic Pantomime; 3 acts; **First Performance, London:** 1794/11/17, Covent Garden; **First Performance, America:** 1802/2/22, Philadelphia

*Hero of the North, The; **Subtitle(s):** Gustavus Vasa; The Deliverer of his Country; **Libretto:** William Dimond; **Music:** Michael Kelly; arr. by Alexander Reinagle, R. Chateaudun; **Genre:** Grand Operatic Drama; 5 acts; **First Performance, London:** 1803/2/19, Drury Lane; **First Performance, America:** 1804/4/2, Philadelphia

Heroes of the Lakes; **Subtitle(s):** A Tribute to the Brave; The Glorious Tenth of September; **Libretto:** May be based on a poem of that name "written in the autumn of 1813" and published New York, 1814; **Music:** "Partly compiled"; **Genre:** Comic Opera; 2, 3 acts; **First Performance:** 1813/10/1, Baltimore

Highland Festivity; **Libretto:** James Byrne, arranger; **Genre:** Pantomimic Ballet; **First Performance:** 1797/4/10, Philadelphia

***Highland Reel, The; **Subtitle(s):** The Female Soldier; **Libretto:** John O'Keeffe; add. by Susannah Rowson; **Music:** William Shield; **Genre:** Comic Opera; 3, 2 acts; **First Performance:** 1786, Dublin; 1788/11/6, London, Covent Garden; **First Performance, America:** 1793/2/11, Charleston

Highland Wedding; **Genre:** Pantomime; **First Performance:** 1795/9/28, Hartford, Conn., Old American

Hit or Miss; **Libretto:** Isaac Pocock; **Music:** Charles Smith; **Genre:** Comic Opera; 2 acts; **First Performance, London:** 1810/2/26, Lyceum; **First Performance, America:** 1810/12/5, New York

Hob in the Well—See *Flora*

Homeward Bound; **Genre:** Pantomime; **First Performance:** 1800/4/14, Charleston, City Theatre

Honest Yorkshireman, An; **Subtitle(s):** A Wonder; **Libretto:** Henry Carey; **Music:** Selected by Henry Carey; **Genre:** Ballad Opera; 1 act; **First Performance, London:** 1735/7/11, Lincoln's Inn Fields; **First Performance, America:** 1752/3/2, New York, Kean and Murray

Honey Moon, The; **Libretto: John Tobin, orig. titled *Matrimony;* **Music:** Michael Kelly; James Hewitt; **Genre:** Comedy, Incidental Music; 5 acts; **First Performance, London:** 1805/1/31, Drury Lane; **First Performance, America:** 1805/5/29, New York

House to Be Sold, A; **Libretto:** James Cobb, from Alexandre Duval's *La Maison à vendre;* **Music:** Michael Kelly; arr. by Alexander Reinagle; **Genre:** Comic Opera; 2 acts; **First Performance, London:** 1802/11/17, Drury Lane; **First Performance, America:** 1803/5/25, New York

Humors of Billy Bristle; **Genre:** Musical Interlude; **First Performance:** 1794/8/ 27, Portsmouth, N. H.

Humours of Bartholemew Fair; **Genre:** Pantomime; **First Performance:** 1797/ 7/7, New York, Ricketts Circus

Hunt the Slipper; **Libretto:** Henry Knapp; **Music:** Samuel Arnold; **Genre:** Musical Farce; 2 acts; **First Performance, London:** 1784/8/21, Little Theatre, Haymarket; **First Performance, America:** 1793/5/31, New York

Hunter of the Alps; **Libretto: William Dimond; **Music: Michael Kelly; James Hewitt; **Genre:** Comic Opera; 3, 2 acts; **First Performance, London:** 1804/7/3, Little Theatre, Haymarket; **First Performance, America:** 1805/5/ 22, New York

Hunters—See *The Birdcatchers*

Hunters and the Milk Maid—See *Two Huntsmen and the Milk Maid*

Huntress; **Subtitle(s):** Tammany's Frolics; **Genre:** Pantomime; **First Performance:** 1794/6/11, New York

Hurry Scurry; **Subtitle(s):** The Devil Among the Mechanics; Harlequin's Frolics (cf); **Genre:** Pantomime; **First Performance:** 1811/4/29, Charleston

Huzzah for Commerce; **Subtitle(s):** The Boston Beauty; **Libretto:** A gentleman of Boston; **Music:** Selected from the best composers (pastiche); **Genre:** Musical Farce; 1 act; **First Performance:** 1809/6/5, Boston

Huzzah for the Constitution (Published as *Yankee Chronology;* See also *Constitution and Guerriere*); **Libretto:** William Dunlap; **Music:** Inc. songs "Freedom of the Seas" and "Yankee Tars"; **Genre:** Patriotic Effusion (Musical Interlude); 1 act; **First Performance:** Boston, 1813/2/22

Imaginary Sick Man, The; **Libretto:** Manfredi, arranger (based on Moliere?); **Genre:** Pantomime Farce; **First Performance:** 1811/3/25, Baltimore, Pepin and Breschard

Independence; **Subtitle(s):** Which Do You Like Best, the Peer or the Farmer?; **Libretto:** William Ioor; **Genre:** Comedy with incidental music; 5 acts; **First Performance:** 1805/3/30, Charleston

Independence of America; **Subtitle(s):** The Evermemorable 4th of July, 1776; **Genre:** Splendid Historical National Pantomime; **First Performance:** 1796/ 6/8, New York

Indian Chief—See *Tammany*

Indian Heroine; **Subtitle(s):** Inkle and Yarico (cf); **Genre:** Pantomime; **First Performance:** 1792/11/19, Boston, Joseph Harper, under Blue Laws

Indian Princess, The; **Subtitle(s):** La Belle Sauvage; **Libretto:** James Nelson Barker; **Music:** John Bray; **Genre:** Operatic Melodrame; 3 acts; **First Performance, America:** 1808/4/6, Philadelphia; **First Performance, London:** 1820/12/15, Drury Lane, as *Pocahontas*

Indian War Feast; **Subtitle(s):** The American Heroine; **Libretto:** Burk, arranger; **Genre:** Pantomime; 2 acts; **First Performance, America:** 1797/5/10, Boston

Indiscretion; **Libretto:** Prince Hoare; **Genre:** Comedy, Incidental Music; 5 acts; **First Performance, London:** 1800/5/8, Drury Lane; **First Performance, America:** 1801/1/1, Boston

***Inkle and Yarico; **Subtitle(s):** The Blessings of Liberty; The American Heroine (cf); The Benevolent Maid; A School for Avarice; **Libretto:** George Colman, jr.; **Music:** Samuel Arnold; arr. by Victor Pelissier; **Genre:** Comic Opera; 3, 2 acts; **First Performance, London:** 1787/8/4, Little Theatre, Haymarket; **First Performance, America:** 1789/7/6, New York

Intrigues of Bayard, The; **Libretto:** L. Gleise, arranger; **Genre:** Pantomime; **First Performance:** 1798/6/8, Philadelphia, Lailson's Circus

Invasion of the Realms of Shakespeare; **Genre:** Pantomime; **First Performance:** 1786/6/5, New York

Invisible Girl, The; **Libretto:** Theodore Hook; based on M. C. Maurice's *Le Babillard;* **Music:** Thomas Attwood, Matthew Peter King; **Genre:** Musical Entertainment; 1 act; **First Performance, London:** 1806/4/28, Drury Lane; **First Performance, America:** 1807/1/26, New York

Irish Fair; **Subtitle(s):** St. Patrick's Day in the Morning; Whit-Monday Frolics; **Genre:** Comic Dance; **First Performance:** 1805/3/18, Philadelphia

Irish Lilt; **Libretto:** William Francis, arranger; **Genre:** Pantomime; **First Performance:** 1794/7/9, Philadelphia

Irish Taylor(s); **Subtitle(s):** The Humours of the Thimble; **Music:** Rayner Taylor; **Genre:** Burletta; 1 act; **First Performance, London:** 1791/10/5, Sadler's Wells; **First Performance, America:** 1796/4/7, Charleston, City Theatre

Irish Widow, The; **Libretto:** David Garrick; **Music:** With epilogue song by the Widow Brady; **Genre:** Comedy; 2 acts; **First Performance, London:** 1772/10/23, Drury Lane; **First Performance, America:** 1773/6/28, New York

Irishman in London; **Subtitle(s): The Happy African; **Libretto:** William Macready; **Genre:** Comedy with songs; 2 acts (see 1811/6/21, Philadelphia, Southwark); **First Performance, London:** 1792/4/21, Covent Garden; **First Performance, America:** 1793/6/5, New York

Iron Chest, The; **Subtitle(s):** Honor's Victim; The Mysterious Murder; **Libretto:** George Colman, jr.; based on William Godwin's novel, *Things as They Are;* **Music:** Stephen Storace; Rayner Taylor; **Genre:** Play interspersed with songs; 3 acts; **First Performance, London:** 1796/3/12, Drury Lane; **First Performance, America:** 1797/4/17, Philadelphia

Iron Mask (See also *Island of St. Marguerite*); **Subtitle(s):** Destruction of the

Bastille; **Music:** Robert Leaumont; **Genre:** Musical Entertainment; **First Performance:** 1797/4/3, Boston

Island of Calypso, The (See also *Telemachus in the Island of Calypso*); **Subtitle(s):** The Adventures of Telemachus; **Libretto:** Rénaud, arranger; **Genre:** Pantomime-Ballet; **First Performance:** 1797/4/5, Boston

Island of St. Marguerite, The; **Subtitle(s):** The Iron Mask (cf); **Libretto:** John St. John; based on *The Man in the Iron Mask* (cf); **Music:** Thomas Shaw; **Genre:** Comic Opera; 2 acts; **First Performance, London:** 1789/11/13, Drury Lane; **First Performance, America:** 1800/3/28, Charleston

Italian Monk, The; **Libretto:** James Boaden; based on Ann Ward Radcliffe's *The Italian*; **Music:** Samuel Arnold; arr. by Alexander Reinagle; **Genre:** Drama, Incidental Music; 3 acts; **First Performance, London:** 1797/8/15, Little Theatre, Haymarket; **First Performance, America:** 1798/4/25, Philadelphia

Jack in Distress; **Subtitle(s):** The Sailor's Landlady (cf); Preparations for a Cruise Against the Tripolitanians; American Tars on Shore; **Genre:** Pantomimic Interlude; 1 act; **First Performance:** 1796/7/14, Newport, R. I.

Jeanne d'Arc; **Subtitle(s):** The Siege of Orleans; **Genre:** Pantomime; **First Performance:** 1795/5/4, New York

Joanna of Montfaucon; **Libretto:** A. F. F. Kotzebue; adapted by Richard Cumberland; **Music:** Thomas Busby; add. by Alexander Reinagle; **Genre:** Dramatic Romance; 5 acts; **First Performance, London:** 1800/1/16, Covent Garden; **First Performance, America:** 1800/5/28, New York

Jockey and Jenny; **Genre:** Pastoral Scotch Pantomime Ballad; **First Performance:** 1799/2/26, Philadelphia, Ricketts Circus

***John Bull; **Subtitle(s):** An Englishman's Fireside; The Tradesman's Fireside (Boston, 1813); **Libretto:** George Colman, jr.; **Music:** Charles Dibdin; **Genre:** Comedy, Incidental Music; 5 acts; **First Performance, London:** 1803/3/5, Covent Garden; **First Performance, America:** 1803/5/23, Baltimore

Jovial Crew, The (See also *The Country Wake*); **Subtitle(s):** Humours of a Country Wake; **Libretto:** William Francis, arranger (based on 1751 ballad opera?); **Genre:** Comic Ballet; **First Performance:** 1813/3/10, Philadelphia

Jubilee, The (Shakespeare Jubilee); **Subtitle(s):** Shakespeare's Garland; **Libretto:** David Garrick; **Music:** Charles Dibdin (pastiche); arr. by Victor Pelissier, Beaumont; **Genre:** Musical Entertainment; 2 acts; **First Performance, London:** 1769/10/14, Drury Lane; **First Performance, America:** 1795/6/1, Philadelphia

Jugement de Midas, Le; **Libretto:** Thomas d'Hèle; **Music:** André E. M. Grétry; **Genre:** Comic Opera; 3 acts; **First Performance:** 1778/6/27, Paris; **First Performance, America:** 1808/6/11, New Orleans

Jupiter and Europa; **Subtitle(s):** The Jealousy of Juno; The Intrigues of Harlequin; **Libretto:** Alexander Placide, arranger; **Genre:** Serious Pantomime; **First Performance:** 1795/3/8, Charleston

*Killing No Murder; **Libretto:** Theodore E. Hook; **Music:** James Hook; arr. by Victor Pelissier; **Genre:** Musical Farce; 2 acts; **First Performance, London:** 1809/8/21, Little Theatre, Haymarket; **First Performance, America:** 1810/1/19, Philadelphia

King Arthur; **Subtitle(s):** The British Worthy; Arthur and Emmeline; The British Enchanter; The Promise of Columbia's Future Glory; **Libretto:** John Dryden; altered by David Garrick; further altered for performance in New York; **Music:** Henry Purcell; Thomas Arne; **Genre:** Masque; 5 acts; **First Performance, London:** 1770/12/13, Drury Lane; **First Performance, America:** 1800/4/25, New York

King of the Genii; **Subtitle(s):** Harlequin Neptune; **Genre:** Pantomime; **First Performance:** 1792/1/2, New York

King's Bench—See *Abroad and at Home*

Kiss; **Subtitle(s):** The Perplexed Husband; Beware of Jealousy; **Libretto:** Stephen Clarke; based on Fletcher and Massinger's *The Spanish Curate*; **Music:** added in Boston, "Will Thou Say Farewell Love" and "The Soldier Tired of Wars Alarms"; **Genre:** Comedy; 5 acts; **First Performance, London:** 1811/10/31, Lyceum; **First Performance, America:** 1812/5/15, Charleston

Knight of Guadalquiver; **Subtitle(s):** Spanish Castle; **Libretto:** William Dunlap; **Music:** James Hewitt; **Genre:** Comic Opera; **First Performance:** 1800/12/5, New York

Knight of Snowdoun; **Libretto:** Thomas Morton; based on Walter Scott's poem, *Lady of the Lake* (cf); **Music:** Henry R. Bishop, in the style of Scottish airs; **Genre:** Musical Drama; 3 acts; **First Performance, London:** 1811/2/5, Covent Garden; **First Performance, America:** 1811/6/12, New York

Knights of Calatrava; **Subtitle(s):** The Bridal Spectre; **Libretto:** From Thomas Dibden's *Alonzo and Imogen?* (cf); **Music:** John Moorehead; **Genre:** Heroic Pantomimical Romance; **First Performance:** 1803/11/4, Baltimore

Ladies Frolic; **Subtitle(s):** Beggar's Opera Revers'd; **Genre:** Comic Opera; **First Performance, London:** 1781; **First Performance, America:** 1796/5/25, Charleston

*Lady of the Lake; **Subtitle(s):** The Knight of Snowden; **Libretto:** Edmund John Eyre, 1811; based on Walter Scott; William Francis, arranger (another version by T. J. Dibdin with music by James Sanderson probably not acted in America); **Music:** J. Jones, add. by Pelissier; **Genre:** Melo-dramatic Romance; 3 acts; **First Performance:** 1811/1/15, Edinburgh; **First Performance, America:** 1812/1/1, Philadelphia

*Lady of the Rock; **Libretto:** Thomas Holcroft; **Music:** Fanny Holcroft; Alexander Reinagle; James Hewitt; **Genre:** Melodrama; 3, 2 acts; **First Performance, London:** 1805/2/12, Drury Lane; **First Performance, America:** 1805/6/17, New York

Lafitte, and Pirates of Barataria; **Libretto:** By a native of Boston; **Genre:** Melodrama; 2 acts; **First Performance:** 1814/11/28, Boston

Lake of Lausanne—See *Out of Place*

Landing of our Forefathers at Plymouth Rock—See *The Pilgrims*

Launch, The; **Subtitle(s):** Huzza for the Constitution (cf); **Libretto:** John Hodgkinson; **Music:** Victor Pelissier (pastiche), "the music selected from the best composers"; **Genre:** Musical Entertainment; 1 act; **First Performance, America:** 1797/9/20, Boston, Haymarket

Lethe; **Subtitle(s):** Aesop in the Shades (cf); **Libretto:** David Garrick; **Music:** Thomas Arne; **Genre:** Musical Entertainment; **First Performance, London:** 1740/4/15, Drury Lane; **First Performance, America:** 1759/6/29, Philadelphia, Society Hill Theatre

Lewis of Monte Blanco; **Subtitle(s):** The Transplanted Hibernian; The Transplanted Irishman; **Libretto:** William Dunlap; **Music:** Victor Pelissier; **Genre:** Comedy, Incidental Music; 5 acts; **First Performance, America:** 1804/3/12, New York

Life; **Subtitle(s):** A Trip to Margate; Hypocrisy Detected; The World As It Goes; **Libretto:** Frederick Reynolds; **Music:** Joseph Mazzinghi; Victor Pelissier; **Genre:** Comedy, Incidental Music; 5 acts; **First Performance, London:** 1800/11/1, Covent Garden; **First Performance, America:** 1801/4/24, New York

Life and Death of Harlequin; **Genre:** Comic Pantomime; **First Performance:** 1803/7/27, New York, Mount Vernon Gardens

Lilliputian Frolic; **Subtitle(s):** The Metamorphosed Old Woman of Eighty; **Genre:** Pantomimical Dance; **First Performance:** 1807/7/30, Philadelphia, Southwark

Linco's Travels; **Libretto:** David Garrick; **Music:** Michael Arne, Joseph Vernon; **Genre:** Musical Interlude; **First Performance, London:** 1767/3/6, Drury Lane; **First Performance, America:** 1791/12/17, Philadelphia, Kenna Company

Lion with the Thorn; **Subtitle(s):** Harlequin protected by Neptune; **Genre:** Pantomime; **First Performance:** 1795/3/9, Charleston

Lionel and Clarissa; **Subtitle(s):** School for Fathers; **Libretto:** Isaac Bicker-staffe; **Music:** Charles Dibdin (pastiche); arr. by Trille Labarre; **Genre:** Comic Opera; 3, 2 acts; **First Performance, London:** 1768/2/25, Covent Garden; **First Performance, America:** 1772/12/14, Philadelphia

Lise et Colin; **Subtitle(s):** The Reapers; **Libretto:** J. K. Labottierre, arranger; **Genre:** Ballet Pantomime; 2 acts; **First Performance:** 1804/12/24, New York

Lisette and Annette—See *Birdcatchers*

Little Bob and Little Ben; **Subtitle(s):** The Poor Sailor; Little Ben and Little Bob; **Libretto:** John O'Keeffe (credited to John Bernard, Boston); **Music:** Thomas Attwood; **Genre:** Musical Entertainment; 2 acts; **First Performance, London:** 1795/5/12, Covent Garden; **First Performance, America:** 1810/4/11, Boston

Little Fanny's Love—See *Scotch Ghost*

Little Red Riding Hood; **Libretto:** Based on Perrault's *Le Petit Chapeau Rouge;* Abercrombie and William Francis, arrangers; **Genre:** Ballet; **First Performance, London:** 1812/1/6, Surrey Theatre; **First Performance, America:** 1812/12/7, Phiadelphia, Southwark

Little Yankee Sailor; **Subtitle(s):** Nature Without Art; **Music:** Selected from William Shield, James Hook, Rayner Taylor, Charles Dibdin, etc.; arr. by George Gillingham; **Genre:** Pantomime; 2 acts; **First Performance:** 1795/5/27, Philadelphia

***Lock and Key, The; **Libretto:** Prince Hoare; **Music:** William Shield (pastiche); arr. by Victor Pelissier; **Genre:** Musical Entertainment; 2 acts; **First Performance, London:** 1796/2/2, Covent Garden; **First Performance, America:** 1796/7/7, Hartford, Conn., Old American

*Lodoiska; **Subtitle(s):** The Rescue of the Princess of Poland; The Captive Princess; **Libretto:** Jean E. B. Dejaure; tr. by John P. Kemble; **Music:** Stephen Storace (pastiche, utilizing early works by Rodolphe Kreutzer and Luigi Cherubini); arr. by Mumbler and Frederick Granger; **Genre:** Musical Romance; 3 acts; **First Performance, London:** 1794/6/9, Drury Lane; **First Performance, America:** 1806/3/3, Boston

Lord of the Manor, The; **Subtitle(s):** The Discarded Son; **Libretto:** John Burgoyne; altered by Charles Dibdin, jr.; **Music:** William Jackson; **Genre:** Comic Opera; 3 acts; **First Performance, London:** 1780/12/27, Drury Lane; **First Performance, America:** 1805/3/8, Philadelphia

Lost and Found; **Subtitle(s):** The Black Forest; **Libretto:** Martin K. Masters; **Genre:** Comedy with incidental music; 5 acts; **First Performance, London:** 1811/1/2, Lyceum; **First Performance, America:** 1812/4/29, New York

Love and Magic; **Libretto:** Perhaps based on Garrick's musical drama, *The Enchanter; or, Love and Magic* (1760); see also *Cymon and Sylvia;* **Genre:**

Pantomime; **First Performance:** 1800/7/11, New York, Mt. Vernon Gardens

Love and Money; **Subtitle(s):** The Fair Caledonian; **Libretto:** Benson; **Music:** Samuel Arnold; **Genre:** Musical Farce (also pantomime); 1 act; **First Performance, London:** 1795/8/29, Little Theatre, Haymarket; **First Performance, America:** 1797/10/10, Boston, Haymarket

Love for Love I Promise Him; **Subtitle(s):** Arbitration; **Libretto:** Claimed to be by James Kenney; **Music:** "with the original music"; **Genre:** Music Entertainment; 2 acts; **First Performance:** 1808/3/19, Philadelphia

Love in a Camp—See *Patrick in Prussia*

Love in a Village; **Libretto: Isaac Bickerstaffe; based on Marivaux, *Le jeu de l'amour et du hasard;* **Music:** Thomas A. Arne (pastiche); arr. by Victor Pelissier; **Genre:** Comic Opera; 3 acts; **First Performance, London:** 1762/12/8, Covent Garden; **First Performance, America:** 1766/6/9, Philadelphia, Society Hill

Love Laughs at Locksmiths; **Subtitle(s): The Guardian Outwitted; **Libretto:** J. N. Bouilly, *Une Folie* (cf); tr. by George Colman, jr.; **Music:** Étienne Méhul; arr. by Michael Kelly; Alexander Reinagle; **Genre:** Operatic Farce; 2 acts; **First Performance, London:** 1803/7/25, Little Theatre, Haymarket; **First Performance, America:** 1804/5/23, New York

Love of Country; **Subtitle(s):** Army and Navy; **Genre:** Interlude, interspersed with song and dance; **First Performance:** 1813/7/5, Philadelphia, Commonwealth, Southwark

Love Triumphant; **Subtitle(s):** Columbine Revived; **Genre:** Pantomime; **First Performance, London:** 1788/6/11, Royal Circus; **First Performance, America:** 1802/6/2, New York

Love's Offering; **Libretto:** J. K. Labottierre, arranger; **Genre:** Anacreontic Ballet; **First Performance:** 1804/6/7, Charleston

Love's Stratagem; **Genre:** Ballet Pantomime (performed by children); **First Performance:** 1807/9/21, New York

Lovers' Frolicks; **Genre:** Pantomime Ballet; **First Performance:** 1807/11/20, Boston

Lovers' Jest, The; **Genre:** Petit Divertissement (ballet); **First Performance:** 1806/11/5, Boston

Lucille and Lauzdeman; **Subtitle(s):** The Natural Son; **Genre:** Pantomime; **First Performance:** 1811/8/26, New York, Pepin and Breschard Circus

Lucky Escape; **Subtitle(s):** The Ploughman Turned Sailor; **Libretto:** William Francis, arranger; "founded on Dibdin's ballad of that name; **Music:** Charles Dibdin, Alexander Reinagle; **Genre:** Pantomime; **First Performance:** 1796/3/14, Philadelphia

M.P.; **Subtitle(s):** The Bluestocking; **Libretto:** Thomas Moore; **Music:** Thomas

Moore; add. by Arthur Clifton (Philip Antony Corri); **Genre:** Comic Opera; **First Performance, London:** 1811/9/9, Lyceum; **First Performance, America:** 1812/6/12, New York

Ma Tante Aurore; **Subtitle(s):** Le Roman impromptu; **Libretto:** C. de Long-champs; **Music:** F. A. Boieldieu; **Genre:** Opera; 2 acts; **First Performance:** 1803/1/13, Paris; **First Performance, America:** 1810, New Orleans

***Macbeth; **Libretto:** William Shakespeare; altered by William Davenant (1673); **Music:** Matthew Locke; perf. at New York, Philadelphia, and Baltimore with Locke's orig. music; with Scottish music between the acts adapted by Benjamin Carr, 1795/1/14, New York; with Alexander Reinagle's *Scotch Medley Overture,* Baltimore, 1814/11/5; also with music by William H. Ware of Drury Lane (Philadelphia, 1815/12/18); **Genre:** Tragedy, incidental music; **First Performance, America:** 1759/10/26, Philadelphia, Society Hill; with Locke's music, 1790/4/5, Philadelphia

Madcap (See also *The Country Madcap*); **Subtitle(s):** The Sailor's Courtship; **Libretto:** Altered from Henry Fielding, *Miss Lucy in Town;* **Genre:** Ballad Farce; 2 parts; **First Performance, London:** 1770/12/12, Covent Garden; **First Performance, America:** 1788/2/11, New York

Magic Chamber, The; **Subtitle(s):** Harlequin Junior (cf); **Genre:** Comic Pantomime; **First Performance:** 1799/12/23, Charleston, City Theatre

Magic Feast; **Genre:** Comic Pantomime; **First Performance:** 1797/1/14, Philadelphia, Pantheon

Magic Fight, The; **Subtitle(s):** The Little Cripple Devil; **Libretto:** Spinacuta, arranger; **Genre:** Pantomime; **First Performance:** 1797/2/14, Philadelphia, Pantheon

Magic Fire; **Subtitle(s):** The Origin of Harlequin (cf); **Music:** William Linley; **Genre:** Pantomime; **First Performance, London:** 1796/1/18, Drury Lane; **First Performance, America:** 1799/4/29, Philadelphia

Magic Oak, The; **Subtitle(s):** Harlequin Woodcutter (cf); **Libretto:** Thomas Dibdin; Charles Farley; **Music:** Thomas Attwood, pastiche; **Genre:** Pantomimical Entertainment; **First Performance, London:** 1799/1/29, Covent Garden; **First Performance, America:** 1805/11/23, Baltimore

Magic Rock, The; **Subtitle(s):** Harlequin Woodcutter (cf); **Genre:** Pantomime; 1 act; **First Performance:** 1815/5/29, Boston

Magic Shades; **Genre:** Grand Magical Pantomime (with transparencies); **First Performance:** 1814/3/2, Baltimore, Pepin and Breschard Circus

Magic Statue; **Genre:** Pantomime; **First Performance:** 1797/10/6, Hartford, Conn., Old American

Magic Tower, The; **Subtitle(s):** The Reward of Virtue; **Libretto:** C. J. Delacroix; **Genre:** Historical Melodrama; 2 acts; **First Performance:** 1808/8/15, New York, Vauxhall Gardens

Magic Tree, The; **Subtitle(s):** Neptune's Favor; **Libretto:** John Durang, arranger; **Genre:** Pantomime; **First Performance:** 1797/4/4, Ricketts Circus, New York

Magician No Conjurer, The; **Subtitle(s):** Harlequin's Release (cf); **Music:** May be based on comic opera, music by Joseph Mazzinghi (1792); **Genre:** Pantomime; **First Performance:** 1803/6/4, Baltimore

Magician of the Cave; **Subtitle(s):** Harlequin's Frolic (cf); **Genre:** Pantomime; **First Performance:** 1787/4/20, New York

Magician of the Enchanted Castle (Magician of the Enchanted Island); **Subtitle(s):** Harlequin Conqueror; **Libretto:** "Partly compiled from the most favorite pantomimes"; William Francis, arranger; **Genre:** Pantomime; **First Performance:** 1797/4/24, Philadelphia

Mahmoud the Robber; **Subtitle(s):** Americans in Tripoli; **Music:** "new music"; **Genre:** Pantomime; 2 acts; **First Performance:** 1804/5/31, Charleston

Maid of Hungary, The—See *La Fille d'Hungerie*

Maid of Orleans; **Subtitle(s):** Joan of Arc; **Libretto:** Alexander Placide, arranger; **Genre:** Grand French Military Pantomime; 3 acts; **First Performance:** 1796/4/8, Charleston

Maid of the Mill, The; **Libretto:** Isaac Bickerstaffe, based on Richardson's *Pamela;* **Music:** Samuel Arnold (pastiche); arr. by Victor Pelissier; Robert Leaumont (Boston); **Genre:** Comic Opera; 3 acts; **First Performance, London:** 1765/1/31, Covent Garden; **First Performance, America:** 1769/5/4, New York

Maid of the Oaks; **Subtitle(s):** A Fete Champetre; **Libretto:** John Burgoyne; **Music:** F. H. Barthélémon (pastiche); **Genre:** Dramatic Entertainment, incidental music; 5, later 2 acts; **First Performance, London:** 1774/11/5, Drury Lane; **First Performance, America:** 1796/5/23, Philadelphia

Maison à vendre—See *A House to Be Sold*

Man in the Iron Mask (See also *Iron Mask*); **Genre:** Pantomime; **First Performance:** 1799/3/25, Charleston, City Theatre

Man of the Times; **Subtitle(s):** A Scarcity of Cash; **Libretto:** John Beete; **Genre:** Musical Farce; **First Performance:** 1797/5/92, Charleston

Manhattan Stage, The; **Subtitle(s):** Cupid in His Vagaries; **Libretto:** John Williams (Anthony Pasquin); **Music:** John Williams (pastiche); **Genre:** Grand Local Historical Pantomimic Melodrame; 3 acts; **First Performance:** 1806/4/11, New York

Marchande de Mode, Les—See *The Milliners*

Maréchal de Logis, Le; **Subtitle(s):** The Two Thieves; **Libretto:** Mestayer, arranger; **Genre:** Historical Pantomime; 2 acts; **First Performance:** 1797/4/27, Philadelphia, Lailson's Circus

Marian; **Libretto:** Frances Brooke; **Music:** William Shield; **Genre:** Comic Opera; 2 acts; **First Performance, London:** 1788/5/22, Covent Garden; **First Performance, America:** 1798/4/21, Philadelphia

*Marmion; **Subtitle(s):** (a) A Tale of Flodden Field; (b,c) The Battle of Floddenfield; **Libretto:** Based on Sir Walter Scott; (a) author unknown; (b) William Dunlap, New York (advertised as Thomas Morton); (c) James Nelson Barker; **Music:** (c) John Bray; **Genre:** (a, b) Melodramatic Romance, interspersed with songs; (c) Grand Heroic Tragedy; 5 acts; **First Performance, London:** (a) 1810/10/25, New Theatre, Tottenham St.; **First Performance, America:** (a) 1812/3/30, Philadelphia, Olympic Theatre; (b) 1812/4/13, New York; (c) 1813/1/1, Philadelphia

Marriage Promise, The; **Libretto:** John Till Allingham; **Music:** Michael Kelly; **Genre:** Comedy, Incidental Music; 5 acts; **First Performance, London:** 1803/4/16, Drury Lane; **First Performance, America:** 1803/10/31, Baltimore

*Matrimony; **Subtitle(s):** The Test of Love; Two Prisoners; The Castle of Linburg; Adolphe et Clara; **Libretto:** James Kenney, from B. J. Marsollier, *Adolphe et Clara;* **Music:** Matthew Peter King (pastiche); arr. by James Hewitt; **Genre:** Petite Opera; 2 acts; **First Performance, London:** 1804/11/20, Drury Lane; **First Performance, America:** 1805/5/17, New York

May Day Dower—See *The Quaker*

May-day in Town; **Subtitle(s):** New-York in an Uproar; **Libretto:** Royall Tyler; **Music:** Pastiche "compiled from the most eminent masters"; **Genre:** Comic Opera; 2 acts; **First Performance:** 1787/5/19, New York

Medea and Jason; **Subtitle(s):** The Golden Fleece; **Music:** James Hewitt; **Genre:** Serious Pantomime; 1 act; **First Performance, London:** 1781/8/8, King's Theatre, Haymarket; **First Performance, America:** 1797/6/2, Boston, Haymarket

Medley, The; **Subtitle(s):** The Taylor and Cobler; **Genre:** Pantomime Dance; **First Performance:** 1795/6/3, New York

Medley, The—See *Harlequin's Invasion of the Realms of Shakespeare*

Mélomanie; **Subtitle(s):** Musical Madness; **Libretto:** Grenier and Duveyrier; **Music:** Stanislas Champein; **Genre:** Comic Opera; 1 act; **First Performance:** 1781/1/23, Paris; **First Performance, America:** 1795/7/16, Charleston

Merry Gardener, The; **Subtitle(s):** The Night of Adventures; **Libretto:** William Dunlap (from the French); **Music:** Victor Pelissier; **Genre:** Comic Opera; 2 acts; **First Performance:** 1802/2/3, New York

Merry Girl—See *Two Philosophers*

Merry Hunters, The (See also *Two Huntsmen and the Milkmaid; The Bear Hunters*); **Subtitle(s):** The Death of the Bear; The Flight to Piccadilly; **Genre:** Pantomime; 1 act; **First Performance:** 1811/4/10, Baltimore, Pepin and Breschard Circus

Merry Hunters of Ardanne; **Genre:** Pantomime; **First Performance:** 1808/11/ 30, New York, Pepin and Breschard Circus

Merry Little Girl; **Genre:** Pantomime; **First Performance:** 1796/6/10, Philadelphia

Merry Rustics; **Subtitle(s):** Trick upon Trick (cf); **Genre:** Pantomime; **First Performance:** 1794/11/10, Charleston

Metamorphoses of the Gardner [*sic*]; **Genre:** Comic Pantomime; 1 act; **First Performance:** 1813/8/17, Philadelphia, Columbian Gardens

Metamorphosis, The; **Subtitle(s):** Harlequin Barber (cf); **Genre:** Pantomime; **First Performance:** 1799/2/14, New York, Lailson's Circus

*Midas; **Subtitle(s):** Prejudice Punished; The Assembly of the Gods; The Dieties Assembled; Olympus in an Uproar; **Libretto:** Kane O'Hara; **Music:** Kane O'Hara, compiler; **Genre:** Burletta; 2 or 3 acts; **First Performance:** 1762/1/22, Dublin; 1764/2/22, London, Covent Garden; **First Performance, America:** 1769/11/24, Philadelphia, Southwark

Midnight Wanderers, The; **Subtitle(s):** The Shipwreck; **Libretto:** William Pearce; **Music:** William Shield (pastiche); **Genre:** Comic Opera; 2 acts; **First Performance, London:** 1793/2/25, Covent Garden; **First Performance, America:** 1796/6/1, Philadelphia

*Miller and His Men, The; **Libretto:** Isaac Pocock; **Music:** (a) Henry R. Bishop; (b) Rayner Taylor (Philadelphia); (c) Vocal music by John Bray, music for the action compiled and adapted by Dupuy (Boston); **Genre:** Grand Melodrama; 2 acts; **First Performance, London:** 1813/10/21, Covent Garden; **First Performance, America:** 1814/7/4, New York

Millers, The; **Subtitle(s):** Le Rondevous [*sic*] Nocturne; Revels by Moonlight; The Run-away Girl; Village Frolics; **Libretto:** J. K. Labottierre, arranger; **Music:** Arr. by James Hewitt; **Genre:** Pantomime-Ballet; **First Performance, London:** 1804/5/1, Sadler's Wells; **First Performance, America:** 1804/11/7, Boston

Milliners, The (Les marchande de mode); **Subtitle(s):** The Wooden Block; The Suspicious Husband; The Jealous Husband; **Music:** Victor Pelissier; **Genre:** Pantomimical afterpiece with singing and dancing; 2 acts; **First Performance:** 1794/5/6, Charleston

*Miraculous Mill; **Subtitle(s):** The Old Ground Young; **Libretto:** William

Francis, arranger; **Music:** DeMarque; Louis Boullay (pastiche); **Genre:** Pantomimical Dance; **First Performance:** 1795/6/26, Philadelphia

Mirth and Magic; **Subtitle(s):** Harlequin's Gambols; **Music:** Pastiche; **Genre:** Pantomime; 2 acts; **First Performance, London:** 1795/7/15, Astley's Circus; **First Performance, America:** 1809/5/31, Boston

Mirth by Moonlight; **Libretto:** William Francis, arranger; **Genre:** Comic ballet; **First Performance:** 1813/3/5, Philadelphia

Mirth's Medley; **Genre:** Pantomime; **First Performance:** 1796/10/22, Philadelphia, Pantheon

Mirza and Lindor; **Subtitle(s):** The Traitor Punished; The Ungrateful Commander; **Libretto:** Alexander Placide, arranger; **Genre:** Grand Historical Pantomime, with vocal and instrumental music and combats; 2 or 3 acts; **First Performance:** "As performed in Paris"; **First Performance, America:** 1794/7/8, Charleston

Mistress and the Maid (See also *The Servant Mistress*); **Subtitle(s):** La Serva Padrona; **Libretto:** Federico, tr. Baurons; in French; **Music:** Pere Golaise [*sic*, Pergolesi]; **Genre:** Opera; Intermezzo; **First Performance:** 1733/8/28, Naples; **First Performance, America:** 1790/6/14, Baltimore, French company

*Mock Doctor, The; **Subtitle(s):** The Dumb Lady Cured; **Libretto:** Henry Fielding, based on Molière's *Le médecin malgré lui;* **Music:** Seedo, compiler; **Genre:** Ballad Opera; 1, 2 acts; **First Performance, London:** 1732/6/23, Drury Lane; **First Performance, America:** 1750/4/30, New York, Kean and Murray

Modern Amazons; **Genre:** Pantomime; 2 acts; **First Performance:** 1797/7/27, Philadelphia, Lailson's Circus

Modern Love(rs); **Subtitle(s):** Generosity Rewarded; **Libretto:** Altered from Charles Dibdin's *Lionel and Clarissa* (cf); **Genre:** "Comic lecture in two parts"; **First Performance:** 1787/7/28, Philadelphia

Mother Bunch; **Subtitle(s):** The Yellow Dwarf; **Genre:** Grand Pantomime; **First Performance, London:** 1807/3/30, Royal Amphitheatre; **First Performance, America:** 1813/1/21, Philadelphia, Olympic

Mother Goose; **Subtitle(s):** The Golden Egg; **Libretto:** Thomas Dibdin (as *Harlequin and Mother Goose*); **Music:** William Henry Ware; arr. by Victor Pelissier; **Genre:** Pantomimical Operatic Romance; **First Performance, London:** 1806/12/26, Covent Garden; **First Performance, America:** 1809/3/3, Charleston

Mother Pitcher; **Genre:** Pantomime; **First Performance:** 1794/5/30, Boston

Motley Group; **Subtitle(s):** Harlequin's Invitation; **Libretto:** William Francis, arranger; **Genre:** Pantomime; **First Performance:** 1796/5/4, Philadelphia

***Mountaineers, The; **Subtitle(s):** Love and Madness; **Libretto:** George Colman, jr.; **Music:** Samuel Arnold; arr. by Victor Pelissier, Rayner Taylor, Alexander Reinagle; **Genre:** Comic Opera; 5 or 3 acts; **First Performance, London:** 1793/8/3, Little Theatre, Haymarket; **First Performance, America:** 1795/4/6, Boston

Mouth of the Nile; **Subtitle(s):** The Glorious first of August; **Libretto:** Thomas J. Dibdin; **Music:** Thomas Attwood; **Genre:** Musical Entertainment; 1 act; **First Performance, London:** 1798/10/25, Covent Garden; **First Performance, America:** 1799/5/13, New York

Music Mad; **Libretto:** Theodore E. Hook; **Music:** James Hook; acc. by Frederick Granger; **Genre:** Petit Comedy; 1 act; **First Performance, London:** 1807/8/27, Little Theatre, Haymarket; **First Performance, America:** 1811/12/20, Boston

Musical Lady, The; **Libretto:** George Colman; **Genre:** Musical Farce; **First Performance, London:** 1762/3/6, Drury Lane; **First Performance, America:** 1769/6/26, Philadelphia, Assembly Room

My Grandmother; **Subtitle(s): The Living Picture; **Libretto:** Prince Hoare; **Music:** Stephen Storace; arr. by Victor Pelissier; **Genre:** Musical Farce; 2 acts; **First Performance, London:** 1793/12/16, Little Theatre, Haymarket; **First Performance, America:** 1795/4/27, Philadelphia

Mysteries of the Castle; **Subtitle(s):** Virtue Rewarded; The Victim of Revenge; **Libretto:** Miles Peter Andrews and Frederick Reynolds; also John Blake White (Charleston, 1807); based on Ann Ward Radcliffe's novel, *The Mysteries of Eudolpho;* **Music:** William Shield (pastiche); **Genre:** Dramatic Tale interspersed with singing; 3 acts; **First Performance, London:** 1795/1/31, Covent Garden; **First Performance, America:** 1796/4/15, Boston

Mysterious Marriage, The; **Subtitle(s):** The Heirship of Roselva; **Libretto:** Harriet Lee; **Music:** James Hewitt; **Genre:** Drama, Incidental Music; 3 acts; **First Performance:** 1799/4/5, Philadelphia; **First Performance, London:** Printed in 1798, but not performed in England till 1821/7/16, Surrey

Mysterious Monk (Ribbemont); **Subtitle(s):** The Feudal Baron; **Libretto:** William Dunlap; **Music:** Victor Pelissier; **Genre:** Tragedy, Incidental Music; **First Performance:** 1796/10/31, New York

Mystery of the Cottage; **Subtitle(s):** The Brave Rewarded; **Libretto:** Mestayer, arranger; **Genre:** Pantomime; **First Performance:** 1814/3/4, Baltimore, Circus

Naval Frolic; **Subtitle(s):** A Tribute of Respect to American Tars; **Genre:** Grand Local Patriotic Ballet; **First Performance:** 1812/12/17, Philadelphia, Southwark

Naval Glory; **Music:** Finale, "Yankee Doodle," "Hail Columbia"; **Genre:** Patriotic Spectacle; **First Performance:** 1812/9/29, Philadelphia, Olympic

Naval Gratitude; **Subtitle(s):** The Generous Tar; **Music:** includes song "Hail Columbia"; **Genre:** Dramatic Sketch; **First Performance:** 1798/5/23, New York

Naval Pillar, The (See also *Tars from Tripoli*); **Subtitle(s):** The American Sailor's Garland; American Tars Triumphant; **Libretto:** Thomas Dibdin; **Music:** John Moorehead (pastiche); arr. by Alexander Reinagle; **Genre:** Musical Entertainment; 2 acts; **First Performance, London:** 1799/10/7, Covent Garden; **First Performance, America:** 1800/4/23, Philadelphia

Naval Volunteers, The—See *American True Blues*

Necromancer, The; **Subtitle(s):** Trick Upon Trick (cf); **Genre:** Pantomime; 2 acts; **First Performance:** 1801/9/11, New York, Mount Vernon Gardens

Needs Must; **Subtitle(s):** The Ballad Singer; **Libretto:** Anne Julia Hatton; **Music:** Mary Ann Pownall, compiler and performer; **Genre:** Musical Entertainment (skit); **First Performance:** 1793/12/23, New York

Neptune and Amphitrite; **Libretto:** Part of Thomas Shadwell's version of Shakespeare's *The Tempest* (cf); **Music:** Pelham Humfrey; Henry Purcell; **Genre:** Masque; **First Performance, London:** 1694; **First Performance, America:** 1770/1/19, Philadelphia

Netley Abbey; **Libretto:** William Pearce; **Music:** William Shield (pastiche); **Genre:** Operatic farce; 2 acts; **First Performance, London:** 1794/4/10, Covent Garden; **First Performance, America:** 1800/12/8, Philadelphia

New Deserter; **Subtitle(s):** The Supposed Marriage; **Libretto:** Based on A. E. M. Grétry; **Genre:** Pantomime; **First Performance:** 1797/11/2, New York, Lailson's Amphitheatre

New French Deserter; **Subtitle(s):** The Supposed Wedding; **Libretto:** Francesquy, arranger; **Music:** A. E. M. Grétry; **Genre:** TragiComic Pantomime interspersed with dances; 3 acts; **First Performance:** Paris; **First Performance, America:** 1797/1/13, Boston, Haymarket

New Hay at the Old Market—See *Sylvester Daggerwood*

New Way to Pay Reckoning During the Embargo, A; **Genre:** Pantomimic Interlude; **First Performance:** 1808/4/18, Boston

New Wreath for American Tars (See also *Constellation; Enterprize*); **Genre:** Musical Entertainment; 1 act; **First Performance:** 1804/5/23, Baltimore

New Year's Gift, The; **Subtitle(s):** Highland Frolicks; **Libretto:** James Byrne, arranger; **Genre:** Pantomime Ballet; **First Performance:** 1797/1/2, Philadelphia

New Year's Gig (The Gig); **Subtitle(s):** Harlequin's Frolics (cf); **Genre:** Pantomime; **First Performance:** 1802/1/2, New York

Nina; **Subtitle(s):** La folle par amour; **Libretto:** B. J. Marsollier; **Music:** Nicholas Dalayrac; **Genre:** Comic Opera; 1 act; **First Performance:** 1786/5/15, Paris; **First Performance, America:** 1794/7/23, Charleston

Nina; **Subtitle(s):** Distracted Lover; The Love Distracted Maid; Love and Madness; The Madness of Love; **Libretto:** B. J. Marsollier; tr. by (a) John Wolcot, (b) William Dunlap; **Music:** Nicolas Dalayrac; (a) adapted by William Parke; **Genre:** Opera; 2 acts; Comedy; 1 act; **First Performance, London:** (a) 1787/4/24, Covent Garden; **First Performance, America:** (b) 1805/2/4, New York

***No Song, No Supper; **Subtitle(s):** The Lawyer in the Sack; **Libretto:** Prince Hoare; **Music:** Stephen Storace (pastiche); **Genre:** Opera; 2 acts; **First Performance, London:** 1790/4/16, Drury Lane; **First Performance, America:** 1792/11/30, Philadelphia, Southwark

Noble Peasant; **Libretto:** Thomas Holcroft; **Music:** William Shield; **Genre:** Comic Opera; 3 acts; **First Performance, London:** 1784/8/2, Little Theatre, Haymarket; **First Performance, America:** 1795/5/8, Philadelphia

Nootka Sound; **Subtitle(s):** The Adventures of Captain Douglas; Harlequin Indian; **Music:** James Hewitt; **Genre:** Pantomime; **First Performance, London:** 1790/6/4, Covent Garden; **First Performance, America:** 1794/6/5, New York

*Obi; **Subtitle(s):** Three-Fingered Jack; **Libretto:** John Fawcett; **Music:** Samuel Arnold; Victor Pelissier; **Genre:** Grand Pantomimical Drama, with songs; 2 acts; **First Performance, London:** 1800/7/2, Little Theatre, Haymarket; **First Performance, America:** 1801/3/31, Boston

Of Age Tomorrow; **Libretto: Thomas Dibdin; based on A. F. F. Kotzebue's *Der Wildfang;* **Music:** Michael Kelly; add. by John Bray; **Genre:** Comic Opera; 2 acts; **First Performance, London:** 1800/2/1, Drury Lane; **First Performance, America:** 1806/1/31, Boston

Offering of Love, An (Offrande a L'Amour); **Libretto:** J. K. Labottierre, arranger; **Music:** James Hewitt; **Genre:** "Anacreontic ballet"; 1 act; **First Performance:** 1804/10/15, Boston

Oh! This Love!; **Subtitle(s):** The Masqueraders; Love's Mysteries; **Libretto:** James Kenney; **Music:** M. P. King; **Genre:** Comic Opera; **First Performance, London:** 1810/6/12, Lyceum, London; **First Performance, America:** 1812/2/26, New York

L'Oiseleur—See *The Bird Catchers*

Old Ground Young—See *Miraculous Mill*

Old Man and Piero Out-done, The; **Genre; Length:** Pantomime; **First Performance:** 1814/11/2, Philadelphia, Villalave at Olympic Theatre

Old Man Taught Wisdom, An—See *The Virgin Unmasked*

Old Schoolmaster Grown Young, The (The Old Man Grown Young); **Genre:** Pantomime; **First Performance:** 1792/4/13, New York

Old Sergeant; **Genre:** Pantomime; **First Performance:** 1795/9/28, Hartford, Conn., Old American

Old Soldier (The Soldier and the Robbers; See also *The Valiant Soldier*); **Subtitle(s):** The Two Thieves; The Two Robbers; The Happy Deliverance; Whitsun Festival; **Music:** James Hewitt; **Genre:** "Historical pantomime"; **First Performance:** 1792/2/15, New York

Old Woman of Eighty (Old Woman of Eighty-Three); **Libretto:** Charles Dibdin; **Music:** Charles Dibdin; Rayner Taylor; **Genre:** All-Sung, Burletta; **First Performance, London:** 1777, Sadler's Wells; **First Performance, America:** 1793/2/28, Annapolis

Old Woman, Weather Wise, The; **Libretto:** Miles Peter Andrews; **Music:** With a Song; **Genre; Length:** Comic Interlude; **First Performance:** 1798/4/20, Charleston

One O'Clock—See *The Wood Demon*

Origin of Harlequin; **Genre:** Pantomime; **First Performance:** 1798/4/14, Philadelphia

Orpheus and Euridice (See also *Peep Behind the Curtain*); **Libretto:** May be based on Robert Houlton's burletta with music by T. Giordani, perf. Dublin, 1784; **Genre:** Pantomime; **First Performance:** 1788/11/1, Philadelphia

Oscar and Malvina; **Subtitle(s): The Hall of Fingal; **Libretto:** "Taken from Ossian"; James Byrne, arranger; **Music:** William Reeve; "Ancient Scots Music selected by [William] Shield"; Union Pipes played by Mr. Bunyie, Philadelphia, 1811; **Genre:** Ballet Pantomime; **First Performance, London:** 1791/10/20, Covent Garden; **First Performance, America:** 1796/3/14, Boston

Out of Place; **Subtitle(s):** Lake of Lausanne; **Libretto:** Frederick Reynolds; **Music:** John Braham, William Reeve; **Genre:** Operatic Farce; **First Performance, London:** 1805/2/28, Covent Garden; **First Performance, America:** 1812/10/9, New York

***Padlock, The; **Subtitle(s):** Fruitless Precaution; **Libretto:** Isaac Bickerstaffe; based on Miguel Cervantes *El zeloso Estemeno* (The Jealous Husband); **Music:** Charles Dibdin; **Genre:** Comic Opera; 2 acts; **First Performance, London:** 1768/10/3, Drury Lane; **First Performance, America:** 1769/5/29, New York

Painters, The; **Subtitle(s):** The Animated Statue (cf); **Genre:** Pantomimic Ballet; 1 act; **First Performance:** 1807/3/18, Boston

Pantaloon Duped; **Subtitle(s):** The Forced Marriage; **Genre:** Pantomime; **First Performance:** 1797/6/17, Philadelphia, Lailson's Circus

Pantaloon in the Suds; **Subtitle(s):** Eastern Gambols; **Genre:** Comic Pantomime; **First Performance:** 1815/3/27, New York

Paragraph, The; **Subtitle(s):** A Recipe for the Nervous; Dine at My Villa; **Libretto:** Prince Hoare; **Music:** John Braham; arr. by Alexander Reinagle; Frederick Granger; **Genre:** Comic Opera; 2 acts; **First Performance, London:** 1804/3/8, Covent Garden; **First Performance, America:** 1804/11/23, Baltimore

Patie and Peggy; **Subtitle(s):** Part Them Who Can; **Libretto:** Based on characters from Allan Ramsay's *The Gentle Shepherd* (cf); **Genre:** Pantomimic Ballet; **First Performance:** 1807/1/30, Boston

Patie and Roger—See *The Gentle Shepherd*

*Patrick in Prussia (Love in a Camp); **Subtitle(s):** Darby Turn'd Soldier; **Libretto:** John O'Keeffe (sequel to *Poor Soldier* (cf); **Music:** William Shield; **Genre:** Comic Opera; 2 acts; **First Performance, London:** 1786/2/17, Covent Garden; **First Performance, America:** 1787/4/9, New York

Patriot, The; **Subtitle(s):** Liberty Asserted; Liberty Attained; **Libretto:** Based on the story of William Tell; **Music:** James Hewitt; Benjamin Carr; **Genre:** Drama, Incidental Music; 3 acts; **First Performance:** 1794/6/5, New York

Paul and Alexis; **Subtitle(s):** The Orphans of the Rhine; **Libretto:** Mordecai M. Noah; tr. from Pixérécourt, *Le Pelerin blanc;* later revised and published as *The Wandering Boys; or The Castle of Olival;* **Genre:** Afterpiece, interspersed with songs and dances; 2 acts; **First Performance:** 1810, Paris, Imperial Theatre; **First Performance, America:** 1812/4/20, Charleston

Paul and Virginia; **Libretto: James Cobb; from the French of Bernardine St. Pierre, by Helen Marie Williams; **Music:** William Reeve, Joseph Mazzinghi; arr. by Alexander Reinagle; James Hewitt; **Genre:** Musical Entertainment; 2 acts; **First Performance, London:** 1800/5/1, Covent Garden; **First Performance, America:** 1801/3/18, Boston

Paul and Virginia; **Libretto:** Based on St. Pierre; Legé, arranger; **Music:** Joseph Mazzinghi; **Genre:** Pantomime; **First Performance, London:** 1795/3/26, King's Theatre, Haymarket; **First Performance, America:** 1797/5/10, Boston

Pawlo and Petrowna; **Subtitle(s):** The Force of Jealousy; **Genre:** Pantomime; 3 acts; **First Performance:** Charleston, 1812/5/15

Peasant Boy; **Subtitle(s):** Innocence Protected; **Libretto:** William Dimond; William Francis, arranger; **Music:** Michael Kelly; Arr. by Victor Pelissier; **Genre:** Melo-Dramatic Romance; 3 acts; **First Performance, London:** 1811/1/31, Lyceum; **First Performance, America:** 1812/3/11, Philadelphia

Peasant of the Alps; **Subtitle(s):** The Wood Cutter; **Genre:** Ballet Pantomime; **First Performance:** 1797/3/16, New York, Ricketts Circus

Pedlar, The; **Genre:** Pantomimic Ballet; **First Performance:** 1801/4/27, Charleston

Peep Behind the Curtain; **Subtitle(s):** Orpheus and Euridice; The New Rehearsal; **Libretto:** David Garrick; **Music:** François Barthélémon; **Genre:** Burletta *(Orpheus and Euridice)* within a 2-act play; **First Performance, London:** 1767/10/23, Drury Lane; **First Performance, America:** 1787/5/14, New York

Peeping Tom of Coventry; **Libretto:** John O'Keeffe; **Music:** Samuel Arnold; **Genre:** Comic Opera; 2 acts; **First Performance, London:** 1784/9/6, Little Theatre, Haymarket; **First Performance, America:** 1793/2/18, Charleston

Perouse (Peyrouse), La; **Subtitle(s): The Desolate Island; **Libretto:** Charles Smith; John Fawcett, 1801; Smalley, arranger (1812); tr. from A. F. F. Kotzebue; **Music:** John Moorehead and John Davy; arr. by Alexander Reinagle, Frederick Granger; **Genre:** Pantomime; 2 acts; **First Performance, London:** 1801/2/28, Covent Garden; **First Performance, America:** 1803/5/10, Charleston

Peru Avenged—See *Alzuma*

Petite Espiegle, La; **Libretto:** Legé, arranger; **Genre:** Ballet; **First Performance:** 1797/4/17, Boston

Petite Piedmontese—See *Travellers Preserved*

Petite Savoyards, The (See also *Deux Petite Savoyards*); **Genre:** Pantomime Ballet (performed by children); **First Performance:** 1806/3/21, Charleston

Petite Trompeuse; **Genre:** Ballet Dance; **First Performance:** 1814/4/13, Philadelphia

Philadelphia Volunteers; **Subtitle(s):** Who's Afraid; **Genre:** National Patriotic Piece, interspersed with Songs and Choruses; 2 acts; **First Performance:** 1812/10/5, Philadelphia, Commonwealth

Piero's [*sic*] Disgrace; **Genre:** Pantomime; **First Performance:** 1814/10/26, Philadelphia, Olympic Theatre, Villalave Company

Pierre de Provençe and La Belle (The Beautiful) Maguelone; **Subtitle(s):** Rival Knights; **Music:** Alexander Reinagle; **Genre:** Heroic, Historical Ballet; 3 acts; **First Performance:** 1796/5/2, Philadelphia

Pigmalion (See also *Pygmalion*); **Libretto:** Jean-Jacques Rousseau; **Music:** Jean-Jacques Rousseau, Horace Coignet; **Genre:** Melodrama (scène lyrique); **First Performance:** 1775/10/30, Paris; 1793/3/18, London, Covent Garden; **First Performance, America:** 1790/10/0, Charleston

Pilgrims, The; **Subtitle(s):** The Landing of our Forefathers at Plymouth Rock; Harlequin Indian; **Libretto:** A gentleman of Boston; **Genre:** Historic Serio-Comic Pantomimic Entertainment; 3 acts; **First Performance:** 1802/4/30, Boston

Pinxter Monday; **Subtitle(s):** Harlequin's Frolics (cf); **Genre:** Pantomime Interlude; **First Performance:** 1804/5/21, New York

***Pizarro; **Subtitle(s):** The Spaniards in Peru; The Death of Rolla; **Libretto:** A. F. F. Kotzebue; tr. by Richard B. Sheridan (also Charles Smith); **Music:** Composed and selected by Michael Kelly; arr. by Alexander Reinagle, Rayner Taylor; **Genre:** Tragedy, Incidental Music; 5 acts; **First Performance, London:** 1799/5/24, Drury Lane; **First Performance, America:** 1800/5/19, Philadelphia

Pizarro in Peru; **Subtitle(s):** The Death of Rolla; **Libretto:** A. F. F. Kotzebue; tr. by William Dunlap, a "continuation of" *The Virgin of the Sun* (cf); (this title and subtitle also used by Thomas Hutton, London, 1799; Dunlap's tr. is based on those of R. B. Sheridan and Benjamin Thompson); **Music:** James Hewitt; **Genre:** Tragedy, Incidental Music; **First Performance:** 1800/3/26, New York

Plymouth Rock; **Subtitle(s):** Harlequin Released from Bondage; **Genre:** Pantomime; **First Performance:** 1796/6/11, Portsmouth, N. H.

Poor Jack; **Subtitle(s):** The Sailor's Return (cf); The Sailor's Landlady (cf); The Generous Sailor; The Shipwrecked Sailor; **Music:** Benjamin Carr; **Genre:** Pantomime; 1 act; **First Performance:** 1795/4/7, New York

Poor Jack (See also *Shipwrecked Tar*); **Subtitle(s):** The Sailor's Return (cf); **Libretto:** Bologna, jr.; **Genre:** Interlude; **First Performance, London:** 1807; **First Performance, America:** 1811/6/14, New York

Poor Lodger; **Libretto:** W. C. White; based on novel, *Evelina;* **Music:** An original song by Mr. Entwisle; **Genre; Length:** Comedy with incidental music; 5 acts; **First Performance:** 1811/2/6, Boston

Poor Sailor—See *Little Bob and Little Ben*

***Poor Soldier, The (Darby and Patrick); **Subtitle(s):** The Shamrock; St. Patrick's Day; **Libretto:** John O'Keeffe, rev. from his *The Shamrock;* **Music:** William Shield (pastiche); add. George Nicks; **Genre:** Comic Opera; 2 acts; **First Performance:** 1783/3/28, Dublin; 1783/11/4, London, Covent Garden; **First Performance, America:** 1785/12/2, New York

Poor Vulcan; **Subtitle(s):** Gods Upon Earth; **Libretto:** Charles Dibdin; **Music:** Charles Dibdin; arr. by Victor Pelissier; **Genre:** Burletta (All-Sung); 2 acts; **First Performance, London:** 1778/2/4, Covent Garden; **First Performance, America:** 1793/2/22, Charleston

Positive Man, The; **Libretto:** John O'Keeffe; an alteration of *The She Gallant;* **Music:** Michael Arne, Samuel Arnold; **Genre:** Musical Farce; 2 acts; **First Performance, London:** 3/16/1782, Covent Garden; **First Performance, America:** 1802/5/10, New York

Power of Love, The; **Subtitle(s):** The Vicissitudes of Fortune; **Genre:** Pantomime; **First Performance:** 1796/5/11, New York

Power of Magic; **Subtitle(s):** Harlequin Everywhere (cf); **Genre:** Pantomime; **First Performance:** 1796/7/25, New York, Ricketts Amphitheatre

Preparations for Privateering—See *The American Tars*

Press Gang, The; **Subtitle(s):** Harlequin Aeronaut; **Genre:** Comic Pantomime; **First Performance:** 1812/3/30, Charleston

Princess and No Princess—See *Forest of Hermanstadt*

Princess of Babilone (Babylon); **Subtitle(s):** Zilia; **Libretto:** Lavalette, arranger; **Music:** Pastiche, selected from French operas; **Genre:** Grand Pantomime; 2 acts; **First Performance:** 1797/5/15, Charleston, City Theatre

Prisoner, The; **Subtitle(s):** Female Heroism; **Libretto:** John Rose; **Music:** Thomas Attwood; add. by T. Andrews; arr. by Trille Labarre (Boston); arr. by Victor Pelissier (New York); **Genre:** Musical Romance; 3 acts; **First Performance, London:** 1792/10/18, King's Theatre, Haymarket; **First Performance, America:** 1795/5/29, Philadelphia

Prisoner at Large, The; **Subtitle(s): The Humours of Killarney; **Libretto:** John O'Keeffe; **Genre:** Musical Entertainment; 2 acts; **First Performance, London:** 1788/7/2, King's Theatre, Haymarket; **First Performance, America:** 1789/11/30, New York

***Prize, The; **Subtitle(s):** 2, 5, 3, 8; Ten Thousand Pounds; **Libretto:** Prince Hoare; **Music:** Stephen Storace; **Genre:** Musical Farce; 2 acts; **First Performance, London:** 1793/3/11, King's Theatre, Haymarket; **First Performance, America:** 1794/5/26, Philadelphia

Proctor's Defeat by General Harrison; **Music:** includes a new march composed for the occasion, called "Harrison's March"; **Genre:** Grand Pantomime; **First Performance:** 1813/11/3, Philadelphia, Columbian Gardens

***Purse, The; **Subtitle(s):** The Benevolent Tar; The Generous Tar; The American Tar; American Tar's Return; American Tar Returned from Tripoli; **Libretto:** John C. Cross; adapted by John Hodgkinson; **Music:** William Reeve; Rayner Taylor; add. by Victor Pelissier; arr. by Alexander Reinagle; **Genre:** Musical Drama; 1 act; **First Performance, London:** 1794/2/8, Little Theatre, Haymarket; **First Performance, America:** 1795/1/7, Philadelphia

Pygmalion ("englished") (See also *Pigmalion*); **Subtitle(s):** The Sculptor in Love with his Statue; **Libretto:** Jean-Jacques Rousseau; tr. St. Aivre; **Music:** Rousseau, Horace Coignet; **Genre:** Lyric scene (melodrama); 1 act; **First Performance:** 1770/5/0, Lyons, France; **First Performance, America:** 1790/11/9, New York, City Tavern

Pyrame and Thisbe; **Music:** Baudron; **Genre:** Melodrama; **First Performance:** 1783, Paris; **First Performance, America:** 1794/9/20, Charleston

Quadrupeds Of Quedlinburg; **Subtitle(s):** The Rovers of Weimar; **Libretto:** George Colman, jr.; **Music:** "With appropriate overture and music"; **Genre:** Grand Tragico, Comico, Anglo, Germanico, Hippo, Melo-Dramatic Romance; **First Performance, London:** 1811/7/26, Little Theatre, Haymarket; **First Performance, America:** 1813/4/19, Philadelphia

Quaker, The; **Subtitle(s): Benevolent Friend; Benevolent Quaker; May-Day Dower; **Libretto:** Charles Dibdin; **Music:** Charles Dibdin; arr. by Rayner Taylor; **Genre:** Comic Opera; 2 acts; **First Performance, London:** 1775/5/3, Drury Lane; **First Performance, America:** 1791/9/16, Fredericksburg, Va., West-Bignall company

Quakers; **Genre:** Ballet; **First Performance:** 1797/3/13, Charleston, City Theatre

Quatre Fils Aymond—See *Four Valiant Brothers*

Quinquette, The; **Subtitle(s):** The Good Humored Girl; **Genre:** Ballet; **First Performance:** 1797/5/4, Philadelphia, Lailson's Circus

Ramah Droog; **Subtitle(s):** Wine Does Wonders; **Libretto:** James Cobb; **Music:** Joseph Mazzinghi, William Reeve; **Genre:** Comic Opera; 2 acts; **First Performance, London:** 1798/11/12, Covent Garden; **First Performance, America:** 1803/3/18, Philadelphia

Rambles of Dennis Brulgruddery (Birth, Parentage, Education, and Rambles of Dennis Brulgruddery); **Libretto:** A gentleman of Boston; **Music:** "with a song"; **Genre:** Musical Interlude; **First Performance:** 1806/3/21, Boston

Raymond and Agnes; **Subtitle(s):** The Bleeding Nun; The Castle of Lindenbergh; **Libretto:** Based on M. G. Lewis's novel, *The Monk;* **Music:** William Reeve; Alexander Reinagle; Victor Pelissier; Frederick Granger; **Genre:** Pantomime; 2 acts; **First Performance, London:** 1797/3/16, Covent Garden; **First Performance, America:** 1802/5/7, Boston

Recapture of Toulon by the French Army; **Subtitle(s):** The Young Female Soldier; **Genre:** Pantomime; **First Performance:** 1795/6/20, Charleston

Reconciliation, The; **Subtitle(s):** The Triumph of Nature; **Libretto:** Peter Markoe; **Music:** Uses 7 ballad airs; **Genre:** Ballad Opera; 2 acts; **First Performance:** Accepted Philadelphia, Southwark, 1790; not performed

Recruit, The; **Subtitle(s):** Domestic Folly; **Libretto:** John D. Turnbull; **Music:** Alexander Reinagle; **Genre:** Musical Interlude; **First Performance:** 1796/3/12, Charleston, City Theatre

Recruiting Sergeant; **Libretto:** Isaac Bickerstaffe; **Music:** Charles Dibdin; **Genre:** Musical Entertainment, All-Sung; 1 act; **First Performance, London:** 1770/7/20, Ranelagh Gardens; **First Performance, America:** 1799/3/15, Boston

Red Cross Knights, The; **Libretto:** Joseph G. Holman; based on Schiller's *Die*

Rauber; **Music:** Thomas Attwood; add. by Benjamin Carr; **Genre:** Play, incidental Music; 5 acts; **First Performance, London:** 1799/8/21, Little Theatre, Haymarket; **First Performance, America:** 1802/7/12, Philadelphia, Southwark

Red Riding Hood—See *Little Red Riding Hood*

Rehearsal Disappointed, The; **Subtitle(s):** The Music Master in Distress; **Genre:** Interlude; **First Performance:** 1812/3/18, Charleston

Rejected Fool; **Subtitle(s):** Fortunate Recruit; **Genre:** Pantomime Ballet; **First Performance:** 1796/3/0, Charleston

Renegade, The; **Libretto:** Frederick Reynolds; based on John Dryden's *Don Sebastian* and *The Spanish Friar;* **Music:** Henry R. Bishop; **Genre:** Grand Historical Drama, interspersed with songs; 3 acts; **First Performance, London:** 1812/12/2, Covent Garden; **First Performance, America:** 1813/2/24, New York

Restoration of Harlequin; **Genre:** Pantomime; **First Performance, London:** 1746; **First Performance, America:** 1792/2/13, New York

Return from a Cruise; **Subtitle(s):** More Laurels for American Tars; **Music:** Includes songs "Columbia's Naval Annals" and "Huzza for the Brave Decatur"; **Genre:** Patriotic Sketch; 1 act; **First Performance:** 1812/12/11, Philadelphia

Return of the Laborers; **Subtitle(s):** The Castle Beseiged (cf); **Genre:** Pantomime interspersed with dances; **First Performance:** 1792/2/8, New York

***Review, The (The Wags of Windsor); **Subtitle(s):** The Wags of Windsor; Windsor Wags; The Man of All Trades; **Libretto:** George Colman, jr.; **Music:** Samuel Arnold; arr. by Alexander Reinagle; James Hewitt (with a grand military overture); **Genre:** Operatic Farce; 2 acts; **First Performance, London:** 1798/7/6, King's Theatre, Haymarket; **First Performance, America:** 1802/3/19, Philadelphia

Ribbemont—See *The Mysterious Monk*

Rich and Poor; **Subtitle(s):** The Father Restored; **Libretto:** M. G. Lewis, based on his comedy, *East Indian;* **Music:** Charles E. Horn; arr. James Hewitt; **Genre:** Comic Opera; 3 acts; **First Performance, London:** 1812/7/22, Lyceum; **First Performance, America:** 1812/11/23, Boston

Richard Coeur de Lion; **Subtitle(s):** The Triumph of Love; **Libretto:** M. J. Sedaine; (a) tr. by Leonard MacNally; (b) tr. by John Burgoyne; **Music:** A. E. M. Grétry; arr. by (a) William Shield (pastiche); (b) Thomas Linley, sr.; (c) Trille Labarre; (d) Victor Pelissier; **Genre:** Grand Historical Romance; 3 acts; **First Performance, London:** (a) 1786/10/16, Covent Garden; (b) 1786/10/24, Drury Lane; **First Performance, America:** (c) 1797/1/23, Boston

Richard Coeur de Lion; **Libretto:** Based on Grétry; **Genre:** Pantomime; **First Performance:** 1793/5/29, Boston, Alexander Placide troupe

Richard the First; **Subtitle(s):** Perfidious Duke; **Genre; Length:** Tragic Pantomime; **First Performance:** 1796/4/18, Charleston

Rinaldo and Armida; **Subtitle(s):** The Assembly of the Christians for the Conquest of Jerusalem; **Libretto:** May be from a work in 3 scenes described in a London publication of 1783; **Genre:** Grand Heroic Pantomime; 3 acts; **First Performance, London:** 1783?; **First Performance, America:** 1796/5/30, Charleston

Rinaldo Rinaldini; **Subtitle(s):** The Secret Avengers; **Libretto:** John C. Cross; **Music:** William Reeve; **Genre:** Pantomime; 2 acts; **First Performance, London:** 1801/4/6, Royal Circus; **First Performance, America:** 1811/4/15, Baltimore, Pepin and Breschard Circus

Rival Candidates, The; **Libretto:** Henry Bate Dudley; **Music:** Thomas Carter; **Genre:** Comic Opera; 2 acts; **First Performance, London:** 1775/2/1, Drury Lane; **First Performance, America:** 1787/3/1, New York

Rival Chiefs, The; **Subtitle(s):** Perea and Emai; **Genre:** Pantomimical Interlude; **First Performance:** 1808/3/16, Boston

Rival Harlequins; **Genre:** Pantomime; **First Performance:** 1798/4/13, Philadelphia

Rival Knights—See *Pierre de Provence*

Rival Sisters, The; **Genre:** Ballet Dance; **First Performance:** 1807/4/3, Philadelphia

***Rival Soldiers, The (Sprigs of Laurel); **Subtitle(s):** Sprigs of Laurel; **Libretto:** John O'Keeffe; **Music:** William Shield (pastiche); **Genre:** Comic Opera; 2 acts; **First Performance, London:** 1793/5/11, Covent Garden (as *Sprigs of Laurel*); 1797/5/17, Covent Garden (as *Rival Soldiers*); **First Performance, America:** 1799/4/5, Philadelphia

Rival Twins, The; **Subtitle(s):** The Lover's Mistake; **Genre:** Serious Pastoral Dance; **First Performance:** 1807/11/4, Boston

Robber of Genoa, The—See also *Great Devil;* **Subtitle(s):** The Black Forest (cf); **Libretto:** From the French; **Genre:** Grand Pantomime; **First Performance:** 1813/10/23, Baltimore

Robin Hood; **Subtitle(s): Sherwood Forest; Love in Sherwood Forest; Love in a Forest; Merry Sherwood; **Libretto:** Leonard MacNally; 2-act version compressed by John Hodgkinson; **Music:** William Shield (pastiche); add. by Alexander Reinagle; James Hewitt; **Genre:** Comic Opera; 3, 2 acts; **First Performance, London:** 1784/4/17, Covent Garden; **First Performance, America:** 1793/2/16, Charleston

Robinson Crusoe; **Subtitle(s): Harlequin Friday; Friday's Deliverance; The Happy Return; The Genius of Columbia; **Libretto:** R. B. Sheridan; **Music:** Thomas Linley, sr.; Victor Pelissier; **Genre:** Pantomime; 2 parts; **First Performance, London:** 1781/1/29, Drury Lane; **First Performance, America:** 1786/1/11, New York

Roman Museum; **Subtitle(s):** Harlequin a Robber Through Love; **Genre:** Pantomime; **First Performance:** 1805/6/28, New York, Italian theatre

Romeo et Juliette; **Libretto:** L. P. de Ségur; **Music:** Daniel Steibelt; **Genre:** Opera; 3 acts; **First Performance:** 1793/9/10, Paris, Théâtre Feydeau; **First Performance, America:** 1810/8/6, New Orleans

***Romp, The; **Subtitle(s):** A Cure for the Spleen; **Libretto:** John Lloyd, from Isaac Bickerstaffe *Love in the City;* **Music:** Isaac Bickerstaffe, Charles Dibdin (pastiche); **Genre:** Musical Entertainment; 2 acts; **First Performance, London:** 1778/3/28, Drury Lane; **First Performance, America:** 1791/ 8/5, Fredericksburg, Va., West-Bignall company

Rose Bush of Salency; **Libretto:** Based on Grétry's *La Rosière de Salenci* (1773); **Genre:** Ballet; **First Performance:** 1795/7/1, Charleston

Rose et la Bouton, La; **Libretto:** Based on Monsigny's *Rose et Colas;* **Genre:** Pantomime; **First Performance:** 1794/4/25, Charleston

***Rosina; **Subtitle(s):** The Reapers, Love in a Cottage; **Libretto:** Frances Brooke; **Music:** William Shield; arr. by Victor Pelissier; **Genre:** Comic Opera; 2 acts; **First Performance, London:** 1782/12/31, Covent Garden; **First Performance, America:** 1786/4/19, New York

Rosina; **Genre:** Pantomime; **First Performance:** 1798/1/10, Ricketts Circus, Philadelphia

Rudolph; **Subtitle(s):** The Robbers of Calabria; **Libretto:** John D. Turnbull; adapted from the French; **Music:** "with marches, combats, and choruses"; **Genre:** Melodrama; 3 acts; **First Performance:** 1804/12/4, New York, Bedlow Street

Rugantino; **Subtitle(s):** The Bravo of Venice; **Libretto:** Matthew G. Lewis; tr. from Pixérécourt, *L'homme à trois visagés; ou, le proscrit de Venise;* **Music:** Thomas Busby; James Byrne, arranger; **Genre:** Melodrama; 2 acts; **First Performance, London:** 1805/10/18, Covent Garden; **First Performance, America:** 1810/3/21, Philadelphia

Rural Grace; **Subtitle(s):** William Francis, arranger; **Genre:** Pantomime; **First Performance:** 1813/2/12, Philadelphia

Rural Merriment; **Subtitle(s):** The Humors of a Country Wake; **Libretto:** William Francis, arranger; **Music:** DeMarque; **Genre:** Pantomime; **First Performance:** 1796/1/4, Philadelphia

Rural Revels; **Subtitle(s):** The Easter Holiday; **Libretto:** William Francis, arranger; **Music:** DeMarque; **Genre:** Pantomime; **First Performance:** 1795/4/6, Philadelphia

Rural Waggish Tricks; **Subtitle(s):** The Enraged Musicians; **Libretto:** Francisquy, arranger; **Music:** Ended with a country dance to "Yankee Doodle"; **Genre:** Comic Pantomime Ballet; **First Performance:** 1796/4/21, New York

Sailor's Daughter, The; **Libretto:** Richard Cumberland; **Music:** Alexander Reinagle; **Genre:** Comedy, Incidental Music; 5 acts; **First Performance, London:** 1804/4/7, Drury Lane; **First Performance, America:** 1804/11/14, Baltimore

Sailor's Festival (Poor Jack's Return to Boston); **Genre:** Comic Pantomime; 1 act; **First Performance:** 1802/2/24, Boston

Sailor's Frolic; **Subtitle(s):** Hearts of Oak; **Genre:** Pantomime; 1 act; **First Performance:** 1799/4/4, Boston

Sailor's Garland; **Subtitle(s):** The Family Picture; **Genre:** Interlude; 1 act; **First Performance:** 1801/6/2, Baltimore

*Sailor's Landlady; **Subtitle(s):** Jack in Distress (cf); Sailor's Return from Tripoli; **Music:** Alexander Reinagle; later versions contain song "America, Commerce, and Freedom"; **Genre:** Pantomime; **First Performance:** 1794/3/3, Philadelphia

Sailor's Return; **Subtitle(s):** Thomas and Sally (cf); **Libretto:** William Francis, arranger; **Genre:** Pantomime; **First Performance:** 1795/5/13, Philadelphia

Sailor's Triumph; **Subtitle(s):** The Family Picture; **Genre:** Pantomime; **First Performance:** 1800/5/12, New York

Saint David's Day; **Subtitle(s):** The Honest Welshman; **Libretto:** Thomas Dibdin; **Music:** Thomas Attwood; **Genre:** Musical Entertainment; 2 acts; **First Performance, London:** 1800/3/25, Covent Garden; **First Performance, America:** 1801/4/22, Baltimore

*Saint Patrick's Day; **Subtitle(s):** The Scheming Lieutenant; **Libretto:** Richard Brinsley Sheridan; **Genre:** Play with added music; 2 acts; **First Performance, London:** 1775/5/2, Covent Garden; **First Performance, America:** 1793/4/15, New York

Saint Tammany's Festival in the Temple of Liberty; **Music:** Pastiche; **Genre:** Occasional Interlude with Songs, Dances, and Spectacle; **First Performance:** 1798/5/1, Philadelphia

Sampson; **Subtitle(s):** The Treachery of Delilah; **Genre:** Pantomime; **First Performance:** 1795/4/29, Charleston

Savoyard; **Subtitle(s):** The Repentant Seducer; **Music:** Alexander Reinagle; **Genre:** Musical Farce; 2 acts; **First Performance:** 1797/7/12, Philadelphia

Scheming Clown; **Subtitle(s):** The Sportsman Deceived; **Libretto:** William Francis, arranger; **Genre:** Comic Dance; **First Performance:** 1794/2/28, Philadelphia

Scheming Millers; **Genre:** Pantomime; **First Performance:** 1811/7/12, New York, Pepin and Breschard Circus

Scheming Milliners; **Subtitle(s):** The Beau New Trimm'd; **Libretto:** William Francis, arranger; **Genre:** Comic Dance; **First Performance:** 1794/7/7, Philadelphia

School for Greybeards; **Subtitle(s):** The Mourning Bride; **Libretto:** Hannah Cowley; **Music:** Benjamin Carr; **Genre:** Comedy, Incidental Music; 5 acts; **First Performance, London:** 1786/11/25, Drury Lane; **First Performance, America:** 1795/4/20, New York

School for Prodigals, The; **Libretto:** Joseph Hutton; **Music:** John Bray; **Genre:** Comedy, Incidental Music; 5 acts; **First Performance:** 1809/2/20, Philadelphia

Scotch Ghost, The; **Subtitle(s):** Fanny's Love; Little Fanny's Love; **Music:** Giuseppe Capelletti; **Genre:** Comic Scotch Ballet; **First Performance, London:** 1796, Drury Lane; **First Performance, America:** 1798/4/27, Philadelphia

Scots Milleners, The; **Genre:** Dance; **First Performance:** 1806/3/21, Boston

Sculptor; **Genre:** Ballet; **First Performance:** 1798/3/13, Charleston, City Theatre

Sea-side Story, The; **Libretto:** William Dimond; **Music:** Thomas Attwood; **Genre:** Comic Opera; 2 acts; **First Performance, London:** 1801/5/12, Covent Garden; **First Performance, America:** 1809/4/1, Philadelphia

Secret, Le; **Libretto:** F. B. Hoffman; **Music:** Jean Pierre Solié; **Genre:** Opera; 1 act; **First Performance:** 1796/4/20, Paris; **First Performance, America:** 1808/9/4, New Orleans

Secret, The; **Subtitle(s):** Partnership Dissolved; Hole in the Wall; Natural Magic; **Libretto:** Edward Morris; **Music:** Alexander Reinagle; **Genre:** Comedy, Incidental Music; 5 acts; **First Performance, London:** 1799/3/2, Drury Lane; **First Performance, America:** 1799/12/30, Philadelphia

Selima and Azor; **Subtitle(s):** The Power of Enchantment; A Persian Tale; **Libretto:** J. F. Marmontel *Zemire et Azor* (cf); tr. by Sir George Collier, with "several judicious alterations" by R. B. Sheridan; **Music:** A. Grétry; adapted by Thomas Linley, sr. (pastiche); add. by Alexander Reinagle; **Genre:** Comic Opera; 3 acts; **First Performance, London:** 1776/12/5, Drury Lane; **First Performance, America:** 1787/6/1, New York

Seraglio, The; **Libretto:** Charles Dibdin; **Music:** Charles Dibdin (pastiche); **Genre:** Comic Opera; 2 acts; **First Performance, London:** 1776/11/14, Covent Garden; **First Performance, America:** 1794/5/19, Philadelphia

Servant Mistress (Le Servante Maîtresse); **Libretto:** Tr. of *La serva Padrona;* **Music:** Pergolesi?; **Genre:** Opera; 2 acts; **First Performance, America:** 1790/ 12/9, New York, City Tavern

Shakespeare's Garland, Shakespeare's Jubilee—See *Jubilee*

Shamrock, The—See *The Poor Soldier*

Shamrock; **Subtitle(s):** St. Patrick's Day; St. Patrick's Day in the Morning; **Libretto:** William Francis, arranger; **Music:** Alexander Reinagle; **Genre:** Speaking Pantomime; **First Performance:** 1796/3/18, Philadelphia

She Would and She Would Not; **Subtitle(s):** The Kind Imposter; **Libretto:** Colley Cibber; **Genre:** Comedy, Incidental Music; 5 acts; **First Performance, London:** 1702/11/26, Drury Lane; **First Performance, America:** 1794/5/26, Philadelphia

Shelty's Frolic; **Subtitle(s):** Caledonian Fling; Caledonian Girls; **Genre:** Comic Ballet; **First Performance:** 1800/5/17, Philadelphia

Shelty's Travels; **Libretto:** William Dunlap (sequel to *Highland Reel* [cf]); **Genre:** Burletta; **First Performance:** 1794/4/24, New York

Shepherd of the Alps, The; **Subtitle(s):** The Woodman; **Libretto:** This is the original title of Charles Dibdin's comic opera, *Shepherdess of the Alps,* Covent Garden, 1780; **Music:** Charles Dibdin?; **Genre:** Pantomimical Ballet; **First Performance:** 1798/1/16, Philadelphia, Ricketts Circus

Shipwreck, The; **Subtitle(s): The Female Sailor; After the Storm; **Libretto:** Samuel James Arnold; **Music:** Samuel Arnold; **Genre:** Comic Opera; 2 acts; **First Performance, London:** 1796/12/10, Drury Lane; **First Performance, America:** 1798/3/2, Philadelphia

Shipwreck; **Subtitle(s):** Le Chef Sauvage; **Libretto:** Allport, arranger; **Genre:** Pantomime Spectacle; **First Performance:** 1814/7/15, New York, Circus

Shipwreck; **Subtitle(s):** Harlequin Fisherman (cf); Benevolent Fisherman; **Libretto:** "Taken from the French"; **Genre:** Pantomime; 1 act; **First Performance:** 1802/5/17, New York

Shipwreck; **Subtitle(s):** The Hermit of Mt. Vesuvius; **Genre:** Pantomime; **First Performance:** 1804/5/16, New York

Shipwreck, The; **Subtitle(s):** Neptune's Favor; **Genre:** Pantomime; **First Performance:** 1799/2/26, Philadelphia, Ricketts Circus

Shipwrecked Mariners Preserved, The (The Shipwrecked Mariners); **Subtitle(s):** La Bonne Petite Fille; **Libretto:** Susannah Rowson; Legé, arranger; **Music:** Rayner Taylor; **Genre:** Speaking Pantomime; Marine Spectacle; **First Performance:** 1795/11/26, Baltimore

Shipwrecked Tar (See also *Poor Jack*); **Subtitle(s):** Poor Jack's Return; Ungrateful Landlady; **Genre:** Pantomime; **First Performance:** 1804/3/15; New York, Grove Theatre

Sicilian Romance, The; **Subtitle(s):** The Apparition of the Cliffs; The Spectre of the Cliffs; **Libretto:** Henry Siddons; based on Horace Walpole's romance, *The Castle of Otranto* (cf); **Music:** William Reeve; add. by Victor Pelissier; arr. by Alexander Reinagle; **Genre:** Opera; 3, 2 acts; **First Performance, London:** 1794/5/28, Covent Garden; **First Performance, America:** 1795/5/6, Philadelphia

*Siege of Belgrade, The; **Libretto:** James Cobb; **Music:** Stephen Storace (pastiche); arr. by Victor Pelissier; **Genre:** Comic Opera; 3 acts; compressed to an afterpiece, 1801; **First Performance, London:** 1791/1/1, Drury Lane; **First Performance, America:** 1796/12/30, New York

Siege of Gibralter; **Genre:** Pantomime; **First Performance:** 1793/6/7, New York

Siege of Quebec; **Subtitle(s):** Death of General Wolfe; **Libretto:** Giles L. Barrett, arranger; **Genre:** Grand Pantomime Ballet; **First Performance, London:** 1784/5/31, Royal Grove; **First Performance, America:** 1797/2/6, Boston, Haymarket

Sighs; **Subtitle(s):** The Daughter; Poverty and Honor; **Libretto:** Prince Hoare; based on A. F. F. Kotzebue, *Armuth and Sinn;* **Music:** Maria T. Bland; James Hewitt; **Genre:** Comedy, Incidental Music; 5 acts; **First Performance, London:** 1799/7/30, Little Theatre, Haymarket; **First Performance, America:** 1800/4/16, New York

Sisters of the Rocks, The; **Libretto:** Sully, arranger; **Genre:** Comic Pantomime; **First Performance:** 1797/7/22, Philadelphia, Lailson's Circus

Silver Rock; **Genre:** Pantomime; **First Performance:** 1792/3/26, New York

*Sixty-Third Letter, The; **Libretto:** Walley C. Oulton; **Music:** Samuel Arnold; add. by Rayner Taylor, Alexander Reinagle; arr. by Victor Pelissier; **Genre:** Musical Entertainment; 2 acts; **First Performance, London:** 1802/7/28, Little Theatre, Haymarket; **First Performance, America:** 1803/1/21, Philadelphia

Slaves in Algiers; **Subtitle(s):** A Struggle for Freedom; A Struggle for Liberty; **Libretto:** Susannah Rowson; **Music:** Alexander Reinagle; **Genre:** Play interspersed with songs; 3 acts; **First Performance:** 1794/6/30, Philadelphia

Smugglers, The; **Subtitle(s):** A Generous Tar; **Libretto:** Samuel Birch; **Music:** Thomas Attwood; **Genre:** Musical Drama; 2 acts; **First Performance, London:** 1796/4/13, Drury Lane; **First Performance, America:** 1799/5/13, Boston, Haymarket

Soldier's Daughter; **Libretto: Andrew Cherry; **Music:** Dibdin's "Flowing Can" introduced in title role, Philadelphia, 1805; **Genre:** Comedy, incidental music; 5 acts; **First Performance, London:** 1804/2/7, Drury Lane; **First Performance, America:** 1804/4/18, New York

Soldier's Return; **Subtitle(s):** What Can Beauty Do?; **Libretto:** Theodore E. Hook; **Music:** James Hook; arr. by Victor Pelissier; **Genre:** Comic Opera; 2 acts; **First Performance, London:** 1805/4/23, Drury Lane; **First Performance, America:** 1807/11/23, Baltimore

Son-in-Law, The; **Subtitle(s):** Blunder upon Blunder; **Libretto:** John O'Keeffe; **Music:** Samuel Arnold; arr. by Victor Pelissier; **Genre:** Comic Opera; 2 acts; **First Performance, London:** 1779/8/14, Little Theatre, Haymarket; **First Performance, America:** 1793/3/8, Charleston

Sons of Anacreon—See *Catch Club*

Sons of Apollo—See *Catch Club*

Sophia of Brabant; **Subtitle(s):** The False Friend; **Music:** Victor Pelissier; **Genre:** Serious Pantomime; **First Performance, America:** 1794/11/1, Philadelphia, Southwark

Sorcerer's Apprentice, The; **Subtitle(s):** Harlequin Woodcutter (cf); **Genre:** Pantomime; **First Performance:** 1792/7/2, Philadelphia, Southwark

Souliers mors-dorés, Les; **Subtitle(s):** Le cordonniere allemande; **Libretto:** A. de Ferrières; **Music:** Alessandro Fridzéri; **Genre:** Opera; 2 acts; **First Performance:** 1776/1/11, Paris; **First Performance, America:** 1796/12/24, Philadelphia

*Spanish Barber, The; **Subtitle(s):** Fruitless Precaution; **Libretto:** P. A. C. Beaumarchais; tr. by George Colman, sr.; **Music:** Samuel Arnold; arr. by Benjamin Carr, Alexander Reinagle; **Genre:** Comedy with music; 3, 2 acts; **First Performance, London:** 1777/8/30, Little Theatre, Haymarket; **First Performance, America:** 1794/7/7, Philadelphia

Spanish Castle—See *The Knight of Guadalquiver*

Spanish Dollars; **Subtitle(s):** The Priest of the Parish; **Libretto:** Andrew Cherry; **Music:** John Davy; **Genre:** Musical Entertainment; 2, 1 acts; **First Performance, London:** 1805/5/9, Covent Garden; **First Performance, America:** 1807/4/3, Philadelphia

Spanish Miller; **Genre:** Pantomime; **First Performance:** 1792/3/13, Portsmouth, N. H.

Spanish Patriots; **Subtitle(s):** Royal Restoration; **Libretto:** Edward Riley; **Music:** Charles Gilfert; **Genre:** Musical Entertainment; **First Performance:** 1809/1/4, New York

Spinster's Lottery, The; **Libretto:** James Byrne, arranger; **Genre:** Comic Ballet; **First Performance:** 1797/9/6, New York, Wignell and Reinagle, Greenwich St.

***Spoil'd Child, The; **Libretto:** Attributed to Prince Hoare, Isaac Bickerstaffe, Dorothy Bland Jordan, or Richard Ford; **Genre:** Musical Farce;

2 acts; **First Performance, London:** 1790/3/22, Drury Lane; **First Performance, America:** 1794/3/5, Philadelphia

Sportsman Outwitted, The; **Genre:** Pantomimical Ballet; **First Performance:** 1797/5/12, Boston, Haymarket

Sprigs of Laurel—See *The Rival Soldiers*

Sterne's Maria; **Subtitle(s):** The Vintage; **Libretto:** William Dunlap; based on Laurence Sterne's *Sentimental Journey;* **Music:** Victor Pelissier; **Genre:** Comic Opera; 2 acts; **First Performance:** 1799/1/14, New York

Stranger, The; **Subtitle(s): Misanthropy and Repentance; **Libretto:** A. Kotzebue; tr. by (a) William Dunlap; (b) Benjamin B. Thompson; (c) John Hodgkinson; **Music:** Thomas Shaw; Alexander Reinagle; **Genre:** Drama, Incidental Music; 5 acts; **First Performance, London:** (b) 1798/3/17, Drury Lane; **First Performance, America:** (a) 1798/12/10, New York

Sultan, The; **Subtitle(s): Peep Into the Seraglio; The Triumphs of Love; American Captive (cf); Roxalana; Female Captive; **Libretto:** Isaac Bickerstaffe; based on J. F. Montmartel; **Music:** Charles Dibdin; **Genre:** Farce; 2 acts; **First Performance, London:** 1775/12/12, Drury Lane; **First Performance, America:** 1794/5/3, New York

*Surrender of Calais; **Subtitle(s):** The Patriot Citizens; Gallic Heroism; **Libretto:** George Colman, jr.; **Music:** Samuel Arnold; **Genre:** Comic Opera; 3 acts; **First Performance, London:** 1791/7/30, Little Theatre, Haymarket; **First Performance, America:** 1793/4/29, Charleston

Sylvester Daggerwood; **Subtitle(s): The Mad Dunstable Actor; The Mad American Actor; **Libretto:** George Colman, jr. (orig. title: *New Hay at the Old Market;* **Genre:** Interlude, often with music added; 1 act; **First Performance, London:** 1795/6/9, King's Theatre, Haymarket; **First Performance, America:** 1796/12/24, Philadelphia, Pantheon

Tableau Magique; **Subtitle(s):** The Comic Shadows; **Libretto:** Probably utilized transparencies; **Genre:** Pantomime; 2 acts; **First Performance:** 1813/8/6, Philadelphia, Columbian Garden

Tableau Parlant, Le (Speaking Picture); **Libretto:** Louis Anseaume; **Music:** André E. M. Grétry; **Genre:** Opera; 1 act; **First Performance:** 1769/9/20, Paris; **First Performance, America:** 1794/5/17, Charleston

Taking of Yorktown, The; **Genre:** Pantomime; 2 acts (equestrian combat); **First Performance:** 1812/2/22, Philadelphia, Olympic

Tale of Mystery, A; **Subtitle(s): The Dumb Man of Arpenay; **Libretto:** Thomas Holcroft; from Pixérécourt, *Coeline, ou, l'enfant du mystère,* Paris, 1800; **Music:** Thomas Busby; Victor Pelissier; add. by James Hewitt; arr. by Alexander Reinagle; **Genre:** Melodrama; 3, 2 acts; **First Performance,**

London: 1802/11/13, Covent Garden; **First Performance, America:** 1803/3/ 16, New York

Tale of Terror, A; **Subtitle(s):** A Tale of Pleasure; **Libretto:** Henry Siddons; based on Moliere, *The Feast of the Statue;* **Music:** Alexander Reinagle; Victor Pelissier; **Genre:** Dramatic Romance; 5, 3, 2 acts; **First Performance, London:** 1803/5/12, Covent Garden; **First Performance, America:** 1803/11/ 18, Baltimore

Tammany (America Discovered); **Subtitle(s):** The Indian Chief; **Libretto:** Anne Julia Hatton; **Music:** James Hewitt; **Genre:** A "serious opera"; 3, 2 acts; **First Performance:** 1794/3/3, New York

Tars from Tripoli (The American Naval Pillar); **Subtitle(s):** A Tribute of Respect to the Mediterranean Heroes; Our Gallant Navy; **Libretto:** H. Charnock; based on Thomas Dibdin's *Naval Pillar* (cf); **Music:** James Hewitt (pastiche); **Genre:** Musical Entertainment; 2, 1 acts; **First Performance:** 1806/2/24, New York

Taste of the Times; **Subtitle(s):** Laugh! Laugh! Laugh!; **Libretto:** Robert Treat Paine; **Music:** New music; **Genre:** Comic Local Pantomime; **First Performance:** 1797/5/24, Boston

Tekeli; **Subtitle(s): The Siege of Montgatz; **Libretto:** Theodore E. Hook; adapted from Pixérécourt, *Tékéli; ou, le siège de Montgatz* (Paris, 1803/12/ 29); **Music:** James Hook; arr. by Victor Pelissier; **Genre:** Melodrama; 3, 2 acts; **First Performance, London:** 1806/11/24, Drury Lane; King's Theatre, Haymarket; **First Performance, America:** 1807/12/21, New York

Telemachus in the Island of Calypso (See also *Island of Calypso);* **Libretto:** Perhaps based on Gardel's Ballet-héroique, *Télémaque dans l'isle de Calipso;* **Genre:** Grand Historical Pantomime; 2 acts; **First Performance:** 1790/2/23, Paris; **First Performance, America:** 1798/3/29, Charleston, City Theatre

Tempest, The; **Subtitle(s):** The Enchanted Island; **Libretto:** William Shakespeare; add. by John Dryden and William Davenant; compiled by J. P. Kemble; **Music:** Henry Purcell; adapted by Thomas Arne; Thomas Linley; new music in Boston; add. by Victor Pelissier; **Genre:** Comedy, Incidental Music (announced as an opera due to blue laws); 5 acts; **First Performance, London:** Kemble version: 1789/10/13, Drury Lane; **First Performance, America:** 1787/7/14, Philadelphia, Southwark (as an opera)

Tempest of Harlequin; **Subtitle(s):** The Clown Turn'd Miller; **Genre:** Pantomime; **First Performance:** 1792/1/23, Philadelphia, French company, Northern Liberties

Temple of American Independence; **Music:** Victor Pelissier; **Genre:** Musical Interlude; **First Performance:** 1794/2/21, New York

Temple of Dullness—See *Capocchio and Dorinna*

Temple of Liberty; **Subtitle(s): Warrior's Welcome Home (cf); Music:** Alexander Reinagle; **Genre:** Ballet-divertissement; **First Performance:** 1796/3/28, Philadelphia

Theatrical Candidates, The; **Subtitle(s):** The Election; **Libretto:** David Garrick; **Music:** William Bates; Alexander Reinagle; **Genre:** Musical Prelude; **First Performance, London:** 1775/9/23, Drury Lane; **First Performance, America:** 1801/10/14, Philadelphia

Thesis and Ariadne (See also *Ariadne Abandoned by Theseus in the Isle of Naxos*); **Libretto:** Tr. from French; **Music:** Victor Pelissier; **Genre:** Serious Pantomimical MeloDrame; 1 act; **First Performance:** Paris; **First Performance, America:** 1807/3/16, Philadelphia

Thirty Thousand, The; **Subtitle(s):** Who's the Richest?; **Libretto:** Thomas Dibdin; based on Maria Edgeworth's *The Will;* **Music:** William Reeve, John Davy, John Braham; arr. by Rayner Taylor; **Genre:** Comic Opera; 3 acts; **First Performance, London:** 1804/12/10, Covent Garden; **First Performance, America:** 1806/2/15, Philadelphia

Thomas and Sally; **Subtitle(s):** The Sailor's Return (cf); **Libretto:** Isaac Bickerstaffe; **Music:** Thomas Arne; **Genre:** Musical Entertainment; 2, 1 acts; **First Performance, London:** 1760/11/28, Covent Garden; **First Performance, America:** 1766/11/14, Philadelphia, Southwark

Three and the Deuce, The; **Subtitle(s): Which is Which?; **Libretto:** Prince Hoare; **Music:** Stephen Storace; **Genre:** Comic Opera; 3, 2 acts; **First Performance, London:** 1795/9/2, Little Theatre, Haymarket; **First Performance, America:** 1797/5/26, Boston, Haymarket

Three Philosophers (Two Philosophers, Three Quakers, Two Quakers); **Subtitle(s):** The Dutch Coffee House; **Genre:** Ballet-Pantomime; **First Performance:** 1794/5/20, Charleston

Three Quakers—See *Three Philosophers*

Three Savoyards—See *Trois Savoyards*

Time's a Tell-Tale; **Libretto:** Henry Siddons; **Music:** Michael Kelly; **Genre:** Comedy, Incidental Music; 5 acts; **First Performance, London:** 1807/10/27, Drury Lane; **First Performance, America:** 1808/3/4, Philadelphia

Timour the Tartar; **Libretto: M. G. Lewis; **Music:** Matthew Peter King; arr. James Hewitt; **Genre:** Grand Romantic Melodrama; **First Performance, London:** 1811/4/29, Covent Garden; **First Performance, America:** 1812/9/25, Philadelphia, Olympic Theatre

Tit for Tat; **Genre:** Comic Pantomime; **First Performance:** 1797/4/29, New York, Ricketts Circus

Tom Thumb the Great (The Tragedy of Tragedies); Subtitle(s): Tom Thumb the Great; The Life and Death of Tom Thumb the Great; The Lilliputian Hero; **Libretto:** Henry Fielding; Kane O'Hara; *Tom Thumb* (1730) was enlarged to *Tragedy of Tragedies* (1731), then redone by O'Hara in 1780; **Music:** J. Markordt (pastiche); **Genre:** Burletta (Tragical, Comical, Farcical, Operatical, Pantomimical Entertainment); 2 acts; **First Performance, London:** 1780/10/3, Covent Garden; **First Performance, America:** 1767/6/1, Philadelphia, Southwark

Tonnelier, Le; **Subtitle(s):** The Cooper (cf); **Libretto:** Nicolas Médard Audinot; revised by François Quétant; **Music:** Audinot, François J. Gossec; **Genre:** Comic Opera; 1 act; **First Performance:** 1765/3/16, Paris; **First Performance, America:** 1790/10/7, New York, City Tavern

*Too Many Cooks; **Libretto:** James Kenney; **Music:** Matthew Peter King; add. by Alexander Reinagle; **Genre:** Comic Opera; 2 acts; **First Performance, London:** 1805/2/12, Covent Garden; **First Performance, America:** 1805/10/25, Boston

T'other Side of the Gutter; **Libretto:** Attacks Ricketts Circus; features the acrobatics of Joseph Doctor (See *Poor Old Haymarket; or, Two Sides of the Gutter,* 1792/6/15, London, Little Theatre, Haymarket); **Genre:** Pantomime; **First Performance:** 1795/12/26, Philadelphia

Touchstone, The (The Touchstone of Truth); **Subtitle(s):** Harlequin Traveller; Harlequin's Rambles; **Libretto:** Charles Dibdin; **Music:** Charles Dibdin; John Bentley; **Genre:** Operatical (Speaking) Pantomime; **First Performance, London:** 1779/1/4, Covent Garden; **First Performance, America:** 1785/9/1, New York

Tournament, The; **Subtitle(s):** Agnes of Bernauer; **Libretto:** Marianne Starke; from *Agnes Bernauer,* adapted from the German; **Music:** Victor Pelissier; **Genre:** Tragedy, Incidental Music; 5 acts; **First Performance:** 1801/3/92, Boston

Town and Country; Subtitle(s): Which is Best?; **Libretto:** Thomas Morton; **Music:** Michael Kelly; **Genre:** Comedy, Incidental Music; 5 acts; **First Performance, London:** 1807/3/10, Covent Garden; **First Performance, America:** 1807/10/9, Boston

Tragedy of Tragedies—See *Tom Thumb the Great*

Transformation; **Subtitle(s):** Love and Law; **Libretto:** J. T. Allingham; **Genre:** Operatic Farce; **First Performance, London:** 1810/11/30, Lyceum; **First Performance, America:** 1814/3/14, Philadelphia

Travellers, The; **Subtitle(s):** Music's Fascination; **Libretto:** Andrew Cherry; James Nelson Barker; **Music:** Domenico Corri; add. Alexander Reinagle;

arr. Victor Pelissier; **Genre:** Comic Opera; 5 acts; **First Performance, London:** 1806/1/22, Drury Lane; **First Performance, America:** 1807/4/20, Philadelphia

Travellers Preserved; **Subtitle(s):** Petite Piedmontese; **Music:** Entirely new music by Rayner Taylor; **Genre:** Pantomime; **First Performance:** 1795/6/19, Philadelphia

Trick upon Trick; **Subtitle(s):** Harlequin Shepherd; **Genre:** Pantomime; **First Performance:** 1783/2/21, Baltimore, Dennis Ryan Company

Tricks Upon Travellers; **Libretto:** Sir James Bland Burges; **Music:** Charles E. Horn, William Reeve; **Genre:** Comic Opera; 3 acts; **First Performance, London:** 1810/7/9, Lyceum; **First Performance, America:** 1811/3/18, New York

Triomphe de l'Amour, La; **Subtitle(s):** La Precaution Inutile; **Libretto:** William Francis, arranger; **Genre:** Pastoral Ballet; **First Performance:** "As performed in Paris"; **First Performance:** 1813/6/7, Baltimore

Trip to Curro; **Music:** Mr. Warrell, jr.?; **Genre:** Ballet; **First Performance:** 1799/6/13, Alexandria, Virginia

Trip to Fontainbleau, A—See *Fontainbleau*

Tripolitan Corsair—See *The Corsair*

Tripolitan Tar, Tripolitan Prize—See *Veteran Tar*

Triumph of Mirth; **Subtitle(s):** Harlequin's Vagaries (cf); Harlequin's Wedding; **Music:** Thomas Linley, sr.; **Genre:** Pantomime; **First Performance, London:** 1782/12/26, Drury Lane; **First Performance, America:** 1794/5/21, Philadelphia

Triumph of Virtue (See also *Harlequin in Philadelphia; Harlequin in Hartford*); **Subtitle(s):** Harlequin in New York; **Libretto:** John William Ricketts, arranger; **Music:** "entirely new"; **Genre:** Pantomime; **First Performance:** 1796, New York, Ricketts Amphitheatre

Triumph of Washington; **Subtitle(s):** His Return from Mt. Vernon; **Genre:** Pantomime; **First Performance:** 1797/4/5, Boston

Trois Savoyards (See also *Cinque Savoyards*); **Subtitle(s):** The Magic Lantern; **Libretto:** J. K. Labottierre, arranger; **Music:** James Hewitt; **Genre:** Pastoral Ballet; 1 act; **First Performance:** 1804/10/22, Boston

Turn Out! (Turn Him Out!); **Libretto:** James Kenney; **Music:** Matthew Peter King; **Genre:** Musical Farce; 2 acts; **First Performance, London:** 1812/3/7, Lyceum; **First Performance, America:** 1813/12/8, New York

Turnpike Gate, The; **Subtitle(s): The New Road to Mirth; **Libretto:** Thomas Knight; **Music:** Joseph Mazzinghi, William Reeve; arr. by James Hewitt, R. Chateaudun; **Genre:** Comic Opera; 2 acts; **First Performance, London:** 1799/11/14, Covent Garden; **First Performance, America:** 1801/1/5, Boston

Tuteur Trompé; **Subtitle(s):** Il maestro di musica; **Genre:** Pantomime; **First Performance:** 1784, Florence; **First Performance, America:** 1795/6/12, Philadelphia

Twenty-eighth of June, The; **Subtitle(s):** The Attack on Fort Moultrie; **Genre:** Pantomime; **First Performance:** 1794/8/4, Charleston

Twenty Years Ago!; **Libretto:** Isaac Pocock; based on Amelia Opie's story, "Love and Duty"; **Music:** Thomas Welsh; **Genre:** Melodramatic Entertainment; 2 acts; **First Performance, London:** 1810/7/21, Lyceum; **First Performance, America:** 1811/2/22, New York

Two Country Squires; **Subtitle(s):** The Justice of a Lord; **Libretto:** Cuvallier; **Genre:** Pantomime; 2 acts; **First Performance:** Paris; **First Performance, America:** 1814/3/8, Baltimore, Circus

Two Faces Under a Hood; **Libretto:** Thomas Dibdin; **Music:** William Shield (pastiche); **Genre:** Comic Opera; 3 acts; **First Performance, London:** 1807/11/17, Covent Garden; **First Performance, America:** 1809/2/22, Boston

Two Hunters (Huntsmen) and the Milkmaid (See also *The Bear Hunters; The Merry Hunters*); **Subtitle(s):** The Death of the Bear; **Libretto:** Based on Louis Anseaume, *Les Deux Chasseurs et la Laitière* (cf); Legé, arranger (Boston); Francisquy, arranger (Boston Haymarket, New York); **Genre:** Comic Pantomime Ballet; 1 act; **First Performance:** 1794/7/12, Charleston

Two Jealous Lovers; **Subtitle(s):** The Transformation of Harlequin; **Genre:** Pantomime; **First Performance:** 1803/8/5, New York, Mount Vernon Gardens

Two Misers, The; **Subtitle(s):** The Mufti's Ghost; **Libretto:** Kane O'Hara; from Fenouillot Falbairé, *Les deux avares;* **Music:** Pastiche; **Genre:** Musical Farce; 2 acts; **First Performance, London:** 1775/1/21, Covent Garden; **First Performance, America:** 1775/4/17, New York

Two Misers—See *Two Philosophers*

*Two Philosophers (Two Quakers; Two Misers; See also *Three Philosophers*); **Subtitle(s):** The Merry Girl; The Magic Pye; **Libretto:** Legé, arranger; **Genre:** Pantomimical Ballet; **First Performance:** 1792/2/3, New York

Two Quakers—See *Two Philosophers*

Two Woodcutters; **Genre:** Pantomime; **First Performance:** 1792/9/5, Boston, Joseph Harper, under Blue Laws

Tyranny Suppressed; **Subtitle(s):** Freedom Triumphant; **Music:** James Hewitt; **Genre:** Grand Serious Pantomime; **First Performance:** 1795/6/23, New York

Unfortunate Family; **Genre:** Pantomime; **First Performance:** 1797/7/10, Boston, Haymarket

Vagaries, The; **Subtitle(s):** Harlequin Triumphant (cf); **Genres:** Pantomime

Sketch; **First Performance:** 1787/8/31, New York, Vandewater's Long Room

Valcour and Emelia—See *Amelia and Valcour*

Valentine and Orson; Subtitle(s): The Downfall of Agramant; The Wild Man of the Woods; **Libretto:** Thomas Dibdin; **Music:** Joseph Juove; add. by Alexander Reinagle; Victor Pelissier; **Genre:** Melodrama; 3, 2 acts; **First Performance, London:** 1804/4/3, Covent Garden; **First Performance, America:** 1805/4/15, New York

Valiant Officer; **Subtitle(s):** The Rescue of Columbus; **Genre:** Pantomime; **First Performance:** 1796/6/10, Philadelphia

Valiant Soldier, The (The Brave Soldier; See also *The Old Soldier*); **Subtitle(s):** The Two Robbers; Innocence Protected; **Genre:** Serious Pantomime; **First Performance:** 1796/10/24, Philadelphia, Pantheon

Veteran Tar, The (Tripolitan Tar); **Subtitle(s):** American Tars on an English Shore; American Tars Triumphant; Tripolitan Prize; **Libretto:** Samuel James Arnold (altered for local use); **Music:** Samuel Arnold; arr. by Victor Pelissier; Alexander Reinagle; **Genre:** Comic Opera; 2 acts; **First Performance, London:** 1801/1/29, Drury Lane; **First Performance, America:** 1802/11/24, New York

Vicissitudes of Harlequin; **Genre:** Pantomime; **First Performance:** 1804/4/5, New York, Grove Theatre

Village Gambols; **Subtitle(s):** The Cooper Outwitted; **Genre:** Comic Ballet; **First Performance:** 1812/12/17, Philadelphia, Southwark

Village Ghost, The; **Subtitle(s):** The Affrighted Lover; The Cooper Outwitted; **Genre:** Ballet; **First Performance:** 1812/12/26, Philadelphia, Southwark

Village Sports; **Genre:** Ballet; **First Performance:** 1800/2/4, Charleston, City Theatre

Vintagers, The; **Libretto:** Edmund J. Eyre; tr. from French; **Music:** Henry R. Bishop; **Genre:** Musical Romance; 2 acts; **First Performance, London:** 1809/8/1, Little Theatre, Haymarket; **First Performance, America:** 1814/3/10, Philadelphia, Theatrical Commonwealth, Olympic

*Virgin of the Sun; **Libretto:** A. Kotzebue; tr. by William Dunlap, 1800 (based on Anne Plumptre's tr., 1799); tr. for Covent Garden by Frederick Reynolds, 1812; another tr. by Charles Smith; **Music:** Victor Pelissier (NY); Henry Rowley Bishop (CG); Charles Gilfert (Phila. Olympic); **Genre:** Grand Operatic Drama; 3, 5 acts; **First Performance, London:** 1812/1/31, Covent Garden; **First Performance, America:** 1800/3/12, New York; CG version 1813/11/15, New York

Virgin Unmasked, The; **Subtitle(s):** An Old Man Taught Wisdom; A Medley of Lovers; **Libretto:** Henry Fielding; **Genre:** Ballad Opera; 2, 1 acts; **First**

Performance, London: 1735/1/6, Drury Lane; **First Performance, America:** 1751/4/22, New York, Kean and Murray

Visionary Shadows; **Genre:** Pantomime; **First Performance:** 1808/5/17, New York, Pearl St. Theatre

*Voice of Nature, The; **Libretto:** L. C. Caigniez, *Le Jugement de Salomon;* tr. by James Boaden; tr. by William Dunlap; **Music:** Victor Pelissier; Alexander Reinagle; **Genre:** Drama with music; 3 acts; **First Performance, London:** 1802/7/31, Little Theatre, Haymarket; **First Performance, America:** 1803/2/4, New York

Volunteers, The; **Libretto:** Susannah Rowson; **Music:** Alexander Reinagle; **Genre:** Comic Opera; **First Performance:** 1795/1/21, Philadelphia

Vulcan's Gift; **Subtitle(s):** The Bower of Hymen; Harlequin Humorist; **Genre:** Pantomime; **First Performance:** 1796/3/12, Philadelphia, Pantheon

Wags of Windsor, The—See *The Review*

Wanderer, The; **Libretto:** Eugenius, a gentleman of New York; **Genre:** Comedy with songs; **First Performance:** 1806/2/7, New York

Wanderer, The; **Subtitle(s):** The Rights of Hospitality; **Libretto:** A. F. F. Kotzebue; tr. by Charles Kemble; **Music:** Victor Pelissier; **Genre:** Drama, Incidental Music; 3 acts; **First Performance, London:** 1808/1/12, Covent Garden; **First Performance, America:** 1808/12/16, Charleston

Wandering Boys (See *Paul and Alexis)*

Wapping Landlady (See also *Sailor's Landlady*); **Subtitle(s):** Jack in Distress (cf); **Libretto:** Charles Dibdin; based on his *General Election;* **Music:** Charles Dibdin; **Genre:** Pantomimical Dance; Musical Entertainment; **First Performance:** 1783/8/6, New York, Dennis Wall Company

Warrior's Welcome Home, The; **Libretto:** William Francis, arranger; **Music:** Alexander Reinagle; **Genre:** Pantomime; Divertissement; **First Performance:** 1796/2/10, Philadelphia

*Waterman, The; **Subtitle(s):** The First of August; **Libretto:** Charles Dibdin; **Music:** Charles Dibdin (pastiche); arr. by Victor Pelissier; **Genre:** Ballad Opera; 2 acts; **First Performance, London:** 1774/8/8, Little Theatre, Haymarket; **First Performance, America:** 1791/4/8, Philadelphia, Kenna company, Northern Liberties

*We Fly By Night; **Subtitle(s):** Long Stories; **Libretto:** George Colman, jr.; **Music:** Michael Kelly; arr. by Alexander Reinagle; **Genre:** Musical Entertainment; 2 acts; **First Performance, London:** 1806/1/28, Covent Garden; **First Performance, America:** 1806/11/27, Baltimore

Weathercock, The; **Subtitle(s): What Next?; Love Alone Can Fix Him; **Libretto:** John Till Allingham; **Music:** Matthew Peter King; **Genre:** Musical

Entertainment; 2 acts; **First Performance, London:** 1805/11/18, Drury Lane; **First Performance, America:** 1806/6/9, New York

Wedding in Wales, The; **Subtitle(s):** Which is the Bridegroom?; **Libretto:** Thomas Stock; **Music:** Thomas Stock; **Genre:** Musical Farce; 5 acts; **First Performance:** 1799/3/11, Philadelphia

Wedding Ring, The; **Libretto:** Charles Dibdin; based on C. Goldoni, *Il Filosofo di Campagna;* **Music:** Charles Dibdin; **Genre:** Comic Opera; 2 acts; **First Performance, London:** 1773/2/1, Drury Lane; **First Performance, America:** 1793/3/20, Charleston

Weird Sisters, The; **Subtitle(s):** The Abduction of Harlequin; **Genre:** Pantomime; **First Performance:** 1797/6/27, Philadelphia, Lailson's Circus

Welsh Opera—See *Gray Mare's the Best Horse*

Western Exhibitions, The; **Subtitle(s):** The Liberty Boys Pole; **Genre:** Pantomime; **First Performance:** 1797/7/12, New York, Ricketts Circus

Wheel of Truth, The; **Subtitle(s):** The Trial of Character; **Libretto:** James Fennell; **Music:** Victor Pelissier; **Genre:** Farce, Incidental Music; 2 acts; **First Performance:** 1803/1/12, New York

Whim Upon Whim; **Subtitle(s):** Harlequin Skeleton (cf); Harlequin Pastry Cook (cf); Harlequin Rambler; **Genre:** Pantomime; **First Performance:** 1804/2/8, Charleston

Whims of Galatea, The; **Subtitle(s):** Pastoral Love; **Libretto:** Francisquy, arranger; **Genre:** Grand Pastoral Pantomime Ballet Dance; **First Performance:** 1794/10/11, Charleston

Whitsun Frolic; **Subtitle(s):** Harlequin Gladiator; **Genre:** Pantomime; **First Performance:** 1800/6/2, New York

Whitsuntide Frolics; **Subtitle(s):** Harlequin Hurry Scurry (cf); Harlequin's Holiday; **Music:** John Bray; **Genre:** Interlude, 1 act; **First Performance:** 1809/5/22, Baltimore

Who Pays the Piper?; **Subtitle(s):** My Lord Knows Who; **Libretto:** John Bray (tr. from the French); see also T. J. Dibdin's *Blind Man's Buff; or, Who Pays the Piper?,* Musical Farce, 1802/2/1, Royalty (London); **Music:** John Bray; **Genre:** Comic Opera; 2 acts; **First Performance:** 1809/3/25, Philadelphia

Who Wins?; **Subtitle(s):** The Widow's Choice; **Libretto:** John Till Allingham (published as *The Widow; or Who Wins?*); **Music:** Henry Condell; add. by James Hewitt; **Genre:** Comic Opera; 2 acts; **First Performance, London:** 1808/2/25, Covent Garden; **First Performance, America:** 1810/3/7, Philadelphia

Who's to Have Her?; **Libretto:** Thomas J. Dibdin; **Music:** William Reeve and Whitaker; **Genre:** Musical Farce; **First Performance, London:** 1813/11/22, Drury Lane; **First Performance, America:** 1814/11/16, New York

Wicklow Mountains; **Subtitle(s):** Lad of the Hills; The Gold Mine; **Libretto:** John O'Keeffe; altered from *The Lad of the Hills; or, The Wicklow Gold Mines;* **Music:** William Shield; **Genre:** Musical Entertainment; 3, 2 acts; **First Performance, London:** 1796/7/10, Covent Garden; **First Performance, America:** 1810/3/14, Philadelphia

*Wife of Two Husbands, The; **Libretto:** Guilbert Pixérécourt, *La Femme à deux Maris;* tr. by (a) James Cobb; (b) Prince Hoare; (c) William Dunlap; **Music:** Joseph Mazzinghi; new music by Alexander Reinagle, Benjamin Carr, Rayner Taylor, Michault; (b) Frederick Granger, Francis Schaffer; (c) Victor Pelissier; **Genre:** Musical Entertainment; 5, 3 acts; **First Performance, London:** 1803/11/1, Drury Lane; **First Performance, America:** 1804/4/4, New York

Wild Goose Chase, The; **Subtitle(s):** Mad Cap of Age Tomorrow; **Libretto:** William Dunlap; based on A. F. F. Kotzebue, *Der Wildfang;* **Music:** James Hewitt; **Genre:** Comic Opera; 3, 2 acts; **First Performance:** 1800/1/24, New York

William Tell; **Libretto:** James Byrne, arranger; **Genre:** Historical Pantomime; **First Performance:** 1799/4/6, Philadelphia

William Tell; **Subtitle(s):** The Patriots of Switzerland; **Genre:** Historical Play interspersed with music; **First Performance:** 1812/12/26, Philadelphia

Windsor Wags—See *The Review*

Wishes, The; **Subtitle(s):** South-Carolinian Peasant; **Libretto:** By a Gentleman of Charleston; **Genre:** Musical Farce; **First Performance, America:** 1796/5/19, Charleston, City Theatre; **First Performance, London:** 1802

Witches (Witches' Cave; Witches of the Cave); **Subtitle(s):** Harlequin Restored (cf); Harlequin in the Moon (cf); Harlequin Salamander (cf); **Libretto:** May be based on Dance/Clagget, London, 1762; **Genre:** Pantomime; **First Performance:** 1767/4/2, Philadelphia, Southwark

Witches of the Rock, The; **Subtitle(s):** Harlequin Everywhere (cf); **Libretto:** Millbourne, William Francis, arrangers; **Music:** Alexander Reinagle; **Genre:** Pantomime; **First Performance:** 1796/2/26, Philadelphia

Wives Metamorphosed—See *Devil to Pay*

Wood Cutters; **Subtitle(s):** The Militia Man; The Cottage Maid; The Pot Broken; **Libretto:** Based on F. A. D. Philidor's *Le Bucheron* (1763); Francisquy, arranger, Boston; **Genre:** Pantomime Ballet; 1 act; **First Performance:** 1792/2/10, New York

Wood Demon, The (Wood Daemon); **Subtitle(s): The Clock Has Struck; **Libretto:** Matthew G. Lewis; expanded by John D. Turnbull; also known as *One O'Clock; or, The Knight and the Wood Daemon,* 1811/8/1, Lyceum; **Music:** Michael Kelly and M. P. King; add. by James Hewitt; arr. by

Victor Pelissier; **Genre:** Melodrama; Grand Cabalistic Pantomimic Romance; 2, 3 acts; **First Performance, London:** 1807/4/1, Drury Lane; **First Performance, America:** 1808/3/18, Boston

Woodman, The; **Subtitle(s):** Female Archery; **Libretto:** Henry Bate Dudley; **Music:** William Shield; **Genre:** Comic Opera; 3 acts; **First Performance, London:** 1791/2/26, Covent Garden; **First Performance, America:** 1793/5/13, Charleston

Wounded Hussar, The; **Subtitle(s):** The Rightful Heir; **Libretto:** Joseph Hutton; **Music:** James Hewitt; **Genre:** Comic Opera; 2 acts; **First Performance:** 1809/3/29, Philadelphia

Yankee Chronology—See *Huzzah for the Constitution*

Yes or No?; **Libretto:** Isaac Pocock; **Music:** Charles Smith; **Genre:** Musical Afterpiece; 2 acts; **First Performance, London:** 1808/8/31, Little Theatre, Haymarket; **First Performance, America:** 1809/11/20, New York

Young Hussar, The; **Subtitle(s):** Love and Mercy; **Libretto:** William Dimond; **Music:** Michael Kelly; John Bray; **Genre:** Musical Entertainment; 2 acts; **First Performance, London:** 1807/3/12, Drury Lane; **First Performance, America:** 1808/3/26, Philadelphia

Youth, Love, and Folly; **Subtitle(s):** The Little Jockey; **Libretto:** William Dimond; **Music:** Michael Kelly; **Genre:** Comic Opera; 2 acts; **First Performance, London:** 1805/5/24, Drury Lane; **First Performance, America:** 1807/3/11, Philadelphia

Youthful Tar; **Subtitle(s):** The Glorious Tenth of September; **Genre:** Afterpiece; **First Performance:** 1813/11/25, New York

Zembuca; **Subtitle(s):** The Net-maker and His Wife; **Libretto:** Isaac Pocock; **Music:** William H. Ware; **Genre:** Grand Melodramatic Romance; 4 acts; **First Performance, London:** 1815/3/13, Covent Garden; **First Performance, America:** 1815/11/22, Baltimore

Zemire et Azor (Zemire and Azor)—See also *Selima and Azor;* **Libretto:** J. F. Marmontel; **Music:** A. E. M. Grétry; **Genre:** Comédie Ballet; 4 acts; **First Performance:** 1771/11/9, Fontainebleau; **First Performance, America:** 1794/8/4, Charleston, City Theatre

Zorinski; **Subtitle(s):** Freedom to the Slaves; Liberty in Poland; Struggle for Liberty; The Preserver of his Country; Freedom to the Brave; **Libretto:** Thomas Morton; **Music:** Samuel Arnold; **Genre:** Play interspersed with songs, duets, and choruses; 3 acts; **First Performance, London:** 1795/6/20, Little Theatre, Haymarket; **First Performance, America:** 1797/5/15, Boston, Haymarket

APPENDIX B
Musical Theatre Performances in Five American Cities, 1801–15

This listing is intended to supplement those already available for eighteenth-century performances in such sources as Sonneck, *Early Opera in America;* Pollock, *The Philadelphia Theatre in the Eighteenth Century;* and Odell, *Annals of the New York Stage.* With the exception of Charleston records from Hoole, *The Antebellum Charleston Theatre,* all entries in this checklist come from contemporary newspapers and periodicals from the city in question. Charleston records have been verified with playbills in Charleston newspapers when they have been available and when there has been reason to question or expand Hoole's information. Because full runs of newspaper playbills are not always available, because of last-minute cancellations and substitutions in the original bills, and because of human error in the present author, there is ample room for errata, but every care has been taken to make these lists as accurate and complete as possible.

Refer to Appendix A for alternate titles.

Unless otherwise noted, New York performances are at the Park Theatre; Philadelphia performances are at the New Chestnut Street Theatre; Boston performances are at the Federal Street Theatre; and Charleston performances are at the Charleston Theatre. Exceptions are noted with the following abbreviations:

Baltimore:	C	Circus
	O	Olympic Theatre at Circus
	P	Pepin and Breschard at Circus
Boston:	C	Circus, Haymarket Place, bottom of the Mall
	H	Haymarket
New York:	A	Anthony Street theatre (later called Commonwealth Theatre, Anthony St.)
	Be	Bedlow St. (formerly Grove)
	C	City Hotel
	Cr	New York Circus (replaced Pepin and Breschard)
	Cw	Commonwealth Theatre, Broadway
	G	Grove Theatre
	I	Italian Theatre
	L	Lyceum
	MV	Mount Vernon Gardens
	O	Olympic Theatre; formerly the Pepin and Breschard Circus
	P	Pepin and Breschard Circus
	Pl	Pearl Street Theatre
	U	Union Hotel
	V	Vauxhall Gardens
	W	Washington Hotel
Philadelphia:	A	Apollo Theatre under Webster at Southwark
	C	Pepin and Breschard at Circus
	Cw	Commonwealth Theatre at Southwark (1813), Olympic (1814)
	G	Columbia Gardens
	O	Olympic Theatre, 9th and Walnut (former Circus)
	S	Southwark Theatre
	V	Villalave at Olympic Theatre

Abaellino, The Great Bandit: Baltimore, 1803/4/25, 4/29, 5/2, 5/21, 1804/5/29, 1805/5/20, 1806/10/20, 1808/5/30, 1809/5/22, 1810/5/12, 1811/5/27, 1812/5/18, 1813/10/6, 1814/5/13, 1815/5/27; Boston, 1802/11/19, 11/22, 11/24, 11/26, 11/29, 12/1, 12/3, 12/8, 12/10; 1803/1/7, 1/10, 1/28, 2/28, 4/20, 12/28, 1804/1/4, 1805/3/22, 10/25, 1806/2/5, 1807/5/18, 11/2, 1809/2/10, 1811/2/8, 2/11, 12/18, 1812/1/15, 1813/3/1, 1814/1/3, 2/21, 10/24, 11/30, 1815/1/11; Charleston, 1802/2/8, 2/15, 3/1; 1804/1/31, 2/13, 1805/2/8, 1806/5/14, 1807/3/18, 5/8, 11/23; 1808/12/14, 1810/2/7, 1811/4/6,

1812/2/24, 4/17, 1815/12/27; New York, 1801/2/11, 2/13, 2/16, 2/20, 2/25, 3/2, 3/11, 4/10, 6/5, 12/14, 1802/1/6, 1/22, 7/2, 11/12, 1803/4/15, 1805/2/8, 2/15, 11/18, 1806/3/3, 10/15, 1807/9/25, 1808/10/31, 1809/9/18, 1810/7/2, 1811/1/14, 3/13, 12/02, 12/23, 1812/3/30, 6/10-O, 6/17, 9/7, 9/30, 1813/3/12, 7/2, 9/17, 1814/6/4-A, 10/17, 12/14, 1815/1/16, 9/11, 10/30; Philadelphia, 1803/1/12, 1/17, 1/28, 3/14, 1805/1/12, 1806/3/7, 1807/2/27, 1808/1/22, 11/14, 1809/12/1, 1811/2/22, 10/9, 1812/1/22, 3/12-O, 10/1-O, 12/24, 1814/1/28, 3/30, 1815/1/27, 2/17

Adelgitha, or the Fruits of a Single Error: Baltimore, 1809/4/21, 1812/4/29; Boston, 1809/12/11, 12/13, 12/14, 12/20, 1810/1/15, 2/2, 1812/2/26, 1814/10/14, 1815/1/9; Charleston, 1809/2/13, 1810/2/21, 1812/1/31; New York, 1808/11/14, 11/16, 11/21, 12/5, 12/12, 1809/4/12, 6/26, 9/22, 10/13, 11/22, 1810/5/14, 9/28, 1811/5/3, 11/13, 1812/11/13, 1813/12/10-Cw, 12/15, 1814/5/11-A, 5/16-A, 9/10-A; Philadelphia, 1809/1/20, 1/23, 3/1, 1810/1/12, 4/6, 12/1, 1811/10/11, 1812/4/24-O, 12/21, 1813/11/29

Adelmorn, the Outlaw: Baltimore, 1802/6/10, 12/3, 1803/6/2, 12/7, 1804/5/19, 1805/10/9, 1806/10/22, 1809/5/5, 1815/6/5; Boston, 1802/5/24, 5/26, 5/28, 5/31, 6/2, 1803/3/9, 3/11, 1805/3/1, 1806/4/18, 1808/3/14, 1811/12/26, 1812/4/22, 1814/11/16, 1815/3/1; Charleston, 1803/3/21, 3/25, 4/18, 1806/2/12, 1808/5/6; New York, 1802/2/25, 2/26, 3/1, 3/5, 3/22, 4/7, 1814/6/22, 7/1; Philadelphia, 1802/4/12, 12/17, 1804/1/3, 1809/3/30, 1810/1/24, 1815/4/1, 12/22

Adopted Child: Baltimore, 1803/10/26, 1804/4/27, 10/15, 1805/5/1, 1806/5/5, 10/6, 1812/4/22; Boston, 1801/5/1, 1802/11/10, 12/6, 1803/12/26, 1804/4/20, 1805/3/1, 11/15, 1807/4/15, 10/7, 1808/3/14, 1810/2/12, 1811/2/27, 1813/4/21, 1815/1/18, 1815/11/20; Charleston, 1801/1/23, 4/24, 1802/2/22, 1803/2/7, 1804/4/9, 6/12, 11/12, 1805/2/8, 1806/12/1, 1807/11/23, 1808/1/2, 1809/3/18, 1810/4/6, 1811/1/9, 1/12, 1812/5/1; New York, 1804/4/5-G, 11/9, 11/19, 1805/11/18, 12/20, 1806/5/23, 7/28-V, 8/1-V, 1807/8/8-V, 1813/9/29, 10/6; Philadelphia, 1803/12/19, 1804/12/31, 1806/3/3, 1811/2/20, 4/1, 11/25, 1812/3/14-O, 2/22, 1814/1/31

Adrian and Orrila: Baltimore, 1808/5/18, 5/23, 10/28; 1810/11/21, 1814/5/9, 10/15, 1815/10/16, 1815/11/1; Boston, 1808/1/18, 1/20, 1/22, 11/11, 1811/3/15, 10/25; Charleston, 1807/12/7, 12/12, 1808/1/1, 1/16, 4/8, 1810/2/10, 1812/12/9, 12/11, 12/21; New York, 1807/9/2-V, 12/11, 12/26, 1814/5/9-A, 6/17-A; Philadelphia, 1808/2/12, 2/15, 2/22, 2/29, 3/14, 4/1, 4/9, 11/16, 1809/12/23, 1810/12/10, 1811/3/13, 1812/3/18-O, 1814/3/21, 4/13, 12/9, 1815/12/13

Aethiop: Baltimore, 1814/11/18, 11/19, 11/21, 1815/5/1; Boston, 1815/3/27,

3/29, 3/31, 4/3, 4/5, 4/7, 4/10, 4/14, 4/17, 4/21, 5/8, 6/7, 11/3, 11/6, 12/4; New York (Dimond/Ferrossier), 1813/4/5, 4/7, 4/12, 4/19, 4/21, 4/30, 5/12, 6/30, 1814/3/2, 3/9, 11/28, 1815/9/27, 11/4; Philadelphia (Dimond/Taylor), 1814/1/1, 1/3, 1/5, 1/7, 1/31, 2/5, 2/14, 3/2, 12/16, 12/19, 1815/1/13

Africans: Baltimore, 1810/6/9; Boston, 1814/2/2, 2/4, 4/22; New York, 1810/1/1, 1/3, 1/5, 1/8, 1/10, 1/16, 2/22, 4/4, 6/11; Philadelphia, 1810/4/18, 4/19

Agreeable Surprise: Baltimore, 1804/5/29, 1806/11/21, 1807/6/5, 12/2, 1808/5/7, 1809/4/17, 10/16, 1810/10/27, 1811/5/4, 1812/4/6, 1813/5/28, 1814/6/6; Boston, 1802/1/18, 1804/1/2, 1/11, 1805/4/1, 11/29, 1807/4/22, 11/20, 1808/1/15, 10/14, 1815/12/14, 12/21; Charleston, 1801/4/27, 11/23, 1802/2/11, 11/12, 1803/11/9, 12/21, 1805/4/17, 1806/3/14, 1807/5/2, 5/13, 1808/3/4, 1811/3/25, 3/29, 1812/2/22, 1815/11/29, 12/2, 12/16; New York, 1801/7/8, 1802/2/23, 2/27, 3/3, 10/20, 1803/6/20, 1805/7/1, 1806/5/7, 6/2, 8/13-V, 10/18, 1807/1/5, 11/2, 1808/5/30, 10/12, 11/23, 1809/5/31, 9/11, 9/27, 10/23, 1810/3/16, 6/22, 1811/6/19, 6/26, 1812/4/3, 1813/12/6-Cw, 1815/1/30, 3/3, 11/13; Philadelphia, 1801/10/28, 1804/1/2, 1806/12/12, 1807/4/10, 7/10, 12/26, 1808/4/11, 11/26, 1810/2/22, 4/25, 11/26, 1811/10/26, 1813/1/7-S, 1/8, 4/7, 1815/2/22

Aladdin (O'Keeffe/Shield): Baltimore, 1801/6/5, 1802/11/27; Philadelphia, 1801/3/14, 4/16, 11/2

Aladdin (Farley, CG, 1813): New York, 1815/11/25, 11/27, 11/29, 12/13

Alberto Albertini: New York, 1811/1/25, 1/28

Algerine Pirates: Boston, 1807/5/1

Alzuma (Peru Avenged): Boston: 1801/5/1, 1802/4/19; New York, 1801/3/23, 3/27; Philadelphia, 1801/3/2

Ambrosia and Matilda: Charleston, 1811/4/22

Amelia and Valcour: New York, 1811/7/10-P, 7/31-P; Philadelphia, 1813/3/24-G, 9/7-G

America, Commerce and Freedom: Boston, 1813/4/12, 4/19, 4/21, 12/22; New York, 1812/12/18, 12/19, 12/21, 12/23, 12/25, 12/28, 1813/1/7, 2/22, 2/24, 2/26

American Camp: Boston, 1812/10/8

American Captive (Ellison): Boston, 1811/12/11, 12/13, 12/16, 12/27, 1814/1/5

American Farmer: New York, 1808/9/5-V

American Generosity: Boston, 1810/10/24, 10/26, 10/29, 11/21; New York, 1812/6/9-O; Philadelphia, 1812/4/29-O, 5/15-O, 10/1-O

American Heroine (Harlequin Neptune): 1806/4/11; New York, 1811/7/22-P, 7/24-P, 9/3-P; Philadelphia, 1801/3/30

American in London: Boston, 1805/3/4

American Tars: Boston, 1812/12/16, 12/23, 1813/1/1, 1/29, 11/15; Charleston, 1812/4/8

American Volunteer: Philadelphia, 1813/4/3

American Volunteers: Philadelphia, 1813/5/12-C, 5/22-C

Amour dans les Rose: New York, 1812/6/5-O, 6/6-O, 6/9-O

Amour et la Marriage: Philadelphia, 1815/4/17

Amour Trouve les Moyens: New York, 1807/9/7-V

Amour Vient a bout de tout: Baltimore, 1814/5/21; Philadelphia, 1813/2/24, 3/3, 1814/3/21

Anniversary of Shelah: Philadelphia, 1808/3/18

Any Thing New?: Boston, 1814/4/11, 1815/1/16

Arbitration (Free and Easy): Charleston, 1808/3/14, 3/16, 3/21, 1809/2/17; New York, 1808/5/25, 5/27

Arlequin dans la Lune (Harlequin in the Moon): Philadelphia, 1813/3/26

Asylum: Boston, 1804/4/16, 4/23

At Home: New York, 1814/2/23

Auld Robin Gray (ballet): Boston, 1804/4/27, 1805/3/22, 1807/12/23; New York, 1804/3/22-G, 4/24-G; Philadelphia, 1807/8/3-S

Battle of Eutaw Springs: Charleston, 1807/1/10, 1/14, 2/23, 1808/5/9; Philadelphia, 1813/6/9-Cw

Battle of Hexham: Baltimore, 1802/4/26, 5/1, 1809/10/3, 1812/5/9; Boston, 1803/11/7, 11/9, 1805/2/6, 1807/4/29, 1808/12/26, 1810/4/30, 1812/4/17; New York, 1802/7/26-MV, 11/24, 1803/4/23, 1806/3/22, 1814/11/16; Philadelphia, 1801/7/17, 9/14-S, 12/16, 1807/4/8, 1813/1/7-S

Battle of Lodi: Philadelphia, 1812/4/18-O

Battle of Savanna: New York, 1808/11/25-P

Battle of York (Fall of York; Capture of York): Baltimore/1/17-P, 1/19-P, 1/22-P; Boston, 1814/4/11, 4/15, 4/18, 5/25, 7/4-A, 10/14, 10/21; Philadelphia, 1813/11/17-C, 11/19-C, 11/23-C, 11/30-C

Bear Hunters: Boston, Charleston, 1812/5/6

Bee Hive: Baltimore, 1812/5/1, 5/6, 1813/10/18, 1814/6/4; Charleston, 1812/5/12; New York, 1811/10/23, 10/28, 11/11, 11/23, 1812/5/11; Philadelphia, 1812/11/4, 11/13, 11/23, 12/18, 1813/12/17, 1814/2/4, 12/5, 1815/1/4

Beggar's Opera: Baltimore, 1807/6/3; Boston, 1809/10/2; Charleston, 1809/3/6; Philadelphia, 1808/3/18

Belle Dorothée: Charleston, 1805/3/19

Bird Catchers: Charleston, 1804/4/16, 4/30, 1807/6/1; New York, 1801/7/22, 1806/8/2-V, 8/6-V

Birth, Death and Renovation of Harlequin: Charleston, 1805/5/9, 5/20, 1806/2/7

Black Beard: Baltimore, 1804/6/8, 6/9, 10/24; Boston, 1811/2/18, 2/20, 2/22, 2/25, 3/1, 3/13; Charleston, 1811/5/14, 5/20; New York, 1804/7/7, 10/26, 12/10; Philadelphia, 1804/4/2, 4/3, 1805/3/2, 1812/5/11-O, 5/13-O

Black Castle: Baltimore, 1807/5/29, 11/21; Boston, 1809/5/8; Philadelphia, 1807/3/20

Black Forest: Baltimore, 1811/4/3-P, 4/8-P

Blind Bargain: Baltimore, 1806/5/5, 10/4; Boston, 1808/4/25; Charleston, 1805/12/6, 12/13, 1806/2/18, 12/1; New York, 1805/5/13, 5/22, 12/30; Philadelphia, 1806/2/26, 6/23

Blind Boy: Baltimore, 1810/5/4, 5/7, 11/9, 1811/5/6, 1812/5/15, 1813/5/28; Boston, 1810/4/16, 4/18, 12/7, 12/10, 12/12, 1811/1/17, 11/4, 1812/1/13; Charleston, 1812/4/10, 4/13; New York, 1808/12/7, 12/12, 12/16, 1809/3/3, 5/17, 1814/6/17, 6/27, 6/29, 1815/2/1; Philadelphia, 1810/1/1, 1/15, 1/26, 2/2, 2/23, 1811/1/18, 1812/3/9, 1813/1/9, 2/1, 1814/2/11, 1815/4/3

Blind Cupid: New York, 1809/1/24-L; 2/21-L, 9/13

Blind Girl, The: Baltimore, 1803/5/6, 5/11; Boston, 1808/10/12, 10/14, 10/17, 10/31, 12/21, 1809/4/10; Philadelphia, 1802/3/10, 1804/1/30

Blue Beard: Baltimore, 1801/6/10, 1802/5/19, 6/4, 1803/4/22, 1808/10/21, 10/24, 10/29, 1809/4/19, 4/28, 1810/5/11, 11/20, 1812/5/9; Boston, 1801/4/27, 5/4, 12/9, 12/21, 1802/2/23, 6/7, 1803/4/29, 1804/3/19, 3/21, 3/28, 1805/1/9, 1/11, 2/4, 11/13, 11/18, 1806/3/31, 11/14, 1807/1/2, 1808/3/11, 1811/4/5, 4/17, 5/15, 1812/10/7, 12/14, 1813/11/1, 11/10, 12/20, 1814/3/14, 12/26, 1815/1/11; Charleston, 1801/3/20, 3/25, 3/27, 4/22, 11/27, 1802/2/12, 4/2, 1803/3/18, 1804/12/26, 12/28, 1805/2/23, 1806/1/15, 2/18, 5/13, 5/15, 1807/2/27, 2/28, 3/12, 1808/1/27, 4/8, 1809/3/1, 1810/4/25, 1811/5/2; New York, 1802/3/8, 3/10, 3/12, 3/15, 3/17, 3/20, 3/24, 4/2, 4/10, 5/5, 6/9, 6/30, 1803/1/1, 1/10, 1/15, 4/12, 1804/1/2, 3/24, 11/26, 1805/1/2, 3/6, 4/5, 12/26, 1806/3/26, 6/6, 10/24, 1807/1/2, 3/30, 9/23, 11/9, 12/26, 1808/3/18, 9/28, 1812/1/1, 1/3, 1/4, 1/6, 1/8, 1/10, 1/13, 1/15, 2/10, 2/26, 6/1, 10/12; Philadelphia, 1801/1/1, 2/18, 4/7, 11/6, 11/13, 11/30, 12/18, 1802/1/16, 3/12, 1803/3/19, 1808/4/13, 4/14, 4/18, 11/11, 11/21, 11/30, 12/23, 1809/1/14, 2/8, 1810/2/2, 3/2, 1811/2/13, 3/20, 9/23, 12/20, 1812/1/20, 1/25, 2/3, 12/19

Boarding House: Baltimore, 1814/5/13, 5/21, 5/30; Boston, 1814/10/10, 10/21, 11/16, 12/30, 1815/2/20, 5/3, 10/30, 12/18; New York, 1812/6/5, 6/10, 6/17; Philadelphia, 1814/4/2, 4/13, 1815/2/6, 3/3, 4/15

Bondocani: Baltimore, 1802/5/5, 11/24, 1803/4/30; Boston, 1809/4/19, 4/24;

Charleston, 1803/4/12; New York, 1815/2/10, 2/13; Philadelphia, 1801/12/
11, 12/14, 1802/1/13, 12/20

Bonne Fille: Charleston, 1804/5/3, 1808/5/6; New York, 1804/12/22-Be,
1806/8/18-V

Boston Sailors: Boston, 1807/5/4, 5/25

Bravo of Spain: Baltimore, 1814/3/24-P, 3/25-P

Brazen Mask: Baltimore, 1806/6/9, 6/10, 10/4, 11/17, 1811/3/7-P, 3/11-P, 3/
18-P, 1813/11/18, 1814/2/26-P, 2/28-P; Boston, 1809/1/4, 1/6, 1/9, 1/11, 1/
13, 1/20, 1/23, 1/30, 2/8, 2/20, 4/12, 4/28, 10/4, 10/9, 11/8, 12/26, 1811/3/
18, 3/20, 3/25, 10/18; Charleston, 1808/2/1; New York, 1807/8/25-V, 8/
26-V, 1808/7/20-V, 1811/7/15-P, 7/17-P, 8/19-P, 1813/3/8, 3/10, 3/29, 4/9,
1814/6/13; Philadelphia, 1806/3/1, 4/7, 4/8, 1812/3/23-O, 3/25-O, 1813/1/
18, 1/25

Bridal Ring: Baltimore, 1812/3/28; Philadelphia, 1812/2/10, 2/14, 2/21

Buxom Joan: Baltimore, 1801/5/1, Philadelphia, 1801/1/30, 2/6

Cabinet: Baltimore, 1807/5/22; Charleston, 1809/3/27; New York, 1814/5/
25, 6/1; Philadelphia, 1807/3/28

Caledonian Frolic: Philadelphia, 1801/3/9, 1807/8/17S, 1811/10/7, 10/9

Caledonian Girls: Philadelphia, 1814/3/25

Caledonian Lasses: Charleston, 1810/4/27

Caledonian Lovers: Boston, 1808/11/25, 1809/3/13; New York, 1808/8/22-V,
8/26-V

Camp: Charleston, 1806/12/15, 12/22, 1808/1/18, 1/21, 12/14; Philadelphia,
1814/12/26, 12/28, 12/30

Captain Smith and the Princess Pocahontas: Philadelphia, 1806/3/5

Captive of Spilberg: New York, 1801/3/25, 3/27, 3/30, 4/6, 4/10, 5/13, 1802/
4/5

Capture of York: New York, 1814/7/4-A

Caravan: Baltimore, 1810/6/1; Boston, 1812/5/13, 5/15, 5/18, 5/27, 1813/5/
5; New York, 1810/6/29, 7/4, 9/10, 9/12, 1815/6/12, 10/9, 10/30; Philadelphia, 1810/3/23, 3/26

Care and Mirth: Charleston, 1802/5/12, 5/17, 1803/11/14, 1804/5/25, 1805/
4/8, 4/25, 1806/12/15, 1808/1/11, 2/19, 1810/5/16; New York, 1801/9/7-
MV, 9/21-MV, 1802/8/13-MV

Castle of Andalusia: Charleston, 1802/2/1, 2/10, 4/7, 1806/1/27, 2/28, 1808/
12/23, 12/28; New York, 1801/2/20, 2/27

Castle of Sorrento: Baltimore, 1805/5/25; Boston, 1801/4/13; Charleston,
1806/3/24; Philadelphia, 1805/3/9

Castle Spectre: Baltimore, 1801/5/4, 5/11, 1802/5/27, 11/26, 1803/5/13, 11/

30, 1804/6/6, 1805/5/18, 1806/5/2, 11/22; 1807/6/1, 10/31, 1809/4/28, 1811/5/18, 1812/3/25, 1814/5/30; Boston, 1801/1/9, 3/16, 5/15, 1802/1/1, 2/8, 4/28, 12/27, 1803/1/24, 1804/2/6, 10/17, 1805/4/8, 1806/12/26, 1807/ 1/19, 2/11, 1809/2/17, 1811/2/1, 10/16, 1812/10/9, 1813/11/10, 1814/3/ 11, 10/5; Charleston, 1801/2/4, 2/6, 2/12, 2/16, 2/23, 3/23, 11/25, 1802/3/ 26, 11/13, 1803/12/22, 1805/3/9, 1806/5/9, 12/5, 12/27, 1807/11/24, 11/ 28, 1808/2/13, 1815/12/13, 12/29; New York, 1801/4/15, 6/8, 11/27, 12/ 26; 1802/10/20, 1803/6/22, 12/5, 12/7, 1804/6/29, 1805/4/29, 1806/2/24, 1807/4/15, 9/21; 1808/4/16, 8/22-V, 1809/9/6, 1811/6/21, 1812/5/22, 1814/3/28, 8/10-Cr, 10/31, 1815/7/3, 9/6; Philadelphia, 1801/1/30, 1802/ 3/15, 4/5, 1803/1/15, 1805/1/7, 1806/2/17, 3/28, 1807/1/9, 1808/1/18, 12/ 28, 1810/1/20, 12/31, 1811/4/22, 7/22-A, 9/21, 1812/3/14-O, 5/15-O, 10/ 3, 12/10-S, 1815/2/15

Catch Club (Sons of Apollo; Feast of Anacreon): Baltimore, 1807/5/25, 6/5; Philadelphia, 1801/3/21, 1804/3/23, 1805/3/11, 1807/3/11, 3/14, 1808/3/ 28, 1815/3/20

Catch Him Who Can: Baltimore, 1809/5/1, 5/26, 1810/6/4, 1813/11/15; Charleston, 1810/5/9; Philadelphia, 1809/3/8, 3/27, 1810/2/28, 1811/1/21, 12/7, 1812/10/31, 1814/2/25, 1815/4/8

Celebrated London Shoemaker: New York, 1808/5/7-Pl

Chains of the Heart: Boston, 1810/1/19, 1/26; New York, 1804/2/1, 2/3, 2/6, 2/8, 2/17, 2/24, 1805/1/1, 3/11

Champlain and Plattsburgh: New York, 1814/11/18, 11/25, 12/9, 1815/1/5

Children in the Wood: Baltimore, 1804/5/31, 1806/5/26, 1807/11/9, 1813/5/ 14, 1815/5/26; Boston, 1801/1/20-H, 4/15, 4/24, 1802/1/8, 2/15, 5/21, 10/ 29, 12/1, 1803/4/22, 1805/12/11, 12/18, 1807/5/20, 12/16, 1808/2/12, 1811/3/27, 3/29, 1815/10/9; Charleston, 1803/4/14, 11/17, 12/3, 1804/2/ 16, 4/16, 12/21, 1805/2/7, 1806/3/10, 11/21, 1807/2/9, 5/18, 12/12, 1808/ 2/22, 1810/2/19, 1811/2/23, 4/6, 1812/2/5, 2/7, 1813/1/1, 1/13; New York, 1801/6/12, 1802/1/18, 1803/5/27, 1804/5/24-G, 12/21, 1805/1/1, 2/22, 3/ 13, 12/9, 1806/3/22, 1807/9/4-V, 1808/7/27-V, 1809/10/13, 10/18, 11/1, 12/29, 1810/6/15, 1811/4/15, 4/24, 5/29, 1812/6/20-O, 1813/7/7, 7/14, 1814/4/1, 1815/4/19, 5/24; Philadelphia, 1801/3/7, 7/8, 1802/4/5, 1803/2/ 16, 1804/3/21, 1806/1/31, 1807/2/6, 7/8, 1808/1/6, 11/14, 1811/3/8, 4/24, 10/21, 1812/2/7, 4/29-O, 5/9-O, 1813/1/20, 2/10, 1814/1/5, 3/3-Cw, 3/17-Cw, 1815/3/13

Chinese in Boston: Boston, 1808/2/22, 2/24

Christmas Box: Philadelphia, 1812/12/24-S, 12/28-S, 12/30-S, 1813/1/2-S, 1/9-S

Christmas Frolick: Philadelphia, 1813/12/29

Christmas Gambols: New York, 1801/12/26; Philadelphia, 1801/1/2, 2/14

Chrononhotonthologos: Charleston, 1807/3/18, 1808/4/1; New York, 1804/12/4-Be, 1806/8/11-V

Cinderella: Baltimore, 1806/4/25, 4/26, 4/28, 5/3, 10/10, 10/15, 10/25, 11/20, 1807/5/2, 5/6, 1814/6/9, 6/10, 10/17, 10/22; Boston, 1807/12/7, 12/9, 12/11, 12/14, 12/16, 12/21, 12/28, 1808/1/13, 1/22, 3/2, 3/7, 5/25, 7/4, 10/7, 10/10, 10/21, 11/16, 12/21, 1809/1/27, 3/1, 9/22, 10/6, 1812/2/28, 3/2, 3/4, 3/6, 3/9, 3/11, 4/6, 4/30, 5/29, 10/14, 1813/4/26, 1814/1/26, 3/9; Charleston, 1807/2/13, 2/14, 2/16, 2/17, 2/18, 2/25, 3/6, 4/15, 5/15, 12/26, 1808/1/6, 2/18, 1809/1/2, 2/18, 1811/4/26; New York, 1807/8/17-V, 8/19-V, 8/22-V, 8/27-V, 1808/4/1, 4/5, 4/7, 4/8, 4/11, 4/13, 4/14, 4/16, 4/18, 4/20, 4/29, 5/20, 6/10, 12/30, 1813/1/1, 1/2, 1/4, 1/6, 1/8, 1/15; Philadelphia, 1806/1/1, 1/3, 1/6, 1/8, 1/13, 1/17, 2/1, 2/8, 2/15, 2/21, 3/15, 4/5, 12/26, 12/27, 1807/2/11, 2/21, 3/7, 12/28, 1808/1/23, 1/30, 12/27, 1809/2/27, 1810/1/22, 1812/2/26, 1813/4/9, 4/10, 4/12, 4/15, 4/17, 4/23, 12/1, 12/8, 12/18

Cinque Savoyards, Les: New York, 1811/10/25

Clown's Triumph: Baltimore: 1807/11/6, 1811/3/15-P; Charleston, 1802/3/26; New York: 1801/6/8, 6/15, 7/13, 1802/6/30, 12/27, 1805/1/19-Be, 1807/9/2-V, 9/3-V, 1811/08/23-P; Philadelphia, 1801/9/16-S, 1813/7/29-G, 8/6-G

Coal Man of the Jura Mountains: New York, 1808/12/8-P

Cobler's Frolic: Baltimore, 1811/3/1-P; Boston, 1815/12/13-C, 12/20-C

Columbine's Choice: Charleston, 1808/4/18

Columbus: Baltimore: 1801/6/10, 1803/5/14, 10/22, 1811/5/22, 5/24, 1812/4/10; Boston, 1802/2/10, 2/12, 2/15, 3/29, 11/8, 1803/1/31, 1804/2/1, 1807/3/25, 1811/4/22; Charleston, 1807/4/6, 1809/3/8, 1812/4/30; New York, 1801/4/17, 4/20, 4/22, 4/25, 1802/1/1, 2/3, 12/30, 1804/5/28, 6/18, 1805/1/21, 3/29, 1808/11/25, 2/2, 1814/2/22, 2/25, 1815/5/8, 9/13; Philadelphia, 1801/7/4, 1802/1/2, 4/9, 1803/1/7, 1811/1/1, 1/5, 1/12, 1/26, 2/2, 3/18, 12/26, 1812/1/15, 1814/12/17

Comet: Baltimore, 1812/4/24, 5/2, 5/16, 1814/10/31, 1815/11/23; Charleston, 1805/4/15; New York, 1802/5/28, 6/14, 8/20-MV, 11/8, 1803/2/23; Philadelphia, 1812/2/17, 2/24, 10/23, 12/5, 1813/12/24, 1814/12/24

Comus: Boston, 1801/1/19, 1/21, 1/23; Charleston, 1805/4/22; New York, 1801/9/7-MV

Confusion: New York, 1807/9/9

Constitution: Philadelphia, 1812/9/28, 10/3

Constitution Again: Philadelphia, 1813/2/22, 3/1

Constitution and Guerriere: Boston, 1812/10/2, 10/5, 10/9

Constitution and Java: Boston, 1813/3/5, 4/9

Constitution and Wasp: Baltimore, 1813/5/12

Cooper (Cooper Outwitted): Charleston, 1806/3/24, 4/23; New York, 1801/9/23-MV, 1806/7/25-V; Philadelphia, 1815/4/10

Coronation of Napoleon Bonaparte, Emperor of the Gauls: New York, 1805/5/31

Corsair: Baltimore, 1802/6/8, 6/9, 6/10, 1803/5/11, 1814/5/14; Philadelphia, 1803/1/1, 1/19, 1814/2/22, 3/5

Cottagers: New York, 1801/5/6

Count Benyowsky: Baltimore, 1804/5/30, 10/10, 1813/11/5, 11/15, 1814/10/19, 1815/4/28; Boston, 1803/1/17, 1/19; Charleston, 1801/4/15, 1802/2/5, 2/13, 1807/5/25; New York, 1802/5/7, 1814/11/25, 11/30; Philadelphia, 1804/3/23, 1805/3/2, 1813/12/27, 1814/2/12, 12/5

Country Mad-cap: Philadelphia, 1803/4/1

Curfew: Baltimore, 1807/6/10, 11/30, 1815/10/13; Boston, 1807/5/6, 5/15, 5/22, 9/28, 11/4, 1808/11/7, 12/23, 1809/10/4, 1810/4/27, 1811/10/28, 1812/4/8, 1813/4/28, 11/12, 1814/12/30, 1815/1/18, 12/18; Charleston, 1808/1/8, 1/11, 4/25, 1809/4/7, 1810/5/12; New York, 1808/3/4, 3/9, 1812/2/7, 1814/1/19, 1815/3/1; Philadelphia, 1807/12/16, 12/21, 1812/2/19, 1813/3/8

Cymon and Sylvia: Baltimore, 1803/5/28; Boston, 1805/3/29, 1807/4/20; Charleston, 1801/4/11, 1805/2/20, 3/11, 1809/3/20; Philadelphia, 1803/1/26, 1808/3/11

De Montfort: Baltimore, 1810/11/12; New York, 1801/4/13, 1809/11/8, 11/10, 11/17; Philadelphia, 1811/2/8

Dead Alive: Baltimore, 1805/5/15; New York, 1809/4/21, 4/26, 5/3, 1813/4/26, 5/5, 5/12; Philadelphia, 1801/2/4, 1805/1/11

Deaf and Dumb: Baltimore, 1802/4/28, 6/7; Charleston, 1802/1/23, 1/25, 1/29; New York, 1814/6/8-A, 6/13-A, 1815/1/18, 1/25; Philadelphia, 1802/1/27, 1/29, 2/12, 2/24, 3/8, 1803/1/3, 1815/3/25

Deaf Lover: Baltimore: 1801/5/9, 1803/4/29, 1806/4/21, 1812/4/11; Boston, 1804/1/16, 1805/1/7, 1807/5/6, 9/30, 1809/10/16, 12/14, 1810/3/21; New York: 1804/6/6, 6/29, 10/31, 12/19; Philadelphia, 1801/2/11, 1803/1/17, 1806/2/5, 1808/4/16, 12/9, 1810/1/3, 1811/1/5, 10/2, 1812/11/14, 1813/3/3

Death of Captain Cook: Baltimore, 1809/4/26, 5/6, 1811/2/18-P, 2/25-P, 1814/4/11-P; Boston, 1802/12/22, 12/24, 12/27, 1803/2/22, 7/6, 11/18,

1815/12/8, 12/13; Charleston, 1801/4/15, 1802/5/5, 1806/3/17, 5/12, 1807/1/26, 1808/3/7, 1810/3/21; New York, 1801/6/10, 1802/11/5, 11/6, 1805/12/6, 12/27, 1807/10/12, 10/16, 1811/8/12-P, 8/14-P; Philadelphia, 1807/9/7S, 1809/2/17, 2/20

Death of Harlequin: Boston, 1801/1/6H, 1/8H, 1/13H; New York, 1801/5/8, 5/13

Delays and Blunders: Baltimore, 1804/4/13, 5/28; Boston, 1804/1/25, 1/27, 1/30; Charleston, 1803/4/25; New York, 1803/5/11; Philadelphia, 1804/3/5, 12/12

Dermot and Kathleen: Boston, 1806/12/17, 12/22, 1807/1/9, 1/26, 1808/2/19, 1809/2/1; Charleston, 1806/4/11, 4/21

Deserter: Charleston, 1801/3/11; Philadelphia, 1807/3/23, 1812/2/11-O, 2/13-O

Deserter (pant.): New York, 1811/8/5-P, 8/7-P, 8/28-P

Deserter of Naples: Charleston, 1808/5/2; New York, 1801/5/6

Devil to Pay: Baltimore, 1801/5/25, 1806/5/19, 1807/10/31, 1809/10/14, 1812/5/18, 1813/11/13, 1815/11/18; Boston, 1802/3/5, 1806/3/24; Charleston, 1805/5/27, 1810/2/26, 1811/1/21; New York, 1804/5/14, 1806/8/8-V, 1808/11/4, 11/9, 11/25, 1809/4/28, 1810/6/13, 1814/5/9, 10/5, 1815/7/17, 10/18, 11/17, 12/22; Philadelphia, 1801/3/6, 1802/1/2, 1807/2/23, 1808/2/19, 1809/3/1, 12/30, 1811/11/22, 1812/10/26, 12/3-S, 1813/12/13, 1814/2/10-Cw, 3/1-Cw, 1815/1/20, 3/1, 12/8

Devil's Bridge: New York, 1815/7/4, 7/5, 7/24, 12/1, 12/16

Doctor and Apothecary: Baltimore, 1803/5/9, 5/18, 11/21; Philadelphia, 1803/3/4, 3/12, 1804/2/6

Dominion of Fancy: Charleston, 1807/3/30, 7/1

Don Juan: Baltimore, 1804/11/7, 11/9, 11/16, 1805/4/15, 10/12, 11/2, 1806/4/19, 11/1, 1808/6/9, 1809/10/27, 1810/10/13, 1811/2/4-P, 2/6-P, 2/22-P, 3/13-P, 5/20, 11/9-O, 1813/10/13, 1814/2/18-P, 2/21-P; Boston, 1804/3/26, 4/2, 6/1, 1805/2/11, 2/13, 11/11, 11/20, 1806/11/7, 1809/1/18, 1810/2/16, 1811/3/15; Charleston, 1801/2/13, 4/8, 1802/2/17, 1803/4/14, 11/19, 1804/12/24, 1805/12/23, 1806/5/5, 12/12, 1807/2/21, 1809/1/23, 1810/2/27, 1811/4/19; New York, 1801/1/1, 3/28, 12/9, 1802/4/30, 10/25, 1803/5/11, 1804/4/2, 1805/3/20, 4/3, 11/22, 1806/10/20, 1807/1/7, 2/13, 3/11, 9/30, 11/4, 12/16, 1809/7/3, 10/20, 11/15, 12/28, 1811/3/22, 3/27, 7/3-P, 7/26-P, 8/31-P, 11/1, 11/27, 12/27, 1812/6/20-O, 1813/7/5, 1814/4/18, 8/13-Cr, 1815/3/15, 5/31, 7/24, 9/11; Philadelphia, 1805/4/3, 12/26, 1806/3/26, 1808/11/23, 1809/12/2, 1810/12/8, 1811/4/29, 9/14, 1812/4/11-O, 12/16, 1813/4/19, 1814/3/5-Cw

Don Quixote de la Mancha: Baltimore, 1811/2/20-P, 12/24-O, 1814/2/14-P; Boston, 1811/4/10-C, 4/18-C, 1815/11/29-C, 11/30-C, 12/4-C, 12/6-C, 12/8-C, 12/25-C, 12/27-C; New York, 1811/07/29-P, 1812/9/8-Cr, 9/10-Cr, 1813/8/4-Cr, 8/6-Cr; Philadelphia, 1812/5/1-O, 1813/8/20-G, 8/31-G, 11/15-C

Double Disguise: Baltimore: 1804/4/30; Boston, 1802/12/3, 1803/2/2, 1804/4/30, 10/22, 12/3; New York, 1801/4/8, 4/15, 1802/1/4; Philadelphia, 1804/2/22, 1812/3/6

Douglas: Baltimore: 1801/5/8, 1805/5/29, 6/7, 1806/4/30, 1807/10/16, 1809/10/20, 1810/5/19, 1812/4/20, 1815/10/23; Boston, 1802/12/29, 1803/10/17, 1804/1/11, 1805/3/25, 3/25, 10/2, 1807/4/22, 1808/2/22, 1809/4/3, 4/28, 1810/11/9, 1811/1/10, 1812/2/14, 3/4; Charleston, 1802/2/24, 11/17, 1805/4/29, 5/17, 1806/4/23, 1807/4/30, 1808/4/13, 12/10, 12/17, 1810/3/26; New York, 1801/1/19, 7/24, 1802/10/15, 11/6, 1804/1/9, 6/6, 1805/2/14, 1806/5/5, 5/23, 1807/8/24-V, 1808/6/3, 8/5-V, 1809/2/24, 5/17, 1810/3/10, 12/3, 1811/2/25, 9/2, 1813/12/10, 1814/8/1-Cr, 1815/5/15; Philadelphia, 1801/10/30, 1803/2/4, 1805/12/18, 1806/2/1, 6/20, 1807/9/26-S, 10/5-S, 1809/12/6, 12/16, 1811/1/23, 4/13, 12/14, 1812/2/12, 10/21, 1813/4/17, 1814/2/11, 1815/3/18

Dramatist: Baltimore, 1802/6/8, 1803/12/8, 1804/10/12, 1806/11/25, 1808/5/25, 1809/11/1, 1810/10/31, 1813/6/8, 1815/6/9; Boston, 1802/11/10, 1804/5/30, 10/19, 1808/11/23, 1809/11/1, 1811/2/18, 1812/10/8, 1813/4/5, 1815/10/9; Charleston, 1802/11/5, 1804/4/26, 1807/2/13, 1808/11/18, 1811/1/30, 1812/12/28; New York, 1802/8/9-MV, 9/1-MV, 9/10-MV, 1807/4/13, 10/21, 1810/4/6, 1814/9/16; Philadelphia, 1802/3/19, 1803/2/16, 1804/2/15, 1807/1/10, 1808/2/26, 1809/1/11, 1810/2/7, 4/26, 1812/3/23-O, 12/19, 1813/4/10, 1814/2/24-Cw

Drunken German: Boston, 1807/4/22

Duel: Boston, 1812/4/27

Duenna: Baltimore, 1807/5/27, 1811/12/19-O; Boston, 1807/9/21, 1809/9/29; Charleston, 1806/1/3, 2/21, 1808/11/28, 12/7, 1809/2/8; New York, 1802/5/13, 1806/1/27, 2/5, 2/12, 1807/9/28; Philadelphia, 1803/3/30, 1807/3/18, 1808/1/20, 1812/4/8-O

Easter Frolics: Charleston, 1805/4/15; Philadelphia, 1813/4/19, 4/21, 1815/3/29

Easter Gambols: Philadelphia, 1807/3/30

Edgar and Emmeline: New York, 1808/7/27-V; Philadelphia, 1801/8/7-S

Edwy and Elgiva: Baltimore, 1801/5/18; Philadelphia, 1801/4/2, 4/6

Ella Rosenberg: Baltimore, 1809/11/3, 11/6, 11/13, 1810/11/3, 1811/5/15,

1812/6/5, 1813/6/4, 1815/5/17, 11/11; Boston, 1808/4/18, 4/20, 1809/4/
26, 1814/4/20, 4/25, 12/22, 1815/2/10; Charleston, 1809/3/22, 3/24, 1810/
5/5, 1811/1/5; New York, 1808/6/15, 1810/4/9, 4/11, 4/13, 4/18, 6/18, 10/
24, 11/9, 12/21, 12/26, 1811/6/14, 1812/6/15, 11/11, 1813/3/5, 1814/5/4-
A, 6/30-A, 8/22-Cr, 1815/6/19; Philadelphia, 1809/11/27, 12/4, 1810/1/17,
2/9, 12/12, 1811/2/15, 10/25, 11/1, 1812/1/4, 3/4, 10/3-O, 10/6-O, 12/2,
1813/5/8, 1814/4/16

Elopement: Baltimore, 1812/5/11; Philadelphia, 1812/2/5, 2/12

Embarassments of Harlequin: New York, 1803/6/6

Embargo: Baltimore, 1808/5/30; Boston, 1808/4/22; Charleston, 1808/4/27;
Philadelphia, 1808/3/16

Enchanted Island: Philadelphia, 1813/1/1-S

Enraged Musician: Philadelphia, 1802/3/20

Enterprize: Philadelphia, 1803/3/14

Erl King: Baltimore, 1807/11/28

Escape of Adelina (Adelina): Baltimore, 1811/3/4-P, 3/9-P, 11/23-O, 1814/1/
24-P, 1/26-P, 1/28-P, 3/2-P; New York, 1812/6/1-O, 6/11-O; Philadelphia,
1812/1/20-O, 1/21-O, 1/23-O, 1/25-O, 2/1-O, 2/4-O, 2/8-O, 2/10-O, 2/29-
O, 4/6-O, 10/15-O, 1813/11/10-C, 11/12-C, 1815/7/21-S

Exile (Exile of Siberia): Baltimore, 1811/12/17-O, 1814/5/18, 5/20, 5/23, 5/
25, 6/10, 11/14, 11/16, 1815/5/13, 10/7, 10/21, 11/8; Boston, 1811/11/20,
11/22, 11/25, 11/27, 12/2, 1812/1/13, 3/13, 9/28, 1813/10/8, 12/17, 1815/
3/8; Charleston, 1812/4/20, 4/24, 4/30; New York, 1810/4/27, 4/30, 5/7, 6/
8, 1811/1/9, 1/16, 1814/10/26, 10/28, 11/2, 11/7, 11/14, 11/21, 12/19,
1815/1/6, 3/22, 5/5, 11/1, 12/8; Philadelphia, 1812/2/22-O, 2/24-O, 2/27-
O, 2/29-O, 3/9-O, 1814/2/18, 2/19, 2/21, 2/26, 2/28, 3/7, 3/12, 4/15, 12/
23, 12/31, 1815/2/25, 12/9, 12/30

Fairies Rivals: New York, 1805/6/19

Faithful Wife: Boston, 1814/4/13

False Alarms: Boston, 1809/2/6, 2/8, 2/15, 2/24, 4/14

False and True: Baltimore, 1805/4/20, 1809/11/14; Charleston, 1809/1/12;
Philadelphia, 1805/3/13, 1808/3/21, 1809/11/29, 1812/2/5

Farmer: Baltimore, 1802/5/21, 1803/11/23, 1805/4/11, 11/15, 1806/4/16,
1809/11/1; Boston, 1801/3/4, 3/6, 5/15, 1802/4/5, 1803/4/13, 10/19, 1804/
11/9, 1805/10/9, 1807/5/4, 1810/11/12, 1813/11/24; Charleston, 1802/2/5,
5/1, 1803/11/11, 1804/1/31, 12/7, 1805/11/18, 1806/4/30, 1807/5/30, 11/
18, 1808/1/8, 1809/1/16, 1810/4/4, 1811/3/15, 1812/2/24; New York,
1802/6/16, 1806/3/28, 4/8, 6/18, 1807/10/28, 1808/6/17, 1811/12/2, 1812/
5/8; Philadelphia, 1804/3/24, 1805/1/18, 1806/2/19, 1809/3/30, 12/18,
1813/5/15, 1815/4/7

Farmer's Wife: New York, 1814/9/26, 9/28, 10/3, 10/21, 12/9

Fashionable Barber: Baltimore, 1811/2/13-P, 2/15-P; New York, 1803/8/1-MV; Philadelphia, 1813/8/3-G

Federal Oath (pant.): Philadelphia, 1802/7/7-S

Festival of Peace: New York, 1815/2/20, 2/22, 2/23, 2/27

Fete des Vendanges: Philadelphia, 1802/4/12

Feudal Times: Boston, 1809/3/20; Philadelphia, 1812/3/13

Fille d'Hungerie: Boston, 1807/1/14, 5/13; Charleston, 1806/3/26; New York, 1805/5/24

Fille Hussar (Female Hussar): Baltimore, 1814/2/5-P, 2/7-P, 2/9-P, 2/12-P; New York, 1803/6/13, 6/15, 6/17; Philadelphia, 1812/3/7-O, 3/9-O, 3/10-O, 3/16-O, 5/2-O

Finger Post: Baltimore, 1807/5/6, 10/5; Boston, 1806/12/26, 12/31, 1807/1/2; Charleston, 1806/12/10, 12/15, 12/22, 1807/2/20; New York, 1806/11/26, 12/3; Philadelphia, 1807/1/28, 2/7, 1808/2/12

Fire King: Boston, 1806/3/17

Flitch of Bacon: Baltimore, 1801/5/11, 1804/10/10, 1805/5/3, 1807/11/6; Boston, 1807/5/25, 12/14, 1809/12/11; Charleston, 1805/5/6; Philadelphia, 1804/12/29, 1807/12/30

Flora: Baltimore, 1806/5/23; Boston, 1802/3/19; Charleston, 1806/3/5

Follies of a Day: Baltimore, 1804/11/19, 11/24, 1805/10/19, 1806/4/25, 1807/6/9, 1809/5/12; Boston, 1804/4/16; Charleston, 1801/3/30, 1805/4/29; New York, 1806/5/5; Philadelphia, 1801/3/2, 1805/2/23, 1806/1/17, 1809/1/4, 1810/2/12, 1813/3/5, 1814/3/16

Fontainebleau (A Trip to Fontainebleau): Baltimore, 1801/4/25, 5/16, 1805/11/22, 1806/5/7, 10/24; Charleston, 1808/5/25; Philadelphia, 1801/2/25, 11/11, 12/23, 1806/2/14

For Freedom Ho: New York, 1815/4/5, 4/10, 4/17

Forest of Hermanstadt: Baltimore, 1814/5/9, 1815/6/3; New York, 1809/9/29, 10/2, 10/9, 12/2, 1810/3/19; Philadelphia, 1814/4/15, 1815/1/11

Forêt Noire: Baltimore, 1802/4/19; Boston, 1802/4/7, 1803/1/28, 2/4, 1804/3/16, 1805/1/14, 12/20, 1806/10/17, 1809/3/17; Charleston, 1803/3/14, 1807/5/27; New York, 1801/1/28, 1/30, 2/11, 2/25, 1803/12/2, 1804/6/4, 1811/7/4, 7/5, 1814/7/20-Cr; Philadelphia, 1802/4/7, 1811/2/16, 3/11

Fortress: Baltimore, 1808/5/16, 5/25, 1809/5/6, 11/6, 1814/5/27, 11/12, 1815/10/27; Boston, 1811/3/29, 4/1, 4/3, 4/22, 1812/1/23, 3/16, 4/24, 10/12; Charleston, 1809/1/14, 1/19, 3/14; New York, 1808/4/22, 4/25, 5/2, 5/26, 1815/3/17, 3/20; Philadelphia, 1808/2/26, 3/2, 3/16, 4/1, 4/21, 12/24, 1809/1/6, 1810/3/10, 1812/3/11, 11/2, 1814/3/28, 1815/2/27

Forty Thieves: Baltimore, 1809/5/12, 5/13, 5/15, 5/17, 5/20, 11/14, 1810/5/
26, 11/16, 1811/5/11, 1812/4/4; Boston, 1810/3/12, 3/14, 3/16, 3/19, 3/21,
3/23, 3/26, 3/28, 3/30, 4/4, 4/9, 4/13, 5/2, 5/30, 6/1, 6/4, 10/31, 11/14, 11/
16, 11/28, 12/12, 12/26, 1811/1/2, 1/28, 2/13, 2/14, 3/4, 3/25, 4/3, 4/19, 5/
29, 11/29, 12/6, 12/23, 1812/11/25, 11/27, 12/23, 1813/1/27, 5/31, 12/27,
12/29, 1814/1/3, 1/10, 1/19, 1/28, 1/31, 2/7, 3/18, 4/4, 4/27, 11/11, 11/21,
1815/1/2, 1/20, 2/8; Charleston, 1807/12/18, 12/19, 1808/2/3, 2/19, 1809/
2/16, 1/25, 1810/3/14, 3/26; New York, 1809/3/20, 3/22, 3/24, 3/27, 3/29,
4/3, 4/5, 4/7, 4/14, 4/21, 5/1, 5/12, 6/2, 7/4, 9/15, 9/20, 10/4, 10/11, 10/16,
1811/11/15, 11/16, 11/18, 11/20, 11/22, 11/23, 11/25, 11/29, 12/7, 12/11,
12/20, 12/26, 1812/2/7, 5/22, 5/29, 6/8, 9/23, 10/21, 1813/6/11, 6/28, 9/
13, 11/10, 12/25, 1814/12/24, 12/26, 12/31, 1815/1/11, 4/3, 5/10, 6/9, 9/9,
9/29, 10/13, 10/28; Philadelphia, 1809/1/2, 1/4, 1/6, 1/9, 1/11, 1/13, 1/16,
2/3, 2/13, 2/24, 3/3, 4/3, 12/26, 12/27, 1810/1/26, 2/23, 3/10, 4/23, 12/26,
1811/2/8, 3/16, 12/2, 12/6, 12/27, 1812/1/18, 2/1, 4/13-O, 10/10, 10/17,
12/28

Foundling of the Forest: Baltimore, 1810/5/1, 5/2, 5/9, 5/14, 5/28, 10/26, 11/
10, 1811/5/8, 1812/4/1, 1813/5/21, 1814/5/11, 1815/5/8, 11/4; Boston,
1809/11/20, 11/22, 11/24, 12/26, 1810/5/4, 12/14, 1811/1/30, 1812/4/13,
10/2, 1813/4/30, 10/20, 1814/11/2, 1815/5/1, 10/18, 11/8; Charleston,
1810/4/11, 4/27, 1811/3/20, 3/27, 1812/2/27, 5/4; New York, 1809/11/27,
11/29, 12/1, 12/4, 12/13, 12/22, 12/27, 12/29, 1810/2/23, 3/2, 5/9, 6/25, 9/
12, 9/21, 1811/1/7, 5/1, 10/11, 11/9, 1812/1/27, 6/5, 1813/3/10, 6/18,
1814/6/10-A, 6/24, 1815/1/13, 2/23; Philadelphia, 1810/2/24, 2/16, 2/19,
2/26, 3/5, 3/9, 3/12, 3/19, 3/23, 3/31, 4/16, 12/3, 1811/1/19, 2/9, 2/20, 9/
18, 12/30, 1812/2/8, 3/10-O, 11/4, 1813/3/29, 4/30, 12/22, 1814/1/29-Cw,
12/12, 1815/12/6

Four Seasons: Boston, 1806/3/19, 4/14, 4/21, 11/19, 12/24, 1807/2/9, 4/9,
1810/4/6, 1811/2/1

Fourth of July: Philadelphia, 1803/3/9

Fourth of July (America, Commerce, and Freedom): New York, 1815/7/4

Free Knights: New York, 1810/6/13, 7/4

Freemen in Arms: Baltimore, 1813/5/24, 6/8; New York, 1813/7/5

Frolics in the Moon: Boston, 1807/5/15, 10/12

Fusilier: Charleston, 1808/4/18

Garden of Love: Boston, 1801/4/15

Generous Farmers: Charleston, 1803/3/28; New York, 1805/5/6; Philadelphia, 1807/3/16

Genii: Boston, 1815/4/28, 5/5, 6/12, 11/15; (Harlequin Fisherman) New
York, 1812/2/21, 2/22, 2/24

Genius of America: Boston, 1814/6/6, 10/12

Gentle Shepherd (Patie and Roger): Charleston, 1801/4/22; New York, 1803/5/23; Philadelphia, 1805/3/30

Gil Blas: Charleston, 1806/1/1, 1/6, 2/21, 5/14, 12/26; New York, 1802/12/10, 12/15, 12/24, 1803/1/29, 1814/6/24-A, 6/25-A

Glory of Columbia: Baltimore, 1807/10/24, 1809/5/1; Boston, 1807/5/8, 1812/6/1, 1814/10/26; Charleston, 1805/4/8, 4/17, 1807/12/22, 1812/5/4; New York, 1803/7/4, 7/6, 11/25, 12/24, 1804/5/12, 7/4, 1808/7/4, 1812/6/24, 1812/7/1, 1813/7/5, 1814/8/31, 11/18; Philadelphia, 1807/3/25, 7/4, 1808/1/30, 1809/2/22

Good Neighbor: New York, 1803/2/28, 3/9, 3/21, 3/23, 5/30

Grateful Lion: Baltimore, 1804/11/21; Philadelphia, 1805/3/18

Great Battle of Marengo: New York, 1805/5/15

Great Devil: New York, 1811/9/14-P

Gretna Green: Baltimore, 1803/4/23, 5/14, 10/24; Philadelphia, 1803/3/11

Hamlet Travestie: Baltimore, 1812/5/13, 5/22; Boston, 1813/4/19, 4/28, 5/31, 1814/3/16, 1815/4/19; Philadelphia, 1812/3/7

Harlequin: Philadelphia, 1814/10/28-V

Harlequin Apprentice: Philadelphia, 1813/11/5-C

Harlequin Cook: New York, 1805/11/30-I

Harlequin Doctor: Baltimore, 1811/4/19-P; New York, 1801/9/2-MV, 1804/5/14, 1814/7/11-Cr, 7/13-Cr; Philadelphia, 1801/8/19-S

Harlequin Dr. Faustus: Baltimore, 1808/6/8; Boston, 1808/12/5, 12/7; Charleston, 1809/3/23; Philadelphia, 1808/1/1, 1/2, 1/15, 12/10

Harlequin Freemason: Boston, 1802/4/9, 5/5, 5/17, 7/5, 1803/3/21, 4/6, 4/15, 4/27, 1805/4/10; Charleston, 1806/3/31, 5/22; New York, 1806/7/2

Harlequin Highlander: New York, 1812/6/13-O; Philadelphia, 1812/4/24-O, 5/14-O

Harlequin Hostler: New York, 1803/1/10

Harlequin Hurry-scurry: Baltimore, 1802/5/22, 1805/10/19; Charleston, 1810/3/20; New York, 1802/7/2, 1805/6/3, 1807/9/7-V; Philadelphia, 1801/3/13, 8/10-S, 9/28-S, 1802/1/1, 1803/3/25, 1808/3/26

Harlequin in Despair: New York, 1808/5/3-Pe

Harlequin in the Moon: Baltimore, 1806/5/26; Boston, 1807/5/1, 1808/4/22; Philadelphia, 1804/3/28, 7/4-S, 1806/2/26, 7/4, 1807/2/13, 1808/3/7, 1811/3/4, 3/13, 1812/1/22

Harlequin Junior: New York, 1804/5/3-G, 5/5-G, 5/8-G, 5/10-G, 5/12-G

Harlequin Magician: New York, 1815/7/4, 9/25, 10/16

Harlequin Magician Apprentice: Baltimore, 1811/3/29-P

Harlequin Mariner: Charleston, 1809/4/3

Harlequin Panattaha: New York, 1809/1/4, 1/5, 2/22, 3/13, 4/17

Harlequin Pastry-Cook: Baltimore, 1811/4/17-P; Philadelphia, 1813/7/20-G, 9/11-G

Harlequin Patriot: New York, 1814/8/26-Cr

Harlequin Pluto: New York, 1815/1/2, 1/4, 1/9

Harlequin Prisoner: Baltimore, 1803/10/22, 10/26, 11/21; Philadelphia, 1803/ 3/16, 4/1, 1804/2/13

Harlequin Prodigal: New York, 1814/1/3-Cw

Harlequin Protected by a Lion: New York, 1805/8/28-I

Harlequin Protected by Cupid: Philadelphia, 1813/7/30-G

Harlequin Ranger: Boston, 1803/3/7, 3/18, 4/1, 4/18

Harlequin Recruit: New York, 1801/7/4, 7/17, 1803/1/19; Philadelphia, 1801/9/21-S

Harlequin Restored: Baltimore, 1804/6/5; Philadelphia, 1803/12/26

Harlequin Sailor: Boston, 1807/5/11

Harlequin Salamander: Boston, 1812/4/29, 6/1

Harlequin Shipwrecked: New York, 1814/1/1, 1/7, 1/10; Philadelphia, 1809/ 3/15

Harlequin Skeleton: Baltimore, 1813/4/8-C; Boston, 1810/4/27; Charleston, 1806/1/13, 1/29, 4/21; New York, 1811/8/2-P; Philadelphia, 1813/7/16-G, 9/2-G

Harlequin Statue: Baltimore, 1811/3/27-P, 4/1-P, 11/30-O, 1813/3/17-C, 3/ 26-C; New York, 1811/07/19-P; Philadelphia, 1803/8/23-S, 1813/8/10-G

Harlequin Tammany: Philadelphia, 1801/7/4

Harlequin the English Dog: New York, 1805/11/28-I

Harlequin the Magicians's Apprentice: New York, 1805/5/10-I

Harlequin Transformed Into a Dog: Philadelphia, 1813/7/13-G

Harlequin Turn'd Barber: New York, 1804/5/28

Harlequin Turned Washerwoman: Philadelphia, 1802/4/9

Harlequin Valetudinarian: New York, 1805/8/2-I

Harlequin Volunteer: New York, 1804/5/23

Harlequin Woodcutter: New York, 1814/7/25-Cr, 7/27-Cr

Harlequin's Almanac: Philadelphia, 1803/4/2, 4/4

Harlequin's Choice: Boston, 1808/3/25, 4/14, 4/25

Harlequin's Frolic: Boston, 1801/2/9, 3/29, 1806/12/15, 1807/11/11, 12/2, 1809/5/5, 1814/1/5; New York, 1804/5/24-G

Harlequin's Invasion: Baltimore, 1805/6/1, 1806/11/25; Boston, 1801/4/27, 12/28; Charleston, 1801/2/25; New York, 1805/5/13, 12/24; Philadelphia, 1801/12/21, 1807/3/9

Harlequin's Jubilee: Boston, 1809/3/6, 4/24, 11/3
Harlequin's Medley: Boston: 1808/10/17
Harlequin's Release: Boston, 1804/4/13, 5/4
Harlequin's Restoration: Charleston, 1811/5/7
Harlequin's Statue: New York, 1804/4/25, 4/27, 4/28, 4/30, 5/2, 5/4
Harlequin's Triumph in War and Love: New York, 1810/1/22-C
Harlequin's Vagaries: Baltimore, 1805/5/29; Boston, 1806/10/22, 11/10,
    1808/7/4; New York, 1805/6/10; Philadelphia, 1805/3/23, 1807/7/4
Haunted Tower: Charleston, 1802/3/8, 1809/1/12, 2/1; New York, 1807/4/3;
    Philadelphia, 1808/3/21
Hear Both Sides: Baltimore, 1804/4/16; Boston, 1804/3/23, 3/28; Charleston,
    1803/5/3; New York, 1803/5/2; Philadelphia, 1804/2/27
Heiress: New York, 1801/5/1
Hercules and Omphale: Baltimore, 1802/5/8, 5/12, 5/13, 5/17, 6/7, 12/1,
    1803/5/4, 6/9, 10/15, 1806/5/31, 1815/5/29; Philadelphia, 1802/2/22, 2/24,
    2/27, 3/3, 3/4, 3/5, 12/27, 12/29, 1803/1/22, 1808/3/14, 1812/12/26, 12/
    30, 1814/1/24
Hero of the North: Baltimore, 1804/6/7, 11/2, 1812/4/24, 1814/6/8; Boston,
    1814/4/27, 5/30, 11/18, 1815/1/13; New York, 1804/5/7, 5/9, 1814/4/22,
    4/25, 4/27, 5/2, 5/6, 6/3, 10/14, 12/26, 1815/1/5, 6/21, 12/13; Philadelphia,
    1804/4/2, 4/3, 12/19, 1812/2/17, 1814/3/23
Heroes of the Lakes: Baltimore, 1813/10/1, 10/4; Boston, 1813/10/15, 10/18,
    10/25, 1814/1/12; New York, 1813/10/20, 10/23, 10/27; Philadelphia,
    1813/11/22
Highland Reel: Baltimore, 1801/6/6, 1802/5/24, 1803/11/12, 1805/11/4,
    1810/6/6, 11/7, 1811/6/3, 12/26-O, 1814/4/25, 6/1, 10/12, 1815/6/7, 10/
    11; Boston, 1801/3/11, 1802/1/27, 3/4, 12/8, 1803/2/9, 11/21, 1804/4/9,
    11/30, 1805/2/8, 3/25, 1807/3/13, 11/23, 1808/11/9, 1809/4/5, 11/29,
    1810/2/13, 1812/2/19, 1814/11/18; Charleston, 1801/5/1, 1802/1/20, 2/3,
    11/17, 1803/2/17, 12/16, 1804/2/6, 12/27, 1806/3/3, 4/18, 12/6, 12/10,
    1807/1/23, 12/2, 12/28, 1808/5/23, 12/16, 1810/4/13, 1811/4/29, 1815/12/
    13; New York, 1801/1/9, 3/9, 4/24, 6/29, 9/1-MV, 12/16, 1802/2/19, 3/31,
    5/5, 6/9, 9/20-MV, 10/27, 1803/1/26, 3/25, 3/26, 7/20-MV, 1805/5/8, 1806/
    5/21, 1807/1/19, 2/9, 2/20, 1809/6/9, 1812/1/31, 3/30, 10/7, 1813/2/22,
    1814/2/25, 1815/3/13, 4/7, 5/12; Philadelphia, 1801/9/7S, 1802/1/25, 12/
    22, 1804/3/3, 1805/3/25, 1808/2/6, 1809/3/20, 1810/3/24, 12/7, 1811/4/
    15, 9/16, 1812/2/6-O, 1813/12/15, 1814/1/21, 12/10, 1815/1/18
Hit or Miss: Baltimore, 1811/5/8; Charleston, 1811/4/15; New York, 1810/
    12/5, 12/10, 12/17; Philadelphia, 1810/12/29, 1811/1/9

Honest Yorkshireman: 1807/5/18; Philadelphia, 1807/4/8

Honey Moon: Baltimore, 1806/4/18, 4/21, 5/7, 5/16, 5/26, 10/13, 10/24, 11/
10, 1807/5/11, 10/7, 1809/4/7, 1811/5/20, 12/18-O, 1812/5/29, 1813/11/
17, 1814/10/22; Boston, 1805/11/1, 11/4, 11/6, 11/8, 11/11, 11/13, 11/25,
1806/1/22, 12/1, 1807/3/26, 10/2, 1808/11/18, 12/5, 1810/1/10, 10/15,
1811/4/29, 11/15, 1812/9/30, 1813/1/25, 3/5, 1814/2/23, 12/22, 1815/2/
22, 12/14; Charleston, 1805/12/28, 1806/1/22, 11/26, 4/25, 1807/2/25, 4/
24, 1808/12/19, 2/22, 1/14, 1809/2/25, 1810/2/14, 1812/4/2, 4/4; New
York, 1805/5/29, 6/10, 1806/5/12, 11/5, 11/10, 12/1, 12/26, 1807/9/14, 10/
9, 12/16, 1808/9/16, 1809/4/19, 11/6, 1810/6/6, 10/8, 10/13, 10/29, 1811/
1/11, 10/9, 12/26, 1812/10/9, 12/4, 1813/5/19, 9/29, 10/29, 1814/1/10-Cw,
1/24, 5/13, 6/6, 1815/1/9, 3/6, 4/5, 5/1, 7/10, 9/8, 10/4, 11/10; Philadelphia,
1806/2/24, 3/15, 4/2, 4/7, 12/8, 12/29, 1807/1/21, 2/14, 7/8, 12/28, 1808/
2/24, 12/10, 1809/4/1, 1810/4/2, 1811/10/5, 1812/1/20, 1/25, 1/28-O, 6/
29-O, 10/10, 12/4, 1813/5/3, 1814/1/17-Cw, 1/21, 1/21-Cw, 1815/2/6

House to be Sold: Baltimore, 1804/5/14, 5/26, 11/2, 1805/5/27, 1807/6/8;
Charleston, 1807/2/2, 2/6, 4/22, 1810/2/12, 3/23; New York, 1803/5/25,
12/28, 1804/1/4, 1/13, 1807/6/26-U, 1809/1/26-L, 2/2-L; Philadelphia,
1804/2/1, 2/3, 2/24, 12/7, 1805/1/5, 1807/3/21

Hunt the Slipper: Boston: 1801/12/30, 1802/1/13, 5/12, 11/15, 1803/12/16,
1804/1/6, 12/19, 1805/1/18, 1809/12/18, 1810/1/12, 5/18, 1811/4/15;
Charleston, 1806/1/22

Hunter of the Alps: Baltimore, 1805/11/6, 11/11, 11/28, 1806/6/4, 10/3,
1810/10/24, 1815/4/26; Boston, 1807/10/21, 10/23, 10/26, 11/11, 11/18,
12/9, 1808/1/11, 7/4, 10/28, 1809/10/20, 1810/6/1, 12/17, 1812/2/24,
1813/3/1, 1814/5/30; Charleston, 1807/1/8, 1/12, 2/20, 3/14, 4/19, 1808/2/
26, 12/19, 1810/5/3, 1811/4/8; New York, 1805/5/22, 1807/8/10-V, 8/22-
V, 11/11, 11/13, 11/30, 1808/3/21, 7/20-V, 1810/3/26, 4/6, 9/21, 1812/2/3;
Philadelphia, 1805/12/11, 1806/1/10, 3/8, 4/9, 1807/2/9, 4/13, 1808/1/16,
1810/3/16, 1811/1/23, 3/29, 11/4, 11/15, 1814/1/15, 2/26, 1815/4/10,
12/29

Hurry Scurry: Boston, 1811/12/27, 1812/3/18; Charleston, 1811/4/29

Huzza for Commerce: Boston, 1809/6/5, 7/4

Huzza for the Constitution: Boston, 1813/2/22, 2/24, 3/19, 3/29

Imaginary Sick Man: Baltimore, 1811/3/25-P, 4/5-P; Philadelphia, 1813/
7/9-G

Independence: Charleston, 1805/3/30, 1806/2/26

Indian Princess: Baltimore, 1808/6/4; Charleston, 1809/4/11, 1810/3/16;
New York, 1809/6/14, 6/23; Philadelphia, 1808/4/6, 1809/2/1

Indiscretion: Boston, 1801/1/1, 1/5
Inkle and Yarico: Baltimore, 1803/11/19, 1811/12/7-O; Boston, 1801/1/2, 1/
    12, 12/4, 1802/2/3, 11/5, 1803/2/14, 1804/1/30, 7/6, 1805/1/16, 10/23,
    1807/11/6, 1808/2/17, 1809/7/4, 1812/2/14, 12/21, 1813/10/22; Charles-
    ton, 1801/4/25, 1802/2/22, 3/15, 12/10, 12/11, 1806/2/10, 1807/5/8; New
    York, 1801/6/19, 1804/4/2-G, 4/14-G, 5/8-G, 5/10-G, 1806/6/9, 6/16, 10/
    31, 11/25, 1807/9/18, 12/4, 1808/3/4, 10/19, 1809/4/19, 1810/7/2, 1815/6/
    21, 10/20; Philadelphia, 1801/9/21-S, 1802/2/8, 1804/2/29, 1807/3/13,
    1812/12/5-S, 1813/6/19-Cw, 1814/2/24-Cw, 1815/3/25
Invisible Girl: Baltimore, 1807/6/9, 6/10, 11/28, 1808/4/25, 1810/10/20,
    1811/5/31, 1812/4/8, 1813/5/17; Charleston, 1809/4/11; New York, 1807/
    1/26, 1/30, 2/18; Philadelphia, 1807/12/11, 1808/2/8, 1810/11/30, 1811/
    10/4, 1812/2/12, 1813/2/15
Irish Fair: Baltimore, 1805/6/3; Philadelphia, 1805/3/18
Irish Widow: Baltimore, 1804/6/1, 1811/5/24; Charleston, 1801/1/24, 11/27,
    1804/11/26, 1807/12/26; New York, 1815/12/11, 12/20; Philadelphia,
    1804/3/14, 1811/2/11, 3/1, 9/27
Irishman in London: Baltimore, 1803/11/14, 1804/4/23, 1805/4/8, 1807/5/27,
    10/9, 1811/12/20-O, 1813/5/29, 1814/11/19, 1815/11/3; Boston, 1802/4/
    14, 12/31, 1806/2/12, 1807/9/21, 1813/12/1, 12/15, 1814/10/7, 1815/1/13,
    12/4; Charleston, 1801/4/29, 5/6, 1802/3/10, 3/24, 1805/11/15, 12/24,
    1808/11/11, 11/28, 1809/2/13, 1811/2/26, 1812/2/19; New York, 1801/9/
    28-MV, 1802/1/29, 1805/6/3, 1806/7/11-V, 1809/3/1, 3/24, 1811/1/9, 1/14,
    2/11, 10/7, 11/9, 11/20, 1812/2/5, 1814/6/6-A, 1815/9/6-Cw; Philadelphia,
    1801/8/31-S, 1803/12/28, 1804/6/25-S, 1805/3/13, 1806/4/5, 1810/2/14, 2/
    19, 4/18, 1811/2/6, 4/30, 6/21-A, 7/4-A, 11/18, 1812/1/11-O, 11/30-S, 12/
    18-S, 1813/1/6, 5/28, 1814/2/5-Cw, 3/19
Iron Chest: Baltimore, 1805/5/31, 1810/11/14, 1815/10/11; Boston, 1806/11/
    21, 11/24, 11/26, 1812/11/6, 11/13, 1814/12/19, 12/26; Charleston, 1807/
    3/16, 1815/12/18; New York, 1807/1/9, 1/12, 10/12, 1812/1/29, 1813/3/
    26, 1814/3/11, 1815/3/10; Philadelphia, 1810/3/16, 1814/3/19
Italian Monk: Charleston, 1803/3/4, 3/9, 3/16
Jack in Distress: Baltimore, 1811/3/15-P; Boston, 1804/4/20, 1805/3/25;
    Charleston, 1809/1/27, 3/18, 1810/3/12, 4/4
Joanna of Montfaucon: Baltimore, 1802/5/21; New York, 1801/1/23, 1/26;
    Philadelphia, 1802/2/5, 2/13
John Bull: Baltimore: 1803/5/23, 5/25, 6/8, 10/24, 10/28, 11/7, 1804/5/2, 5/
    12, 10/15, 1805/6/3, 10/30, 1806/5/23, 11/15, 1808/6/1, 1809/4/22, 1810/
    11/17; Boston, 1803/11/25, 11/28, 11/30, 12/2, 12/5, 12/7, 1804/1/23, 2/8,

3/16, 11/28, 12/17, 1805/2/20, 10/4, 1806/11/19, 1808/10/5, 3/22, 1810/
10/17, 1813/11/15, 11/22, 1814/1/24, 11/7, 1815/1/23, 12/1; Charleston,
1803/11/23, 11/28, 12/3, 1804/2/8, 2/18, 5/28, 12/14, 1805/12/4, 1806/11/
21, 1807/1/12, 1808/1/20, 2/26, 12/12, 1810/3/21, 1811/1/16, 1815/11/10;
New York, 1803/11/21, 11/23, 11/28, 12/2, 12/12, 12/19, 12/26, 1804/1/4,
1/18, 2/15, 3/17, 3/23, 5/16, 6/13, 11/2, 12/24, 1805/3/22, 1806/4/9, 6/21,
1807/2/2, 2/13, 1808/5/2, 5/6, 11/18, 1809/1/4, 6/10, 1810/6/20, 1811/1/
30, 6/28, 1814/4/6, 1815/3/15; Philadelphia, 1804/1/2, 1/6, 1/11, 2/8, 7/6S,
12/3, 1805/2/16, 1806/3/5, 1807/1/31, 1808/2/1, 1809/1/25, 1810/1/27,
1811/3/9, 1812/1/11-O, 3/9, 1815/2/24

Jovial Crew: Baltimore, 1813/5/26; Philadelphia, 1813/3/10, 3/15

Jubilee: Baltimore, 1802/6/3; Boston, 1803/4/11; Charleston, 1804/4/30,
1812/4/28; New York: 1801/5/18, 1802/5/24, 1803/4/11, 1805/11/25; Philadelphia, 1801/3/11, 1802/3/31, 1805/3/15, 1807/2/14, 1808/3/23, 1814/
3/21

Jupiter and Europa: Charleston, 1803/3/2, 3/7, 3/11, 3/23, 3/24, 4/28, 12/5,
1804/2/13, 12/10, 1805/2/19, 1806/1/8, 1/11, 1808/4/6; New York, 1806/
7/4, 10/17

Killing No Murder: Baltimore, 1810/5/21, 5/28, 10/15, 1811/5/3, 1812/4/10,
1813/10/11, 1814/10/19; New York, 1812/1/24, 1/27, 1/29, 1814/3/14, 3/
18, 3/25, 4/27, 6/3, 11/11, 12/12, 1815/3/1, 4/24, 10/7; Philadelphia, 1810/
1/19, 1/24, 1/29, 2/10, 3/31, 12/1, 1811/4/6, 12/23, 1812/10/19, 1813/1/1,
1814/1/14, 2/19, 11/30, 1815/1/25

King Arthur (Arthur and Emmeline): Baltimore, 1805/6/5; Philadelphia,
1805/3/22

Kiss: Baltimore, 1813/11/18, 1814/4/29; Boston, 1812/10/12, 10/14, 10/19,
10/28, 12/16, 1814/11/9; Charleston, 1812/5/15; New York, 1812/6/8, 6/
10; Philadelphia, 1813/12/3, 12/15, 1814/4/11, 1815/4/8

Knight of Snowdoun: Boston, 1812/3/30, 4/1, 4/3, 4/30, 10/7; New York,
1811/6/12

Knights of Calatrava: Baltimore, 1803/11/4, 11/9, 11/16; Philadelphia, 1803/
12/27

Lady of the Lake: Baltimore, 1812/4/3, 4/6, 4/13, 5/2, 6/3, 1813/10/8, 10/15,
10/25, 1814/4/27, 5/7, 1815/6/9, 6/10, 10/14, 11/3, 11/18; Charleston,
1812/2/28, 3/2, 3/13; New York, 1812/5/8, 5/11, 5/15, 6/15, 9/25, 1814/6/
24, 1815/10/7, 10/14; Philadelphia, 1812/1/1, 1/3, 1/6, 1/10, 1/24, 1/29, 2/
10, 10/24, 11/7, 1813/12/27, 1814/2/2, 1815/4/14, 1815/12/16, 12/23

Lady of the Rock: Baltimore, 1809/5/19, 5/22, 5/27, 6/7, 1810/11/14; Boston,
1809/5/12, 6/5, 9/20, 11/15; Charleston, 1807/3/16, 4/1; New York, 1805/

6/17, 1806/6/13; Philadelphia, 1809/3/17, 3/24, 3/29, 4/7, 12/1, 1810/1/12, 1/31, 1811/2/1, 4/22, 11/30, 1813/3/31, 1815/3/27

Lafitte: Boston, 1814/11/28

Lewis of Monte Blanco: New York, 1804/3/12, 3/14, 3/19, 4/2, 4/9, 4/13, 11/9, 12/26; Philadelphia, 1806/3/10

Life: Baltimore, 1802/5/19; Boston, 1801/12/11, 12/16, 1802/2/1, 1804/1/20, 1808/6/6, 1809/1/20, 1814/4/11; Charleston, 1802/5/3, 5/17, 1803/2/12, 2/14, 3/24; New York, 1801/4/24, 4/27, 4/29, 5/22; Philadelphia, 1802/1/1, 1/4, 1/18

Life and Death of Harlequin: Baltimore, 1811/2/8-P, 2/27-P, 12/14-O, 1813/3/22-C, 1814/1/15-P, 1/21-P; New York, 1803/7/27-MV, 1811/7/4-P, 9/7-P; Philadelphia, 1812/2/27-O, 1813/8/13-G

Lilliputian Frolic: Philadelphia, 1807/7/30-S

Lionel and Clarissa: Baltimore, 1806/5/19; Philadelphia, 1806/3/12

Lise et Colin: New York, 1804/12/24, 12/26, 12/28

Little Bob and Little Ben: Boston, 1810/4/11

Little Red Riding Hood: Baltimore, 1813/5/14, 5/17, 5/31, 10/22, 1814/5/28, 10/26, 1815/5/17, 10/28; Boston, 1815/4/26, 10/11, 12/15; Philadelphia, 1812/12/7-S, 12/12-S, 1813/3/31, 4/2, 4/7, 4/14, 12/3, 1814/1/14, 2/11, 1815/1/7, 3/27

Lock and Key: Baltimore, 1801/5/6, 1802/4/28, 11/22, 1803/10/6, 1805/6/4, 1806/6/2, 11/24, 1807/12/1, 1815/11/1, 11/22; Boston, 1801/2/2, 2/4, 2/6, 2/13, 1802/4/28, 11/24; Charleston, 1802/2/17, 5/7, 12/15, 12/16, 1803/2/26, 1805/11/25, 1806/2/24, 1807/5/20, 1808/5/2, 12/17, 1810/3/2, 4/14, 1812/3/20, 3/21, 4/2, 4/8, 1815/11/24, 12/1, 12/30; New York, 1802/6/25, 1803/2/2, 2/5, 2/25, 11/18, 11/25, 1806/3/21, 1807/3/20, 4/10, 9/4-V, 10/5, 11/23, 1808/6/20, 10/31, 1809/4/5, 5/15, 11/19, 1810/11/19, 1811/2/6, 3/1, 4/19, 5/3, 5/8, 7/1, 9/2, 1812/3/16, 6/26, 9/7, 12/19, 12/21, 1814/1/8, 1/26, 1815/7/19, 9/13; Philadelphia, 1801/10/21, 1803/1/5, 12/14, 1806/2/24, 1807/4/15, 1812/2/21, 3/12-O, 3/20-O

Lodoiska: Boston, 1806/3/3, 3/5, 3/7, 3/10, 3/12, 3/14, 12/26, 12/31, 1807/1/5, 3/30, 10/19, 11/9, 11/13, 1808/1/20, 1809/5/1, 1811/5/3, 5/13, 1812/10/16, 11/20, 1813/10/11, 12/10, 1814/11/4; Charleston, 1807/3/20, 3/23; New York, 1808/6/13, 6/17, 7/4, 9/21; Philadelphia, 1810/3/28

Lord of the Manor: Philadelphia, 1805/3/8

Lost and Found: Boston, 1812/11/16, 11/18, 11/30; New York, 1812/4/29

Love and Money: Baltimore, 1807/6/1; New York, 1806/6/11; Philadelphia, 1807/3/18, 1815/2/24

Love for Love I Promise Him: Baltimore, 1808/5/11; Philadelphia, 1808/3/19

Love in a Village: Baltimore, 1807/4/29, 10/1; Boston, 1807/9/14, 1814/1/7;

Charleston, 1801/11/21, 1805/3/15, 1806/2/14, 1808/11/11, 11/23; New York, 1801/8/25-MV, 9/11/-MV, 1802/6/5, 1805/12/16; Philadelphia, 1806/12/17, 1807/2/16, 1812/3/5-O

Love Laughs at Locksmiths: Baltimore, 1804/5/25, 5/28, 10/22, 1808/5/23, 10/17, 1809/5/3, 6/6, 1810/10/31, 1815/10/16; Boston, 1805/12/23, 12/27, 1806/1/8, 1/20, 1/29, 2/26, 3/28, 4/16, 1807/4/13, 5/8, 12/30, 1808/12/28, 1810/10/8, 11/7, 1811/5/1, 1812/4/29, 1813/2/26, 4/12, 11/3, 12/13, 1814/2/25; Charleston, 1805/5/31, 12/9, 12/14, 1806/2/20, 4/25, 12/27, 1807/2/4, 12/16, 1808/1/9, 12/10, 12/21, 1810/2/10, 1811/1/11, 5/9, 1815/11/3, 11/17, 12/23; New York, 1804/5/23, 1806/12/26, 12/31, 1807/1/16, 2/4, 2/16, 4/8, 9/21, 11/20, 1808/3/9, 5/18, 9/14, 10/21, 11/7, 1809/12/4, 12/20, 1810/4/2, 1811/3/25, 9/23, 10/4, 10/16, 1812/9/11, 10/28, 1814/8/24-Cr, 10/10, 1815/1/16, 2/15, 2/24, 5/15; Philadelphia, 1805/2/11, 2/15, 2/27, 3/16, 1808/12/19, 1/28, 1809/1/23, 12/22, 1810/4/16, 1811/1/25, 1812/1/17, 2/8-O, 4/3-O, 10/5, 1813/4/22, 1814/2/14-Cw, 1815/3/29

Love of Country: Philadelphia, 1813/7/5-Cw

Love Triumphant: New York, 1802/6/2

Love's Offering: Charleston, 1804/6/7

Love's Stratagem: New York, 1807/9/21, 9/25, 10/9

Lovers' Frolicks: Boston, 1807/11/20

Lovers' Jest: Boston, 1806/11/5, 11/26, 1807/1/7, 3/20

Lucille and Lauzdeman: New York, 1811/8/26-P, 1811/8/30-P

Lucky Escape: Philadelphia, 1801/3/27

M.P.: New York, 1812/6/12

Macbeth: Baltimore, 1801/5/25, 1802/5/7, 1803/5/31, 1805/5/17, 1808/4/25, 1810/10/17, 1812/4/11, 5/20, 1814/11/5; Boston, 1801/5/11, 1802/11/15, 1803/7/8, 1804/11/5, 12/21, 1805/3/13, 10/28, 1806/1/15, 1807/1/26, 2/20, 9/28, 1808/2/15, 1809/12/4, 1811/1/18, 1812/1/27, 2/7, 1813/2/15, 1814/2/14, 12/12, 1815/1/30, 12/22; Charleston, 1801/3/2, 1802/2/9, 12/8, 1803/12/9, 1804/12/15, 1806/1/24, 4/16, 5/13, 5/15, 1807/1/6, 4/28, 1808/11/21, 1809/2/10, 1810/2/28; 1811/4/8, 4/19, 1812/4/16, 4/22; New York, 1801/11/30, 12/24, 1802/10/18, 1803/1/5, 11/30, 1804/5/11, 10/29, 11/19, 12/12, 1806/1/15, 3/10, 12/29, 1807/1/5, 1/16, 10/26, 1808/5/16, 10/17, 12/7, 1809/4/24, 9/29, 1810/5/18, 12/10, 1811/2/13, 4/10, 9/20, 12/13, 12/30, 1812/10/2, 12/30, 1813/5/21, 5/24, 9/20, 10/22, 12/1, 1814/4/20, 10/5, 1815/3/8, 11/8; Philadelphia, 1801/2/6, 1802/1/22, 1803/1/1, 2/12, 1805/1/16, 1806/1/27, 3/17, 1807/1/12, 12/11, 1808/12/21, 1810/1/5, 11/28, 1811/1/28, 4/11, 10/4, 11/13, 1812/2/15, 10/28, 1813/12/6, 1815/2/8, 12/18

Magic Chamber: New York, 1801/7/15, 7/24

Magic Oak: Baltimore, 1805/11/23

Magic Rock: Boston, 1815/5/29

Magic Shades: Baltimore, 1814/3/2-P

Magic Tower: New York, 1808/8/15-V, 8/17-V, 8/19-V

Magician No Conjuror: Baltimore, 1803/6/4

Magician of the Enchanted Castle: Philadelphia, 1813/3/17

Mahmoud the Robber: Charleston, 1804/5/31

Maid of the Mill: Charleston, 1802/4/26

Maid of the Oaks: Boston, 1801/1/28, 1804/4/11, 1805/2/20, 3/22, 1806/11/
   17, 1807/12/11, 1812/5/4, 10/26; Charleston, 1802/4/12, 1804/3/13; New
   York, 1801/1/26, 12/18, 1806/4/21, 1814/5/20-A; Philadelphia, 1801/11/
   25, 1810/12/19, 1812/1/14-O, 1/16-O

Manhattan Stage: New York, 1806/4/11

Mareschal de Logis: Philadelphia, 1813/8/27-G

Marian: Baltimore, 1807/5/1; Philadelphia, 1807/1/30, 2/2

Marmion: Baltimore, 1813/11/10, 11/12, 11/16, 1814/4/30; Boston, 1815/4/
   26, 5/3; New York, 1812/4/13, 4/15, 4/17, 4/22, 4/24, 4/27, 5/1, 5/4, 5/6,
   11/9, 1815/1/23, 1/27, 3/27, 6/28, 11/3, 11/14; Philadelphia, 1812/3/30-O,
   4/1-O, 4/3-O, 4/4-O, 1813/1/1, 1/2, 1/4, 1/11, 1/18, 2/5, 2/15, 12/10, 12/
   24, 1814/1/10, 2/8, 3/9

Marriage Promise: Baltimore, 1803/10/31, 11/2, 1804/10/13; Boston, 1804/
   2/24, 2/27, 2/29; Charleston, 1804/3/5, 3/9, 1807/1/30, 2/14, 11/30, 12/18;
   New York, 1804/1/11, 1/13, 1/16, 1/25, 1/30, 3/21, 10/31, 1806/5/21; Philadelphia, 1803/12/28, 1804/1/4

Matrimony: Baltimore, 1806/5/14, 5/16, 1807/10/23, 1812/4/20; Boston,
   1808/11/11, 11/14, 12/12; Charleston, 1807/3/9, 1808/4/6; New York,
   1805/5/17, 6/12, 1808/7/15-V, 7/22-V, 9/5-V, 1811/2/4, 2/8, 4/8, 1813/12/
   6, 1814/8/17-Cr; Philadelphia, 1806/3/7, 1807/3/26, 1811/2/18, 3/27, 11/
   2, 11/16, 1812/12/23, 1814/3/9, 1815/1/23

Medea and Jason: Charleston, 1807/3/9; New York, 1801/5/20, 6/1, 1803/6/
   27, 1805/6/3, 6/21

Merry Gardener: New York, 1802/2/3, 2/5, 2/12, 2/17, 4/9

Merry Hunters: Baltimore, 1811/4/10-P; New York, 1811/8/21-P; Philadelphia, 1812/3/21-O, 1813/12/4-C

Merry Hunters of Ardanne: New York, 1808/11/30-P

Metamorphoses of the Gardner [sic]: Philadelphia, 1813/8/17-G

Midas: Boston, 1804/5/7, 1805/2/27, 1809/2/13, 2/24, 3/3, 10/2, 1810/2/26;
   Charleston, 1804/5/7, 5/21, 12/17, 1809/4/7, 1810/3/6; Philadelphia, 1807/
   3/30

Miller and His Men: Baltimore, 1815/5/19, 5/20, 10/25; Boston, 1815/1/23,

1/25, 1/27, 2/3, 2/17, 3/3, 4/12, 5/24, 10/20, 11/27; Charleston, 1815/12/
20, 12/22, 12/26, 12/27; New York, 1814/7/4, 8/31, 9/12, 1815/6/16, 9/22;
Philadelphia, 1815/3/1, 3/4, 3/11, 3/18, 12/2

Millers: Boston, 1804/11/7, 11/16; New York, 1805/3/27, 1811/9/19-P

Milliners: Boston, 1804/10/26, Charleston, 1804/4/12, 1805/3/15, 1806/3/10,
1810/2/26

Miraculous Mill: Baltimore, 1803/10/14, 10/29, 11/18, 1804/4/27, 1805/4/
13, 1812/4/20, 1813/6/5, 10/30, 11/15, 1815/4/29, 10/23; Philadelphia,
1803/12/23, 1804/1/13, 3/2, 1805/2/20, 1813/2/19, 2/20, 12/13, 1814/1/
29, 2/16, 1815/4/5, 12/2

Mirth and Magic: Boston, 1809/5/31

Mirth by Moonlight: Baltimore, 1813/6/2; Philadelphia, 1813/3/5, 3/8, 3/22

Mirza and Lindor: 1804/11/19; Charleston, 1806/3/12, 4/28; New York,
1805/2/18

Mock Doctor: Baltimore, 1807/11/11; Boston, 1802/1/20, 1810/5/28;
Charleston, 1803/2/12, 2/14, 3/5, 1806/4/16, 12/23; New York, 1801/9/25-
MV, 1804/3/20-G, 1806/7/23-V, 8/2-V, 8/6-V, 1809/3/10, 3/20, 5/26, 11/3,
11/8; Philadelphia, 1808/1/13, 2/27, 4/14, 12/17

Mother Bunch: Philadelphia, 1813/1/21-O

Mother Goose: Baltimore, 1810/6/8, 6/9, 11/17, 1812/6/6; Charleston, 1809/
3/3; Philadelphia, 1810/2/5, 2/7, 2/9, 2/12, 2/21

Mountaineers: Baltimore, 1801/5/15, 1803/4/11, 10/15, 1804/4/21, 1805/4/
10, 5/25, 11/2, 1806/11/1, 1809/5/17, 10/27, 1811/11/18-O, 11/30-O,
1813/5/12, 1815/10/6; Boston, 1801/3/13, 12/24, 1802/2/19, 4/12, 4/15, 6/
9, 1803/3/4, 4/27, 1804/3/9, 1805/3/15, 10/18, 12/27, 1807/9/23, 1809/1/
6, 4/12, 11/6, 1810/2/16, 11/2, 11/7, 1812/2/12, 3/2, 1814/2/11, 12/9,
1815/12/26; Charleston, 1801/2/14, 11/13, 1802/11/15, 1803/4/21, 1804/
11/21, 1805/2/23, 1806/1/6, 5/12, 11/10, 1807/11/13, 1808/3/9, 11/14,
1810/3/28, 4/27, 1811/2/16, 2/27, 1812/3/13, 1815/11/13, 11/22, 12/23;
New York, 1801/2/6, 1802/7/21-MV, 12/28, 1805/2/20, 7/8, 12/23, 1806/
2/10, 10/11, 11/24, 1807/7/24-V, 10/14, 12/30, 1808/5/27, 7/1, 12/14,
1809/3/3, 5/22, 10/16, 12/20, 1810/3/30, 1811/4/22, 11/6, 1812/6/6-O, 6/
19, 11/23, 1813/3/29, 10/1, 10/23, 12/24, 1814/1/14, 3/25, 6/10, 8/19-Cr,
9/7, 1815/11/22, 12/27; Philadelphia, 1801/2/14, 7/8, 1803/1/26, 1804/2/
1, 1805/3/20, 1806/4/8, 7/7, 1807/9/16S, 1808/1/23, 1809/1/13, 12/8,
1810/12/24, 1811/7/12-A, 12/9, 1812/1/29, 3/21-O, 5/14-O, 9/30, 12/12-
S, 1814/2/9, 1815/2/11, 11/29

Music Mad: Boston, 1811/12/20, 12/27, 1812/1/22, 12/16; New York, 1814/
5/20, 6/10

My Grandmother: Baltimore, 1803/5/31, 11/28, 1804/4/20, 1806/11/19,

1807/10/10; Boston, 1801/4/20, 1802/3/15, 1803/12/7, 1804/4/25, 11/28, 1805/10/7, 11/4, 1808/1/13, 1809/12/4, 1810/1/1, 3/23, 1811/1/7, 1/25, 10/21, 1812/1/8, 1813/3/3, 1814/2/23, 1815/1/10, 2/22, 10/13; Charleston, 1802/2/19, 3/1, 4/28, 11/24, 12/20, 1805/11/13, 1806/4/14, 1811/3/20, 1812/2/14, 1813/1/15, 1815/11/25; New York, 1806/1/31, 2/10, 2/17, 2/26, 3/14, 4/14, 4/25, 5/7, 11/21, 1807/11/27, 1809/12/27, 1810/1/8, 1811/3/29, 1812/9/28, 1813/3/31, 5/24, 12/17-Cw, 1814/1/7-Cw, 4/6, 5/16, 9/5; Philadelphia, 1803/3/28, 1804/1/27, 1806/12/10, 1807/12/12, 1810/4/6, 1811/1/19, 1813/4/27, 5/24, 1814/1/26-Cw

Mysteries of the Castle: Baltimore, 1805/4/24; Charleston, 1806/12/26, 12/29, 1807/2/19; Philadelphia, 1805/3/25

Mysterious Monk: New York, 1803/1/31

Mystery of the Cottage: Baltimore, 1814/3/4-P

Naval Frolic: Philadelphia, 1812/12/17-S, 12/18-S

Naval Glory: Philadelphia, 1812/9/29-O

Naval Pillar: Philadelphia, 1814/4/7

Necromancer: New York, 1801/9/11-MV, 9/18-MV, 1802/7/26-MV

Netley Abbey: Philadelphia, 1813/3/15

New Way to Pay Reckoning During the Embargo: Boston, 1808/4/18, 6/6

New Wreath for American Tars: Baltimore, 1804/5/23; Philadelphia, 1804/7/6S

New Year's Gig: New York, 1802/1/2, 1/30

Nina: Charleston, 1805/4/3, 5/14; New York, 1805/2/4, 2/6

No Song, No Supper: Baltimore, 1802/6/1, 1803/5/23, 11/2, 1805/5/29, 1806/11/15, 1807/11/7, 1808/4/29, 1809/10/18, 1811/11/20-O; Boston, 1801/11/30, 1802/3/1, 11/29, 1803/2/18, 11/14, 1805/12/4, 1806/12/1, 1807/4/17, 10/16, 1810/1/29, 11/30, 1811/1/3, 10/16, 1812/1/1, 1813/1/8, 2/8, 10/8, 1814/2/9, 2/14, 1815/10/25; Charleston, 1801/2/10, 11/16, 11/18, 1802/2/24, 12/6, 1804/5/3, 12/12, 1805/12/2, 1806/12/20, 1807/5/25, 11/27, 1808/12/12, 1810/2/7, 5/11, 1811/3/27, 1812/4/16, 1813/1/15; New York, 1801/4/27, 5/8, 7/13, 12/28, 1802/3/22, 10/22, 1803/6/29, 1806/2/14, 6/21, 1807/1/14, 1808/1/6, 7/13, 1809/5/22, 12/13, 1810/3/14, 1813/9/27, 10/4, 10/20, 11/29-Cw, 12/17, 1814/1/8-Cw, 4/20-A, 5/4, 8/5-Cr, 10/31, 12/7, 1815/3/29, 11/18; Philadelphia, 1802/1/20, 7/12-S, 1803/2/18, 1804/3/2, 1806/12/8, 1807/7/1, 1808/3/4, 11/7, 1810/2/21, 4/13, 1812/1/9-O, 12/14-S, 1813/5/14, 1814/1/31-Cw, 1815/4/5

Obi: Boston, 1801/3/31, 4/2, 4/3, 4/22, 1802/4/2, 4/15, 12/15, 1803/1/26, 12/23, 1804/12/31, 1807/12/24, 1808/1/27, 1809/5/10; New York, 1801/5/27, 6/5, 11/20, 1802/4/7, 4/19, 1803/1/3, 1814/8/15-Cr, 8/17-Cr, 8/19-Cr; Philadelphia, 1801/12/26, 12/28, 12/30, 1802/1/4, 1/11, 1/18, 3/8, 1812/5/6-O

Of Age Tomorrow: Baltimore, 1808/5/30, 6/3, 6/10, 10/14, 10/22, 1809/10/
20, 1813/10/29, 1815/11/10; Boston, 1806/1/31, 2/3, 2/5, 2/10, 2/19, 1807/
1/4, 1810/10/12, 10/17, 11/2, 1811/10/28, 12/13, 1812/1/9, 1813/1/22, 3/
15; Charleston, 1811/2/1, 2/20, 3/1, 5/7, 1812/3/6, 5/6, 1813/1/18; New
York, 1806/11/5, 11/17, 1807/3/9, 12/11, 12/18, 1808/4/22, 1809/3/6, 4/7,
5/19, 1810/6/6, 6/27, 10/17, 10/26, 1811/10/21, 1813/12/29-Cw, 1814/5/
13, 5/16-A, 9/8-A, 1815/5/22, 10/11; Philadelphia, 1808/4/4, 11/16, 12/21,
1809/11/20, 1810/4/7, 12/22, 1811/4/8, 9/9, 1812/2/29, 1813/1/22, 12/20,
1814/1/18-Cw, 2/26-Cw, 1815/4/1, 12/30
Offering to Love (Offrande a L'Amour): Boston, 1804/10/15, 10/19, 11/19;
New York, 1805/5/15, 5/22, 5/24, 1811/9/24-P, 10/16; Philadelphia, 1812/
12/14-S
Oh! This Love!: New York, 1812/2/26, 2/28
Old Man and Piero Out-done: Philadelphia, 1814/11/2-V
Old Soldier: Boston, 1806/3/24; Charleston, 1804/4/19; New York, 1801/5/
1, 5/29, 1802/6/7, 7/14-MV, 1805/6/7, 1806/8/27V
Oscar and Malvina: Baltimore, 1812/6/1; Boston, 1801/5/8, 5/13, 12/24,
1803/1/14, 1/21, 1/24, 1805/4/19, 1806/1/27, 2/17, 1807/4/27, 10/2, 1809/
2/15, 2/27, 1810/1/26, 2/2, 1811/1/30, 3/11, 1812/4/22; Charleston, 1803/
3/31, 4/18, 1807/4/3, 4/24, 1808/3/30; New York, 1801/1/2, 1/5, 3/21,
1813/11/25, 11/26; Philadelphia, 1811/2/23, 9/30, 10/5, 1813/1/13, 1/30
Out of Place: New York, 1812/10/9, 10/19, 10/30, 11/6, 11/18, 1814/5/23,
9/2
Padlock: Baltimore, 1807/6/1, 10/24, 1808/10/12, 1809/6/9, 11/4, 1811/12/
21-O; Boston, 1802/3/31, 11/1, 12/17, 1803/10/17, 12/12, 1804/12/26,
1806/1/13, 10/29, 1807/3/18, 10/30, 1809/9/27, 1810/2/9, 5/23, 10/10,
1811/1/11, 1814/4/1; Charleston, 1801/3/23, 1802/2/8, 1803/2/18, 1804/
11/19, 1805/11/20, 12/28, 1807/5/22, 1808/11/16, 1811/2/9, 1812/4/10;
New York, 1801/7/6, 1803/3/11, 1804/11/5, 11/30, 1805/2/13, 2/14, 11/
27, 1806/1/29, 8/11V, 12/12, 1808/2/24, 9/9, 1810/12/12, 1812/5/27,
1813/12/30-Cw, 1814/9/30; Philadelphia, 1801/3/13, 4/4, 11/9, 1807/10/7-
S, 1808/4/8, 12/7, 1811/6/14-A, 7/1-A, 1812/1/7-O, 1813/4/13, 5/1, 1814/
1/17-Cw, 3/8-Cw
Painters: Boston, 1807/3/18
Pantaloon in the Suds: New York, 1815/3/27, 3/31
Paragraph: Baltimore, 1804/11/23, 11/27, 1805/5/11; Boston, 1810/12/14,
1812/2/17, 4/8; Philadelphia, 1805/2/1, 2/25
Patie and Peggy: Boston, 1807/1/30, 2/3
Patrick in Prussia: Baltimore, 1803/5/13, 6/10, 1806/11/14; Philadelphia,
1803/3/25, 1807/1/19, 1/26

Paul and Alexis (Wandering Boys): Charleston, 1812/4/20, 4/22, 5/20

Paul and Virginia: Baltimore, 1804/5/11, 1805/6/3, 10/21, 10/28, 11/20, 1806/5/2, 10/8, 1807/10/7, 1808/5/14; Boston, 1801/3/18, 3/25, 3/27, 4/8, 1803/3/2, 3/4, 3/11, 3/16, 1804/2/3, 2/29, 3/14, 7/2, 12/7, 12/24, 1805/2/1, 3/18, 11/25, 12/6, 1806/1/22, 4/18, 10/20, 11/12, 1807/2/27, 9/16, 1808/3/4, 1809/3/13, 9/18, 1810/10/15, 11/9, 1811/3/6, 1812/11/30, 1814/3/21, 1815/4/24, 6/14, 11/24; Charleston, 1805/4/25, 5/2, 1807/3/2, 1808/4/22; New York, 1802/5/7, 6/2, 6/18, 6/28, 10/5, 10/29, 1805/4/22, 4/26, 6/7, 1806/5/16, 6/4, 11/14, 11/19, 12/8, 1807/3/18, 4/6, 9/9, 10/21, 11/6, 12/30, 1808/6/6, 1810/6/25, 1811/10/30, 1812/12/9, 1813/5/19, 1814/4/15, 5/14, 9/9, 10/17, 11/30, 12/31, 1815/1/25, 4/14, 6/2, 9/1, 9/5, 10/2; Philadelphia, 1804/3/28, 1805/3/30, 12/9, 12/20, 1806/1/29, 3/28, 12/15, 1807/1/31, 1808/3/12, 1809/2/15, 1810/1/10, 1813/1/27, 3/8, 1814/3/10-Cw

Pawlo and Petrowna: Charleston, 1812/5/15

Peasant Boy: Baltimore, 1812/3/30, 4/4, 1813/5/15; Boston, 1814/1/17, 1/21, 1/28, 4/18, 1815/3/3, 4/19, 6/9; New York, 1812/6/26, 7/1, 9/9; Philadelphia, 1812/3/11, 3/14, 4/24, 1814/4/6

Peasant of the Alps: Philadelphia, 1807/7/25-S, 10/2-S, 10/12-S

Pedlar: Charleston, 1801/4/27, 1803/3/16, 1804/5/11; New York, 1801/8/27-MV

Peep Behind the Curtain: Baltimore, 1801/6/4; Philadelphia, 1801/3/27, 4/10

Peeping Tom of Coventry: Baltimore, 1806/5/21, 11/26; Philadelphia, 1807/3/2

Perouse (Peyrouse): Baltimore, 1805/6/7, 6/10, 10/23, 10/26, 11/16, 1806/5/10, 10/29, 1814/1/10-P, 1/12-P, 1/14-P, 2/11-P; Boston, 1807/1/16, 1/19, 2/13, 3/23, 4/3, 9/28, 11/2, 1808/1/18, 12/2, 12/9, 12/16, 1809/2/10, 10/23, 1812/11/4, 11/6, 11/11, 12/2, 1813/1/20, 2/3, 12/3, 1814/1/21, 10/24, 11/23; Charleston, 1803/5/10, 12/1, 1804/2/25, 1805/2/9, 1806/5/16, 1807/12/5, 12/14, 1808/4/4; New York, 1811/1/1, 1/2, 1/4, 1/7, 2/1; Philadelphia, 1804/12/26, 12/27, 1805/1/2, 2/18, 3/4, 12/18, 1806/1/24, 3/29, 1807/1/21, 1812/4/10-O, 4/20-O, 4/27-O, 1813/11/25-C, 11/27-C, 12/2-C

Petite Savoyards: Charleston, 1806/3/21

Petite Trompeuse: Philadelphia, 1814/4/13

Philadelphia Volunteers: Philadelphia, 1812/10/5-O, 10/8-O

Piero's Disgrace: Philadelphia, 1814/10/26-V

Pigmalion: Baltimore, 1805/4/17; New York, 1809/1/26-L, 1/28-L, 2/9-L

Pilgrims: Boston, 1802/4/30, 1808/12/23, 12/26, 1809/1/2, 2/17, 1810/1/10

Pinxter Monday: New York, 1804/5/21

Pizarro: Baltimore, 1803/5/26, 10/17, 1804/5/14, 1805/5/4, 11/25, 1806/5/

12, 11/3, 1807/5/18, 10/12, 1808/10/7, 1809/5/24, 10/21, 1810/5/5, 5/23, 1811/5/17, 1812/4/25; Boston, 1801/2/16, 2/18, 2/20, 2/23, 3/2, 3/6, 3/23, 1802/5/14, 5/19, 1803/3/14, 1804/2/22, 1805/4/15, 11/29, 1806/10/31, 11/5, 1807/4/17, 11/30, 1808/2/26, 1809/2/27, 4/19, 1810/1/12, 11/21, 1811/10/21, 1812/2/17, 4/10, 1814/12/2, 1815/5/10; Charleston, 1801/2/20, 3/9, 1802/1/27, 2/11, 3/29, 3/31, 11/22, 12/3, 1803/11/11, 1804/2/17, 1805/2/19, 1806/5/5, 11/28, 12/8, 1807/5/18, 11/25, 1808/5/9, 11/16, 1810/2/9, 3/3, 3/5, 4/9, 1811/1/9, 1/12, 3/29, 1812/3/21, 5/1; New York, 1807/2/25, 5/6, 1808/3/7, 3/21, 5/25, 10/12, 1809/5/15, 5/26, 9/8, 9/27, 12/11, 1810/5/5, 9/19, 1811/3/29, 9/23, 10/14, 11/8, 1813/12/3, 12/8, 1814/3/18, 5/27, 6/15-A, 12/7, 1815/6/19, 9/18, 9/30, 10/11, 10/21; Philadelphia, 1801/2/9, 1802/3/10, 3/13, 12/23, 1804/1/16, 1805/1/25, 1806/2/28, 3/31, 1807/1/7, 12/23, 1808/11/9, 1809/3/27, 11/22, 12/15, 1810/12/21, 1811/1/30, 9/13, 11/1, 12/18, 1812/10/5, 12/7, 1813/1/9-S, 5/24, 1814/1/19, 2/19-Cw, 12/24, 1815/2/10

Pizarro in Peru: New York, 1801/2/4, 3/18, 12/7, 1802/1/2, 4/20, 11/3, 1803/4/11, 1804/3/16, 4/7, 4/14, 12/14, 1805/7/4, 1806/3/24

Poor Jack (pant.): New York, 1801/6/12, 1802/6/18, 1803/1/1, 1804/1/2, 6/29, 1805/5/27, 1806/6/16

Poor Jack (interlude): New York, 1811/6/14

Poor Soldier: Baltimore, 1802/6/5, 1803/6/7, 10/7, 1804/5/5, 11/10, 1805/5/28, 10/30, 1806/5/28, 1807/5/11, 10/26, 1808/5/2, 1811/3/23-P, 11/8-O, 11/23-O, 1813/4/12-C, 1814/6/3, 11/21, 1815/6/5; Boston, 1801/1/16, 1802/2/17, 12/10, 1804/1/27, 2/24, 4/23, 1806/1/1, 2/24, 11/3, 1807/2/25, 11/27, 1808/10/3, 1810/1/15, 2/5, 1813/10/13, 1814/3/4, 11/23, 12/23, 1815/5/22; Charleston, 1801/2/18, 5/18, 1802/1/29, 2/13, 3/12, 3/29, 3/31, 12/8, 1803/12/7, 1804/3/26, 1805/12/18, 1806/2/22, 1807/2/19, 5/16, 11/16, 1808/12/9, 1809/2/25, 1812/3/9, 1815/12/4; New York, 1801/8/27-MV, 1802/1/1, 3/29, 1803/4/27, 5/6, 11/16, 1804/4/3-G, 4/12-G, 11/7, 1805/3/13, 1806/2/19, 7/2-V, 11/7, 1809/6/19, 1810/12/24, 12/28, 1811/9/6, 9/18, 1812/6/12-O, 1813/10/15, 12/13, 12/18-Cw, 1814/3/4, 9/6-A, 9/14, 9/27, 1815/2/3, 8/30-Cw; Philadelphia, 1801/3/23, 9/18-S, 1802/4/3, 12/24, 1804/1/4, 1806/2/10, 1807/8/17, 1808/3/2, 1809/2/22, 1810/1/27, 1811/3/6, 7/10-A, 11/6, 1812/1/1-O, 1/27-O, 1813/5/17, 1814/3/7-Cw, 3/28, 11/28, 1815/1/16

Positive Man: New York, 1802/5/10

Press Gang: Charleston, 1812/3/30, 4/6

Prisoner: Boston, 1802/4/23, 5/24

Prisoner at Large: Baltimore, 1802/11/26, 1803/5/2, 1804/10/13, 1805/4/22,

10/9, 1813/6/9, 1814/11/7, 1815/6/2; Boston, 1813/3/26, 4/7, 1815/3/6, 4/10; Charleston, 1808/4/29, 5/4, 12/23, 1809/2/14, 1812/3/4, 1815/12/15; New York, 1805/6/19, 1808/5/13, 6/3, 12/26, 1809/6/2, 6/23, 1811/5/17, 5/22, 6/21, 9/13, 11/16, 1812/1/10, 4/24, 9/25, 1813/12/31-Cw, 1814/9/23, 1815/8/30-Cw; Philadelphia, 1801/12/16, 1803/3/7, 1805/1/23, 1808/3/13, 1810/2/26, 11/28, 1811/1/1, 4/19, 10/12, 11/13, 1812/12/4, 1813/5/7, 1814/1/21-Cw, 4/6, 1815/4/14

Prize: Baltimore, 1802/4/26, 1803/10/14, 10/29, 1804/10/6, 1805/6/6, 1807/11/2, 1808/5/13, 10/4, 1809/5/2, 1815/10/2, 10/21; Boston, 1801/2/25, 2/27, 4/29, 1802/2/8, 5/10, 11/3, 1803/2/21, 1804/4/18, 1807/1/6, 1/25, 1808/10/19, 1810/1/8, 1815/10/23, 11/6; Charleston, 1805/3/21, 3/30, 12/20, 1806/2/3, 12/19, 1807/5/6, 1809/1/19, 1810/3/3, 1811/1/14; New York, 1801/11/18, 1802/12/17, 12/22, 1804/1/9, 4/18, 11/12, 1805/12/30, 1806/1/13, 3/19, 10/6, 10/10, 1807/8/8-V, 8/19-V, 9/14, 1808/9/16, 1809/1/31-L, 5/29, 1810/11/30, 1811/12/4, 12/17, 1812/5/15, 5/25, 9/30, 1813/10/25, 1814/1/5-Cw, 5/11, 6/20-A, 1815/5/8, 5/17, 7/12; Philadelphia, 1802/3/15, 1803/2/14, 12/12, 1805/2/13, 1807/6/26, 12/7, 1808/4/20, 11/9, 1809/1/18, 1810/2/16, 1811/1/7, 1813/2/12, 1814/2/21-Cw, 1815/11/29

Proctor's Defeat by Gen. Harrison: Baltimore, 1814/2/24-P; Philadelphia, 1813/11/3-C

Purse: Baltimore, 1801/5/23, 1802/11/8, 1803/5/7, 1805/5/6, 10/11, 1806/4/18, 1811/11/20-O, 1813/4/8-C, 5/28, 10/2; Boston, 1801/1/1, 1/14, 12/18, 1802/10/27, 11/12, 1803/11/30, 1804/2/15, 11/5, 1805/1/4, 4/16, 10/4, 1806/2/14, 1807/1/9, 1/21, 4/10, 1808/2/11, 1809/1/27, 1810/1/3, 1812/1/24, 2/10, 1813/2/15, 3/17, 12/22, 1815/5/31; Charleston, 1801/2/9, 11/7, 1802/11/22, 1803/2/4, 1804/2/20, 1805/11/28, 1806/4/23, 5/27, 1807/4/20, 11/28, 1809/1/30, 1810/2/21, 1811/1/25, 1812//3/18; New York, 1801/4/22, 7/3, 8/12-MV, 9/21-MV, 12/11, 1802/1/20, 8/18-MV, 9/3-MV, 12/28, 1803/12/30, 1804/2,22, 3/9-G, 3/12, 3/17-G, 4/7G, 5/12-G, 1805/6/5, 1806/7/11-V, 10/8, 1808/7/18-V, 12/21, 1809/3/10, 1810/11/24, 12/1, 12/14, 1811/1/25, 8/21-P, 9/10-P, 11/22, 1812/1/1, 1/10, 5/13, 11/20, 1813/5/3, 9/24, 10/23, 12/7-Cw, 1814/1/5, 1/8, 4/18, 4/22-A, 5/9-A, 9/10-A, 9/19, 11/16, 1815/1/4; Philadelphia, 1801/1/23, 8/21-S, 11/18, 1805/1/19, 1806/1/27, 3/10, 1807/3/4, 7/25, 1808/2/22, 1810/3/30, 1812/1/4-O, 2/20-O, 7/1-O, 11/30-S, 12/5-S, 1813/5/3, 6/4, 11/24, 1814/2/22-Cw, 12/14

Quadrupeds of Quedlinburg: Philadelphia, 1813/4/19

Quaker: Baltimore, 1803/4/13, 10/21, 1805/10/7, 1807/6/10, 1811/12/14-O; Boston, 1801/12/11, 1802/3/8, 1803/2/25, 10/28, 1804/10/15, 1806/10/15, 12/8, 1809/1/16, 1811/1/21, 12/11, 1812/1/31, 1814/2/16; Charleston, 1801/1/26, 5/22, 1802/1/22, 2/26, 11/19, 1803/2/9, 1804/3/23, 1805/3/23,

11/27, 1806/11/17, 1808/12/30, 1809/1/9, 2/3, 1810/3/12; New York, 1801/5/29, 11/27, 1802/2/10, 1806/2/3, 3/12, 3/24, 1811/1/21, 1/28, 1812/ 12/23; Philadelphia, 1802/7/16-S, 12/17, 1805/12/2, 1811/6/26-A, 7/3-A

Quakers (ballet): Charleston, 1812/4/20

Ramah Droog: Baltimore, 1803/5/30; Boston, 1807/4/24; Philadelphia, 1803/ 3/18

Rambles of Dennis Brulgruddery: Boston, 1806/3/21, 3/28, 1807/4/24; Philadelphia, 1808/2/8

Raymond and Agnes: Baltimore, 1804/4/18, 4/21, 4/28, 10/12; Boston, 1802/ 5/7, 1803/4/4; New York, 1804/1/16, 1/18, 1/20, 1/27, 3/17, 11/28, 1811/ 9/17-P; Philadelphia, 1804/3/19, 1805/1/28, 2/23, 1811/12/24

Recruit: Charleston, 1802/4/23, 1807/5/30

Recruiting Sergeant: Baltimore, 1806/5/9; Philadelphia, 1806/2/26

Red Cross Knights: Baltimore, 1803/4/13, 11/5, 1804/4/28; Philadelphia, 1802/7/12-S, 1803/3/18, 4/2

Rehearsal Disappointed: Charleston, 1812/3/18, 4/4

Renegade: Baltimore, 1815/5/24; New York, 1813/2/24, 2/26; Philadelphia, 1815/1/2, 1/4, 1/6

Restoration of Harlequin: New York, 1802/7/21-MV

Return from a Cruise: Philadelphia, 1812/12/11, 12/12

Review (Wags of Windsor): Baltimore, 1802/5/1, 5/29, 11/17, 1803/6/1, 11/ 25, 1804/4/16, 5/18, 11/5, 1805/5/18, 11/27, 1807/6/3, 10/19, 1808/10/28, 1810/10/17, 11/19, 1811/11/13-O, 12/23-O, 1812/4/29, 1813/5/24, 1814/ 10/14, 1815/5/6, 10/2; Boston, 1804/2/20, 3/7, 3/12, 4/27, 1805/2/18, 3/ 13, 9/30, 10/30, 1806/3/26, 4/9, 1807/3/20, 1808/1/1, 2/22, 11/30, 1812/4/ 20, 10/8, 1813/10/4, 10/14, 1814/4/18, 10/5, 1815/5/1, 12/11; Charleston, 1804/12/5, 12/20, 1805/2/16, 2/27, 1806/1/17, 1/31, 5/10, 1807/1/21, 2/ 23, 11/30, 1808/1/23, 11/21, 12/24, 1809/1/21, 1810/3/1, 1811/3/6, 5/20, 1812/3/2, 1815/12/8; New York, 1803/5/13, 5/16, 5/20, 6/1, 6/10, 6/25, 7/ 1, 1804/1/30, 2/20, 4/4, 12/7, 1805/2/11, 3/29, 6/26, 1806/5/2, 5/14, 10/ 22, 11/12, 12/15, 1807/1/23, 2/11, 2/23, 4/17, 9/16, 10/19, 11/18, 1808/5/ 16, 6/27, 9/12, 10/3, 1809/2/2-L, 5/5, 6/28, 10/6, 1810/6/1, 1811/5/20, 5/ 24, 5/27, 9/26-P, 10/11, 1812/4/1, 11/16, 1814/1/21, 6/22, 8/22-Cr, 1815/ 2/17, 3/10, 6/5, 9/8; Philadelphia, 1802/3/19, 4/9, 1803/12/16, 12/23, 1804/1/18, 7/4S, 12/10, 1805/1/7, 1806/2/28, 1807/3/25, 12/14, 1808/11/ 25, 1809/1/30, 11/22, 1810/12/31, 1811/3/25, 9/11, 10/30, 1812/1/18-O, 3/2, 11/21, 1813/1/28-O, 4/2, 1814/4/7, 12/3, 1815/3/15, 11/27

Rich and Poor: Boston, 1812/11/23, 11/27, 12/4, 1813/5/3, 10/18, 12/31, 1814/6/6, 1815/5/26

Richard Coeur de Lion: Charleston, 1801/5/11, 5/15; New York, 1801/12/23, 12/30, 1802/2/1, 4/28, 5/3; Philadelphia, 1811/3/1

Rinaldo Rinaldini: Baltimore, 1811/4/15-P

Rival Chiefs: Boston, 1808/3/16

Rival Sisters: Boston, 1809/3/24; Philadelphia, 1807/4/3, 1809/3/24

Rival Soldiers (Sprigs of Laurel): Baltimore: 1801/5/13, 1803/4/16, 12/5, 1804/5/12, 10/1, 10/19, 11/14, 1805/5/24, 1808/6/1, 10/10, 1809/4/29, 10/9, 1813/6/2, 1814/3/10-P, 3/19-P, 1815/10/28, 11/4; Boston, 1803/12/30, 1804/1/4, 1/25, 4/4, 10/17, 12/28, 1805/4/5, 11/8, 12/30, 1806/10/27, 11/10, 1807/3/25, 10/5, 10/22, 1808/2/18, 1809/3/10, 12/8, 1810/3/28, 5/21, 1811/1/18, 1812/4/15, 1814/12/12, 1815/1/6, 4/5, 6/5; Charleston, 1805/12/16, 1807/1/28, 1808/1/18, 5/28, 1809/2/10, 1815/11/15, 12/6; New York, 1805/3/22, 3/25, 4/1, 4/19, 5/1, 6/21, 6/28, 1806/4/30, 6/13, 8/25-V, 12/5, 1807/1/28, 1808/2/22, 5/4, 11/14, 1809/2/27, 5/1, 1811/12/13, 12/16, 12/23, 1812/2/14, 3/18, 5/4, 10/26, 12/30, 1813/1/7, 6/7, 6/30, 9/22, 12/3, 1814/1/12, 9/16, 1815/2/20, 5/26, 9/23; Philadelphia, 1801/1/5, 2/20, 1802/1/27, 7/7-S, 1803/1/7, 1/29, 12/30, 1804/3/17, 12/21, 1806/2/17, 1808/2/5, 12/3, 1813/2/3, 6/7, 1814/1/10, 2/15-Cw, 1815/12/15

Rival Twins: Boston, 1807/11/4, 11/18

Robber of Genoa (Black Forest): Baltimore, 1813/10/23; Philadelphia, 1813/12/11, 1814/4/6

Robin Hood: Baltimore: 1803/12/8, 1808/10/26; Boston, 1805/3/27, 1806/3/21, 1807/1/12, 9/18, 1810/1/17, 2/14, 1811/4/1; Charleston, 1801/11/20, 1802/2/17, 1804/2/21, 3/3, 3/15, 5/28, 12/22, 1805/2/18, 1806/3/7, 1807/3/4, 1808/3/28, 1809/1/7, 1/20; New York, 1801/1/7, 2/9, 3/13, 9/4-MV, 12/21, 1802/1/11, 4/21, 1803/1/24, 1806/5/30, 6/11, 1807/1/21, 1809/6/30, 1812/5/30; Philadelphia, 1801/1/21, 1805/3/23, 1806/12/22, 1808/12/24

Robinson Crusoe: Baltimore, 1802/5/28, 11/20, 1803/4/11, 11/12, 1807/6/9; Boston, 1801/4/27, 1802/5/19, 1803/3/30, 1810/4/30; Charleston, 1803/4/25, 12/16, 1807/4/6; New York: 1801/5/11, 5/15, 1802/1/6, 1/27, 4/26, 11/1, 11/26, 1803/1/31, 1812/6/19-O, 1814/5/30-A, 6/4-A, 6/11-A, 7/2-A; Philadelphia, 1802/3/24, 12/31, 1807/8/27-S, 9/14-S, 1814/3/17-Cw

Roman Museum: New York, 1805/6/28, Italian Theatre

Romp: Baltimore, 1802/4/30, 1805/10/19, 11/8, 1806/4/14, 1807/11/4, 1808/10/15, 1813/6/9, 11/10; Boston, 1801/12/14, 1803/3/9, 12/21, 1804/2/1, 1805/1/25, 4/17, 10/14, 1806/1/10, 10/22, 10/31, 12/5, 1807/4/6, 9/25, 1808/2/3, 12/30, 1809/4/7, 1810/4/19, 5/25, 1813/4/23, 10/27, 1814/1/19, 6/6, 10/28, 12/16; Charleston, 1801/2/16, 1802/1/21, 3/3, 1804/11/28, 1805/3/13, 12/13, 1806/12/8, 1807/11/25, 12/7, 1808/1/21, 2/20, 1809/2/

6; New York, 1801/1/21, 4/13, 8/12-MV, 12/1, 1802/11/15, 1803/1/5, 1805/5/29, 6/12, 11/29, 1806/1/6, 1/17, 3/15, 7/16-V, 1807/7/27-V, 9/11, 1809/9/6, 9/18, 9/25, 11/6, 1811/3/8, 10/18, 10/25, 1812/3/20, 5/1, 6/24, 11/9, 1813/7/9, 11/5, 1815/5/19, 9/30, 10/23, 12/9; Philadelphia, 1801/8/ 28-S, 12/2, 1802/12/23, 1805/12/30, 1806/3/17, 6/23, 1808/2/10, 1809/2/ 6, 1812/12/10-S, 12/17-S, 1813/2/24, 1815/12/1

Rosina: Baltimore, 1802/4/22, 11/15, 1806/11/12, 1807/10/30, 1809/10/25, 1815/5/31, 10/6; Boston, 1802/5/3, 11/17, 1803/1/5, 10/12, 12/14, 1804/ 10/19, 1805/11/1, 1806/10/13, 1807/9/18, 1808/9/30, 1810/5/28, 12/21, 1813/10/6, 1814/3/2; Charleston, 1801/1/30, 11/11, 1802/1/23, 1/25, 11/8, 12/18, 12/24, 1803/11/23, 1804/11/14, 1805/11/16, 12/4, 1806/5/9, 12/29, 1808/5/6, 11/18, 11/25, 1809/2/22, 1810/5/12, 1811/2/8, 1812/2/20; New York, 1801/7/1, 11/30, 1802/6/21, 1803/3/2, 1804/10/24, 11/16, 1805/3/8, 12/2, 12/13, 1806/1/10, 1/24, 7/18-V, 1807/8/6-V, 10/30, 1808/8/15-V, 1809/9/8, 10/27, 1811/2/20, 1812/6/10-O, 1813/12/27-Cw, 1814/4/20, 1815/11/27; Philadelphia, 1801/10/19, 11/16, 1802/4/14, 12/13, 1803/2/9, 1806/6/20, 12/3, 1807/4/17, 6/24, 9/26-S, 1809/12/9, 1811/6/12-A, 6/17- A, 7/4-A, 1812/1/2-O, 3/2-O, 1813/4/15, 4/20

Rudolph: Boston, 1807/5/13; New York, 1804/12/4-Be, 12/8-Be, 12/22-Be

Rugatino: New York, 1815/6/7; Philadelphia, 1810/3/21, 1814/2/22-Cw, 2/ 26-Cw, 3/3-Cw

Rural Grace: Baltimore, 1813/5/12; Boston, 1814/12/23; Philadelphia, 1813/ 2/12, 2/15, 3/12, 3/24

Rural Merriment: Philadelphia, 1801/3/16

Sailor's Daughter: Baltimore, 1804/11/14, 11/16, 1805/4/15, 11/18, 1806/4/ 28, 1807/5/23; Boston, 1808/3/16, 3/23, 1813/5/7, 11/26, 1814/5/9; Charleston, 1805/3/23, 3/27; New York: 1805/3/15, 3/18; Philadelphia, 1804/12/10, 12/17, 1805/2/1, 1806/1/8, 1807/1/1, 1808/1/15, 1813/3/13, 3/19

Sailor's Festival: Boston, 1802/2/24, 3/4, 5/21

Sailor's Frolic: Boston, 1804/7/4

Sailor's Garland: Baltimore, 1801/6/2; Philadelphia, 1813/5/19, 1814/1/ 28-Cw

Sailor's Landlady: Baltimore, 1802/5/31, 1803/10/7; Charleston, 1806/1/24, 1/27, 2/17, 2/22, 5/2, 1807/1/21, 3/2, 4/28, 12/16, 1808/12/30; New York, 1807/7/25-V, 7/27-V; Philadelphia, 1801/3/6, 10/2-S, 1802/4/2, 1808/4/8, 1812/1/31

Sailor's Return: Baltimore, 1805/10/11, 10/16, 10/25; Boston, 1815/6/2; Phil- adelphia, 1805/12/24, 1806/2/7, 1807/1/23, 1/30

Saint David's Day: Baltimore, 1801/4/22; Philadelphia, 1801/12/7, 1802/3/1

Saint Patrick's Day: Baltimore, 1806/11/5, 1807/10/28, 1811/6/5; Boston, 1802/2/1, 3/17; Charleston, 1804/3/19; New York, 1802/5/26, 12/6, 1803/ 5/2, 1809/3/17, 1813/3/17, 3/22, 1814/4/27-A, 6/10-A, 1815/3/17, 12/8; Philadelphia, 1801/3/18, 1802/3/17, 1805/3/16, 1807/1/10, 1808/3/18, 1811/3/2, 4/20, 12/11, 1812/10/15-O, 11/9, 1813/6/5

Scheming Millers: New York, 1811/7/12-P

Scheming Milliners: Baltimore, 1802/6/5, 1803/10/10; New York, 1805/1/15-Be, 1807/7/22-V, 7/31-V; Philadelphia, 1803/3/11, 3/30, 12/30, 1804/2/15, 1809/3/17, 1813/8/10-G

School for Greybeards: Charleston, 1803/3/31; New York, 1803/7/1

School for Prodigals: Philadelphia, 1809/2/20

Scotch Ghost: Boston, 1810/4/30; New York, 1807/9/1; Philadelphia, 1813/ 1/28-O

Scots Milleners: Boston, 1806/3/21

Sea Side Story: Baltimore, 1809/5/8; Philadelphia, 1809/4/1

Secret: Baltimore, 1802/11/24, 1803/11/11, 1805/10/11; Boston, 1804/4/2, 1807/1/12; Charleston, 1806/3/3; New York, 1808/2/26; Philadelphia, 1801/11/2, 1802/12/20, 1804/2/3, 1807/4/13

Selima and Azor: Baltimore, 1805/6/8; Philadelphia, 1805/3/6

Shamrock: Baltimore, 1813/5/28, 5/29, 1814/6/3; Philadelphia, 1813/3/17, 3/ 20, 1814/3/19

She Would and She Would Not: Baltimore, 1803/10/12, 1804/10/24; Boston, 1804/4/18; Charleston, 1805/5/2; New York, 1803/5/9, 5/25, 11/14, 11/18, 12/20, 1805/5/27, 1813/3/3, 3/8, 10/18; Philadelphia, 1803/12/30

Shelty's Frolic: Baltimore, 1809/5/27, 1812/5/16; Philadelphia, 1801/3/23, 1802/4/7, 1811/3/8

Shelty's Travels: Philadelphia, 1807/9/18-S

Shipwreck: Baltimore, 1801/5/18, 1802/5/14, 11/12, 1803/5/25, 10/28, 1804/ 4/13, 11/12, 1805/4/13, 1806/10/17, 1810/5/16, 11/2, 1815/5/15, 10/18, 11/21; Boston, 1803/2/7, 2/23, 11/2, 1804/5/30, 1805/3/20, 11/22, 1806/ 10/24, 1807/1/23, 1808/3/9, 1811/11/15, 12/4, 1812/10/21, 1813/1/6, 3/ 29, 1814/2/21; Charleston, 1801/4/13, 1804/4/19, 5/14, 1805/4/19, 1806/ 2/5, 1808/4/1, 4/21; New York: 1801/3/16, 1804/6/8, 1805/6/14, 1806/5/ 19, 11/3, 1809/6/26, 1812/1/22, 1/24, 10/14, 12/28, 1813/5/4, 1814/11/4, 12/14; Philadelphia, 1801/3/9, 11/4, 1803/1/15, 1804/1/13, 2/20, 12/17, 1806/2/3, 1809/12/6, 1810/4/2, 1812/2/29, 1814/11/7-V, 1815/2/1

Shipwreck (Le Chef Sauvage): New York, 1814/7/15-Cr, 7/18-Cr

Shipwreck (Harlequin Fisherman): Baltimore, 1811/3/16-P; New York, 1802/ 5/17, 5/26, 1811/8/16-P

Shipwreck (Harlequin of Mt. Vesuvius): New York, 1804/5/16, 5/18, 6/13, 6/15

Shipwrecked Mariners Preserved: Boston, 1804/4/30

Shipwrecked Tar: Baltimore, 1813/3/17-C; New York, 1804/3/15-G, 3/20-G, 4/2-G

Sicilian Romance: Boston, 1810/4/23, 5/2; New York, 1814/5/20-A; Philadelphia, 1802/3/27, 1812/12/17-S, 12/18-S

Siege of Belgrade: Baltimore, 1801/5/20, 5/30, 6/3; Charleston, 1802/3/19, 3/24, 4/9, 1803/2/23, 1809/3/16; New York, 1807/4/17, 10/7, 11/25, 1808/1/6, 12/16, 1813/1/8, 1/18, 11/22; Philadelphia, 1801/2/11, 2/13, 2/23, 2/27, 1802/5/26, 1812/4/17-O

Siege of Quebec: Baltimore, 1802/5/29, 1803/11/19; Boston, 1803/3/23; Charleston, 1801/5/4; Philadelphia, 1804/3/3

Sighs: Boston, 1801/5/6, 1802/2/17, 11/3; Charleston, 1802/4/19, 12/13, 12/22, 1803/3/23, 1809/4/3

Sixty-Third Letter: Baltimore, 1803/4/15, 4/18, 12/6, 1804/4/25; Boston, 1804/12/10, 12/12, 12/14, 12/17, 1805/1/2, 2/6, 12/16, 1806/2/7, 1807/3/6, 3/16, 11/16, 1808/11/28, 1809/12/13, 1810/3/14, 1811/1/14, 1813/10/20, 1814/2/4; New York, 1803/11/30, 12/5, 12/9, 1804/4/20, 5/11, 12/12, 1805/2/20, 1806/8/18-V, 1808/3/14, 1813/5/28, 6/2; Philadelphia, 1803/1/21, 1/24, 2/28, 2/28, 1804/1/25

Soldier's Daughter: Baltimore, 1804/5/18, 5/23, 10/8, 11/23, 1805/10/14, 1807/11/20, 1808/10/12, 1812/3/26, 1813/10/25, 1814/10/21, 1815/5/31; Boston, 1804/5/7, 1807/5/20, 12/18, 1808/3/2, 9/26, 1810/10/10, 1813/5/5, 10/25, 1814/10/3, 1815/4/24; Charleston, 1804/12/24, 1805/2/15, 3/25, 1807/2/4, 2/18, 12/9, 1808/2/24, 1809/3/10, 1811/1/7, 1815/12/4; New York, 1804/4/18, 4/20, 4/23, 4/27, 5/4, 1805/3/4, 1806/5/30, 1808/12/23, 1809/10/27, 1870/2/26, 10/5, 10/20, 11/19, 1811/6/10, 1812/6/1, 9/11, 1813/12/7-Cw, 1814/6/20-A, 11/11, 1815/6/23; Philadelphia, 1804/12/21, 1805/1/2, 1/28, 3/4, 12/6, 1806/4/3, 1808/11/7, 1811/9/11, 1812/1/6, 3/13, 9/28, 1813/4/13, 6/5, 1814/2/22

Soldier's Return: Baltimore, 1807/11/23, 11/25, 1808/10/19; Philadelphia, 1807/12/9, 1808/1/4, 3/30, 1809/1/20

Son-in-Law: Baltimore, 1807/5/4, 11/30; Boston, 1801/3/9, 1803/4/20; Charleston, 1809/1/25, 2/15; Philadelphia, 1807/1/9

Spanish Barber: Baltimore, 1801/5/8, 1803/10/4, 1811/5/25; Boston, 1802/4/26, 1803/4/25; New York, 1803/4/18, 4/29, 6/1, 1808/4/27, 4/29, 6/13, 1814/4/13, 4/18, 4/29; Philadelphia, 1801/10/26, 1811/3/1, 3/15, 1814/2/8, 3/16

Spanish Dollars: Baltimore, 1807/5/30; Boston, 1808/3/16; New York, 1807/4/6; Philadelphia, 1807/4/3

Spanish Patriots: New York, 1809/1/4, 1/5, 4/3, 1814/5/23-A, 5/27-A, 5/28-A

Spoiled Child: Baltimore, 1801/5/4, 1805/10/18, 11/1, 1806/10/1, 1807/11/18, 1808/5/9, 1809/4/21, 11/11, 1810/5/1, 1811/11/16-O, 1814/5/28, 1815/5/24; Boston, 1801/4/13, 4/29, 1802/1/6, 11/26, 1803/1/31, 10/14, 12/9, 1804/12/21, 1807/3/2, 3/4, 3/11, 10/14, 1808/9/26, 1809/3/15, 10/13, 11/27, 1810/3/16, 1812/10/30, 12/11, 1813/3/24, 1814/3/30, 1815/1/30, 2/15; Charleston, 1802/1/27, 11/5, 1804/4/4, 12/1, 1805/2/11, 11/22, 1807/11/24, 12/9, 1808/2/18, 1809/2/1, 1810/2/9, 3/30, 1811/1/30, 1812/12/7, 1815/11/27; New York, 1810/7/20, 9/9-MV, 1802/6/11, 1804/3/24-G, 4/3-G, 4/12-G, 11/14, 1805/2/8, 3/15, 12/4, 12/13, 12/23, 1806/1/1, 1/8, 1/22, 2/7, 3/7, 4/9, 4/23, 7/4, 1807/7/22-V, 1808/7/22-V, 9/19, 9/23, 10/24, 1809/3/8, 10/25, 10/30, 1810/1/16, 2/28, 1811/9/20, 9/25, 12/28, 1812/4/13, 5/22-O, 1813/7/7, 1814/4/4, 4/11, 9/21, 12/30, 1815/2/8, 11/10, 11/24, 12/15; Philadelphia, 1801/7/27, 9/28-S, 1803/2/11, 8/18-S, 1804/10/16-S, 1805/12/6, 12/16, 1806/12/1, 1807/6/29, 9/16-S, 12/21, 1809/1/16, 4/8, 12/11, 1810/3/5, 1811/1/28, 4/10, 1812/1/6-O, 6/29-O, 1813/4/17, 1814/1/22-Cw, 1/29-Cw, 2/8-Cw, 3/10-Cw, 1815/4/12

Stranger: Baltimore, 1801/5/20, 1802/6/3, 1803/10/4, 1804/5/16, 1808/6/3, 1812/6/3, 1813/10/9; Boston, 1801/2/4, 1802/1/29, 12/24, 1804/3/7, 5/2, 1807/3/23, 4/8, 11/9, 1810/4/2, 1811/12/9, 1813/4/23, 1815/1/6; Charleston, 1801/3/11, 4/18, 1802/3/12, 5/5, 1803/12/21, 1806/5/16, 1807/3/14, 5/15, 11/11, 1811/4/3, 1812/3/18; New York, 1801/1/16, 6/12, 1802/6/18, 1803/6/20, 12/22, 12/30, 1806/5/16, 11/14, 1808/6/24, 1810/9/26, 1812/12/14, 12/21, 1813/10/11, 11/1, 12/31, 1814/5/18-A, 6/18-A, 8/20-Cr; Philadelphia, 1801/12/11, 12/18, 1804/3/2, 1805/3/30, 1811/1/4, 2/23, 9/30, 12/7, 1812/10/2, 12/14-S, 12/28, 1813/4/22, 1814/2/2, 1815/3/17, 12/20

Sultan: Baltimore, 1805/5/31, 11/16, 1806/5/24, 1810/11/21, 1811/12/11-O, 1814/11/16; Boston, 1801/12/7, 1804/3/23, 1806/12/19, 1807/1/7, 10/9, 12/14, 1811/11/1, 11/8, 1813/1/25, 1814/3/28, 1815/2/27; Charleston, 1806/5/22, 1811/3/13; New York, 1805/7/5, 1806/1/27, 1807/7/22-V, 1808/12/19, 12/28, 1812/5/25-O, 10/23, 11/4, 1813/5/10, 1814/4/25-A, 8/10-Cr, 1815/12/1; Philadelphia, 1805/3/11, 1806/2/21, 1808/12/5, 1810/3/28, 12/5, 12/17, 1811/6/19-A, 7/17-A, 1812/1/13-O, 7/1-O, 12/9, 1814/2/7-Cw, 1815/3/22

Surrender of Calais: Baltimore, 1807/5/25; Charleston, 1801/4/29, 1808/5/11; New York, 1802/5/19, 1812/1/31, 1814/11/9, 11/23; Philadelphia, 1807/3/11, 1809/3/18, 1811/3/2

Sylvester Daggerwood: Baltimore, 1803/6/1, 11/26, 12/6, 1804/5/19, 11/17, 1805/4/17, 6/5, 1806/5/28, 6/4, 1807/6/6, 11/13, 1808/5/11, 1809/5/31, 10/30, 1810/10/12, 1812/3/28, 4/15, 5/30, 6/1, 1814/3/12-P, 3/22-P; Boston, 1806/4/2, 4/11, 1807/5/11, 1811/5/15, 1812/4/20; Charleston, 1807/3/6, 11/18; New York, 1804/12/4-Be, 1805/7/5, 1806/5/16, 6/2, 8/13-V, 1807/1/14, 3/16, 1808/1/27-W, 2/5-W, 8/8-V, 1809/6/12, 1811/6/10, 7/4, 8/2-P, 11/18, 11/20, 1812/1/3, 1813/6/11, 11/5, 12/8, 1814/1/21, 1/26, 8/22-Cr, 1815/10/3-Cw, 12/27; Philadelphia, 1803/3/28, 12/21, 1804/2/13, 3/7, 3/14, 3/24, 7/18-S, 1805/1/19, 3/15, 1806/6/30, 1807/1/14, 4/1, 12/18, 1809/1/16, 1810/2/2, 1811/1/23, 4/5, 9/28, 12/11, 1812/3/2, 3/4, 4/18-O, 11/14, 1813/7/24-G, 8/27-G, 12/15, 1815/4/1, 7/21-S

Tableau Magique: Philadelphia, 1813/8/6-G, 8/13-G

Taking of Yorktown: Philadelphia, 1812/2/22-O, 2/25-O

Tale of Mystery: Baltimore, 1804/5/4, 5/7, 5/16, 5/26, 10/5, 10/31, 1805/4/26, 11/18, 1806/5/17, 10/18, 1808/5/27, 1809/6/2, 1813/5/31, 1814/10/29; Boston, 1804/2/10, 2/13, 2/15, 2/17, 2/20, 3/21, 10/24, 1805/1/4, 2/18, 1808/3/21, 4/8, 10/24, 11/21, 1811/4/24, 1812/1/17, 1/29, 11/23; Charleston, 1803/5/3, 5/6, 12/19, 1804/2/2, 2/14, 1805/2/26, 12/6, 1806/5/7, 11/12, 1807/4/30, 1808/1/4, 11/30; New York, 1803/3/16, 3/18, 3/21, 3/23, 3/24, 3/25, 4/1, 4/18, 4/29, 5/18, 1804/3/21, 1805/6/10, 12/11, 12/18, 1806/6/22, 1809/11/25, 12/15, 12/26, 1810/3/10, 1812/1/20, 1814/1/17, 6/22-A, 6/27-A; Philadelphia, 1804/1/20, 1/24, 1/30, 2/10, 2/17, 3/12, 1805/1/30, 2/6, 1806/3/14, 4/3, 1808/3/9, 1809/3/22, 1810/3/17, 4/2, 1811/10/16, 1812/3/6, 4/15-O, 10/7, 11/28, 1813/3/19, 12/4, 1814/4/1, 1815/1/14

Tale of Terror: Baltimore, 1803/11/18, 11/21, 11/26; Boston, 1806/4/7; Charleston, 1805/4/15, 4/25; New York, 1804/1/25, 2/13, 2/15; Philadelphia, 1803/12/21, 12/23, 1811/2/22

Tars from Tripoli: New York, 1806/2/24, 2/28, 3/3, 3/8, 4/18, 1808/6/24, 10/3, 11/25, 1809/6/10, 1812/7/4; Philadelphia, 1812/7/4-O

Tekeli: Baltimore, 1809/6/3, 10/13, 11/3, 1811/5/29, 1812/4/18, 5/23, 1813/11/1; Boston, 1809/10/11, 10/13, 10/16, 10/18, 10/25, 10/27, 10/30, 11/1, 11/10, 11/13, 11/17, 11/24, 12/19, 12/27, 12/29, 1810/1/22, 1/31, 2/28, 4/16, 5/4, 10/19, 10/22, 11/19, 12/24, 1811/2/6, 2/8, 6/3, 10/23, 1812/4/27, 5/29, 11/18, 12/28, 1813/11/17, 12/8, 1814/4/29, 10/19, 11/25, 1815/3/1; Charleston, 1808/1/23, 1/29, 2/17, 3/16, 12/21, 12/30, 1809/1/6, 1810/4/2, 1811/3/23, 1812/5/8; New York, 1807/12/21, 12/23, 12/28, 1808/1/1, 1/4, 1/8, 3/16, 6/1, 1813/7/16, 9/15, 10/18, 11/3, 1814/2/4, 10/24, 12/2, 12/28, 1815/5/1, 6/23, 9/15, 10/6, 11/15; Philadelphia, 1809/2/6, 2/10, 2/15, 2/24, 3/3, 12/23, 1812/11/11, 1814/4/11, 1815/3/23

Telemachus in the Isle (Island) of Calypso: Charleston, 1801/5/13, 1804/3/9,

3/21, 1808/5/21, 1811/2/4, 4/3; New York, 1801/7/29; Philadelphia, 1812/5/8-O

Tempest: Baltimore, 1812/6/5; Boston, 1803/4/6, 4/15, 1807/4/24; Charleston, 1802/5/12, 1806/3/31; New York, 1801/1/7, 1808/6/8; Philadelphia, 1803/3/16, 1812/2/7, 2/14, 1813/1/6

Theatrical Candidates: Baltimore, 1802/11/8; Philadelphia, 1801/10/14, 10/19, 1815/4/12

Thesis and Ariadne: Philadelphia, 1807/3/16

Thirty Thousand: Baltimore, 1806/4/23; Philadelphia, 1806/2/15

Thomas and Sally: Baltimore, 1807/5/30; Charleston, 1802/5/14, 1808/4/8, 4/21, 5/25, 1811/5/18

Three and the Deuce: Baltimore, 1808/6/6, 1812/5/23, 5/27, 6/1, 1813/5/22, 10/2, 1815/11/6, 11/21; Boston, 1803/3/28, 1811/4/29, 5/20, 11/11, 12/2, 1812/3/18, 9/30; New York, 1812/4/20, 4/29, 5/13, 6/19, 11/20, 1813/7/9, 11/8, 1814/1/14, 1/24; Philadelphia, 1808/3/7, 1812/2/21, 2/26, 2/29, 3/4, 10/7, 10/17, 10/31, 11/14, 12/18, 1813/1/9, 2/13, 3/6, 5/19, 5/22, 11/24, 12/11, 1814/1/8, 2/9, 3/30, 12/17, 12/21, 1815/1/7, 2/13, 12/2

Time's a Tell-Tale: Baltimore, 1808/5/20; Boston, 1808/4/8, 4/11, 4/20, 1813/12/15, 1814/1/14; Charleston, 1808/11/25, 11/30, 1809/3/18; New York 1808/4/18, 4/20, 1813/11/12; Philadelphia, 1808/3/4

Timour the Tartar: Baltimore, 1813/6/9, 6/10, 10/20, 10/27, 11/3, 1814/5/2, 5/16, 1815/5/27, 10/13; Boston, 1813/3/15, 3/17, 3/19, 3/22, 3/24, 3/26, 4/2, 4/5, 5/7, 5/26, 10/22, 11/5, 11/26, 1814/1/14, 3/23, 5/9, 1815/3/10, 12/26; New York, 1812/11/20, 11/23, 11/25, 11/27, 12/4, 12/11, 12/25, 1815/7/21, 12/25; Philadelphia, 1812/9/25-O, 10/3-O, 10/6-O, 1813/2/10, 2/13, 2/17, 2/20, 2/27, 3/6, 3/13, 4/5, 1814/3/16, 3/25, 1815/3/10

Tom Thumb the Great: Baltimore, 1803/10/19, 1804/6/6, 1806/10/31, 11/22, 1807/5/22, 1808/6/4, 1809/11/15, 1810/5/25, 1812/4/25, 1813/5/19, 1814/10/21, 1815/5/10; Boston, 1807/5/18, 5/22, 11/4, 11/25, 1808/11/18, 12/14, 1810/11/23, 1812/2/26, 4/10, 10/28, 1813/1/29, 12/6, 1815/11/15; Charleston, 1805/5/14, 5/20, 1806/1/20, 2/26, 11/24, 1808/5/11; New York, 1801/2/2, 2/18, 11/25, 1802/4/20, 1803/6/22, 1806/4/28, 5/26, 12/17, 12/19, 1808/11/30, 1810/10/29, 10/31, 11/5, 11/14, 1811/1/11, 6/17, 11/8, 11/13, 1812/9/14, 10/5, 1814/4/13, 1815/7/3; Philadelphia, 1804/6/29-S, 1807/2/18, 2/25, 4/11, 4/18, 1808/1/18, 1/29, 4/9, 11/19, 1810/1/20, 1811/1/4, 10/28, 11/9, 1813/1/11, 5/21, 1814/1/26, 2/12-Cw, 1815/1/21

Too Many Cooks: Baltimore, 1806/10/22, 10/27, 11/7, 1809/11/8, 1810/6/2, 11/22; Boston, 1805/10/25, 10/28, 11/6, 1806/1/6; Charleston, 1807/12/23, 12/26, 1808/3/18; New York, 1805/12/13, 12/16; Philadelphia, 1807/

1/7, 1/12, 4/1, 1808/4/2, 12/12, 1809/12/20, 1810/12/28, 1811/4/11, 1812/
11/25, 1813/2/6

Touchstone: Charleston, 1804/4/2

Tournament: Boston, 1801/3/9; New York, 1803/4/20, 4/22, 4/25, 5/2, 5/6, 5/
30, 1804/1/27

Town and Country: Baltimore, 1807/11/4, 11/9, 11/18, 11/28, 1808/5/13, 6/
9, 10/15, 1809/4/29, 10/11, 1810/11/9, 1812/3/23, 1813/5/26, 1815/4/24;
Boston, 1807/10/9, 10/12, 10/16, 10/21, 11/18, 1809/2/13, 3/24, 1810/10/
26, 1811/5/13, 1814/4/13, 5/25, 1815/1/27, 4/28, 6/2; Charleston, 1807/
12/30, 1808/1/4, 2/16, 3/11, 1809/3/1, 1811/4/26, 1812/4/24, 5/20; New
York, 1807/11/2, 11/4, 11/6, 11/11, 11/20, 12/4, 1808/4/13, 1809/1/2,
1810/6/11, 1811/6/14, 1812/1/15, 1813/1/20, 11/3, 1814/5/30, 1815/1/11,
5/12, 9/25; Philadelphia, 1807/12/26, 12/30, 1808/1/11, 2/10, 2/19, 3/23,
4/11, 11/11, 1809/2/17, 11/24, 1811/3/11, 9/9, 1812/12/16, 1813/3/31,
1814/3/25, 11/30

Transformation: Baltimore, 1814/4/22, 4/29, 1815/5/22, 10/9; Philadelphia,
1814/3/14, 3/18, 1815/2/8, 2/17

Travellers: Baltimore, 1807/11/13, 11/14, 11/16, 6/10; Charleston, 1808/3/
14, 3/18, 3/23, 12/5; Philadelphia, 1807/4/20, 4/22, 4/23, 1808/12/26, 12/
30, 1809/1/21

Tricks Upon Travellers: New York, 1811/3/18, 3/20

Triomphe de l'Amour: Baltimore, 1813/6/7

Trois Savoyards: Boston, 1804/10/22, 10/29, 11/9, 1808/11/11; New York,
1805/1/21, 2/1, 2/8, 3/11, 1811/9/28-P

Turn Out!: Baltimore, 1815/5/8, 5/12, 10/14, 11/20; Boston, 1814/11/9, 11/
14, 11/30, 12/28, 1815/2/13, 5/10; New York, 1813/12/8, 12/10, 12/22,
12/31, 1814/3/16, 3/30, 7/1, 1815/7/10, 12/18; Philadelphia, 1815/3/17, 3/
20, 12/11

Turnpike Gate: Baltimore, 1802/5/3, 5/10, 11/10, 12/4, 1803/4/27, 1804/10/
27, 1805/4/24, 11/9, 1806/5/12, 11/8, 1815/4/21, 11/17; Boston, 1801/1/5,
4/17, 12/16, 1802/1/22, 3/10, 1803/1/10, 10/10, 1805/4/11, 10/2, 12/2,
1806/2/28, 1807/2/4, 1810/12/31, 1811/2/11, 1812/1/20, 2/7, 1813/1/4,
1814/2/18, 3/25, 10/31, 12/19, 1815/12/22; Charleston, 1802/5/3, 1805/
12/30; New York, 1801/6/8, 7/11, 1806/7/31-V, 1809/6/5, 1814/5/13-A, 5/
14-A, 5/18, 6/8, 8/24-Cr; Philadelphia, 1802/2/10, 2/12, 2/15, 2/26, 3/29,
12/15, 1803/1/12, 3/26, 1805/1/9, 2/2, 1806/3/31, 12/29, 1814/12/2

Twenty Years Ago: New York, 1811/2/22, 3/4, 1814/12/23, 1815/2/8

Two Country Squires: Baltimore, 1814/3/8-P

Two Faces Under a Hood: Boston, 1809/2/22

Two Hunters (Huntsmen) and the Milkmaid: Charleston, 1801/1/28, 1804/2/11, 1810/2/21, 1812/4/4, 4/10, 12/7; Philadelphia, 1803/9/10-S, 1807/8/20-S

Two Jealous Lovers: New York, 1803/8/5-MV

Two Merry Hunters: Baltimore, 1814/2/16-P, 1814/3/12-P

Two Misers: Boston, 1809/11/8, 11/10, 11/15, 12/20, 1810/4/18

Two Philosophers (Two Misers, Two Quakers): Baltimore, 1813/3/26-C, 4/12-C; Charleston, 1805/4/22, 1812/12/28; New York, 1801/7/27, 9/1-MV, 9/4-MV, 1804/6/8, 1806/6/4, 8/20-V, 1815/8/31-Cw; Philadelphia, 1807/3/20, 1807/7/30-S, 1808/6/28-S, 1809/3/10, 1812/2/28, 1813/7/24-G

Valentine and Orson: Baltimore, 1807/5/13, 5/15, 5/20, 5/23, 10/5, 10/17, 1808/5/21, 10/8, 1812/3/30, 1813/10/16; Boston, 1810/2/7, 2/9, 2/19, 2/23, 2/28, 4/2, 11/26, 12/3, 1811/2/4, 1812/12/4, 12/7, 12/18, 1813/2/12, 10/29, 11/29, 1814/1/24, 3/11, 10/17, 12/21; Charleston, 1806/3/21, 1808/2/8; New York, 1805/4/15, 4/16, 4/17, 4/19, 4/24, 5/1, 5/3, 5/10, 1806/1/1, 4/7, 11/10, 1814/6/15, 6/20, 7/4, 10/21, 11/23, 1815/7/7, 9/16, 10/27; Philadelphia, 1807/1/1, 1/3, 1/5, 1/14, 1/28, 2/7, 2/28, 12/24, 1808/2/13, 1811/2/25, 3/9, 12/14, 12/21, 1812/10/16, 1813/4/3, 12/29, 1814/12/7, 1815/12/26

Valiant Soldier: Philadelphia, 1807/8/7-S, 9/18-S, 1808/6/28-S

Veteran Tar: Baltimore, 1804/4/11; Boston, 1803/10/21, 10/24, 10/26, 10/31; Charleston, 1807/3/20, 4/11; New York, 1802/11/24, 11/25, 12/3, 12/27; Philadelphia, 1804/3/7, 3/23

Vicissitudes of Harlequin: New York, 1804/4/5-G, 4/7-G, 4/10-G, 4/14-G

Village Gambols: Philadelphia, 1812/12/17-S

Village Ghost: Boston, 1815/10/27; Philadelphia, 1812/12/26-S

Vintagers: Philadelphia, 1814/3/10-Cw

Virgin of the Sun: Baltimore, 1801/5/27, 5/29, 1802/5/10, 11/10, 1803/11/14, 1804/5/25, 1805/5/3, 1806/6/2; Boston, 1808/3/21; Charleston, 1807/3/12; New York, 1801/3/30, 12/4; (Reynolds) 1813/11/15, 11/16, 11/17, 11/19, 11/24, 11/29, 12/20, 12/29, 1814/3/30, 4/11, 4/29, 12/16, 12/21, 1815/4/12, 7/7, 9/23, 12/2, 12/15; Philadelphia, 1801/4/10, 4/11, 1802/2/3, 2/15, 1803/3/23, 1804/1/27, 1805/1/23, 1806/3/14, 1807/3/9; (Reynolds) 1814/1/17, 2/2-Cw, 2/4-Cw, 2/5-Cw, 2/8-Cw

Virgin Unmasked: New York, 1806/8/16-V; Philadelphia, 1803/9/10-S, 1807/8/7-S, 8/15-S, 9/22-S, 9/30-S

Visionary Shades: New York, 1808/5/17-Pe

Voice of Nature: Baltimore, 1803/6/10, 10/7, 11/16; Boston, 1803/10/26, 10/28, 10/31, 11/2, 11/4, 11/21, 1804/1/2, 3/19, 1806/3/10, 1807/1/14, 1811/4/19, 12/6, 1812/5/15, 1814/11/21; Charleston, 1804/2/14, 2/21, 3/2,

1805/5/14; New York, 1803/2/4, 2/5, 2/21, 2/23, 2/28, 3/9, 3/18, 1805/12/9, 1812/1/4, 1813/1/2, 1/4, 10/27, 1814/12/30, 1815/3/17, 11/25; Philadelphia, 1804/1/13, 1/24, 2/10, 1805/1/30, 1806/1/31, 1807/1/30, 1812/3/6

Vulcan's Gift: Charleston, 1804/4/23, 5/17, 11/21, 1805/2/22, 1806/2/14, 1807/1/1, 1808/1/1, 1/20, 12/26, 1810/4/23; New York, 1806/6/20, 6/23, 6/30

Wanderer (Eugenius): New York, 1806/2/7

Wanderer (Kotzebue): Baltimore, 1809/4/19, 4/26, 5/13; Boston, 1810/10/29, 10/31; Charleston, 1808/12/16, 1809/1/6, 3/24; Philadelphia, 1809/3/6

Waterman: Baltimore, 1802/4/23, 1805/11/13, 1806/6/7, 1807/11/27; Boston, 1801/2/18; Charleston, 1801/2/20, 1803/2/2, 12/22, 1809/3/22; New York, 1802/11/22, 1806/4/7; Philadelphia, 1801/9/16-S, 11/23, 1806/4/2, 1807/1/23, 1811/7/15-A, 7/19-A

We Fly By Night: Baltimore, 1806/11/27; Boston, 1809/3/24, 4/3, 11/22; Charleston, 1807/6/1, 6/5, 1808/2/6, 2/10, 2/17, 3/9, 12/2; New York, 1807/2/27, 3/2, 3/6, 3/13, 9/25, 10/26, 12/9, 1808/3/7, 5/23, 11/2, 12/9, 1809/11/4, 11/11, 12/1, 1812/6/29, 1814/4/25; Philadelphia, 1807/1/16, 1808/2/24, 3/25, 1809/3/18

Weathercock: Baltimore, 1807/4/27, 5/9, 5/25, 10/1, 12/3, 1808/4/27, 10/5, 1809/4/22, 10/30, 1810/5/14, 10/26, 1812/3/23, 5/29, 1814/11/12, 1815/11/8; Boston, 1807/11/30, 12/4, 12/9, 12/23, 1808/2/26, 10/17, 1809/3/22, 9/29, 1810/3/26, 1811/1/9, 3/8, 1812/1/6, 1/28, 1813/2/10, 1815/10/11, 11/10; Charleston, 1806/11/10, 11/18, 1807/1/6, 4/9, 11/11, 1808/1/16, 1809/1/27, 1810/4/7, 1811/1/16; New York, 1806/6/9, 6/13, 7/4, 8/20-V, 1807/2/25, 3/4, 6/26-U, 10/2, 12/7, 1808/7/11-V, 8/17-V, 1810/9/24, 9/28, 10/12, 1811/4/29, 10/14, 11/18, 1812/1/3, 1/17, 5/20, 1813/5/31, 1814/4/18-A, 9/20-A, 1815/9/4; Philadelphia, 1807/2/4, 2/13, 2/20, 2/27, 3/18, 4/6, 12/23, 1808/1/11, 11/12, 1809/3/30, 12/13, 1810/3/19, 12/21, 1811/1/26, 4/3, 9/13, 10/9, 1812/1/8, 11/18, 1813/3/24, 1814/1/7, 1815/1/30, 12/18

Wedding in Wales: Baltimore, 1804/4/27; Philadelphia, 1801/12/21, 1802/2/8

Wheel of Truth: New York, 1803/1/12, 1/14, 1/17, 1/21; Philadelphia, 1804/3/16

Whim Upon Whim: Charleston, 1804/2/8, 2/15, 1805/12/26, 1806/12/17, 1807/1/19, 12/22, 12/30, 1808/2/24, 1811/4/15

Whitsuntide Frolics: Baltimore, 1809/5/22, 1814/5/30

Who Pays the Piper?: Philadelphia, 1809/3/25

Who Wins?: Baltimore, 1810/5/23, 10/29; New York, 1810/3/12, 3/23; Philadelphia, 1810/3/7, 4/4, 12/14

Who's to Have Her?: New York, 1814/11/16, 11/21

Wicklow Mountains: Baltimore, 1810/5/30; Philadelphia, 1810/3/14, 4/9

Wife of Two Husbands: Baltimore, 1805/4/22, 11/22, 1806/5/10; Boston, 1805/1/18, 1/21, 1/23, 1/25, 1/28, 1/30, 2/1, 2/8, 2/11, 2/22, 1806/3/7, 11/14, 1809/3/10, 1814/4/29, 10/21, 1815/6/14; Charleston, 1805/11/20, 11/25, 1806/2/20; New York, 1804/4/4, 4/6, 4/11, 4/16, 11/14, 1805/1/2; Philadelphia, 1805/3/1, 1806/1/1

Wild Goose Chase: Baltimore, 1802/5/27; Boston, 1802/5/7; Charleston, 1804/3/2, 3/7, 1805/2/15; New York, 1801/1/12, 3/20, 8/19-MV, 1802/2/8, 2/15, 1803/1/28, 2/4; Philadelphia, 1801/3/21

William Tell: Baltimore, 1813/10/16; Philadelphia, 1812/12/26, 1813/12/31

Witches (Witches Cave): Boston, 1805/2/25, 4/8, 4/15, 11/27, 12/26, 1814/10/28, 12/2, 12/14, 1815/12/27; New York, 1801/5/25, 6/3

Wood Cutters: Boston, 1808/11/18; Charleston, 1809/1/16, 2/22, 1810/4/7, 1811/4/26; New York, 1808/8/29

Wood Daemon: Baltimore, 1809/11/13, 11/16, 1810/5/7; Boston, 1808/3/18, 3/23, 4/11, 10/28, 10/31, 11/2, 11/7, 11/23, 12/19, 1809/3/8, 9/25, 11/6, 1811/11/13, 11/18, 1815/5/12, 5/26, 11/1, 11/22; Charleston, 1809/3/27, 1810/3/10, 4/16; New York, 1808/5/9, 5/11, 5/13, 5/18, 5/23, 6/29, 10/7, 10/14, 1810/11/12, 11/14, 11/16, 11/17, 11/26, 12/31, 1811/1/23, 1/30, 3/18, 4/1, 6/10, 6/28, 9/16, 9/30, 10/9, 11/6, 1812/6/12, 9/9, 1813/6/14, 1815/1/13, 2/27, 3/6, 6/30; Philadelphia, 1809/4/10, 4/12, 4/13, 11/27, 1810/1/17

Wounded Hussar: Philadelphia, 1809/3/29

Yes or No?: Boston, 1811/12/18, 12/31, 1812/11/2, 1813/2/5; Charleston, 1811/3/11; New York, 1809/11/20, 11/22, 11/27, 12/6, 1810/2/26, 1813/3/26

Young Hussar: Baltimore, 1808/5/28; New York, 1811/5/31, 6/3, 6/5, 9/4, 1812/5/16; Philadelphia, 1808/3/26, 1809/3/11

Youth, Love, and Folly: Baltimore, 1807/5/8, 5/16, 10/14, 1809/5/29, 10/13; New York, 1815/5/29, 7/14; Philadelphia, 1807/3/11, 3/14, 1808/3/16, 1809/12/16

Youthful Tar: New York, 1813/11/25, 12/1, 1814/1/5, 2/21

Zembuca: Baltimore, 1815/11/22, 11/23

Zemire and Azor: Charleston, 1805/3/8, 3/25

Zorinski: Boston, 1801/1/30, 1802/5/17, 12/15; Charleston, 1808/5/17; New York, 1802/5/31, 1815/2/22; Philadelphia, 1815/3/31

NOTES

CHAPTER 1: HISTORICAL OVERVIEW

1. *The Mirror of Taste and Dramatic Censor* 1, no. 1 (January 1810), p. 18.
2. Oscar George Theodore Sonneck, *Early Opera in America* (1915; reprint, New York: Benjamin Blom, 1963), pp. 10, 137.
3. Ibid., pp. 35–36.
4. See David McKay, "The Fashionable Lady: The First Opera by an American," *Musical Quarterly* 65, no. 3 (July 1979), pp. 360–67, for a discussion of an opera written in London in 1762 by the American-born James Ralph.
5. For additional information about this opera see Patricia Virga, *The American Opera to 1790* (Ann Arbor: UMI Research Press, 1982), pp. 17–148; and Carolyn Rabson, "*Disappointment* Revisited: Unweaving the Tangled Web," *American Music* 1, no. 1 (Spring 1983), pp. 12–35, and 2, no. 1 (Spring 1984), pp. 1–28. Virga's book provides thorough and complete information concerning all the ballad and pastiche operas composed in America until 1790.
6. Louis C. Madeira, *Annals of Music in Philadelphia and the Musical Fund Society* (Philadelphia: J. B. Lippincott, 1896), p. 32.

7. Irving Lowens, *Music and Musicians in Early America* (New York: W. W. Norton, 1964), p. 93.

8. Ibid.

9. William Dunlap, *History of the American Theatre,* (2 vols.; New York, 1832; reprint, New York: Burt Franklin, 1963), vol. 1, p. 101.

10. These bills are located at the Maryland Historical Society, Baltimore.

11. Bills for October 1, 3, Fell's Point; November 19, Annapolis.

12. Bills in the *Pennsylvania Journal and the Weekly Advertiser* and *The Independent Gazateer; or, the Chronicle of Freedom,* 1787–88.

13. George O. Seilhamer, *History of the American Theatre* (3 vols.; Philadelphia: Globe Printing House, 1888–91), vol. 1, p. 176.

14. John Fanning Watson, *Annals of Philadelphia, and Pennsylvania, in the Olden Time; being a Collection of Memoirs, Anecdotes, and Incidents of the City and its Inhabitants . . . , 1842* (enlarged, with many additions and revisions, by Willis P. Hazard; 3 vols.; Philadelphia: Edwin S. Stuart, 1884), p. 473. Watson also says that when Washington attended the theatre "the Poor Soldier was invariably played by his desire," but this is not true. When Washington visited the theatre, he witnessed a variety of plays and operas.

15. *The New-York Journal, and Weekly Register,* May 17, 1787.

16. David P. McKay and the American Antiquarian Society presented a concert version in Worcester, Massachusetts, on November 8, 1985. See the notice by Arthur Schrader in *The Sonneck Society Newsletter* 12, no. 2 (Summer 1986), p. 59.

17. John Bernard, *Retrospections of America: 1797–1811* (New York: Harper and Brothers, 1887), p. 265.

18. *The New York Magazine or Literary Repository* 5 (December 1794), p. 718.

19. Though the Southwark Theatre was occasionally used for traveling troupes, summer theatre, and exhibitions of various kinds, its days as a regular theatre were done; it eventually became a warehouse, and burned in 1821. The Old American Company granted the superiority of the Wignell-Reinagle company on its own ground; the Wignell-Reinagle company traveled to New York once, in 1797, then ceded that field to the Old Americans.

20. Bernard, *Retrospections of America,* p. 259.

21. William Arms Fisher, *Notes on Music in Old Boston* (Boston: Oliver Ditson Co., 1918), p. 18.

22. *American Mercury,* Hartford, Conn., July 4, 1796.

23. Sonneck, *Early Opera in America,* tables B, C, D, E, I, J. These numbers are conservative; I've found performances of other works, especially pantomimes, not listed by Sonneck.
24. See appendix B.
25. Edward E. Hipsher, *American Opera and Its Composers* (New York: Theodore Presser, 1927), p. 25. The surviving songs are included in Victor Pelissier, *Pelissier's Columbian Melodies: Music for the New York and Philadelphia Theatres,* ed. Karl Kroeger (Madison, Wis.: A-R Editions, 1984).
26. "Why Huntress, Why" was published in the *Musical Journal* (Vol. 2, Philadelphia, 1801), and Rondo in the *Musical Miscellany* in 1813. Excerpts from all of the three operas mentioned are readily accessible in W. Thomas Marrocco and Harold Gleason, *Music in America: An Anthology from the Landing of the Pilgrims to the Close of the Civil War, 1620–1865* (New York: W. W. Norton and Co., 1964). Another work about William Tell, *The Patriot,* had been performed in New York on June 6, 1794, with music by James Hewitt. The libretto may have been by William Bates. No music or text survives.
27. See Wiley H. Hitchcock, "An Early American Melodrama: *The Indian Princess* of J. N. Barker and John Bray." *Notes* 12 (June 1955), pp. 375–88; also Hitchcock's edition of the music and libretto of *The Indian Princess* (New York: Da Capo Press, 1972).
28. *Poulson's American Daily Advertiser,* February 9, 1813.
29. Recorded by New World Records in an edition by Victor Fell Yellin. See also Yellin, "Rayner Taylor's Music for *The Æthiop:* Part I, Performance History," *American Music* 4, no. 3 (Fall 1986), pp. 249–67; "Part II, The Keyboard Score *(The Ethiop)* and Its Orchestral Restoration," 5, no. 1 (Spring 1987), pp. 20–47.

CHAPTER 2: GENRES AND STYLES

1. Thomas Holcroft, "Essay on Dramatick Criticism," quoted in *Polyanthos* 4, no. 2 (January 1807), p. 117.
2. Joseph Addison, *The Spectator* (March 21, 1711), ed. by Donald F. Bond (Oxford: Clarendon Press, 1964), p. 32.
3. Richard Graves, "English Comic Opera: 1760–1800," *Monthly Musical Record* 87 (1957), pp. 208–9.
4. Donald J. Grout, *A Short History of Opera,* 2d ed. (New York: Columbia University Press, 1965), p. 263.

5. From "Essay on Dramatick Composition," quoted in *Polyanthos* 4, no. 1 (December 1806), p. 52.

6. John Durang, *The Memoir of John Durang, American Actor 1785–1816*, ed. Alan S. Downer (Pittsburgh: University of Pittsburgh Press, 1966), pp. 122–26.

7. W. J. Lawrence, "Early Irish Ballad Opera and Comic Opera," *Musical Quarterly* 8 (July 1922), p. 398.

8. Roger Fiske, *English Theatre Music in the Eighteenth Century* (London: Oxford University Press, 1973), p. 274.

9. Edmond McAdoo Gagey, *Ballad Opera* (New York: Columbia University Press, 1937), p. viii.

10. Fiske, *English Theatre Music*, p. 104.

11. *General Advertiser*, Philadelphia, October 16, 1794.

12. *Columbian Centinel*, Boston, January 6, 1796.

13. Michael Winesanker, "Musico-Dramatic Criticism of English Comic Opera, 1750–1800," *Journal of the American Musicological Society* 2 (1949), p. 87. Lawrence, "Early Irish Ballad Opera and Comic Opera," p. 399. George Hogarth uses the term "pasticcio" to describe this style in his *Memoirs of the Musical Drama* (2 vols.; London: Richard Bentley, 1838), vol. 2, 100.

14. Lawrence, "Early Irish Ballad Opera and Comic Opera," p. 399.

15. A complete list of the borrowings is found in Appendix E of Fiske, *English Theatre Music*, pp. 605–6. See also Fiske's theory that one tune is the king's, pp. 330–31.

16. Ibid., p. 328.

17. Arne also wrote a full-length all-sung opera, *Artaxerxes,* in 1762.

18. See table in Fiske, *English Theatre Music*, p. 607.

19. In four major American cities (New York, Baltimore, Boston, and Philadelphia) during the first decade of the nineteenth century, a day-by-day survey of playbills in newspapers throughout each season found the term "comic opera" used 553 times, "musical entertainment" 363, "musical farce" 144, "play interspersed with songs" 94, "opera" 85, and "musical drama" 69. Though all these terms were used interchangeably, the term "ballad opera" was never used to describe any work performed.

20. Sheldon Cheney, *The Theatre: Three Thousand Years of Drama, Acting and Stagecraft* (New York, 1929; reprint, London: Vision Press, 1972), p. 409.

21. Frederick W. Bateson, *English Comic Drama, 1700–1750* (Oxford: Clarendon Press, 1929), pp. 7, 13. Bateson here speaks of the sentimen-

talizing of Restoration comedy in the early part of the eighteenth century, but the sense of the quote applies also to post-Revolutionary sentimentalism.

22. *The Port Folio* 1, no. 9 (February 28, 1801), p. 68.
23. George C. D. Odell, *Annals of the New York Stage* (New York: Columbia University Press, 1927), vol. 1, 424–25.
24. Rey M. Longyear, "Notes on the Rescue Opera," *Musical Quarterly* 45 (1959), p. 50.
25. Richard Moody, *America Takes the Stage: Romanticism in American Drama and Theatre, 1750–1900* (Bloomington: Indiana University Press, 1955), pp. 2–3.
26. *Polyanthos* 1, no. 1 (October 1812), p. 54.
27. *The Mirror of Taste and Dramatic Censor* 1, no. 1 (January 1810), p. 80.
28. Ibid., 3, no. 6 (June 1811), pp. 367, 369.
29. *The Emerald* 1, no. 26 (October 25, 1806), p. 304.
30. *The Comet*, November 2, 1811, p. 33.
31. George Colman, *Blue Beard. A Dramatic Romance*, W. Oxberry's edition (London: W. Simpkin, R. Marshall, and C. Chapple, 1823), p. iv.
32. *The Mirror of Taste and Dramatic Censor* 3, no. 6 (June 1811), p. 371.
33. Ibid., 1, no. 3 (March 1810), p. 252.
34. Ibid., 3, no. 1 (January 1811), p. 55.
35. Quoted in Fiske, *English Theatre Music*, p. 71.
36. *The Maryland Journal and Baltimore Advertiser*, March 31, 1783.
37. Drury Lane, too, had its *Harlequin Dr. Faustus* that season, but the two productions were unrelated; Samuel Arnold also wrote a *Harlequin Dr. Faustus* in 1766.
38. Oscar George Theodore Sonneck, *Early Opera in America* (1915; reprint, New York: Benjamin Blom, 1963), p. 92.
39. Fiske, *English Theatre Music*, pp. 92, 166.
40. Tom Davies, 1780, quoted in Fiske, *English Theatre Music*, p. 76.
41. *Gazette of the United States*, February 28, 1799; this is not the playwright Susannah Rowson, whose husband was William.
42. *The Port Folio* 2, no. 3 (January 23, 1802), pp. 17–18.
43. *Gazette of the United States*, July 18, 1797.
44. *New York Packet*, October 10, 1785.
45. *Charleston Courier*, March 12, 24, 1804.
46. *The Emerald* 1, no. 9 (December 19, 1807), p. 99.
47. Henry Barton Baker, *History of the London Stage and its Famous Play-*

ers (1576–1903) (1904; reprint, New York: Benjamin Blom, 1969), p. 110. Said of the London patent houses.

48. *Daily Advertiser,* New York, March 15, 1803.

49. Karl Kroeger lists a *Shantreuse* published by James Hewitt in 1803 (W6927), and includes a Dance published in 1812 (W6888) in his edition of Victor Pelissier's *Columbian Melodies* (Madison, Wis.: A-R Editions, 1984). The dance has no indication of movement nor of its position in the play.

50. Description of a New York performance of the tragedy *The Tournament,* playbill, May 2, 1803, Harvard Theatre Collection.

51. *The Mirror of Taste and Dramatic Censor* 1, no. 4 (April 1810), pp. 345–46.

52. *The Emerald* 1, no. 21 (March 12, 1808), p. 251.

53. *American Citizen,* New York, April 11, 1806; *Polyanthos* 2, no. 1 (April 1806), p. 71. The composer and compiler of this work was apparently John Williams (Anthony Pasquin).

54. *The Emerald* 1, no. 50 (October 1, 1808), p. 598.

55. *Polyanthos* 5, no. 2 (May 1807), pp. 139–40. Brackets original.

56. Fiske, *English Theatre Music,* pp. 171–72.

57. *Daily Advertiser,* New York, May 19, 1800; complete bill reproduced in Sonneck, *Early Opera in America,* pp. 94–95; *Poulson's American Daily Advertiser,* Philadelphia, March 22, 1805.

58. Sonneck, *Early Opera in America,* p. 95.

59. Quoted in Eric Walter White, *The Rise of English Opera* (London: John Lehmann, 1951), p. 65.

60. Fiske, *English Theatre Music,* pp. 171–72.

61. Allardyce Nicoll, *A History of Late Eighteenth Century Drama, 1750–1800* (Cambridge: University Press, 1927), p. 194.

62. Allardyce Nicoll, *A History of Early Nineteenth Century Drama, 1800–1850* (Cambridge: University Press, 1930), p. 139.

63. See the article on "New Orleans" in *The New Grove Dictionary of American Music,* eds. H. Wiley Hitchcock and Stanley Sadie (London: Macmillan Press; New York: Grove's Dictionaries of Music, 1986); also see Sonneck, *Early Opera in America,* pp. 197–219.

CHAPTER 3: THE PARTS AND THE WHOLE

1. "Upon the Relation of Music to the Drama," *The Euterpeiad: or Musical Intelligencer* 1, no. 12 (June 17, 1820), p. 47; apparently quoted from an earlier, unnamed, English source.

2. Quoted by Roger Fiske in "The Operas of Stephen Storace," *The Proceedings of the Royal Musical Association* 86 (1959–60), pp. 39–40.

3. *Gentleman's Magazine* 34 (March 1764), p. 110; *European Magazine* 9 [March 1786], p. 182. These and other criticisms are quoted in Michael Winesanker, "Musico-Dramatic Criticism of English Comic Opera, 1750–1800," *Journal of the American Musicological Society* 2 (1949), pp. 87–96.

4. George Hogarth, *Memoirs of the Musical Drama* (2 vols.; London: R. Bentley, 1838), vol. 2, p. 101.

5. Quoted in Fiske, "The Operas of Stephen Storace," p. 39.

6. *The Port Folio*, 1, no. 7 (February 14, 1801), p. 50.

7. *Dramatic Censor*, June 5, 1800, quoted in Roger Fiske, *English Theatre Music in the Eighteenth Century* (London: Oxford University Press, 1973), p. 266.

8. "Upon the Relation of Music to the Drama," *The Euterpeiad: or Musical Intelligencer* 1, no. 12 (June 17, 1820), p. 47.

9. George Colman, *Blue Beard. A Dramatic Romance*, W. Oxberry's edition (London: W. Simpkin, R. Marshall, and C. Chapple, 1823), p. iv.

10. Fiske, *English Theatre Music*, p. 262.

11. John O'Keeffe, *Recollections of the Life of John O'Keeffe, written by himself* (2 vols.; London: Henry Colburn, 1926), vol. 2, p. 12. See also Fiske, *English Theatre Music*, p. 454, concerning financial problems with this opera.

12. *The Ramblers' Magazine* 4 (February 2, 1810), pp. 8–9. The term "Maecenas" refers to a patron of the arts; Gaius Maecenas was an eighth-century B.C. Roman statesman and patron of literature.

13. *New-York Journal and Patriotic Register*, March 8, 1794.

14. William Dunlap, *Diary of William Dunlap (1766–1839)*, ed. Dorothy C. Barck (3 vols.; New York: New York Historical Society, 1930), vol. 1, p. 75.

15. *New-York Evening Post*, February 24, 1806. William Charles White received the second performance of his tragedy *Orlando* as a benefit in 1797 (*Columbian Centinel*, March 8, 1797). William Ioor of South Carolina wrote a comedy called *Independence; or, Which Do You Like Best, the Peer or the Farmer?* which was performed at Charleston on March 29, 1805. The second performance, April 1, was a benefit for him (*Charleston Courier*, March 31, 1805).

16. William Dunlap, *History of the American Theatre* (2 vols.; New York, 1832; reprint, New York: Burt Franklin, 1963), vol. 2, p. 292.

17. Frederick Corder, "The Works of Sir Henry Bishop," *Musical Quarterly* 4 (1918), p. 91.

18. Fiske, *English Theatre Music*, p. 520.

19. Ibid., p. 292.

20. Such "Turkish" marches—though actually French bagpipe tunes—were well known in the English theatre; Stephen Storace actually borrowed parts of Mozart's "Rondo alla turca" for the "Dance of the Turkish Soldiers" in *The Siege of Belgrade*. See Richard Graves, "The Comic Operas of Stephen Storace," *The Musical Times* 95 (October 1954), p. 531.

21. From the score.

22. Richard Graves, "English Comic Opera: 1760–1800," *Monthly Musical Record* 87 (1957), pp. 208–15, contains a good discussion of musical forms used.

23. Since the first violin normally doubles the voice, it is cued on the middle staff, while the second violin part, which is usually supplied only if there is an additional staff, is cued on the top line.

24. Fiske, *English Theatre Music*, p. 351.

25. *Carr's Musical Miscellany* 28 (Baltimore: J. Carr, ca. 1815).

26. Haydn also provided a setting of "Ay, wakin' oh!" in a version similar to Arnold's.

27. William Shield, *An Introduction to Harmony* (London: G. G. and J. Robinson, 1800), p. 84.

28. *Aurora. General Advertiser*, Philadelphia, March 20, 1795. Italics mine.

29. This influence was direct. Storace and his sister Nancy were close friends of Mozart in Vienna, and Stephen may even have studied with him. Nancy created the role of Susanna in *Le Nozze di Figaro;* she and tenor Michael Kelly provided the acting experience for Stephen's action ensembles and finales.

30. *The Comet*, December 21, 1811, p. 117.

31. *Aurora. General Advertiser*, February 2, 1811.

32. Oscar George Theodore Sonneck, "Early American Operas," *Sämmelbande der Internationalen Musik Gesellschaft*, 1904–1905, pp. 486, 487, 483.

33. Playbill, September 26, 1795, Maryland Historical Society.

34. *The Daily Advertiser*, New York, November 29, 1803.

35. Playbill, October 19, 1795, Maryland Historical Society.

36. *Boston Daily Advertiser*, February 16, 1815.

37. *Federal Orrery*, Boston, November 9, 1795.

38. *The Children in the Wood. A Musical Piece in two acts. With the Additions and alterations as performed by the Old American Company* (New York: Columbian Press, 1795). Hereafter cited as New York, 1795. Other New York librettos, published in 1805, 1808, and 1816, contain similar texts.

39. "When Nights Were Cold" is found in all American librettos, including New York, 1795, and *The Children in the Wood. A Musical Piece in two acts. With the additions and alterations as performed at Boston* (Boston: Jno. and Jos. N. Russell, 1795). Hereafter cited as Boston, 1795.

40. "Mark My Alford" is found in the New York and Boston librettos, 1795. The variation sets are "Mark Me Alfred, A Favorite French Air with Variations" (Albany: J. C. Goldberg, n.d.) and "Mark My Alford, a Favorite Air with Variations for the Piano Forte," composed by J. Hewitt (Philadelphia: G. Willig, [1812–15]).

41. Found in New York, 1795, but not in Boston. Also performed in Charleston in 1796. *City Gazette and daily advertiser,* Charleston, March 17, 1796.

42. New York, 1795; Boston, 1795.

43. *City Gazette and daily advertiser,* Charleston, March 17, 1796.

44. *The Comet,* October 26, 1811, p. 14.

45. *New York Magazine or Literary Repository* 5 (December 1794), p. 719.

46. *Polyanthos* 4, no. 2 (January 1807), p. 136.

47. *Polyanthos* 3, no. 4 (November 1806), p. 281.

48. William B. Wood, *Personal Recollections of the Stage, embracing notices of actors, authors and auditors during a period of forty years* (Philadelphia: H. C. Baird, 1855), pp. 93–94.

49. *New-York Journal and Patriotic Register,* March 8, 1794.

50. *The Theatrical Censor* 7 [January 1806], p. 58.

51. *The Ramblers' Magazine* 3 [December 1809], p. 194. This was the first performance on November 20.

52. *The Mirror of Taste and Dramatic Censor* 1, no. 1 (January 1810), p. 66.

53. *The Comet,* December 7, 1811, p. 90.

54. *Polyanthos* 1, no. 5 (February 1812), p. 66.

55. *The Theatrical Censor* 5 [December 1805], p. 44.

56. *The Theatrical Censor and Critical Miscellany* 8 (November 15, 1806), p. 115.

57. *Charleston Courier,* March 19, April 29, 1805.

58. *The Comet,* October 26, 1811, p. 16.

59. Oscar George Theodore Sonneck, *Early Opera in America* (1915; reprint, New York: Benjamin Blom, 1963), p. 145.

60. *American Mercury,* Hartford, November 7, 1799.

61. *Federal Orrery,* Boston, January 14, 1796.

62. *Charleston Courier,* February 23, 1804.

63. *Polyanthos* 1, no. 4 (January 1813), p. 216.

64. *The Theatrical Censor* 9 [January 1806], p. 78.

65. *The Emerald* 2, no. 46 (March 14, 1807), p. 126.

66. Ibid. 2, no. 73 (September 14, 1807), p. 450.

67. *Polyanthos* 1, no. 1 (December 1805), p. 61.

68. *The Ramblers' Magazine* 3 [December 1809], p. 201.

69. *The Emerald* 1, no. 26 (April 16, 1808), p. 310. This performance was "the first for many years."

70. *Charleston Courier,* February 21, 1804.

71. *The Emerald* 2, no. 42 (February 14, 1807).

72. Ibid. 2, no. 46 (March 14, 1807), p. 127.

73. Playbill, New York John St. Theatre, January 14, 1795, Harvard Theatre Collection.

74. *Commercial Advertiser,* New York, June 3, 1799.

75. Ibid., November 28, 1799.

76. Prince Pückler-Muskau, *A Tour in England, Ireland and France in 1828 and 1829* (London, 1832), quoted in Eric Walter White, *The Rise of English Opera* (London: John Lehmann, 1951), p. 89. According to Loewenberg, the first New York performance in 1824 also used Bishop's arrangement. In his article, "The Works of Sir Henry Bishop," p. 87, Frederick Corder described this version, first performed on March 6, 1819: "The Overture and eight of Mozart's best numbers are omitted and ten vile songs and six dances by Bishop substituted. There is a dreadful song for *Susanna* with a Cadenza for voice and Clarinet, a Scotch song transcribed, besides pointless alterations in the original numbers retained. A really shocking affair." The entire catalog of Bishop's works serves as a compilation of the alteration practices of the early nineteenth century.

CHAPTER 4: THE THEATRES

1. For U.S. total figures: *Historical Statistics of the United States: Colonial Times to 1790,* U.S. Bureau of the Census, 1975. For 1790: *A Cen-*

tury of Population Growth 1790–1900, U.S. Bureau of the Census, 1909. For 1800: Tertius Chandler and Gerald Fox, *3,000 Years of Urban Growth* (New York: Academic Press, 1974). For 1810: George Rogers Taylor, *The Transportation Revolution 1815–1860,* vol. 4 (New York: Rinehart and Co., 1951).

2. Washington Irving, "Letters of Jonathan Oldstyle, Gent.," *Morning Chronicle,* New York, 1802. In *The Works of Washington Irving* (London: George Bell and Sons, 1890), vol. 11, p. 188.

3. *The Ramblers' Magazine* 1 (October 6, 1809), p. 13.

4. *American Citizen,* New York, September 1, 1808.

5. Royall Tyler, *The Contrast* (1790; reprint, New York: AMS Press, 1970), p. 77.

6. A. N. Vardac, *Stage to Screen: Theatrical Method from Garrick to Griffith* (Cambridge: Harvard University Press, 1949), p. 7.

7. An early act curtain, used in Providence on August 8, 1812, and painted by Warrell of Boston, ca. 1810, survives. Brooks McNamara, *The American Playhouse in the Eighteenth Century* (Cambridge: Harvard University Press, 1969), p. 94.

8. Irving, "Jonathan Oldstyle," pp. 183–84.

9. McNamara, in *The American Playhouse in the Eighteenth Century,* claims that these spikes were no longer used in the new playhouses built at the end of the eighteenth century. John Durang's story in *The Memoir of John Durang, American Actor 1785–1816,* ed. Alan S. Downer (Pittsburgh: University of Pittsburgh Press, 1966), p. 23 (hereafter cited as *Memoir*), however, describes injuring himself on the spikes of the orchestra pit—evidence that spikes were used in American theatres as late as 1785, when Durang joined the Old American Company in Philadelphia. The gallery at the Chestnut Street Theatre in Philadelphia was still separated from the boxes by spikes; it is not unreasonable to assume they were also used to protect the orchestra.

10. *The Theatrical Censor and Critical Miscellany* 7 (November 8, 1806), p. 108.

11. *Commercial Advertiser,* New York, December 4, 1798.

12. *Gazette,* New York, November 19, 1750.

13. Henry Pitt Phelps, *Players of a Century: A Record of the Albany Stage, including notices of prominent actors who have appeared in America* (Albany: J. McDonough, 1880), p. 20.

14. *Columbian Centinel,* Boston, January 22, 1794.

15. *Providence Gazette and Country Journal,* November 14, 1801.

16. *New-York Evening Post,* November 15, 1813.

17. *City Gazette and Daily Advertiser,* Charleston, June 23, 1794.

18. Oscar George Theodore Sonneck, *Early Opera in America* (1915; reprint, New York: Benjamin Blom, 1963), p. 84. The "wind sail" was also used in New York in late May 1793 (*New-York Journal and Patriotic Register,* May 29, 1793).

19. *Aurora. General Advertiser,* Philadelphia, July 10, 1802. The innovation was contrived by a contingent from the New Theatre who had rented the Southwark for a summer season.

20. *The Mirror of Taste and Dramatic Censor* 2, no. 4 (October 1810), p. 297.

21. *New York Magazine or Literary Repository* 3 (September 1792), p. 573.

22. Ibid. Brooks McNamara points out that a print of the exterior of this theatre, reproduced in Eola Willis, *The Charleston Stage in the XVIII Century, with Social Settings of the Time* (Columbia, S.C., 1924; reprint, New York: Benjamin Blom, 1968), p. 152, is actually a view of the Arch Street Theatre in Philadelphia after 1829.

23. Quoted in Sonneck, *Early Opera in America,* p. 169.

24. *Charleston Courier,* November 14, 1804.

25. *Charleston Courier,* January 31, 1804.

26. *Charleston Daily Courier,* February 6, 1812.

27. *Aurora. General Advertiser,* June 29, 1813.

28. Durang, *Memoir,* p. 106. Charles Durang reported that he often saw the model lying in the property room over the dome.

29. Arthur Hobson Quinn, *A History of the American Drama from the Beginning of the Civil War* (2 vols.; New York: Harper and Brothers, 1923), p. 82.

30. *Moreau de St. Méry's American Journey (1793–1798),* trans. and eds. Kenneth and Anna M. Roberts (Garden City, N.Y.: Doubleday and Co., 1947), p. 348.

31. *The Port Folio* 1, no. 8 (February 21, 1801), p. 60. It is not clear if this were true, or if the comment was intended as a suggestion.

32. McNamara, *The American Playhouse in the Eighteenth Century,* p. 108.

33. James Mease, *The Picture of Philadelphia* (Philadelphia: B. & T. Kite, 1811), p. 330.

34. Ibid., p. 330. The 1800 picture of the exterior of the theatre which is referred to may be found in Brooks McNamara, pp. 109.

35. *The Emerald* 1, no. 26 (April 16, 1808), p. 311; Durang, *The Philadelphia Stage,* chapter 19.

36. *The Thespian Monitor and Dramatick Miscellany* 1, no. 1 (November 25, 1809), p. 4.

37. Quoted in Sonneck, *Early Opera in America,* pp. 113–14. The letter is dated 1793 in error, but obviously dates from the following year.

38. The engraving seems to have been made before the interior decorations were complete; no chandeliers are shown, either overhead or on the fronts of the boxes.

39. *Moreau de St. Méry's American Journey,* p. 346.

40. *New York Magazine or Literary Repository* 4, no. 4 (April 1794), p. 195.

41. Forman, quoted in Sonneck, *Early Opera in America,* p. 114.

42. *Moreau de St. Méry's American Journey,* p. 346.

43. *General Advertiser,* Philadelphia, January 29, 1793.

44. *Moreau de St. Méry's American Journey,* p. 346.

45. *New York Magazine or Literary Repository* 4, no. 4 (April 1794), p. 195.

46. *Moreau de St. Méry's American Journey,* p. 347.

47. Ibid., p. 346.

48. *New York Magazine or Literary Repository* 4, no. 4 (April 1794), p. 195.

49. Forman, quoted in Sonneck, *Early Opera in America,* p. 114.

50. *Moreau de St. Méry's American Journey,* p. 346.

51. Forman, quoted in Sonneck, *Early Opera in America,* p. 114.

52. *Moreau de St. Méry's American Journey,* p. 346.

53. Mease, *The Picture of Philadelphia,* p. 331.

54. Forman, quoted in Sonneck, *Early Opera in America,* p. 114. The internal quote is from Shakespeare's *Titus Andronicus.*

55. *Moreau de St. Méry's American Journey,* p. 347.

56. Mease, *The Picture of Philadelphia,* p. 330. The floor plan in figure 6 dates from after the introduction of gas stage lighting at the house in 1816 and before the 1820 fire.

57. Charles Durang, *The Philadelphia Stage . . . Partly compiled from the papers of his father, the late John Durang; with notes by the editors* (seven looseleaf notebooks clipped from the *Sunday Dispatch,* Philadelphia; first series, 1749–1821, published in 75 chapters, beginning May 7, 1854; Harvard Theatre Collection), chapter 19.

58. *The Port Folio* 1, no. 44 (October 31, 1801), p. 349; *The Mirror of Taste and Dramatic Censor* 2, no. 4 (October 1810), p. 295.

59. *The Thespian Monitor, and Dramatick Miscellany* 1, no. 1 (November 25, 1809), p. 4.

60. *The Mirror of Taste and Dramatic Censor* 2, no. 4 (October 1810), pp. 297.

61. Mease, *The Picture of Philadelphia*, p. 331.

62. *The Mirror of Taste and Dramatic Censor* 2, no. 4 (October 1810), pp. 297–98.

63. *Boston Gazette*, January 29, 1798.

64. William W. Clapp, Jr., *A Record of the Boston Stage* (Boston, 1853; reprint, New York: Greenwood Press, 1969), p. 19.

65. These contrasting views of the exterior can be seen in McNamara, *The American Playhouse in the Eighteenth Century*, pp. 121–23.

66. Clapp, Jr., *A Record of the Boston Stage*, p. 19.

67. John Alden, *A Season in Federal Street; J. B. Williamson and the Boston Theatre, 1796–1797* (Worcester: American Antiquarian Society, 1955), p. 12.

68. Clapp, Jr., *A Record of the Boston Stage*, p. 19.

69. Alden, *A Season in Federal Street*, pp. 11–12.

70. *Polyanthos* 3, no. 1 (October 1813), p. 56.

71. Henry Wansey, *The Journal of an Excursion of the United States of North America in the Summer of 1794* (Salisbury: J. Eaton, 1796), p. 126.

72. John Bernard, *Retrospections of America: 1797–1811* (New York: Harper and Brothers, 1887), p. 292.

73. McNamara, *The American Playhouse in the Eighteenth Century*, pp. 134–35. In his letters concerning the Hartford Theatre (Harvard Theatre Collection), John Hodgkinson also spoke of a Mr. Wilson who was an architect on the Park Theatre.

74. *The Argus*, New York, November 30, 1798.

75. The facade is pictured in an 1809 watercolor by John C. Hind owned by Harvard Theatre Collection, and reproduced as the frontispiece of McNamara, *The American Playhouse in the Eighteenth Century*.

76. T. B. Thorpe, "The Old Theatres of New York, 1750–1827," *Appleton's Journal* 8 (November 23, 1872), p. 578; quoted in McNamara, p. 5.

77. Joseph N. Ireland, *Fifty Years of a Play-goers Journal; or Annals of the New York Stage, from A.D. 1798 to A.D. 1848, with Biographical Sketches of the Principal Performers* (New York: Samuel French, 1860), p. 7.

78. *New-York Evening Post,* August 23, 1807.

79. *The Ramblers' Magazine* 1 (October 6, 1809), p. 10.

80. Thomas Allston Brown, *History of the New York Stage from the first performance in 1732 to 1901* (3 vols.; New York: Dodd, Mead and Co., 1903), vol. 2, p. 12.

81. *Daily Advertiser,* New York, January 31, 1798.

82. *Commercial Advertiser,* New York, January 31, 1798.

83. William Dunlap, *History of the American Theatre* (2 vols.; 1832; reprint, New York: Burt Franklin, 1963), vol. 2, p. 247.

84. Brown, *New York Stage,* vol. 2, p. 12.

85. *Commercial Advertiser,* New York, December 4, 1798.

86. Ibid., January 31, 1798.

87. *The Theatrical Censor and Critical Miscellany* 7 (November 8, 1806), p. 102.

88. Brown, *New York Stage,* vol. 2, p. 12.

89. *Commercial Advertiser,* New York, January 31, 1798. The statement about the gallery implies that the front of the topmost tier was used as boxes, which were separated by a partition and passageway from the gallery above and behind them on the same tier. This separating partition was apparently removed on June 5 (*Daily Advertiser,* June 4, 1798).

90. Dunlap, *The Diary of William Dunlap,* ed. Dorothy C. Barck (3 vols.; New York: New York Historical Society, 1930), vol. 1, p. 207.

91. Dunlap, *History of the American Theatre,* vol. 2, p. 247. Odell, vol. 2, p. 291, says this box was demolished in the 1807 remodeling.

92. Letter of December 11, 1802; Irving, "Jonathan Oldstyle," pp. 187–88.

93. William Dunlap, *Memoirs of a Water Drinker* (2 vols.; New York: Saunders & Otley, 1837), vol. 1, p. 28; vol. 2, p. 31.

94. *New-York Evening Post,* August 23, 1807.

95. Dunlap, *History of the American Theatre,* vol. 2, pp. 245–47. Dunlap says "We copy the following description of it," and places it all in quotes, but gives no source. All the preceding information concerning the 1807 remodeling is taken from Dunlap or from the *New-York Evening Post,* August 23, 1807.

96. *The Ramblers' Magazine* 1 (October 6, 1809), pp. 17–18. The quotes are used without attribution, but the material is taken from a letter by "Fillullee" printed in the *New-York Commercial Advertiser,* September 8, 1809.

97. Dunlap, *History of the American Theatre,* vol. 2, p. 249.

98. James Moreland, "The Theatre in Portland in the Eighteenth Century," *New England Quarterly* 11, no. 2 (June 1938), pp. 333–34. Moreland's source is the *Eastern Herald and Gazette of Maine.*

99. George O. Willard, *History of the Providence Stage, 1762–1891* (Providence: Rhode Island News Co., 1891), pp. 22–25 passim. Providence, too, was still under an antitheatre law but it seems to have been largely ignored. The General Assembly voted to allow the licensing of theatres in 1793, and the law was repealed in 1798.

100. *Providence Gazette and Country Journal,* August 1, 1795.

101. Durang, *Memoir,* pp. 96ff. passim.

102. *Providence Gazette and Country Journal,* August 8 and 29, 1795.

103. Willard, *History of the Providence Stage, 1762–1891,* p. 26.

104. Ibid., p. 75.

105. *The Albany Register,* August 16, 1803. On the 19th this venue was described as the "Thespian Hotel, north end of Pearl-Street."

106. *Polyanthos* 1, no. 4 (January 1813), p. 220.

107. *Augusta Herald,* January 31, 1805.

108. West T. Hill, Jr., *The Theatre in Early Kentucky, 1790–1820* (Lexington: University Press of Kentucky, 1971), p. 9.

109. *Kentucky Gazette,* Lexington, November 14, 1799.

110. Hill, *The Theatre in Early Kentucky,* p. 5.

111. *Kentucky Gazette,* February 28 and December 29, 1807.

112. Ibid., October 11, 1808.

113. Ibid., October 18, 1808.

114. Noah Miller Ludlow, *Dramatic Life as I Found It* (St. Louis: G. I. Jones and Co., 1880; reprint New York: Benjamin Blom, 1966), p. 89.

115. Ibid., p. 55.

116. Durang, *Memoir,* pp. 113, 114, 116, 120, 130-31, 136. All spellings original.

117. Hodgkinson may have originally intended to simply transfer the old scenery from the John Street Theatre to Hartford on completion of the Park Theatre—but the Park was, of course, delayed far longer than expected.

118. Alfred L. Bernheim, *The Business of the Theatre: An Economic History of the American Theatre, 1750–1932* (New York: Actors Equity Association, 1932; reissued New York: Benjamin Blom, 1964), p. 13.

119. Ibid., p. 14. See also Odell, vol. 1, p. 361; vol. 2, p. 1.

120. *Columbian Museum and Savannah Advertiser,* Savannah, January 23, 1804.

121. Ibid., February 8, 1804.
122. *American and Commercial Advertiser,* May 8, 1813.
123. Ibid., April 17, 1813.
124. Ibid., May 8, 1813.
125. Ibid., April 11, 1814.
126. Ibid., June 16, 1814.
127. Ibid., September 28, 1815.

CHAPTER 5: AND ALL THE TRIMMINGS

1. Quoted in Allardyce Nicoll, *A History of Late Eighteenth Century Drama 1750–1800* (Cambridge: University Press, 1927), p. 26.
2. John Alden, *A Season in Federal Street: J. B. Williamson and the Boston Theatre, 1796–1797* (Worcester: American Antiquarian Society, 1955), p. 34.
3. See, for example, the "Articles of Agreement" for the Hartford Theatre, August 15, 1795, located in the Harvard Theatre Collection.
4. The custom of referring to actors and other stage personnel by last name only in playbills creates many problems for historians. First names are supplied here whenever they are known. Spellings also vary from bill to bill.
5. Washington Irving, for example, speaks of the "good folks of the gallery, who have the privilege of demanding a bow from John (by which name they designate every servant of the theatre who enters to move a table or snuff a candle)." "Letters of Jonathan Oldstyle, Gent.," *Morning Chronicle,* New York, 1802. In *The Works of Washington Irving* (London: George Bell and Sons, 1890), vol. 11, p. 184. Hereafter cited as "Jonathan Oldstyle."
6. *New York Evening Post,* November 15, 1813.
7. *Commercial Advertiser,* New York, June 30 and July 3, 1800. Much of this scenery was used for productions of *Count Benyowsky* and *Pizarro in Peru.*
8. These are all listed among "Incidental Current Expences of accumulating Property" in Alden, *A Season in Federal Street,* p. 36.
9. "Report of the Committee of Investigation" into a December 16 fire, *Virginia Argus,* Richmond, January 2, 1812. Same report printed in the *Enquirer.*
10. *Polyanthos* 5, no. 4 (July 1807), p. 284.
11. *The Port Folio* 1, no. 46 (November 14, 1801), p. 365. Brackets origi-

nal. While the correspondent's point is to show that the scenery is not really flammable, he does not mention transparent scenes, which were "coated with varnish and extremely flammable" (*Virginia Argus,* Richmond, January 2, 1812).

12. Edwin Duerr, "Charles Ciceri and the Background of American Scene Design," *Theatre Arts Monthly* 16 (December 1932), p. 988.

13. Charles Durang, *The Philadelphia Stage . . . Partly compiled from the papers of his father, the late John Durang; with notes by the editors* (seven looseleaf notebooks clipped from the *Sunday Dispatch,* Philadelphia; first series, 1749–1821, published in 75 chapters, beginning May 7, 1854; Harvard Theatre Collection), chapter 18.

14. Richard Southern, *Changeable Scenery: Its Origin and Development in the British Theatre* (London: Faber and Faber, 1952), p. 104.

15. *Daily Advertiser,* New York, April 4, 1787.

16. Abraham Rees, *Cyclopaedia, or Universal Dictionary of Arts, Sciences and Literature, illustrated with numerous engravings* (London, 1803–1819), quoted in Southern, *Changeable Scenery,* p. 174. This observation is borne out in the Boston inventory.

17. *Virginia Argus,* Richmond, January 2, 1812.

18. Rees, *Cyclopaedia,* quoted in Southern, *Changeable Scenery,* p. 273. A good illustration of the mechanical workings of these various scene pieces is found in figure 39 of Southern. Southern's book is so thorough, well-documented, and orderly as to make it almost indispensable to anyone interested in technical details of this type of scenery.

19. Rees, *Cyclopaedia,* quoted in Southern, *Changeable Scenery,* p. 273.

20. Duerr, "Charles Ciceri," p. 989.

21. John O'Keeffe, *Recollections of the Life of John O'Keeffe, written by himself* (2 vols.; London: Henry Colburn, 1826), vol. 2, p. 114.

22. George C. D. Odell, *Annals of the New York Stage* (16 vols.; New York: Columbia University Press, 1927), vol. 1, p. 165.

23. Eola Willis, *The Charleston Stage in the XVIII Century, with Social Settings of the Time* (Columbia, S.C., 1924; reprint, New York: Benjamin Blom, 1968), p. 90.

24. *American Citizen,* New York, July 1, 1801.

25. *The Ramblers' Magazine* 3 [December 1809], p. 195.

26. *Aurora. General Advertiser,* February 18, 1811.

27. John Durang, *The Memoir of John Durang, American Actor 1785–1816,* ed. Alan S. Downer (Pittsburgh: University of Pittsburgh Press, 1966), p. 126.

28. *The Theatrical Censor* 7 [January 1806], pp. 67–68.

29. *Polyanthos* 1, no. 6 (March 1813), p. 332.

30. *Daily Advertiser,* New York, April 4, 1787.

31. William Dunlap, *History of the American Theatre* (2 vols.; New York, 1832; reprint, New York: Burt Franklin, 1963), vol. 1, p. 210.

32. *New York Magazine or Literary Repository,* April 1794, p. 195.

33. Henry Wansey, *The Journal of an Excursion of the United States of North America in the Summer of 1794* (Salisbury: J. Eaton, 1796), p. 126.

34. Richard Stoddard, "Stock Scenery in 1798," *Theatre Survey* 13 (November 1972), pp. 102–103.

35. William B. Wood, *Personal Recollections of the Stage, embracing notices of actors, authors and auditors during the period of forty years* (Philadelphia: H. C. Baird, 1855), p. 236. Wansey, in his *Journal,* p. 127, says "the greatest part of the scenes . . . belonged to Lord Barrymore's Theatre, at Wargrave." John Bernard, in his *Retrospections of America: 1797–1811* (New York: Harper and Brothers, 1887), p. 69, says the scenery was "painted from designs of Loutherbourg."

36. Wood, *Personal Recollections,* p. 205.

37. Bernard, *Retrospections of America,* p. 291.

38. *Daily Advertiser,* New York, May 10, 1788.

39. *Commercial Advertiser,* New York, February 18, 1799.

40. *Aurora,* Philadelphia, May 7, 1795. The story had been told in the London papers as an example of the naiveté and gullibility of the American, but was apparently retold in Philadelphia to show the effect achieved in the theatre.

41. Percy Fitzgerald, *The World behind the Scenes* (London: Chatto and Windus, 1881), p. 71.

42. A. N. Vardac, *Stage to Screen: Theatrical Method from Garrick to Griffith* (Cambridge, Mass.: Harvard University Press, 1949), p. 104.

43. Fitzgerald, *The World behind the Scenes,* p. 71.

44. *Charleston Courier,* November 19, 1803.

45. *Daily Advertiser,* New York, March 9, 1802.

46. Quoted in Duerr, "Charles Ciceri," p. 989–90. This description reminds me of the methods used by scenic artist Elizabeth Lloyd in a recent production of Menotti's *Amahl and the Night Visitors* at The Ohio State University in Lima. Ingenuity on a budget repeats itself.

47. *American Citizen,* New York, June 4, 1806.

48. Ibid., June 6, 1806.

49. *Polyanthos* 3, no. 2 (November 1813), p. 115.

50. *Herald and Public Advertiser,* Norfolk, April 16, 1801, quoted in McNamara, *The American Playhouse in the Eighteenth Century,* p. 95.

51. Southern, *Changeable Scenery,* p. 166.

52. George Owen Willard, *History of the Providence Stage: 1762–1891* (Providence: Rhode Island News Co., 1891), p. 26.

53. Irving, "Jonathan Oldstyle," p. 178.

54. *The Theatrical Censor* 7 [January 1806], p. 61.

55. *Herald and Public Advertiser,* Norfolk, June 8, 1802. Quoted in McNamara, *The American Theatre in the Eighteenth Century,* p. 102.

56. *The Mirror of Taste and Dramatic Censor* 1, no. 2 (February 1810), p. 160.

57. "Articles to be strictly observ'd, by the Managers and Performers belonging to the Maryland Company of Comedians," [1782], Maryland Historical Society.

58. William Dunlap, *Memoirs of a Water Drinker* (2 vols.; New York: Saunders and Otley, 1837), vol. 2, pp. 31–32.

59. [Thomas Morton,] *The Children in the Wood. A Musical Piece in two acts. With the additions and alterations as performed at Boston* (Boston: Jno. and Jos. N. Russell, 1795).

60. Fitzgerald, *The World behind the Scenes,* p. 35.

61. W. J. Lawrence, "Early American Playgoing," *The Theatre* 24 (December 1916), p. 404.

62. Theron R. McClure, "A Reconstruction of Theatrical and Musical Practice in the Production of Italian Opera in the Eighteenth Century" (Ph.D. diss., Ohio State University, 1956), p. 82.

63. John Fanning Watson, *Annals of Philadelphia, and Pennsylvania, in the Olden Time; being a Collection of Memoirs, Anecdotes, and Incidents of the City and its Inhabitants . . . 1842,* enlarged, with additions and revisions, by Willis P. Hazard (3 vols.; Philadelphia: Edwin S. Stuart, 1884), vol. 1, p. 473.

64. *Moreau de St. Méry's American Journey (1793–1798),* trans. and eds. Kenneth and Anna M. Roberts (Garden City, N.Y.: Doubleday and Co., 1947), p. 346.

65. *The Mirror of Taste and Dramatic Censor* 2, no. 4 (October 1810), p. 298.

66. *Columbian Centinel,* October 12, 1811.

67. *Boston Daily Advertiser,* October 1, 1814.

68. Willard, *History of the Providence Stage: 1762–1891,* p. 75.

69. Thomas Allston Brown, *History of the New York Stage from the first performance in 1732 to 1901* (3 vols.; New York: Dodd, Mead and Co., 1903), vol. 2, p. 24.

70. Lawrence, "Early American Playgoing," p. 368.

71. "Report of the Committee of Investigation," *Virginia Argus*, Richmond, January 2, 1812.

72. Roger Fiske, *English Theatre Music in the Eighteenth Century* (London: Oxford University Press, 1973), p. 255.

73. McClure, "Theatrical and Musical Practice," p. 83. When St. Méry visited the Philadelphia Theatre in 1794, he remarked that "The wings have illumination lights." (*Moreau de St. Méry's American Journey*, p. 346.) In 1810 *The Mirror of Taste and Dramatic Censor* said, "The illuminated wings recently exhibited in some of the pieces last produced, are new to this country, and have a very brilliant effect: they do much credit to Messrs. Robins and Stewart in the painting-room." This seems to imply that the wings sometimes used transparencies as a decorative effect. 1, no. 2 (February 1810), p. 160.

74. John Bernard, *Retrospectives of the Stage* (2 vols.; London: Henry Colburn and Richard Bentley, 1830), vol. 1, p. 241.

75. Lawrence, "Early American Playgoing," p. 404; see also William Dunlap, *Memoirs of a Water Drinker*, vol. 1, p. 76.

76. McClure, "Theatrical and Musical Practice," p. 83.

77. Vardac, *Stage to Screen*, p. 11.

78. Fitzgerald, *The World behind the Scenes*, pp. 62–63.

79. Henry Phillips, *Musical and Personal Recollections during half a century* (London: C. J. Skeet, 1864), p. 11.

80. Vardac, *Stage to Screen*, p. 10.

81. Fitzgerald, *The World behind the Scenes*, p. 62. This, too, may have been created with magnesium.

82. Ibid., p. 70.

83. O'Keeffe, *Recollections*, vol. 1, p. 17.

84. Fitzgerald, *The World behind the Scenes*, pp. 61–62.

85. Dunlap, *History of the American Theatre*, vol. 2, p. 273.

86. William Dunlap, *Life of Cooke*, quoted in a review in *The Port Folio* 1, no. 6 (June 1813), pp. 547–48.

87. *Commercial Advertiser*, New York, March 25, 1801.

88. Vardac, *Stage to Screen*, p. 12.

89. Fitzgerald, *The World behind the Scenes*, p. 62; Vardac, *Stage to Screen*, p. 12.

90. Fitzgerald, *The World behind the Scenes,* p. 77.
91. Ibid., p. 13, quoting, but no indication of source; he is discussing the effects used by Loutherbourg.
92. Ibid., p. 18.
93. Ibid., p. 73.
94. *Boston Gazette,* May 5, 1812.
95. *Boston Daily Advertiser,* June 3, 1814.
96. Willis, *Charleston Stage,* p. 263.
97. *The Ramblers' Magazine* 4 (February 2, 1810), p. 25.
98. Vardac, *Stage to Screen,* p. 11.
99. Fitzgerald, *The World behind the Scenes,* p. 52.
100. Dunlap, *History of the American Theatre,* vol. 1, pp. 312–14.
101. *Charleston Courier,* March 19, 1805.
102. *The Theatrical Censor* 5 [December 1805], p. 39.
103. Franklin Fyles, "Behind the Scenes During a Play," *Ladies Home Journal* 17, no. 5 (April 1900), p. 8; quoted in Vardac, *Stage to Screen,* p. 13.
104. *Aurora. General Advertiser,* Philadelphia, February 1, 1797.
105. Durang, *Memoir,* p. 18.
106. *The Mirror of Taste and Dramatic Censor* 1, no. 2 (February 1810), p. 182.
107. *General Advertiser,* Philadelphia, January 8, 1793.
108. Durang, *Memoir,* p. 23.
109. *The Theatrical Censor* 8 (January 16, 1806), p. 75.
110. *Boston Gazette,* December 7, 1807. Ellipses original.
111. *The Theatrical Censor* 7 [January 1806], p. 65.
112. Ibid., 8 (January 16, 1806), p. 76.
113. *Polyanthos* 1, no. 2 (March 1812), pp. 136–37.
114. Playbill, November 24, 1795, Maryland Historical Society.
115. *Charleston Courier,* April 25, 1805.
116. McNamara, *The American Playhouse in the Eighteenth Century,* p. 98.
117. Alden, *A Season in Federal Street,* pp. 44–51 passim.
118. John Hodgkinson, *A Narrative of his Connection with the Old American Company, from 5 September, 1792–31 March, 1797* (New York: J. Oram, 1797), p. 12.
119. Dunlap, *Diary of William Dunlap,* entry for May 24, 1797, vol. 1, pp. 47–48.
120. Ibid., vol. 1, p. 267.
121. Oral Sumner Coad, "Stage and Players in Eighteenth Century

America," *The Journal of English and Germanic Philology* 19 (1920), pp. 216, 217; Durang, *The Philadelphia Stage,* chapter 31.

122. Wood, *Personal Recollections,* p. 236.

123. Alden, *A Season in Federal Street,* pp. 37–43 passim.

124. Playbill, New York Park Theatre, 7th performance, March 24, 1802, Harvard Theatre Collection; *Aurora. General Advertiser,* Philadelphia, April 13, 1808.

125. *Aurora. General Advertiser,* December 31, 1811.

126. *Poulson's American Daily Advertiser,* January 1, 1813.

127. Ibid., February 17, 1814.

128. Walter J. MacQueen-Pope, "James Quin," *Encyclopaedia Britannica* (1968), vol. 18, p. 966.

129. *The Emerald* 1, no. 9 (December 19, 1807), p. 100.

130. Wood, *Personal Recollections,* p. 25.

131. *Polyanthos* 1, no. 4 (January 1813), p. 219.

132. Ibid., 2, no. 1 (March 1813 [corrected in next issue to April]), p. 42.

133. Dunlap, *History of the American Theatre,* vol. 1, p. 155.

134. James Fennell, *An Apology for the Life of James Fennell, Written by Himself* (Philadelphia, 1814; reprint, New York, Benjamin Blom, 1969), pp. 183–84.

135. *The Mirror of Taste and Dramatic Censor* 3, no. 5 (May 1811), p. 309; Henry Barton Baker, *History of the London Stage and its Famous Players (1576–1903)* (1904; reprint, New York: Benjamin Blom, 1969), p. 119. This was during the period (1745–82) when the kilt was banned in Scotland.

136. Charles Blake, *An Historical Account of the Providence Stage* (Providence, 1868; reprint, New York: Benjamin Blom, 1971), p. 65.

137. Alden, *A Season in Federal Street,* p. 40.

138. Wood, *Personal Recollections,* p. 46.

139. Irving, "Jonathan Oldstyle," p. 187.

140. *The Emerald* 1, no. 15 (January 30, 1808), p. 177.

141. *The Ramblers' Magazine* 3 [December 1809], pp. 188–89.

142. Ibid., p. 190.

143. Nicoll, *Late Eighteenth Century Drama,* p. 35.

144. *The Mirror of Taste and Dramatic Censor* 3, no. 5 (May 1811), p. 309.

145. *Commercial Advertiser,* New York, April 28, 1798.

146. *The Ramblers' Magazine* 4 (February 2, 1810), p. 25.

147. *The Comet,* November 30, 1811, pp. 90–91.

148. Dunlap, *History of the American Theatre,* vol. 2, p. 96.

149. *The Ramblers' Magazine* 4 (February 2, 1810), p. 16.

150. *Polyanthos* 3, no. 1 (October 1813), p. 57. When the piece was played again in December, Mrs. Young had corrected the fault; "a pelisse trimmed with fur, with a comfortable pair of sleeves, looked something like a dress for a Siberian winter." *Polyanthos* 3, no. 3 (December 1813), p. 170.

151. *New-York Evening Post*, December 14, 1801.

152. *The Theatrical Censor* 13 (February 22, 1806), p. 119.

153. Anthony Pasquin [pseud. for John Williams], *Eccentricities of John Edwin, comedian. A Calm Inquiry into the present state of our theatres* (2 vols.; London: J. Strahan, 1791), vol. 2, p. 13.

154. George Daniels, ed., *Cumberland's Plays* (London: G. H. Davidson, ca. 1827), vol. 30, p. 8.

155. [Thomas Morton,] *The Children in the Wood. A Musical Piece in two acts. With the additions and alterations as performed by the Old American Company* (New York: Columbian Press, 1795).

156. William Priest traveled in Pennsylvania during the summer of 1794, giving concerts with a group of players: "At our first concert [in Lancaster], three clownish-looking fellows came into the room, and after setting a few minutes, (the weather being *warm*, not to say *hot*) very composedly took off their coats: they were in the usual summer dress of farmers servants in this part of the country; that is to say *without* either stockings or breeches, a loose pair of trowsers being the only succedaneum. As we fixed our Admission at a dollar each, (here seven shillings and sixpence,) we expected this circumstance would be sufficient to exclude such characters, but on inquiry, I found (to my very great surprise!) our three *sans culottes* were german *gentlemen* of considerable property in the neighborhood." Priest found some consolation in the fact that at the dancing assemblies in Hanover, no gentlemen could enter the ballroom without breeches (i.e., no pantaloons or trowsers) or dance without his coat. William Priest, *Travels in the United States of America commencing in the year 1793, and ending in 1797, . . .* (London: J. Johnson, 1802), pp. 60–61.

157. Alden, *A Season in Federal Street*, pp. 37–43 passim.

158. *Charleston Courier*, December 25, 1804.

159. *The Mirror of Taste and Dramatic Censor* 4, no. 2 (August 1811), p. 106.

160. *The Theatrical Censor and Critical Miscellany* 7 (November 8, 1806), p. 102.

161. *The Theatrical Censor* 3 [December 1805], p. 18.

162. *The Thespian Mirror* 10 (March 1, 1806), p. 104.

163. *The Emerald* 1, no. 34 (December 20, 1806), p. 399.

164. *The Ramblers' Magazine* 1 (October 6, 1809), p. 14.

165. Inkle and Yarico's country was inhabited by cannibals, crocodiles, leopards, tigers, and bears. Perhaps Scott Joplin rediscovered it in *Treemonisha,* with its bears and giant beehives, and perhaps Dorothy got there from Kansas somehow when she discovered (or expected) "lions and tigers and bears" in Oz.

166. *Connecticut Courant,* Hartford, September 2, 1799.

167. *The Ramblers' Magazine* 4 (February 2, 1810), p. 25.

168. *The Ramblers' Magazine* 2 [November 1809], p. 94.

169. *The Theatrical Censor* 11 [February 1806], p. 100.

170. *The Comet,* January 11, 1802, p. 172.

171. Wansey, *Journal,* p. 42.

172. *General Advertiser,* Philadelphia, October 2, 1792.

173. Fennell, *Apology,* p. 337.

174. *Charleston Courier,* February 9 and 13, 1804; Watson, *Annals of Philadelphia,* pp. 193, 197.

175. Dunlap, *Memoirs of a Water Drinker,* vol. 2, p. 31.

176. *Polyanthos* 4, no. 1 (December 1806), p. 61.

177. *The Emerald* 1, no. 6 (November 18, 1807), p. 65.

178. *The Ramblers' Magazine* 1 (October 6, 1809), p. 19.

179. "Articles to be strictly observ'd, by the Managers and Performers belonging to the Maryland Company of Comedians," [1782], Maryland Historical Society.

180. Watson, *Annals of Philadelphia* vol. 1, pp. 185–86; Lucy Barton, *Historic Costumes for the Stage* (Boston: Walter H. Baker Co., 1935, rev. 1961), pp. 334–35, 262–63.

181. Watson, *Annals of Philadelphia,* vol. 1, p. 187.

182. James Boaden, *Memoirs of Mrs. Siddons* (London, 1827), vol. 2, 188–292, quoted in A. M. Nagler, *A Source Book for Theatrical History* (New York: Dover Publications, 1952), p. 416.

183. Thomas Campbell, *Life of Mrs. Siddons* (London, 1834), vol. 1, pp. 244–45; quoted in Nagler, *A Source Book for Theatrical History,* p. 417.

184. Watson, *Annals of Philadelphia,* vol. 1, p. 187.

185. Barton, *Historic Costumes for the Stage,* p. 368.

186. Watson, *Annals of Philadelphia,* vol. 1, p. 182.

187. *The Emerald* 1, no. 9 (December 19, 1807), p. 100.

188. *The Ramblers' Magazine* 1 (October 6, 1809), p. 54.

189. *Charleston Courier*, December 20, 1804.

190. Alden, *A Season in Federal Street*, pp. 19, 21, 29, 34.

191. *The Comet*, December 7, 1811, p. 94.

CHAPTER 6: THE ACTING COMPANY

1. *Polyanthos* 2, no. 1 (June 1812), pp. 65–66.

2. John Bernard, *Retrospections of America: 1797–1811* (New York: Harper and Brothers, 1887), p. 263.

3. *Polyanthos* 5, no. 3 (June 1807), p. 215.

4. John Durang, *The Memoir of John Durang, American Actor 1785–1816*, ed. Alan S. Downer (Pittsburgh: University of Pittsburgh Press, 1966), pp. 110–11.

5. John Alden, *A Season in Federal Street; J. B. Williamson and the Boston Theatre, 1796–1797* (Worcester: American Antiquarian Society, 1955), pp. 32–35.

6. William W. Clapp, Jr., *A Record of the Boston Stage* (Boston, 1853; reprint, New York: Greenwood Press, 1969), p. 85.

7. Alfred Bunn, *The Stage: both before and behind the Curtain from "Observations taken on the Spot"* (3 vols.; London: Richard Bentley, 1840), vol. 1, p. 27. It is interesting to contrast Bunn's comments above with his later (sour grapes?) comments about the relative merits of English and American actors: "With the exception of Mr. Forrest, there is no American performer, whom I have seen, that has any right to expect of the London stages the favour which has been extended to English performers on the principal stages in America. . . . Most of our performers who have visited our transatlantic allies, have been persons of high station and acknowledged attainments, and admitted to be so by the most enlightened audience of Europe; and as it is not yet heresy to say that neither the patrons of New York, Philadelphia, Boston, Baltimore, &c., can lay claim to the same degree of refinement, nor their performers to the same order of ability as ours, the case is very different" (pp. 135–36).

8. *Moreau de St. Méry's American Journey*, trans. and eds. Kenneth and Anna M. Roberts (New York: Doubleday & Company, 1947), p. 157. For an approximation of modern dollar values, multiply by 6.5.

9. William Dunlap, *The Diary of William Dunlap*, ed. Dorothy C. Barck (3 vols.; New York: New York Historical Society, 1930), vol. 1, p. 82.

10. Oscar George Theodore Sonneck, *Early Opera in America* (1915; reprint, New York: Benjamin Blom, 1963), p. 128.

11. Alden, *A Season in Federal Street,* pp. 32–33.

12. William Dunlap, *History of the American Theatre* (2 vols.; New York, 1832; reprint, New York: Burt Franklin, 1963), vol. 2, pp. 70, 120.

13. Ibid., vol. 2, p. 114.

14. "Articles to be strictly observ'd, by the Managers and Performers belonging to the Maryland Company of Comedians," [1782], Maryland Historical Society.

15. *Connecticut Courant,* Hartford, August 29, 1796.

16. H. Earle Johnson, *Musical Interludes in Boston, 1795–1830* (New York: Columbia University Press, 1943), p. 36.

17. Bernard, *Retrospections of America,* p. 263. One benefit occurred during the regular season and one or more on tour.

18. *The Theatrical Censor* 15 (March 15, 1806), p. 134.

19. *Polyanthos* 1, no. 2 (March 1812), p. 143.

20. Dunlap, *Diary,* vol. 1, pp. 259, 296.

21. *Poulson's American Daily Advertiser,* March 17, 1814.

22. *The Mirror of Taste and Dramatic Censor* 3, no. 1 (January 1811), p. 62.

23. Dunlap, *History of the American Theatre,* vol. 1, pp. 316–17.

24. Dunlap, *Diary,* vol. 1, p. 296 and elsewhere passim.

25. *Aurora. General Advertiser,* April 8, 1813.

26. Ibid., April 26, 1813.

27. *National Advocate,* December 23, 1813.

28. In Charleston, for example, Stephen Cullen Carpenter denounced this custom: "Politicians and legislators, fie upon it; you wring a heavy impost, by way of tax, upon this playwork—a thing unk[n]own in any other part of the world." *Charleston Courier,* February 11, 1805.

29. John Hodgkinson, *A Narrative of his Connection with the Old American Company, from 5 September 1792–31 March, 1797* (New York: J. Oram, 1797), p. 12.

30. Clapp, *Boston Stage,* p. 33.

31. Dunlap, *Diary,* vol. 1, p. 45.

32. *The Port Folio* 1, no. 13 (March 28, 1801), p. 102.

33. *Polyanthos* 4, no. 1 (December 1806), p. 61.

34. George C. D. Odell, *Annals of the New York Stage* (16 vols.; New York: Columbia University Press, 1927), vol. 2, p. 341.

35. *The Ramblers' Magazine* 2 [November 1809], p. 107.

36. *The Theatrical Censor* 1 (December 9, 1805), p. 2.

37. The last three quotations from Charles William Janson, *The Stranger in America: 1793–1806* (1807; ed. Carl S. Driver, New York: Lenox Hill, 1979), p. 262.
38. Alden, *A Season in Federal Street*, p. 30.
39. Dunlap, *Diary*, vol. 1, pp. 79, 208.
40. *Poulson's American Daily Advertiser*, January 20, 1814.
41. Bernard, *Retrospections of America*, pp. 262–63.
42. Ibid., p. 273.
43. Ibid., p. 340.
44. *Aurora. General Advertiser*, July 17, 1812.
45. Ibid., April 29, 1815.
46. Ibid., Philadelphia, February 24, 1803.
47. Entry for May 24, 1797, Dunlap, *Diary*, vol. 1, p. 47.
48. Ibid., vol. 1, pp. 261, 298.
49. Alden, *A Season in Federal Street*, p. 35.
50. *Columbian Centinel*, Boston, January 29, 1794. On February 5 Col. Tyler assured patrons that the rule was "not intended to prevent their appearance in hats and bonnet" but only to discourage bonnets that obscured the vision of the rest of the audience.
51. *Polyanthos* 1, no. 3 (April 1812), p. 215.
52. About $6.50 in present-day dollars.
53. *Columbian Centinel*, Boston, January 29, 1794.
54. Durang, *Memoir*, p. 117.
55. Ibid., p. 118. Charles Durang says this was the Columbia Garden, owned by Thomas Leahman, with a stage erected in 1804.
56. *Charleston Courier*, December 1812; February 1813 passim.
57. *The Mirror of Taste and Dramatic Censor* 1, no. 5 (May 1810), p. 368; John Hodgkinson related his early dramatic training at the hands of the prompter.
58. Ibid., p. 415, commenting on the Old American Company.
59. Charles Durang, *The Philadelphia Stage . . . Partly compiled from the papers of his father, the late John Durang; with notes by the editors* (seven looseleaf notebooks clipped from the *Sunday Dispatch*, Philadelphia; first series, 1749–1821, published in 75 chapters, beginning May 7, 1854; Harvard Theatre Collection), chapter 29.
60. Dunlap, *History of the American Theatre*, vol. 2, p. 273.
61. *Polyanthos* 3, no. 3 (October 1806), p. 207.
62. *Commercial Advertiser*, New York, June 30, 1805; Dunlap, *Diary*, vol. 1, p. 80.
63. Bernard, *Retrospections of America*, p. 259.

64. Ibid., p. 164.

65. Playbill, July 20, 1797, described in a clipping from an apparent sale prospectus for the Charles N. Mann Collection, 1907, Maryland Historical Society.

66. *The Mirror of Taste and Dramatic Censor* 3, no. 2 (February 1811), p. 81.

67. *The New York Magazine or Literary Repository* 5 (December 1794), p. 717.

68. Durang, *Memoir*, p. 115. Durang's own spelling is preserved throughout.

69. Ibid., p. 116.

70. Ibid., pp. 122–26.

71. Ibid., p. 119.

72. Ibid., p. 121.

73. Ibid., p. 129–30.

74. Ibid., p. 132.

75. Ibid., pp. 131, 133.

76. Ibid., pp. 128, 131.

77. William B. Wood, *Personal Recollections of the Stage, embracing notices of actors, authors and auditors during a period of forty years* (Philadelphia: H. C. Baird, 1855), p. 55.

78. Bernard, *Retrospections of America*, p. 116.

79. Durang, *Memoir*, p. 41.

80. Bernard, *Retrospections of America*, p. 318.

81. Ibid., p. 319.

82. William Priest, *Travels in the United States of America Commencing in the year 1793, and ending in 1797* (London: J. Johnson, 1802), p. 13. This notion was by no means confined to rural audiences. A letter in the *Boston Gazette* on October 26, 1795, reiterates this reasoning.

83. Related by Janson, *Stranger in America*, p. 266.

84. Bernard, *Retrospections of America*, p. 117.

85. Ibid., p. 121.

86. Ibid., p. 122.

87. Dunlap, *History of the American Theatre*, vol. 2, p. 149.

88. Wood, *Personal Recollections*, p. 132.

89. Alden, "A Season in Federal Street," p. 22. This amount is listed among weekly salaries ranging from $10 to $27 (pp. 32–33). Alden believes that Whitlock had received $275 each week; it seems more likely that this was the fee for her total engagement (not including her benefit).

90. Thomas Allston Brown, *History of the New York Stage from the first*

performance in 1732 to 1901 (3 vols.; New York: Dodd, Mead and Co., 1903), vol. 2, p. 13.

91. Odell, *Annals of the New York Stage*, vol. 2, p. 581.

92. James C. Burge, *Lines of Business: Casting Practice and Policy in the American Theatre 1752–1899* (New York: Peter Lang, 1986), p. 127.

93. Wood, *Personal Recollections*, pp. 446–47.

94. *The Mirror of Taste and Dramatic Censor* 1, no. 1 (January 1810), p. 44. In this context, the word "cattle" means horses.

95. Janson, *Stranger in America*, pp. 259–60.

96. *Polyanthos* 4, no. 3 (February 1807), p. 216.

97. Wood, *Personal Recollections*, p. 440.

98. *Polyanthos* 1, no. 4 (January 1813), p. 219.

99. Wood, *Personal Recollections*, p. 442.

100. Ibid., p. 447.

101. *The Mirror of Taste and Dramatic Censor* 1, no. 5 (May 1810), pp. 415–16.

102. *The Emerald* 2, no. 73 (September 19, 1807), p. 451.

103. Theophilus Cibber, *Dissertations on Theatrical Subjects . . . ,* 1756, no. 2, pp. 14–15; quoted in Allardyce Nicoll, *A History of Late Eighteenth Century Drama 1750–1800* (Cambridge: University Press, 1927), p. 11.

104. Wood, *Personal Recollections*, pp. 437, 450.

105. Ibid., p. 453.

106. *The Comet*, November 9, 1811, p. 40.

107. Wood, *Personal Recollections*, p. 262.

108. *The Cynick* 1, [no. 10] (November 30, 1811), pp. 170–71.

109. Theatre programs of the late eighteenth and early nineteenth centuries almost never gave the first names of actors and actresses; as a result many are known to history only as Mr. Jones or Mrs. Smith. The indication "jr." that followed a name did not necessarily indicate that father and son shared the same first name, but rather that "jr." was the younger actor in the family. Nor did the title "Mrs." always indicate that the recipient was married, but rather that she had reached an age where the title was given as a mark of respect—or of respectability.

110. Her arrival from London is mentioned in the *Columbian Centinel*, Boston, January 6, 1796.

111. All information concerning Portsmouth taken from the *New Hampshire Gazette*, quoted in Louis Pichierri, *Music in New Hampshire: 1623–1800* (New York: Columbia University Press, 1960), pp. 100–102.

112. James Moreland, "The Theatre in Portland in the Eighteenth Century," *New England Quarterly* 11, no. 2 (June 1938), p. 335.

113. *Eastern Herald and Gazette of Maine*, December 22, 1796. Quoted in Moreland, "The Theatre in Portland in the Eighteenth Century," p. 337.

114. Sonneck, *Early Opera in America*, p. 151.

115. Moreland, "The Theatre in Portland in the Eighteenth Century," p. 333.

116. Sonneck, *Early Opera in America*, p. 173.

117. Dunlap, *History of the American Theatre*, vol. 1, p. 275.

118. *Philadelphia Repository and Weekly Register* 1, no. 20 (March 28, 1801), p. 3.

119. *Polyanthos* 5, no. 3 (June 1807), p. 216.

120. *The Mirror of Taste and Dramatic Censor* 1, no. 5 (May 1810), p. 417.

121. *Federal Orrery*, Boston, November 5, 1795.

122. *The Thespian Mirror* 5 (January 25, 1806), pp. 33–35.

123. Dunlap, *History of the American Theatre*, vol. 1, p. 343.

124. *The Thespian Mirror* 5 (January 25, 1806), pp. 33–35.

125. *The Port Folio* 3, no. 5 (January 31, 1807), p. 66.

126. Bernard, *Retrospections of America*, p. 267.

127. Dunlap, *History of the American Theatre*, vol. , p. 236.

128. *The Euterpeiad: or Musical Intelligencer* 3, no. 1 (March 30, 1822), p. 3.

129. The eldest sister, Juliana Westray, married William Wood; the youngest, Elizabeth A. Westray, married first Mr. Villiers, then William Twaits.

130. Dunlap, *History of the American Theatre*, vol. 2, p. 72.

131. *Boston Gazette*, October 28, 1802.

132. Ibid., November 22, 1802.

133. Charles Blake, *An Historical Account of the Providence Stage* (Providence, 1868; reprint, New York: Benjamin Blom, 1971), p. 86.

134. *Polyanthos* 3, no. 3 (October 1806), p. 148.

135. Dunlap, *History of the American Theatre*, vol. 2, p. 211.

136. *Polyanthos* 5, no. 2 (May/June 1807), p. 143; 5, no. 3 (June 1807), p. 215.

137. *The Port Folio* 3, no. 5 (January 31, 1807), p. 67.

138. Joseph Ireland, *Fifty Years of a Play-Goer's Journal; or Annals of the New York Stage, from A.D. 1798 to A.D. 1848, with Biographical Sketches of the Principal Performers* (New York: Samuel French, 1860), p. 61.

139. *Polyanthos* 2, no. 1 (April 1806), p. 66. Cooper was the leading tragedian and Twaits the leading comic actor of the day. Darley had been
praised earlier in the season for his singing of "Let fame sound the
trumpet," which he added to *Love Laughs at Locksmiths. Polyanthos* 1, no. 1 (December 1805), p. 137.

140. For additional information about Mrs. Darley, see "Memoir of Mrs.
Darley," *Polyanthos* 3, no. 3 (October 1806), pp. 145–49.

141. Dunlap, *History of the American Theatre,* vol. 1, p. 368.

142. *Polyanthos* 4, no. 2 (January 1807), p. 136.

143. "Theatrical Sketch," *Columbian Centinel,* Boston, December 31, 1794.

144. "Theatric," *Columbian Centinel,* January 7, 1795.

145. *Boston Gazette,* April 26, 1810.

146. *The Emerald* 2, no. 73 (September 19, 1807), p. 451.

147. *New York Magazine and Literary Repository* 5 (December 1794),
p. 720.

148. *New-York Evening Post,* quoted in *The Port Folio* 2, no. 7 (February 20, 1802), p. 54.

149. Clapp, *Boston Stage,* p. 33.

150. *The Mirror of Taste and Dramatic Censor* 1, no. 3 (March 1810),
p. 204.

151. *The Euterpeiad: or Musical Intelligencer* 3, no. 1 (March 30, 1822),
p. 3.

152. *The Mirror of Taste and Dramatic Censor* 1, no. 3 (March 1810),
p. 240.

153. *The Port Folio* 2, no. 7 (February 20, 1802), p. 54.

154. Washington Irving, "Letters of Jonathan Oldstyle, Gent.," *Morning
Chronicle,* New York, 1802. In *The Works of Washington Irving*
(London: George Bell and Sons, 1890), vol. 11, p. 178.

155. *The Mirror of Taste and Dramatic Censor* 1, no. 3 (March 1810),
p. 240 passim.

156. Ibid., p. 238.

157. Ibid., p. 244.

158. *Columbian Centinel,* Boston, September 21, 1805; quotation from
Hamlet.

159. Dunlap, *History of the American Theatre,* vol. 1, p. 281.

160. Ibid.

161. Wood, *Personal Recollections,* p. 378.

162. Montrose J. Moses, *Famous Actor-families in America* (New York:
Thomas Y. Crowell and Co., 1906), p. 65.

163. Wood, *Personal Recollections,* p. 375.

164. *The Theatrical Censor and Critical Miscellany* 7 (November 8, 1806), p. 186; quoted and corrected in *Polyanthos* 4, no. 1 (December 1806), p. 38; quoted in *The Thespian Monitor, and Dramatick Miscellany* 1, no. 1 (November 25, 1809), pp. 10–12. Dunlap wrote that Mrs. Jones was a sister of the Wallack acting family, had played at Norwich and Covent Garden, and left a daughter who married Mr. Simpson, manager at the Park Theatre (Dunlap, *History of the American Theatre,* vol. 2, p. 235).

165. *The Thespian Monitor, and Dramatick Miscellany* 1, no. 1 (November 25, 1809), pp. 10–12.

166. *The Port Folio* 1, no. 44 (October 31, 1801), p. 349; 1, no. 46 (November 14, 1801), p. 365.

167. *Polyanthos* 4, no. 1 (December 1806), p. 38.

168. Dunlap, *History of the American Theatre,* vol. 2, p. 235.

169. *Polyanthos* 4, no. 1 (December 1806), p. 38.

170. Ibid., 2, no. 1 (April 1806), p. 71.

171. Ibid., 4, no. 1 (December 1806), p. 38; Dunlap, *History of the American Theatre,* vol. 2, p. 240.

172. *Polyanthos* 1, no. 1 (December 1805), p. 68.

173. Ibid., 2, no. 1 (April 1806), pp. 70–71.

174. *New-York Evening Post,* December 11, 1805.

175. *The Thespian Mirror* 6 (February 1, 1806), p. 51.

176. *Polyanthos* 3, no. 3 (October 1806), p. 211.

177. *The Theatrical Censor and Critical Miscellany* 12 (December 13, 1806), p. 185.

178. *Polyanthos* 4, no. 1 (December 1806), p. 39.

179. *The Theatrical Censor and Critical Miscellany* 12 (December 13, 1806), p. 185.

180. *Polyanthos* 4, no. 1 (December 1806), p. 66.

181. Ibid., pp. 38–39.

182. All information about Mrs. Merry to this point is from Dunlap, *History of the American Theatre.* Quote from vol. 2, p. 111.

183. Ibid., vol. 2, p. 169.

184. *The Emerald* 1, no. 6 (November 28, 1807), p. 65.

185. Dunlap, *History of the American Theatre,* vol. 2, p. 255.

186. *The Port Folio* 1, no. 16 (April 18, 1801), p. 127; 1, no. 46 (November 14, 1801), p. 349.

187. *The Ramblers' Magazine* 1 (October 6, 1809), p. 37.

188. Dunlap, *History of the American Theatre,* vol. 1, p. 228.

189. Ibid., vol. 2, pp. 23–24; see also Dunlap, *Diary,* vol. 1, pp. 242–43.

190. *American Citizen,* New York, January 20, 1809.

191. Dunlap, *History of the American Theatre,* vol. 1, p. 228.

192. Ireland, *Journal,* p. 31.

193. *Charleston Courier,* November 1, 1805.

194. *The Euterpeiad: or Musical Intelligencer* 2, no. 26 (March 16, 1822), p. 202; see also *The Port Folio* 2, no. 7 (February 20, 1802), p. 54.

195. Ireland, *Journal,* p. 30.

196. Dunlap, *History of the American Theatre,* vol. 1, pp. 213–14.

197. *The Euterpeiad: or Musical Intelligencer* 2, no. 24 (February 16, 1822), p. 187.

198. James M. Barriskill, "The Newburyport Theatre in the 18th Century," *Essex Institute Historical Collection* 91 (July 1955), p. 223.

199. Dunlap, *History of the American Theatre,* vol. 1, p. 261.

200. *Aurora. General Advertiser,* Philadelphia, March 20, 1795.

201. Alden, *A Season in Federal Street,* p. 32.

202. Dunlap, *History of the American Theatre,* vol. 2, p. 216.

203. Ibid., vol. 2, p. 217. See also the description of Twaits as Zebediah Spiffiard in Dunlap's *Memoirs of a Water Drinker* (New York: Saunders and Otley, 1837), vol. 1, pp. 8–9.

204. *The Ramblers' Magazine* 2 [November 1809], p. 89.

205. *The Port Folio* 3, no. 10 (March 7, 1807), p. 147.

206. Ibid.

207. *National Advocate,* December 14, 1813.

208. Dunlap, *History of the American Theatre,* vol. 2, p. 296; *Virginia Argus,* Richmond, January 2, 1812.

209. *Polyanthos* 2, no. 1 (May 1806), p. 214.

210. *The Mirror of Taste and Dramatic Censor* 1, no. 5 (May 1810), p. 416.

211. Dunlap, *History of the American Theatre,* vol. 2, p. 205.

212. Ireland, *Journal,* p. 14.

213. Dunlap, *Diary,* vol. 1, p. 222.

214. *The Thespian Mirror* 6 (February 1, 1806), p. 48.

215. Bernard, *Retrospections of America,* p. 66.

216. Dunlap, *History of the American Theatre,* vol. 1, p. 171.

217. *Federal Orrery,* Boston, November 5, 1795.

218. Dunlap, *History of the American Theatre,* vol. 1, p. 375.

219. Ibid., vol. 1, p. 195.

220. *Polyanthos* 4, no. 3 (February 1807), p. 215.

221. *Boston Gazette*, October 16, 1812.

222. *New York Evening Post*, August 30, 1815.

223. Some material for this chapter was previously used in the author's article, "The Actor-Singer in America at the Turn of the Nineteenth Century," *Musicology at the University of Colorado* (Boulder: University of Colorado), 1978.

CHAPTER 7: ACTING TRADITIONS

1. *The Monthly Register and Review of the United States* 1, no. 4 (April 1805), p. 159.

2. John Durang, *The Memoir of John Durang, American Actor 1785–1816*, ed. Alan S. Downer (Pittsburgh: University of Pittsburgh Press, 1966), p. 121.

3. *Charleston Courier*, May 21, 1805.

4. *The Mirror of Taste and Dramatic Censor* 1, no. 1 (January 1810), p. 37.

5. *Polyanthos* 4, no. 1 (December 1806), p. 70.

6. *The Mirror of Taste and Dramatic Censor* 1, no. 4 (April 1810), pp. 283–94.

7. *The Monthly Register and Review of the United States* 1, no. 1 (January 1805), pp. 39–48; 1, no. 2 (February 1805), pp. 84–88.

8. *The Ramblers' Magazine* 4 (February 2, 1810), p. 27.

9. Ibid.

10. *The Mirror of Taste and Dramatic Censor* 4, no. 3 (September 1811), pp. 194, 197; 4, no. 5 (November 1811), p. 378.

11. *Aurora. General Advertiser*, Philadelphia, January 16, 1795.

12. *The Mirror of Taste and Dramatic Censor* 2, no. 3 (September 1810), p. 222.

13. William B. Wood, *Personal Recollections of the Stage, embracing notices of actors, authors and auditors during a period of forty years* (Philadelphia: H. C. Baird, 1855), p. 120.

14. *Daily Advertiser*, New York, March 9, 1801.

15. *The Mirror of Taste and Dramatic Censor* 2, no. 6 (December 1810), p. 473. Melpomene was the Greek muse of tragedy.

16. *Daily Advertiser*, New York, March 9, 1801. The quote at the end is taken from Robert Lloyd, "The Actor."

17. Henry Siddons, *Practical Illustrations of Rhetorical Gesture and Action*, after a work on the subject by T. T. Engel, Berlin, 1802 (London:

Sherwood, Neely, and Jones, 1822). See also Washington Irving, "Letters of Jonathan Oldstyle, Gent.," *Morning Chronicle,* New York, 1802. In *The Works of Washington Irving* (London: George Bell and Sons, 1890), vol. 11, p. 186.

18. *New-York Evening Post,* December 9, 1801.

19. *The Theatrical Censor and Critical Miscellany* 12 (December 13, 1806), p. 187.

20. *Charleston Courier,* December 10, 1803.

21. *The Mirror of Taste and Dramatic Censor* 3, no. 1 (January 1811), p. 50.

22. *The Emerald* 1, no. 6 (November 28, 1807), p. 66.

23. *Daily Advertiser,* New York, March 9, 1801.

24. *Polyanthos* 1, no. 4 (March 1806), pp. 280–81.

25. *The Mirror of Taste and Dramatic Censor* 1, no. 4 (April 1810), p. 339.

26. *The Enquirer,* Richmond, August 29, 1806.

27. *The Ramblers' Magazine* 4 (February 1810), p. 29.

28. *The Thespian Monitor, and Dramatick Miscellany* 1, no. 1 (November 25, 1809), p. 8.

29. Henry Barton Baker, *History of the London Stage and its Famous Players (1576–1903)* (1904; reprint, New York: Benjamin Blom, 1969), p. 69.

30. Richard Cumberland, *Memoirs of Richard Cumberland, Written by Himself. Containing an Account of his Life and Writings, interspersed with Anecdotes and Characters of several of the most distinguished persons of his time, with whom he has had intercourse and connexion* (London: Lackington, Allen and Co., 1806), p. 60.

31. Ibid., p. 366.

32. *Daily Advertiser,* New York, March 9, 1801.

33. Ibid.

34. *Federal Orrery,* Boston, November 12, 1795.

35. *The Ramblers' Magazine* 2 [November 1809], p. 82.

36. John Bernard, *Retrospections of America: 1797–1811* (New York: Harper and Brothers, 1887), p. 26.

37. *Aurora. General Advertiser,* Philadelphia, January 16, 1795.

38. *The Mirror of Taste and Dramatic Censor* 2, no. 6 (December 1810), pp. 467–68.

39. Ibid., 3, no. 1 (January 1811), pp. 22–23.

40. Ibid., 2, no. 5 (November 1810), p. 377.

41. *Federal Orrery,* Boston, November 12, 1795. This example also required a distinction between "upper-class" and "lower-class" speech patterns.

42. *The Thespian Mirror* 13, (March 22, 1806), p. 104.

43. *The Mirror of Taste and Dramatic Censor* 3, no. 4 (April 1811), p. 252.

44. *Aurora. General Advertiser,* Philadelphia, March 20, 1795.

45. *Daily Advertiser,* New York, March 9, 1801.

46. *The Thespian Mirror* 5 (January 25, 1806), p. 39.

47. Bernard, *Retrospections of America,* p. 257.

48. *New York Magazine or Literary Repository* 5 (December 1794), p. 720.

49. *Polyanthos* 2, no. 1 (April 1806), p. 71; Durang, *Memoir,* p. 108.

50. Thomas Holcroft, "The Art of Acting, No. 1," quoted in *The Thespian Mirror* 5 (January 25, 1806), pp. 35–39. Unattributed, but taken from Holcroft's *Theatrical Recorder* 1 (London, 1805), pp. 62–67.

51. Bernard, *Retrospections of America,* pp. 367–68.

52. *Polyanthos* 1, no. 1 (December 1805), p. 59.

53. Ibid.

54. Durang, *Memoir,* p. 107.

55. *The Theatrical Censor* 14 [March 1806], p. 130; 8 (January 16, 1806), pp. 70–71.

56. *The Comet,* October 26, 1811, p. 15.

57. *Charleston Courier,* December 25, 1804.

58. *The Theatrical Censor* 5 [December 1805], p. 42.

59. *The Ramblers' Magazine* 2 [November 1809], p. 92.

60. Ibid., 4 (February 2, 1810), p. 15.

61. *Polyanthos* 1, no. 4 (March 1806), p. 282.

62. Durang, *Memoir,* p. 107.

63. *The Theatrical Censor* 6 (January 2, 1806), p. 52.

64. Even though Walter is the principal character of *Children in the Wood,* it should be clearly understood that this role is *not* in the hero line.

65. *The Ramblers' Magazine* 4 (February 2, 1810), p. 31.

66. *The Theatrical Censor* 8 (January 16, 1806), p. 71.

67. Joseph N. Ireland, *Fifty Years of a Play-Goer's Journal; or Annals of the New York Stage, from A.D. 1798 to A.D. 1848, with Biographical Sketches of the Principal Performers* (New York: Samuel French, 1860), p. 19.

68. *The Theatrical Censor* 7 [January 1806], p. 62. A similar description of

Walter in *Children in the Wood* as a "good boy" instead of a drunken idiot is found in the *New-York Evening Post,* December 11, 1805.

69. Ibid., 8 (January 16, 1806), p. 70.

70. *The Port Folio* 1, no. 12 (March 12, 1801), p. 93.

71. *Polyanthos* 3, no. 2 (November 1813), p. 119.

72. John Hodgkinson, *A Narrative of his Connection with the Old American Company, from 5 September, 1792, to 31 March, 1797* (New York: J. Oram, 1797) p. 11.

73. Ireland, *Journal,* p. 17.

74. *Columbian Centinel,* Boston, January 17, 1795.

75. *Philadelphia Repository and Weekly Register* 1, no. 5 (December 13, 1800), p. 37.

76. *Polyanthos* 4, no. 1 (December 1806), p. 66.

77. *Columbian Centinel,* Boston, November 1796; *Independent Chronicle and the Universal Advertiser,* Boston, November 28, 1796; *The Emerald* 1, no. 51 (October 8, 1808), p. 610.

78. *Polyanthos* 4, no. 4 (March 1807), p. 278.

79. *The Theatrical Censor* 2 (December 12, 1805), p. 12.

80. Wood, *Personal Recollections,* p. 69.

81. Ireland, *Journal,* p. 38.

82. Ibid., p. 18.

83. Ibid., pp. 29, 41.

84. *The Port Folio* 2, no. 41 (October 16, 1802), p. 325.

85. *The Theatrical Censor* 3 [December 1805], p. 18.

86. *The Ramblers' Magazine* 4 (February 2, 1810), p. 13.

87. *The Theatrical Censor* 8 [January 16, 1806], p. 71.

88. *Polyanthos* 2, no. 1 (April 1806), p. 10.

89. Bernard, *Retrospections of America,* p. 257.

90. Ireland, *Journal,* pp. 12, 13.

91. *The Euterpeiad: or Musical Intelligencer* 2, no. 26 (March 26, 1822), p. 202.

92. James Fennell, *An Apology for the Life of James Fennell, Written by Himself* (Philadelphia, 1814; reprint, New York, Benjamin Blom, 1969), p. 218.

93. William Dunlap, *History of the American Theatre* (2 vols.; 1832; reprint, New York: Burt Franklin, 1963), vol. 1, p. 29.

94. *Charleston Courier,* March 19, 1805.

95. Hodgkinson, *Narrative,* p. 11.

96. Hodgkinson, *Narrative,* p. 11.

97. Dunlap, *History of the American Theatre,* vol. 2, p. 114.

98. George O. Seilhamer, *History of the American Theatre* (3 vols.; Philadelphia: Globe Printing House, 1888–1891), vol. 3, p. 246.

99. Fennell, *Apology*, p. 220.

100. *The Port Folio* 1, no. 5 (February 8, 1806), p. 75.

101. *The Theatrical Censor and Critical Miscellany* 12 (December 13, 1806), p. 190.

102. Dunlap, *History of the American Theatre*, vol. 2, p. 114.

103. Oral Sumner Coad, "Stage and Players in Eighteenth Century America," *The Journal of English and Germanic Philology* 19 (1920), p. 210.

104. *Charleston Courier*, February 13, 1804.

105. Coad, "Stage and Players in Eighteenth Century America," p. 210.

106. *The Emerald* 2, no. 75 (October 3, 1807), p. 472.

107. *The Ramblers' Magazine* 3 [December 1809], p. 201.

108. William Charles White papers, 1771–1813, American Antiquarian Society, Worcester, Massachusetts. The young man ignored all his father's pleas (while writing dutiful and reassuring letters home) and is listed on the payroll of the Boston Theatre in the 1796–97 season at $12 a week. He later played for a time in New York, but eventually fulfilled family expectations by becoming a respectable lawyer.

109. *The Comet*, December 14, 1811, p. 100.

110. *The Theatrical Censor and Critical Miscellany* 13 (December 20, 1806), p. 210. The play was *The Honeymoon*, but the actress's name was not given.

111. *Columbian Centinel*, Boston, February 11, 1797.

112. *Polyanthos* 1, no. 3 (April 1812), p. 212.

113. *The Thespian Mirror* 4 (January 18, 1806), p. 29.

114. *The Comet*, November 9, 1811, p. 43.

115. *Polyanthos* 1, no. 2 (March 1812), p. 137.

116. *The Mirror of Taste and Dramatic Censor* 3, no. 3 (March 1811), p. 178.

117. *Maryland Journal*, Baltimore, March 11, 1783.

118. *The Newport Mercury*, July 19, 1796.

119. Henry Saxe Wyndham, *Annals of Covent Garden* (2 vols.; London: Chatto and Windus, 1906), vol. 1, p. 419.

120. William Dunlap, *The Diary of William Dunlap (1766–1839)*, ed. Dorothy C. Barck (3 vols.; New York: New York Historical Society), vol. 1, p. 164. Dunlap received the letter about this incident in New York on October 17; it must have occurred during the October 7 performance.

121. *The Port Folio* 1, no. 6 (February 7, 1801), p. 45. The accident oc-

curred during the February 2 performance, while Thomas Cooper played Richard, Duke of Gloucester, and William Wood portrayed Richmond. The accident must not have been serious, since both were advertised to repeat their roles on the fourth (*Poulson's American Daily Advertiser*, Philadelphia, February 2, 4, 1801).

122. *The Thespian Mirror* 7 (February 8, 1806), p. 55.

123. *Boston Gazette*, February 1, 1803; *Providence Gazette and Country Journal*, July 7, 1804; *Charleston Courier*, November 28, 1804.

124. Thomas Holcroft, *The Theatrical Recorder*, vol. 1 (1805), pp. 345–49; quoted in A. M. Nagler, *A Source Book in Theatrical History* (New York, Dover Publications, 1959), p. 421.

125. *The Mirror of Taste and Dramatic Censor* 1, no. 3 (March 1810), p. 230.

126. *The Ramblers' Magazine* 1 (October 6, 1809), p. 24. The actor was Joseph Tyler; the work was the melodrama *Forty Thieves*.

127. *Polyanthos* 4, no. 1 (December 1806), p. 64.

128. *The Theatrical Censor and Critical Miscellany* 13 (December 20, 1806), p. 190.

129. *The Mirror of Taste and Dramatic Censor* 2, no. 5 (November 1810), p. 377. Supposedly first said by Macklin to Quick.

130. Ibid., 3, no. 2 (February 1811), p. 118.

131. Ibid., 1, no. 3 (March 1810), p. 230.

132. *The Thespian Mirror* 7 (February 8, 1806), p. 55.

133. *The Theatrical Censor* 1 (December 9, 1805), p. 7; 2 (December 12, 1805), p. 13.

134. *New-York Evening Post*, December 11, 1805.

135. *The Theatrical Censor* 6 (January 2, 1806), p. 53.

136. *Federal Orrery*, Boston, November 12, 1795.

137. *The Theatrical Censor* 11 [February 1806], p. 101.

138. *Polyanthos* 5, no. 1 (April 1807), p. 63.

139. Thomas Holcroft, *The Theatrical Recorder*, vol. 1, quoted in Nagler, *A Source Book in Theatrical History*, pp. 420–21.

140. *Polyanthos* 3, no. 5 (February 1814), p. 293.

141. *New-York Journal and Patriotic Register*, February 2, 1793.

142. *The Ramblers' Magazine* 1 (October 6, 1809), p. 54.

143. *The Mirror of Taste and Dramatic Censor* 4, no. 3 (September 1811), p. 165; *The Ramblers' Magazine* 2 (1809), p. 79; *The Theatrical Censor* 3, p. 23, 5, p. 39.

144. *The Mirror of Taste and Dramatic Censor* 4, no. 3 (September 1811), p. 199.

145. *The Theatrical Censor* 3 [December 1805], p. 23.

146. *The Theatrical Censor and Critical Miscellany* 8 (November 15, 1806), p. 114.

147. *The Ramblers' Magazine* 3 [December 1809], p. 191.

148. *Polyanthos* 3, no. 2 (November 1813), p. 116.

149. *The Theatrical Censor* 3 [December 1805], p. 23.

150. *The Mirror of Taste and Dramatic Censor* 4, no. 4 (October 1811), p. 232.

151. Ibid., p. 301.

152. *The Emerald* 2, no. 36, (January 3, 1807), p. 5.

153. *The Mirror of Taste and Dramatic Censor* 3, no. 5 (May 1811), p. 326.

154. *The Comet,* January 11, 1812, p. 170.

155. *The Mirror of Taste and Dramatic Censor* 3, no. 3 (March 1811), pp. 185, 197.

156. Ibid., 3, no. 2 (February 1811), p. 119.

157. *Charleston Courier,* December 17, 1803.

158. *Polyanthos* 2, no. 1 (April 1806), pp. 66–67.

159. Charles Durang, *The Philadelphia Stage . . . Partly compiled from the papers of his father, the late John Durang; with notes by the editors* (seven looseleaf notebooks clipped from the *Sunday Dispatch,* Philadelphia; first series, 1749–1821, published in 75 chapters, beginning May 7, 1854; Harvard Theatre Collection), chapter 22.

160. *The Theatrical Censor* 1 (December 9, 1805), p. 7.

161. *Polyanthos* 1, no. 4 (January 1813), p. 218.

162. *The Theatrical Censor* 11 [February 1806], p. 105.

163. *Charleston Courier,* December 14, 1805.

164. *The Theatrical Censor* 3 [December 1805], p. 20.

165. *The Ramblers' Magazine* 2 [November 1809], p. 77.

166. *Federal Orrery,* Boston, November 16, 1796. The first criticism was of Mrs. Hodgkinson's singing of an aria in *The Purse;* the second line comes from Otway's *The Orphan.*

167. *The Mirror of Taste and Dramatic Censor* 1, no. 1 (January 1810), pp. 76–78; *Charleston Courier,* November 15, 1803, February 13, 1804, and December 25, 1804.

168. *Polyanthos* 3, no. 1 (August 1806), p. 49.

169. *Federal Orrery,* Boston, Monday, January 11, 1796 [misdated January 7].

170. Ibid., November 16, 1795.

171. Dunlap, *History of the American Theatre,* vol. 1, p. 205.

172. *The Mirror of Taste and Dramatic Censor* 1, no. 2 (February 1810), p. 155.

173. *The Theatrical Censor* 1 (December 9, 1805), p. 6.

174. *Federal Orrery,* Boston, November 16, 1796; *Polyanthos* 1, no. 2 (January 1806), p. 139.

175. *Polyanthos* 4, no. 1 (December 1806), p. 70.

176. Ibid., 2, no. 2 (May 1806), pp. 94–96.

177. Dunlap, *Diary,* vol. 1, pp. 297, 299.

178. Durang, *The Philadelphia Stage,* chapter 30.

179. Durang, *The Philadelphia Stage,* chapter 29; William Dunlap, *Memoirs of a Water Drinker* (New York: Saunders and Otley, 1837), vol. 1, p. 22.

180. Dunlap, *Diary,* vol. 1, pp. 260, 290.

181. Bernard, *Retrospections of America,* p. 27. Bernard claims (second hand) that Hodgkinson was negligent while he was manager at New York, but Dunlap's eyewitness account reports he was always there to direct the stage business. When Hodgkinson returned to the company strictly as an actor, he was probably as lax about rehearsals as anyone else.

182. Wood, *Personal Recollections,* p. 138.

183. "Articles to be strictly observ'd, by the Managers and Performers belonging to the Maryland Company of Comedians," [1782], Maryland Historical Society.

184. Dunlap, *History of the American Theatre,* vol. 1, p. 317.

185. Wood, *Personal Recollections,* p. 441. The reason for the difference is that tragedy had to be learned verbatim because of the verse, while comedy could be paraphrased if needed.

186. Dunlap, *History of the American Theatre,* vol. 1, p. 190.

187. *The Mirror of Taste and Dramatic Censor* 2, no. 2 (August 1810), p. 104.

188. *The Port Folio* 1, no. 7 (February 14, 1801), p. 50.

189. Ibid., 1, no. 13 (March 28, 1801), p. 102.

190. Dunlap, *History of the American Theatre,* vol. 2, pp. 21–22.

191. Wood, *Personal Recollections,* p. 76.

192. Ibid., p. 77. The lady referred to may be Mrs. Poe.

193. *Charleston Courier,* May 17, 1804.

194. *The Spectator,* New York, February 28, 1801.

195. *The Ramblers' Magazine* 1 (October 6, 1806), p. 22.

196. *New York Magazine or Literary Repository* 5 (December 1794), p. 722; 6 (February 1795), p. 68.

197. *The Ramblers' Magazine* 4 (February 2, 1810), p. 19.

198. *American Citizen,* New York, March 10, 1809.

199. *The Port Folio* 1, no. 3 (January 17, 1801), p. 21.

200. *Polyanthos* 5, no. 2 (May 1807), p. 141.

201. Ibid., 4, no. 3 (February 1807), p. 214.

202. *The Comet,* November 16, 1811, p. 51.

203. *Polyanthos* 4, no. 1 (December 1806), p. 64.

204. *The Theatrical Censor* 7 [January 1806], pp. 57–58.

205. *Polyanthos* 1, no. 3 (April 1812), p. 212.

206. *Charleston Courier,* February 10, 1804.

207. *The Ramblers' Magazine* 2 [November 1809], p. 109.

208. *The Comet,* November 23, 1811, p. 65.

209. *New-York Evening Post,* December 10, 1801.

210. "Articles to be strictly observ'd, by the Managers and Performers belonging to the Maryland Company of Comedians," [1782], Maryland Historical Society.

211. *The Mirror of Taste and Dramatic Censor* 4, no. 5 (November 1811), p. 380.

212. *Polyanthos* 4, no. 4 (March 1807), p. 284.

213. Holcroft, *The Theatrical Recorder* 1, quoted in Nagler, *A Source Book in Theatrical History,* p. 421.

214. *The Comet,* December 21, 1811, p. 118.

215. Durang, *The Philadelphia Stage,* chapter 19.

216. *The Mirror of Taste and Dramatic Censor* 1, no. 1 (January 1810), p. 104.

217. *Charleston Courier,* November 15, 1803. The New York system is described in the *Minerva,* New York, January 20, 1795.

218. *Moreau de St. Méry's American Journey (1793–1798),* trans. and eds. Kenneth and Anna M. Roberts (Garden City, N.Y.: Doubleday and Co., 1947), p. 347.

219. *Connecticut Courant,* Hartford, August 10, 1795; *Charleston Courier,* February 24, 1804.

220. *Connecticut Courant,* Hartford, August 5 and 12, 1799; *American Mercury,* Hartford, August 8, 1799.

221. *The Cynick,* Philadelphia 1, no. 5 (October 19, 1811), p. 81.

222. *Charleston Courier,* November 1, 1815.

223. *Virginia Argus,* Richmond, January 2, 1812. (There were also fifty people in the gallery.)

224. *Moreau de St. Méry's American Journey,* p. 347.

225. *Virginia Gazette and General Advertiser,* Richmond, February 8, 1806.
226. *Charleston Courier,* November 14, 1804.
227. *New-York Evening Post,* November 16, 1801.
228. *The Mirror of Taste and Dramatic Censor* 1, no. 1 (January 1810), p. 59.
229. *Moreau de St. Méry's American Journey,* pp. 186, 323.
230. *New-York Evening Post,* December 9, 1801.
231. *General Advertiser,* Philadelphia, October 25, 1794.
232. Irving, "Jonathan Oldstyle," p. 181.
233. Ibid., p. 184.
234. *The Mirror of Taste and Dramatic Censor* 1, no. 1 (January 1810), p. 104.
235. Irving, "Jonathan Oldstyle," p. 185.
236. *The Mirror of Taste and Dramatic Censor* 1, no. 1 (January 1810), p. 106.
237. Ibid., 2, no. 4 (October 1810), p. 296; 2, no. 5 (November 1810), p. 382.
238. *Minerva,* New York, January 10, 1795.
239. Thomas Allston Brown, *History of the New York Stage, from the first performance in 1732 to 1901* (3 vols.; New York: Dodd, Mead, and Co., 1903), vol. 2, p. 12.
240. According to Brooks McNamara, *The American Playhouse in the Eighteenth Century* (Cambridge, Mass.: Harvard University Press, 1969), p. 58, it was common eighteenth-century practice to paint the auditorium green, and to line the lower boxes with red draperies (in better houses) or red paper (in lesser houses). The upper boxes were left unpapered, and this led to the term "green boxes" which eventually came to describe the upper boxes occupied by the prostitutes.
241. *The Thespian Mirror* 7 (February 8, 1806), p. 60.
242. *Boston Daily Advertiser,* January 17, 1814.
243. *Mirror of Taste and Dramatic Censor* 2, no. 5 (November 1810), p. 380.
244. *The Ramblers' Magazine* 2 [November 1809], p. 100.
245. *The Port Folio* 1, no. 7 (February 14, 1801), p. 52.
246. *General Advertiser,* Philadelphia, October 25, 1794.
247. *Aurora,* Philadelphia, December 16, 1795; *Columbian Centinel,* Boston, January 7, 1795.
248. *The Argus, or Greenleaf's New Daily Advertiser,* New York, November 28, 1796.

249. *Polyanthos* 1, no. 3 (February 1806), p. 216.

250. Seilhamer, *History of the American Theatre*, vol. 3, p. 96.

251. William W. Clapp, Jr., *A Record of the Boston Stage* (1853; reprint, New York: Greenwood Press, 1969), pp. 27–28.

252. Bernard, *Retrospections of America*, p. 290.

253. *The Rambler's Magazine* 3 [December 1809], p. 191. The term "raising the wind" means "coming up with the cash."

254. *Polyanthos* 1, no. 2 (March 1812), p. 138.

255. *New-York Journal and Patriotic Register*, March 12, 1794.

256. I am indebted to Margaret MacArthur of Marlboro, Vermont, for copies of two songs called "Constitution and Guerriere" and to Arthur Schrader of Singing History, Sturbridge, Massachusetts, for the information that neither of them is necessarily a part of the afterpiece.

257. *Polyanthos* 1, no. 5 (February 1813), p. 274.

258. Ibid., 3, no. 1 (October 1813), p. 61.

CHAPTER 8: THE SINGER AND THE SONG

1. George Hogarth, *Memoirs of the Musical Drama* (2 vols.; London: R. Bentley, 1838), vol. 2, p. 435.

2. *The Theatrical Censor* 8 (January 16, 1806), p. 71.

3. *The Theatrical Censor and Critical Miscellany* 13 (December 20, 1806), p. 210.

4. *The Comet*, November 30, 1811, p. 80.

5. Ibid., December 14, 1811, p. 101.

6. *The Theatrical Censor* 8 (January 16, 1806), p. 70.

7. Ibid., p. 71.

8. Eric Walter White, *The Rise of English Opera* (London: John Lehmann, 1959), p. 192.

9. *The Mirror of Taste and Dramatic Censor* 1, no. 5 (May 1810), p. 380.

10. Ibid., 1, no. 3 (March 1810), p. 243.

11. *Charleston Courier*, April 22, 1805.

12. Playbill, Maryland Historical Society.

13. *The Mirror of Taste and Dramatic Censor* 1, no. 5 (May 1810), p. 416.

14. Ibid., 1, no. 2 (February 1810), p. 160.

15. In James Hewitt's *New Federal Overture*, he included an "Air from Rosina" ("Lads and Lasses All Advance"); in the chorus sections his piano arrangement includes appoggiaturas not written into the vocal score.

16. *Columbian Centinel*, January 25, 1797.

17. William Dunlap, *The Diary of William Dunlap*, ed. Dorothy C. Barck (3 vols.; New York: New York Historical Society, 1930), vol. 1, p. 275.
18. *The Theatrical Censor* 13 (February 22, 1806), p. 119.
19. Ibid., 6 (January 2, 1806), p. 55.
20. *The Comet*, December 7, 1811.
21. Giacomo Gotifredo Ferrari, *A concise treatise on Italian singing elucidated by Rules, Observations and Examples; succeeded by a New Method of Instruction, comprising Scales, Exercises, Intervals and Solfeggios, Peculiarly arranged and harmonized*, trans. William Shield (London: Chappell and Co., ca. 1818), p. 8.
22. *The Euterpeiad: or Musical Intelligencer* 2, no. 25 (March 2, 1822), p. 194.
23. Michael Winesanker, "Musico-Dramatic Criticism of English Comic Opera, 1750–1800," *Journal of the American Musicological Society* 2 (1949), p. 91.
24. *Polyanthos* 3, no. 4 (November 1813), p. 120.
25. *The Comet*, November 9, 1811.
26. *Federal Orrery*, Boston, November 12, 1795.
27. "When Love Gets You Fast in Her Clutches," "Mark the True Test of Passion," and "When First to Helen's Lute."
28. *The Thespian Mirror* 6 (February 1, 1806), p. 51.
29. *Polyanthos* 2, no. 1 (April 1806), p. 69.
30. James Boaden, quoted by Roger Fiske, *English Theatre Music in the Eighteenth Century* (London: Oxford University Press, 1973), p. 273.
31. *The Thespian Monitor, and Dramatick Miscellany* 1, no. 1 (November 25, 1809), p. 7.
32. Michael Kelly, *Reminiscences of Michael Kelly of the King's Theatre and Theatre Royal Drury Lane* (2 vols.; London, 1826; reprint, New York: Da Capo Press, 1968), vol. 2, p. 132.
33. Washington Irving, "Letters of Jonathan Oldstyle, Gent.," *Morning Chronicle*, New York, 1802. In *The Works of Washington Irving* (London: George Bell and Sons, 1890), vol. 11, p. 179.
34. *Charleston Courier*, March 24 and April 5, 1804.
35. *The Theatrical Censor* 13 (February 22, 1806), p. 119.
36. *The Thespian Monitor, and Dramatick Miscellany* 1, no. 1 (November 25, 1809), p. 10; *The Mirror of Taste and Dramatic Censor* 1, no. 1 (January 1810), p. 68.
37. *Polyanthos* 3, no. 1 (October 1813), p. 57.
38. *Charleston Courier*, February 29, 1804.

39. John Durang, *The Memoir of John Durang, American Actor 1785–1816*, ed. Alan S. Downer (Pittsburgh: University of Pittsburgh Press, 1966), p. 19.

40. *Polyanthos* 1, no. 4 (May 1812), p. 274.

41. Thomas Busby, *Concert Room and Orchestra Anecdotes of Music and Musicians, Ancient and Modern* (3 vols.; London: Clementi and Co. and Knight and Lacey, 1825), vol. 1, pp. 304–5.

42. *The Euterpeiad: or Musical Intelligencer* 2, no. 25 (March 2, 1822), p. 194.

43. Ibid., 2, no. 26 (March 16, 1822), p. 202.

44. William T. Parke, *Musical Memoirs: an Account of the General State of Music in England from the First Commemoration of Handel, in 1784, to the year 1830* (2 vols.; London, 1830; reprint, New York: Da Capo Press, 1970), vol. 1, p. 128.

45. Henry Saxe Wyndham, *The Annals of Covent Garden Theatre from 1732 to 1897* (2 vols.; London: Chatto and Windus, 1906), p. 241.

46. James Nares, *A Treatise on Singing* (London: Longman and Broderip, [ca. 1785]), p. 37. Nares (1715–83) was organist at the Chapel Royal and composer of a masque, *The Royal Pastoral* (1769).

47. Quoted in Roger Fiske, *English Theatre Music*, p. 270.

48. Entry for December 10, 1791; quoted in Henry Edward Krehbiel, *Music and Manners in the Classical Period* (New York: Scribner, 1899), pp. 86–87.

49. *Post*, New York, October 21, 1817.

50. *The Euterpeiad: or Musical Intelligencer* 2, no. 15 (October 13, 1821), p. 114. See also William Oxberry, *Oxberry's Dramatic Biography and Histrionic Anecdotes* (6 vols.; London: G. Virtue, 1825), vol. 4, pp. 77–78.

51. Fiske, *English Theatre Music*, p. 630.

52. Quoted, Ibid., p. 270.

53. Quoted, Ibid., p. 621.

54. Quoted in Mollie Sands, "These Were Singers," *Music and Letters* 225 (April 1944), p. 106.

55. Parke, *Musical Memoirs*, vol. 1, p. 33.

56. Quoted in Fiske, *English Theatre Music*, p. 271.

57. *Boston Gazette*, April 18, 1803, p. 44.

58. Nares, *A Treatise on Singing*, p. 37.

59. John Mewburn Levien, *The Singing of John Braham* (London: Novello and Company, 1944), p. 34.

60. Nares, *A Treatise on Singing*, p. 37.
61. Benjamin Carr, *Lessons and Exercises in Vocal Music, Opus VIII* (Baltimore: Carr's Music Store, n.d.). Probably published about 1811 (Opus VII was published in 1810 and Opus IX in 1812).
62. Nares, *A Treatise on Singing*, p. 37.
63. Fiske, *English Theatre Music*, p. 270; paraphrasing from "Observations on the Present State of Music in London."
64. *Musical Quarterly*, 1818, quoted in Sands, "These Were Singers," p. 106.
65. *Aurora. General Advertiser*, Philadelphia, January 19, 1795.
66. Nares, *A Treatise on Singing*, p. 39.
67. Ibid., p. 38.
68. Levien, *The Singing of John Braham*, p. 32.
69. *Aurora. General Advertiser*, Philadelphia, October 22, 1794.
70. *The Comet*, December 7, 1811, p. 93.
71. Nares, *A Treatise on Singing*, p. 40.
72. Levien, *The Singing of John Braham*, p. 33.
73. Thomas Moore, *The Memoirs of the Life of the Right Honourable Richard Brinsley Sheridan* (2 vols.), quoted in Roger Fiske, "A Score for the Duenna," *Music and Letters* 42 (1961), p. 133.
74. *Polyanthos* 3, no. 4 (November 1813), p. 120.
75. *The Comet*, Boston, October 26, 1811, p. 16.
76. *Charleston Courier*, May 17, 1804.
77. Oxberry, *Dramatic Biography*, vol. 4, p. 133.
78. Fiske, *English Theatre Music*, p. 269.
79. Charles Dibdin, *The Professional Life of Mr. Dibdin, written by himself* (4 vols.; London: published by the author, 1803), vol. 2, pp. 113–14.
80. Busby, *Anecdotes*, vol. 1, pp. 166–67.
81. Nares, *A Treatise on Singing*, p. 35.
82. Nares uses the syllables "Do re mi fa sol la si"; Carr uses "ut" for "do" but otherwise uses the same seven-note system.
83. Carr, *Lessons and Exercises in Vocal Music*, p. 21.
84. Ibid., pp. 37–38.
85. Ibid., p. 38.
86. Ibid., p. 48.
87. [Giusto Tenducci], *The Instruction of Mr. Tenducci to his Scholars* (London: Longman and Broderip, [1785]), p. 2.
88. *The Euterpeiad: or Musical Intelligencer* 1, no. 36 (December 2, 1820), p. 142.

89. Domenico Corri, *A Select Collection of the Most Admired Songs, Duetts, &c. From Operas in the highest esteem and from other Works in Italian, English, French, Scotch, Irish, &c., &c., in three books* (3 vols.; Edinburgh: John Corri, [1779]); Idem, *A New and Complete Collection of the most favorite Scots Songs including a few English and Irish with proper Graces and Ornaments peculiar to their character, likewise the new method of accompanyment of Thorough Bass* (2 vols.; Edinburgh: Corri and Coy, n.d.).

90. *The Euterpeiad: or Musical Intelligencer* 1, no. 36 (December 2, 1820), p. 142.

91. Henry Phillips, *Musical and Personal Recollections during half a century* (2 vols.; London: Charles J. Skeet, 1864), vol. 1, p. 37.

92. Oxberry, *Dramatic Biography*, vol. 3, p. 59; O'Keeffe, *Recollections of the Life of John O'Keeffe, written by Himself* (2 vols.; London: Henry Colburn, 1826), vol. 2, pp. 71–72. I have been unable to locate the third quote in either the 1802 or 1805 editions of *The Thespian Dictionary* (London: J. Cundee) in the Bannister, Billington, or other related entries. All quotations regarding Mrs. Bannister are from Fiske, *English Theatre Music*, p. 276.

93. Oxberry, *Dramatic Biography*, vol. 5, p. 245.

94. James Boaden, *Life of John Philip Kemble*, vol. 1, p. 122. Quoted in Fiske, *English Theatre Music*, p. 276.

95. *The Port Folio* 1, no. 9 (February 28, 1801), p. 68.

96. *The Emerald* 29 (November 15, 1806), p. 341.

97. *Polyanthos* 3, no. 1 (October 1813), p. 57.

98. *The Ramblers' Magazine* 4 (February 2, 1810), p. 20.

99. Fiske, *English Theatre Music*, p. 276.

100. *The Euterpeiad: or Musical Intelligencer* 2, no. 1 (March 31, 1821), p. 2.

101. Levien, *The Singing of John Braham*, p. 13.

102. Oxberry, *Dramatic Biography*, vol. 3, p. 59.

103. Fiske, *English Theatre Music*, pp. 277–78.

104. Parke, *Musical Memoirs*, vol. 1, p. 127.

105. John R. Parker, *A Musical biography: or, Sketches of the lives and writings of eminent musical characters. Interspersed with an epitome of interesting musical matter* (Boston: Stone and Tovell, 1824), pp. 112–13.

106. William Shield, *An Introduction to Harmony* (London: G. G. and J. Robinson, 1800), p. 84.

107. Carr, *Lessons and Exercises in Vocal Music*, p. 29. See also Tenducci's Rule 21, above.

108. Sands, "These Were Singers," p. 104.

109. See, for example, "The Bird When Summer Charms No More" from *Edwin and Angelina* (Mrs. Hodgkinson) and "At First How Humble" from *The Merry Gardener* (Miss Brett), in Victor Pelissier, *Pelissier's Columbian Melodies: Music for the New York and Philadelphia Theatres,* ed. Karl Kroeger (Madison: A-R Editions, 1984), pp. 26, 52.

110. Busby, *Anecdotes,* vol. 1, p. 216.

111. Sands, "These Were Singers," p. 104.

112. Nares, *A Treatise on Singing,* p. 38.

113. Pier Francesco Tosi, *Observations on the Florid Song,* trans. J. E. Galliard (London, 1743; reprint, London: W. Reeves, 1926), pp. 128–29.

114. Richard, second Earl of Mount Edgcumbe, *Musical Reminiscences of an old Amateur chiefly respecting the Italian Opera in England for fifty years from 1773 to 1823* (London: John Andrews, 1827), p. 271.

115. Reprinted in James Hewitt, *Selected Compositions,* ed. John W. Wagner (Madison: A-R Editions, 1980), pp. 21–26.

116. Samuel Arnold, *A Set of Progressive Lessons, for the Harpsichord, or the Piano Forte calculated for the ease of beginners,* Opus 12 (London: printed for the author, ca. 1777).

117. Benjamin Carr, *The Analytical instructor for the piano forte,* Opus 15 in 3 parts (Philadelphia: Lee and Walker, 1826).

118. John Wall Callcott (1766–1821) was a close associate of Samuel Arnold and a student of Haydn (London, 1791); his compositions were principally vocal, and he published a *Musical Grammar* in 1806. His mind failed in 1807; thus this table can be assumed to be contemporary with the operas being discussed.

119. General information and terminology used in this section are based on Putnam Aldrich's articles on ornamentation in Willi Apel, *Harvard Dictionary of Music,* 2d edition (Cambridge, Mass.: Harvard University Press, 1969).

120. Carr, *Lessons and Exercises in Vocal Music,* p. 29.

121. Based on Corri, *Select Collection,* vol. 1, p. 8, with additions from *New and Complete Collection,* vol. 2, p. 31.

122. Corri, *Select Collection,* vol. 1, p. 8.

123. Arnold, *Progressive Lessons,* p. 38.

124. Carr, *Lessons and Exercises in Vocal Music,* pp. 30–31.

125. Corri, *New and Complete Collection,* vol. 2, p. 31.

126. Corri, *Select Collection,* vol. 1, p. 8.

127. Carr, *Lessons and Exercises in Vocal Music,* pp. 32–33.

128. Shield, *An Introduction to Harmony,* p. 84.

129. Carr, *Lessons and Exercises in Vocal Music,* pp. 33–34.

130. *The British Magazine* 1 (June 1760), pp. 349–50; quoted in Wine-sanker, "Musico-Dramatic Criticism, " p. 91. A similar effect is called for—instrumentally—at the beginning of Air No. 1 of *No Song, No Supper.*

131. Ferrari, *Treatise,* p. 8. See also the *Euterpeiad* definition of *Messa di Voce* quoted above on p. 371.

CHAPTER 9: THE ORCHESTRA IN THE THEATRE

1. The term "orchestra" had three separate connotations in the eighteenth century: (*a*) the entire musical establishment, both vocal and instrumental; (*b*) the area in which the "band" of instrumentalists played; and (*c*) the same as modern usage.

2. This is the way the orchestra sat at Philadelphia, according to Moreau de St. Méry, *Moreau de St. Méry's American Journey (1793–1798),* trans. and eds. Kenneth and Anna M. Roberts (Garden City, N.Y.: Doubleday and Co., 1947), p. 346, and was standard in European pit orchestras during the eighteenth century. The small orchestra at the Little Theatre in the Haymarket is pictured facing the stage in Roger Fiske, *English Theatre Music in the Eighteenth Century* (London: Oxford University Press, 1973), plate facing p. 49. The orchestra at the Park Theatre in New York also faced the stage in 1822; see *New Grove Dictionary of American Music,* eds. H. Wiley Hitchcock and Stanley Sadie (London: Macmillan Press and New York: Grove's Dictionaries of Music, 1986), vol. 3, p. 437.

3. Fiske, *English Theatre Music,* gives examples of the types of music used in English theatres for this purpose; see pp. 259–61.

4. *New-York Evening Post,* January 11, 1802.

5. *Columbian Centinel,* Boston, February 1, 1794.

6. Ibid., February 5, 1794.

7. Ibid., February 6, 1794.

8. Ibid., February 22, 1794.

9. *The Daily Advertiser,* March 7, 1794.

10. *New York Magazine or Literary Repository* 5 (December 1794), p. 718; *Aurora. General Advertiser,* Philadelphia, September 20, 1794. The title applied to both parties—the Federalists as well as the opposing Federal Republicans.

11. *Providence Gazette and Country Journal,* September 19, 1795.

12. *Columbian Centinel,* Boston, October 31, 1795, describing a performance on November 2.

13. *Boston Gazette,* June 4, 1798.

14. John Wagner, "New York City Concert Life, 1801–05," *American Music* 2, no. 2 (Summer 1984), p. 63. This may be the *New Federal Overture* performed at the United States Gardens in New York on July 4, 1801, by a band led by Mr. Nicholas. *Commercial Advertiser,* New York, July 3, 1801.

15. From the score, Library of Congress.

16. *Federal Orrery,* Boston, January 21, 1796.

17. Ibid., January 25, 1796.

18. John Durang, *The Memoir of John Durang, American Actor 1785–1816,* ed. Alan S. Downer (Pittsburgh: University of Pittsburgh Press, 1966), pp. 27–28.

19. This incident was reported in the *City Gazette and Daily Advertiser,* Charleston, on January 12, 1796, under a dateline of "London, Nov. 2, Drury Lane—."

20. *The Theatrical Censor* 4 [December 1805], p. 32.

21. *New-York Evening Post,* December 7, 1805.

22. *The Theatrical Censor and Critical Miscellany* 7 (November 8, 1806), p. 102. From a correspondent in New York.

23. *The Comet,* December 7, 1811, p. 93.

24. *Polyanthos* 1, no. 2 (March 1812), p. 111. The letter was intended to expose "vulgarisms" in speech and grammar found in Boston; italics are original and all words in italics were deliberately misused.

25. *Charleston Courier,* November 16, 1803.

26. *The Enquirer,* Richmond, October 11, 1805.

27. *Daily Advertiser,* New York, April 4, 1787.

28. *The Theatrical Censor* 2 (December 12, 1805), p. 13.

29. *The Cynick* 1, no. 3 (October 5, 1811), p. 40.

30. *The Mirror of Taste and Dramatic Censor* 4, no. 5 (November 1811), p. 400.

31. Fiske, *English Theatre Music,* p. 436, indicates that there was room for six winds; however, in his edition of *No Song, No Supper,* Fiske indicates that music was written for six woodwinds in addition to the horns. Illustrations of the tiny pit, with players facing the stage for ensemble, may be found in Fiske in the plate facing p. 49, and in Sheldon Cheney, *The Theatre: Three Thousand Years of Drama, Acting and Stagecraft* (New York, 1929; reprint, London: Vision Press, 1972), p. 413.

32. Alfred Loewenberg, *Annals of Opera, 1597–1940* (2 vols.; London, 1955; reprint, St. Clair Shores, Mich.: Scholarly Press, 1971), p. 5.

33. William C. Smith, *The Italian Opera and Contemporary Ballet in London, 1789–1820: A Record of Performances and Players with Reports from the Journals of the Time* (London: Society for Theatre Research, 1955), pp. 12, 16.

34. Adam Carse, *The Orchestra in the XVIII Century* (Cambridge: W. Heffer and Sons, 1940), p. 79.

35. Ibid.

36. Henry Saxe Wyndham, *The Annals of Covent Garden Theatre from 1732 to 1897* (2 vols.; London: Chatto and Windus, 1906), vol. 1, p. 336.

37. William Dunlap, *History of the American Theatre* (2 vols.; New York, 1832; reprint, New York: Burt Franklin, 1963), vol. 1, p. 391. Dunlap explains earlier that Pelham was the entire orchestra in Williamsburg, Virginia, in 1752 (vol. 1, p. 15), and that William Hewlet [Hulett, Hulet, or Hewlett] joined the company as dancer and violinist, arriving in New York in 1753 (vol. 1, p. 25).

38. *Moreau de St. Méry's American Journey*, pp. 187, 323. Perhaps some of the rancor against the orchestra—and the demands for Jacobin tunes—was specifically aimed at these former French noblemen by Republicans in the gallery.

39. *Charleston Courier*, April 3, 1805.

40. Durang, *Memoir*, p. 20.

41. John Hodgkinson, *A Narrative of his Connection with the Old American Company, from 5 September, 1792–31 March, 1797* (New York: J. Oram, 1797), p. 4.

42. *New York Magazine or Literary Repository* 5 (December 1794), p. 718.

43. Dunlap, *History of the American Theatre*, vol. 2, p. 71. William Dunlap, *The Diary of William Dunlap*, ed. Dorothy C. Barck (3 vols.; New York: New York Historical Society, 1930), vol. 1, p. 268. The *Diary* lists all but George Ulschoeffer in an estimate of expenses for 1798–99 made in the spring of 1798.

44. Olive d'Auliffe, letters in French, quoted by Julian Mates, *The American Musical Stage before 1800* (New Brunswick, N.J.: Rutgers University Press, 1962), p. 94.

45. Victor Pelissier, incidental music for *The Voice of Nature*, manuscript score and parts in the New York Public Library; excerpt printed in Anne Dhu Shapiro, "Action Music in American Pantomime and

Melodrama, 1730–1913," *American Music* 2, no. 4 (Winter 1984), pp. 58–61.

46. Reproduced in *New Grove Dictionary of American Music,* vol. 4, p. 437.

47. Louis C. Elson, *The History of American Music* (New York: Macmillan, 1904), p. 100.

48. Sonneck, *Early Opera in America,* p. 114.

49. Durang, *Memoir,* p. 108.

50. *The Euterpeiad: or Musical Intelligencer* 2, no. 7 (June 22, 1821), p. 52.

51. Ibid., 2, no. 22 (January 19, 1822), p. 170.

52. Based on Robert A. Gerson, *Music in Philadelphia* (Philadelphia: Theodore Presser, 1940), pp. 38–42, 62. Gerson's information, marked with asterisks, has been supplemented from other sources, particularly Oscar George Theodore Sonneck, *Early Concert-Life in America, 1731–1800* (Leipzig: Breitkopf and Hartel, 1907), p. 144.

53. *The Port Folio* 1, no. 16 (April 18, 1801), p. 127.

54. Ibid., 1, no. 52 (December 26, 1801), p. 412.

55. Gerson, *Music in Philadelphia,* p. 42.

56. *Aurora. General Advertiser,* Philadelphia, June 20, 1810.

57. *The Mirror of Taste and Dramatic Censor* 1, no. 1 (January 1810), p. 74.

58. Ibid., 1, no. 2 (February 1810), p. 160.

59. *The Cynick* 1, no. 1 (September 21, 1811), p. 10.

60. Sonneck, *Early Concert-Life,* p. 304.

61. John Alden, *A Season in Federal Street: J. B. Williamson and the Boston Theatre, 1796–1797* (Worcester, Mass.: American Antiquarian Society, 1955), p. 33.

62. *Federal Orrery,* Boston, January 21, 1796; Alden, *A Season in Federal Street,* p. 33.

63. Irving Lowens, *Music and Musicians in Early America* (New York: W. W. Norton, 1964), p. 196.

64. Eola Willis, *The Charleston Stage in the XVIII Century, with Social Settings of the Time* (Columbia, S.C., 1924; reprint, New York: Benjamin Blom, 1968), p. 92.

65. Sonneck, *Early Opera in America,* p. 104.

66. Willis, *Charleston Stage,* p. 211.

67. Ibid., p. 292.

68. Sonneck, *Early Concert-Life,* p. 34.

69. *American and Commercial Advertiser,* January 10, 1811.

70. *Charleston Courier,* November 17, 1803.

71. Ibid., February 29, 1804.

72. Ibid., June 6, 1804.

73. Ibid., November 15, 1804.

74. John Max Patrick, *Savannah's Pioneer Theatre from Its Origins to 1810* (Athens: University of Georgia Press, 1953), pp. 12, 27.

75. *Kentucky Gazette,* Lexington, February 28, 1807; see also concert announcements on March 5, June 10, November 20, 1806.

76. *Eastern Herald of Maine,* quoted in Sonneck, *Early Opera in America,* p. 51.

77. Sonneck, *Early Opera in America,* p. 192.

78. *Albany Register,* September 23, 1803, concerning a performance on September 16. Perhaps the accompaniment was performed by Mr. Loss and Mr. Gilford, the gentlemen who performed "The Battle of Prague" that evening with "four hands on the Piano-Forte."

79. John Bernard, *Retrospections of America: 1797–1811* (New York: Harper and Brothers, 1887), p. 122.

80. Catherine Graupner Stone, "Gottlieb Graupner, the pioneer of classical music in America . . . ," (typescript, 1906, Boston Public Library), p. 14.

81. Alden, *A Season in Federal Street,* pp. 28, 53.

82. Dunlap, *History of the American Theatre,* vol. 2, p. 71.

83. Dunlap, *Diary,* vol. 1, p. 274.

84. Alden, *A Season in Federal Street,* pp. 32–33.

85. Dunlap, *History of the American Theatre,* vol. 2, p. 249.

86. William B. Wood, *Personal Recollections of the Stage, embracing notices of actors, authors and auditors during a period of forty years* (Philadelphia: H. C. Baird, 1855), pp. 421–23.

87. From playbills in New York's *American Citizen* and the *Commercial Advertiser,* as well as in *L'Oracle and Daily Advertiser* for all the above dates. I am indebted to Vera Brodsky Lawrence for her tip concerning the advertisements in the French newspapers.

88. Dunlap, *Diary,* vol. 1, pp. 293, 295.

89. Willis, *Charleston Stage,* p. 238.

90. *City Gazette and Daily Advertiser,* Charleston, April 10 and 11, 1794; quoted in Willis, *Charleston Stage,* pp. 210–12.

91. *Aurora. General Advertiser,* March 30, 1812.

92. Dunlap, *History of the American Theatre,* vol. 1, p. 401.

93. Dunlap, *Diary,* vol. 1, pp. 208, 226.

94. Ibid., vol. 1, pp. 402–6.

95. *The Euterpeiad: or Musical Intelligencer;* quoted in Johnson, *Musical Interludes in Boston,* p. 251.

96. Alden, *A Season in Federal Street,* p. 33.

97. *The Euterpeiad: or Musical Intelligencer* 2, no. 22 (January 19, 1822), p. 170.

98. The term "leader" is still used to designate the concertmaster of English orchestras.

99. *The Euterpeiad: or Musical Intelligencer* 2, no. 22 (January 19, 1822), p. 170.

100. *The Theatrical Censor* 2 (December 12, 1805), p. 13.

101. John R. Parker, *A Musical Biography: or Sketches of the lives and writings of eminent musical characters. Interspersed with an epitome of interesting musical matter* (Boston: Stone and Tovell, 1824), p. 194.

102. John Sullivan Dwight, "History of Music in Boston," *Memorial History of Boston,* vol. 4, p. 415; quoted in Stone, "Gottlieb Graupner, the pioneer of classical music in America . . . ," p. 20.

103. These general comments concerning the role of director and leader in the eighteenth-century orchestra are based on Carse, *The Orchestra in the XVIII Century,* pp. 88–109.

104. This and the next three musical examples are from *Children in the Wood* (London: Longman and Broderip, 1795).

105. Roger Fiske, preface to Stephen Storace, *No Song, No Supper,* in *Musica Britannica,* vol. 16 (London: Stainer and Bell, 1959), p. xvii.

106. John S. Sainsbury, *A Dictionary of Musicians from the earliest ages to the present time* (2 vols.; London: Sainsbury and Co., 1824), vol. 1, p. 433.

107. Thomas Busby, *Concert Room and Orchestra Anecdotes of Music and Musicians, Ancient and Modern* (3 vols.; London: printed for Clementi and Co. and Knight and Lacey, 1825), vol. 1, p. 187.

108. String ranges from Busby, *Anecdotes,* vol. 1, pp. 304–5.

109. Willi Apel, *Harvard Dictionary of Music,* 2d edition (Cambridge, Mass.: Harvard University Press, 1969), p. 321, has pictures of both recorder and flageolet.

110. My thanks to the Dayton C. Miller Flute Collection at the Library of Congress for permitting me to see and play this instrument and another flageolet in 1974.

111. Henry Charles Lahee, *Annal of Music in America: A Chronological Record of Significant Musical Events, from 1640 to the Present Day, with Comments on the Various Periods into which the work is divided* (Boston, 1922; reprint, New York: AMS Press, 1969), p. 3.

112. *Philadelphia Gazette,* April 18, 1796.

113. Johnson, *Musical Interludes in Boston, 1795–1830,* p. 59.

114. Fiske, *English Theatre Music,* p. 283.

115. Said of Grétry; quoted in Wallace Brockway and Herbert Weinstock, *The Opera: A History of Its Creation and Performance, 1600–1941* (New York: Simon and Schuster, 1941), p. 184.

116. *Polyanthos* 2, no. 1 (April 1806), p. 68.

117. William Shield, *An Introduction to Harmony* (London: G. G. and J. Robinson, 1800), p. 163.

118. John O'Keeffe and William Shield, *The Poor Soldier,* eds. William Brasmer and William Osborne (Madison, Wis.: A-R Editions, 1978), p. 26.

119. Fiske, *English Theatre Music,* p. 283.

120. Wyndham, *The Annals of Covent Garden Theatre from 1732 to 1897,* vol. 1, p. 336.

121. See specific examples in Fiske, *English Theatre Music,* p. 284.

122. Quoted in Carse, *The Orchestra in the XVIII Century,* p. 143.

123. *Commercial Advertiser,* New York, August 14, 1800.

124. In February 1771 Thomas Jefferson ordered an instrument from London, but in June he wrote that he had "since seen a Fortepiano and am charmed with it. Send me this instrument, then, instead of the clavicord." Quoted in Oscar George Theodore Sonneck, *Suum cuique; essays in music* (New York: G. Schirmer, 1916), p. 51.

125. *Aurora. General Advertiser,* Philadelphia, November 24, 1794.

126. Wood, *Personal Recollections,* p. 93. During the early part of the eighteenth century, large European orchestras used two harpsichords for sufficient volume; it is possible that these pianofortes were also used simultaneously.

127. Alden, *A Season in Federal Street,* pp. 28–29.

128. Daniel Spillane, *History of the American Pianoforte; Its Technical Development, and the Trade* (New York: D. Spillane, 1890), pp. 52–53.

129. Ibid., p. 125.

130. Sonneck, *Early Concert-Life,* p. 29.

131. Spillane, *American Pianoforte,* p. 61.

132. Ibid., p. 66.

133. Ibid., p. 70.

134. Ibid., p. 99.

135. *Daily Advertiser,* New York, June 9, 1795.

136. Shield, *An Introduction to Harmony,* p. 84.

137. Ibid., p. 89.

138. Ibid., p. 90.

139. Fiske, *English Theatre Music,* p. 286.
140. Domenico Corri, *A Selected Collection of the Most Admired Songs, Duetts, &c . . .* (Edinburgh: John Corri, [1779]), vol. 1, p. 10.
141. See, for example, *No Song, No Supper,* Air No. 2, measures 38 and 42, and the ornamentation of the final cadence at measure 44. Also see the trill added in Air No. 3, measures 12 and 14, and the appoggiatura on the final note.
142. Compare, for example, the ornamented version of the ballad tune "O Ponder Well" in the overture to *Children in the Wood* (ex. 3) with Linley's setting (ex. 51).
143. Shield, *An Introduction to Harmony,* p. 100.

CHAPTER 10: THE MODERN PERFORMANCE

1. *New-York Journal and Patriotic Register,* March 8, 1794.
2. *L'Oracle and Daily Advertiser,* New York, March 21, 1808.
3. Ibid., March 31, 1808.
4. Roger Fiske, *English Theatre Music in the Eighteenth Century* (London: Oxford University Press, 1973), p. 301.
5. *Columbian Centinel,* Boston, February 8, 1797.
6. According to the 1737 Licensing Act.
7. These were Charles Dibdin's *The Recruiting Sergeant* (1770) and J. C. Smith's *The Enchanters* (1760), both all-sung operas. All information about opera publication in England during the eighteenth century is taken from Fiske, *English Theatre Music.*
8. The following theatres were destroyed by fire: Boston Federal Street, 1798; London Covent Garden, 1808, and Drury Lane, 1809; Chestnut Street Theatre in Philadelphia, 1820; and New York Park Theatre in 1820. The Charleston Theatre had its backstage areas severely damaged by fire in 1793. All English and American theatres of this era not destroyed by fire were eventually demolished, or (as at Bristol and at Richmond in Yorkshire) were so severely rebuilt and remodeled as to have lost all their original properties and libraries.
9. William B. Wood, *Personal Recollections of the Stage, embracing notices of actors, authors and auditors during a period of forty years* (Philadelphia: H. C. Baird, 1855), p. 239.
10. John Durang, *The Memoir of John Durang, American Actor 1785–1816,* ed. Alan S. Downer (Pittsburgh: University of Pittsburgh Press, 1966), p. 37.

11. William Wood, *Personal Recollections,* pp. 98–99. On January 21, 1801, for example, when Thomas Dibdin's comedy *Liberal Opinions* was presented at Philadelphia, the bill stated "The managers are indebted to the liberality of the Patentee [at Covent Garden], (who favoured them with a manuscript copy) for the purpose of giving to the public this celebrated performance." *Poulson's American Daily Advertiser,* Philadelphia, September 21, 1801.

12. Eola Willis, *The Charleston Stage in the XVIII Century with Social Settings of the Time* (Columbia, S.C., 1924; reprint, New York: Benjamin Blom, 1968), p. 387. Since Williamson had supposedly sold all costumes and properties to the proprietors in Boston at the end of the 1796–97 season, this might be considered justification for their suspicions of larceny! It did, however, save at least some music, temporarily, from the fire that destroyed the Federal Street Theatre in 1798.

13. William Dunlap, *History of the American Theatre* (2 vols.; New York, 1832; reprint, New York: Burt Franklin, 1963), vol. 1, p. 404; John Max Patrick, *Savannah's Pioneer Theatre from Its Origins to 1810* (Athens: University of Georgia Press, 1953), p. 60.

14. Dunlap, *History of the American Theatre,* vol. 2, p. 114.

15. Letter from Barker to Dunlap, quoted in Dunlap, *History of the American Theatre,* vol. 2, p. 313.

16. "Pitch," in Willi Apel, *Harvard Dictionary of Music,* 2d ed., (Cambridge, Mass.: Harvard University Press, 1969), pp. 678–79.

17. John R. Parker, *A Musical Biography: or Sketches of the lives & writings of eminent musical characters. Interspersed with an epitome of interesting musical matter* (Boston: Stone and Tovell, 1824), pp. 42–44.

18. William Shield, *An Introduction to Harmony* (London: G. G. and J. Robinson, 1800), p. 90.

19. Ibid., p. 104.

SELECTED BIBLIOGRAPHY

BOOKS AND MULTIVOLUME SETS

Addison, Joseph. *The Spectator.* Edited by Donald F. Bond. Oxford: Clarendon Press, 1964.

Alden, John. *A Season in Federal Street; J. B. Williamson and the Boston Theatre, 1796–1797.* Worcester, Mass.: American Antiquarian Society, 1955. Reprinted from the *Proceedings of the American Antiquarian Society* 65 (April 1955).

Apel, Willi. *Harvard Dictionary of Music.* 2d ed. Cambridge, Mass.: Harvard University Press, 1969.

Arnold, Samuel. *A Set of Progressive Lessons, for the Harpsichord, or the Piano Forte expressly calculated for the ease of beginners, Opus 12.* London: printed for the author, [1777].

———. *The Children in the Wood.* Piano-vocal score. London: Longman and Broderip, [1794].

Baker, David E., Isaac Reed, and Stephen Jones. *Biographica Dramatica, or A Companion to the Playhouse.* 3 vols. London, 1812; reprint, New York: AMS Press, 1966.

Baker, Henry Barton. *History of the London Stage and Its Famous Players (1576–1903).* 1904; reprint, New York: Benjamin Blom, 1969.

Barton, Lucy. *Historic Costume for the Stage.* Boston: Walter H. Baker, 1935; revised, 1961.

Bateson, Frederick W. *English Comic Drama, 1700–1750.* Oxford: Clarendon Press, 1929.

Bernard, John. *Retrospections of America: 1797–1811.* New York: Harper and Brothers, 1887.

———. *Retrospections of the Stage.* 2 vols. London: Henry Colburn and Richard Bentley, 1830.

Bernheim, Alfred L. *The Business of the Theatre: An Economic History of the American Theatre, 1750–1932.* New York: Actors Equity Association, 1932; reprint, New York: Benjamin Blom, 1964.

Blake, Charles. *An Historical Account of the Providence Stage.* Providence, R.I., 1868; reprint, New York: Benjamin Blom, 1971.

Brede, Charles F. *The German Drama in English on the Philadelphia Stage from 1794 to 1830.* Philadelphia: Americana Germanica Press, 1918.

Brockway, Wallace, and Herbert Weinstock. *The Opera: A History of Its Creation and Performance, 1600–1941.* New York: Simon and Schuster, 1941.

Brown, Thomas Allston. *History of the American Stage, containing biographical sketches of nearly every member of the profession that has appeared on the American Stage, from 1733 to 1870.* 1870; reprint, New York: Burt Franklin, 1969.

———. *History of the New York Stage from the first performance in 1732 to 1901.* 3 vols. New York: Dodd, Mead and Co., 1903.

Bunn, Alfred. *The Stage: both before and behind the Curtain from "Observations taken on the Spot."* 3 vols. London: Richard Bentley, 1840.

Burge, James C. *Lines of Business: Casting Practice and Policy in the American Theatre 1752–1899.* New York: Peter Lang, 1986.

Busby, Thomas. *Concert Room and Orchestra Anecdotes of Music and Musicians, Ancient and Modern.* 3 vols. London: Clementi and Co. and Knight and Lacey, 1825.

———. *The Overture, Marches, Dances, Symphonies, and Songs in the Melo Drame, called A Tale of Mystery.* London: E. Riley, [1802].

Carr, Benjamin. *The analytical instructor for the piano forte, Op. 15 in three parts.* 3 volumes in 1. Philadelphia: Lee and Walker, [1826].

———. *Lessons and exercises in Vocal Music, Op. VIII.* Baltimore: Carr's Music Store, [c. 1811].

Carse, Adam. *The Orchestra in the XVIII Century.* Cambridge: W. Heffer and Sons, 1940.

Cheney, Sheldon. *The Theatre: Three Thousand Years of Drama, Acting and Stagecraft.* New York, 1929; reprint, London: Vision Press, 1972.

Clapp, William W., Jr. *A Record of the Boston Stage.* Boston, 1853; reprint, New York: Greenwood Press, 1969.

Colman, George. *Blue Beard. A Dramatic Romance.* William Oxberry's edition. London: W. Simpkin, R. Marshall, and C. Chapple, 1823.

Corri, Domenico. *A new and complete collection of the most favorite Scots Songs including a few English and Irish with proper Graces and Ornaments peculiar to their character, likewise the new method of accompanyment of Thorough Bass.* 2 vols. Edinburgh: Corri and Coy, n.d.

———. *A Select Collection of the Most Admired Songs, Duetts, &c. From Operas in the highest esteem and from other Works in Italian, English, French, Scotch, Irish, &c., &c., In Three Books.* 3 vols. Edinburgh: John Corri [1779].

Cumberland, Richard. *Memoirs of Richard Cumberland, Written by Himself. Containing an Account of his Life and Writings, interspersed with Anecdotes and Characters of several of the most distinguished persons of his time, with whom he has had intercourse and connexion.* London: Lackington, Allen and Co., 1806.

Daniels, George, ed. *Cumberland's Plays.* London: G. H. Davidson, 1822–55.

Dibdin, Charles. *The Professional Life of Mr. Dibdin, written by Himself.* 4 vols. London: published by the author, 1803.

Dunlap, William. *Diary of William Dunlap (1766–1839).* Edited by Dorothy C. Barck. 3 vols. New York: New York Historical Society, 1930.

———. *History of the American Theatre.* 2 vols. New York, 1832; reprint, New York: Burt Franklin, 1963.

———. *Memoirs of a Water Drinker.* 2 volumes in 1. New York: Saunders and Otley, 1837.

Durang, John. *The Memoir of John Durang, American Actor, 1785–1816.* Edited by Alan S. Downer. Published for the Historical Society of York County and for the American Society for Theatre Research. Pittsburgh: University of Pittsburgh Press, 1966.

Elson, Louis C. *The History of American Music.* New York: Macmillan, 1904.

Fennell, James. *An Apology for the Life of James Fennell, Written by Himself.* Philadelphia, 1814; reprint, New York: Benjamin Blom, 1969.

Ferrari, Giacomo Gotifredo. *A concise treatise on Italian singing elucidated by Rules, Observations and Examples; succeeded by a New Method of Instruction, comprising Scales, Exercises, Intervals and Solfeggios, Peculiarly arranged and harmonized.* Translated by William Shield. London: Chappell and Co., preface dated 1818.

Fisher, William Arms. *Notes on Music in Old Boston.* Boston: Oliver Ditson Co., 1918.

Fiske, Roger. *English Theatre Music in the Eighteenth Century*. London: Oxford University Press, 1973.

Fitzgerald, Percy. *The World behind the Scenes*. London: Chatto and Windus, 1881.

Gagey, Edmond McAdoo. *Ballad Opera*. New York: Columbia University Press, 1937.

Genest, John. *Some Account of the English Stage from the Restoration in 1660 to 1830*. 10 vols. Bath, England, 1832; reprint, New York: Burt Franklin, 1965.

Gerson, Robert A. *Music in Philadelphia*. Philadelphia: Theodore Presser, 1940.

Grout, Donald Jay. *A Short History of Opera*. 2d ed. New York: Columbia University Press, 1965.

Hewitt, James. *Selected Compositions*. Edited by John W. Wagner. Madison, Wis.: A-R Editions, 1980.

Hill, West T., Jr. *The Theatre in Early Kentucky, 1790–1820*. Lexington: University of Kentucky Press, 1971.

Hipsher, Edward E. *American Opera and Its Composers*. New York: Theodore Presser, 1927.

Hitchcock, H. Wiley, and Stanley Sadie, eds. *The New Grove Dictionary of American Music*. London: Macmillan Press and New York: Grove's Dictionaries of Music, 1986.

Hixon, Donald L. *Music in Early America: A Bibliography of Music in Evans*. Metuchen, N.J.: Scarecrow Press, 1970.

Hodgkinson, John. *A Narrative of his Connection with the Old American Company, from 5 September, 1792–31 March, 1797*. New York: J. Oram, 1797; reprint, New York: Burt Franklin, 1963 (bound with Dunlap, *History of the American Theatre*).

Hogan, Charles Beecher, ed. *The London Stage 1660–1800*. Part 5, vol. 3, *1776–1800*. Carbondale: Southern Illinois University Press, 1960–70.

Hogarth, George. *Memoirs of the Musical Drama*. 2 vols. London: R. Bentley, 1838.

Hoole, W. Stanley. *The Ante-Bellum Charleston Theatre*. Tuscaloosa: University of Alabama Press, 1946.

Hornblow, Arthur. *A History of the Theatre in America*. 2 vols. Philadelphia: J. B. Lippincott, 1919.

Ireland, Joseph N. *Fifty Years of a Play-Goers' Journal; or Annals of the New York Stage, from A.D. 1798 to A.D. 1848, with Biographical Sketches of the Principal Performers*. New York: Samuel French, 1860.

————. *Records of the New York Stage from 1750 to 1860.* 2 vols. 1866; reprint, New York: Benjamin Blom, 1966.

Irving, Washington. "Letters of Jonathan Oldstyle." In *The Works of Washington Irving,* vol. 11. London: George Bell and Sons, 1890.

Janson, Charles William. *The Stranger in America: 1793–1806.* Edited by Carl S. Driver. New York: Lenox Hill, 1971.

Johnson, H. Earle. *Musical Interludes in Boston, 1795–1830.* New York: Columbia University Press, 1943.

Kelly, Michael. *Reminiscences of Michael Kelly of the King's Theatre and Theatre Royal Drury Lane.* 2 vols. London, 1826; reprint, New York: Da Capo Press, 1968.

Krehbiel, Henry. *Music and Manners in the Classical Period.* New York: Scribner, 1899.

Kroeger, Karl. Preface to *Pelissier's Columbian Melodies: Music for the New York and Philadelphia Theaters.* Edited by Karl Kroeger. Madison, Wis.: A-R Editions, 1984.

Lahee, Henry Charles. *Annals of Music in America: A Chronological Record of Significant Musical Events, from 1640 to the Present Day, with Comments on the Various Periods into which the work is divided.* Boston, 1922; reprint, New York: AMS Press, 1969.

Levien, John Mewburn. *The Singing of John Braham.* London: Novello and Company, 1944.

Lippincott, Horace Mather. *Early Philadelphia, Its People, Life, and Progress.* Philadelphia: J. B. Lippincott, 1917.

Loewenberg, Alfred. *Annals of Opera, 1597–1940.* 3d ed. 2 vols. London, 1955; reprint, St. Clair Shores, Mich.: Scholarly Press, 1971.

Lowens, Irving. *Music and Musicians in Early America.* New York: W. W. Norton, 1964.

Ludlow, Noah. *Dramatic Life as I Found It: A Record of Personal Experience.* St. Louis: G. I. Jones and Co., 1880.

McClure, Theron Reading. "A Reconstruction of Theatrical and Musical Practice in the Production of Italian Opera in the Eighteenth Century." Diss., Ohio State University. Ann Arbor, Mich.: University Microfilms, 1956.

McNamara, Brooks. *The American Playhouse in the Eighteenth Century.* Cambridge, Mass.: Harvard University Press, 1969.

Madeira, Louis C. *Annals of Music in Philadelphia and the Musical Fund Society.* Philadelphia: J. B. Lippincott, 1896.

Marrocco, W. Thomas, and Harold Gleason. *Music in America: An Anthol-*

ogy *from the Landing of the Pilgrims to the Close of the Civil War, 1620–1865.* New York: W. W. Norton, 1964.

Mates, Julian. *The American Musical Stage before 1800.* New Brunswick, N.J.: Rutgers University Press, 1962.

Mease, James. *The Picture of Philadelphia.* Philadelphia: B. & T. Kite, 1811.

Moody, Richard. *America Takes the Stage: Romanticism in American Drama and Theatre, 1750–1900.* Bloomington: Indiana University Press, 1955.

Morton, Thomas. *The Children in the Wood. A Musical Piece in two acts. With the additions and alterations as performed at Boston.* Boston: Jno. and Jos. N. Russell, 1795.

———. *The Children in the Wood. A Musical Piece in two acts. With the additions and alterations as performed by the Old American Company.* New York: Columbian Press, 1795.

Moses, Montrose J. *Famous Actor-Families in America.* New York: Thomas Y. Crowell and Co., 1906.

Mount Edgcumbe, Richard, second Earl of. *Musical Reminiscences of an old Amateur chiefly respecting the Italian Opera in England for fifty years from 1773 to 1823.* London: John Andrews, 1827.

Nagler, A. M. *A Source Book in Theatrical History.* New York: Dover Publications, 1959.

Nares, James. *A Treatise on Singing.* London: Longman and Broderip, [c. 1785].

Nicoll, Allardyce. *A History of the English Drama: 1660–1900.* Part 3, *A History of Late Eighteenth Century Drama, 1750–1800;* Part 4, *A History of Early Nineteenth Century Drama, 1800–1850.* Cambridge, England: Cambridge University Press, 1927, 1930.

Odell, George C. D. *Annals of the New York Stage.* 16 vols. New York: Columbia University Press, 1927.

O'Keeffe, John. *Recollections of the Life of John O'Keeffe, written by himself.* 2 vols. London: Henry Colburn, 1826.

Oxberry, William. *Oxberry's Dramatic Biography and Histrionic Anecdotes.* 6 vols. London: G. Virtue, 1825.

Parke, William T. *Musical Memoirs: an Account of the General State of Music in England from the First Commemoration of Handel, in 1784, to the year 1830.* 2 vols. London, 1830; reprint, New York: Da Capo Press, 1970.

Parker, John R. *A Musical biography: or, sketches of the lives and writings of eminent musical characters. Interspersed with an epitome of interesting musical matter.* Boston: Stone and Tovell, 1824.

Patrick, John Max. *Savannah's Pioneer Theatre from Its Origins to 1810.* Athens: University of Georgia Press, 1953.

Phelps, Henry Pitt. *Players of a Century: A Record of the Albany Stage, including notices of prominent actors who have appeared in America.* Albany, N.Y.: J. McDonough, 1880.

Phillips, Henry. *Musical and Personal Recollections during half a century.* 2 vols. London: Charles J. Skeet, 1864.

Pichierri, Louis. *Music in New Hampshire: 1623–1800.* New York: Columbia University Press, 1960.

Pollock, Thomas Clark. *The Philadelphia Theatre in the Eighteenth Century.* Philadelphia: University of Pennsylvania Press, 1933.

Porter, Susan L. "Performance Practice in American Opera at the Turn of the Nineteenth Century as Seen in *Children in the Wood,* a Representative Musical Entertainment." Ph.D. diss., University of Colorado, 1977.

Priest, William. *Travels in the United States of America commencing in the year 1793, and ending in 1797. With the author's Journals of his Two Voyages Across the Atlantic. By William Priest, musician, late of the Theatres Philadelphia, Baltimore and Boston.* London: J. Johnson, 1802.

Quinn, Arthur Hobson. *A History of the American Drama, from the Beginning to the Civil War.* 2 vols. New York: Harper and Brothers, 1923.

Redway, Virginia Larkin. *Musical Directory of Early New York City.* New York: New York Public Library, 1941.

Sainsbury, John S. *A Dictionary of Musicians, from the earliest ages to the present time.* 2 vols. London: Sainsbury and Co., 1824.

St. Méry, Moreau de. *Moreau de St. Méry's American Journey (1793–1798).* Translated and edited by Kenneth and Anna M. Roberts. New York: Doubleday and Co., 1947.

Seilhamer, George O. *History of the American Theatre.* 3 vols. Philadelphia: Globe Printing House, 1888–91.

Shield, William. *An Introduction to Harmony.* London: G. G. and J. Robinson, 1800.

Shield, William, and John O'Keeffe. *The Poor Soldier.* Edited by William Brasmer and William Osborne. In *Recent Researches in American Music,* vol. 6. Madison, Wis.: A-R Editions, 1978.

Siddons, Henry. *Practical Illustrations of Rhetorical Gesture and Action.* London: Sherwood, Neely and Jones, 1822.

Smith, William C., compiler. *The Italian Opera and Contemporary Ballet in London, 1789–1820: A Record of Performances and Players with Reports from the Journals of the Time.* London: Society for Theatre Research, 1955.

Sonneck, Oscar George Theodore. *Catalogue of Opera Librettos Printed before 1800.* 3 vols. 1914; reprint, New York: Burt Franklin, 1967.

————. *Early Concert-Life in America, 1731–1800.* Leipzig: Breitkopf and Hartel, 1907.

————. *Early Opera in America.* 1915; reprint, New York: Benjamin Blom, 1963.

————. *Suum Cuique; Essays in Music.* New York: G. Schirmer, 1916.

————. *A Bibliography of Early American Secular Music (18th Century).* Revised and enlarged by William Treat Upton. New York: Da Capo Press, 1964.

Southern, Richard. *Changeable Scenery: Its Origin and Development in the British Theatre.* London: Faber and Faber, 1952.

Spillane, Daniel. *History of the American Pianoforte; Its Technical Development, and the Trade.* New York: D. Spillane, 1890.

Storace, Stephen. *No Song, No Supper.* Edited by Roger Fiske. In *Musica Britannica,* vol. 16. London: Stainer and Bell, 1959.

[Tenducci, Giusto.] *The Instruction of Mr. Tenducci to his Scholars.* London: Longman and Broderip, [1785].

Tosi, Pier Francesco. *Observations on the Florid Song.* Translated by J. E. Galliard. London, 1743; reprint, London: W. Reeves, 1926.

Tyler, Royall. *The Contrast.* 1790; reprint, New York: AMS Press, 1970.

Vardac, A. N. *Stage to Screen: Theatrical Method from Garrick to Griffith.* Cambridge, Mass.: Harvard University Press, 1949.

Vernon, Grenville. *Yankee Doodle-Doo: A Collection of Songs of the Early American Stage.* New York: Payson and Clarke, 1927.

Virga, Patricia H. *The American Opera to 1790.* Ann Arbor, Mich.: UMI Research Press, 1982.

Wansey, Henry. *The Journal of an Excursion of the United States of North America in the Summer of 1794.* Salisbury, England: J. Easton, 1796.

Watson, John Fanning. *Annals of Philadelphia, and Pennsylvania, in the Olden Time; being a Collection of Memoirs, Anecdotes, and Incidents of the City and its Inhabitants . . . , 1842.* Enlarged, with many additions and revisions, by Willis P. Hazard. 3 vols. Philadelphia: Edwin S. Stuart, 1884.

Wegelin, Oscar. *Early American Plays, 1714–1830.* Edited by John Malone. New York: Dunlap Society Publication, 1900.

Wemyss, Francis C. *Chronology of the American Stage from 1752 to 1852.* New York, 1852; reprint, New York: Benjamin Blom, 1968.

White, Eric Walter. *The Rise of English Opera.* London: John Lehmann, 1951.

Willard, George Owen. *History of the Providence Stage, 1762–1891.* Providence: Rhode Island News Co., 1891.

Williams, John (Anthony Pasquin, pseud.). *Eccentricities of John Edwin, Comedian. A Calm Inquiry into the present state of our theatres.* 2 vols. London: J. Strahan, 1791.

Willis, Eola. *The Charleston Stage in the XVIII Century, with Social Settings of the Time.* Columbia, S.C., 1924; reprint, New York: Benjamin Blom, 1968.

Wolfe, Richard J. *Secular Music in America, 1801–1825: A Bibliography.* 3 vols. New York: New York Public Library, 1964.

Wood, William B. *Personal Recollections of the Stage, embracing notices of actors, authors and auditors during a period of forty years.* Philadelphia: H. C. Baird, 1855.

Wyndham, Henry Saxe. *The Annals of Covent Garden Theatre from 1732 to 1897.* 2 vols. London: Chatto and Windus, 1906.

Zimmerman, Elena I. "American Opera Librettos, 1767–1825: The Manifestation and Result of the Imitative Principle in American Literary Form." Ph.D. diss., University of Tennessee, 1972.

ARTICLES IN PERIODICALS AND MULTIVOLUME WORKS

Barriskill, James M. "The Newburyport Theatre in the 18th Century." *Essex Institute Historical Collection* 91 (July 1955), pp. 211–95.

Coad, Oral Sumner. "Stage and Players in Eighteenth Century America." *Journal of English and Germanic Philology* 19 (1920), pp. 210–23.

Corder, Frederick. "The Works of Sir Henry Bishop." *Musical Quarterly* 4 (1918), pp. 78–97.

Dent, Edward J. "The Nomenclature of Opera," *Music and Letters* 25 (1944), pp. 132–40, 213–26.

Duerr, Edwin. "Charles Ciceri and the Background of American Scene Design." *Theatre Arts Monthly* 16 (December 1932), pp. 983–90.

Fiske, Roger. "The Operas of Stephen Storace." *Proceedings of the Royal Musical Association* 86 (1959–60), pp. 29–44.

———. "A Score for *The Duenna*." *Music and Letters* 62 (1961), p. 133.

Graves, Richard. "The Comic Operas of Stephen Storace." *Musical Times* 95 (October 1954), pp. 530–32.

———. "English Comic Opera: 1760–1800." *Monthly Musical Record* 87 (1957), pp. 208–15.

Hamar, Clifford E. "Scenery on the Early American Stage." *Theatre Annual* 7 (1948–49), pp. 84–103.

Hauger, George. "William Shield." *Music and Letters* 31 (1950), pp. 337–42.

Hitchcock, H. Wiley. "An Early American Melodrama: *The Indian Princess* of J. N. Barker and John Bray." *Notes* 12 (June 1955), pp. 375–88.

Lawrence, W. J. "Early American Playgoing." *The Theatre* 24 (December 1916), pp. 368, 404.

———. "Early Irish Ballad Opera and Comic Opera." *Musical Quarterly* 8 (July 1922), pp. 397–412.

Longyear, Rey M. "Notes on the Rescue Opera." *Musical Quarterly* 45 (1959), pp. 49–66.

McKay, David. "The Fashionable Lady: The First Opera by an American." *Musical Quarterly* 63 (July 1979), pp. 360–67.

Macqueen-Pope, Walter J. "James Quin." *Encyclopaedia Britannica*, 200th anniversary ed. (1968), vol. 18.

Moreland, James. "The Theatre in Portland in the Eighteenth Century." *New England Quarterly* 11, no. 2 (June 1938), pp. 331–42.

Pritner, Calvin L. "William Warren's Financial Arrangements with Traveling Stars—1805–1829." *Theatre Survey* 6 (1965), pp. 83–90.

Rabson, Carolyn. "*Disappointment* Revisited: Unweaving the Tangled Web." *American Music* 1, no. 1 (Spring 1983), pp. 12–35, and 2, no. 1 (Spring 1984), pp. 1–28.

Redway, Virginia Larkin. "The Carrs, American Music Publishers." *Musical Quarterly* 18 (1932), pp. 150–77.

Rimbault, Edward F. "Samuel Arnold, Mus. Doc." *Grove's Dictionary of Music and Musicians*. Edited by J. A. Fuller Maitland. 5 vols. New York: Macmillan, 1904.

Sands, Mollie. "These Were Singers." *Music and Letters* 25 (April 1944), pp. 103–9.

Shapiro, Anne Dhu. "Action Music in American Pantomime and Melodrama, 1730–1913." *American Music* 2, no. 4 (Winter 1984), pp. 49–72.

Sonneck, Oscar George Theodore. "Early American Operas." *Sammelbande der Internationalen Musik Gesellschaft* (1904–5), pp. 429–92.

Stoddard, Richard. "Stock Scenery in 1798." *Theatre Survey* 13 (November 1972), pp. 102–3.

Swanson, Wesley. "Wings and Backdrops: The Story of American Stage Scenery from the Beginnings to 1875." *The Drama* 18, no. 1 (October 1927), pp. 5–7, 30; no. 2 (November 1927), pp. 41–42, 63–64; no. 3 (December 1927), pp. 78–80; no. 4 (January 1928), pp. 107–10.

Todt, William Charles. "Stage Lighting." *Encyclopaedia Britannica*, 200th anniversary ed. (1968), vol. 21.

Tufts, George. "Ballad Operas: A List and Some Notes." *Musical Antiquary* 4 (January 1913), pp. 61–86.

Wagner, John. "New York City Concert Life, 1801–05." *American Music* 2, no. 2 (Summer 1984), pp. 53–69.

Winesanker, Michael. "Musico-Dramatic Criticism of English Comic Opera, 1750–1800." *Journal of the American Musicological Society* 2 (1949), pp. 87–96.

Yellin, Victor Fell. "Rayner Taylor's Music for *The Æthiop:* Part 1, Performance History," *American Music* 4, no. 3 (Fall 1986), pp. 249–67; "Part 2, The Keyboard Score *(The Ethiop)* and Its Orchestral Restoration," 5, no. 1 (Spring 1987), pp. 20–47.

EIGHTEENTH- AND NINETEENTH-CENTURY NEWSPAPERS AND PERIODICALS

The Albany Register, Albany, N.Y.

American and Commercial Advertiser, Baltimore.

American and Daily Advertiser, Baltimore.

American Citizen, New York.

American Mercury, Hartford, Conn.

The Argus, or Greenleaf's New Daily Advertiser, New York.

Augusta Herald, Augusta, Ga.

Aurora. General Advertiser, Philadelphia.

Boston Daily Advertiser, Boston.

Boston Gazette and Weekly Republican Journal, Boston.

Boston Gazette. Commercial and Political, Boston.

Carr's Musical Miscellany. Baltimore: J. Carr, 1815.

Charleston Courier, Charleston, S.C.

City Gazette and Daily Advertiser, Charleston, S.C.

Claypoole's American Daily Advertiser, Philadelphia.

Columbian Centinel, Boston.

Columbian Museum and Savannah Advertiser, Savannah, Ga.

The Comet. [J. T. Buckingham, ed.] Boston, 1811–12.

Connecticut Courant, Hartford.

The Cynick. Philadelphia, 1811.

The Daily Advertiser, New York.

Dunlap and Claypoole's American Daily Advertiser, Philadelphia.

The Emerald, or, Miscellany of Literature, containing Sketches of the Manners, Principles and Amusements of the Age. Boston: Belcher and Armstrong, 1806–October 10, 1807. *The Emerald.* New series, Boston: Oliver C. Greenleaf, October 31, 1807–1808.

The Enquirer, Richmond.

The Euterpeiad: or, Musical Intelligencer. Boston: John R. Parker, ed., 1820–23.

Federal Gazette, Baltimore.

Federal Gazette and Baltimore Daily Advertiser, Baltimore.

Federal Orrery, Boston.

Gazette, New York.

Gazette of the United States and Daily Evening Advertiser, Philadelphia.

General Advertiser, Philadelphia.

Herald; a Gazette for the Country, New York.

Independent Chronicle and the Universal Advertiser, Boston.

The Independent Gazetteer; or The Chronicle of Freedom, Philadelphia.

Jenks' Portland Gazette, Portland, Me.

Kentucky Gazette, Lexington.

The Maryland Journal and Baltimore Advertiser, Baltimore.

Massachusetts Mercury, Boston.

Minerva, New York.

The Mirror of Taste and Dramatic Censor. 4 vols. Stephen Cullen Carpenter, ed. Philadelphia, Boston, and New York, 1810–11.

The Monthly Register and Review of the United States. Stephen Cullen Carpenter, ed., 1805–6.

Morning Chronicle, New York.

National Advocate, New York.

New England Palladium, Boston.

The Newport Mercury, Newport, R.I.

New-York Commercial Advertiser, New York.

New-York Evening Post, New York.

New York Gazette and General Advertiser, New York.

New-York Journal and Patriotic Register, New York.

The New York Journal, and Weekly Register, New York.

New York Magazine or Literary Repository. New York, 1792–95.

New York Packet, New York.

L'Oracle and Daily Advertiser, New York.

Pennsylvania Journal and the Weekly Advertiser, Philadelphia.

Philadelphia Gazette (Pennsylvania Gazette), Philadelphia.

Philadelphia Repository and Weekly Register. Philadelphia: E. Conrad, 1800–1802.

Piano-Forte Magazine. 15 vols. London: Harrison, [1797–1802].

Polyanthos. Boston, 1805–7. Title varies: *The Polyanthos. A Monthly Maga-*

zine, consisting of original performances and selections from works of
merit. New series, Boston: February–September 1812. *The Polyanthos*. Enlarged, Boston: October 1812–September 1814.

The Port Folio. Oliver Oldschool, Esq., ed. Philadelphia, 1801–3. New series,
1806–7. Third series, 1813.

Post, New York.

Poulson's American Daily Advertiser, Philadelphia.

Providence Gazette and Country Journal, Providence, R.I.

The Ramblers' Magazine. New York: D. Longworth, 1809–10.

Republican, or anti-democrat, Baltimore.

South Carolina State Gazette, Charleston, S.C.

South Carolina State Gazette and Timothy's Daily Advertiser, Charleston,
S.C.

The Spectator, New York.

The Theatrical Censor. Philadelphia, 1805–6.

The Theatrical Censor and Critical Miscellany. Gregory Gryphon, Esq., ed.,
Philadelphia, 1806.

The Thespian Mirror. John Howard Payne, ed. New York, 1806.

The Thespian Monitor, and Dramatick Miscellany. Barnaby Bangbar, Esq.,
ed. Philadelphia, 1809.

United States Chronicle, Providence, R.I.

Virginia Argus, Richmond.

Virginia Gazette and General Advertiser, Richmond.

MANUSCRIPTS AND UNPUBLISHED MATERIALS

"Articles of agreement between proprietors of the theatre, Joseph Bull, Timothy Burr and Ephraim Root and the managers Messrs. Hallam and Hodgkinson," Hartford, Conn., August 15, 1795. Harvard Theatre Collection.

"Articles to be strictly observ'd, by the Managers and Performers belonging
to the Maryland Company of Comedians." [1782.] Maryland Historical
Society, Annapolis.

Durang, Charles. *The Philadelphia Stage . . . Partly compiled from the papers
of his father, the late John Durang; with notes by the editors.* Seven looseleaf notebooks clipped from the *Sunday Dispatch*, Philadelphia. First series
(1749–1821) published in 75 chapters, beginning May 7, 1854. Harvard
Theatre Collection.

Hodgkinson, John. Letters concerning the establishment of a theatre in Hartford, Conn. December 15, 1794, and March 25, 1795. Harvard Theatre
Collection.

Pelissier, Victor. *The Voice of Nature.* Score and parts. New York Public Library.

"Rules to be Observed in the Baltimore Theatre, respecting Benefits." [1782.] Maryland Historical Society, Annapolis.

Stone, Catherine Graupner. "Gottlieb Graupner, the pioneer of classical music in America . . . " Typescript, 1906. Boston Public Library.

Wall, Thomas. Personal collection of playbills for Annapolis and Baltimore, 1781–82, with autograph notations. Maryland Historical Society, Annapolis.

White, William Charles. Papers, 1771–1813. American Antiquarian Society, Worcester, Mass.

INDEX

Titles of works included only in the appendixes are not indexed. First-word articles "The" and "A" are omitted from titles of works. Sources' spellings of personal names vary widely; cross references and parentheses are used for clarification. Page references to figures are in italics.

617